OXFORD

HANN

BOOKS TWENTY-ONE

TITUS LIVIUS (LIVY), the historian, was born in Patavium (modern Padua) in 64 or 59 BC and died in AD 12 or 17 in Patavium, surviving therefore into his late seventies or early eighties. He came to Rome in the 30s BC and began writing his history of Rome not long after. There is no evidence that he was a senator or held other governmental posts, although he was acquainted with the emperor Augustus and his family, at least by his later years. He appears to have had the means to spend his life largely in writing his huge history of Rome, *Ab Urbe Condita* or 'From the Foundation of the City', which filled 142 books and covered the period from Rome's founding to the death of the elder Drusus (753–9 BC). Thirty-five books survive: 1–10 (753–293 BC) and 21–45 (218–167 BC).

J. C. YARDLEY has been Professor and Head of Classics at the Universities of Calgary and Ottawa and is a former President of the Classical Association of Canada. He has also translated *The Dawn of the Roman Empire* (Books 31–40 of Livy's history) for Oxford World's Classics, as well as Quintus Curtius' *History of Alexander* for Penguin Classics (1984) and Justin for the American Philological Association Classical Resources series (1994) and (Books 11–12) for the Clarendon Ancient History series (1997). His most recent books are *Justin and Pompeius Trogus* (2003) and (with Waldemar Heckel) *Alexander the Great* (2004).

DEXTER HOYOS was born in Barbados, studied at Oxford, and teaches Roman history and historians, and Latin, at Sydney University. His most recent publications include *Unplanned Wars* (1998), on the causes of the first two Punic Wars, and *Hannibal's Dynasty: Power and Politics in the Western Mediterranean 247–183 B.C.* (2003).

OXFORD WORLD'S CLASSICS

For over 100 years Oxford World's Classics have brought readers closer to the world's great literature. Now with over 700 titles—from the 4,000-year-old myths of Mesopotamia to the twentieth century's greatest novels—the series makes available lesser-known as well as celebrated writing.

The pocket-sized hardbacks of the early years contained introductions by Virginia Woolf, T. S. Eliot, Graham Greene, and other literary figures which enriched the experience of reading. Today the series is recognized for its fine scholarship and reliability in texts that span world literature, drama and poetry, religion, philosophy and politics. Each edition includes perceptive commentary and essential background information to meet the changing needs of readers.

OXFORD WORLD'S CLASSICS

LIVY

Hannibal's War
Books Twenty-One to Thirty

Translated by
J. C. YARDLEY

With an Introduction and Notes by
DEXTER HOYOS

OXFORD
UNIVERSITY PRESS

OXFORD
UNIVERSITY PRESS

Great Clarendon Street, Oxford OX2 6DP

Oxford University Press is a department of the University of Oxford.
It furthers the University's objective of excellence in research, scholarship,
and education by publishing worldwide in

Oxford New York

Auckland Cape Town Dar es Salaam Hong Kong Karachi
Kuala Lumpur Madrid Melbourne Mexico City Nairobi
New Delhi Shanghai Taipei Toronto

With offices in

Argentina Austria Brazil Chile Czech Republic France Greece
Guatemala Hungary Italy Japan Poland Portugal Singapore
South Korea Switzerland Thailand Turkey Ukraine Vietnam

Oxford is a registered trade mark of Oxford University Press
in the UK and in certain other countries

Published in the United States
by Oxford University Press Inc., New York

Translation © J. C. Yardley 2006
Introduction, Notes and other editorial matter © Dexter Hoyos 2006

The moral rights of the authors have been asserted
Database right Oxford University Press (maker)

First published as an Oxford World's Classics paperback 2006

British Library Cataloguing in Publication Data

Data available

Library of Congress Cataloging in Publication Data

Data available

Typeset in Ehrhardt
by RefineCatch Limited, Bungay, Suffolk
Printed in Great Britain by
Clays Ltd, St Ives plc, Suffolk

ISBN 0–19–283159–3   978–0–19–283159–0

1

For
Andrea, Elaine, Jane, Camilla, Jann, and Barbara

CONTENTS

INTRODUCTION

Livy and his history

Titus Livius was born at Patavium in northern Italy, today's Padua, probably in 64 BC, and died there probably in AD 12; his family's communal epitaph may still be seen. He began writing his history *From the Foundation of the City* (*Ab Urbe Condita*) around 27 BC, just as Rome's latest supreme leader, Augustus, was consolidating his primacy over the city and the empire. Starting with the origins of Rome, he concluded with the year 9 BC in Book 142, an average yearly output of nearly four sizeable books. Of these, only 35 (1–10 and 21–45) survive, though luckily a collection of epitomes or résumés of nearly all 142 is extant.

The history made Livy famous in his own lifetime: there is a story of an admirer from Gades (Cádiz) in Spain who travelled to Rome simply to see the man of renown, and then went home. Livy was on friendly terms with Augustus, but *From the Foundation of the City* was not a commissioned work or propaganda piece for the new regime: Livy openly wondered whether it would have been worse or better for the Roman people if Julius Caesar had never been born, and accorded enough praise to Caesar's foe Pompey for Augustus to tease him with being a 'Pompeian'—perhaps a punning joke based on his Patavine origin.[1]

Books 21–30 of *From the Foundation* comprise our most detailed and exciting ancient account of the Second Punic War, Hannibal's war against Rome.[2] The two warring states, Rome and Carthage, were supposedly founded within a few decades of each other: Carthage in 814, Rome in 753. It will help a better understanding of Livy's narrative to summarize the events that led to their rivalry.

---

[1] Doubt about Caesar: Seneca, *Natural Questions* 5.18. Friendship with Augustus, and the joke: Tacitus, *Annals* 4.34; perhaps a pun on Livy's origin—not really a 'Patavine' but a 'Pompeian' (Pompeii being the well-known town in Campania).

[2] 'Punic' (Latin *Punicus* or *Poenicus*) is an alternative term for 'Carthaginian', recalling the city's Phoenician ancestry.

Rome and Carthage: two republics

Both Rome and Carthage had traditions of eastern ancestry—Rome descended from Trojan refugees, Carthage the creation of Dido, a princess of Tyre in Phoenicia (roughly today's Lebanon), fleeing tyranny at home. The favourable geography of both cities made them locally powerful from early times. Rome's strong site on seven hills beside the Tiber commanded the best routes along that section of Italy's coast and between sea and interior. Carthage, on a diamond-shaped peninsula overlooking the narrowest stretch of the Mediterranean, was not the oldest Phoenician colony but the best positioned for western commerce and communications.

By 270 the Romans dominated peninsular Italy. Roughly its central third had become actual Roman territory, including the wealthy region of Campania whose cities—notably Capua—enjoyed much local autonomy. Many strategic sites elsewhere were occupied by 'Latin colonies', cities founded by the Romans and holding a privileged status akin to Roman citizenship. The rest of Italy was a political quilt of states, all bound to Rome by alliance treaties, which left them (like the Latins) self-governing but inflexibly subordinate to her in foreign relations and military activities. The Romans had also developed significant international trade (as had many maritime Italian cities) from Spain to Greece and including Punic North Africa. They had also undergone a first encounter with an overseas foe: Pyrrhus, king of Epirus, who brought over a professional Greek army in 280 to aid the Greek city of Tarentum against them. With Greek military science at its peak, Pyrrhus inflicted the expected defeats on Roman armies, only to find himself no better off. When the Romans finally drove him out of Italy and forced Tarentum into their alliance system, it was a portent of the future.

The Carthaginians built their hegemony mainly by sea, from the profits of trade and then from dependent territories. From the mid-sixth century they controlled the western quarter of Sicily, sharing the island with numerous, often squabbling, Greek city-states like Syracuse, Agrigentum, and Messana. They also occupied the fertile lowlands of Sardinia and places in Corsica; and maintained close contacts with the old Phoenician colonies on the coasts of Spain, notably Gades. They tried to enforce a monopoly on the trade in tin that came from beyond the Straits of Gibraltar, and sometimes regulated other dealings through agreements with trade-partners: the second-century Greek historian Polybius quotes the texts of two early treaties with Rome, struck in 509 and 348. Carthage also imposed control over her fertile North African hinterland, including other old Phoenician cities like Utica which were treated as privileged allies; by contrast, the surrounding North African populations were taxed and conscripted as subjects.

Third-century Carthage and Rome shared many general political features. After early monarchies, both had developed as republics. Their systems included male-only citizens' assemblies which enacted laws and elected magistrates (see Glossary), a senate made up of leading men including ex-magistrates, and the magistrates themselves who had fixed tenures of office. In both republics, it was the senate and magistrates who between them decided most questions, with the citizens' ratification usually a formality. Closer comparisons are difficult, for details of politics at Carthage are few, but at Rome some leading families enjoyed prominence—thanks to recurrent electoral success—for generations, like those of the Hannibalic war's heroes Fabius, Marcellus, and Scipio. But there was room for men from less distinguished backgrounds to attain rank and influence, too: for instance Flaminius, the energetic though brash consul whose career ended in disaster at Lake Trasimene in 217 (but whose son in turn would one day be consul), and Cato, a newcomer from Tusculum near Rome, consul in 195, censor, proponent in old age of Carthage's destruction, founder of Latin history writing, and much else.

With only two consuls a year, very few reached that ultimate height. But as the detailed notices in Livy and other authorities show, Roman voters at elections were capable both of loyalty to generations of the same families and of choosing virtual unknowns; there were enough magistracies, particularly at the lower levels, to allow this range of selection. The citizen body in turn, meeting in various formal assemblies, usually followed the Senate's lead but occasionally enacted otherwise. The result was a vigorous and versatile political life of blended conservatism and innovation.

The Punic republic, too, had well-established political families, but they are much harder to trace. With much of the city's wealth based on the risks of maritime trading, and with wealth (according to Aristotle, writing around 330) no less important than birth for political success, it was a challenge for competitive families to maintain the standing won by successful ancestors. Hamilcar Barca's supposed descent from a brother of Queen Dido is no guide to whether his family had enjoyed recent eminence. All the same, one family or clan, the Magonids, had enjoyed not only eminence but practical dominance over the state starting around 550 with Mago— a successful general—and lasting until 396, while another family (thanks to a leader termed Hanno 'the Great') managed similar leadership from about 350 to 310.[3]

Aristotle regarded Carthage as mostly a well-governed state, and it is the only non-Greek city to be discussed in his *Politics*. The chief magistrates were two annual 'sufetes', whose role was chiefly to consult the senate of Carthage on matters of government. For its wars, though, the republic elected generals with wide and open-ended tenure. The senate of Carthage, in turn, bore the engaging title of The Mighty Ones and had a select inner 'council of thirty'; but how this council and The Mighty Ones themselves were recruited is unknown. No doubt money talked again. As for the assembly of citizens, Polybius rather disapprovingly remarks that it had more real power than the citizen body at Rome, but what that means in practical terms is opaque. We find the senate of Carthage, in practice anyway, as the organ still authorizing war and ratifying peace during Hannibal's war. Polybius' comment may be a censorious Greek oligarch's exaggeration.

Unlike Rome, whose 'foreign' relations until 280 were almost entirely with other Italian states, Carthage had to deal from early on with overseas powers, and especially the Greek cities of Sicily because of her own territorial interests there. A long series of wars, invariably ending in a stalemated return to the status quo, was fought with Sicilian Greek coalitions usually led by Syracuse. During the greatest such war, from 317 to 306, the Syracusan leader Agathocles turned the tables at one desperate stage by invading Punic Africa (310–307), winning a series of successes, and, though finally forced to retire to Sicily, weakening the Carthaginians enough to secure peace soon after. Thirty years later Pyrrhus of Epirus, frustrated in his Roman war, took up the Sicilian Greek cause to overrun most of

---

[3] On Carthaginian names, often confusingly similar, see Glossary under 'Hanno'.

the Punic west, but the struggle ended as before. Carthage's next Sicilian war, however, was a serious shock.

The First Punic War

In 264 Rome and Carthage suddenly went to war. The circumstances were odd. Both had stepped in to protect Messana—a Sicilian city now occupied by renegade Italian mercenaries, the Mamertines— from falling into the grip of a resurgent Syracuse, yet the would-be protectors soon found themselves in a confrontation. The Carthaginians' concern over possible Roman intrusion into Sicily led them into an unprecedented alliance with Syracuse, but the Syracusan king, Hiero II, quickly made his peace with the intruders, accepting second-rank status for his city in return for a long and prosperous reign until 215. Rome and Carthage, by contrast, remained at war for nearly a quarter of a century (264–241).

The war ebbed and flowed, largely fought in western Sicily but with a number of major naval operations beyond. The Romans not only launched a grand fleet (261) but surprised the world by repeatedly defeating the Carthaginians at sea. They eventually invaded Africa under the consul Regulus, who forced the Carthaginians to sue for peace; but when talks broke down he, like Agathocles, suffered a disastrous reverse (256–255). The Romans then lost several fleets between 255 and 249, along with tens of thousands of Roman and allied lives, through storms or enemy action. The Carthaginians in their turn eventually found themselves deprived of all their Sicilian province save the fortress-ports of Lilybaeum (modern Marsala) and Drepana (Trápani). Their defence of these was helped, from 247 on, by the agile guerrilla warfare carried on by a new commanding general, Hamilcar, nicknamed Barca ('lightning'); but after a new Roman fleet was launched by public subscription in 242, the consul Lutatius Catulus crushed its clumsily handled Punic counterpart at the Aegates Islands off Drepana (March 241). Hamilcar was instructed to seek terms, and after some difficult negotiations the war ended with Carthage abandoning Sicily and agreeing to pay a large indemnity.

The Romans became effective masters of all Sicily save Syracuse's small kingdom, but did little with the island. The Carthaginians meanwhile, unable (or unwilling) to pay their professional troops what they owed them, were put in mortal danger by a mutiny of these troops followed by a general revolt of the oppressed North African population; this savage 'Truceless' War (241–238) was finally won under Hamilcar Barca's leadership, and with help from Rome and Syracuse. But, just after it ended, the Romans abruptly annexed Sardinia and extracted another large indemnity from Carthage— perhaps as an afterthought from the peace of 241, or because a Carthage revived by the indomitable Hamilcar looked as if it would threaten the hard-won Roman supremacy over Sicily. That done, however, they paid Carthage little notice for a dozen years.

The Barcid ascendancy

With Hamilcar and his supporters at the helm, the Carthaginians turned to Spain to build new dominions. Hamilcar's sole office was the open-ended one of general—in effect, generalissimo of all Carthaginian forces, military and naval—but in practice the Barcids ('Barca' was Hamilcar's nickname alone, but it is convenient to give his family this name) dominated all the republic's affairs, like the Magonids two centuries before. To restore his city's fortunes and, of course, to keep his kinsmen and allies in office, Hamilcar brought wide areas of southern Spain (roughly modern Andalusia) under his control, levying tribute, developing resources like mines, founding cities—one was probably at the site of today's Alicante—and taking care to create a powerful army of Spanish and North African levies along with foreign mercenaries. Much of the new wealth was, in turn, redirected to Carthage. When Hamilcar was killed on campaign in early 228, he was followed by his son-in-law Hasdrubal as general in Spain and overall leader of the Carthaginian republic.

Other aristocrats found it politic to cooperate with the Barcids for their own advancement, for instance Hasdrubal, son of Gisgo, a man of vigour and patriotism, who played a major part in the second half of Hannibal's war. Opposition to the Barcid juggernaut rallied round an ex-general named Hanno, whom some writers—not Livy or Polybius—term 'the Great' (perhaps a descendant of the fourth-century leader Hanno the Great), but his supporters won few offices after 237 and they must have shrunk in prestige and influence.

Hasdrubal the son-in-law, the new leader of the republic, extended Punic (in practice, Barcid) rule to the River Tagus, maintained an even larger army—reportedly with 200 elephants—and founded the most brilliant of Spanish-Punic colonies, which he named 'Carthage', on a natural harbour on the south-eastern coast ('New Carthage' to the Romans, modern Cartagena). The Romans, threatened with Gallic attacks, worried that his expansion might further disturb the situation if he reached the Pyrenees; but a simple agreement struck with them in early 225 assured them that Barcid arms would stop at the River Ebro. Serving in Spain under Hasdrubal were Hamilcar's sons, Hannibal (born in 247) and two younger brothers; and when Hasdrubal fell to an assassin in late 221, the Carthaginians appointed Hannibal as the new generalissimo and de facto leader of the republic.

Like his father and brother-in-law, Hannibal had been elected by the Carthaginians. His brothers and various kinsmen, too, held high military commands; and a non-Barcid aristocrat like Hasdrubal, son of Gisgo, achieved his own high rank in alliance with them. All the available evidence shows Barcid domination of the republic continuing through the years of victory that followed Hannibal's invasion of Italy. The only recorded opposition, that of Hanno the Great, was as sidelined and impotent as ever, even after setbacks began to weaken the Barcids' predominance. But once the war was plainly lost—from 203 on—it suited all non-Barcid grandees at Carthage to blame it entirely on Hannibal and claim that the rest of the elite had always opposed both it and him. At the same time Hannibal and his history-writing friends (see below), keen to set his reputation in the best light, insisted that he would have won the war if the authorities at home had sent him proper reinforcements and supplies, instead of constantly withholding them out of party spite.

Their contemporary Fabius Pictor, who had family contacts among the Carthaginian elite, in turn told his readers that the Barcids had made themselves independent lords in Spain and that Hannibal, flushed with arrogance and greed, had launched the war in the teeth of aristocratic opposition. This view of Barcid political relationships and Hannibal's own role in the war continues to be widely held, but is implausible.

Rome in the interwar years

The Romans were in an assertive mood after 241. After annexing Sardinia, and Corsica with it, they intermittently sent troops over to cow the warlike natives (with middling success); but more important was their interest in north Italy, then called Cisalpine Gaul. Domestic pressures for land-grants to poorer citizens caused a vigorous tribune of the plebs in 232, Gaius Flaminius, to enact such grants in Roman-held territory in the north, which in turn antagonized the warlike Gallic peoples in the Cisalpine region. A great Gallic invasion of the peninsula ensued in 225, but was decisively crushed in the battle of Telamon in Etruria; then a series of campaigns, under leaders like Flaminius (consul in 223) and Marcus Claudius Marcellus (consul in 222), extended Roman control to the River Po with a fuzzier zone of influence beyond. To strengthen this control, two new Latin colonies by the Po were initiated in 218, Placentia and Cremona.

As early as 229–228, moreover, the Romans extended their influence across another body of water, the Adriatic, to the piratically inclined communities of Illyria opposite the heel of Italy. A powerful expedition, involving both consuls with appropriate armies and a fleet, imposed terms on the Illyrian monarchy and a measure of influence (often termed a 'protectorate') over the coastal Greek cities like Epidamnus and Apollonia. Another large expedition in 219, under the consuls Lucius Aemilius Paullus and Marcus Livius, reasserted Roman influence; while a couple of years earlier Rome had intervened in the Istrian peninsula further north. All these activities in turn brought the Roman republic into formal diplomatic relations with the states of Greece for the first time.

Hannibal's war: causes and theories

It was after Hannibal became general that the Romans showed a new interest in Spain, prompted perhaps by the broad conquest-campaigns which he waged across central Spain in 221 and 220. The previously ignored town of Saguntum, on the Mediterranean coast, suddenly found it was a Roman protégé; and the agreement with Hasdrubal about the Ebro was equally suddenly set before Hannibal, with orders to abide by it. The Romans perhaps supposed that, young and theoretically inexperienced, he would acquiesce in this double démarche by an embassy in 220, and thus save them from needing to notice Spain or Carthage further (they then turned to launch their second Illyrian war). Certainly the Romans seem to have been unprepared for the attack on Saguntum, for they did nothing throughout 219, even though Hannibal took seven months to capture the city, well after the Illyrian war had ended in victory.

Hannibal had treated their démarche as a provocation, noisily signalled that he would reject it, and then besieged and sacked Saguntum, as Livy vividly reports in Book 21. As soon as sailing conditions permitted in early 218, a new Roman embassy went to Carthage (significantly, not to Spain) to demand that he be surrendered for punishment—a demand obviously unacceptable—or that war be accepted instead. The chief envoy, another Fabius, then duly declared war, to loud acclaim from the Carthaginian senate.

The reasons for the war have been explored from that day to this. Ancient explanations included Hannibal's family-nurtured greed and arrogance (monarchic vices, stressed by the contemporary historian Fabius Pictor); a long-standing plan of revenge devised by the Barcid leaders to reverse the outcome of the previous war (the view put by Livy and his predecessor Polybius); and reciprocal greed, mistrust, and fear felt by both republics (urged by the later historian Cassius Dio). Modern observers hold to a still wider range of explanations. Some stress the economic attractions of Punic Spain to the proverbially booty-hungry Romans; others highlight the factors of mistrust and fear; and a few argue for the deadly combination of great-power assertiveness (especially by the Romans towards a state they had defeated), mutual mistrust, and miscalculation on both sides. On this last view, the war was neither planned nor wanted but the démarche from Rome, instead of restraining the Carthaginians and their new leader, fatally aroused them into standing their ground over Saguntum and, in effect, daring the Romans to respond.

The rival military systems

The Romans levied their armies from their own citizens and from the Latin and other Italian states, while their navy was manned largely by crews from their maritime Italian allies. Normally each consul commanded two legions for the main effort, and if necessary one or more praetors could be given a legion apiece for other theatres. During Hannibal's war, many more than the traditional four to six legions were in service to meet military needs; in 212 there were twenty-five under arms around Italy and in Cisalpine

Gaul, Sicily, Spain, and elsewhere, and even ten years later there were still fourteen. In 218 a legion (see Glossary) theoretically had 4,200 infantry and 300 cavalry, and was accompanied by allied horse and foot who could be twice as numerous. A consular army thus could involve up to 25,000 men, though at Cannae the legions were extra large and the Roman army under the two consuls is reported as over 80,000 strong—a number not reached again until the later second century. The demands put on Italy's manpower by such forces, and the war fleets, were enormous, as were the needs of payment and supply.

There was not a lot of tactical or strategic doctrine, partly because there was no professional soldiery. Generals and officers were men with political careers, soldiers were levied from among ordinary working citizens. Discipline emphasized obedience, cohesion, and stamina, for the goal of a campaign was to crush the enemy's army and scour his territory to force a surrender. Complex manœuvres and specialized military devices were unusual in a Roman army in 218; normal battle tactics were to attack, with infantry in the centre and cavalry on either wing, and seek to defeat the other side with one or more such blows. The enemy, of course, were seeking the same result in reverse.

Legionary and allied infantry wore protective armour (coat of chain-mail or leather, and helmet), carried oblong wooden shields, and used two hurling-javelins and the short, two-edged 'Spanish' sword. They were arranged in maniples, small units each consisting of two centuries (see Glossary), and in three lines: an array that allowed flexible movement and considerable shock absorption. The army's light troops, wearing less armour, were used to open a battle with skirmishing tactics, and for pursuit after victory. Against a Greek phalanx formation, like Pyrrhus'—a division or divisions of closely packed pikemen, charging with their pikes levelled and supported by cavalry—the Roman manipular army could have problems, but superior flexibility and the phalanx's own tendency to loosen ranks in charging could turn the tide. Similarly with the enthusiastic but ill-disciplined mass of a Gallic army, whose onrush could usually be checked by javelins and the light infantry, and then be broken by the legions countercharging with cavalry support.

The Carthaginian armies of 218 were made up largely of North African and Spanish levies, with Carthaginian senior officers. In earlier times the North Africans had been complemented by units of foreign professionals on contract—Greeks, Gauls, and Campanians among them—but the trauma of the 'Truceless War' perhaps prompted Hamilcar and his successors to reshape their forces. At all events, Hannibal in Italy and his brothers and colleagues elsewhere seem to have had few mercenaries of the old style, except Numidian cavalry and some Spanish infantry (certainly no Greeks, who still formed the elite of eastern Mediterranean mercenaries). Hannibal filled out his ranks with recruits from the Italian states that joined his side after Cannae.

Until the later third century, a Punic army's battle array had been the infantry phalanx plus cavalry. But with troops equipped along national lines, and therefore with notable variety of weapons, tactical array needed to be adaptable. Spanish infantry, for instance, used not pikes but a sword, either the straight two-edged type or a menacingly curved version called a *falcata*. When Hannibal re-equipped his troops after Trasimene with captured Roman arms (as we learn from Polybius, not Livy), and acquired Italian recruits, swordplay in closely ordered lines must have been the rule—if not in manipular formation, then rather like the hoplite array of older Greece. This was not intrinsically superior to the manipular formation: it was not his line-array as such that won Hannibal's battles, but his combination of steady infantry with highly skilled cavalry, and (whenever possible) some form of surprise stroke.

Hannibal's tactical genius, the greatest since Alexander, enabled him, like his Macedonian predecessor, to inflict crushing defeats on larger forces, and at Cannae he established a model of battle which has inspired military planners ever since (reportedly even General Norman Schwarzkopf in Iraq). His strategic and geopolitical skills were less fortunate: he invaded Italy without a fallback plan in case the Romans refused to come to terms, could not create a viable alliance system with the defecting Italians, allowed his administrators at Carthage and in Spain to disperse available forces unproductively, and performed far below par in 207 when his brother arrived over the Alps. Scipio Africanus, his admirer and ultimate nemesis, used equally varied and inspired tactics, and was just as charismatic if not more so, but did not have the problem of building up and then defending a broad alliance system, or coordinating the entire national war effort.

A further advantage for the Romans was that they had several
other capable commanders (though no other genius), like Fabius,
Marcellus, Gracchus, and Nero. By contrast, the other Carthaginian
generals were definitely second-rate or even third-rate: the one great
victory they won, over the elder Scipio brothers in Spain (211), was
partly owing to the brothers' own strategic mistakes. The once
mighty Punic navy performed miserably throughout the war. Such
limitations among the Carthaginians and in their leader himself led
to misjudgements and missed opportunities, which in the end cost
them victory.

Hannibal's war

The war of 218–201 was conditioned by several factors, including
Hannibal's military genius and limited geopolitical skills, Carthage's
renewed wealth, the lack of a vigorous Carthaginian navy—ironic,
in view of her centuries of maritime expertise—and the Romans'
stubborn resourcefulness under pressure. Like his father and
brother-in-law, Hannibal was a land warrior. Punic naval inferiority
after two decades of Barcid rule practically dictated a land invasion
of Italy, unless he were to await enemy invasions of both Spain and
Africa. His grand strategy clearly aimed at inflicting shattering
defeats on the Romans on their home ground, so as to win over the
Italian allies and press the Romans themselves into a peace on his
terms. Victory would, in turn, have made Carthage the dominant
power across the Mediterranean west and—with a subservient Rome
and Italy at her side—potentially the arbiter of the east as well.

The strategic scheme began less than brilliantly, however. Marching out of Spain with 59,000 cavalry and infantry, Hannibal arrived
in Cisalpine Gaul with 26,000. Whatever the reasons—much
debated ever since—he had lost nearly 60 per cent of his troops; and
though he recruited Gallic warriors, these proved less disciplined
and reliable than his lost Spanish and North African effectives.
(Had he arrived with his original 59,000, all subsequent history
might have been different.) Yet he won a spectacular series of victories, climaxing at Cannae on 2 August 216, when more Romans
and allies were killed, on even the lowest estimate, than on the first
day of the Somme in 1916. Defections from the losing side began,
including the major and discontented city of Capua in Campania, so

that by 212 most of southern Italy's states were Punic allies. Moreover, Cannae brought an eastern great power, Macedon, into alliance, for King Philip V disliked the Roman 'protectorate' in Illyria; and by 214 Syracuse, too, had joined. Rome and her remaining allies were all but encircled.

After Cannae Hannibal expected the Romans to seek peace talks. His treaty with Macedon implicitly forecast that they would be weakened, but not obliterated (contrary to what the Romans later claimed). Instead, they multiplied their armies and maintained their fleets: by 213, more than a quarter of all available manpower was in military service. Armies operated in Spain and, when destroyed in 211, were replaced. Philip V was contained; Syracuse was besieged and taken; and in Italy Hannibal found his grand alliance as much a hindrance as a help. He was shadowed by Roman armies while other armies operated against his allies, who then called for his protection. Despite some further gains, he never won another major victory, whereas his allies were subjugated one after another by the remorseless Romans. Spain was lost by 206 after a spectacular series of victories won by the new, and surprisingly young, Roman general Publius Scipio. A fresh Punic army, under Hannibal's middle brother, did make it from Spain to Cisalpine Gaul in 207, but Hannibal was now penned in southern Italy, and his brother's reinforcements were cut off in the far north and destroyed.

Hannibal's grand strategy foundered on Roman endurance and resource. This had always been the risk. Every Punic leader knew how the same qualities had taken the Romans through to unexpected victory in the First Punic War. His calculated hope had to be that massive defeats and defections on their very doorstep would produce a different result. When this failed to happen, he lacked a practicable alternative. The enemy refused further pitched battles, finding ways instead to harass and frustrate his army in southern Italy—the Roman general Marcellus grew particularly skilled at this—while reconquering defected allies and simultaneously putting unbearable pressure on Carthage's supporters elsewhere. By 206 Hannibal was virtually a prisoner, in strategic terms, in what was left of his southern Italian province, and when Scipio undertook the invasion of Punic Africa in 204 the grand strategy was in ruins. The best that Hannibal and Carthage could now hope for was to defeat the homeland's invaders and try to salvage a compromise peace; but at the battle of Zama, in October 202, Scipio's generalship proved more than equal to the Carthaginian's.

The war terminated Carthage as a great power. Her territories in North Africa were left to her, but nothing beyond; a heavy war-indemnity was imposed, the navy was burned, and any future war, even within Africa, required Roman permission. On her western border lay the now-united kingdom of Numidia under a ruler of genius, Masinissa, who enjoyed all the favour from Rome that Carthage could never earn, and who had designs on Punic territories. Yet, helped by political and financial reforms that Hannibal enacted as sufete in 196–195, and because it no longer had naval and large military costs, the much-buffeted republic regained prosperity in astonishingly short order. Despite Masinissa's provocations, Carthage embarked on forty years of peaceful growth and wealth.

The victors did even better, of course. Far more than the First Punic War, the Second made Rome an imperial state. Not only was Cisalpine Gaul reconquered and southern and central Spain taken over (with immense profits), but the Romans could once more direct their attentions across the Adriatic. A decade and a half after Zama, every eastern great power had been taught a hard lesson in the superiority of Roman arms and had learned that their unfettered days of Hellenistic rivalry were over. Roman domination, potential if not always exercised, extended from the Atlantic to the Euphrates. Hannibal was there to see it, for he lived until 183. It was an ironic outcome to the grand enterprise that had started with his epic march across the Alps, thirty-five years before; but the memory of that enterprise has remained vivid and instructive to this day, and much of this is thanks to Livy's artistry and devotion.

Books 21–30: structure and ideals

Livy had recorded the first war with Carthage (264–241) in the lost Books 16–19, then in Book 20 alone the almost equally long interwar period (241–219). By contrast, the ten sizeable books on Hannibal's war cover two years each on average.

Livy treats events year by year, a format termed 'annalistic' (from Latin *annus*, 'year'), and necessary because there was no simple chronological indicator—each year was identified by the names of its consuls. For detailed history, this layout was undeniably convenient, but, with plenty of sources to work from, composing a coherent account sometimes gave trouble. Books 21–30 provide many illustrations. An event might be put into different years by different annalists, which could puzzle a later author (e.g. 27.7). Different sources could vary greatly in their details of army figures, booty items, and other statistics (see for instance 22.36, 26.49). Again, when non-Roman sources were used, they used quite different systems of dating, which required working out how their dates fitted Roman chronology—something not always accurately done. This may partly explain Livy's problems with dating the siege of Saguntum (21.6, 15). What complicated his task was that his dominant concerns were the same as in most of his Latin and many of his Greek predecessors: literary art, psychological description, and moralizing comment.[4]

Livy employs a carefully structured, elegantly balanced, and versatile Latin style, very much like the style 'flowing on with a certain even smoothness' that Cicero had demanded as the ideal for history writing. Vivid narrative, memorably described places and characters, and strong moral assessments were the desiderata. This was well suited, too, to speech-writing, and Livy takes care to give to all his leading characters—and some minor ones—carefully crafted orations (see for instance 21.40–4, 25.6, 28.40–4). Speeches give emotional depth to a situation, illustrate a person's character, or dramatize the pros and cons in a difficult debate. For Quintilian, the expert on oratory a century later, Livy the speech-writer is 'more eloquent than can possibly be described'.

Quintilian succinctly describes Livy's overall style as 'milky richness'. Even so, this is an inadequate description of a versatility that can move from the harrowing vividness of Hannibal's Alpine march (Book 21) to the excitement of battle narratives like Lake Trasimene in Book 22, where the doomed valour of the Roman army is unforgettably painted, and to the plain factual accounts of election results and administrative business (as in 23.30 or 26.23); and from Maharbal's memorably pithy riposte to Hannibal following Cannae, when the general refused to march on Rome ('You know how to win a battle, Hannibal; you do not know how to use the victory!': 22.51) to the romantic tragedy of Sophoniba in Book 30—

---

[4] On passages referred to, see Explanatory Notes.

the beautiful Carthaginian girl married to one Numidian king and then to his victorious rival, only to be forced into suicide to escape the shame of Roman captivity. Not only is *From the Foundation* a masterpiece of thoroughly poised writing but it is shot through with constantly varying expressive colour.[5]

To Livy as to others, Hannibal's war was the zenith of Roman heroism, virtue, and toughness. After recording the catastrophe of Cannae he declares: 'There is surely no other nation that would not have been crushed by such an overwhelming disaster.' The Carthaginians' final defeats in both Punic wars 'can in no respect be compared with Cannae—except to say that they were borne with less strength of character than the Romans bore theirs' (22.54). The Italian allies remained loyal 'evidently because the authority to which they were subject was just and tolerant, and they did not refuse obedience to a superior people—the only real bond of loyalty' (22.13). The high-principled behaviour of Roman voters, in a contested election at a tense moment, brings out even greater enthusiasm:

So much for the disdain some feel for admirers of the past! If there does exist a philosopher state somewhere—a product of our scholars' imagination rather than their knowledge—I certainly would not believe its leaders could be more serious-minded or restrained in their ambition, or the commons more principled, than in this case. (26.22)

Serious-mindedness and its parent qualities—determination, patriotic devotion, and unselfish virtue—represent for Livy the essence of Roman character in that era. When a Roman prisoner of Hannibal's breaks parole after Cannae and remains at Rome, the Senate sternly sends him back (22.60–1); revealingly, Livy himself (22.58) condemns the parole-breaker as 'a person of truly un-Roman character'. The Roman leaders in this time of testing are largely portrayed with admiration, some solid and forbearing, like the elder Publius Scipio in 218 and that byword for prudence Fabius the Delayer, whom Livy shows patiently weathering firebrands' criticisms, repeatedly proving the soundness of his judgement, and managing a dry joke to deflate a foolish braggart (27.25). His skilful

---

[5] Cicero's discussion of history: *Laws* 1.5–9. Quintilian on Livy: *Training of the Orator* 8.1.3, 10.1.32, 10.1.101.

recapture of Tarentum prompts Hannibal to the implausible comment, 'The Romans have *their* Hannibal, too' (27.16). Marcellus, in his turn, is an appealingly combative risk-taker: after one drawn battle Livy gushes: 'the achievement of that day was enormous, and possibly the greatest of that war. For it was more difficult to avoid defeat by Hannibal at that time than it was to defeat him later on' (23.16).

Scipio Africanus is almost Livy's perfect hero. Resourceful, self-controlled, charismatic, fully aware of his own genius, and industrious in self-promotion (26.19), 'destined by fate to be the leader in this war' (22.53), he completes the work of Fabius and Marcellus, finally proving he is more than a match for Hannibal himself. He deals firmly but moderately with mutinous troops (28.24–9), is chaste towards women (much to the surprise of his solicitous troops whose gift, a beautiful Spanish girl, he instead restores to her fiancé: 26.49–50), and generous to the defeated Carthaginians in spite of all their acts of bad faith (30.37).

Yet Livy does not invariably whitewash facts less flattering to the 'superior people'. The common folk at Rome (in contrast to their wise leaders) give way to unseemly panic on the news of the disasters at Lake Trasimene (22.7) and Cannae (22.54), and again when Hannibal marches on Rome in 211 (26.9, 10). Some young officers do the same after Cannae, until pulled into line by the teen-aged Scipio (22.53). And, despite first praising the patriotic generosity and exemplary honesty of army suppliers (23.49), Livy later records unsavoury frauds by some of them—even a concerted act of public thuggery aimed at disrupting their ensuing trial (25.3–4). The heroes, too, show human flaws. Marcellus, as commander in Sicily, condones a treacherous Roman massacre (24.39) and later plunders Syracuse so thoroughly for Rome's adornment that, Livy remarks severely, 'this was what first started the appreciation for Greek works of art, and the licence we now see in the widespread looting of all manner of things sacred and profane' (25.40). Marcellus' death in an avoidable ambush earns censure: 'he had blindly thrown himself, his colleague, and, one might almost say, the entire republic into a reckless situation, and that was not in keeping with his age—he was then more than sixty—or the caution one would have expected from a veteran commander' (27.27). Claudius Nero and Marcus Livius, who as consuls gloriously defeat the invading Barcid brother

Hasdrubal, later indulge in an absurd and demeaning feud when censors, to Livy's clear annoyance (29.37). Fabius the Delayer, cautious and bitter, unimaginatively opposes Scipio's brilliant plan of invading Africa while Hannibal remained in Italy (28.40–2); and Scipio himself proves scandalously indifferent to the criminal acts of his commandant Pleminius at Locri in southern Italy (29.16).

Enemies and friends in Hannibal's War

Enemies of Rome generally labour under a Livian cloud. Hostile generalizations dominate. Gauls are big and noisy but fickle in loyalty, lack staying power and have no patience or skill with sieges (21.25, 22.2, 27.48). The Campanians—more precisely, Capua and her satellite towns—share citizenship with the Romans but, dissatisfied, defect to Hannibal's side after Cannae, so they are depicted as criminally ungrateful and foolishly arrogant (23.6, 25.18), not to mention sunk in luxurious degeneracy (23.18).

The Carthaginians are the prime foe in *Hannibal's War*. They are treacherous (of course), vengeful, and cruel, as they and their leader demonstrate by a long sequence of bad behaviour. Hannibal treacherously attacks Saguntum and they stand by him. Roman troops who surrender on terms to a subordinate of Hannibal's are enslaved by the faithless general (22.6), he crucifies a local guide for misunderstanding his words (22.14), and takes vengeance on an Italian defector by burning the man's wife and children alive (24.45). In Africa, during a truce with Scipio, the Carthaginians treacherously attack and plunder a Roman supply convoy and follow this up by trying to drown Scipio's protesting envoys (30.24–5). Many allegations look like Roman exaggeration if not invention, but Livy presents them as simple facts.

Yet, despite war crimes real and alleged, Hannibal is a compelling and often attractive figure in *Hannibal's War*, as in later books. Even more than Scipio, he is the war's dominant individual. A famous character-portrait—as revealing of Livy as of Hannibal—introduces him at the age of 23 (21.4): first a lively description of the young man's appearance, leadership, and charismatic virtues, then a broadly vague list of 'enormous vices: pitiless cruelty, a treachery worse than Punic, no regard for truth, and no integrity', and so on—for the reader is not to think of the young Carthaginian as a virtual

Roman hero. But his energy and military genius are fully brought out (even if Livy has nothing like his predecessor the Greek historian Polybius' understanding of military technicalities), his piety is more than once illustrated—including not long after the character-portrayal (21.21–2)—and Livy takes care to mention his efforts to honour the slain Roman commanders Flaminius, Aemilius Paullus, Tiberius Gracchus, and Marcellus (22.7, 22.52, 25.17, 27.28). When final defeat looms, he becomes a positively sympathetic figure, giving a speech of world-weary wisdom to his younger opponent Scipio before the last battle and, after it, statesmanlike support to making peace (30.30–1, 37–8). Significantly, Scipio admires him as much as he admires Scipio (30.30).

When his interest is aroused Livy brings lesser figures to life too. Hannibal's youngest brother Mago is a vigorous, ruthless, but less talented version of the general. At Rome, there is the splendidly irascible Marcus Livius who, after sulking in the Senate for some years, is forced to become consul and win the battle of the Metaurus along with a fellow consul he despises; then, as censor later on with the same colleague, he makes a farce of their revered office by berating voters for fickleness and reducing almost the entire citizen body to the inferior rank of 'poll-tax payers'. Livy's dramatic account, brief as it is (30.12–15), of the beautiful Sophoniba, Carthaginian wife of two successive Numidian kings and forced into suicide to save her honour, would inspire much later literature, including a tragedy by Voltaire. Of all the minor figures, perhaps the most interesting is the Numidian prince Masinissa, first an enemy and then a friend to Rome, whose exciting adventures, valour, and passion win over not only Scipio but Livy himself.

Facts and flaws: Livy and history writing

All of Livy's literary sources (see below) had their own points of view, many of them held very pronounced biases and there were plenty of discrepancies small and large between them. As a result, his job was not at all straightforward. Two factors complicated matters further: Livy's genius was literary, not analytical, and he was a patriotic Roman.

His basic procedure was to follow one chosen source fairly closely for a section of narrative, but add—or change—various details based

on what he read in others. We can see this practice at work in many
sections of *Hannibal's War* where Polybius' history is also available.
Livy may, of course, have taken some of these blended accounts
ready-made from one or other earlier writer, but the variety of passages (not solely in *Hannibal's War*) where he stops to discuss con-
tradictions in his sources, and his own personal bafflement, indicates
that he did much of his own reading and compiling. The difficulty
for him is that he is not very good at source analysis.

His methods with sources are illustrated, for instance, in the
account of Hannibal's march to Italy (see also Appendix 2). Though
mainly Polybian, it includes Hannibal's famous dream, in which the
general meets a godlike youth who guides his steps amidst awe-
inspiring portents (21.22)—according to Cicero this tale went back
via the historian Coelius to Silenus (see below). Polybius merely
scoffs at sensationalist writers who equipped Hannibal with divine
pathfinders. Both Polybius' and other writers' versions are given,
unnamed, of how the Punic elephants crossed the River Rhône
(21.28); in the Alps, Livy accurately names several Gallic tribes not in
Polybius (21.31); and the well-known story of Hannibal using hot
vinegar to shatter fallen rocks blocking the army's path in the Alpine
pass (21.37) is from elsewhere too. When he goes on to discuss
Hannibal's army-strength on arriving in north Italy (21.38), he shows
that the reported figures varied wildly, with the lowest being 20,000
foot and 6,000 horse. This number, we know from Polybius, was what
Hannibal himself recorded in his Cape Lacinium inscription, but
Livy mentions neither Hannibal nor Polybius, nor the issue of
assessing evidence from, so to speak, the horse's mouth. Such
assessment seems simply not to occur to him. He prefers to discuss
(critically) the figures supplied by Cincius Alimentus, who had discussed the topic with Hannibal—but who, according to Livy, made
his own computing mistakes. As a result, our historian offers no final
figure at all.

Meeting other divergences in his sources, Livy has to keep deciding which version looks the most credible. This could come down to
a mere headcount, as seems to happen when he accepts the patriotic
Roman report that an embassy was sent to Hannibal during the siege
of Saguntum: he ignores Polybius' account dating the mission
earlier, to autumn 220 (21.6). Again, Roman tradition, presumably to
show the republic acting promptly on behalf of wronged allies, chose

to date the siege to 218, the first year of actual war; Livy accepts this too. Only later does he concede that a seven-month siege, a winter, a five-month march to Italy and then the north Italian campaign of late 218 were impossible to fit into one year. 'Either all these events took a shorter time, or else it was the capture of Saguntum, not the start of the siege, that took place at the beginning of the consular year [of 218]', he rather lamely concludes (21.15). Working out a more reasoned sequence of events is beyond his powers.

Sometimes he does advise his readers that there is trouble: for instance over Hannibal's army-strength in 218 and over his Alpine pass (21.38), over the Roman forces at Cannae (22.36), and about the route of Hannibal's march on Rome in 211 (26.11). His limited skill in deciding on the most credible version is illustrated again when he is faced with enormous discrepancies in the sources' figures for prisoners and booty from New Carthage—from the low numbers in Silenus (and Polybius, whom he does not mention) to the surreal fantasies of Valerius Antias (26.49). Livy feebly suggests a math-ematical compromise: 'figures halfway between the extremes seem closest to the truth.'

He himself perpetuates some falsehoods despite having the means to correct them. He reports the young Hannibal going to Spain, both when aged 9, with his father in 237 (21.1), and in 224 to serve under brother-in-law Hasdrubal (21.3). The reason for this second report is literary: to allow Hanno the Great to deliver a dramatic prophecy of the catastrophic war to come. Much later, Livy goes back to the original date, following Polybius (30.37). Similarly but less excus-ably, he (like his Roman predecessors) could read, in Polybius at least, the verbatim Greek text of the treaty Hannibal made in 215 with Macedon; but he chooses instead (23.34) to purvey a hostile distorted version found in some Roman predecessors—again maybe on a headcount.

Military technicalities are not a Livian strong point either, and he never lets them stand in the way of telling a story. All save one of Hannibal's elephants were dead before Cannae but, when the general follows up his victory by attacking places in Campania, elephants briefly turn up to assist (23.18). Accustomed to armies in battle having a centre and two wings, Livy provides each army at the Metaurus with a quite imaginary and therefore inactive centre (27.48). His version of Zama (30.32–4) adapts Polybius' account but contradicts various items in it; presumably he is drawing from another account or accounts, but he does not appreciate the resulting blend of inconsistency and incoherence.

Despite such faults, a blanket condemnation of Livy as a historian would be mistaken. With all his sources, Latin and Greek, written in cumbrous papyrus book-rolls (like his own), with no easy system of reference or indexing (in fact, with virtually no system at all), and light largely restricted to daytime, his sheer output is impressive, and that is the least of what he achieved. Often his narrative is admirable, including sections where he may be drawing closely on parts of Polybius that we no longer have: for instance, the gripping account of political machinations and upheavals at Syracuse in Books 24–5, and the complicatedly adventurous struggles of Masinissa with his Numidian rival Syphax (29.29–33). In certain places, Livy's information looks better than Polybius': for example, the casualties at Cannae (22.49), and Naraggara—a genuine and suitable place in ancient North Africa—as the name of the town where Scipio camped before the battle of Zama (30.29). Other invaluable information abounds: crucial details of administration, Senate business, troop levies, elections and appointments, religious matters, censuses, finance, and even economics (24.11 and 28.45, for instance)—presumably from Roman sources, for few are in Polybius.

Livy's sources

Official chronicles and lists, historical accounts in Greek and Latin, and other sources all provided Livy directly or indirectly with his information. The pontifical annals, which yearly recorded important religious and secular events down to the later second century, had since been published in eighty books as the *Annales Maximi* ('Principal Yearbooks'). From 200 BC on, literary history was written, beginning with Quintus Fabius Pictor, one of Fabius the Delayer's kinsmen, who paid much attention, naturally, to modern times. His close contemporary was Lucius Cincius Alimentus, who had fought against Hannibal, been taken prisoner late in the war, and enjoyed some conversations with the general; his Roman history again came down to his own times. They and several others wrote in Greek, not only because Greek historians were models, but probably also in order to put 'correct' views of Rome's history to the international, and therefore Greek-reading, educated community. They could take for granted that educated Romans also read Greek.

Marcus Porcius Cato, another war veteran, initiated history writing in Latin, narrating from the earliest origins down to his own old age, and Latin now became the norm for Roman historians. Another important predecessor of Livy's—he cites him several times—was Lucius Coelius Antipater, the first Roman to write a historical monograph, soon after 120 and on the Second Punic War at that. Coelius drew on earlier accounts, not just Roman authors but also, for instance, Hannibal's friend Silenus. Two voluminous first-century annalists, Claudius Quadrigarius and Valerius Antias, are also often cited by Livy (if sometimes critically). It is often held that these more recent historians were Livy's real authorities, along with Polybius; supposedly, he mentions earlier ones only if Coelius, Quadrigarius, or Antias did—this because he cites Cincius and Fabius only once each (21.38, 22.7). But he does so with Polybius as well; and a remark in 29.14 does imply he consulted 'writers living close to the time' of the events. Certainly the later authors cannot have provided him with most of his annalistic information: Coelius' history was in seven books; Quadrigarius, who began his work with the Gauls' sack of Rome in 390, was at Cannae by Book 5; and Antias (starting in legendary times) reached the year 137 in his Book 23— while Livy got there, as the epitomes show, only in Book 56. All that remains, though, of these historians' extensive output is a few references or quotations in later authors, including Livy. (Cornelius Nepos, a friend of Cicero and Catullus, consulted both Roman and pro-Hannibalic sources for his uneven thirteen-paragraph *Life of Hannibal*, but Livy does not use it.)[6]

Pro-Carthaginian writers included Hannibal himself. At Cape Lacinium (Capo Colonna in Calabria), he set up what Livy notes as 'a large inscription, written in both Punic and Greek, which listed his achievements' (28.46). All that we know from it are some troop-numbers: the forces he stationed in Spain and in Africa early in 218, and those he had on reaching Cisalpine Gaul late that year. So it may have been a fairly detailed narrative, but we cannot be certain. He was accompanied to war by two Greek friends, Sosylus of Sparta—

---

[6] The early Roman historians are brilliantly treated by E. Badian in *Latin Historians*, ed. T. A. Dorey (London, 1966), 1–38.

who had taught him Greek, according to Nepos—and Silenus, a Sicilian. Both remained with him 'as long as fortune permitted' (writes Nepos rather obscurely) and both later wrote 'Hannibal-histories', Sosylus devoting seven books to his. Neither confined himself to Hannibal's own campaigns; a papyrus fragment of Sosylus, for instance, narrates a naval battle in Spanish waters. As eyewitnesses, and with access to participants and other eyewitnesses, their reliability was high but need not be romanticized: it is hard to imagine either depicting their friend and patron unfavourably, or being partial to the Roman side on any major issue, such as responsibility for the war.

Among Livy's sources, Polybius (*c.*200–118) is a special case. Not only was he a great historian and extensively used by our author, but much of his forty-book *Histories* survives and thus, uniquely, allows comparisons. A leading citizen of the Achaean League in the Peloponnese, Polybius had to spend seventeen adult years (167–150) as a privileged hostage at Rome. He found the Romans and their political system almost wholly admirable, and wrote his analytical history to explain to Greek readers how, in little more than half a century, Rome had won herself unchallengeable dominance over the Mediterranean world. The work was a 'universal history' of the Mediterranean world from 264 to 146—originally from 220 to 167, but then chronologically extended in both directions. Only Books 1–5, down to Cannae, exist complete, but a very large number of extracts, long and short, survive from the others (many extracts were made in tenth-century Constantinople).

Experienced in military and political life, widely travelled, a rationalist interested in philosophy, geography, and practical mechanics, and pugnaciously certain of his own merits, Polybius narrates military and diplomatic events judiciously as a rule, admitting different points of view and by no means hostile towards the enemies of Rome. But his Mediterranean scope means that he includes relatively few of the internal political, administrative, religious, and other events which bring the Roman republic to life in Livy (though there are rather more of these in Polybius' later books, on the Rome he knew personally). Livy used his work extensively, particularly on military events, even if the one mention of him in *Hannibal's War* is the famously tepid 'by no means a source to be disregarded' (30.45).

Livy's achievement is to present, along with the detailed historical record, a gallery of unforgettable men and women, all slightly larger than life but each with very human touches, and a long series of memorably told episodes—from Hannibal crossing the Alps to the drama of Sophoniba. It is not Polybius' methodical telling of events that has seized imaginations and inspired creative artists for two millennia, but Livy's literary genius. He provides a powerful panorama of societies in war which, faults and all, makes *Hannibal's War* one of the most outstanding narratives in ancient historiography.

NOTE ON THE TEXT AND TRANSLATION

The text on which the translation is based is that of the Teubner editions of Dorey and Walsh (see Select Bibliography). There are a few places where I have diverged from this, and they are to be found in Appendix 1.

A translator of a Latin text inevitably finds that he or she must steer a course between literal translation and paraphrase, and I have attempted to make the English readable for the Latinless reader, while staying close enough to the text to help those with some Latin to understand the original. But the fate of translations is always to be too literal for some readers, and too free for others. For those trying to follow the Latin I have used the sigla † and <. . .> to indicate respectively where the text is thought to be uncertain or lacunose, but I have not indicated where the two editors have supplemented the text if I feel the supplements are certain, or close enough to what Livy must have written for them not to affect the translation.

I have not retained Livy's spelling of place names where another spelling is more familiar and generally accepted (e.g. 'Rhegium' instead of Livy's 'Regium', 'Lemnos' for his 'Lemnus', 'Balearic' for 'Baliaric') and I have standardized where the editors/manuscripts give different spellings of the same name (e.g. Centumalus/ Centimalus).

I have consulted numerous other translations, including the various Budé and Loeb editions, de Sélincourt's very readable Penguin, and Canon Roberts's elegant Everyman's Library version. Sometimes I have coincidentally arrived at the same, or a similar, translation as one or more of these translators, but on other occasions I have merely resisted the temptation to alter what I believed to be the *mot juste* simply because I did not arrive at it first.

J. C. Y.

A debt of gratitude is owed to a number of people. In the first place we both offer our thanks to Judith Luna, general editor of the series, for her unfailing efficiency and courtesy in seeing this project through from beginning to end, and to Elizabeth Stratford for her remarkably thorough copy-editing of the volume. The translator also expresses his gratitude to Laura Gagné, his research assistant at the University of Ottawa, for various forms of assistance in the project's early days, for her help with proofreading, and especially for her compilation of the index.

J. C. Y., D. H.

SELECT BIBLIOGRAPHY

Texts

T. Livius, *Ab Urbe Condita*, Libri XXI–XXII, ed. T. A. Dorey (Teubner: Leipzig, 1971).

T. Livius, *Ab Urbe Condita*, Libri XXIII–XXV, ed. T. A. Dorey (Teubner: Leipzig, 1976).

T. Livius, *Ab Urbe Condita*, Libri XXVI–XXVII, ed. P. G. Walsh (Teubner: Leipzig, 1989).

T. Livius, *Ab Urbe Condita*, Libri XXVIII–XXX, ed. P. G. Walsh (Teubner: Leipzig, 1986).

Translations

Livy: The War with Hannibal, trans. Aubrey de Sélincourt (Harmondsworth, 1965).

Livy: The History of Rome, trans. Canon W. M. Roberts, 6 vols., Everyman's Library (London, 1912–31); vols. 3–4 comprise Books XXI–XXX.

Livy: Books XXI–XXII, ed. and trans. B. O. Foster, Loeb Classical Library (Cambridge, Mass., 1929).

Livy: Books XXIII–XXV, ed. and trans. Frank Gardner Moore, Loeb Classical Library (Cambridge, Mass., 1940).

Livy: Books XXVI–XXVII, ed. and trans. Frank Gardner Moore, Loeb Classical Library (Cambridge, Mass., 1943; revised and reprinted 1950).

Livy: Books XXVIII–XXX, ed. and trans. Frank Gardner Moore, Loeb Classical Library (Cambridge, Mass., 1949).

There are also useful French translations (with extensive notes) for each of the books of this decade in the Budé series of the Presses Universitaires de France. [At this point (January, 2005), only Books 22, 24, and 30 have yet to appear.]

Commentaries

The best complete commentary on Books XXI–XXX is still that by W. Weissenborn and H. J. Müller, in German: it forms vols. IV–VI of their complete text and commentary on Livy (10 vols., various edns., Berlin, 1878–94). Selected English commentaries are:

Livy Book XXI, ed. P. G. Walsh (Bristol Classical Press, 1997; originally published 1973).

Livy Book XXII, ed. John Pyper (Oxford, 1919).

Livy Book XXII, ed. W. W. Capes and J. E. Melhuish (Macmillan, 1890).

Livy Book XXII, ed. John Thompson and F. G. Plaistowe (University Tutorial Press, London; reprinted Bristol Classical Press, 1991).

Livy Books XXII–XXIV, ed. G. C. Macaulay (Macmillan, 1885).

Livy Book XXVII, ed. S. G. Campbell (Cambridge, 1913).

Livy Book XXIX, ed. T. A. Dorey and C. W. F. Lydall (Kenneth Mason: Havant, Hampshire, 1968; reprinted University Tutorial Press, London, 1971).

Livy, Book XXX, ed. H. E. Butler and H. H. Scullard (Bradda Books, Letchworth, 1939; 6th edn., Methuen, London, 1953).

Modern studies

Broughton, T. R. S., *The Magistrates of the Roman Republic*, vols. i–ii, with the collaboration of Marcia L. Patterson (New York, 1951, 1952); vol. iii, *Supplement* (Atlanta, 1986).

Brunt, P. A., *Italian Manpower, 225 BC–AD 14* (Oxford, 1971).

Cambridge Ancient History, 1st edn.: vols. 7 and 8 (Cambridge, 1928, 1930).

Cambridge Ancient History, 2nd edn.: vol. 7 part 2, vol. 8 (Cambridge, 1989).

Cambridge History of Classical Literature, ed. P. E. Easterling, E. J. Kenny, et al., 2 vols. (Cambridge 1982, 1985).

Caven, B., *The Punic Wars* (London, 1980).

Connolly, P., *Greece and Rome at War* (London and New York, 1981).

Cornell, T., Rankov, B., and Sabin, P. (eds.), *The Second Punic War: A Reappraisal* (London, 1996).

Daly, G., *Cannae: The Experience of Battle* (London and New York, 2003).

Decret, F., *Carthage ou l'empire du mer* (new edn., Paris, 1977).

De Sanctis, G., *Storia dei Romani*, 2nd edn., vol. 3, parts 1 and 2 (Florence, 1967, 1968).

Dorey, T. A. (ed.), *Livy* (London, 1971).

Erdkamp, P., *Hunger and the Sword: Warfare and Food Supply in Roman Republican Wars (264–30 BC)* (Amsterdam, 1998).

Fornara, C. W., *The Nature of History in Ancient Greece and Rome* (Berkeley, Los Angeles, London, 1983).

Frederiksen, M. W., *Campania*, ed. N. Purcell (Rome, 1984).

Goldsworthy, A., *The Punic Wars* (London, 2000; reissued in paperback as *The Fall of Carthage: The Punic Wars*, 2003).

—— *Cannae* (London, 2003).

Harris, W. V., *War and Imperialism in Republican Rome, 327–70 BC* (Oxford, 1979).

Hoyos, B. D., *Unplanned Wars: The Origins of the First and Second Punic Wars* (Berlin and New York, 1998).

—— *Hannibal's Dynasty: Power and Politics in the Western Mediterranean, 247–183 BC* (London and New York, 2003; paperback, with maps, 2005).

Keppie, L., *The Making of the Roman Army* (London, 1984).

Lancel, S., *Carthage* (Paris, 1992; English translation as *Carthage: A History*, London, 1995).

—— *Hannibal* (Paris, 1995; English translation, London, 1999).

Lazenby, J., *Hannibal's War: A Military History* (Warminster, 1978).

—— *The First Punic War: A Military History* (London, 1995).

Lloyd, A. B. (ed.), *Battle in Antiquity* (London and Swansea, 1996).

Luce, T. J., *Livy: The Composition of his History* (Princeton, 1979).

Nicolet, C. (ed.), *Rome et la conquête du monde méditerranéen*, 2 vols. (Paris, 1977, 1978).

Picard, G. C., *Daily Life at Carthage in the Time of Hannibal* (London, 1964; original French edition, 1958; revised German edn. (with C. Picard), *Karthago: Leben und Kultur*, Berlin, 1983).

—— *Hannibal* (Paris, 1967).

—— and Picard, C., *The Life and Death of Carthage* (London, 1968).

Scullard, H. H., *The Elephant in the Greek and Roman World* (London, 1974).

—— *Scipio Africanus: Soldier and Politician* (London, 1970).

Seibert, J., *Forschungen zu Hannibal* (Darmstadt, 1993).

—— *Hannibal* (Darmstadt, 1993).

Sekunda, N., et al., *Republican Roman Army 200–104 BC* (London, 1996).

Starr, C. G., *The Beginnings of Imperial Rome: Rome in the Mid-Republic* (Ann Arbor, 1980).

Tränkle, H., *Livius und Polybios* (Basle, 1977).

Walbank, F. W., *A Historical Commentary on Polybius*, 3 vols. (Oxford, 1957, 1967, 1979).

—— *Polybius* (Berkeley, Los Angeles and London, 1972).

Walsh, P. G., *Livy: His Historical Aims and Methods* (Cambridge, 1963).

Warmington, B. H., *Carthage* (Harmondsworth, 1964).

Wise, T., *Armies of the Carthaginian Wars, 265–146 BC* (London, 1982).

Wiseman, T. P., *Roman Drama and Roman History* (Exeter, 1998).

Further reading in Oxford World's Classics

Livy, *The Dawn of the Roman Empire (Books 31–40)*, trans. J. C. Yardley, introduction by Waldemar Heckel.

—— *The Rise of Rome (Books 1–5)*, trans. T. J. Luce.

Plutarch, *Roman Lives*, trans. Robin Waterfield, ed. Philip A. Stadter.

A CHRONOLOGY OF EVENTS

All dates are BC. (II) means consul for the second time, (III) consul for the third time, etc.

814   Carthage founded by Dido (traditional date).

753   Rome founded by Romulus (traditional date).

550s–396 Dominance of the Magonid family at Carthage.

509   Expulsion of the kings from Rome; first consuls elected. First Rome–Carthage treaty (Polybius' date).

480–275 Recurrent wars between Carthage and Sicilian Greeks.

390   Sack of Rome by Gauls (traditional date; real date 387).

348   Second Rome–Carthage treaty (probable date).

280   Pyrrhus of Epirus arrives in Italy to aid Tarentum against the Romans.

278   Pyrrhus arrives in Sicily to aid the Greeks against the Carthaginians.

276   Pyrrhus leaves Sicily (leaves Italy 275).

276/5–215 Rule of Hiero II at Syracuse (king from 264).

264   Outbreak of First Punic War.

256–255 Roman invasion of North Africa under Regulus, ultimately defeated.

247   Birth of Hannibal, eldest son of Hamilcar Barca. Hamilcar appointed general in Sicily.

241   (10 March) Romans defeat Carthaginians at Aegates Islands; peace treaty negotiated for Carthage by Hamilcar.

241–238 'Truceless War' of rebel mercenaries and African subjects against Carthage; war won by Hamilcar.

237   Romans seize Sardinia, impose new indemnity on Carthage. Hamilcar's expedition to southern Spain; Hannibal accompanies him.

237–228 Hamilcar builds new Punic province in Spain.

232   Flaminius' law granting land in northern Italy to poor Romans.

229–228 First Illyrian War. Roman 'protectorate' established over coastal Greek cities in Illyria.

early 228	Hamilcar killed in combat; Hasdrubal, his son-in-law, is elected the new general.
226(?)	Hasdrubal founds (New) Carthage, modern Cartagena.
225	Hasdrubal makes Ebro agreement with Rome. Gallic invasion of Italy; defeated at Telamon, Etruria.
224–222	Roman subjugation of Cisalpine Gaul.
221	Romans intervene in Istria (northern Adriatic). Hasdrubal is assassinated; Hannibal is elected new general.
221–220	Hannibal campaigns victoriously in central and northern Spain.
220	Autumn: Roman envoys sent to New Carthage urge Hannibal to keep the Ebro agreement and not molest Saguntum; Hannibal accuses the Romans of improper interference.
219	*Consuls: Marcus Livius, Lucius Aemilius Paullus.* Hannibal besieges Saguntum and captures it in eighth month of the siege (April–Nov.?). Second Illyrian War waged by Rome.
218	*Consuls: Publius Cornelius Scipio, Tiberius Sempronius Longus.* Spring: Roman embassy to Carthage declares war. May: Hannibal sets out from New Carthage to subdue north-east Spain and then march to Italy. Aug.(?): the consul Publius Scipio sets out for Spain. Late Oct.–early Nov.: Hannibal crosses the Alps into Cisalpine Gaul; skirmish with the consul Scipio at the River Ticinus. Gnaeus Scipio's operations in north-east Spain. *c.*21 Dec.: battle of the Trebia.
217	*Consuls: Gnaeus Servilius Geminus, Gaius Flaminius (II). Consul suffect (replacing Flaminius): Marcus Atilius Regulus.* 22 June: battle of Lake Trasimene. Fabius Maximus is elected dictator, Minucius as his master of horse (then co-dictator). Hannibal marches into southern Italy, then into Campania. Fabius' entrapment of Hannibal circumvented; Carthaginian army returns to Apulia. Operations around Gereonium; Minucius saved from disaster by Fabius. Gnaeus and Publius Scipio's campaign in north-east Spain; victory near Hibera.
216	*Consuls: Lucius Aemilius Paullus (II), Gaius Terentius Varro.* Lengthy Roman preparations for decisive blow against Hannibal. 2 Aug.: battle of Cannae. Hannibal re-enters Campania; defection of Capua. Hannibal captures Nuceria and Acerrae; attacks Nola, Naples, and other cities unsuccessfully. Consul-elect Lucius Postumius Albinus and army annihilated in Cisalpine Gaul.

215   *Consuls: Tiberius Sempronius Gracchus, Marcus Claudius Marcellus (II; abdicated). Consul suffect: Quintus Fabius Maximus (III).* Hannibal operates in Campania against Casilinum, Cumae, and Nola. Hannibal makes an alliance with Philip V of Macedon; the Romans capture Philip's envoys. Scipio brothers' victory at River Ebro in Spain. Hiero II of Syracuse dies, aged 90; succeeded by his grandson Hieronymus.

214   *Consuls: Quintus Fabius Maximus (IV), Marcus Claudius Marcellus (III).* Hannibal operates in Campania against Puteoli and Nola. Tiberius Gracchus defeats Hanno at River Calor in Samnium. Assassination of Hieronymus; political strife at Syracuse. Marcellus in Sicily captures Leontini. Syracuse allies with Carthage. Roman operations in Illyria against Philip V of Macedon.

213   *Consuls: Quintus Fabius Maximus (junior), Tiberius Sempronius Gracchus (II).* Arpi in Apulia recaptured by Fabius. Roman operations in Sicily; Marcellus and Appius Claudius Pulcher begin siege of Syracuse by land and sea.

212   *Consuls: Appius Claudius Pulcher, Quintus Fulvius Flaccus (III).* Hannibal wins over Tarentum, Metapontum, Heraclea, and Thurii. Consuls begin siege of Capua. Hanno is defeated at Beneventum. Gracchus is killed in ambush. First battle of Herdonea. Marcellus captures Syracuse; Archimedes killed. The Scipio brothers carry out new operations in Spain; restoration of Saguntum.

211   *Consuls: Publius Sulpicius Galba, Gnaeus Fulvius Centumalus.* Hannibal's march on Rome; Capua capitulates to Fulvius Flaccus. The Scipio brothers defeated and killed in southern Spain. Roman remnants retreat to River Ebro under Lucius Marcius; Gaius Claudius Nero sent out to take command. Aetolians ally themselves with Rome; Roman operations in Illyria. Roman and Carthaginian operations in Sicily.

210   *Consuls: Marcus Valerius Laevinus, Marcus Claudius Marcellus (IV).* Marcellus retakes Salapia in Apulia. Second battle of Herdonea; death of the proconsul Centumalus. Indecisive battle of Numistro between Hannibal and Marcellus. Laevinus captures Agrigentum in Sicily. Operations in central Greece and the Aegean. Publius Scipio, aged 24, appointed commander for Spain.

209   *Consuls: Quintus Fabius Maximus (V), Quintus Fulvius*

Flaccus (IV). Twelve Latin colonies refuse further contributions to war effort. Operations of Hannibal and Marcellus in southern Italy. Fabius retakes Tarentum. Scipio captures New Carthage.

208   *Consuls: Marcus Claudius Marcellus (V), Titus Quinctius Crispinus*. Marcellus killed, Crispinus mortally wounded in an ambush near Venusia. Further operations in southern Italy. Battle of Baecula in Spain: Scipio defeats Hasdrubal, brother of Hannibal. Hasdrubal departs for Italy.

207   *Consuls: Gaius Claudius Nero, Marcus Livius (Salinator) (II)*. Hasdrubal enters Cisalpine Gaul, advances southwards. Hannibal's indecisive movements around southern Italy. 23 June: consuls defeat and kill Hasdrubal at battle of River Metaurus.

206   *Consuls: Quintus Caecilius Metellus, Lucius Veturius Philo*. Indecisive small operations in southern Italy. Scipio defeats the Carthaginians at Ilipa; the Carthaginian forces abandon Spain. Mutiny of Roman troops at Sucro is quelled by Scipio. Struggles of Masinissa against Syphax in Numidia. The Aetolians make peace with Philip V.

205   *Consuls: Publius Cornelius Scipio, Publius Licinius Crassus*. Mago lands in Liguria with an army. Scipio in Sicily prepares an invasion army for Africa. Scipio captures Locri, in southern Italy, despite Hannibal's efforts. Atrocities of Pleminius at Locri. Revolt of Mandonius and Indibilis in north-east Spain is defeated. Peace of Phoenice between Rome and Macedon.

204   *Consuls: Marcus Cornelius Cethegus, Publius Sempronius Tuditanus*. Hannibal confined to part of Bruttium. Scipio lands in Africa; alliance with Masinissa. Negotiations outside Utica between Scipio, Hasdrubal son of Gisgo, and Syphax.

203   *Consuls: Gnaeus Servilius Caepio, Gaius Servilius Geminus*. Scipio attacks enemy camps outside Utica and destroys their armies. Late May/early June: battle of the Great Plains; Scipio is victorious over Hasdrubal and Syphax. 23 June: Masinissa captures Syphax. Masinissa captures Cirta; the tragedy of Sophoniba. Scipio recognizes Masinissa as king of all Numidia. Carthaginians agree to Scipio's peace-terms; Senate at Rome ratifies them. Carthaginians renew hostilities

in anticipation of Hannibal's return. Hannibal lands at Leptis on Emporia coast. Death of Quintus Fabius Maximus, the Delayer.

202   *Consuls: Tiberius Claudius Nero, Marcus Servilius Geminus.* Roman and Carthaginian armies in Africa move inland towards Naraggara. (18?) Oct.: meeting between Hannibal and Scipio. 19 Oct.: battle of 'Zama' (actually near Sicca). 17 Dec.: defeat of Syphax's son Vermina. Winter 202–201: Carthaginians accept Scipio's terms.

201   *Consuls: Gnaeus Cornelius Lentulus, Publius Aelius Paetus.* Peace terms ratified at Rome. Scipio returns to hold a triumph; accorded celebratory *cognomen* Africanus.

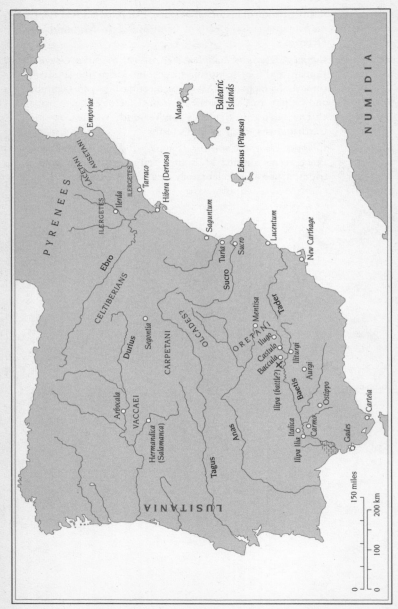

MAP I. Spain at the time of Hannibal's war

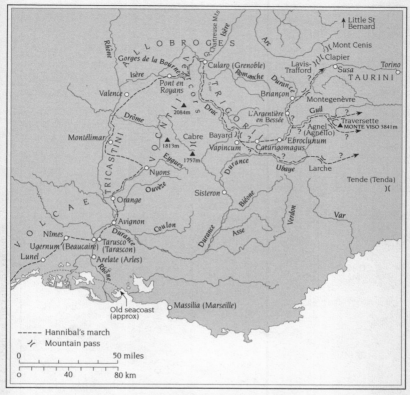

MAP 2. Hannibal's route over the Alps

MAP 3. Italy and the islands during Hannibal's war

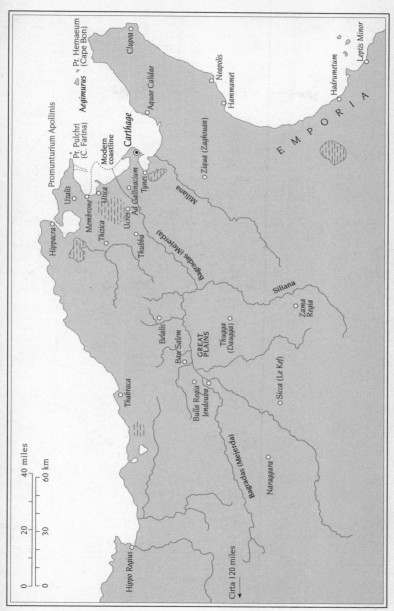

MAP 4. North Africa at the time of Hannibal's war

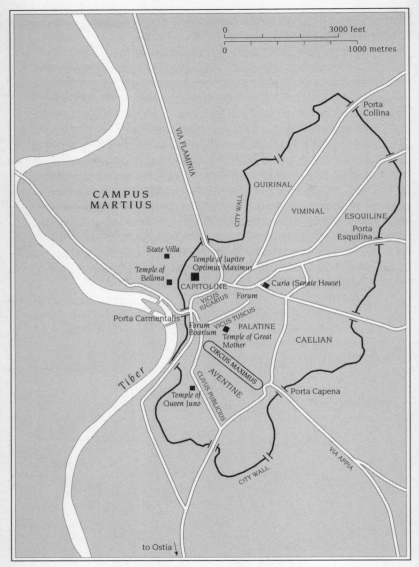

MAP 5. Rome in the third century BC

HANNIBAL'S WAR

BOOK TWENTY-ONE

1. In a preface to just a section of my work I am able to make the claim that most historians have made at the beginning of their entire opus: I can say that I am going to provide an account of the most momentous war ever fought. This is the war the Carthaginians, led by Hannibal, waged against the Roman people. For no other states or nations that have come into conflict had greater resources than these two peoples, nor had the combatants themselves ever been stronger or more powerful than they were at that time. They also brought to the struggle strategies and tactics familiar to each other, both having had experience of them in the First Punic War; and so changeable were the fortunes of the war, and so evenly matched the fighting, that it was the eventual victors who came closer to ruin. In addition, the conflict was marked by the hatred the adversaries felt for each other which was almost greater than their might. The Romans were indignant that a vanquished people was presuming to attack its victors, the Carthaginians because they thought that the authority wielded over them in defeat was high-handed and rapacious.

There is a story that Hannibal, at about the age of nine, was in a boyish fashion trying to coax his father Hamilcar into taking him to Spain. Hamilcar, who had finished off the war in Africa and was on the point of taking his army across to Spain, was offering sacrifice. He brought Hannibal to the altar and there made him touch the sacred objects and swear to make himself an enemy of the Roman people at the earliest possible opportunity.* Hamilcar was a man of great pride, and the loss of Sicily and Sardinia vexed him greatly. He thought that Sicily had been ceded only because the Carthaginians had too quickly abandoned hope, and that Sardinia had been dishonestly filched from them by the Romans—who had even gone so far as to impose an indemnity on them—during the upheavals in Africa.*

2. Such were the concerns that beset Hamilcar. For the five years of the African War (which closely followed the peace treaty with Rome), and then for the nine years he spent extending Punic authority in Spain, his conduct made it evident that he had ambitions transcending the war he was fighting.* Had he lived longer, the

Carthaginians would clearly have launched under Hamilcar the invasion that they actually launched under the command of Hannibal.

Hamilcar's timely death, and the fact that Hannibal was just a boy, deferred hostilities, and in the interval between father and son Hasdrubal held office for some eight years. Hasdrubal had initially attracted Hamilcar's interest, they say, by his youthful good looks, and was subsequently invited to become his son-in-law on the basis of other qualities, no doubt intellectual. Thanks to being Hamilcar's son-in-law, he had risen to power through the influence of the Barca faction—a faction which exercised a considerable degree of influence amongst the armed forces and Carthaginian commons—and certainly against the wishes of the Carthaginian establishment. Hasdrubal's administration was characterized by diplomacy rather than force; eschewing armed conflict, he extended the authority of Carthage more by fostering relations with chieftains, and by enlisting the support of fresh tribes through friendship with their leaders. Peace, however, afforded him no more security: he was assassinated in public by a barbarian incensed over his execution of his master. The killer was caught by bystanders, but his expression remained that of a man who had made good his escape. Even under torture, the look on his face was such that he actually appeared to be smiling, his joy surmounting his suffering.

Because Hasdrubal had possessed an amazing talent for winning over tribes and attaching them to his empire, the Roman people had renewed their treaty with him. The basis of the agreement was that the limit of the authority of each would be the River Ebro, and that Saguntum, lying between the domains of the two peoples, would retain its independence.*

3. There was no doubt about who would succeed Hasdrubal. The soldiers' choice came first—the young Hannibal had been immediately carried into the general's tent where the men noisily and unanimously acclaimed him as commander—and the endorsement of the commons followed.

When Hannibal was barely an adolescent Hasdrubal had summoned him by letter,* and the matter of his future had even been discussed in the Carthaginian senate. The Barca faction insisted that Hannibal be familiarized with military life, and that he succeed to his father's authority. But Hanno, who led the opposing faction,* demurred. 'Hasdrubal seems to be making a reasonable request,' he said, 'but I am against granting what he is asking for.' Hanno caught everyone's attention, such an inconsistent comment taking them all by surprise.

'Hasdrubal thinks that he offered up the good looks of his youth for the gratification of Hannibal's father, and that now it's fair for him to take the son's in return,' he said. 'However, it is most inappropriate for us to subject our young soldiers to the sexual appetite of their officers as though that were military training. Or is this our fear, that Hamilcar's son must wait too long to look upon the father's unlimited authority and apparently regal power, and that we too late become slaves to the son of that *king*, whose son-in-law was left our armies as a bequest? No, in *my* opinion, that young man should be kept at home and taught to live in obedience to the laws and the magistrates, on an equal footing with everyone else. Otherwise, this small flame may one day start a huge conflagration.'

4. A small number, including all the most right-thinking men, agreed with Hanno, but, as usual, the bigger party triumphed over the better.

Hannibal was sent to Spain where he won the hearts of the entire army immediately upon his arrival. The older soldiers thought that a young Hamilcar had been brought back to them; they saw that same dynamism in his expression, the same forcefulness in his eyes, the same facial expression and features. Then, in a short while, he saw to it that his father counted for little in winning him support. Never was one character so amenable to the two extremes of obedience and command, and as a result one would have found it hard to tell whether he was better liked by the commander or by the army. There was no one whom Hasdrubal preferred to put in command when a gallant or enterprising feat was called for, while there was no other officer under whom the rank and file had more confidence and enterprise.

Hannibal was possessed of enormous daring in facing dangers, and enormous resourcefulness when in the midst of those dangers. He could be physically exhausted or mentally cowed by no hardship. He had the ability to withstand heat and cold alike; his eating and drinking depended on the requirements of nature, not pleasure. His times for being awake and asleep were not determined by day or night. Only the time which he had left from discharging his duties was given to sleep, and it was not brought on by a soft bed or silence—many often observed him lying on the ground, amidst the sentry-posts and pickets, wrapped in a soldier's cloak. His dress was no better than that of his comrades, but his weapons and horses marked him out. On horse or foot he was by far the best soldier; the first to enter battle, he was the last to leave once battle was joined.

The man's great virtues were matched by his enormous vices: pitiless cruelty, a treachery worse than Punic, no regard for truth, and no integrity, no fear of the gods or respect for an oath, and no scruples. With such a combination of virtues and vices, Hannibal served under Hasdrubal's command for three years, overlooking nothing needing to be done or seen by a man who was to be a great leader.

5. From the day Hannibal was declared commander it was as if Italy had been decreed his area of responsibility, and the war with Rome his assignment. He thought there should be no delay in case, like his father Hamilcar, and Hasdrubal after him, he too be over-taken by some accident while he wavered. He therefore determined to launch an attack on Saguntum. Because there was no doubt that such an attack would elicit an armed response from the Romans, he first led his army into the territory of the Olcades, a people south of the Ebro,* and more aptly described as being in the zone of the Carthaginians rather than under their control. By doing this Hannibal could appear not to have specifically targeted the Saguntines but to have been drawn into that conflict in the course of events, that is, in the conquest of neighbouring tribes and annexation of their territories.

Hannibal took by storm and pillaged the rich city of Cartala, the tribal capital, and the fear this inspired drove the smaller com-munities to capitulate and accept the imposition of an indemnity. The triumphant army, rich with booty, was led back to winter in New Carthage. There, by generously dividing up the booty and scrupulously discharging any arrears in pay, Hannibal consolidated the loyalty of all, citizens and allies alike, and in the early spring he marched on the Vaccaei.* Hermandica and Arbocala, cities of the Vaccaei, were taken by storm, but there was prolonged resistance from Arbocala, thanks to the townspeople's courage and their large population. The refugees from Hermandica then joined forces with exiles of the Olcades, the tribe that had been crushed the previous summer. They roused the Carpetani to action and, not far from the River Tagus, launched an attack on Hannibal as he was returning from the Vaccaei, throwing into confusion his column which was heavily burdened with plunder.

Hannibal refused to engage. He pitched camp on the river-bank, and as soon as all was calm and silent on the side of the enemy he forded the river. He then extended his entrenchment in such a way as to leave the enemy room to cross, for he had determined to attack them as they made their way over. As soon as they saw that the enemy had entered the water, the cavalry were under orders to attack their column while it was hampered with the crossing, and Hannibal deployed his elephants—there were forty of them—on the bank. With supplementary detachments from the Olcades and Vaccaei, the Carpetani were 100,000 strong, an unbeatable army were the battle fought on a level field. They were ferocious by nature and confident in their superior numbers; and, believing the enemy had fallen back from fear, they thought that the only thing impeding this victory was the fact that a river lay between them. They raised a shout and, without awaiting anyone's command, all rushed into the river at the point closest to them. From the other bank a huge contingent of horsemen was sent into the river, and the engagement that ensued midstream was by no means evenly matched. The infantryman, unsteady on his feet and wary of the ford, could easily have been thrown off balance even by the random charges of a cavalryman without weapons. As it was, the cavalrymen could move freely themselves, and had free use of their weapons, and were fighting, at close quarters or at a distance, from mounts that remained stable even in the midst of the swirling waters.

Most of the enemy were swept away by the river; some were borne into their foes by the churning current and then trampled under by the elephants. The rearmost could return more safely to their side of the river but, as they tried to regroup after their alarm, and before they could recover from their desperate panic, Hannibal entered the stream with a company in battle formation, driving the enemy in flight from the bank. He ravaged their fields and, within a few days, accepted the surrender of the Carpetani, as well. And now everything south of the Ebro was under Carthaginian control—except Saguntum.

6. To this point there was no war with Saguntum, but already

quarrels were being fomented between her and her neighbours, the Turdetani in particular, in order to provoke a war.* The Turdetani were receiving assistance from the instigator of the conflict, and it was clear that the goal was not a fair settlement but violent confrontation. And so a delegation was sent to Rome by the Saguntines with an appeal for assistance for a war that was clearly on the horizon. Publius Cornelius Scipio and Tiberius Sempronius Longus, the consuls in Rome at the time, brought the delegates into the Senate and opened the matter up for official debate, and it was decided that ambassadors be dispatched to Spain to examine the plight of the allies. If they felt the situation warranted it, the ambassadors were to issue a formal caution to Hannibal to leave in peace the people of Saguntum, allies of the Roman people. They were also to cross to Carthage in Africa, and deliver the grievances of the allies of the Roman people. This embassy had been authorized, but not yet sent, when, sooner than anyone had anticipated, word was brought that Saguntum was under attack.

The matter was brought anew before the Senate. Some recommended assigning Spain and Africa to the consuls as their areas of responsibility, and opening operations against them on land and sea; others advocated focusing the entire campaign on Spain and Hannibal. There were also some who felt that such a critical step should not be taken hastily, and that they should await the return of the ambassadors from Spain. This last view seemed the safest course and won the day, and the dispatch of the ambassadors—Publius Valerius Flaccus and Quintus Baebius Tamphilus—was accordingly accelerated. These men were to go to Hannibal at Saguntum and, if he failed to break off hostilities, to proceed from Saguntum to Carthage. There they were to demand the surrender of the commander himself as redress for the infraction of the treaty.*

7. While the Romans were engaged in these preparations and deliberations, Saguntum was already facing an all-out assault. This city-state, lying about a mile from the sea, was by far the most prosperous south of the Ebro. The Saguntines are said to hail from the island of Zacynthos, some also being of mixed race from the Rutulian city of Ardea. At all events, they had in a short time come to possess great wealth thanks to their maritime or agricultural activities, to their increase in population, or to their high moral values— which led them to remain loyal to their allies even when faced

with destruction themselves.* Hannibal entered their territory with an invading force, laid waste their agricultural lands, and made a three-pronged attack on the city.

There was a corner of the city wall, contiguous to the valley, where the ground became more level and open than the other land surrounding the town. It was towards this that Hannibal decided to advance his siege-sheds, under the cover of which the ram could be brought up to the walls. But, while the terrain some distance from the wall was level enough for moving up the siege-sheds, the Carthaginian efforts met with no success at all once it came to the actual execution of the manœuvre. There was a huge tower overlooking the spot, and the wall there, as one might expect at an insecure point, had been built up higher than elsewhere. In addition, an elite detachment was there to provide stiffer resistance at a spot seen to be particularly dangerous and vulnerable. At first, these men kept the enemy at bay with projectiles, and left those involved in the works with no security. Later, not only were their missiles flying before the walls and the tower, but the Saguntines found the courage to make forays against their enemy's sentry-posts and siege-works—and in these spontaneous engagements Saguntine casualties slightly outnumbered the Punic. But then Hannibal himself, approaching the wall with insufficient caution, collapsed with a serious spear-wound to the front of his thigh, and with that his men fled in panic from their positions, leaving the earthworks and siege-sheds well-nigh abandoned.

8. To give the general's wound time to heal, it was siege tactics rather than direct assault for the next few days. But while there was a lull in the fighting during this time, there was no let-up in the construction of siege-works and of fortifications to protect the city. As a result, when hostilities resumed it was with greater determination than before, and the siege-sheds began to be advanced and the rams brought up in more locations, although a number of places scarcely accommodated such operations. The Carthaginians had abundant manpower—they are fairly estimated to have had some 150,000 under arms*—while the townspeople, starting to be drawn off in different directions in order to defend and patrol all points, had not the resources for the fight.

The walls were now being pounded by the rams, and many sections had been damaged. In one area a line of breaches, one after the other, had laid bare the city—three towers in a row and the wall running between them had collapsed with a deafening roar. The Carthaginians had expected that the collapse meant the town was captured, but then the two sides rushed into the fray just as if the wall had been offering *both* of them protection. It was nothing like the scrappy fighting that usually arises during assaults on cities, when one side grasps an opportunity; rather, two regular fighting-lines had taken up a position in what was virtually an open field between the collapsed wall and the city buildings a short distance away. On one side hope, on the other desperation, fired spirits. The Carthaginian thought that with a little push he had the city captured, and the Saguntines set their bodies before their native town that was stripped of its walls, not one of them giving ground for fear of letting an enemy into the spot he had vacated. Thus, the more fiercely the two fought, and the more densely packed they were, the greater the number of wounds inflicted, since no weapon fell without effect, striking either a soldier's armour or his body.

The Saguntines had a weapon for throwing called a *phalarica*. This had a fir shaft that was cylindrical except for the tip where the iron head protruded. This section, cube-shaped as on a javelin, they would wrap with tow and smear with pitch. The head was three feet long, and so able to pass through a man's body as well as his shield. But even if it stuck in the shield without penetrating the body it still caused immense alarm, for it was discharged with its centre set alight, and the forward motion itself further magnified the flames, which then made the soldier drop his shield and exposed him to the weapons that followed.

9. The battle had long hung in the balance. The Saguntines' confidence soared because their resistance was more effective than they could have hoped, while the Carthaginians' failure to secure victory left them feeling beaten. Suddenly the townspeople raised a shout and pushed the enemy back to where the wall had collapsed. Dislodging them from there in disorder and panic, they finally routed and scattered them, driving them back to their camp.

Meanwhile, word came that the ambassadors had arrived from Rome, and men were sent by Hannibal to meet them on the seashore. They were to tell the Romans that they would not have a safe passage through all the violent tribes in the area, who were now up in arms, and that Hannibal had no time at such a critical juncture to listen to embassies. It was evident that, refused a hearing, the ambassadors would carry straight on to Carthage. Hannibal accordingly sent written and verbal instructions ahead to the leaders of the Barca faction, telling them to mentally prepare his supporters, and prevent the opposition from making any concession to the Roman people.

10. So, apart from the fact that it was received and given a hearing in Carthage, this delegation also served no purpose whatsoever. Hanno stood alone in challenging the senate and defending the treaty. Because of the respect he commanded he was heard in hushed silence, but not with the approval of his audience, as he implored the senate in the name of the gods who oversee and witness treaties not to precipitate hostilities with Rome as well as with Saguntum. He had advised them, he had warned them, not to send the child of Hamilcar to the army, he said; Hamilcar's ghost could not remain calm, nor could any son of his, and, while anyone of Barca bloodline or name remained, the treaty with Rome would never remain undisturbed.

'A young man with a burning desire for power and seeing only one way to it, that is, by living surrounded by weapons and legions, and by following one war with another—that is what you have sent out to your armies, virtually adding fuel to the flames. So you have fed this fire in which you are now being consumed. Your armies are blockading Saguntum, from which they are debarred by treaty, and soon Roman legions will be blockading Carthage, led by the same gods through whom the Romans exacted revenge for broken treaties in the last war. Is it your enemy you do not know, or your own selves, or the destinies of the two peoples? Ambassadors came from your allies on behalf of allies, and your fine commander refused to admit them to his camp, thereby violating international convention. Excluded from what is not even denied to embassies of a declared enemy, these men have come to you. They are claiming reparations in accordance with their treaty; they demand that our state clear itself of responsibility by surrendering the guilty party, the man accused of the crime.

'The softer their approach, the slower their initial moves, the more unrelenting, I fear, will be their wrath once they have begun. Bear in mind the Aegates Islands and Eryx—those twenty-four years of tribulation that you suffered on land and sea. And your leader was not this boy, but his father, Hamilcar himself, a second Mars, according to those supporters of his. We had not kept our hands off Tarentum, which is to say off Italy, as the treaty required, just as now we are not keeping our hands off Saguntum. And so the gods prevailed over men and, to settle the argument over which of the two peoples had broken the treaty, the outcome of hostilities stood as a disinterested judge, giving victory to the one with right on its side.*

'It is against Carthage that Hannibal now brings up his siege-sheds and assault-towers. It is the walls of Carthage that he batters with his ram. The collapse of Saguntum—how I wish my prophecy may prove false!—will come crashing down on *our* heads, and the war we started with Saguntum will have to be fought against the Romans. "Well, then, are we to surrender Hannibal?" someone will ask. I am aware that my influence in his case is slight, because of my differences with his father. But just as I was pleased with Hamilcar's death because if he were alive we should already be at war with the Romans, so I hate and abhor this young man as the fury that is firing this conflict. Nor is it simply a matter of his having to be surrendered to atone for the broken treaty. No, even if no one were demanding his punishment, I think he should be hauled off to the remotest limits of sea and land—banished to some place from which his name or news of him could not reach us, and where he could not upset the tranquillity our nation now enjoys. I vote that we immediately send ambassadors to Rome to make amends to the Senate, and send others to tell Hannibal to withdraw his army from Saguntum —and these should also surrender Hannibal himself to the Romans as the treaty requires. I further recommend a third delegation be sent to pay compensation to the people of Saguntum.'

11. When Hanno wound up his speech, there was no need for anyone to debate him—so completely was the senate, practically to a man, in support of Hannibal. Hanno had been even more vitriolic in his remarks than the Roman envoy, Valerius Flaccus, they claimed. The reply then given to the Roman embassy was that the war had been initiated by the people of Saguntum, not by Hannibal, and that the Roman people were in the wrong if they held Saguntum in higher regard than their time-honoured alliance with the Carthaginians.

Hannibal's men, meanwhile, were exhausted from battle and constructing siege-works and, while the Romans were frittering away time in sending off embassies, the commander gave them a few days' respite, setting up sentry-posts to protect his siege-sheds and other installations. And all the while he was whetting their spirit, by turns provoking them to anger against the enemy and then promising rewards. In fact, when, in an assembly, he proclaimed that the spoils from the captured city would go to the men, they were all so fired up that it looked as if they would have been completely unstoppable had the signal been immediately given. As for the Saguntines, they had enjoyed several days' rest from fighting, neither launching nor facing attack. But they had never halted work on the defences by night or day, trying as they were to construct a new wall at the point where the town had been exposed when the old one collapsed.

Then the assault recommenced, with considerably more ferocity than before, and the confused uproar and shouting everywhere made it impossible for the townspeople to be sure where to bring help first, or in the fullest measure. Hannibal was on hand in person to give encouragement at a point where a movable tower that rose above all the city's defences was being pushed forward. When this was brought up, it swept the walls clean of defenders with catapults and slings that were deployed on all its platforms, and at that moment Hannibal, sensing an opportunity, sent some 500 Africans with pick-axes to burrow under the wall. That was not a difficult operation because the stones were not set with mortar but merely lined with clay in the old-fashioned manner of building. As a result, the wall caved in beyond the section where it was being cut away, and packs of armed Carthaginians streamed into the city through the gaps left by the collapse. The Carthaginians also seized some higher ground, where they brought together catapults and ballistas, and surrounded it with a wall so that they would have a stronghold within the actual city, overlooking it like a citadel. The Saguntines, on their side, built an inner wall to encompass the section of their city not yet taken.

On both sides the building and fighting went on with maximum intensity, but the Saguntines, by focusing on the defence of the interior sections of their city, were every day decreasing its size. At the same time, there was an increasing shortage of all supplies because of the length of the siege, while the prospects of assistance from without became dimmer—the Romans, their only hope, were far off, and everything in the vicinity was in enemy hands. Even so, the townspeople's flagging spirits were raised briefly when Hannibal suddenly marched off against the Oretani* and Carpetani. These two peoples, galled by the severity of the troop-levies amongst them, had seized the recruiting officers and so raised fears of insurrection. But, taken by surprise by Hannibal's swift response, they abandoned the fight they had started.

12. In fact, the blockade of Saguntum proved no less vigorous under Maharbal, son of Himilco, whom Hannibal had left in command. Maharbal operated with such energy that neither his fellow citizens nor the enemy felt the commander's absence. He fought a number of successful engagements, and shattered a section of the wall with three battering rams, offering the returning Hannibal a prospect of the whole area strewn with fresh rubble. Accordingly, the Carthaginian troops were immediately led against the citadel itself. A furious engagement ensued, with heavy losses on both sides, and part of the citadel was captured.

Hopes for a negotiated peace were slim, but efforts to attain it were made by two men, the Saguntine Alco and the Spaniard Alorcus. Alco felt he could achieve something by entreaty, and crossed over to Hannibal at night without the knowledge of the people of Saguntum. Tears had no effect and the conditions offered him were severe, coming as they did from an exasperated victor. Alco therefore became a deserter instead of a spokesman, and remained with the enemy, claiming that anyone who negotiated a peace on such terms faced certain death. The Carthaginian demands were that the Saguntines make full restitution to the Turdetani, that they surrender all their gold and silver, and that they leave the city with a single article of clothing, to settle wherever the Carthaginian decreed. Alco replied that the Saguntines would not accept such peace-terms, but Alorcus claimed that when everything else is crushed the spirit, too, is crushed, and he engaged to broker the peace. Alorcus was at that time a soldier of Hannibal's, but he was officially regarded as a friend and foreign representative of the people of Saguntum.

Alorcus openly surrendered his weapon to the sentries, passed the defence-works, and was escorted, at his request, to the Saguntine general. A horde of people of every class immediately converged on the spot, but the crowd was pushed aside and Alorcus was granted an audience with the senate. His address was as follows:

13. 'Your fellow-citizen Alco came to Hannibal to sue for peace. If he had also brought Hannibal's conditions for peace back to you, this mission of mine would have been unnecessary, a mission on which I have come neither as Hannibal's representative nor as a deserter. But

Alco has stayed behind with your enemy, and the fault is either yours or his—his, if his fear is just a pretence, but yours if bringing you the truth is dangerous. It is I who have come to you, in consideration of my long-established ties of guest-friendship with you, and I do so in order that you not be unaware of terms that can bring you salvation and peace. And you can take this fact as assurance that what I say I say for your own sake and no one else's: I never made any mention of peace to you the whole time you had the strength to resist, or were still expecting assistance from Rome. It is only now that you can expect nothing from the Romans, and have insufficient protection from your own arms and defences, that I am bringing you peace-terms which are not equitable but which you must accept. You have some hope of concluding this peace if you listen, as the defeated party, to the terms that Hannibal dictates to you as the victor. And when everything is in that victor's hands, you must not regard what is removed from you as a loss, but consider whatever is left to you as a gift. Hannibal is taking from you your city—most of it he has destroyed, anyway, and practically all of it he has captured—but he leaves you your lands, on which he will assign to you a location for building a new town. All gold and silver, state- or privately owned, he orders to be brought to him. Yourselves, along with your wives and children, he spares, if you are prepared to leave Saguntum unarmed and with two articles of clothing each. Such are your instructions from a victorious enemy; harsh and grievous though they are, your circumstances press you to accept. In fact, I am not without hope that Hannibal will ease the conditions somewhat once he is in full control. But, in my view, you should put up with them even as they are, rather than allow yourselves to be butchered and have your wives and children seized and dragged away before your eyes, in accordance with the rules of war.'

14. A crowd had gradually come together to hear these words and the general assembly of the people had merged with the senate. Suddenly the leading men split away and, before a reply could be given to Alorcus, they brought together in the forum all the silver and gold from public and private buildings. This they threw into a fire, hurriedly built for the purpose, many of them flinging themselves in as well. The resulting fear and panic swept through the city and then another clamour was heard coming from the citadel. A tower that had taken a long pounding had collapsed, and a company of Carthaginians

had forced its way through the breach, signalling back to their commander that the city was now deprived of its customary sentry-posts and guards. Hannibal thought such an opportunity did not brook delay. Giving the word for all of fighting age to be put to death, he attacked in full force, and took the city in an instant.

Hannibal's order was callous but was seen to be almost necessary in the event. Men who shut themselves away with their wives and children, and burned their homes over their own heads, or who took up their weapons and allowed only death to put an end to their resistance—such men simply could not be spared.

15. The town was taken with an enormous amount of plunder. Most personal property had been systematically destroyed by the owners; in the killing, exasperation had barely allowed for differentiation in ages; and the captives had become the booty of the rank and file. Nevertheless, it is well established that a considerable sum of cash was realized from the sale of goods, and that a great deal of expensive furniture and clothing was shipped to Carthage.

Some authors have dated the capture of Saguntum to the eighth month after the commencement of the siege. They have stated that, after it, Hannibal withdrew to winter quarters in New Carthage, and that he then arrived in Italy four months after leaving New Carthage. If that is so, then Publius Cornelius and Tiberius Sempronius cannot have been the consuls to whom the Saguntine envoys were sent when the siege began, and who also engaged with Hannibal during their term of office (one at the River Ticinus, and both somewhat later at the Trebia). Either all these events took a shorter time, or else it was the capture of Saguntum, not the start of the siege, that took place at the beginning of the consular year of Publius Cornelius and Tiberius Sempronius. For the battle of the Trebia cannot have been as late as the consular year of Gnaeus Servilius and Gaius Flaminius, because Gaius Flaminius entered his consulship at Ariminum and his election was supervised by the consul Tiberius Sempronius. Sempronius had come to Rome after the battle of the Trebia, to oversee the consular elections, and when the elections were completed he returned to his army in its winter quarters.*

16. News of the destruction of Saguntum reached Rome at about the time that the envoys came back from Carthage with the report that everything pointed to war. Various emotions gripped the senators at the same moment: sorrow and pity for the heinous massacre of

their allies, shame at their own failure to bring assistance, fury with the Carthaginians, and fear for the security of the state—it was as if the enemy were already at the gates. So many emotions arising together threw them off balance, making them dither rather than deliberate. They realized that they had never come to grips with a more ruthless or combative foe, and Rome had never been in such a shiftless and enervated condition. The Sardinians, the Corsicans, the Istrians, and the Illyrians had teased Roman military power but not really put it to the test, and with the Gauls there had been desultory rather than regular warfare. But the Carthaginians were their enemy of old and they had spent twenty-three years in the hardest kind of campaigning amidst the Spanish tribes, campaigns from which they had always emerged the victors. They were used to the harshest leadership, and they were crossing the Ebro fresh from the destruction of a prosperous city. They had roused to arms, and were dragging along with them, large numbers of Spanish peoples, and they would now stir into action the ever-belligerent Gallic tribes. The Romans would have to fight the whole world, and do so in Italy and before their city walls.*

17. The consular spheres of authority had already been defined, and the consuls were now instructed to proceed to the sortition. Spain fell to Cornelius, and Africa, along with Sicily, to Sempronius. It was decided that six legions be levied that year, together with as many allied troops as the consuls should deem appropriate, and as great a fleet as could be mustered. Twenty-four thousand Roman infantry were conscripted and 1,800 cavalry, together with 40,000 infantry and 4,400 cavalry from the allies, and, on the naval front, two hundred and twenty quinqueremes and twenty cutters were launched. The question was then put before the people whether it was their wish and command that war be declared on the people of Carthage. The Roman people approved the war, and public prayers for it were held throughout the city, with entreaties made to the gods for a victorious and happy outcome.

The division of troops between the consuls was as follows. Sempronius was given two legions, each comprising 4,000 infantry and 300 cavalry, together with 16,000 allied infantry and 1,800 allied cavalry. He was also assigned one hundred and sixty warships and twelve cutters. With such land and naval forces Tiberius Sempronius was dispatched to Sicily. From there he was to cross to Africa, but only if the other consul proved to have the strength to stop the Carthaginian from entering Italy.

Cornelius was assigned fewer troops because the praetor Lucius Manlius was also being sent to Gaul with a force of considerable strength. In particular, the number of Cornelius' vessels was curtailed: he was given just sixty quinqueremes, for the Senate believed the enemy would not come by sea or employ that mode of warfare. He also received two Roman legions with their regular complement of cavalry, and 14,000 allied infantry along with 1,600 allied cavalry. The province of Gaul, which would also be a theatre in the war with Carthage, also received two Roman legions plus 10,000 allied infantry, and 1,000 allied and 600 Roman cavalry.

18. These preparations finished, the senators wanted to have all protocols observed before hostilities commenced, and they sent to Africa an embassy of older men—Quintus Fabius, Marcus Livius, Lucius Aemilius, Gaius Licinius, and Quintus Baebius.* The ambassadors were to enquire of the Carthaginians whether Hannibal's assault on Saguntum had been officially authorized, and to declare war on the people of Carthage if, as seemed likely, they acknowledged the fact, and if they defended Hannibal's action as being state policy. On their arrival in Carthage, the Romans were granted an audience with the senate, and Quintus Fabius did nothing more than put forward the one question the deputation had been instructed to ask. One of the Carthaginians then replied:

'Romans, your earlier delegation, when you demanded that Hannibal be surrendered to you for blockading Saguntum on his own initiative, was presumptuous enough. But this delegation, while it has been more restrained in its language up to this point, is actually more unreasonable. On that occasion Hannibal was being accused, and a demand was being simultaneously made for his surrender. On this, a confession of wrongdoing is being wrung from us, and immediate satisfaction is also demanded—as though we had already confessed. To my mind, the pertinent question is not whether the assault on Saguntum came from individual initiative or state policy, but whether the attack was or was not justified. For the investigation and punishment of a citizen with respect to what he has done with our blessing or on his own account is our prerogative and ours alone. The only matter to discuss with *you* is whether the action was permissible under the treaty.

'And, by the way, since you want a distinction made between what commanders do as a matter of state policy and what they do independently, we have a treaty with you that was struck by your consul Gaius Lutatius. In this treaty, provision was made for the allies of both parties, but not for the people of Saguntum, who were not at that point allied to you. But I suppose you will argue that the Saguntines are covered in the treaty that was struck with Hasdrubal, and to this my reply will simply be the one that I have learned from you. For you claimed that you were not bound by the treaty that Gaius Lutatius first concluded with us because it was not concluded with the sanction of the Senate and at the command of the people. As a result, a second, new treaty that had official approval was concluded. If you are not bound by your treaties unless they are struck with your authority, and at your command, then Hasdrubal's treaty, which he concluded unbeknownst to us, could not bind us, either. So drop all this talk of Saguntum and the Ebro, and deliver at last the thought that has long been gestating in your minds!'

At this the Roman gathered his toga into a fold and said: 'Here we bring you war and peace. Take whichever you please!' A shout, no less defiant, came back immediately—he could *give* whichever he pleased. Fabius shook out the fold and said he gave them war. In reply, the Carthaginians to a man declared that they accepted it, and that they would fight it in the spirit in which they were accepting it.

19. This direct question, and the formal declaration of war, seemed more in keeping with the dignity of the Roman people than a debate over legal niceties in treaties, especially now that Saguntum had been destroyed. In fact, if it came to a discussion of the wording, there was no comparison to be made between the treaty concluded by Hasdrubal and the earlier one of Lutatius that was subsequently changed. In Lutatius' treaty, there was a rider explicitly stating that its validity was contingent on the approval of the people, while Hasdrubal's contained no such escape clause.* Furthermore, all the years of silence on the matter while Hasdrubal was alive had indicated that it was officially approved, so much so that no change was made even on the death of its author. But even if the former treaty remained in effect, the people of Saguntum were sufficiently safeguarded by the stipulation that excepted the allies of both parties. There was no rider specifying 'those who were allies at that time' or 'not those taken on as allies later'. It was permissible to take on new allies; so one could not consider it fair that no people could be accepted into friendship for services rendered, or that they could not be defended once they were given treaty-status. The only proviso should be that no effort be made either to incite Carthaginian allies to defect, or to accept them into an alliance if they detached themselves of their own accord.

In accordance with the instructions given to them in Rome, the Roman ambassadors crossed from Carthage to Spain, with the aim of approaching the various city-states to draw them into an alliance, or at least to dissuade them from joining the Carthaginians.* They came first to the Bargusii, who gave them a warm welcome, sick as they were of Carthaginian rule; and so they went on to foment revolution amongst a large number of tribes south of the Ebro. They then reached the Volciani, but these gave them a reply that became famous throughout Spain and discouraged all the other states from allying themselves with Rome. This was how the eldest of them responded to the delegation in a meeting of their council:

'Romans, are you not embarrassed to ask us to set friendship with you above friendship with Carthage? You betrayed men who did just that—you, their allies!—acting more callously than the Punic foe who destroyed them. I think you should be looking for allies in some place where the catastrophe of Saguntum is not known. To the peoples of Spain the ruins of Saguntum will stand as an object lesson, as harrowing as it is striking, not to put one's trust in Roman loyalty or a Roman alliance.'

With that, the ambassadors were told to leave the territory of the Volciani at once, and they received no more favourable a response thereafter from any other tribal council in Spain. Accordingly, after a fruitless journey through Spain, they crossed into Gaul.

20. In Gaul the embassy was presented with a strange and alarming spectacle: the Gauls, after their tribal custom, came to meetings under arms. The ambassadors sang the praises of the glory and valour of the Roman people, and asked the Gauls not to grant the Carthaginian passage through their lands and cities, if he attempted to carry hostilities into Italy. This, they say, raised such noisy guffaws that the younger warriors could barely be brought to order by the magistrates and older men. It seemed such a stupid and impudent request—to suggest that the Gauls, to prevent a war from passing

into Italy, should bring it on themselves, and expose their own farmlands to devastation rather than someone else's. When the commotion was finally brought to order, the envoys were given the answer that the Romans had not done the Gauls so much good, and the Carthaginians had not done them so much harm, as to justify their taking up arms on behalf of Rome, or against Carthage. On the contrary, they said, they were receiving reports of men of their race being driven by the Roman people from the frontiers of Italian territory, and of these men paying tribute and suffering other such indignities.

Much the same sort of exchange occurred in the other tribal councils in Gaul, and not a word of a hospitable or friendly nature was heard until the envoys reached Massilia. There they learned the whole story from their allies, who had made careful and precise enquiries. Hannibal, they were told, had anticipated them and already enlisted the support of the Gauls. But, added the Massiliots, even Hannibal himself would not find them a very easy people to deal with, naturally aggressive and violent as they were, unless he repeatedly conciliated their chieftains with gold, for which the race had an enormous appetite.

Their round of the peoples of Spain and Gaul complete, the envoys returned to Rome, arriving not long after the consuls had left to take up their responsibilities. They found the whole community tense with the anticipation of war, for there was a persistent rumour that the Carthaginians had already crossed the Ebro.

21. After taking Saguntum, Hannibal had withdrawn to winter in New Carthage. There he was told of the events, and of the decisions taken, both in Rome and Carthage, and learned that he was the cause of the war as well as its commander-in-chief. He then doled out or sold off the remaining booty and, thinking he should delay no longer, summoned the Spanish troops in his army and addressed them as follows:

'Allies! I think you, too, can see that, after winning over all the tribes of Spain, we must either terminate our campaign and demobilize our armies, or else move our operations into other lands. In fact, these tribes will enjoy the fruits of our victory as well as of peace, but only if we search for plunder and glory amongst other races. And so, as a campaign far from home lies ahead, and as it is unclear when you are going to see your homes, and the things dear to each of you, I am granting leave to any of you wishing to visit his family. I give you notice to be here at the start of spring, so that with heaven's help we may embark upon a war that will bring us immense glory and spoils.'

Almost to a man the soldiers were delighted to be offered the opportunity of visiting their homes without having to ask permission; they had already been missing their loved ones, and saw ahead an even longer separation from them. An entire winter of repose, between hardships experienced and others soon to be faced, revived them physically and psychologically to confront all the new challenges to come. At the start of spring they mustered as instructed.

After a review of all his auxiliary troops, Hannibal set off for Gades. There he discharged his vows to Hercules, and bound himself with further vows for the continued success of his venture. He then divided his attention between offensive and defensive measures. Fearing to leave Africa unprotected, and exposed to Roman attack from Sicily, while he headed for Italy by the overland route through Spain and Gaul, he decided to strengthen the country with a powerful defensive force. To compensate for this, he himself requested troops from Africa, mostly light-armed javelin-throwers. Thus Africans would be serving in Spain, and Spaniards in Africa, both contingents likely to prove the better soldiers for serving far from home, bound by reciprocal obligations, as it were. Hannibal sent to Africa 13,850 infantry armed with the *caetra*, 870 Balearic slingers and 1,200 cavalry made up of many different peoples, and he gave instructions for part of this force to serve as a garrison for Carthage, with the rest deployed throughout Africa. At the same time he sent recruiting officers to the various African communities with orders for 4,000 handpicked men of military age to be conscripted and brought to Carthage. There they would strengthen the garrison, and also serve as hostages.

22. Hannibal felt Spain should not be neglected, either, the more so since he was aware that the Roman ambassadors had done the rounds of it to enlist the support of tribal chieftains. He assigned responsibility for this to a man of great energy, his brother Hasdrubal. The military strength that Hannibal gave his brother lay mostly in African troops: 11,850 African infantry, 300 Ligurians and 500 from the Balearic Islands. To this infantry force the following cavalry was added: 450 Libyphoenicians (a race of mixed Punic and African

blood), some 1,800 Numidians and Moors, who live by the Ocean, and a small detachment of 300 Ilergetan cavalry from Spain. Finally, to ensure that no form of land force was lacking, there were twenty-one elephants. Hasdrubal was also assigned a fleet to protect the coastline, for it could be supposed that the Romans would then, too, operate in the military sphere in which they had earlier been victors. There were fifty quinqueremes, two quadriremes, and five triremes, but of these only thirty-two of the quinqueremes and the five triremes were fitted out and furnished with crews.*

From Gades, Hannibal returned to the army's winter quarters in New Carthage. On leaving New Carthage he marched along the coast, past the city of Onussa, to the Ebro. There is a tale* that here he saw in a dream a young man of godlike appearance who claimed he had been sent by Jupiter to guide Hannibal to Italy. The young man told him to follow, and not take his eyes off him at any point. At first, they say, Hannibal was frightened, and he followed without letting his gaze wander around, or back, at any stage; but then, with the curiosity of a human being, he began to wonder what it could be that he was forbidden to look back at. He could not help looking, and saw behind him a snake of an amazing size sliding along, and causing massive destruction to trees and bushes, a deafening thunderstorm following in its wake. Hannibal asked the young man what the monstrous apparition was and what the portent meant. He was informed that it was the destruction of Italy, and that he should simply proceed on his journey, asking no further questions and leaving destiny shrouded in darkness.

23. Delighted with this vision, Hannibal led his forces across the Ebro in three divisions. He had already sent men ahead to soften up with gifts the Gauls in the areas through which the army was to be led, and also to reconnoitre the Alpine passes, and crossing the Ebro he was at the head of 90,000 infantry and 12,000 cavalry. He then crushed the Ilergetes, the Bargusii, and the Ausetani, and the region of Lacetania, which lies at the foot of the Pyrenees.* He put Hanno in charge of this entire area so as to have in his power the defiles connecting the Spanish and Gallic provinces, and Hanno was assigned 10,000 infantry and 1,000 cavalry to secure the area.

The march of the Carthaginian army through the pass over the Pyrenees had already begun, and by now a rumour that was spreading amongst the barbarians that the war was to be with Rome became more persistent. As a result, 3,000 of the Carpetani abandoned the march. It was clear that their motivation for this was not so much the war as the length of the journey, and the apparent impossibility of crossing the Alps. Calling them back, or keeping them in service under duress, was a risky business, as it might provoke the fiery tempers of the others as well. Hannibal therefore sent home more than 7,000 men whose hearts he had felt were not in the campaign, and he pretended that the Carpetani, too, had been discharged by him.

24. Not to have delay and inactivity sap his men's morale, Hannibal then crossed the Pyrenees with the rest of his forces and encamped at the town of Iliberri.

The Gauls had been repeatedly told that the objective of the campaign was Italy, but there was a rumour that the Spaniards across the Pyrenees had been reduced by force, with powerful garrisons imposed on them. Fear of being subjugated themselves now drove them in panic to arms, and a number of tribes converged on Ruscino. News of this was brought to Hannibal and he, fearing delay more than he did a fight, sent spokesmen to their chieftains to say that he wanted to talk to them in person. Either they could come closer to Iliberri, or he could advance to Ruscino—their meeting would be more easily arranged if they were near each other. He would be happy to welcome them into his camp, he said, and would not himself hesitate to come to them, for he had come to Gaul as a friend, not an enemy, and would not draw his sword before reaching Italy— if the Gauls made that possible. Such was Hannibal's communication by his messengers and, in fact, the chieftains of the Gauls showed no reluctance in moving camp immediately to Iliberri, and coming to the Carthaginian. Here, falling prey to his gifts, they permitted his army to pass quite unmolested through their territory, past the town of Ruscino.

25. Meanwhile, the only news that had reached Italy—it was brought to Rome by ambassadors from Massilia—was that Hannibal had crossed the Ebro. Then, as if it was the Alps that he had crossed, the Boii rose up, having already incited the Insubres to join them. The reason was not so much the long-standing animosity of the Boii towards the Roman people as the rancour they harboured over the establishment of the colonies of Placentia and Cremona on Gallic soil on the banks of the Po. As a result, they quickly took up arms and attacked that very region. Here they caused such panic and chaos that not simply the farming people, but the actual triumvirs who had come to apportion the land (Gaius Lutatius, Gaius Servilius, and Marcus Annius) lost all confidence in Placentia's defences, and fled to Mutina.

The identification of Lutatius in this episode is not in doubt, but in place of Annius and Servilius some annalistic accounts carry the names of Manius Acilius and Gaius Herennius, and others those of Publius Cornelius Asina and Gaius Papirius Maso.* In question, too, is whether the envoys sent to protest to the Boii were man-handled,* and whether the triumvirs were attacked as they surveyed the land.

The Gauls are unskilled in the techniques for besieging cities, and uncommonly idle when it comes to soldierly duties, and so when the Romans were blockaded at Mutina, they sat passively before the walls, which they left intact. They then proceeded to feign interest in peace negotiations. Spokesmen for the Romans were invited to par-ley by the Gallic chieftains, but were then apprehended by them, the Gauls declaring that they would release them only if their hostages were returned. Apart from contravening international convention, this even broke the sworn guarantees given for that particular occa-sion. When the praetor Lucius Manlius was brought the news about the envoys, and about the danger facing Mutina and its garrison, he flew into a rage, and led towards Mutina a poorly ordered column of troops.

At that time woods surrounded the road, the area being mostly uncultivated. Since he had set off without reconnoitring, Manlius fell into an ambush and, after suffering heavy losses, only with dif-ficulty made it through to open country. There he established a fortified camp. The Gauls had not the confidence to attack it, and so the spirits of Manlius' men rose again, though it was known that about 500 had been lost. The march then recommenced, and there was no sign of the enemy while the column was being led through open terrain. When it entered woodlands once more, the Gauls attacked the rear and, in the great confusion and general panic that followed, they killed 700 men and carried off six standards. Only when the Romans emerged from the trackless and difficult woods did the intimidating pressure of the Gauls and the Romans' fear come to an end. In the open country that followed, the Romans easily defended their column as they advanced to Tannetum,* a village close to the Po. There they protected themselves against the daily increasing numbers of the enemy by erecting a temporary fortification, and bringing in provisions by river; and they also had help from the Brixian Gauls.

26. News of this sudden uprising was brought to Rome, and the senators now learned that the war against Carthage had been extended to include Gaul as well. They issued orders for the praetor Gaius Atilius to relieve Manlius with a single Roman legion and 5,000 allied troops, which had been recently conscripted by the consul. Atilius reached Tannetum without a fight, the enemy having withdrawn in fear.

Publius Cornelius Scipio raised a new legion to replace the one that had been sent with the praetor, and he then set out from the city with sixty warships. Skirting the coastline of Etruria and Liguria, and then the mountains of the Saluvi, he reached Massilia and encamped at the closest mouth of the Rhône (for the river divides and runs to the sea by several different channels). Cornelius found it difficult to believe that Hannibal had crossed the Pyrenees, and when he realized that he was now in fact planning his crossing of the Rhône as well, he wondered where he should meet him, as his men were not yet fully recovered from the rigours of their sea voyage. In the meantime he sent out 300 hand-picked horsemen with Massiliot guides, and some Gallic auxiliaries, to reconnoitre the area thoroughly, and take a look at the enemy at a safe remove.

Hannibal had now reached the lands of the powerful tribe of the Volcae, having established peaceful relations with all the other peoples by intimidation or bribery. The Volcae inhabit an area on both banks of the Rhône. However, since they lacked confidence in their ability to keep the Carthaginians out of their western territory, they had ferried almost all their people across the Rhône, so as to have the river as a barrier, and were proceeding to secure the eastern bank with their armed forces. Hannibal bribed the other peoples living along the river, as well as those Volcae who had not left their homes, to bring together boats from all around, and to construct others. And, in fact, it was the wish of the natives themselves to see the army taken across, and their region relieved as soon as possible of the pressure of such large numbers of men. And so there was assembled a massive number of ships and of boats that were rough-hewn for local use. The Gauls then began constructing new vessels, which they hollowed out from individual trees. Their example was followed by the soldiers, who, encouraged by the plentiful supply of wood and the ease of the work, hurriedly constructed formless tubs for transporting them and their equipment across the water—their only concern being that the things could float and carry a load.

27. All was now ready for the crossing, but the Carthaginians were fearful of the enemy opposite, who were policing the entire bank with cavalry and infantry. To dislodge them, Hannibal ordered Hanno son of Bomilcar* to take a division of troops, Spaniards for the most part and, setting off at the first watch of the night,* to make a one-day's journey upstream. Then, at the earliest opportunity, Hanno was to cross the river as unobtrusively as he could, and at the appropriate moment lead the column around to attack the enemy from the rear. The Gauls assigned to him as guides for this manœuvre informed Hanno that, about twenty-five miles upstream from their present location, the river flowed around a small island. As it was broader at the point where it divided, they told him, it was also less deep, and afforded a crossing-place.

At that spot, wood was swiftly cut and rafts constructed, on which horses, men, and other cargo could be ferried over. The Spaniards stuffed their clothing into skins and crossed the river, lying on their shields, with no difficulty at all. The rest of the army crossed on rafts that they lashed together, and they made camp close to the river. The men were exhausted from their overnight march and the hard work, but they were granted only a day's repose to recover, their leader being intent on putting the plan into effect at just the right moment.

Setting off again the next day, they used a smoke-signal from an elevated point, as had been agreed, to show that they had made the crossing, and were not far away; and, not to miss his opportunity, Hannibal gave the order to cross when he received the signal. The infantry had their boats ready and prepared; the cavalry, mostly because of their horses, had larger vessels.* A line of the larger vessels made the crossing upstream to absorb the force of the current, thus providing smooth water for the boats traversing below them. Most of the horses were swimming, pulled along by their reins fastened to the boats' sterns, apart from those that they had boarded already saddled and bridled, ready for use by the cavalry as soon as they set foot on the bank.

28. The Gauls came rushing towards them on the bank with discordant yells and their customary war chants, shaking their shields above their heads and brandishing spears in their hands. But the huge flotilla, along with the loud roar of the river, unnerved them, as did the confused shouting of the sailors and soldiers, both those battling the river-current and those who, from the far bank, were cheering on their comrades who were making the crossing. They were startled enough by the commotion before them, but then a more terrifying uproar arose to the rear, where their camp had been taken by Hanno. Soon Hanno was there in person, and the Gauls faced terror on two fronts: a massive force of armed men was disembarking, and an unexpected army was bearing down on their rear. They attempted resistance on both fronts, but were driven back. They then forced a passage wherever a way seemed most open, and scattered and fled in panic to their villages. Hannibal took his time ferrying over the rest of his troops, no longer concerned about interference from the Gauls, and pitched camp.

I believe different ideas were put forward for bringing the elephants over the river—certainly, there are differing accounts of how it was accomplished.* Some claim that the elephants were brought together on the bank, and that the most fractious of them was goaded to anger by his driver, who then ran off into the water. As he swam off, the beast followed, and drew the rest of the herd after him. All the animals feared the deep water, but as each went out of his depth the very force of the current carried him to the other bank.

The more reliable version, however, is that they were brought over on rafts. This would have appeared the safer plan before the event, and so, after it, it appears the more plausible one. The Carthaginians pushed a single raft, measuring 200 feet by 50, into the river from the shore, and secured it with a number of strong ropes, attached to the bank upstream, so that it would not drift down with the current. On this they laid a carpet of soil to form a sort of bridge, so that the animals could confidently walk on it as on dry land. A second raft of the same width, and a hundred feet in length, and suitable for crossing the river, was fastened to it. Then, females in front, the elephants were driven over the immobile raft, as though it were a road. When they had passed over to the smaller raft that was joined to it, the ropes with which it had been loosely attached to the other were suddenly untied, and the raft was towed to the other bank by a number of swift boats. After disembarking the first animals, the men went back and brought over the others. The elephants showed no real agitation while they were driven over what seemed to be a bridge attached to land, and the first signs of disquiet came only when the raft was disconnected from the other* and the animals were swept into the deep part of the river. Then they began jostling each other, as those on the outside edged back from the water, and that caused some panic, until fear itself calmed them down when they gazed at the water all around them. Some, in their frenzy, even fell into the river. Their riders were thrown off but, buoyed by their own weight, the animals managed to make it ashore by feeling cautiously for the bottom with their feet.

29. While the elephants were being ferried over Hannibal had sent 500 Numidian riders to the Roman camp to investigate the position, strength, and plans of the enemy forces. This cavalry squadron was met by the 300 Roman horsemen who, as stated above, had been sent out from the mouth of the Rhône. The ensuing battle was more ferocious than the number of combatants would have led one to expect. Many were wounded, and the loss of life was also about equal on both sides; and, when the Numidians panicked and fled, they ceded victory to a Roman side that was by then quite exhausted. Of the victors, some 160 fell—not all Romans, but some Gauls as well— and of the defeated, more than 200. This marked the start of the war, and also served as an omen for it, indicating that, while the Romans would have success in the long run, the victory would certainly not be bloodless and would follow a close-fought struggle.

When the men returned to their respective commanders after this engagement, Scipio felt he could not stick to any plan—all he could do was react to the strategy and moves of the enemy. As for Hannibal, he was unsure whether to continue the march on Italy that he had started or to engage with this Roman army, the first that had appeared before him; but he was kept from an immediate confrontation by the arrival of a delegation of Boians with their chieftain, Magalus. These promised to act as guides for the routes to be taken and to share the dangers with him, and they told him that, in their opinion, he should invade Italy before opening hostilities and without weakening his forces in any other theatre before he did so. Most

of Hannibal's men did, indeed, fear their enemy, for the memory of
the last war had not yet been erased; but they dreaded much more
the interminable march over the Alps—and this, for men with no
experience of it, rumour made terrifying,

30. After deciding to go ahead with his march and make for Italy
as planned, Hannibal called a meeting of the men and roused their
spirits with a mixture of criticism and encouragement.

He was shocked, he said, that hearts ever fearless could have been
subject to a panic attack. They had served, and served victoriously,
for so many years, and they had not left Spain before seeing all the
tribes and lands between its two seas under Carthaginian control.
Then, vexed by the demand of the Roman people that any who
had blockaded Saguntum be turned over to them, as though guilty
of some crime, they had crossed the Ebro to wipe out the name of
Rome and set the world free. At that point it seemed to no one to be
a long journey, though they were travelling from where the sun set to
where it rose again. Now they could see that by far the greater part
of their journey was behind them. They could see that they had
climbed the pass through the Pyrenees where they had been surrounded by truly fierce tribes, and that they had crossed the formidable River Rhône, where they had conquered even the violence of
that waterway, in the teeth of so many thousands of Gauls. And
it was only now, when they had the Alps in sight, with Italy on
the other side, and when they were at the very gateway to the
enemy—only now did they halt from weariness.

The Alps—what else did they think them but high mountains? All
right, they might well suppose them higher than the crests of the
Pyrenees, but certainly no points of the earth reached the sky, or
were insurmountable for the human race. In fact, the Alps were
inhabited, and under cultivation. They bore and sustained living
beings, and armies could pass through their gorges. The very envoys
his men saw before them had not come over the Alps flying high on
wings, he said. No, even the ancestors of these men were not natives
of Italy; they were foreign settlers who had safely crossed these very
same Alps on many occasions and in huge numbers, taking children
and wives with them on their migrations. And a soldier carrying
nothing but his implements of war—what is there that he cannot
pass or surmount? Think of the eight months of danger and hardship they had suffered to take Saguntum! Their objective now was

Rome, capital of the world. Can any challenge seem sufficiently daunting or difficult to delay that enterprise? In the past Gauls had captured those very places the Carthaginians were now losing hope of approaching! So, he concluded, they ought to admit that, in spirit and courage, they were inferior to a people they had so often defeated in recent days! Either that or they should expect that the end of their journey would be the plain lying between the Tiber and the walls of Rome.

31. After energizing the men with such words of encouragement, Hannibal told them to take refreshment and ready themselves for the march. The next day he set off upstream, along the bank of the Rhône, heading for the interior of Gaul. This was not because it was a more direct route to the Alps but because he thought that, the further he moved from the sea, the less likely he was to meet the Romans— his intention was not to engage them until he reached Italy.

On the fourth day's march, Hannibal reached the Island. This is the confluence of the River Sarar and the River Rhône, which run down from different Alpine ranges, enclosing a considerable amount of land; and the plains between them have been given the name 'the Island'.* The Allobroges live close by, a tribe that in those days was already second to none of the Gallic tribes in wealth or reputation. At that particular time there was internal strife amongst them, with two brothers locked in a struggle for the throne. The elder brother, whose name was Branceus, had already been the ruler, but was now facing the prospect of being deposed by his younger brother and a clique of younger men, who had greater strength but less justice on their side. Very opportunely for Branceus, adjudication of this dispute was referred to Hannibal, who, having the disposal of the kingdom in his hands, supported the view of the senate and leading citizens, and restored authority to the elder brother. In return for this service, Hannibal was provided with support in the form of all manner of supplies and provisions, clothing in particular, the acquisition of which the infamous cold of the Alps made absolutely necessary.

Hannibal headed for the Alps after settling the Allobrogan dispute, but instead of taking the direct route he veered to the left into the lands of the Tricastini. He then advanced through the border territory of the Vocontii into the lands of the Trigorii, meeting no obstacle anywhere on his route until he reached the River Druentia.

Also an Alpine river, the Druentia is, of all the waterways of Gaul, by far the most difficult to cross. The volume of water it carries is enormous, but it is not navigable because it has no banks to confine it. Its flow is divided amongst a number of channels that never remain the same, and the river is continually forming new shallows and new pools, making passage hazardous also for a foot soldier. In addition, it rolls along gravel, thus providing no steady or secure footing for any one stepping into it. At that time, too, it was in spate from the rains, which caused terrible problems for the men as they tried to cross, for, in addition to everything else, they were also thrown off balance by their own fear and discordant cries.

32. Some three days after Hannibal had moved camp from the bank of the Rhône, the consul Publius Cornelius had come to the enemy encampment with his army in battle formation, intending to engage without delay. But he found their fortifications abandoned, and saw that catching them would not be easy when they had such a head start. He accordingly returned to his ships on the coast, thinking it would be safer and easier to confront Hannibal while he was making his descent from the Alps. But he had gained Spain in the provincial sortition, and was reluctant to leave it lacking Roman aid. He therefore sent most of his troops against Hasdrubal, under his brother Gnaeus Scipio, with the aim not merely of defending longstanding allies of Rome and enlisting new ones, but of actually driving Hasdrubal out of Spain. Cornelius himself headed back to Genua with considerably diminished forces, intending to undertake the defence of Italy with the army now in the vicinity of the Po.

Following a mostly flat route from the Druentia, Hannibal reached the Alps after being granted a safe passage by the Gauls inhabiting those parts. The men had been given some forewarning of their nature from rumour, which usually exaggerates the unknown. But now, seen close-up, everything served to renew their dread. They saw the towering mountains with snow almost blending into the sky; ugly homesteads perched on cliffs; flocks and pack animals shrivelled with cold; human figures shaggy and unkempt; everything, animate and inanimate alike, stiff with frost; and everything else a grimmer sight than words could possibly describe. As the Carthaginians brought the column up the nearest slopes, mountain dwellers came into view, occupying the heights overlooking them. Had these instead positioned themselves in the gorges that provided greater cover, they could have suddenly sprung to the attack and caused a massive flight and loss of life. Hannibal ordered a halt, and sent forward some Gauls to reconnoitre the area. Learning from them that there was no way through, he pitched camp in the most level piece of open ground that could be found in the generally broken and rocky terrain. Then these same Gauls managed to insinuate themselves into conversations with the local mountain men, from whom they differed little in language and customs. Through them Hannibal gained the further information that the pass was guarded only by day, and that at night all the men slipped away to their own homes. And so, at dawn, he approached the heights, apparently intending to force his way through in broad daylight. Then, after a whole day of pretending to achieve a goal other than the true one, the Carthaginians fortified the camp where they had originally halted. As soon as Hannibal perceived that the mountain men had left the heights and relaxed their guard, he created an illusion for the enemy by lighting more fires than were required for the numbers remaining. Then, leaving the baggage behind with all the cavalry and most of the infantry, he took a number of light-armed men, the bravest he had, and swiftly made his way up to the top of the pass. There he took up a position on the very heights that the enemy had held.

33. At dawn, camp was struck and the rest of the army began to advance. By now the mountain men, having been given the signal, were leaving their strongholds and converging on their customary post. Then, all of a sudden, they caught sight of some of the enemy above their heads, occupying the vantage-point that had been theirs, and they saw others coming along the road. Perceiving the two things together, and realizing what they meant, they were left momentarily pinned to the spot, motionless. They then observed some disarray in the pass, with the column thrown into disorder by its own difficulties, and the horses especially panic-stricken. Thinking that whatever they could add to the panic would be enough to finish off their enemy, they came charging down together at various points over the rocks, familiar as they were with the paths and trackless areas alike. At this point the Carthaginians really were under pressure, both from the enemy and from the roughness of the ground, and as they all struggled to be the first out of danger there was more fighting amongst themselves than there was with the enemy. The

horses posed the greatest danger for the column. Startled by the confused shouting, which was intensified by the woods and echoing ravines, they reared up, and those that chanced to be struck or wounded became so frantic as to cause severe damage to the men and all the various kinds of baggage. The pass had precipitously steep cliffs on either side,* and the crowding caused many to be hurled down into a sheer abyss, some of them in armour; but it was just like a building collapsing when pack animals came tumbling down along with their loads.

Frightful as the scene was, Hannibal none the less halted for a short while and held back his men for fear of only worsening the confusion and panic. Then he saw that a break in the column was occurring and that, if the baggage were lost, he faced the risk of having wasted his time in bringing the troops through safely. He therefore swooped down from his higher position and, with his assault, scattered the enemy, though this also increased the commotion amongst his men. That commotion, however, was calmed in an instant when the mountain men fled and left the paths clear, and soon the entire force was brought through not simply unmolested but almost in silence.

After this Hannibal took the stronghold that served as the regional capital, along with the villages around it, and with the food and livestock he captured there he fed his army for three days. No longer troubled by the mountain men, who were cowed by the initial defeat, or by the terrain, he made considerable progress during those three days.

34. The Carthaginians next reached another tribe that was comparatively populous for mountain-dwellers, and here Hannibal almost came to grief, not through open resistance but through duplicity and subterfuge, his own tricks of the trade. The older chieftains of the local strongholds came to the Carthaginian as spokesmen. They had learned a salutary lesson from the suffering of others, they declared, and preferred to try out the friendship of the Carthaginians, rather than their military strength. They would follow Hannibal's instructions to the letter, they said, and he was invited to take from them provisions, guides for his route and hostages as a guarantee of their promises.

Hannibal was polite in his response. He felt he should not put blind faith in them, but that he should not refuse the offer, either, in case rejection made them openly hostile. He accepted the hostages they offered, and availed himself of the provisions, which the spokesmen had personally brought down to the road; but in following their guides he had his column carefully ordered, not assuming he was in friendly country.

The vanguard comprised elephants and cavalry; Hannibal himself brought up the rear with the best of his infantry, anxiously looking about with every step. When the column reached a narrowing of the road, overlooked on one side by a mountain ridge, the barbarians rose up from all their hiding places. They attacked the Carthaginians front and rear, engaging hand-to-hand and from a distance, and rolling huge rocks down on the column. An enormous body of men bore down on the rear, and the infantry wheeled round to face them, leaving no doubt that, had it not been for the reinforcement provided for both ends of the column, the Carthaginians would have suffered a calamitous defeat in that pass. Even as it was, they faced extreme peril and were almost destroyed. For Hannibal hesitated to send down his division into the pass—it would mean leaving the infantry without the support in the rear that he was himself providing for the cavalry. The mountain men thereupon attacked from the side, cutting the column in half, and occupied the road. Hannibal then spent a night cut off from the cavalry and baggage.

35. The next day the barbarian assaults slackened, and the Carthaginian force then reunited and made it through the pass. They suffered losses in the process, but more pack animals were killed than men. After this, the mountain men were less in evidence, and they made predatory raids on the head or the rear of the column, rather than real strikes, wherever the terrain offered an opportunity, or where they could take advantage of some of the Carthaginians going too far ahead, or lagging behind. The elephants could be driven only at a snail's pace because the paths were steep and narrow, but they also provided security from the enemy all the way along: unfamiliar with the beasts, they feared to come too close to them.

On the ninth day they reached the crest of the Alps. They had wandered around over mostly trackless terrain because of the duplicity of their guides or because, distrusting the guides, they strayed blindly into gorges while guessing their way. They encamped on the crest for two days, and the soldiers, exhausted from their exertions and fighting, were given a rest. A number of pack animals that had fallen along the rocky path reached this camp by following the tracks of the column.

The men were sick and tired of all their tribulations, and then a snowfall arrived—for it was now the setting of the constellation Pleiades—filling them with a new and terrible fear. A deep layer of snow covered the entire landscape and, when they struck camp at dawn, the column moved sluggishly, with despondency and despair written on every face. Hannibal rode ahead of the standards and ordered his men to halt on a spur that afforded a deep and broad panorama. Here he pointed out to them Italy, and the plains that surrounded the Po, at the foot of the Alps.* At that moment, he told them, they were crossing the defences not merely of Italy but of the city of Rome. The rest of the way would be flat or downhill; one or at most two battles and they would have that chief bastion of Italy in their hands and at their mercy.

The column went ahead, and now, apart from some stealthy attacks, the enemy did not even take advantage of opportunities to harass them. But the journey was much harder than on the way up, the Alpine slopes on the Italian side being as a rule shorter but also steeper. Almost every step of the way was steep, narrow, and slippery. As a result the men could not keep from falling and, even after losing their balance only slightly, they could not, once in difficulties, keep their footing, so that they would fall over each other, and the pack animals would fall on the men.

36. They next came to a much narrower passageway on the rock face, where the cliff fell away so steeply that a soldier free of baggage could barely make it down by feeling his way and clinging with his hands to shrubs and roots projecting round about him. The spot had been naturally steep before, but it had now also been sheered off by a recent landslide, which had created a drop of fully one thousand feet. The cavalry halted at this point, thinking they had reached the end of the road and, as Hannibal wondered what was holding up the column, word that the cliff was impassable was brought back to him. He then went off to examine the location for himself.

It seemed clear to him that he had to take the column round on a detour—no matter how long it might be—through the surrounding areas, where there was no path and no one had set foot before. But that avenue proved impossible, too. Over an old, untouched layer of snow there was a fresh one of some slight depth. On this layer, since it was soft and not too deep, the feet of the marching men could get a footing. But then it melted as all the men and pack animals walked over it; and the soldiers began to find themselves stepping on the glare ice that lay beneath and on the slush of the thawing snow. This produced a horrific struggle. The slippery path afforded no foothold, and on the incline it made the feet slide all the more quickly. If they used hands or knees to help themselves up, these supports themselves would slither away from under them, and they would fall again. And there were no stumps or roots around to provide leverage for either foot or hand—only glare ice and slushy snow on which they simply slithered about. The pack animals treading the snow would occasionally cut even into the bottom layer. They would then slip forward and, with their hoofs flailing more wildly in their efforts to get up, would break right through. As a result, a number became wedged in the ice, which was hardened and frozen to a great depth, as though they were caught in a snare.

37. Finally, with pack animals and men exhausted to no purpose, they pitched camp on the crest—and they had a very hard time clearing ground even for this, so much snow had to be dug up and removed. The men were then taken off to make a road down the cliff, which was the only possible way to go on. Solid rock had to be cut. They felled some massive trees in the area, stripped the branches from them, and made a huge pile of logs. This they set on fire when a strong breeze arose suitable for whipping up a blaze, and as the rocks became hot they made them disintegrate by pouring vinegar on them.* After scorching the cliff-face with fires in this way, they opened it up with picks and softened the gradient with short zigzag paths so that even the elephants, not just the pack animals, could be brought down.

Four days were spent at the cliff, during which the pack animals almost starved to death. The mountain peaks are practically bare, and the snows cover such pasture as there is. The lower regions have valleys, a number of sunny hillocks, and streams with woods close by—a more suitable habitat for humans. There the pack animals were put out to pasture, and the men, exhausted from their road-building, were given some rest. It took only three days to descend from here into the plains, the environment and the disposition of the inhabitants both being less forbidding.

38. Such were the main features of the journey into Italy. Hannibal

reached it in the fifth month after leaving New Carthage, according
to some authorities, and after spending fourteen days crossing the
Alps. There is no agreement at all amongst the sources on the size of
Hannibal's forces when he crossed into Italy. The highest count is
100,000 infantry and 20,000 cavalry; the lowest 20,000 infantry and
6,000 cavalry. The most authoritative account should be that of
Lucius Cincius Alimentus, who records that he was taken prisoner
by Hannibal, but Cincius makes a mess of the numbers by adding in
Gauls and Ligurians. With these included, Cincius asserts that the
total brought into Italy was 80,000 foot and 10,000 horse, but it is
likely, as some authors in fact affirm, that it was within Italy rather
that these peoples flocked to Hannibal's banner. Cincius also states
that he learned from Hannibal's own lips that he lost 36,000 men and
a huge number of horses and other beasts after crossing the Rhône.*

On coming down into Italy the people Hannibal reached next were
the Taurini Semigalli.* This is universally accepted, which makes me
all the more surprised at the dispute over Hannibal's route over the
Alps, and at the prevailing belief that he crossed by the Poenine Alps
(and that this Alpine range was given its name on that account*). I am
likewise surprised at Coelius' statement that Hannibal crossed by way
of the Cremo ridge. Both of these passes would have brought Hannibal down not amongst the Taurini but amongst the Libuan Gauls,
the route traversing the mountain-dwelling Salassi. Moreover, it is
unlikely that those routes to Gaul would have been open at that time
and, in any case, those leading to the Poenine Alps would have been
blocked by the Half-German tribes. And, indeed, there is another
argument that may have some validity. The Sedunoveragri, who
inhabit that particular Alpine range, are unaware of the derivation of
the name of those mountains from any crossing of the Carthaginians,
and draw it instead from the god whom the mountain people call
Poeninus, whose cult is established on their highest peak.

39. Very convenient for Hannibal at the start of his campaign was
the fact that a war had been launched against the Insubres by the
tribe closest to them, the Taurini. But Hannibal could not put his
force under arms to give assistance to one side or the other—it was
now, in the process of recovery, that his men were experiencing the
worst effects of their earlier tribulations. Rest after hardship, plenty
after privation, comfort after filth and disease—all this was having
various physical effects on men who had been reduced to squalor and

near-brutalization. This was why the consul Publius Cornelius Scipio hastened towards the Po after reaching Pisa by sea, even though the army he had taken over from Manlius and Atilius was one of raw recruits demoralized by their recent discreditable performance—he wanted to engage an enemy whose strength was not yet restored. When the consul reached Placentia, however, Hannibal had already moved from his camp, and had taken by storm a single city of the Taurini—in fact, the tribal capital—because its people would not willingly enter into an alliance with him. Indeed, he could have enlisted the Gauls living around the Po, who would have come to him of their own accord, and without intimidation, but for the prompt arrival of the consul, who checked them as they sought an opportunity for insurrection. Hannibal then moved from the land of the Taurini in the belief that the Gauls, undecided on which side to support, would in fact support whichever was close at hand.

The armies were now almost in sight of each other, and two commanders had been brought face to face who, while not yet knowing each other well, felt a certain admiration for the other. Hannibal's name had been very well known to the Romans even before the destruction of Saguntum; and Hannibal thought Scipio a remarkable man for the sole reason that it was he who had been chosen commander to face him. And their mutual esteem had been increased by recent events: Scipio had been left behind in Gaul, but had come to face Hannibal after his crossing into Italy; and Hannibal had had the nerve to attempt the Alpine crossing, and had actually brought it off.

Scipio crossed the Po before Hannibal. He moved his camp to the River Ticinus and, to encourage the men before leading them into battle, proceeded with the following harangue:*

40. 'Men! Were I leading into battle the army I had with me in Gaul, I could have dispensed with an address before you. What would have been the point of words of encouragement to horsemen who had won a fine victory over the enemy cavalry at the Rhône? Or to legions with which I chased this very enemy as he fled before me, when I interpreted as a victory his avowal of defeat in pulling back and refusing to engage? But that army was mobilized to serve in Spain, and it is there that, under my auspices, it is seeing action with my brother Gnaeus Scipio, in accordance with the wishes of the Roman Senate and People. As for me, I have freely volunteered my

services for this battle so you could have a consul leading you against Hannibal and the Carthaginians and now, as your new commander, I must say a few words to men who are new to me.

'I do not want you to be ignorant of the war and of the enemy you are facing, men. The people you must fight are those whom you defeated on land and sea in the last war, people from whom you wrung tribute over a twenty-year period and from whom you seized Sicily and Sardinia, which you hold now as prizes of war.* So, in this conflict, you and they will both have the level of morale usually found in the victors and the vanquished respectively. And now they are going to fight not because they have confidence, but because they have to. For you cannot believe that men who refused battle when their army was intact have higher hopes after losing almost two-thirds of their infantry and cavalry in crossing the Alps, when those who perished almost outnumber the survivors!

'Ah, you may say, few they may be, but their morale and strength is intact—no force could withstand their toughness and stamina. Not so! They are mere ghosts, insubstantial shadows of men, lifeless from hunger and cold, covered with dirt and filth, and battered and disabled from the rocks and cliffs. In addition, their limbs are frost-bitten, their muscles stiffened by the falling snow, their bodies paralysed with cold. Their weapons are shivered and broken, their horses lame and spent. This is the cavalry, this is the infantry you will fight—you will have not an enemy but the last traces of an enemy. And there is nothing I fear more than this: that after you have fought, it may appear that it was the Alps that actually defeated Hannibal. And yet perhaps that is appropriate. Perhaps it should be the gods themselves who start, and with no human assistance virtually finish, a war with a treaty-breaking commander and people, while we, victims of the outrage next after the gods, should simply mop up after what they began and more or less finished.

41. 'I have no fear of any of you thinking that this is bluster on my part, intended merely to encourage you, while my true feelings are different. I could have gone off to Spain, my area of responsibility, with my own army—I had already set out for it. There I should have had my brother involved in my decisions, and sharing my dangers, and I should have had Hasdrubal rather than Hannibal as my foe, and a war of clearly lesser proportions. But no! As soon as I received the news about *this* enemy, as I skirted the coast of Gaul with my

fleet, I disembarked, sent my cavalry ahead and advanced my camp to the Rhône. I scattered the enemy in a cavalry battle, the only branch of my forces with which I was given the chance to engage. Their infantry column was quickly marched off like an army in flight and, because I could not catch up with it on land, I returned to my fleet. Then I made a long, roundabout journey over sea and land, with all the speed I could muster, and have come to meet this formidable enemy practically in the foothills of the Alps.

'So what do you think I have done? Come upon him accidentally when I was trying to avoid battle? Or, rather, dogged his footsteps, trying to provoke him and draw him into a decisive battle? I want to see for myself whether the earth has, over these past twenty years, suddenly produced Carthaginians of a different kind. I want to know if these are the same as those who fought at the Aegates Islands, and whom you released from Eryx only after setting a price of eighteen denarii apiece on their heads. I want to see if this Hannibal really is, as he himself claims, on a par with Hercules on his travels, or rather has been left by his father as a mere tribute- and tax-payer, indeed a slave, of the Roman people. The crime of Saguntum must have deranged the man. Otherwise he would have given some thought, if not to his defeated country, then at least to his home, his father, and those treaties written down in Hamilcar's hand. It was Hamilcar who withdrew the Carthaginian garrison from Eryx on the order of our consul; it was Hamilcar who accepted with rage and sorrow the harsh conditions imposed on the Carthaginians and who, on his withdrawal from Sicily, agreed to pay tribute to the Roman people.

'And so, men, I should like you to fight, not just with the spirit with which you usually face other enemies, but with resentment and anger—just as though you are looking at your own slaves who are suddenly shouldering arms against you. When we blockaded them at Eryx, we could have starved them to death, the worst of punishments to be inflicted on a human. We could have sent our victorious fleet across to Africa and destroyed Carthage in a matter of days, without a fight. Instead, we showed mercy when they begged for it, raised the siege, and made peace with them after their defeat; and then, when they were in difficulties with a war in Africa, we regarded them as being under our protection. As thanks for these favours, they come following a young maniac to attack our country.

'And I wish that this battle were only for your glory and not for your survival. It is not for the possession of Sicily and Sardinia, our earlier bones of contention, that you now must fight, but for Italy. There is, furthermore, no other army behind us to block the enemy, if we are not victorious, and no other Alps that would give us the time to establish fresh defences while they crossed. This is where we must stop them, men, just as if we were fighting before the walls of Rome.

'Each one of you must imagine that, by his arms, he is protecting not only his own person, but his wife and small children, too. And his thoughts should be focused not merely on his home. Rather, let him time and again bear this in mind, that it is on our hands that the Senate and People of Rome now have their attention fixed, and that the fate of that city and of the Roman empire lies in our strength and courage.'

42. Such were the consul's words to the Roman troops. Hannibal thought his exhortation to his soldiers should take the form of action rather than words. He formed the army into a circle for a demonstration, and set in the middle some captives from the mountains, in chains. He then had some Gallic weapons thrown at their feet, and told an interpreter to ask whether any of them was prepared to fight to the death with a sword, if victory meant being relieved of his chains and given arms and a horse. To a man, they all asked for a sword and the chance to fight, and lots were cast to decide the matter, each of them wishing that he was the one fortune would choose for the fight. As each lot was drawn, the ecstatic winner jumped for joy. He would break into his native dance, and swiftly grab his weapons, while his comrades around him offered congratulations. And, during the fighting, such were the feelings of the spectators at large, and not just the men facing the same ordeal, that the fortunate victors received no more applause than the unfortunates who died well.

43. Hannibal put on show a number of pairs to enliven his men. He then dismissed them and called an assembly, at which he is reported to have addressed them as follows:

'Men! A little while ago you demonstrated your spirit as you watched the fate of others. Demonstrate that same spirit when you consider your own prospects and we are already victors! For that was not simply a show; it virtually mirrored your own position. I wonder, in fact, if fortune has not imposed on you stronger fetters and more pressing demands than she has on your prisoners. To the right and to the left, two seas hem you in, and you have not a single ship even to make an escape. Around you is the River Po, bigger and more violent than the Rhône, and to your rear the barrier of the Alps, which you could barely cross when your strength was unimpaired and robust. Here, men, as soon as you meet the enemy, you must either conquer or die. But, if you prevail, that very same Fortune that has imposed on you the obligation to fight holds out prizes to you—and prizes greater than men usually ask for even in their prayers to the immortal gods! Suppose it were merely Sicily and Sardinia, filched from our fathers, that we were going to recover. Those would be prizes great enough themselves. As it is, whatever all their many triumphs have won and accumulated for the Romans, all that is going to be yours— along with its owners! Come on, then, take up your arms to win this rich reward—the gods are with you! You have spent enough time chasing sheep on the desolate mountains of Lusitania and Celtiberia, seeing no return for all your tribulation and danger. It is now time to make your service rich and profitable and, after that enormous journey over all those mountains and rivers, and through all those belligerent tribes, it is time you earned the great rewards for all your efforts. It is here that Fortune has granted an end to your labours, and here she will give you the reward you deserve when your service is done.

'Do not imagine that victory will be as difficult as the fame of the war might suggest. Often an underrated enemy has put up a bloody fight, and famous peoples and kings have been defeated with little effort. For set aside this one thing, the shining name of Rome, and how are they to be compared with you? I say nothing of the twenty years you have served with the valour and success for which you are famous. Now you have come to this place, triumphant, from the Pillars of Hercules, and from the Ocean and the bounds of the earth, passing through all the most violent tribes of Spain and Gaul. You will fight against an inexperienced army that was massacred, beaten, and blockaded by Gauls this very summer, an army that its commander does not know and which does not know its commander. In my case, I was practically born—and certainly brought up—in the headquarters of a distinguished commander, my father. I am the man who brought Spain and Gaul to heel, and conquered not only the peoples of the Alps but—a much greater achievement—the Alps themselves. Am I then to compare myself with this six-month commander, with this deserter of his own army? If, today, someone should take away the standards and show him Carthaginians and Romans, I am convinced he would have no idea of which army he is the consul! And, personally, I do not judge the following considerations to be of little importance. There is not a man amongst you before whose eyes I have not myself on numerous occasions performed some military exploit. Likewise there is not one whose courage *I* have not personally observed and witnessed, and whose feats I could not recount, with details of time and location. I shall take the field with men I have praised and decorated a thousand times, men to all of whom I was a stepson before becoming their commander, and I shall go into battle against soldiers who simply do not know each other.

44. 'Wherever my eyes have fallen all I see is courage and strength: a veteran infantry; cavalry, with and without bridles, drawn from tribes of noble spirit; you, our allies, loyal and brave; and you Carthaginians, who will not only fight for your country, but fight also with righteous indignation. We are on the offensive; we are going down to attack Italy. We shall fight all the more boldly and courageously—as the invader we have higher hopes, and greater morale, than the defender. In addition, our hearts are afire and spurred on by resentment, by our unjust treatment, and by humiliation.

'The Romans demanded the punishment first of your leader, me, and then of all of you, for your attack on Saguntum. Had we been delivered to them, they would have inflicted on us the cruellest of tortures. They are a barbarous and high-handed nation; they want everything to be theirs and under their control. They think they have the right to decide with whom we are to be at war, and with whom to be at peace. They confine and restrict us, using mountains and rivers as boundaries that we are not to cross, but they themselves do not observe those boundaries that they have defined.

' "Do not cross the Ebro!" they say. "Keep away from the people of Saguntum!" But is Saguntum on the Ebro? "Do not take a step in any direction!" they say. Is it not enough that you have taken from me my oldest provinces, Sicily and Sardinia? Are you taking the Spanish provinces, too? And if I cede these as well, will you cross to Africa? Did I say "*will* cross"? I mean *have* crossed. They have sent out this year's two consuls, one to Africa and the other to Spain. We have been left nothing anywhere apart from what we may defend with our weapons. The people who can afford to be timid and cowardly are those who have a refuge behind them, those who have lands and farms to receive them as they withdraw along safe and peaceful routes. But you, you must be men of courage. You must set aside as absolutely hopeless any result between victory and death, and either win or, if your fortunes waver, meet your end in battle rather than in flight. If you are all firmly resolved on this and if it is fixed in your minds, then—I shall say it again—you are already the victors. Man has been given by the immortal gods no sharper an incentive to conquer than indifference to death.'

45. Such were the words of exhortation by which the men's hearts were fired for battle on the two sides. The Romans then bridged the Ticinus, and set a fort on its bank to protect the bridge. While his enemy was busy with the construction, the Carthaginian sent Maharbal with a company of Numidian cavalry, 500 strong, to conduct raids on the farmland of the allies of the Roman people. Maharbal had orders to spare the Gauls as far as possible, and to induce their chieftains to defect.

When the bridge was completed, the Roman army was marched across into the territory of the Insubres where they encamped five miles from Victumulae. It was at Victumulae that Hannibal had his camp. He now swiftly recalled Maharbal and the cavalry, since he saw a battle was in prospect. Feeling that soldiers could never be given sufficient advice and encouragement to spur them on, he now called them to a meeting where he announced specific rewards that they could hope to win from combat. He would give them land in Italy, Africa, or Spain, he said, wherever an individual chose, and for the man receiving it, and for his children, it would be tax-free. To anyone preferring cash to land he would give the full equivalent in silver. He would make it possible for allies wishing to become Carthaginian citizens to do so, and he would do his utmost to see that those wanting to return to their homes would not wish to change places with any of their compatriots. He also offered their freedom to slaves who had accompanied their masters, undertaking to give the masters two each in their place. Wishing the men to appreciate that these engagements were binding, he held a lamb in his left hand and a stone in his right, and made a prayer to Jupiter and the other gods that they should slay him, as he slew the lamb, if he broke his word. After the prayer, he smashed the animal's head with the stone. At this each man felt the gods were smiling on his hopes, and they all thought that the fact that they were not yet fighting only delayed fulfilment of those hopes. With one heart and one voice they clamoured for battle.

46. There was nothing like as much enthusiasm amongst the Romans. Other concerns apart, they were also frightened by recent portents. A wolf had entered the camp, savaged the people it encountered, and escaped unharmed; and a swarm of bees had settled on a tree overlooking the general's headquarters. After rites to avert these omens, Scipio set off with his cavalry and light-armed javelin-throwers to get a close look at the enemy camp and at the size and make-up of his troops. In so doing he came upon Hannibal, who had himself gone forth with his cavalry to reconnoitre the surrounding area. At first neither party could see the other. Then the dust from so many men and horses on the move rose thicker, indicating the approach of the enemy. Both columns came to a halt and proceeded to prepare for battle.

Scipio positioned his javelin-throwers and Gallic cavalry in front, with the Roman and the cream of the allied cavalry in reserve. Hannibal set his bridled cavalry in the centre, and strengthened the wings with the Numidians. The battle-cry had scarcely gone up when Scipio's javelin-throwers ran back amidst the supporting troops to the second line.* After that there was a cavalry battle, which for some time remained even, but then the infantry became involved in the fighting and this startled the horses. Many riders were thrown from their mounts, or climbed down on seeing their comrades surrounded and under pressure, and it had become mostly a battle fought on foot, until the Numidians on the wings effected a slight encircling manœuvre to appear to the rear of the Romans. At this, panic struck the Romans, and that panic was increased when the consul was wounded, the threat to his life averted only by the intervention of his son (who was at that time just coming to maturity). This was to be the young man who would have the distinction of terminating this war, and who would be called 'Africanus' for his outstanding victory over Hannibal and the Carthaginians.

The disordered flight, however, was mostly confined to the javelin-throwers, whom the Numidians attacked first. The rest of the cavalry closed ranks and brought the consul into their midst, giving him protection with their own bodies as well as their arms, and taking him back to camp, with no hint of panic or disorder in their retreat.

Coelius assigns the glory of the consul's rescue to a slave of Ligurian nationality. I would rather accept the truth of the version concerning the son, an account passed down by several historians and entrenched in popular tradition.*

47. This was the first engagement with Hannibal, and it was patently obvious from it that the Carthaginians had cavalry superiority. It was also clear that, for this reason, the open plains of the kind between the Po and the Alps were not a suitable battleground for the Romans. Accordingly, the following night, Scipio ordered his men to pack up quietly, struck camp from the Ticinus, and marched swiftly to the Po. His intention was to take his army across by the pontoon bridge with which he had spanned the river, and which was not yet dismantled; he could thus avoid confusion and enemy harassment. They reached Placentia before Hannibal had definite word of their leaving the Ticinus, but the Carthaginian still captured some 600 who were too slow in unmooring a pontoon on his side of the river. He could not himself cross by the pontoon bridge since the end sections had been loosened, and the whole structure was floating downstream.

Coelius claims that Mago, his cavalry, and the Spanish infantry swam across immediately, but that Hannibal himself took the main body over by fording the Po upstream, with elephants positioned in a line to take the force of the current. Those who know the river would find it difficult to accept this. It is unlikely that cavalry could have mastered such a strong current while still retaining their arms and horses, even if one assumes that all the Spaniards were floated over on inflated skins. And, secondly, to seek out fords over the Po that would afford a crossing for an army weighed down with baggage would have meant a detour lasting several days.

More credible, in my view, are the historians who record that it took a good two days to find a spot for spanning the river with a pontoon bridge, and that the cavalry and light-armed Spanish troops were sent over it first, under Mago's leadership.*

Hannibal spent some time giving audiences to Gallic embassies before crossing the river. He then took the column of heavy-armed infantry across, and meanwhile Mago and the cavalry marched towards the enemy at Placentia, one day's journey from the river-crossing. A few days later Hannibal established a fortified camp six miles from Placentia, and the following day drew up his line of battle in full view of his enemy, offering them the opportunity to engage.

48. During the night that followed there was a bloody coup in the Roman camp, pulled off by some Gallic auxiliaries, though the commotion was disproportionate to the actual damage. About 2,000 infantrymen and 200 cavalry killed the sentries at the gates, and deserted to Hannibal. The Carthaginian welcomed them with kind words, filled them with expectations of rich rewards, and sent them off to their various communities to enlist the support of their compatriots.

Scipio feared that the coup was a signal for wholesale insurrection by the Gauls, who, becoming infected by this villainous behaviour, would now rush to arms in a fit of madness. He was still in pain from his wound, but he nevertheless slipped quietly away towards the River Trebia with his army at the fourth watch of the following night, and proceeded to move his camp to a higher elevation where the hills would obstruct cavalry. His attempt at concealment was less successful than at the Ticinus. Hannibal sent the Numidians in pursuit first, and then the entire cavalry, and would certainly have created havoc at least at the rear of the Roman column had not greed for plunder sidetracked the Numidians to the now unmanned Roman camp. There they frittered away valuable time rifling through every corner of the camp, without finding any prize worth the delay, and the enemy slipped through their fingers. The Numidians sighted the Romans only when they had already crossed the Trebia, and were measuring off their camp. They did manage to kill a few of the stragglers whom they cut off on their side of the river.

Scipio could no longer bear the discomfort caused by the jolting of his wound on the march; and, besides, he felt he should await his colleague who, he had been told, had, in fact, already been recalled from Sicily. He therefore selected and fortified a spot near the river that seemed the safest location for a stationary camp.

Hannibal dug in not far from there. Elated as he was by the victory of his cavalry, he was also worried by his lack of supplies; this was becoming more acute every day as he passed through enemy territory where no provision had been made for replenishment. He accordingly sent men to the village of Clastidium, where the Romans had stockpiled a large quantity of wheat. The Carthaginians were preparing an assault when the prospect of a sell-out emerged. The price was not high: the garrison commander, Dasius of Brundisium, was bribed with 400 gold pieces,* and Clastidium was handed over to

Hannibal. The town became the granary of the Carthaginians while they remained at the Trebia. So that Hannibal could have a reputation for clemency established right at the start, no harsh treatment was meted to the prisoners from the surrendered garrison.

49. The war on land had now come to a halt at the Trebia. In the meantime there had been land and sea operations conducted by the consul Sempronius*—and some even before Sempronius' arrival—in the area of Sicily and the islands off the Italian coast. Twenty quinqueremes, along with 1,000 marines, had been dispatched by the Carthaginians to conduct raids on the coastal areas of Italy. Nine of these headed for the Lipara Islands, eight for the Island of Vulcan. The other three were swept into the straits by rough seas. These three were sighted off Messana, and twelve ships were sent to intercept them by King Hiero of Syracuse,* who happened to be in Messana at the time awaiting the arrival of the Roman consul. The ships captured the Carthaginian vessels, meeting no resistance, and brought them to the harbour of Messana.

From the prisoners it was learned that, apart from the fleet of twenty ships sent to Italy, to which the prisoners themselves belonged, a further thirty-five quinqueremes were making for Sicily, with the aim of spreading disaffection amongst the former Carthaginian allies. The principal mission of these vessels was to seize Lilybaeum, they said, but they thought that this fleet had also been driven off course, towards the Aegates Islands, by the same bad weather by which they had been scattered themselves. The king made a full report of this, just as it had been told to him, in a letter to Marcus Aemilius, who had responsibility for Sicily; and he advised Aemilius to secure Lilybaeum with a powerful garrison. Officers and tribunes were immediately sent around the various city-states by the praetor, pressing the inhabitants to heighten their caution, and above all to keep Lilybaeum on a war footing. A proclamation was issued that crews should take to their ships cooked rations sufficient for ten days, and that all should immediately embark when the signal was given. In addition, men were sent the length of the coast to keep watch from towers for the coming of the enemy fleet.

The Carthaginians had purposely slowed the progress of their ships in order to arrive at Lilybaeum before dawn, but thanks to this vigilance on shore they were nevertheless detected, as there was a moon throughout the night and they were also coming under sail. A signal was immediately given from the watchtowers, there was a call to arms in the town and the ships were manned. Some of the troops mounted the walls and patrolled the gates, others boarded the ships. The Carthaginians could see they would not be engaging men caught off guard, and they kept their distance from the harbour until daylight, using the time to stow their tackle and ready the fleet for action. At daybreak they backed water into the open sea to allow room for the engagement and ensure that the enemy ships had a clear passage from the harbour. The Romans did not refuse battle, either; they drew confidence from the memory of their past successes in those very waters and from the numbers and fighting ability of their men.

50. When they got out to sea, the plan of the Romans was to join battle and fight at close quarters. The Carthaginians, by contrast, wanted to manœuvre, to use tactics rather than brute force, and to make it a battle of ships rather than of men and weapons. Their fleet was well manned with crews, but short of marines, and any time a ship was grappled the Carthaginians had nothing like the same number of soldiers fighting from it. When this was noticed, the Romans' numerical advantage raised their morale while the Carthaginians' deficiency lowered theirs. Seven Carthaginian vessels were immediately surrounded, and the rest took flight. There were 1,700 marines and sailors in the captured ships, including three Carthaginian noblemen. The Roman fleet returned to port undamaged; just one ship was holed, but even she was brought home.

The consul Tiberius Sempronius came to Messana after this battle, but before news of it reached those in town. As Sempronius entered the strait, King Hiero came to meet him at the head of a fully equipped fleet. Hiero crossed from the royal barge to the Roman flagship, congratulated the consul on having arrived safely with his army and ships, and prayed that he would have a successful and favourable crossing to Sicily. He then explained the situation on the island, and the schemes of the Carthaginians, and promised to be as committed a helper of the Roman people as an old man as he had been as a youth in the earlier war. He would supply the consul's legions and the crews with grain and clothing, and at no cost, he said, adding that Lilybaeum and the coastal city-states were facing great danger and some would be happy to see a regime-change.

The consul therefore felt he should lose no time in heading for Lilybaeum with his fleet, and the king and the royal fleet set off with him. During the voyage from Messana they received news from Lilybaeum of the battle that had been fought there, and of the defeat and capture of the enemy ships.

51. The consul sent Hiero and the royal fleet back from Lilybaeum and, leaving the praetor to protect the Sicilian coastline, himself crossed to the island of Melita, which was occupied by the Carthaginians. On his arrival, Hamilcar son of Gisgo, who commanded the garrison there, surrendered himself, along with slightly fewer than 2,000 men, and the town and the island were turned over to the Romans. A few days later Sempronius returned to Lilybaeum, and there the prisoners, apart from men of noble birth, were all auctioned off by the consul and praetor.

Now that the consul felt that Sicily was well enough protected in that quarter, he crossed to the Island of Vulcan, as there had been a report of a Carthaginian fleet at anchor there. However, no enemy was found in the vicinity of the islands. It so happened that the Carthaginians had already crossed to conduct raids on the coastline of Italy, and after laying waste the agricultural land of Vibo they were even threatening the town of Vibo. News of the enemy raid on the farmland of Vibo reached the consul as he was heading back to Sicily. Sempronius was also brought a letter from the Senate, informing him of Hannibal's crossing into Italy, and instructing him to bring his colleague help at the earliest possible opportunity.

Sempronius now had many simultaneous concerns on his mind. He straight away boarded his army on some ships, and sent it up the Adriatic to Ariminum.* He assigned to his legate Sextus Pomponius the task of patrolling the territory of Vibo and the coastal areas of Italy with twenty-five warships, and he brought the fleet of the praetor Marcus Aemilius up to a full complement of fifty ships. Sempronius himself settled affairs in Sicily, and then came to Ariminum with twelve ships, skirting the Italian coast. He marched off from there with his army, and joined up with his colleague at the River Trebia.

52. At this point the two consuls and all available Roman forces were facing Hannibal, and it was perfectly clear that either the empire of Rome could be defended by those troops, or else there was simply no hope.* However, one of the consuls, disheartened by the single cavalry engagement and by the wound he had suffered, preferred to see things deferred; the other, his drive still fresh, and so all the more audacious, would brook no delay.

In those days, the land between the Trebia and the Po was inhabited by Gauls, and as the two superpowers came into conflict these peoples vacillated in their support, quite clearly with an eye on gaining the eventual winner's favour. The Romans were happy enough with this situation, as long as the Gauls took no action, but the Carthaginian leader was not at all happy—he had come to liberate the Gauls, he would say, and at their request. Hannibal's anger, and at the same time his wish to enrich his men with spoils, led to his ordering 2,000 infantry and 1,000 cavalry (Numidians mostly, but with some Gauls among them) to systematically pillage Gallic farmlands right up to the banks of the Po. The Gauls had been ambivalent up to that point but, with no help at hand, they were now driven to turn from the perpetrators of the wrong done to them to those they hoped would avenge it. They sent a deputation to the consuls and begged for Roman aid for a land that was suffering damage because its inhabitants were simply too loyal to Rome.

Cornelius liked neither the reason for taking action nor the timing. He was wary of the Gallic people because of their many acts of treachery; and, even if the memory of other things had been erased by the passage of time, he remembered the recent duplicity of the Boii. Sempronius, by contrast, was of the opinion that the strongest bond for maintaining the loyalty of the allies was forged by defending the first ones who needed help. While his colleague hesitated, Sempronius sent his cavalry, and some 1,000 javelin-throwing infantry, across the Trebia to defend the Gallic farmlands. These took the Carthaginians by surprise as they were roving around out of formation, most of them also burdened with loot, and created sheer panic and great carnage, chasing them right to the outposts of the enemy camp. From here they were driven back by superior enemy numbers, and only with the arrival of reinforcements did they resume their offensive. Fortunes then alternated, the two sides by turns in pursuit and on the defensive, and, although they finished the combat on even terms, enemy casualties were greater, and the Romans were credited with the victory.

53. But in no one's eyes was the victory greater and more decisive than in the consul's. Sempronius was absolutely delighted—he had carried the day with that branch of the forces with which the other

consul had seen defeat. His men's morale had been restored and strengthened, he claimed, and nobody wanted to delay an all-out battle, apart from his colleague. Cornelius' problem was more psychological than physical, he said; the thought of his wound made him shudder at the prospect of armed engagement. But they should not become decrepit in a sick man's company. Why put things off further, or fritter away valuable time? Were they waiting for a third consul, another army? The Carthaginians were encamped in Italy, he said, almost in sight of the city. What they were after was not Sicily and Sardinia, which had been taken from them by conquest, or Spain north of the Ebro. No, what they wanted was to evict the Romans from their native soil, and from the land in which they had been born. 'Our fathers were used to campaigning around the walls of Carthage,' he declared. 'How they would groan to see us, their descendants—two consuls with consular armies—cowering within their fortifications, in the heart of Italy, when the Carthaginian has brought under his sway the lands between the Alps and the Apennines!'

Such were Sempronius' comments at his colleague's sickbed, and in staff meetings as well, as if he were making a public address. He was egged on, too, by the approaching elections—he feared that the war might drag on into the term of the new consuls—and also by the chance of appropriating to himself all the glory, while his colleague lay ill. Accordingly, while Cornelius remonstrated in vain, he ordered his men to prepare for an imminent engagement.

Hannibal could see what his enemy's best strategy would be, and he could scarcely hope for any impulsive or foolish move on the consuls' part. But he now knew for himself what he had heard earlier, namely that one of the consuls was by nature hot-headed and impetuous; and he also believed that Sempronius would have been made even more impetuous by his successful skirmish with the Punic raiding party. He was therefore not without hope of soon having an opportunity for action. He now focused anxiously on not missing his moment, while his enemy's soldiers lacked experience, while the better of the two generals was out of action with a wound, and while the Gauls were still in good spirits. For he realized that the further their vast horde was drawn from home, the less eager they would be to follow him. For these and other such reasons, he was hoping for an imminent engagement, and he wished to initiate one if the enemy hesitated. Gallic spies were chosen for gathering the intelligence he required—a safer option since Gauls were serving in both camps—and when these brought back news that the Romans were ready for battle he proceeded to seek out a spot for an ambush.

54. Between the two armies was a stream, high-banked on both sides and overgrown with marsh reeds and the shrubs and prickles usually found covering wastelands. Hannibal rode around the area and, after seeing for himself that it provided sufficient cover for concealing even cavalry, he said to his brother Mago: 'This will be the spot to position yourself. Select from your entire force* 100 infantrymen and 100 cavalrymen, and come to me with them at first watch. Now it is time for rest and refreshment.'

With that the officers were dismissed, and shortly afterwards Mago appeared with his handpicked soldiers. 'I see here the toughest of my men,' said Hannibal. 'But to have strength in numbers to match the strength of your courage, you must each choose nine men like yourselves from your respective troops and maniples. Mago will show you the spot for the ambush—you are facing an enemy blind to such military stratagems.'

So saying, Hannibal sent Mago off with his 1,000 horsemen and 1,000 infantry. At dawn he ordered his Numidian cavalry to cross the River Trebia, ride up to the gates of the enemy and entice him out to battle by hurling spears at the sentry-posts. Then, after provoking a confrontation, they were to draw him over the river by gradually ceding ground.

Such were the orders for the Numidians. The other infantry and cavalry officers were instructed to tell all their men to take their meal, and then await the signal under arms and with horses saddled.

When the Numidians struck, Sempronius first led out all his cavalry, supremely confident as he was in that branch of his forces, and then 6,000 infantry, and finally his entire force—he was eager for the battle, and was already decided upon fighting it. It happened to be the winter solstice,* and there was snowy weather in the country between the Alps and the Apennines, an area that is also subject to intense cold from the neighbouring rivers and marshlands. In addition, men and horses had been hurriedly led out, without taking nourishment or any measures to counteract the cold. They were chilled to the marrow and, with every step they took towards the breezes coming from the river, the more intense became the cold blowing in their faces. But then, chasing the retreating Numidians, they plunged into the water, which had been swollen by overnight rain and came up to their chests. At that point, and especially as they emerged from the river, they all felt their limbs so numb with cold that they could scarcely hold their weapons, and at the same time exhaustion and, as the day progressed, hunger also sapped their strength.

55. In the meantime, Hannibal's men had lit fires before their tents, oil had been distributed amongst the companies for softening up the soldiers' limbs, and they had taken a leisurely meal. When news came that the enemy had crossed the river, they took up their weapons, in good form both mentally and physically, and proceeded to the battle line.

Hannibal deployed his Balearic and light-armed troops, some 8,000 men, before the standards, and behind them he placed his heavier infantry, which represented the real strength and kernel of his forces. On the wings he set 10,000 cavalry and, dividing his elephants in two groups, added these to the two wings as well.

The Roman cavalry had been in disorder giving chase, and then they were unexpectedly confronted by the Numidians, who suddenly made a stand. The consul then called them back by signalling the retreat, and stationed them on the flanks of his infantry. There were 18,000 Romans and 20,000 Latin allies, plus some auxiliary forces from the Cenomani, the one Gallic tribe that had remained loyal. Such were the troops that faced each other in battle.

The action was initiated by Hannibal's Balearic troops. However, being confronted with the superior might of the Roman legions, the light-armed force was swiftly withdrawn to the wings, and this had the immediate effect of putting the Roman cavalry under pressure. Even so, the cavalry could, on its own, barely make a stand against the Carthaginian cavalry—4,000 men were facing 10,000, and they were exhausted and facing mostly fresh troops—and now they were also buried under a virtual cloud of missiles hurled by the Balearic forces. In addition to this, the elephants standing at the extremities of the wings caused widespread panic, especially amongst the horses, which were terrified not just by the sight but also by their unfamiliar smell.

As for the infantry, the engagement was more evenly matched in terms of courage than strength. The Carthaginians had come into battle with strength unimpaired, having shortly before taken food and rest; the Romans, by contrast, were hungry and tired, and stiff and numb with cold. Even so, their courage would have enabled them to make a stand—had their fight been only against the infantry. As it was, the Balearic troops, after putting the cavalry to flight, were hurling spears onto the Roman flanks, and the elephants had begun to bear down on the infantry in the centre of the field. Furthermore, as soon as the Roman line had, without realizing it, passed the Carthaginian hiding-place, Mago and his Numidians rose up to their rear, causing enormous confusion and panic. But despite these setbacks all around, the Roman line still held fast for a time, even against the elephants, which no one could have expected. Skirmishers, expressly posted for the job, would turn the beasts with showers of spears; then, when they turned, they would follow and stab them under the tail where, thanks to the softness of the hide, the animals are most vulnerable.

56. The beasts were panic-stricken, and roused to fury against their own side, and so Hannibal ordered them to be driven from the centre of the fight against the Gallic auxiliaries on the far left wing. There they immediately occasioned what was undoubtedly a rout, and this inspired fresh panic in the Romans when they saw their auxiliaries driven off in defeat.

The Romans were now bunched into a circle as they fought. Unable to break out elsewhere, about 10,000 men forced a passage through the African centre, which was reinforced with Gallic auxiliaries, and there they inflicted heavy losses on the enemy. Cut off by the river, they were unable to return to their camp, and because of the rain it was impossible to see where to bring assistance to their comrades. They therefore headed directly for Placentia.

After that more of them broke out, and in all directions. Those who made for the river were either swept away by the waters, or were caught by the enemy as they hesitated to jump in. Those who dispersed in flight through the countryside made for Placentia by following in the tracks of the main body in its retreat. Others again, sufficiently emboldened to plunge into the river by fear of the enemy, reached camp after making it across. Rain mixed with snow, and cold of unbearable intensity, took the lives of large numbers of men and pack animals, and of almost all the elephants.

The Trebia marked the limit of the Carthaginian pursuit of the enemy; and they returned to camp so numb with cold as to barely experience the joy of victory.* On the night that followed, the garrison of the Roman camp and all the soldiers remaining after the defeat—most of them unarmed—crossed the Trebia on rafts. The Carthaginians either heard nothing over the noise of the rain or, unable to stir from exhaustion and wounds, simply pretended to hear nothing. They took no action, either, as the army was led in silence to Placentia by the consul Scipio. Scipio then crossed the Po, and continued to Cremona, to relieve the one colony of the burden of wintering two armies.

57. Such was the panic brought to Rome by this debacle that people believed that the enemy would immediately march on the city, that they had no hope and no means of repelling the attack from their gates and walls. One consul had been defeated at the Ticinus, they said, and the other had been brought back from Sicily. Now both consuls and the two consular armies together had been defeated. So what other commanders, and what other legions, were there to call to their aid? Such was the level of anxiety when the consul Sempronius arrived. He had taken an enormous risk in passing through the enemy cavalry, which was roaming far and wide on marauding expeditions. It had been an act of sheer bravado on his part,* and not a calculated risk, or one taken with some prospect of eluding the enemy, or making a stand should he fail to elude them. Sempronius saw to the consular elections, the one pressing need at the moment, and returned to his winter quarters. The consuls elected were Gnaeus Servilius and Gaius Flaminius.

In fact, there was no peace for the Romans even in winter quarters. Numidian cavalry ranged far and wide and Celtiberians and Lusitanians were doing so wherever the ground proved too difficult for the Numidians. As a result, all Roman supplies were cut off from every quarter, with the exception of those shipped up the Po.

There was a Roman storage-depot near Placentia that was well defended by stout fortifications and a powerful garrison, and Hannibal set out with his cavalry and light-armed infantry in the hope of storming this stockade. Since his greatest chance of success lay in keeping the operation secret, he made the attack at night, but he failed to elude the sentinels. A cry immediately went up, so loud that it was heard even in Placentia. The result was that the consul appeared on the scene at daybreak with his cavalry. He had left instructions for the legions to follow in battle formation, but in the meantime there was a cavalry engagement. Since Hannibal left the fight with a wound, the enemy were filled with alarm, and the post was very successfully defended.

After that, Hannibal took a few days' repose and then, though his wound was not yet properly healed, he proceeded to launch an attack on Victumulae. This had been a storage depot for the Romans during the Gallic War.* The place had been fortified during that period, and subsequently it had been thickly settled by an assortment of inhabitants from the neighbouring tribes. At that time, too, fear of Hannibal's marauding had driven a number of people to the town from the countryside. Such was the make-up of the band that hastily took up arms and advanced to face Hannibal, their spirits fired by word of the resolute defence mounted by the garrison at Placentia. They were ordered as marching columns rather than battle lines when the two forces met on the road. But since there was nothing on one side but a disorganized mob, and on the other a commander with confidence in his soldiers, and soldiers with confidence in their commander, some 35,000 men were routed by a mere handful.

The next day the townspeople capitulated and a garrison was posted within their walls. They were ordered to surrender their weapons and, when they complied, a signal was suddenly given to the conquerors to ransack the place like a captured city. The people were spared none of the atrocities usually recounted by historians as occurring in such circumstances. Indeed, the wretched inhabitants were subjected to every imaginable form of sexual abuse, cruelty, and inhuman oppression. Such were Hannibal's winter operations.

58. The Carthaginian soldiers were now given a respite of no great duration while the weather remained unbearably cold. Then, at the first faint glimmerings of spring, Hannibal left his winter quarters, and struck out into Etruria.* His aim was to enlist the support of its people, too, either by coercion or with their compliance, as he had done with the Gauls and Ligurians. As he crossed the Apennines, he was overtaken by a storm so severe that it was almost worse than the foul weather of the Alps. Wind and rain together blew straight into the men's faces. At first they simply halted, because either they would have had to drop their weapons or, if they struggled on against the blast, they were spun round and bowled over by it. Then, when it began to block their breathing, and prevented them from getting their breath, they turned their backs to the wind and sat for a while.

At that point there came a huge crash from the heavens, and there were flashes of lightning, amidst frightening peals of thunder. Blinded and deafened, they all froze with fear. Finally, there was a torrential downpour, and the force of the wind rose all the more, so that pitching camp in the very spot where they had been caught seemed unavoidable.

That, however, proved to be the start of a fresh set of problems. The men could not unfold, or set up, their tents, and what *was* set up would not stay up, for the wind tore everything apart and swept it away. Soon the water whipped up by the wind froze above the frigid mountaintops, and this brought down so much snow and hail that they dropped everything and fell to the ground, buried under their shelters rather than protected by them. This was followed by temperatures so low that anyone trying to get up, or extricate himself from that sad mess of men and pack animals, could not do so for a long time: their bodies numb with cold, they found they could barely bend their joints. Finally, shaking themselves, they began to move about and pull themselves together, and fires started to appear here and there, but, still helpless, they all looked for help from each other. For two days they remained in that spot, virtually in a state of siege. Many men and beasts of burden were lost, together with seven of the elephants that had survived the battle at the Trebia.

59. After the descent from the Apennines, Hannibal moved his camp back towards Placentia, halting after he had advanced about ten miles. The next day he marched on his enemy with 12,000 infantry and 5,000 cavalry; and the consul Sempronius, who had by now returned from Rome, did not refuse battle.

That day the two camps remained three miles distant from each other, but on the next the sides engaged with great fervour, and with fluctuating results. At the first clash, the Romans were clearly superior, so much so that they not only triumphed in the field but, after driving back the enemy, chased him to his camp, which they soon had under attack. Hannibal stationed a few men to secure the rampart and gateways; the rest he withdrew en masse into the centre of the camp, telling them to be on the alert for the signal for a counterattack.

It was already about the ninth hour of the day, and the Roman commander, his men exhausted to no purpose, saw no prospect of taking the camp. He therefore signalled the recall. Hannibal heard this; he also saw that the fighting had slackened, and that the Romans had fallen back from his camp. Suddenly he unleashed his cavalry against his enemy from right and left, and he himself counter-attacked from the centre of the camp with the elite of his infantry. Seldom could one have found a battle more savage, and more remarkable for losses on both sides, had daylight allowed it to go on. The onset of night, however, broke off an engagement that had started with enormous ferocity. As a result, the clash was marked more by its violence than loss of life, and the two sides left the field with equal losses, after a battle that was pretty much a draw. No more than 600 infantry fell on each side, and only half that number of cavalry, but the Romans suffered greater damage than the numbers would indicate, for the dead included some men of equestrian rank, five military tribunes, and three allied officers.

After the battle Hannibal withdrew into Liguria, and Sempronius to Luca.* On his arrival, Hannibal was presented by the Ligurians with two Roman quaestors, Gaius Fulvius and Lucius Lucretius, who had been taken in an ambush, and with them two military tribunes and five men of equestrian rank, for the most part senators' sons. This gesture was intended to reassure Hannibal of the stability of his peace treaty and alliance with the Ligurians.

60. Meanwhile Gnaeus Cornelius Scipio had been sent to Spain with a fleet and an army and, while these events were taking place in Italy, he had left the mouth of the Rhône and skirted the Pyrenees, putting in at Emporiae.* Disembarking his army there, he had, starting with operations against the Lacetani, brought under Roman control the entire coastline as far as the River Ebro. This he had done partly by renewing old alliances, and partly by forging new ones. The reputation he here established for clemency served him well, not only with the coastal peoples, but also with the more recalcitrant tribes of the interior and the mountains. With them he was able to conclude not just a non-aggression pact but an offensive alliance, as well, and some strong cohorts of auxiliary troops were raised from their number.

Command of the area north of the Ebro lay with Hanno, whom Hannibal had left behind to safeguard the region. Believing he should face the Romans before everything fell into their hands, Hanno now encamped in sight of the enemy, and led his men out for battle. The Roman commander also thought there should be no postponement of hostilities: he knew that he had to fight Hanno and Hasdrubal, and he preferred to take them on one at a time rather than together. The engagement proved to be no great struggle. Six thousand of the enemy were cut down, and 2,000 captured, including the camp garrison—for the camp was stormed, and the commander himself taken prisoner, along with several important people. The town of Cissis, close to the camp, was also taken by storm.* But the booty from the town consisted of articles of little value—some primitive furniture and some worthless slaves. The camp, however, was a source of riches for the soldiers. It was the base not only of the army that had been defeated, but also of the army campaigning in Italy with Hannibal; and almost all valuables had been left south of the Pyrenees, so that the soldiers would not have heavy baggage to carry.

61. Hasdrubal had crossed the Ebro with 8,000 infantry and 1,000 cavalry before he received reliable news of this defeat. His aim had been to meet the Romans as soon as they arrived but, after being told of the debacle at Cissis, and the loss of the Carthaginian camp, he veered towards the coast. Not far from Tarraco he encountered the marines and crews from the Roman fleet, who were wandering aimlessly through the countryside—for success almost inevitably leads to carelessness. Hasdrubal sent out his cavalry in every direction against them, driving them back to their ships and producing great carnage and greater havoc. Not daring to linger in the area any longer for fear of being overtaken by Scipio, he then fell back across the Ebro. When Scipio received word of this new enemy, he did indeed lose no time in bringing up his column. Then, after punishing a few of the officers from the fleet, and leaving a small garrison at Tarraco, he returned with his fleet to Emporiae.

Scipio had scarcely left when Hasdrubal reappeared on the scene. He pushed the Ilergetes, a tribe that had given hostages to Scipio, into insurrection and then, accompanied by soldiers from that tribe, he laid waste the farmlands of allies who had remained loyal to Rome. Scipio was thus drawn from his winter quarters, but Hasdrubal once more retired from all the territory north of the Ebro. Scipio then launched a campaign against the Ilergetes, who were now abandoned by the man responsible for their uprising. He drove them all into their tribal capital of Atanagrus, which he blockaded. In a matter of days he took them back under his authority and control, exacting from them a greater number of hostages than he had on the earlier occasion, and imposing a fine on them as well.*

Scipio next advanced against the Ausetani, close to the Ebro, who were also allies of the Carthaginians, and laid siege to their city. The Lacetani tried to bring them aid (they were their neighbours), but Scipio caught them in an ambush at night not far from the city, which they were intending to enter. About 12,000 were killed; nearly all the others, their weapons thrown aside, dispersed far and wide throughout the countryside, and fled to their homes. As for the Ausetani, now under siege, all that saved them was the winter weather that plagued their assailants. The blockade went on for thirty days, and during that time the depth of the snow was hardly ever less than four feet. Such was the snow-cover on the Roman mantlets and siege-sheds that it alone provided sufficient protection against the occasional fire-brand hurled at them by the enemy. Eventually, their leader Amusicus sought refuge with Hasdrubal, and the Ausetani surrendered, after agreeing to a payment of twenty talents of silver. The Romans then returned to their winter quarters at Tarraco.*

62. In Rome or its environs there were many prodigies that winter, or rather many prodigies were reported, and too readily accepted, the usual experience when people's minds have turned to superstition. They included the following:

A freeborn six-month-old child had shouted 'Triumph' in the vegetable market.

In the Forum Boarium, an ox had of its own accord climbed to the third floor of a building, and then thrown itself off when frightened by the alarmed reaction of the tenants.

Glowing ship-like figures had appeared in the sky.

The temple of Hope in the vegetable market had been struck by lightning.

At Lanuvium, a spear had moved on its own, and a crow had swooped down into the temple of Juno, actually settling on the goddess's couch.

At several places in the countryside of Amiternum, figures of men had been seen in the distance dressed in white, but these had never come into contact with anyone.

In Picenum stones had fallen as a rain shower.

At Caere the oracular lots had shrunk.*

In Gaul, a wolf had unsheathed a sentinel's sword and made off with it.

For all the other prodigies the decemvirs were told to consult the scrolls, but for the shower of stones in Picenum a nine-day sacrifice was officially prescribed. Then almost the entire citizenry promptly set about performing other ceremonies of expiation. First of all, the city was ritually purified, and full-grown sacrificial animals were killed for the gods specified by the decemvirs. A gold gift weighing 40 pounds was transported to Lanuvium for Juno, and the married women dedicated a bronze statue to Juno on the Aventine. A *lectisternium* was prescribed for Caere, where the oracular lots had shrunk, and public prayers were to be made to Fortune on Mt. Algidus. At Rome, too, a *lectisternium* was prescribed, here for Juventas,* and public prayers were to be offered at the temple of Hercules, who was specifically named; but then the whole population was also directed to offer them at all the couches of the gods. Five full-grown animals were sacrificed to the Genius of Rome, and the praetor Gaius Atilius Serranus was ordered to make vows that would be discharged on condition that the republic were in the same position ten years from then. These expiatory rites, and vows, that were performed in accordance with the Sibylline Books* did much to allay religious fears in people's minds.

63. The legions wintering at Placentia had fallen by lot to Flaminius, one of the consuls designate, and he sent written instructions to the consul to have these troops quartered at Ariminum by 15 March.* It was Flaminius' intention to commence his consulship right there, in the province. For he remembered his earlier disagreements with the Senate, when he was tribune of the plebs and, later on, consul—the disagreements first over his entry to the consulship, which the senators tried to revoke, and then over his right to a triumph. But he was also unpopular with the senators because of a new bill, directed against the Senate, which Quintus Claudius had proposed, and which Gaius Flaminius was the only senator to support. The proposed law forbade anyone who was a senator, or whose father had been a senator, to own a sea-going vessel with a capacity of more than 300 amphorae, that being regarded as sufficiently large for transporting produce from a country estate—for all commerce was considered unbecoming for senators. It was a contentious issue which had generated hostility amongst the nobility towards Flaminius, who had spoken for the bill, though it had also won him support amongst the people and, as a result, gained him a second consulship.*

For these reasons Flaminius felt the senators would keep him in the city by deliberately misinterpreting the auspices, or by using the delay imposed by the Latin Festival, or anything else that could retard a consul. Accordingly, he pretended he had a journey to make, and slipped away furtively to his province as a private citizen. When this became public knowledge, it generated fresh anger in the breasts of the already hostile senators. Gaius Flaminius, they declared, was now at war not merely with the Senate, but with the immortal gods. When the auspices were unfavourable on the last occasion that he was made consul, gods and men tried to call him back from the actual battlefield, but he had not listened. Guiltily aware of the disrespect he had shown them, he had this time steered clear of the Capitol and the formal pronouncement of his vows. He did not want to come to the temple of Jupiter Optimus Maximus on the day of his entry into office, and did not want to see and deliberate with the Senate by which he was detested and which he, and he alone, detested. He wished to avoid giving notice of the Latin Festival, offering the customary sacrifice to Jupiter Latiaris on the Alban Mount,* proceeding to the Capitol to make his vows after taking the auspices, and then setting off for his province dressed in his military cloak and accompanied by his lictors. No, they said, he had gone secretly, furtively, without the decorations of office and without lictors, like a camp-follower, and no differently than if he had left the country to become an exile. To enter office at Ariminum rather than Rome, they concluded, and to put on the *praetexta* in an inn rather than before his household gods—this, of course, better suited the majesty of his command!

The vote for recalling Flaminius and making him return was unanimous.* He was to be compelled to present himself for the performance of all his duties towards gods and men before leaving for his army and his province. It was decided that a delegation be sent to him, and Quintus Terentius and Marcus Antistius went as the delegates. However, they made no more impression on him than had the letter sent to him by the Senate during his previous consulship.

A few days later Flaminius entered his consulship. He was offering the sacrifice when the calf, which had already been dealt the blow, charged from the hands of the celebrants, spattering the bystanders with blood. The commotion and alarm was even greater amongst those further away, who had no idea of what was causing the excitement. This was interpreted by a number of people as a frightful omen.

After that Flaminius assumed command of the two legions from Sempronius, and two from the praetor Gaius Atilius, and the army proceeded on its march into Etruria through the Apennine passes.

BOOK TWENTY-TWO

1. Spring was now approaching, and so Hannibal emerged from his winter quarters. His earlier attempt to cross the Apennines had been thwarted by the unbearably cold weather and the waiting period had been very dangerous and fraught with fear. The Gauls had been induced to revolt by hopes of plunder and booty, but now they saw that, instead of taking loot and spoils from the territory of others, their own lands were the theatre of war, and they were burdened with providing winter quarters for the armies of both sides. They therefore transferred their animosity from the Romans back to Hannibal. He had often been a target of the plots of Gallic chieftains, but he had been saved from them by the Gauls' own treachery to each other, since they betrayed a conspiracy as easily as they had formed it. He had also protected himself against their plots by confusing them with various changes of clothing and headgear.* But the fear of such plots was a further reason for his hasty move from his winter quarters.

It was about this time, on 15 March, that the consul Gnaeus Servilius entered office in Rome.* When Servilius opened discussion of the current state of affairs, the senators' resentment towards Gaius Flaminius resurfaced. They had elected two consuls, they said, but had just one—what legal or religious sanction did Flaminius have for his authority? Magistrates took that authority with them from home—when they left the state and their own hearths—only after celebrating the Latin Festival, performing the sacrifice on the Alban Mount, and making vows in accordance with ritual on the Capitol. Auspices did not go with a private individual, they said, nor could someone who had left without them take them for the first time in a foreign land.

Fears were heightened by prodigies that were simultaneously reported from several places. In Sicily, the spears of a number of soldiers had burst into flames, and this also happened in Sardinia to a staff that a horseman had been holding in his hand while he was doing the rounds of the sentries on the wall. In Sardinia, too, beaches had been lit up with numerous fires, two shields had oozed blood, a number of soldiers had been struck by lightning, and the sun's orb appeared to have grown smaller. At Praeneste, burning stones had fallen from the sky. At Arpi, shields had been seen in the sky and the sun seemed to be fighting with the moon. At Capena, two moons had arisen during the daytime. The waters at Caere had flowed mixed with blood, and the spring of Hercules itself had streaks of blood in its flow. In the region of Antium, harvesters found that bloody ears of wheat had fallen into their baskets. At Falerii, a huge fissure seemed to appear in the sky and a blinding light shone out from the opening. The oracular lots had spontaneously shrunk in size, and one of them fell out bearing the words 'Mars is brandishing his spear'. During this same period, in Rome, sweat appeared on the statue of Mars on the Appian Way, and on the figures of the wolves. At Capua, the sky appeared to be on fire, and the moon seemed to fall during a rain shower. Then less spectacular prodigies also won belief—some people's goats growing wool, and a hen turning into a cock and vice versa.

These signs were brought to the Senate's attention just as they had been reported, along with the individuals who had witnessed them, and the consul sought the senators' opinions on the appropriate rites to be observed. Their decision was that full-grown animals should be used for the expiation of some prodigies, and suckling animals for others, and that there be a three-day period of public prayers at all the couches of the gods. For the rest, the decemvirs were to study the Books, and such measures were to be taken as the decemvirs interpreted as pleasing to the gods on the basis of the holy verses.

Following the advice of the decemvirs, the Senate decided that, in the first instance, a gift of a fifty-pound thunderbolt of gold be made to Jupiter, and gifts of silver to Juno and Minerva. Sacrifices of full-grown victims were to be made to Queen Juno on the Aventine and to Juno Sospita at Lanuvium. In addition, the married women were to gather together as much money as each could afford and bear it as a gift to Queen Juno on the Aventine, where a *lectisternium* was also to be held. Even freedwomen were required to contribute money, according to their means, for a gift for Feronia.

When all this was done, the decemvirs held a sacrifice of full-grown victims in the forum at Ardea. Finally, when December came round, a sacrifice was offered at the temple of Saturn in Rome, orders were issued for a *lectisternium*—which the senators conducted—and there was a public feast. Throughout the city, for a day and a night, the cry 'Saturnalia' went up, and the people were instructed to keep the day as a holiday which they were to observe ever after.

2. While the consul was busy at Rome with ceremonies of propitiation and with the mobilization of troops, Hannibal had left his winter quarters. Word had come to him that the consul Flaminius had reached Arretium and so, although he was shown an easier but longer route, he took the shorter path through the marshes of the River Arno, which at that time was unusually high.

Hannibal directed the Spaniards and Africans—the very best of his veteran troops—to lead the line of march, taking their baggage within their ranks so they would not lack vital supplies if compelled to halt at any stage. He ordered the Gauls to follow them, and form the centre of the column, while the cavalry were to be in the last position. Finally, Mago and the light-armed Numidians were to bring up the rear. Mago had the special charge of keeping the Gauls in check, preventing them from slipping away, or stopping, if they tired of the long and gruelling journey (Gauls as a race having little tolerance for hardships of that kind).

The troops in front simply followed the lead of the guides, and they managed to keep up through the deep and almost bottomless morasses left by the river, despite being almost swallowed up by the mud and submerged in water. But the Gauls were unable to remain on their feet once they stumbled, or to extricate themselves from the deep holes; their spirit could not sustain their strength, nor hope their spirit. Some, physically exhausted, had difficulty dragging themselves along, and others, their spirit broken from fatigue, simply collapsed, and perished amongst the beasts of burden that themselves lay dying all around. Most debilitating of all was the sleeplessness they endured for four days and three nights. Everything was covered with water, and finding a dry spot to set down their wearied limbs was impossible. And so they would pile their baggage packs together in the water and lie down on them; or the cadavers of pack animals that were strewn in heaps all along their path provided as much of a bed as they needed. All they sought was something above water that would give them a moment's sleep.

As for Hannibal himself, he had been suffering from an eye-infection since the inclement spring weather with its alternating

hot and cold temperatures, and now he rode the one surviving elephant to keep himself higher above the water. However, the sleep-
deprivation, the damp nights, and the swampy atmosphere all had a
bad effect on his head, and since there was no place and no time for
treatment he went blind in one eye.*

3. Many men and pack animals had died horrible deaths by the
time Hannibal finally emerged from the marshes, and he took the
first possible opportunity of encamping on dry land. Here he was
informed by scouts that the Roman army was close to the walls of
Arretium. He thereupon proceeded with a very thorough and detailed enquiry into the consul's strategy and way of thinking, into the
geography and routes of the area and its capability of providing
supplies, and into everything else that it was valuable for him to know.

The area, the Etruscan plains lying between Faesulae and
Arretium, was amongst the most fertile in Italy, well blessed with
grain, livestock, and all other commodities. The consul had become
headstrong as a result of his earlier consulship, having no respect,
not just for the laws and the Senate, but even for the gods. His
natural recklessness had been further nourished by good luck, which
had secured him success in civilian and in military life. It was therefore perfectly clear that Flaminius would have no regard for god or
man, and that his conduct would be characterized throughout by
arrogance and lack of caution. And, to make him more ready to yield
to his natural defects, the Carthaginian was preparing to stimulate
him and stir him to action. Leaving his enemy to the left, Hannibal
made for Faesulae and went on to conduct raids in central Etruria.
There, with slaughter and burning, he provided the consul with a
distant spectacle of as much devastation as he could.

Even if his enemy had remained inactive, Flaminius would not
have remained inactive himself—and now he saw allied property
hauled off and pillaged almost before his eyes. He took it as a personal insult that the Carthaginian was meandering through central
Italy and meeting no opposition as he advanced to launch an assault
on the very walls of Rome. In council, everybody else was advocating
a prudent rather than a flamboyant course of action. They should
await Flaminius' colleague, they suggested, so as to have combined
forces and a unified plan and strategy for the campaign, and in the
meantime use their cavalry and light infantry to curb the unchecked
raiding of the enemy. Furious, Flaminius stormed out of the council,

and put up the signal simultaneously for marching and engaging the enemy.

'Why, yes,' he said, 'let us just sit before the walls of Arretium! This is where our home and our hearths are! Let us have Hannibal slip through our fingers and make a thorough job of pillaging Italy! Let him reach the walls of Rome, looting and burning everything on his way! And let us not move from here until the senators summon Gaius Flaminius from Arretium, as once they did Camillus from Veii.'*

With this snide remark he gave the order for the standards to be quickly pulled from the ground, and he himself leaped onto his horse. But the horse suddenly took a stumble, throwing the consul over its head. All the bystanders were terrified at this apparently dreadful omen for the start of the campaign but, to add to it, word was brought that, despite the standard-bearer's greatest efforts, one of the standards could not be pulled out of the ground.

Flaminius turned to the messenger. 'It's not as if you are bringing me a letter from the Senate forbidding me to engage, is it?' he asked. 'If the man's hand is too numb with fear to pull it up, go back and tell them to dig up the standard.'

With that the column began to move forward. The officers, as well as disagreeing with Flaminius' strategy, were also dismayed by the twofold portent; but the rank and file in general were delighted with their commander's determination—they felt optimism, without asking themselves what it was based on.

4. Hannibal completely razed the territory between the city of Cortona and Lake Trasimene, using all the atrocities of war to sharpen his foe's resentment and spur him to avenge the injuries inflicted on his allies. The Carthaginians had by now reached a spot naturally suited to an ambush, the area where Trasimene is at its closest to the mountains of Cortona. Between the two there is no more than a narrow pathway, almost as if just enough space had been deliberately left for Hannibal's purpose! After this, the terrain widens a little to form a plain, and beyond that rise some hills. It was there, in the open, that Hannibal established camp. He intended to take up a position in this spot himself, but only with his African and Spanish troops. The Balearic troops and other light infantry he led behind the hills, and the cavalry he stationed right at the entry to the defile, where some hillocks conveniently provided cover. His plan

was for the cavalry to block the defile after the Romans had entered, and the whole enemy force would then be shut in between the lake and the mountains.*

Flaminius had reached the lake at the sunset of one day, and, when it was barely light on that which followed, he went through the defile without reconnoitring. Then, after the column began to spread out as it reached the more open terrain, all he saw of the enemy was what was right ahead of him; the ambush to his rear and above his head remained undetected. The Carthaginian now had his enemy where he had wanted him, squeezed between lake and hills, and surrounded by his troops, and so he gave all his units the signal for a simultaneous attack. These swooped down, each taking the shortest route to the enemy. The attack was all the more surprising and unexpected for the Romans because of a mist which had risen from the lake and which had settled more densely on the level ground than on the heights. As a result, the enemy columns had been quite visible to each other from the various hills, and had better synchronized their downward charge. When the cry went up on every side, the Romans realized they were surrounded before they could actually see it, and fighting broke out at the front and on the flanks before the line could be drawn up, weapons made ready, or swords drawn.

5. There was chaos all around but the consul himself showed considerable composure in such a precarious situation.* The ranks were in disarray, as men turned in the direction of the confused shouts, but he formed them up as well as time and their position permitted. Wherever he could go, and wherever he could make himself heard, he encouraged them and told them to stand and fight. They needed force and courage to get out of there, he said, not prayers and petitions to the gods. It was by the sword that a way could be made through the midst of the enemy line, and in general less fear meant less danger. But, over the din and turmoil of battle, advice and orders were inaudible. So far from recognizing their own standards, or their ranks and their places within them, they had barely the presence of mind to seize their armour and put it on for the fight. In fact, some were cut down when their weapons proved more a hindrance than a means of protection. Furthermore, in such dense fog, ears were more useful than eyes. It was to sounds that they turned their faces and eyes, to sounds of wounds being dealt, of

blows falling on bodies and armour, and of the mingled cries of
confusion and panic. Some tried to flee, only to be brought to a halt
when they ran into batches of comrades still fighting, while others
who were returning to the fray would be driven back by a crowd in
flight. Attempts to force a passage in any direction proved futile.
They were hemmed in on the flanks by the hills and the lake, and to
the front and rear by lines of the enemy. It became clear that they
had no hope of deliverance except by their own right hands and their
swords, and at that point each man became his own leader and
spurred himself to action, and the battle started all over again. It was
not the usual ordered engagement, with *principes*, *hastati*, and *triarii*,
or with the men of the front rank fighting before the standards and
the rest behind, or with soldiers taking their places in the appropriate legion, cohort, or maniple.* Chance threw them together, and
individual courage determined whether each man stood in front or
behind in the fight. So whetted were their spirits, so focused were
they on the fight, that even though there was an earthquake* that
demolished large sections of many Italian cities, made swift rivers
change course, brought tidal waters up rivers, and created huge
landslides on mountains, none of the combatants actually noticed it.

6. The battle went on for some three hours. It was savage at every
point, but around the consul the fighting was even more fierce and
violent. Flaminius had his strongest troops alongside him, and he
was energetically bringing assistance at any point where he had seen
his men under pressure and in difficulties. His armour marked him
out, and so the enemy furiously attacked him, and his own men just
as furiously defended him. Then an Insubrian horseman named
Ducarius recognized the consul by his appearance.

'Look,' he said to his compatriots, 'here's the man who cut our
legions to pieces and sacked our territory and city! Now I shall make
him a sacrificial offering to the shades of our fellow citizens foully
slain.' So saying, he put the spurs to his horse and thrust forward
through the thickest of the enemy. He first cut down Flaminius'
armour-bearer, who had thrown himself in the way of his charge,
then ran the consul through with his lance. The *triarii* raised their
shields to block the man's attempt to strip the body.

The event triggered the flight of most of the Romans, and now
neither lake nor hills stood in the way of their panic. They ran off
blindly, over ground that was nothing but ravines and cliffs, and

arms and men fell tumbling over each other. Most, finding no passage for their flight, waded through the shallows at the edge of the lake into the deeper water, sinking up to their heads and shoulders. Some, in their unthinking panic, were prompted to attempt escape by swimming, but the distance was interminable and the effort hopeless. They drowned in the depths, or else with difficulty scrambled back to the shallows, having exhausted themselves pointlessly, for they were then butchered all along the shore by enemy horsemen who rode out into the water.

About 6,000 at the head of the column had made a spirited charge through the enemy facing them, and thus managed to exit from the defile, unaware of what was happening behind them. They halted on a knoll, but heard only the shouting and clash of arms, and because of the mist they could not see, or know, how the battle was going. It was only when the issue was decided that the sun's heat dispersed the mist, and brought on the light of day. Then, in the now clear sunlight, the hills and plains revealed to them that the battle was lost, and the Roman army hideously slaughtered. Frightened of being spotted and having enemy cavalry dispatched against them, they hurriedly took up the standards, and made off with all possible speed.

The following day, alongside all their other woes, they were facing severe hunger. However, Maharbal had caught up with them when it was still dark, and he gave them an undertaking that, if they surrendered their weapons, he would let them depart with one article of clothing each. At this the Romans capitulated, but the promise was honoured by Hannibal with typical Punic scruple, and they were all clapped in irons.

7. Such was the famous battle of Trasimene; few defeats suffered by the people of Rome have been as memorable. Fifteen thousand Romans fell in action. Ten thousand scattered in flight throughout Etruria, and headed for the city by various roads. Two thousand five hundred of the enemy died in the battle, and many others later succumbed to their wounds. Statistics for the fallen on both sides are many times greater in other authors. Apart from my aversion to the unfounded exaggeration to which historians are all too prone, I have myself accepted Fabius as my main source, since he was contemporary with this war.*

Hannibal released captives of Latin status without ransom, but Romans he put in irons.* He had the corpses of his own men separated from the piles of the enemy dead, and ordered them buried. He also made every effort also to seek out Flaminius' body for burial, but he failed to find it.

When news of the defeat first reached Rome, the people rushed to the Forum in sheer terror and panic. Women roamed the streets, and queried those they met about the unexpected disaster that had been reported, and the fortunes of the army. Then the crowd, like some teeming assembly, turned to the Comitium and the Senate house, and called upon the magistrates. Eventually, not long before sunset, the praetor Marcus Pomponius declared: 'We have lost a great battle.' They heard no further details from Pomponius, but they gleaned snippets of gossip from each other, and took home the news that the consul and most of his army had been killed, and that the few survivors were wandering as fugitives through Etruria, or else were prisoners of the enemy.

Numerous though the misfortunes of the defeated army were, there were just as many anxieties besetting the minds of those whose relatives had been serving under the consul Gaius Flaminius. They were ignorant of what had become of their loved ones, and nobody knew what to hope for, or what to fear. The next day, and on a number of days following, a crowd stood at the gates—and there were almost more women than men—waiting for one of their relatives, or for news of them. They encircled new arrivals and plied them with questions, and could not be torn away from them, at least if they were acquaintances, until they had fully interrogated them on every detail. After that, as they left their informants, one might have seen the different expressions on their faces, according to whether the news each received was good or bad, and one could have seen people gathering round them, as they went home, offering congratulations or sympathy. It was the women's displays of joy and sorrow that were especially striking. They say that one suddenly came face to face with a son who had come home safely, and that she expired in his arms. A second had received a false report of her son's death and sat grieving at home; but the son returned and she died from excessive joy at the sight of him.

The praetors kept the Senate sitting in the Curia for several days, from dawn to dusk, and debated with them which commander and which troops could be used to face the triumphant Carthaginians.

8. Before the senators could come up with any firm plans, news

came of another unexpected reverse, involving 4,000 cavalry that had been sent by the consul Servilius to his colleague, under the command of the propraetor Gaius Centenius. On receiving word of the battle of Trasimene, these had changed course, and had then been cut off in Umbria by Hannibal. The news inspired different reactions. The hearts of some were in the grip of a greater anguish, and this fresh loss of the cavalry they thought of little account compared with what had been lost earlier. Others would not consider the occurrence in isolation. When a body was sick, they said, any upset, however slight, was felt more seriously than a graver one was felt in good health. Likewise, when the commonwealth was ailing and weakened, any stroke of misfortune should be measured not on an absolute scale but with reference to its diminished capacity, which could stand no further burden.

As a result, the citizen body resorted to a measure that had been neither needed nor employed for a long time, namely the appointment of a dictator. But a dictator could, it seemed, be named only by the consul, and he was away from the city. In addition, sending a messenger or letter through Italy, now occupied by the Carthaginian army, was no easy matter. Accordingly, the people took the hitherto unprecedented step of appointing a dictator themselves.* They appointed Quintus Fabius Maximus, and they made Marcus Minucius Rufus his master of horse. These two were charged by the Senate with responsibility for reinforcing the city walls and their towers, for deploying sentries at points they thought appropriate, and for cutting down bridges across the rivers. People felt they now had to fight for their city and homes, since their defence of Italy had been a failure.

9. Hannibal marched straight through Umbria as far as Spoletium.* He wreaked havoc on the surrounding countryside and proceeded with an assault on the city, but was repulsed with heavy losses. He now reflected on the strength of this single colony, which he had attacked with little success, to gauge the difficulty he would have with the city of Rome, and then he changed course into the territory of Picenum. The land here was rich in all manner of produce, and well provided with goods for plunder, as well—and Hannibal's voracious and impoverished troops showed no restraint in seizing them. Hannibal maintained a stationary camp in the region for a number of days, while his soldiers recovered from the

rigours of their winter marches, from their trek through the swamps, and from the battle, which, successful though it proved to be, had been no trivial or easy affair. When the men had been given sufficient rest (and in fact they enjoyed looting and pillaging more than inactivity and rest) Hannibal went ahead again. He laid waste the land around Praetutia and Hadria, and after that the territory of the Marsi, the Marrucini, and the Paeligni, and the parts of Apulia closest to Arpi and Luceria.

The consul Gnaeus Servilius had fought some minor battles with the Gauls, and taken one town of little importance. When he heard that his colleague had been killed, and the army destroyed, he feared for the defences of the capital and headed for Rome. He did not wish to be absent at the moment of her greatest peril.

Quintus Fabius Maximus had now been made dictator for the second time. On the day of his entry into office, he convened the Senate and, opening the session with matters of religion, told the senators that the consul Gaius Flaminius' mistake lay more in his disregard for ritual and auspices than in his recklessness and incompetence. The gods, said Fabius, should themselves be consulted on the means of appeasing heaven's anger, and he convinced the senators to take a decision hardly ever taken, other than when dire prodigies have been reported, namely to have the decemvirs consult the Sibylline Books. After the decemvirs had consulted the oracular writings, they reported back to the senators that there had been some irregularity in the formulation of the vow made to Mars for that war. It should be formulated again, and on a more generous scale, with Great Games vowed to Jupiter and temples to Venus of Eryx and Mens. Public prayers and a *lectisternium* were also to be held, and a vow taken to hold a Sacred Spring, if the campaign turned out successfully, and the republic remained in the same condition in which it had been before the war. Since Fabius was going to be busy with the conduct of the war, the Senate followed the advice of the College of Pontiffs and instructed the praetor Marcus Aemilius to see that all these measures were quickly implemented.

10. When these senatorial decrees had been passed, the praetor consulted the pontifical college, and the *pontifex maximus*, Lucius Cornelius Lentulus, was of the view that their first priority was to put the question of the Sacred Spring before the people. That vow,

he claimed, could not be made without the authority of the people. The question was put to the people in the following words:

'Is it your will and command that such measures be implemented? Should the republic of the Quirites, the Roman people, be kept safe for the next five years, as I wish and pray, throughout these wars— the war of the Roman people with the people of Carthage, and the wars against the Gauls living this side of the Alps—let the Quirites, the people of Rome, offer and make this gift. All pigs, sheep, goats, and cattle that the spring shall have brought forth are to be sacrificed to Jupiter (provided that they are not already consecrated to a god) from the day so decreed by the Senate and people. Let whosoever makes this sacrifice make it when he wishes and in the manner he wishes; and whatever his manner of making it, let the sacrifice be considered duly made. If the animal that is due to be sacrificed dies, let it be considered as unconsecrated, and with no guilt attaching to it. If anyone should unwittingly damage or kill the beast, let him not be regarded as culpable. Should anyone steal it, neither the people of Rome nor the individual from whom it is stolen are to be considered guilty. If the sacrifice is unknowingly performed on a day of ill omen, let it still be considered properly made, and if it is performed by day or night, by a slave or a free man, let it be considered properly made. If it is performed before the time the Senate and people have decreed, let the people be considered exempt and quit of the vow.'

For the same purpose Great Games were included in a vow, and the cost of them was to be 333,333⅓ *asses*. In addition, 300 oxen were to be sacrificed to Jupiter, and white oxen, and other sacrificial animals, to numerous other gods. When the vows had been duly formulated, a period of public prayer was proclaimed, and these were attended not only by the urban populace with their wives and children, but also by such country people as had some property, and consequently took some thought for the public good. Then a three-day *lectisternium* was held under the supervision of the decem-virs for sacrifices. Six couches were put on display: one to Jupiter and Juno, a second to Neptune and Minerva, a third to Mars and Venus, a fourth to Apollo and Diana, a fifth to Vulcan and Vesta, and a sixth to Mercury and Ceres. After this vows of temples were made. The dictator Quintus Fabius Maximus made the vow of a temple for Venus of Eryx, because the oracular books had prescribed that the vow be formulated by the man holding the highest office in the state, and the praetor Titus Otacilius made a vow of the temple for Mens.

11. Religious observances completed, the dictator now opened discussion of the war and the state of the republic, seeking the opinion of the senators on the specific legions, and the number of them, with which they should face their triumphant foe. It was decided that Fabius should take over the army of the consul Gnaeus Servilius, but that he should, in addition, enlist from the citizens and the allies as great a force of cavalry and infantry as he thought appropriate. He was also to take all other measures and decisions as he thought to be in the state's interests.

Fabius declared that he would add two legions to Servilius' army. When he had enlisted these, using the services of the master of horse, he proclaimed a date on which they were to mobilize at Tibur. He also issued an edict for all people whose towns and settlements lacked fortifications to move to places of safety, and for all those in the area along the route Hannibal was likely to take to leave their farms. These people were to burn their buildings and destroy their crops before departing so as to leave the enemy no supplies of any kind. Fabius then set off along the Flaminian Way to meet the consul and his army; and near Ocriculum, on the banks of the Tiber, he caught sight of the column, and of the consul, who was proceeding towards him with his cavalry. He thereupon sent an attendant to inform the consul that he should come to the dictator without his lictors. Servilius complied with the order, and the meeting of the two men did much to alert citizens and allies to the high standing of the office of dictator—with the passage of time they had forgotten the authority it carried.* At this point a letter arrived from the city with news that transport vessels carrying supplies from Ostia to the army in Spain had been captured off the port of Cosa by a Carthaginian fleet.* The consul was ordered to leave for Ostia immediately. He was instructed to man the ships lying at anchor at the city of Rome or at Ostia with marines and crews, and, with these vessels, to give chase to the enemy fleet and patrol the coasts of Italy. Men were conscripted in large numbers in Rome, and even freedmen who had children and were of military age had sworn the oath of allegiance. Members of this urban force who were under thirty-five years of age were assigned to the ships, and the others were left to guard the city.

12. Assuming command of the consul's army from the legate

Fulvius Flaccus, the dictator marched through Sabine territory to Tibur. It was there that he had fixed the rendezvous for his new recruits. He then moved on to Praeneste and, by taking various byways, emerged on the Latin Way. After that, reconnoitring the roads with extreme care, he marched towards the enemy, determined not to trust to luck anywhere unless circumstances forced him to.

On the very first day that Fabius pitched camp within sight of the enemy—it was not far from Arpi—the Carthaginian leader immediately led his troops out for action, and offered battle. But he could see nothing stirring on the enemy side, and no signs of activity in their camp. He therefore returned to camp uttering disdainful comments: the Romans' famed military spirit had been crushed, they were a conquered people and they had openly admitted they were no match for him in valour and glory, he said. But in his heart he felt unspoken concern:* his dealings henceforth would be with a commander nothing like Flaminius or Sempronius, and the Romans had finally been taught by hard experience to choose one who was Hannibal's equal. Indeed, he felt immediate apprehension about the dictator's wariness. But as yet he had not put the man's determination to the test, and so he began to harass and provoke him. He would frequently move camp, and he would lay waste the lands of the allies before his eyes. At one moment he would accelerate his march and disappear from view; then, suddenly, he would take up a concealed position at some curve in the road, hoping to catch Fabius unawares, if he came down to the plain.

Fabius led his column along higher ground, keeping a short distance from the enemy so as not to lose contact with him, but not engage him either. His men were confined to camp except in case of pressing need. Food- and wood-gathering expeditions were not undertaken with small numbers, or over a large area. There was a unit of cavalry and light infantry drawn up ready to meet any sudden assault, and this provided complete security for his own men, and also posed a threat for scattered foragers of the enemy. There was no question of risking everything on an overall engagement, and minor and unimportant brushes with enemy, conducted from points of safety and with shelter close by, brought the men to have fewer concerns about their fighting capabilities and fortunes, after the fright of their earlier defeats.

However, Fabius found no more hostility to this sound strategy

in Hannibal than he did in his master of horse, and this man's
subordinate command was all that held him back from destroying
the republic. He was arrogant and impulsive in judgement, and too
quick with his tongue. Talking first to a few men, and then openly
before the ranks, he began to call Fabius' deliberate hesitation idleness, and his caution cowardice, and he pinned on him faults that
bore some relation to his real virtues. In this way he kept trying to
exalt himself by maligning his superior, a loathsome practice that has
become more widespread because many have found it all too
successful.

13. Hannibal crossed over into Samnium from the territory of the
Hirpini. He laid waste the agricultural land of Beneventum, took the
city of Telesia and deliberately provoked the Roman commander,
hoping to infuriate him with all the humiliation and suffering he
inflicted on the allies, and bring him down to a battle on level
ground.

Large numbers of Italian allies had been taken prisoner by
Hannibal at Trasimene and subsequently released. These included
three Campanian knights, who had been bribed with numerous gifts
and promises from him to enlist the support of their compatriots for
his cause. These men now informed him that he had an opportunity
to capture Capua, if he brought his army into Campania. This was
too important a step to take just on the recommendation of these
men, and Hannibal hesitated, fluctuating between trust and distrust.
Finally, however, they convinced him to make for Campania from
Samnium.

The three men he let go after warning them to strengthen with
actions their repeated promises, and ordering them to return to him
with more of their people, including some prominent citizens. He
then instructed a guide to take him into the territory of Casinum—
he had been told by people familiar with the area that, by seizing
control of the pass there, he could prevent the Romans from getting
through to bring help to their allies. But a Carthaginian speaker has
difficulty in pronouncing Latin names, and this made the guide hear
'Casilinum' rather than 'Casinum'.* He branched off from his correct path, and went down through the territory of Allifae, Caiatia,
and Cales into the plain of Stellas.* Here Hannibal looked around,
and saw the area enclosed by mountains and rivers, and so he called
the guide and asked where on earth he was. It was only when the

guide declared that Hannibal would lodge that day at Casilinum that the mistake became clear, and Hannibal realized that Casinum was far off in another direction. He had the guide flogged and crucified to intimidate the others, established a fortified camp, and sent Maharbal and his cavalry to raid the territory of Falernum. The raid extended all the way to the Baths of Sinuessa, the Numidians causing enormous damage, and spreading panic and fear even further. But even intimidation on that scale, with the whole country aflame with war, failed to shake the loyalty of the allies. That was evidently because the authority to which they were subject was just and tolerant, and they did not refuse obedience to a superior people—the only real bond of loyalty.

14. Hannibal's camp was now pitched at the River Volturnus. The most beautiful countryside of Italy was going up in flames, farmhouses were burning and smoking, and meanwhile Fabius was marching along the heights of Mt. Massicus. At this point, mutiny almost flared up again amongst the troops. For a few days they had been silent; the column had been taken along at a faster pace than usual, and they had believed the object of the speedy advance was to keep Campania from enemy depredations. But now they came to the last heights in the range of Mt. Massicus, and the enemy were, before their eyes, torching the buildings in the Falernian fields and those of the colonists at Sinuessa—and there was still no word of combat.

'Have we come here as spectators?' asked Minucius. 'To enjoy the sight of our allies being butchered and their property burned? Even if we feel no shame before anyone else, do we not at least feel it before these fellow citizens of ours, these men whom our fathers sent to Sinuessa as colonists, to make this area secure from the Samnite foe? But now it is not the neighbouring Samnite who is putting it to the torch, but the Carthaginian from abroad, who, thanks to our indecision and inertia, has made his way here from the very ends of the earth. Ah, is this how far we fall short of our forefathers? They felt that it disgraced their empire to have Punic ships at large along their coastline—and now we see that coast filled with our enemies, and taken over by Numidians and Moors! Recently we protested against the blockade of Saguntum, appealing not only to men, but also to treaties and the gods that protect them—and now we happily watch Hannibal scaling the walls of a Roman colony! The smoke from burning farms and fields comes blowing into our eyes and faces; our ears ring with the weeping and wailing of our allies, who invoke our aid more often than they do heaven's. And here we are, hidden in clouds and forests, leading our army like a flock of sheep through summer pastures and along remote trails.

'Imagine if this was how Marcus Furius had proposed to recover the city from the Gauls—by trailing over hilltops and mountain passes the way this latter-day Camillus, this superlative dictator that we have chosen in our hour of need, is attempting to recover Italy from Hannibal! In that case, Rome would now be in the hands of the Gauls. So many times did our ancestors save it—but if we keep delaying like this I fear that they may have done so only for the benefit of Hannibal and the Carthaginians! But no, Camillus was a hero, and a true Roman. On the day that the news was brought to Veii that he had, on the authority of the Senate and at the bidding of the people, been appointed dictator, he came down into the plain, even though the Janiculum was high enough to let him sit and watch his enemy! And on that very day in the city centre—the site of Gallic graves today—and on the following day this side of Gabii, he cut down the Gallic legions. And remember how years later we were sent beneath the yoke by our Samnite foe at the Caudine Forks. How was it that Lucius Papirius Cursor took the yoke from Roman necks and set it upon the arrogant Samnite? For heaven's sake, was it by ranging the hills of Samnium, or was it by attacking and blockading Luceria, and giving the victorious enemy no rest? More recently, what, other than speed of action, gave victory to Gaius Lutatius? The day after he caught sight of the enemy he crushed their fleet, then laden with supplies and encumbered by its own equipment and weaponry. It is idiocy to believe a war can be won by sitting around or making vows. One has to seize one's arms, go down to the plain, and engage the enemy man to man. It was daring and action that enhanced the power of Rome, not policies of inertia like this that only cowards call "cautious".'

Tribunes and Roman knights* would crowd around Minucius as he made these comments like a public orator in action, and his swaggering comments even made their way to the ears of the common soldiers. Had the matter depended on a poll of the men, they made it quite plain that they would have chosen Minucius as their leader over Fabius.*

15. Fabius had his eyes on his own men as much as on the enemy, and he first of all showed them that he could not be cowed by them. He well knew that his delaying tactics were now discredited in Rome as well as in the camp, but he drew out the rest of the summer sticking resolutely to the same plan of campaign. The result was that Hannibal was deprived of any hope of the engagement which he had made every effort to bring on, and he began to look around for a site for winter quarters. The region he was now in could provision him for the season, but not indefinitely, for it was a land of fruit trees and vines, with all its cultivation given over to fruits that were delicacies rather than basic foodstuff. This was reported to Fabius by his scouts, and Fabius was quite sure that Hannibal would go back by the same passes he had used to enter Falernian territory. He accordingly secured, with small garrisons, Mt. Callicula and Casilinum, a town that is cut in two by the River Volturnus, and marks the boundary between Falernian and Campanian territory. He then sent Lucius Hostilius Mancinus out with 400 allied cavalry to reconnoitre, while he personally led the army back by way of the same heights.

Mancinus had been amongst the crowd of young men listening to the master of horse's ranting diatribes. He at first went forward, as scouts do, trying to spy on the enemy from a secure vantage point. But then he caught sight of some Numidians roaming at large through the villages, and when the opportunity arose he actually killed a few of them. Fabius had ordered him to advance only as far as he could with safety, and to fall back before he could be seen by the enemy, but suddenly Mancinus' thoughts were focused on battle, and the instructions of the dictator slipped from his mind. The Numidians, some charging, some giving ground, lured him on almost to their very encampment, tiring the Roman horses and their riders. Then Carthalo, supreme commander of the Carthaginian cavalry, bore down on them at a gallop, routing them even before they came within javelin-range, and maintaining a non-stop pursuit for about five miles. Seeing that the enemy was not abandoning the chase and that he had no hope of escape, Mancinus encouraged his men, and turned back to give battle, though he was outclassed in all respects. As a result, the commander himself, and his elite cavalry troops, were surrounded and killed. The others made off in scattered flight, escaping first to Cales, and then, by almost impassable trails, to the dictator.

It so happened that this was the day on which Minucius had rejoined Fabius. He had earlier been sent by the dictator to secure with a garrison the pass that contracts to a narrow gorge above Tarracina, and which overlooks the sea—the object was to deny the Carthaginian access to Roman territory from Sinuessa by the Appian Way. The armies now joined up, and the dictator and his master of horse encamped down on the path that Hannibal was going to take. The enemy was two miles away.

16. The following day the Carthaginians filled the entire road between the two camps with their column. The Romans had stationed themselves directly in front of their own rampart, clearly in a more favourable position, but Hannibal nonetheless moved forward with his light infantry and cavalry to challenge his enemy. The Carthaginians attacked at several points, charging and then retreating, but the Roman line remained in position. It was a sluggish battle, more satisfying to the dictator than Hannibal. Casualties numbered 200 on the Roman side, and 800 on the enemy's.

Hannibal then seemed to be cut off, since the road to Casilinum was blocked. Capua, Samnium, and large numbers of produce-rich allies to their rear could provision the Romans, but the Carthaginians would be wintering amidst the rocks of Formiae, the sands and swamps of Liternum, and throughout the inhospitable woodlands. And it did not escape Hannibal's notice that his own strategy was being turned against him. He could not make his way through by way of Casilinum; he would have to head for the hills, and cross the heights of Callicula. Fearing that the Romans might attack his column while it was hemmed in by the valleys, Hannibal thought up a frightening optical illusion to baffle his enemy, and decided to approach the hills furtively during the early hours of the night. His stratagem was set up as follows. Combustible material was collected from all the surrounding fields, and Hannibal had this, together with bunches of twigs and dry vine-shoots, attached to the horns of cattle (he had a large number of these, both domesticated and wild, amongst the spoils taken from the countryside—the total came to some 2,000 head). Hasdrubal was given responsibility for driving the herd at night towards the hills, with their horns alight, and especially, if he could, over the passes occupied by the enemy.

17. When darkness fell, the Carthaginians silently broke camp, and the cattle were driven at some distance ahead of the main body of the army. When they reached the foothills, and the narrow defiles, a signal was immediately given for the horns to be lit, and the cattle driven up the hills facing them. The very panic instilled in them by the flames that flashed from their heads, and the burning that went to the quick at the roots of their horns, drove them into a frenzy. There was an immediate stampede, and it was as if all the brushwood in the area was aflame, with woods and hills set on fire. The beasts shook their heads in vain, merely fanning the flames, and thus created the illusion of men rushing about in all directions. Those stationed to guard the pass could see fires on the hilltops, and some right above their heads. Thinking they were surrounded, they abandoned their posts. They headed for the hilltops, where the blazing flames were least concentrated, assuming this to be the safest path, but even so they ran into a number of cattle that had strayed away from their herd. And when they first saw them in the distance, they froze, astounded by the miraculous sight of animals apparently breathing fire. Then it dawned on them that it was a trick, and man-made, and thinking it was an ambush, they beat a hasty retreat in even greater panic. They also encountered some enemy light-armed infantry, but the darkness spread fear equally on both sides, and kept them there till dawn, with neither opening hostilities. Meanwhile, Hannibal brought his entire column through the pass, taking a number by surprise in the pass itself, and encamped in the region of Allifae.*

18. Fabius heard the commotion, but thought it was a trap, and he was reluctant to fight any battle, especially in the dark. He therefore kept his men within their defence-works. At dawn there was a battle close to the crest of the hill. The Carthaginian light infantry were cut off from their comrades, and the Romans, having some numerical advantage, would easily have crushed them, but for the arrival on the scene of a company of Spaniards, sent back by Hannibal expressly for the purpose of relieving them. These troops had more experience of the mountains, and were better at skirmishing amongst rocks and rough terrain. They were also more nimble, both because of their physical agility and the way they were armed, and thanks to their mode of fighting they easily outmanœuvred an enemy who was used to level ground, and who was also heavily armed and trained only in stationary warfare. Consequently, when they parted after what was not by any measure an even fight, the Spaniards returned to camp with almost no casualties, and the Romans with considerable losses.

Fabius also struck camp and, after making his way through the pass, occupied a high and well-protected position overlooking Allifae. Hannibal then made a pretence of marching on Rome by way of Samnium but in fact he went all the way back to Paelignian territory on a marauding expedition. Fabius kept marching along the heights, midway between the enemy column and the city of Rome, neither losing contact with Hannibal nor engaging him. After leaving Paelignian territory, the Carthaginians changed direction and, heading back to Apulia, arrived at Gereonium, a city abandoned by its inhabitants, who were fearful after the collapse of a section of its walls. The dictator established a fortified camp in the region of Larinum.

Fabius was then recalled to Rome for religious duties. At this point he not only brought the authority of his command to bear on his master of horse, but offered personal advice, too, almost pleading with him, as he tried to persuade him to trust more to planning than luck, and to follow his strategy rather than that of Sempronius and Flaminius. Minucius should not think that almost a summer spent playing cat and mouse with the enemy had been time wasted, he said; physicians have sometime found rest more beneficial than exercise and activity. Besides, he added, it was no small achievement to have put an end to defeats by an enemy who had so often been victorious, and to have recovered their breath after an unbroken string of disasters. Such was the advice Fabius gave the master of horse before he set off for Rome, but it served no purpose.

19. At the start of the summer in which these events took place, land and sea operations also commenced in Spain. Hasdrubal had been given a number of fully manned and fully equipped vessels by his brother. He added a further ten ships to these, and then passed on command of this fleet, now forty strong, to Himilco. Hasdrubal then set off from New Carthage. On the march, he kept close to land with his fleet, and marched the army along the shoreline, ready to engage whatever branch of the enemy forces he encountered. When Gnaeus Scipio heard that his foe had moved from winter quarters, he at first had the same idea. However, at the rumour of a huge mobilization of new auxiliary troops by the Carthaginians, he felt less confident about meeting them on land. Instead, he put some handpicked troops on board ship, and proceeded to meet his enemy with a fleet of thirty-five vessels.

On the second day out of Tarraco, Scipio arrived at an anchorage ten miles from the mouth of the River Ebro. From there he sent out two Massiliot spy-ships, and these came back with the information that the Punic fleet was at anchor in the river-mouth, with its camp pitched on the bank. Scipio weighed anchor and bore down on the enemy, hoping to catch them off guard and unprepared, and to crush them by spreading panic throughout their force.

There are numerous towers on high elevations in Spain that the inhabitants use both as observation posts and as defences against marauders. It was from one of these that the enemy ships were first spotted, and their coming signalled to Hasdrubal. A mad scramble broke out on land, and in the camp, before it did on the ships on the water. For no beating of oars, or any other sounds carried from ships, had been heard, and the promontories still kept the Roman fleet out of view. The crews were sauntering around on the beach, or resting in their tents, and the last thing they had on their minds was the enemy, or fighting that day. Then, suddenly, one horseman after another was sent out by Hasdrubal with orders for them to embark quickly, and take up their arms—the Roman fleet was already close to their harbour. The riders carried these orders to all points, and soon Hasdrubal appeared in person with his entire land force.

The scene was now one of utter confusion and uproar, with oarsmen and marines together running for their vessels, more like men fleeing the land than going into battle. They had all barely got aboard when some of them cast off the stern-cables, and drifted over the anchors; and others hacked through the anchor lines so nothing would be holding them back. And, in their frantic haste to get everything done, the crews were impeded in their duties by the equipment of the marines, while the marines were prevented from taking up and fitting on their armour by the panic of the crews.

By now the Romans were not just approaching but had actually formed up their ships for battle. The Carthaginians were thrown into disarray less by the enemy and the upcoming engagement than by their own panic, and after a token resistance rather than a real fight they turned and fled. The river current was running against them, and for the broad column of ships to enter its mouth was certainly impossible, with so many vessels converging on it simultaneously. And so the Carthaginians drove their ships ashore at various points. Some of the men stepped out into shallow water, others onto dry land, some with weapons and some without, and they ran for cover to the line of their comrades drawn up on the shore. But two Carthaginian ships had been captured at the beginning of the charge, and four had been sunk.

20. The Romans could see that the land was under the control of the enemy and that his armed troops were lined up all along the shore, but they did not hesitate to go after the demoralized Carthaginian fleet. They tied towing ropes to the stern of all those enemy ships that had not shattered their prows on impact with the shore, or did not have their keels stuck fast in the shallows, and they towed them out to sea. In this manner they captured some twenty-five of the forty vessels. But for the Romans this was not the sweetest aspect of that particular victory—it was the fact that, with a single effortless battle, they had gained mastery of that entire seaboard.

They now set sail for Onussa.* Landing there, they took the city by storm, pillaged it after capturing it, and then headed for New Carthage. Here they raided all the farmlands around the city, and eventually set fire to the buildings adjoining the wall and gates. From there, the fleet, well laden with plunder, came to Longuntica, where large quantities of esparto grass had been laid up by Hasdrubal for the use of his fleet. The Romans removed what they could use, and all the rest was put to the torch. In addition to skirting the coastline of the mainland, they now also sailed over to the island of Ebusus. Here they spent two days in an intensive but fruitless assault on the island's capital city, turning then to pillaging the countryside when they realized that their time was being wasted on a futile enterprise. After looting and burning a number of villages, they returned to their ships in possession of greater spoils than they had taken from the mainland, and delegates from the Balearic Islands now came to Scipio suing for peace.

The fleet then turned back and returned to the more northerly parts of the province. Here the Romans were met by numerous ambassadors from all the peoples living north of the Ebro, as well as from many of the peoples of the furthest reaches of Spain. In fact, the number of peoples who actually put themselves under Roman jurisdiction and authority by surrendering hostages came to more than 120. The Roman commander now felt ample confidence in his land forces as well, and he went ahead all the way to the pass of Castulo.* Hasdrubal meanwhile pulled back into Lusitania, closer to the Atlantic.

21. The remainder of the summer, so it seemed, was going to be uneventful, and indeed would have been as far as the Carthaginians were concerned. But the Spaniards are by nature a fractious people, always eager for violent change, and now there was the problem of Mandonius and the former chieftain of the Ilergetes, Indibilis.* As soon as the Romans retired from the pass to the coast, these two roused their compatriots to insurrection, and came to pillage the peaceful lands of the allies of Rome. Some military tribunes and light-armed auxiliaries were sent by Scipio to confront the insurgents, and they easily routed their makeshift force in battle, killing a thousand men, taking some prisoner, and disarming most of the others. Even so, this uprising had the effect of making Hasdrubal, who was now in retreat towards the Atlantic, turn back north of the Ebro to defend his allies. The Punic camp was located in the territory of the Ilergavon-enses, the Roman at Nova Classis,* but a piece of news suddenly arrived that moved the theatre of operations elsewhere.

The Celtiberians had sent the leading men of their territory as spokesmen to the Romans, and had also given hostages. Now, prompted by a message they were sent by Scipio, they took up arms and overran the Carthaginian area with a powerful army. They stormed three towns, and then put up a magnificent fight against Hasdrubal himself in two battles, killing 15,000 of the enemy and capturing 4,000, along with some military standards.

22. This was how matters stood in Spain when Publius Scipio came into the province. His command had been extended after his consulship, and he had been sent by the Senate with thirty warships, 8,000 fighting men, and a large quantity of supplies. This armada, huge thanks to its large column of transport vessels, was seen in the distance, and, to the great jubilation of the Romans and their allies, it came in from the open sea and docked in the harbour of Tarraco.* After disembarking his men, Scipio set out and joined his brother, and from that point they fought the war together, with a joint strategy.

Thus, while the Carthaginians were preoccupied with the war against the Celtiberians, the Scipios lost no time in crossing the Ebro. Seeing nothing of the enemy, they moved on to Saguntum, for rumour had it that the hostages that had been taken from all over Spain had been placed there by Hannibal, and were being guarded in the citadel by a small garrison. All the peoples of Spain were favourable to an alliance with Rome, and the hostages' position as pawns was all that had been holding them back, for they feared that an uprising might be punished with the blood of their children.

One man removed this constraint on Spain, employing a scheme of greater ingenuity than integrity. This was Abelux, a Spanish nobleman then living in Saguntum. He had earlier been a loyal adherent of the Carthaginians, but had changed his allegiance as his own fortunes changed, such being the nature of barbarians. He assumed that, if he came to the enemy as a deserter but with nothing of great value to betray to them, he would be no more than another worthless, discreditable individual. He therefore set his mind on making himself as useful as possible to his new allies. He considered everything that fortune could put within his reach, and settled on returning the hostages as being the best idea. That one thing, more than anything else, he thought, would win for the Romans the support of the Spanish chieftains.

Abelux was well aware, however, that those guarding the hostages would make no move without authorization from Bostar, their commander, and so he craftily approached Bostar himself. The latter had his camp right on the beach outside the city, in order to cut the Romans off from access from that direction. In the camp, Abelux took Bostar aside, and explained to him how matters stood, as though Bostar were ignorant of the fact. Until that day fear had curbed the spirit of the Spaniards because the Romans were far off, said Abelux, but now the Roman camp stood south of the Ebro, providing a secure stronghold and refuge for all who looked for violent change. Accordingly, he concluded, since fear would not keep the Spaniards in check, they should be put under obligation to Carthage by a gesture of generosity and good will.

Bostar, taken aback, asked what offering could now suddenly be so important to the Spaniards. 'Send the hostages back to their communities,' said Abelux. 'That will win you gratitude on a personal level from the parents—the people who have the greatest respect in their communities—and on the official level from the various tribes. Everybody wants to be trusted, and giving a person one's trust generally secures his true loyalty. I claim for myself the duty of returning the hostages to their homes. I should like to assist my own plan with a special effort, and increase as much as I can the gratitude for an act that by its very nature will make people grateful.'

The man was not very quick-witted compared with other Carthaginians, and Abelux managed to win him over. Abelux then set off furtively at night to the enemy outposts, and there was met by a number of Spanish auxiliaries, by whom he was conducted to Scipio. The Spaniard explained his proposition, assurances were exchanged, and the time and location fixed for the transfer of the hostages were arranged. He then returned to Saguntum.

Abelux spent the next day with Bostar, receiving instructions on how the business was to be conducted. He then took his leave, having decided with Bostar that he would make the journey at night, so as not to be spotted by enemy sentinels. At the time he had established with them, he woke the men who were guarding the boys and set off, leading the party into the trap he had treacherously prepared, and of which he pretended to be unaware. They were brought into the Roman camp. After that, all the other measures for returning the hostages were taken in line with the agreement made with Bostar, and in the same sequence as if the affair were under the direction of the Carthaginians.

For the very same service the Romans earned considerably more gratitude than the Carthaginians would have done. For the Spaniards had found the Carthaginians hard to bear and domineering when things were going well for them, and the softening of their attitude could have been attributed to their changing fortunes, and to their fear. The Romans, on the other hand, had been strangers up to that point, and now, at the moment of their arrival, they had begun with an act of kindness and generosity. And Abelux, it would appear, was a prudent man who must have had good reason to change his allies. As a result, there was massive support for the defection which they were all contemplating; and in fact fighting would have broken out immediately but for the intervention of winter, which obliged Romans and Carthaginians alike to retire to their billets.

23. Such were operations in Spain during the second summer of the Punic War. In Italy, meanwhile, the shrewd delaying tactics of Fabius had brought a short interruption to the Roman defeats. This caused Hannibal no small concern: he could see that the Romans had chosen for their campaign the sort of leader who was guided by reason in his conduct of the war and did not trust to luck. At the same time, however, the tactics were unpopular with Fabius' fellow citizens, both military and civilian. This was particularly so during

Fabius' absence, when the recklessness of his master of horse had led to an engagement that I could more honestly say provided short-term joy rather than long-term advantage.

In addition, two incidents had increased the dictator's unpopularity, one of them a crafty scheme on Hannibal's part. A farm that belonged to the dictator had been pointed out to the Carthaginian by some deserters, and he ordered everything in the area to be razed to the ground except the farm—that was to be shielded from fire and the sword, or any kind of damage an enemy might inflict. The object was to create the impression that some secret pact had been made, and this was Fabius' payment for it. For the other incident Fabius was himself responsible and, though it might initially have been questioned because he failed to await senatorial endorsement, the action undoubtedly redounded greatly to his credit in the long run. The Roman and Carthaginian commanders had followed the precedent of the First Punic War with regard to the exchange of prisoners; they had decided between them that the side recovering more prisoners than it gave would pay two and a half pounds of silver for each extra soldier. The Roman commander recovered 247 more than the Carthaginian, but the payment of the money owing for these was, despite numerous debates in the Senate, rather slow in coming, since Fabius had not consulted the senators on the matter. Fabius therefore sent his son Quintus to Rome, sold the land that had been left untouched by the enemy, and then used his private resources to discharge the public debt.

Hannibal was now encamped before the walls of Gereonium. He had captured the city and put it to the torch, but had left a few buildings standing to serve as grain-depots. From there he regularly sent two-thirds of his force on foraging expeditions. To protect the camp and also guard against attacks on his foragers from any direction, Hannibal himself remained on watch with the other third, which was kept ready for action.

24. The Roman army was, at that point, in the territory of Larinum, under the command of Minucius, the master of horse, since the dictator had, as noted above, left for the city. Camp had earlier been pitched in a safe location on a lofty hill, but now it was brought down into the plain. Given the general's disposition, more hot-headed plans were now being mooted—attacking either the scattered Carthaginian foragers, or the camp that had been left only lightly guarded.

Hannibal was aware that the strategy of the war had changed with the commander, and that his enemy's moves would be impulsive rather than cautious. However, Hannibal himself now made a move that it would be hard to credit: despite the proximity of the enemy, he sent a third of his men on a foraging expedition, keeping the other two-thirds in camp. He then moved the actual camp closer to the enemy, establishing himself on a hillock visible to them, about two miles from Gereonium. This was to let them know that he was at the ready to protect his foragers, should they come under attack. From that point, another hillock came into sight, closer to the enemy, and actually overlooking their camp. If Hannibal made a move to seize this in broad daylight, there was no doubt that the enemy would get there before him—their path to it was shorter—and so some of his Numidians were sent out to take it secretly at night.

The following day, with disdain for the slight enemy numbers, the Romans dislodged the Numidians holding the position, and moved their own camp to the hillock. Thus, there was but a short distance between one rampart and the other, and that space had been almost entirely filled by the Roman battle line. At the same time cavalry and light infantry were sent forth from the rear of the camp against the Carthaginian foragers, and these killed or chased off the scattered enemy over a wide area. Hannibal did not dare commit himself to battle because, with numbers so small, he could barely defend the camp if it came under attack. And now he proceeded to fight the war with Fabian tactics, sitting and waiting, and he had drawn his troops back to their earlier camp, before the walls of Gereonium.

Some sources have it that a pitched battle, with lines drawn up, was fought that day. They claim that, at the first clash, the Carthaginians were driven in disarray right back to their camp, but then counter-attacked, suddenly terrifying the Romans in their turn, until the fortunes of the battle were restored by the arrival of the Samnite Numerius Decimus. He was the leading man, in terms of family and wealth, not just of his home town of Bovianum, but of the whole of Samnium. According to this version, Numerius was, at the command of the dictator, bringing to the camp 8,000 infantry and some 500 cavalry. When he appeared to Hannibal's rear, he gave both sides the impression that these were reinforcements coming from Rome with Quintus Fabius. Hannibal also feared it might be some sort of trap, and withdrew his men, and the Romans, pushing ahead with the help of the Samnite, took two strongholds by storm that day. Six thousand of the enemy were reportedly killed, and a good 5,000 Romans. But, though the losses on both sides were so nearly equal, a gushing report was brought to Rome, along with an even more gushing dispatch from the master of horse, of a superlative victory.

25. These events were the subject of frequent discussions in both the Senate and meetings of the people. The community was full of joy; only the dictator would give no credence to the report or the dispatch. Even if it were all true, he said, he feared a success more than he did a reverse. At this the tribune of the plebs, Marcus Metilius, declared that this really was intolerable. Not only had the dictator opposed an operation that promised success when he was present in the field, but now in his absence he was also refusing to recognize success achieved. He was purposely temporizing, in order to stay in office and be the only person with *imperium*, both in Rome and in the field. For, said the tribune, one of the consuls had fallen in action, and the other had been taken far from Italy, ostensibly in pursuit of the Punic fleet; and the two praetors were engaged in Sicily and Sardinia, though neither province was in need of a praetor at that time. And as for Marcus Minucius, the master of horse, he had been virtually kept under lock and key to prevent him getting a glimpse of the enemy, or engaging in any military action!

And so, the tribune continued, it was not just Samnium that had been totally devastated, its territory ceded to the Carthaginians as if it were the other side of the Ebro. So, too, for heaven's sake, had the territory of Campania, of Cales and of Falernum! And, meanwhile, the dictator sat around in Casilinum, using the legions of the Roman people to protect his private lands. The army had been eager to engage, he said, but along with the master of horse it had been virtually kept imprisoned within the rampart, and had been deprived of its weapons, like enemy prisoners. It was only when the dictator left that they had finally emerged from behind their rampart, like men delivered from a blockade—and then they drove back and routed the enemy. In view of which, added Metilius, he would have confidently proposed the annulment of Quintus Fabius' *imperium*—if the Roman people still had its mettle of days gone by. As matters stood, he would bring forward only a modest bill to give the master of horse and the dictator the same constitutional powers.* That notwithstanding, he concluded, Quintus Fabius must not be sent back to his army until he had seen to the election of a consul to replace Gaius Flaminius.

The dictator avoided assemblies of the people, enjoying as he did no popularity in public speaking. Not even in the Senate did he receive an impartial hearing when he paid tribute to his enemy, blamed the defeats of the past two years on the recklessness and incompetence of commanders, and said that the master of horse should be called to account for engaging against his orders. If supreme command and strategic planning lay with him, he said, he would soon make people aware that, when the general is good, luck is of little consequence, and that intelligence and reason are the important factors. Indeed, he added, there was greater glory in having kept the army safe at the appropriate time, and without dishonour, than there was in slaughtering thousands of the enemy.

The speeches that he made in this vein had no effect. He then saw to the election to the consulship of Marcus Atilius Regulus* and, to avoid being present for the squabble over the rights of command, slipped away to his army after dark on the day before the motion was to be brought forward.

The plebs came together for the meeting at dawn. Their inner feelings were animosity towards the dictator, and approval for the master of horse, but men still did not have the nerve to come forward to speak on behalf of a measure that had public support. Thus, in spite of overwhelming enthusiasm for it, the motion lacked substantive endorsement. One man alone was found to speak in favour of the bill: Gaius Terentius Varro, praetor the previous year, a man whose family background was not merely lowly but downright sordid.* They say his father had been a butcher who had kept his own stall, and had employed that very son in the degrading activities of his trade.

26. As a young man, Varro inherited from his father the money that had come from this sort of business, and it gave him the confidence to hope for a more respectable position in the world. Public life and the courts appealed to him and, by using a noisy rhetoric on behalf of disreputable individuals and causes, and against the property and reputations of decent people, he achieved notoriety with the masses, and then civil office. He gained the quaestorship, two aedileships (plebeian and curule), and eventually the praetorship, at which point he presumed to entertain hopes of a consulship. With no lack

of cunning, he now attempted to exploit the animosity against the dictator to win over the wavering support of the masses, and he alone gained the credit for the passing of the resolution.

Whether they were in Rome or in the army, everybody, Fabius' friends and foes alike, took the passing of the bill as a deliberate slap in the face for him. Not so the dictator. He accepted the slight of the people's rage against him with the same dignified composure with which he had borne the slanderous remarks that his enemies made against him before the popular assembly. He was actually on the road when he received the letter from the Senate informing him of the equal division of the command, but he was quite sure that, while there may have been an equal sharing of authority, there was no equal sharing of the general's skills. He returned to his army, his spirit broken neither by his fellow citizens nor by the enemy.

27. Even before this, Minucius' success, and his support from the masses, had made him quite insufferable, but at this juncture he proceeded to boast impudently and arrogantly that Quintus Fabius had come off second best to him no less than Hannibal had done. Fabius, he said, had been chosen in hard times as sole commander, one who could be a match for Hannibal. But now something historically unparalleled had happened—the superior officer had, by order of the people, been put on the same level as the junior, the dictator on the same level as the master of horse. And this had happened in the same society in which it had been the norm for masters of horse to tremble and shake at the sight of the dictator's rods and axes. So brilliant, said Minucius, had been his own success and valour. He was therefore going to follow his own fortunes, he concluded, if the dictator persisted with his policy of delaying and doing nothing, a policy condemned by gods and men alike.

And so, on the day that he first met up with Quintus Fabius, Minucius told him that what needed to be established first was how to put their shared command into effect. The best idea, in his opinion, was for each to have absolute authority and power in turn, either on alternate days or, if longer periods seemed preferable, for equal blocks of time. In this way, he said, each man could hold his own against the enemy numerically as well as tactically, should he have the opportunity for action.

Quintus Fabius did not like this at all: everything would depend on the luck that came his headstrong colleague's way. His *imperium* had been divided between himself and another, he argued, but had not actually been taken from him. He would therefore never willingly relinquish his discretion in directing the campaign, which he could still retain. He would not, he said, agree to a division by periods, or days, of command shared with him. He would, however, split the army, and would use his own strategy to save what he could, since he was not permitted to save everything. With this Fabius gained the division of the legions between the two, after the normal practice of the consuls. The first and fourth legions then fell to Minucius, and the second and third to Fabius, and they similarly split equally the cavalry and the auxiliary troops of the allies, and those with Latin status. The master of horse also wanted separate camps.

28. Nothing taking place amongst the enemy escaped the notice of Hannibal, for he had ample intelligence from deserters, as well as information from his spies. Now he had two reasons to be happy: Minucius' recklessness had been set free for him to capitalize on it as he would; and the effectiveness of Fabius' resourceful strategy had been halved.

Between the camp of Minucius and that of the Carthaginians was a low hill, and it was clear that whoever took it first would have territorial advantage over his enemy. Hannibal's aim was not to take it without a fight, though that in itself was a worthwhile objective, but to use it to bring on a battle with Minucius, since he was well aware that the Roman would sally forth to stop him.

All the land between the two forces looked, at first sight, to be of no use for laying a trap: not only was there no woodland, but it did not even have a covering of bushes. But, for that very reason, it was just the spot for concealing an ambush, for there could be no fear of such a trap in a bare valley; and in fact there were rocky hollows in its ravines, some able to hold 200 men. Five thousand infantry and cavalry were set in these hiding-places, distributed according to how many each hollow could conveniently hold. Fearing that the movement of a man carelessly stepping out, or the glint of armour, might give away the trap in such an open valley, Hannibal distracted the enemy's attention by sending a few men out at dawn to take the hill mentioned above.

At the first sight of these men, the Romans scoffed at their paltry numbers, and all demanded for themselves the task of dislodging the enemy and taking the position. Their leader was himself one of the most senseless and reckless of them, calling the men to arms and hurling empty threats at the enemy. He began by sending out his light infantry, and after them, in close formation, he sent the cavalry. Finally, seeing reinforcements also being brought up for the enemy, he marched forward with his legions in battle order. As the battle gained momentum and his men came under pressure, Hannibal also sent in wave after wave of reinforcements, both infantry and cavalry, until he had brought his battle line up to its full complement. The two sides were now locked in all-out combat.

It was the Roman light infantry that was driven back first, just as they were advancing from lower ground up the hill taken earlier by the enemy. As they were pushed back, they spread panic amongst the cavalry, who were coming up behind them, and then they fled back to the legionary standards. The heavy infantry line alone remained unwavering in the general panic, and it appeared that they would not have been found wanting had it been a regular and straightforward battle—so great was the courage that their success a few days earlier had inspired in them. But the men who were lying in ambush suddenly rose up, and such was the alarm and terror they produced with their attacks on both flanks, and on the rear, that none of the Romans had any spirit left for the fight, or any hope of making good his escape.

29. Fabius heard their cries of panic first; then he saw the line thrown into disorder in the distance. 'Just as I thought,' he said to his men. 'Fortune has overtaken his recklessness, and as quickly as I feared it would. He was made Fabius' equal in command, but he now sees that Hannibal is his superior in valour and fortune. But there will be another time for reproaches and anger. Now carry the standards forward from camp. Let us wrest victory from the enemy, and an admission of their error from our fellow citizens!'

By now large numbers of Minucius' men had been cut down, and others were looking around for a way to escape. Then, suddenly, Fabius' army appeared, as though sent from heaven to help them. Before coming within javelin-range, or getting down to hand-to-hand fighting, Fabius checked his own side's headlong flight, as well as the enemy's furious onslaught. Those who had broken ranks, and scattered far and wide, came running from all parts to join the new line of battle. Others who had turned and run off in large groups now swung round to face the enemy again. They formed a circle, and at one moment slowed their retreat and at the next bunched together to stand their ground. By now what was almost a single line had been formed from the defeated army and the fresh one, and this was advancing on the enemy—but at that moment the Carthaginian commander sounded the retreat. This was Hannibal openly declaring that, while Minucius had been beaten by him, he had been beaten by Fabius.

This day of wavering fortunes was mostly done when the two sides returned to camp. Minucius then summoned his men. 'Men!' he said, 'I have often been told that the best man is he who gives helpful advice, that the man who accepts good advice stands next to him; and that the most inadequate man is he who cannot give advice, but cannot accept it from another, either. We have been denied the top rank of intellect and ability, so let us grasp the second—the intermediate—ranking and, while we learn to command, let us resolve to be guided by a man of good judgement. Let us join our camp with that of Fabius. Let us carry the standards to his head-quarters, where I shall address him with the title "father", as his benefit conferred on us, and his exalted position, requires. You, men, must salute as "patrons" those who just now gave you protection with the weapons in their right hands and, if nothing else, this day will at least have brought us credit for showing our gratitude.'

30. The signal was given, and the call for breaking camp went up. They set off and, in marching order, proceeded to the dictator's encampment, taking the dictator himself and those around him by surprise. The standards were set up before the tribunal, and the master of horse marched forward ahead of the others. He addressed Fabius with the title 'father', and his entire army saluted as 'patrons' those of the dictator's men who were standing around him.

'Dictator,' said Minucius, 'I have just made you equal to my parents in the name I applied to you, the best I can do with language. But to them I owe only my life, whereas to you I owe these men's salvation as well as my own. And so, that decree of the people, onerous to me rather than an honour, I am the first to reject and repeal. I put myself once more under your command and auspices,* and restore to you these standards and legions, praying that this might turn out well for you, for me, and for these armies of yours, the rescued one and the rescuer alike. Please forgive us, and give me the order to hold the position of master of horse, and these men to retain their various ranks.'

Handshakes followed, and at the meeting's end the soldiers received warm and cordial hospitality from acquaintances and strangers alike. And so a festive day emerged from one that, shortly before, had been particularly dismal and almost under a curse.

Word of the episode reached Rome, where it was corroborated by correspondence, not just from the two commanders but from the rank and file in both armies as well. Everybody now praised Maximus to the skies. His prestige was just as high with Hannibal and the Carthaginian foe, who were now finally realizing that their war was against Romans, and that it was being fought in Italy. For they had, over the past two years, developed such a low opinion of the Roman officers and fighting men that they had found it difficult to believe that the war was with the same people about whom they had heard frightening tales from their fathers. And they say, too, that Hannibal, when he was returning from the battle, commented that the cloud that usually sat on the mountaintops had now come down as a rainstorm.

31. While this was going on in Italy, the consul Gnaeus Servilius Geminus sailed around the coastline of Sardinia and Corsica with a fleet of a hundred and twenty ships. He took hostages from both islands, and sailed on to Africa. Before landing on the mainland he laid waste the island of Meninx, and then received ten talents of silver from the inhabitants of Cercina* as the price for not burning and pillaging their land, as well. He proceeded to the coast of Africa where he disembarked his troops. From there, soldiers and ships' crews were led off on plundering expeditions, and they spread out as widely as if their raids were being conducted on uninhabited islands. Their lack of caution soon brought them into an ambush. Stragglers were surrounded by bands of natives, men ignorant of the land surrounded by men who knew it, and they were driven back to the ships in ignominious flight, and with heavy casualties. Some 1,000 men were lost, including the quaestor Tiberius Sempronius Blaesus.

The fleet cast off in panic from shores that were swarming with the enemy, and held a course for Sicily. At Lilybaeum, it was transferred to the praetor Titus Otacilius, to be taken back to Rome by Otacilius' legate, Publius Cincius. The consul himself set off on foot through Sicily, crossing then to Italy by the strait, since he and his colleague Marcus Atilius had been sent for in a dispatch from Quintus Fabius. They were to take over the dictator's armies, since Fabius' six-month *imperium* had almost expired.

Practically all the annalistic accounts record Fabius' position as that of dictator for his Hannibalic campaign, and Coelius also recounts that Fabius was the first dictator appointed by the people. However, Coelius and the others have lost sight of the fact that the right to appoint a dictator lay with the one surviving consul, Gnaeus Servilius, at that time far off in Gaul, his province. Panic-stricken after the defeat it had suffered, the state could not brook the delay this would involve, and so resorted to the measure of having a provisional dictator appointed by the people. Subsequently, Fabius' achievements and outstanding reputation, together with the additions his descendants made to the inscription on his bust, all made it easy to believe that a man who had been made a provisional dictator had actually been dictator.*

32. The consuls Atilius and Geminus Servilius* assumed command of the armies of Fabius and Minucius respectively. They constructed winter quarters early and, in complete harmony, spent the rest of the autumn prosecuting the war with Fabius' tactics. When Hannibal went out to forage, they would appear at the appropriate moment at various points, hounding his column and waylaying stragglers. They would not risk an all-out battle, which the enemy was doing all he could to bring on, and Hannibal was reduced to such a state of deprivation that he would have headed back to Gaul had he not feared that his leaving would be necessarily seen as flight. For he was left with no hope of provisioning his army in those parts, if the incoming consuls followed the same tactics for the war.

The difficulties of winter had now brought the war around Gereonium to a halt, and at this time ambassadors from Neapolis came to Rome. They brought into the Senate forty golden bowls of considerable weight, and made a speech declaring that they were aware that the treasury of the Roman people was being depleted by the war. This war was being fought as much for the cities and farmland of the allies as for the city of Rome—Italy's capital city and bastion—and its empire, they said. Accordingly, the people of Neapolis had voted that it was only right for them to assist the Roman people with gold that had been left them by their ancestors for beautifying their temples, and also as a fund to help them in adversity. Had they believed their personal assistance would help, they would have been just as ready to offer that, they said. The Roman senators and people would be doing them a favour, they declared, if they regarded as their own everything the Neapolitans possessed, and if they saw fit to accept a gift whose value lay more in the good will of those who gladly gave it than in its intrinsic worth. The ambassadors were formally thanked for the generosity and concern, and only the lightest one of their bowls was accepted.

33. At about this time a Carthaginian spy, who had escaped detection for two years, was arrested in Rome; he was released after having his hands cut off. Twenty-five slaves were also crucified for conspiring together in the Campus Martius, and the informer in the affair was given his freedom and 20,000 full *asses*.* A delegation was also sent to King Philip of Macedon to demand the surrender of Demetrius of Pharus, who had sought asylum with him after being defeated in war. Another party of delegates was sent to the Ligurians to complain about the assistance they had given the Carthaginians in material and men, and at the same time to get a close look at what was happening amongst the Boii and Insubres. An embassy was also sent to King Pinnes in Illyria to demand payment of his indemnity,* the due date for which had expired, or to take hostages from him if he wanted the date for payment extended. Such was the extent to which the Romans refused to overlook their interests anywhere in the world, even those far away, despite having the burden of this massive war on their backs.

Religious concerns also arose over a temple of Concord that had been promised in a vow two years earlier in Gaul, during a mutiny of the troops, by the praetor Lucius Manlius. The building of the temple had not to that day been put up for contract. Accordingly, duumvirs were appointed expressly for the purpose by the urban praetor Marcus Aemilius. These were Gaius Pupius and Kaeso Quinctius Flamininus, and they contracted out the building of the temple on the citadel.

A letter from the same praetor, Manlius, was sent to the consuls, on the authorization of the Senate, requesting one of them, if they saw fit, to return to Rome to arrange the consular elections. Manlius added that he would announce the election for the date they ordained. The answer that came back from the consuls was that they could not leave the enemy without prejudice to the state, and so it was preferable for the elections to be held by an *interrex* than for one of the consuls to be called away from the war. The senators felt that it was more appropriate for a dictator to be appointed by one of the consuls to hold the elections.* Lucius Veturius Philo was appointed, and he in turn appointed Marcus Pomponius Matho to be his master of horse. But there was an irregularity in the appointment process, and they were ordered to resign their posts after fourteen days. The state then returned to an interregnum.

34. The consuls had their *imperium* extended for a year, and the *interreges* appointed by the senators were Gaius Claudius Cento, son of Appius, and then Publius Cornelius Asina. The elections were held during Cornelius' interregnum and saw bitter antagonism between the senatorial party and the plebeians.*

The commons were striving to raise to the consulship Gaius Terentius Varro, a man of their own class, who had ingratiated himself with the plebeians by his attacks on leading citizens, and by his crowd-pleasing methods. Indeed, thanks to the attack he had mounted on Quintus Fabius' influence, and on his authority as dictator, Varro had gained some distinction through another man's unpopularity. The senatorial party were using every means to block him; they wanted to prevent it becoming common practice for people to rise to their level by scurrilous attacks on them. Quintus Baebius Herennius, a tribune of the plebs and a kinsman of Gaius Terentius, cast aspersions not only on the senators, but also on the augurs who, he claimed, had stopped the dictator from holding the elections, and by disparaging them he won support for his own candidate. The nobles had been thirsting for war for many a year, he said. It was by them that Hannibal had been brought to Italy, and by them, too, that the war was being fraudulently prolonged when it could be finished off. Operations could be successfully conducted by four united legions, Herennius continued, as had been demonstrated by Marcus Minucius' successful engagement during Fabius' absence. But now two legions had been thrown before the enemy to be slaughtered, and then brought back from the brink of slaughter—just so that the words 'father' and 'patron' could be applied to the man who had prevented the Romans from conquering, before he prevented them from being conquered. After this, the consuls had used Fabian tactics to draw out the war when they could have finished it off. This was a pact the nobles had all made amongst themselves, he said, and the Romans would not see an end to the war until they had elected to the consulship a real plebeian, that is, a 'new man'. For the plebeians who had been made nobles were now initiates in the same rites as them, and they had been looking down on the plebs ever since they had stopped being looked down upon by the senators. The aim of all this activity and manœuvring for an interregnum was clear to see—it was so that the elections would remain under the control of the Senate. That was what lay behind the two consuls' staying behind with the army. Later, when, against the senators' wishes, a dictator was appointed to hold the elections, that was what lay behind their forcing through a declaration by the augurs that the dictator's appointment was invalid. So, he said, the senators now had their interregnum. But one consulship did at least belong to the Roman plebs, and the people would make free use of it, and give it to a man who wanted a quick victory rather than a long tenure of command.

35. The plebeians were inflamed by such speeches. There were three patrician candidates, Publius Cornelius Merenda, Lucius Manlius Volso, and Marcus Aemilius Lepidus, and two plebeian candidates from already ennobled families, Gaius Atilius Serranus and Quintus Aelius Paetus (of whom one was a pontiff, the other an augur). But only one consul, Terentius Varro, was elected, and as a result the elections for the appointment of his colleague lay in his hands.

Discovering that those running against Varro had lacked the necessary electoral strength, the nobles now forced Lucius Aemilius Paulus to stand, though for a long time he steadfastly refused to do so. Paulus had served as consul with Marcus Livius, and he had been a bitter enemy of the plebs ever since the condemnation of his former colleague, an affair in which his own reputation almost went up in flames.* On the next election day all those who had been in competition with Varro withdrew, and Paulus joined the consul less as a colleague than as a rival in opposition to him.

The praetorian elections were held next, and Marcus Pomponius Matho* and Publius Furius Philus were returned. Philus was allotted the urban judicial administration, and Pomponius jurisdiction between citizens and foreigners. There were two additional praetors, Marcus Claudius Marcellus for Sicily, and Lucius Postumius Albinus for Gaul. These magistrates were all elected *in absentia*, and apart from Terentius (the consul elect) none of them was given an office that he had not already held. A number of intrepid and active men were passed over because it was felt that, under the circumstances, no one should be assigned an office that was new to him.

36. There was also a substantial increase in military personnel, but such are the discrepancies in the sources regarding numbers and kinds of troops involved that I would not venture to give precise information on the size of the additions to infantry and cavalry forces. Some record a supplementary mobilization of 10,000 men, others of four new legions, to make a total of eight for the campaign. A number of authors claim that the legionary complement was also increased in terms of infantry and cavalry. According to these, 1,000 infantry and 100 cavalry were added to each legion, bringing the strength of each up to 5,000 foot and 300 horse, with the allies contributing double that number of cavalry and the same number of infantry. There were, they claim, 87,200 men under arms in the Roman camp when the battle was fought at Cannae.* On one point there is no disagreement: the effort and vigour devoted to the campaign was greater than in previous years because the dictator had given reason to hope that the enemy could be defeated.

Before the new legions marched from the city, however, the decemvirs were instructed to go and consult the Sacred Books, for there was general unease over some strange prodigies. There had been reports of showers of stones falling on the Aventine in Rome and also, at about the same time, at Aricia. It was reported, too, that blood had flowed profusely from statues amongst the Sabines, and also amid the waters at Caere; and this caused greater alarm because it had occurred quite frequently. In addition, a number of people had been fatally struck by lightning on the vaulted street that used to lead to the Campus Martius. Expiation for the prodigies was conducted as prescribed by the Books.

Ambassadors from Paestum brought golden bowls to Rome. As in the case of the people of Neapolis, they were formally thanked, but their gold was not accepted.

37. At about this time, a fleet that had been sent by Hiero reached Ostia bearing a large cargo of provisions. Ushered into the Senate, Hiero's ambassadors announced that King Hiero had been extremely distressed by the news of the death of the consul Gaius Flaminius, and the destruction of his army—he could not have been more

distraught at any misfortune that overtook him personally, or his realm. So, they said, while Hiero well knew that the greatness of the Roman people was almost more remarkable in adversity than in good times, he had nevertheless sent all the means of assistance usually provided in wartime by good and faithful allies. These he earnestly begged the senators not to refuse. First of all, they said, they were bringing a 220-pound golden Victory to serve as a good omen, and they asked the senators to accept it, and hold it and keep it as theirs in perpetuity. They had also brought 300,000 measures of wheat and 200,000 of barley, they said, so that the Romans would have no shortage of provisions, and they would ship any further quantities they needed to whatever destination they specified. Hiero was aware that the Roman people made use only of infantry and cavalry that were Roman or of Latin status, they added, but he had also observed foreign light-armed auxiliaries in the Roman camp. He had therefore sent them a thousand archers and slingers, a force well suited to combat Balearic and Moorish troops, and other peoples who fought with projectiles.

To these gifts the ambassadors added a word of advice. The praetor allotted the charge of Sicily should take a fleet across to Africa— the enemy would then be facing hostilities in his own land, as well, and thus be granted less leeway for sending assistance to Hannibal.

The reply given to the king by the Senate was as follows. Hiero was a good man and an outstanding ally, they said, one who had shown unflagging loyalty ever since he had established a treaty of friendship with the Roman people, and who had on every occasion, and in every place, generously supported the Roman cause. The Roman people were grateful to him, as well they should be. Gold had also been brought to them by other communities, they said, but the Roman people had not accepted it, appreciative though they were of the kind gesture. They did, however, accept Hiero's Victory, and the good omen it represented, and they accordingly gave and assigned to her, as her residence, the Capitol, the temple of Jupiter Optimus Maximus. Sanctified in that citadel of the city of Rome, she would be gracious and propitious, and firm and constant, in her support of the Roman people.

The slingers and archers, along with the grain, were passed along to the consuls. The fleet of fifty ships under the command of Titus Otacilius in Sicily was strengthened with twenty-five quinqueremes, and Otacilius was granted permission to sail to Africa with the fleet, if he thought that served the interests of the state.

38. The enrolment of forces completed, the consuls waited a few days for the troops from the allies and men of Latin status to arrive.* At this time an unprecedented step was taken: the oath of allegiance was administered to the enlisted men by the military tribunes. Until that day, there had been only the oath the men took to mobilize when the consuls gave the order and not to disband without their order. When they had mobilized for division into decuries* or centuries, the cavalry (by decuries) and the infantry (by centuries) would simply swear an informal oath amongst themselves. They would swear not to break ranks for flight, or from fear—indeed, for no reason other than to fetch or retrieve a weapon, to strike an enemy, or to rescue a fellow citizen. This discretionary pact, made amongst the men themselves, was now superseded by an official administering of the oath of allegiance by the tribunes.

Before the troops marched from the city, there were a large number of blustering addresses made by the consul Varro. He claimed that the war had been brought on Italy by the nobility, and would remain stuck in the vitals of the state if she had more generals like Fabius. He, however, was going to end the war on the day he set eyes on the enemy. Varro's colleague Paulus made only one speech, the day before he left the city, and it had more truth to it than popular appeal. He had no disrespectful comments about Varro, except one. Varro, he said, did not yet know his own army, or that of his enemy, and did not know the lie of the land and geographical features of the region of his campaign. So, said Paulus, he was amazed that such a leader would know, while still wearing civilian clothes in the city, what his tactics should be when under arms, and that he was even able to predict the day on which he would meet the enemy in pitched battle. As for himself, he continued, he would not formulate plans before the appropriate time; for the situation dictated strategy for men: men could not impose strategy on the situation. His wish was that a strategy of caution and prudence might prove successful; recklessness was intrinsically foolish, and, apart from that, it had to that point achieved nothing. It was quite clear that Paulus would choose safety over impetuous plans and, to make sure that he stuck to it all the more firmly, Quintus Fabius Maximus is said to have addressed him in the following words* on his departure:

39. 'Lucius Aemilius, if you had a colleague like yourself—my own preference—or if you yourself were like your colleague, then what I have to say would be unnecessary. If you were both good consuls, all your actions would be loyally taken for the good of the republic, no matter what I said. Likewise, if you were both bad men, you would not listen to my words, or pay attention to my advice, anyway. As matters stand, as I look at your colleague's qualities, and your own, all my words are directed to you alone. I do, nevertheless, see that your being a good man and good citizen will serve no purpose, if half our state is crippled, and bad policies have the same force and support as good ones. For you are wrong, Lucius Paulus, if you think you will have any less of a fight with Gaius Terentius than you will with Hannibal, and I wonder if you might not in future have this man as a more dangerous adversary than that redoubtable enemy of ours. With Hannibal you will fight only in the battlefield; with Varro you are going to be fighting in all places, and at all times. Against Hannibal and his legions you will have to do battle with your cavalry and infantry; Varro, as commander, is going to attack you with your own soldiers.

'I should not mention Gaius Flaminius—it might prove a bad omen for you. But I must say that *his* delusion took effect only when he was consul, and when he was in his province, and with his army. Varro was out of control before he stood for the consulship, and again during his campaign for it—and is so now, before even setting eyes on his camp and his enemy. And when a man causes such a stir with blustering talk of battles and warfare amongst *civilians*, imagine what he will do when surrounded by young soldiers, and in a situation where action follows hard on the heels of talk! But if he engages immediately, as he threatens to do, then either I have no knowledge of military tactics, or of the nature of this war and of this enemy, or else there is going to be another place more famous for our defeats than Trasimene.

'This is no time for self-glorification before an audience of one, and also I would rather go too far in shunning glory than in courting it. But the fact is this: the only way of fighting the war against Hannibal is as I have fought it. And it is not merely the result—that notorious teacher of fools—which illustrates this. The same reasoning that obtained in the past will remain unchanged in future, as long as the situation remains the same. We are fighting the war in Italy, in our homeland, and on our own soil. All around us there are only fellow citizens and allies, and they are assisting us—and will continue to assist us—with armaments, fighting men, horses, and provisions. Such is the evidence of their loyalty that they have already given us in our times of trouble! And every passing day gives us greater expertise, judgement, and perseverance.

'Hannibal, by contrast, is in a strange and hostile land, facing opposition and peril on every side, and far from his home and country. He has no peace on land or sea, and no cities, no protective walls to shelter him—he sees nothing anywhere that is his. He lives on what he pillages day by day, and has barely a third of the army he took across the Ebro. More have died from starvation than in battle, and for the few that remain food is in short supply. Can you have any doubt, then, that it is by non-aggression that we shall overcome this man, who grows weaker by the day, and has no provisions, no reinforcements, and no money? How long has he been sitting before the walls of that feeble Apulian town of Gereonium as though he were defending the walls of Carthage! I shall not brag about my own performance, not even before you; just see how the last consuls, Servilius and Atilius, toyed with him!

'This is the one road to safety, Lucius Paulus, and it will be your fellow citizens, not your enemy, who will make it difficult and treacherous for you. For your own soldiers will want the same thing as the enemy's soldiers, and the Roman consul Varro will hanker after the same thing as the Carthaginian Hannibal. All on your own you must resist two generals. But resist them you will, if you remain sufficiently unmoved before people's gossip and tittle-tattle, and if you are not influenced by the hollow reputation of your colleague, and by your own ill-deserved notoriety. The truth is all too often in difficulty, but is never extinguished, the saying goes, and the man who despises glory will have *true* glory. *Let* people call you cowardly rather than cautious, lethargic rather than judicious, spineless rather than a shrewd tactician. I prefer to have a discerning enemy fearing you than foolish compatriots praising you. Hannibal will despise the risk-taker, but he will fear the man who makes no foolhardy move. I am not encouraging you to take no action, but to let reason, not chance, direct that action. Always control yourself and all your actions; be under arms and on the alert; do not let slip your own opportunity and do not give the enemy his. Everything is clear and in focus for the man who is not in a rush; haste is improvident and blind.'

40. The consul's response to this was not very promising. While admitting that what Fabius said was true, he added that it was not easy to put into effect. The dictator had been unable to cope with his master of horse, so what power or authority would a consul have over an unruly and reckless colleague? He had in his previous consulship come away badly burned from the fiery wrath of the people, he said, and, while he wanted everything to turn out successfully, he would rather face the spears of the enemy than the votes of the angry citizens.

They say that Paulus left after this conversation, with the leading senators at his side. The plebeian consul was attended by his plebeian adherents, a group impressive in numbers, but lacking men of distinction.

On their arrival in camp, the new and the old forces were combined, and the camp split in two parts. The newer and smaller of the two was closer to Hannibal, but the old one contained the greater part of the troops, and all the best and strongest of them. Marcus Atilius, one of the consuls of the previous year, asked to be relieved of command on grounds of age, and the commanders sent him back to Rome. The other ex-consul, Geminus Servilius, they put in command of a Roman legion, and 2,000 allied infantry and cavalry, in the smaller camp.

Hannibal noted the fifty per cent increase in the enemy's troops, but even so he was remarkably cheered by the arrival of the consuls. Nothing remained of the supplies acquired by his daily pillaging, and there was no place left for him to plunder—throughout the area, the grain had been transported into the fortified towns by all the locals, when the countryside became unsafe. As a result (so it was ascertained later), Hannibal was left with barely enough grain for another ten days, and, because of the shortage of food, his Spaniards were preparing to desert. The Romans, however, did not wait long enough for them to do so.*

41. In fact, fortune also provided fuel for the consul's recklessness and impatient character. While some Carthaginian foragers were being driven off, a haphazard engagement occurred, with a spontaneous charge from the soldiers rather than one planned and ordered by the commanders. In this, the Carthaginians in no way measured up to their enemy. Some 1,700 of them were killed, with no more than 100 Roman and allied casualties. The consul Paulus, however, feared an ambush, and halted a disorderly pursuit by the victors—the consuls were alternating command on a daily basis, and this was Paulus' day. Varro was furious, screaming that the enemy had been allowed to slip through their fingers, and the war could have been finished off if they had not halted.

Hannibal was not too upset by the loss—in fact, he believed that the trap had now been baited for the recklessness of the hot-headed consul, and especially for that of his newly recruited men. He was as fully aware of how matters stood on the enemy side as on his own— he knew that the commanders differed in character and were at loggerheads, and that nearly two-thirds of their army consisted of raw recruits. Accordingly, believing that the place and time were right for an ambush, he set off the following night, his men carrying nothing but their weapons, and he left the camp behind him filled with all manner of property, state- and privately owned. On the other side of some nearby hills he posted his men out of view, and ready for battle, infantry on the left, cavalry on the right, and led the baggage-train along the valley between the two. His aim was to take the enemy by surprise while they were completely preoccupied with ransacking a camp, which they would assume had been abandoned when its occupants fled. Numerous fires were left burning in the camp. This was to make the Romans believe that Hannibal had tried to keep the consuls where they were by creating the illusion of a functioning camp while he, meanwhile, got a good head start in his flight—the same ploy with which he had duped Fabius the previous year.

42. At daybreak, the Romans were taken by surprise, first by the fact that the Carthaginian outposts had been withdrawn, and after that, as they approached, by the unusual silence. Then, when they were quite sure the camp was empty, the men converged on the two headquarters of the consuls. They reported that the enemy had fled in such panic that they left the camp with the tents still standing; and, they added, a large number of fires had also been left burning, to cover up the flight. A cry went up for the consuls to order the advance—they should lead the men in pursuit of the enemy, and pillage their camp immediately. And one of the consuls was acting just like one of the crowd of common soldiers, though Paulus time and time again said that they should show caution, and keep their

wits about them. In the end, however, having no other means to check the mutiny, or the leader of the mutiny, he sent the prefect Statilius to reconnoitre with a squadron of Lucanian cavalry.

Statilius rode up to the camp gates. Telling the rest of his men to remain outside the fortifications, he passed beyond the palisade with two cavalrymen, and, after carefully examining the whole camp, he reported that it had to be a trap. The fires that had been left alight were on the side of the camp facing the Romans, the tents were open and all their precious objects left exposed to view, he said, and in places he had seen silver carelessly strewn about, as if inviting plunder.

The report, which was intended to discourage the men's rapacity, only served to excite them and, when the cry went up from them that, unless the signal were given, they would go without their leaders, a leader was not lacking—for Varro immediately gave the signal to advance. Paulus was holding back in any case, but in addition the chickens refused their approval* when the auspices were taken, and so he ordered the news to be taken to his colleague, who was already marching the troops through the gate. Varro was angry, but Flaminius' recent disaster and the consul Claudius' famous calamity at sea in the First Punic War filled him with superstitious fears.

In fact, it was almost as if, that day, the gods took it upon themselves to defer—but not prevent—the disaster that was awaiting the Romans. For it so happened that two slaves, one belonging to a knight from Formiae, and the other to a knight from Sidicinum, appeared just when the men were refusing to obey the consul's order to return to camp. These men had been amongst a group of foragers intercepted by the Numidians during the consulship of Servilius and Atilius, and on that day they escaped to rejoin their masters. Brought before the consuls, they reported that Hannibal's entire army was lying in ambush on the other side of the nearby hills. The timely arrival of these men re-established the authority of the consuls, but not before one of them, by courting popularity with a misguided permissiveness, had compromised the dignity of his office.*

43. Hannibal saw that, while the Romans had acted imprudently, they had not been completely carried away, and so, his ambush discovered, he returned disappointed to camp. He could not remain there for many days because his grain was running out, and now fresh plans were every day being mulled over, not just by the common soldiers, who were a motley rabble drawn from every race, but even

by the Carthaginian general himself. Amongst the soldiers there had initially been some muttering, and then open protests. They demanded pay that was owing to them, and complained first about the high price of food, and eventually about hunger, and there was also a rumour circulating that the Spanish mercenaries had decided to defect to the enemy. It is said that even Hannibal himself occasionally considered a flight into Gaul by making a swift departure with his cavalry, and leaving behind all his infantry. Such being the ideas bandied about, and such the mood in the camp, Hannibal decided to move to the warmer regions of Apulia where the harvests would be earlier. An additional consideration was that the further he withdrew from the enemy, the more difficult it would be for his less reliable troops to desert. He set off at night after lighting fires as he had done earlier, and leaving a few tents in place for the enemy to see, hoping that fear of an ambush would hold the Romans back as before.

However, the Lucanian Statilius was sent out on reconnaissance again, and after a sweep of all the land beyond the camp and beyond the mountains he reported that the enemy column had been sighted in the distance. This prompted discussion of whether they should pursue it. Each consul stuck to the view he had persistently advocated in the past, but Varro had the support of almost everybody, and Paulus of no one apart from the previous year's consul, Servilius. Thus, accepting the majority vote, and with destiny thrusting them on,* they set off to make Cannae famous as the site of a Roman disaster.

Near that village Hannibal had pitched camp, facing away from the Volturnus wind,* which blows clouds of dust over the dry, torrid plains. While very convenient for the actual encampment, this was to prove especially advantageous when the Carthaginians deployed their battle line. They would be facing away from the wind, which would be only at their backs, and they would be fighting an enemy half-blinded by clouds of dust.

44. After thoroughly reconnoitring the pathways, the consuls proceeded to follow the Carthaginians. Coming into the area of Cannae, and now having them in sight, they fortified two camps roughly the same distance apart as at Gereonium, dividing up the troops in the same manner as before. The River Aufidus flowed close to both encampments, affording their water-carriers more or less convenient access to it, though not without a fight. However, it was from the smaller camp on the far side of the Aufidus that the Romans could more easily provision themselves with water because of the lack of any enemy presence on the far bank.

Hannibal had come to hope that the consuls would give him the chance to do battle, the area being naturally suited for a cavalry engagement, the branch of his forces in which he was unbeatable. He, therefore, deployed his battle line, and provoked his enemy with sudden charges from his Numidian troops. At this, there was upheaval once more in the Roman camps, with the men in an insubordinate mood and the consuls in disagreement. Paulus taunted Varro with the recklessness of Sempronius and Flaminius, and Varro taunted his colleague by citing Fabius as merely a convenient model for leaders who were cowardly and indolent. Varro also called on gods and men to witness that no blame lay with him for Hannibal's occupation of Italy virtually through right of possession. His hands remained tied, thanks to his colleague, he said, and soldiers who were angry and eager to fight were having their swords and weapons taken out of their hands. Paulus replied that, if the legions were betrayed and sacrificed to a hasty and ill-advised engagement, he for his part would be free of all blame for any misfortune befalling them, but he, too, would have to share the consequences with his colleague. So he said that Varro should see to it that those men with glib and impetuous tongues demonstrated as much strength of arm in battle.

45. Rather than being devoted to consultation, time was now being wasted in slanging-matches. Hannibal, meanwhile, who had kept his line in formation till late in the day, took all his other troops back to camp, but sent his Numidians over the river to attack the water detail from the smaller of the Roman camps. The carriers were an ill-ordered crowd, whom the Numidians, on barely reaching the bank, chased off merely with their shouting and clamour. The Numidians then rode on to the guard-emplacement before the Roman rampart, and almost to the very gates of the camp. That a Roman camp should now be threatened by a group of allied irregulars did indeed seem humiliating, and the only thing that kept the Romans from immediately crossing the river, and forming up for battle was the fact that that day's command lay with Paulus.

The next day it was Varro's turn to take charge. Without conferring with his colleague in any way, he put up the signal, and led his troops over the river in battle order. Paulus followed him; he might disapprove of the plan, but he could not refuse assistance. After crossing the river, the two attached to their forces the troops that they had kept in the smaller camp. When the line was deployed, they had the Roman cavalry stationed on the right wing, the one closer to the river, and next to them the Roman infantry. The extreme left flank was made up of the allied cavalry. Further in, adjoining the Roman legions towards the centre, were the allied infantry. The front line comprised javelin-throwers and the other light-armed auxiliary forces. The consuls commanded the wings, Terentius Varro the left and Aemilius Paulus the right, while Geminus Servilius was given charge of the centre.

46. Sending his Balearic troops and other light-armed infantry ahead, Hannibal crossed the river at dawn and placed his men in line in the order in which he had brought them over. The Gallic and Spanish cavalry he set on the left wing, near the river bank, and facing the Roman cavalry. The right wing was assigned to the Numidian cavalry, and the centre was composed of infantry arranged in such a way that there were Africans on both sides, with Gauls and Spaniards between them. One might have taken the Africans to be a Roman battle line, for they were armed with captured weapons, some taken at the Trebia, but most of them at Trasimene. The Gauls and the Spaniards had shields almost identical in shape, but their swords differed in size and appearance. Those of the Gauls were very long and without a point, whereas those of the Spaniard, whose practice was to lunge at his enemy rather than to slash, were short and easy to wield, and were pointed. These tribes provide a more terrifying spectacle than others because of their large physique and general appearance. The Gauls were bare above the navel; the Spaniards took their positions dressed in purple-fringed tunics that shone with an incredible whiteness. The infantry standing in line that day numbered 40,000, the cavalry 10,000. On the wings, the commanders were Hasdrubal (on the left) and Maharbal (on the right), while Hannibal personally held the centre along with his brother Mago.*

Whether they owed their positions to calculation or pure chance, both sides were fortunate enough to have the sun at an angle, the Romans facing south and the Carthaginians north. The wind, locally known as the Volturnus, now rose in the direction of the Romans, rolling large clouds of dust right into their faces, and obstructing their vision.

47. When the battle-cry was raised the auxiliary forces charged forward, and the fighting began with the light infantry of the two sides. Then the Carthaginian left wing, composed of Gallic and Spanish cavalry, clashed with the Roman right; but it was a very atypical cavalry engagement. Because there was no room left for an encircling manœuvre—they were hemmed in by the river on one side, and by the lines of infantry on the other—they were forced to charge head-on. Both sides drove straight ahead but, as horses came to a standstill, and were then crowded together in a mass, rider grappled with rider, each trying to drag the other from his mount. It had now for the most part turned into an infantry engagement, but the fighting was more ferocious than it was long-lived. The Roman cavalry was driven back, and took to flight.

As the cavalry engagement was coming to an end, the infantry battle got under way. This was at first fought with equal strength, and equal confidence, by the two sides, as long as the Gallic and Spanish ranks remained unbroken. But these were standing ahead of the rest of the line, in a wedge-formation that was too thin, and so lacking in strength, and, while the Roman front equalled theirs in length, that line was densely ordered. Thus, after persistent and frequent efforts, the Romans eventually pushed their adversary back. Then, the enemy repelled and retreating in confusion, the Romans charged ahead and, in one surge, drove through the terror-stricken column of fleeing men, and into the Carthaginian centre. Meeting no resistance, they finally reached the African reserves, who had taken up a position on the two wings. The wings had been drawn back from the main body on both sides, while the centre, formed of Gauls and Spaniards, had protruded some way ahead of them. This convex formation had now been driven back, first of all straightening out the Carthaginian front, and then, as the Carthaginian retreat continued, even forming a depression in the centre. The Africans had now completed the crescent-formation at both ends and, as the Romans charged recklessly into the centre, they outflanked them, and soon extended the crescent to enclose them to their rear as well.

At this point the Romans found the one battle they had now finished was to no purpose, and leaving the Gauls and Spaniards, whom they had been cutting down as they retreated, they entered into a fresh combat with the Africans. But the fight was one-sided, not simply because they were penned in by an enemy that completely surrounded them, but also because they were exhausted, and were beginning a struggle with troops that were fresh and full of energy.

48. By this time, battle had also been joined on the Roman left, where the allied cavalry faced the Numidians. The fighting was sluggish at first, and commenced with a Carthaginian trick.* Some 500 Numidians kept swords hidden under their corslets, in addition to their regular weapons and javelins. Pretending to desert, they rode over from their side, keeping their shields behind their backs. Swiftly dismounting, and throwing down their shields and spears at the feet of the enemy, they were welcomed into the centre of the Roman ranks, taken to the rear of the lines and told to wait at the back. While the engagement got under way at all points they remained there quietly. But after everyone's thoughts and eyes had become fixed on the battle, they seized shields that lay scattered here and there amongst the piles of corpses, and attacked the Roman line from behind. Hacking at the soldiers' backs, and cutting their hamstrings, they caused enormous loss of life, and considerably more panic and confusion. In one spot men would be running off in terror, in another fighting on obstinately, when little hope now remained. Then Hasdrubal, commander in that quarter, withdrew the Numidians from the centre of the line since they were showing little spirit in fighting their opponents, and sent them in pursuit of the scattered fugitives. He now brought in the Spaniards and the Gauls to support the Africans, who by this time were well-nigh exhausted, more from massacring their enemy than fighting them.

49. In the other sector of the fighting, Paulus had been seriously wounded, at the very start of the engagement, by a projectile from a sling. Even so, he made frequent charges against Hannibal, his men in a compact body, and restored the battle at several points. Roman horsemen were giving him cover, but eventually these abandoned their mounts, for the consul was now losing the strength even to control his horse. Someone then brought word to Hannibal that the consul had ordered his cavalrymen to dismount, and he is reported to have said: 'I should have prefered him to have handed them to me in irons!' The cavalry were now on foot and fighting as if the enemy victory was no longer in doubt. Though defeated, they preferred to die where they stood rather than to flee, while the victors, furious at the men delaying their victory, massacred those they could not dislodge. They did, however, drive off a few survivors,

exhausted from their efforts and their wounds. All the Romans then scattered, and those who could were chasing after their horses to make their escape.

The military tribune Gnaeus Lentulus was riding by when his eyes fell on the consul sitting on a rock and covered with blood.

'Lucius Aemilius,' he said, 'on you alone the gods should look with favour, the one man free of blame for today's debacle. Take this horse while you still have some strength left. I shall be at your side; I can raise you up and protect you, so that you do not add tragedy to this battle with the death of a consul. Even without that there is enough to weep and grieve for!'

'God bless your courage, Gnaeus Cornelius,' replied the consul, 'but do not waste in useless pity the little time you have to escape the enemy's clutches. Go, take this official message to the Senate: they must see to the fortifications of the city of Rome, and secure them with troops, before the victorious enemy arrives. But take Quintus Fabius aside, and tell him that Lucius Aemilius Paulus lived to this point, and now dies, with his precepts in mind. For myself, let me breathe my last amidst my men, the victims of this massacre. Thus I can avoid standing trial again after my consulship, or coming forward as my colleague's accuser, to defend my innocence by blaming another.'

As they conversed, they were overtaken first by a crowd of their fellow citizens in flight, then by the enemy. The enemy, unaware of his identity, showered the consul with projectiles, and in the confusion Lentulus was whisked away to safety by his horse. With that, there was disordered flight in every quarter. Seven thousand men made good their escape to the smaller camp, 10,000 to the larger. About 2,000 escaped to the actual village of Cannae, but they were immediately surrounded by Carthalo and his cavalry, since the town had no fortifications to protect it. Whether by accident or design, the other consul had joined none of these particular groups of fugitives. He slipped away to Venusia with about 50 cavalrymen.

Roman casualties are reported to have been 45,500 infantry and 2,700 cavalry, with numbers of citizens and allies being roughly the same. They included both quaestors of the consuls, Lucius Atilius and Lucius Furius Bibaculus, as well as 29 military tribunes, some of whom were former consuls, praetors, and aediles. (Numbered amongst these are Gnaeus Servilius Geminus, and Marcus Minucius, who had been master of horse the year before and consul a number of years earlier). There were also 80 senators, or men who had held offices that qualified them for selection for the Senate—these had themselves chosen to serve as soldiers in the legions. Three thousand infantry and 1,500 cavalry were reportedly taken prisoner in the battle.*

50. So went the battle of Cannae. Its fame rivals that of the disaster at the Allia,* and, while it was less critical in its outcome (since the enemy stalled thereafter), it was, in losses, even more serious and appalling. For while the rout at the Allia meant the loss of the city, it still saved the army; at Cannae the fleeing consul had with him barely 50 men, and almost the entire army shared the fate of the other consul who died there.

In the two Roman camps there was now a poorly armed crowd of men without leaders. Those in the larger camp dispatched a message to the smaller asking their comrades to join them while the enemy, exhausted from the battle and from the jubilant feasting that would follow it, would be deep in sleep during the night. They would then leave for Canusium in a single column, they said. Some rejected the suggestion out of hand, asking why the men issuing the invitation could not come themselves, as that would be as good a way of their joining up. The reason was evident, these men said: the ground between them was all in enemy hands, and they preferred to put other people's safety at risk rather than their own. Others were not averse to the suggestion, but lacked the nerve to follow it.

However, the military tribune Publius Sempronius Tuditanus declared: 'So, you prefer to be taken by a greedy and ruthless foe, do you? To have a price set on your heads and payment demanded by men who ask you if you are a Roman citizen or a Latin ally—humiliating and tormenting you to give another man some recognition? No, you do not prefer that, at least not if you are the fellow citizens of the consul Lucius Aemilius—who chose to die well rather than live in disgrace—and of all those courageous men who lie heaped about him. The enemy clamouring before our camp gates are in chaotic disorder. Let us break through them before dawn comes upon us and their troops block our path in greater numbers. With a sword and pluck one can find a way through the thickest enemy line. And with a wedge-formation you could scatter this sprawling and disorganized crowd as though nothing blocked your path. Go with me, then—those of you who want to save yourselves and the republic!'

So saying, he drew his sword, formed up a wedge of men, and marched through the enemy's midst. The right flank was exposed, and at this the Numidians directed their javelins; but the men transferred their shields to their right side and some 600 made good their passage to the larger camp. Then, joined by another large group, they came through directly to Canusium without losses. This was a feat brought off by conquered men, the result of a surge of courage that came from the character of each individual, or from pure chance. It was not planned by the men, or conducted under any one's command.

51. All the Carthaginians were gathered around Hannibal, congratulating him on his victory and urging him, now that he had finished off this great war, to take what remained of that day, and the oncoming night, for rest, both for himself and for his exhausted men. Not so the cavalry commander Maharbal, who was of the opinion that they should not let up for a moment. 'No,' said Maharbal. 'So you may realize the significance of this battle, you will be holding your victory dinner on the Capitol in four days! Follow behind me. I shall go ahead with the cavalry—so the Romans will know of our arrival before they are aware of our coming!'

To Hannibal the idea seemed too good to be true, too great for him to absorb immediately. He declared that, while he appreciated Maharbal's enthusiasm, he would need time to consider his suggestion. Then Maharbal quipped: 'Yes, indeed, the gods do not give everything to the same man. You know how to win a battle, Hannibal; you do not know how to use the victory!'* That day's delay is generally believed to have been the salvation of the city and the empire.*

At first light the next day, the Carthaginians proceeded to gather the spoils and inspect the slaughter, which was a shocking sight even to the enemy. Romans, infantry and cavalry, lay in their thousands all over the field as the fighting, or their flight, happened to have brought them together. Some gory figures rose up from the midst of the carnage when their wounds, smarting in the cool of the morning, roused them to consciousness, and they were cut down by the enemy. Some the Carthaginians found lying there, alive, with thighs and knee-tendons severed, exposing their necks and telling them to shed the last of their blood. Others were discovered with their heads buried in freshly dug earth—they had evidently made holes and suffocated themselves by covering their faces with the soil. What especially caught everybody's attention was a Numidian, with nose and ears torn off, who was pulled out alive from beneath a dead Roman who was lying on top of him. When the Roman found his hands no longer able to hold a weapon, his anger had turned to fury and he had died while he was tearing his enemy apart with his teeth.

52. Hannibal spent most of the day gathering up the spoils. He then led an attack on the smaller camp, where he first of all constructed an earthwork that cut its occupants off from the river. In fact, the Romans were all fatigued from their efforts and sleep-deprivation as well as their wounds, and their capitulation came even sooner than Hannibal had expected. They negotiated an agreement whereby they surrendered their weapons and horses for a ransom price of 300 *quadrigati** per head for Romans, 200 for allies, and 100 for slaves. They would leave with one piece of clothing each once the payment was made. They then admitted the enemy into their camp, and were all put under guard, citizens and allies in their own separate groups.

While time was being spent on this, some 4,000 infantrymen and 200 cavalrymen—those with the strength and nerve for the venture—left the larger camp and escaped to Canusium, some in a body, others randomly drifting through the fields, which proved no less safe an option. The camp itself was surrendered to the enemy, on the same terms as the other, by the wounded and the faint-hearted who were left behind.

The spoils accumulated were enormous. Apart from the horses, prisoners, and whatever silver there was (most of it in the form of trappings from horses, since the Romans used very little silverware at table, at least on campaign), everything else was to be parcelled out as plunder for the army. Hannibal then had the bodies of his men gathered together for burial, and these, it is said, represented some 8,000 of his finest soldiers.* Some sources have it that the Roman consul was also sought out and accorded burial.

Those who had escaped to Canusium were afforded only the shelter of the city walls and plain lodging by the townspeople. However, an Apulian woman called Busa, renowned for her nobility and wealth, also assisted them with gifts of grain, clothing, and money for travelling. Later, on the conclusion of the war, she was honoured by the Senate for her generosity.

53. There were four military tribunes in Canusium: from the first legion Quintus Fabius Maximus, whose father had been dictator the previous year; from the second legion Lucius Publicius Bibulus and Publius Cornelius Scipio; and from the third Appius Claudius Pulcher, who had recently been aedile. But by general agreement supreme command was vested in Publius Scipio, who was just a young man,* and in Appius Claudius. These were discussing with a few others how matters stood for the state when Publius Furius Philus, son of a former consul, announced that they were idly nourishing hopes that were lost—the republic was completely finished, as good as dead! Some young noblemen, with Lucius Caecilius Metellus at their head, were contemplating taking to the sea in ships, leaving Italy to seek asylum with one of the kings, he said.

This terrible news was shocking in itself but, coming also as a fresh blow on top of all the disasters they had suffered, it left all present stunned and numb with astonishment. They voted to hold a meeting on the issue, but the young Scipio, destined by fate to be the leader in this war, declared that it was not a matter for discussion. In such a crisis they needed courage and action, not deliberation, he said, and those who wanted the state out of harm should immediately take up their weapons and go with him. No camp is more truly an enemy camp than one that harbours plans like this within it, he added.

With a few following him, Scipio then made for Metellus' quarters, and there came upon the young men of whom he been informed, holding a meeting. With his sword drawn over their heads as they conferred, he exclaimed: 'On my sacred oath I swear that I myself shall not abandon the republic of the Roman people, nor will I allow any other Roman citizen to do so. If I knowingly break my oath, then, Jupiter Optimus Maximus, visit the most terrible destruction on my home, my family, and my possessions! Lucius Caecilius, I demand that you, and the rest of you here present, take an oath using these words of mine. Anyone not swearing—let him know that this sword is drawn against him!'

They were as frightened as if they were looking upon the victorious Hannibal. They all took the oath, and put themselves under Scipio's charge.

54. At the same time as these events were taking place in Canusium, some 4,500 infantry and cavalry, who had scattered in flight over the countryside, came to the consul in Venusia. The people of Venusia assigned all of them to various households, where they were to be given a warm welcome and looked after. The townspeople also gave each cavalryman a toga, a tunic, and twenty-five *quadrigati*, and each infantryman ten *quadrigati* and such arms as he was lacking. In all other respects, too, the treatment they received was hospitable on both the official and personal level, and every effort was made to ensure that the people of Venusia were not surpassed in acts of kindness by the lady of Canusium.

In fact, the large numbers of refugees were proving too onerous a burden for Busa; the total had now reached close to 10,000 men. When Appius and Scipio were told that the other consul had survived the battle, they immediately sent him a message to report on their infantry and cavalry strength, and to ask whether his instructions were for their army to be brought to Venusia or to remain at Canusium. Varro actually led his own troops to Canusium, and there was now some semblance of a consular army, and it looked as if they would at least be able to defend themselves behind their fortifications, though not in open battle.

The report that had been brought to Rome made no mention of the survival even of these remnants of citizen and allied troops; there it had been reported that the army and its leaders were completely annihilated, their forces totally wiped out. At no time ever was there such panic and uproar within the walls of Rome while the city was still safe. My abilities will not meet the task, and I shall not attempt a description which, whatever details I record, will fall short of the truth. A consul and his army had been lost at Trasimene the year before, and now it was not a case of the blow being followed by another blow, but by a disaster many times greater. Two consular armies, along with the two consuls, were reported lost. They were left with no Roman camp, no commander, no common soldier. Apulia, Samnium, and practically all of Italy were in Hannibal's hands.

There is surely no other nation that would not have been crushed by such an overwhelming disaster. One might think of comparing the defeat of the Carthaginians in the sea battle off the Aegates Islands, which crushed their resolve, and made them abandon Sicily and Sardinia* and accept tax-paying and tributary status. Or

perhaps one might think of the defeat in Africa later sustained by
Hannibal himself. These disasters can in no respect be compared
with Cannae—except to say that they were borne with less strength
of character than the Romans bore theirs.

55. The praetors Publius Furius Philus and Marcus Pomponius
summoned the Senate to the Curia Hostilia to discuss defensive
measures for the city. They were in no doubt that, following the
destruction of the armies, the enemy would advance to assault Rome,
which was all that remained for him to do in the war. They faced a
situation that was critical, but on which intelligence was lacking, and
they could not come up with a plan to meet it. Meanwhile, ears were
ringing with the noisy lamentations of women while, in almost every
house, with the truth not yet known, mourning went on for the
living and the dead alike. At this point Quintus Fabius Maximus
proposed sending some light cavalry along the Appian and Latin
Ways. These men would make enquiries of those whom they met—
some were sure to be soldiers who had scattered after the rout—and
report back on what had befallen the consuls and their armies. Also,
if the immortal gods had shown pity on their empire, and allowed
some Romans to survive, they were to report on where those forces
were located. They were to bring word, too, of where Hannibal had
gone after the battle, what his plans were, what he was then doing,
and what he was likely to do. Active young men should be used for
searching out and retrieving this information, said Fabius, and the
senators, meanwhile, had jobs to do. Given the shortage of magistrates, they had to suppress any public disturbance or panic. They
had to keep women from appearing in public, compel them all to
remain within their homes, and place restrictions on family mourning. They should impose city-wide silence, and see that bearers of
any news were brought before the praetors—people should wait at
home for news touching themselves. In addition, they were to post
sentinels at the gates to stop anyone from leaving the city, and thus
force people to see that their only hope lay in preserving the city and
its defences. Fabius concluded by saying that when the unrest died
down, the senators should be recalled to the house and defensive
measures for the city should then be brought up for discussion.

56. There was unanimous support for this proposal without debate.
The crowds were removed from the Forum by the magistrates, and
the senators went off in different directions to quell the disturbance.

Then, finally, a letter arrived from the consul Gaius Terentius with the report of the death of the consul Lucius Aemilius and the destruction of his army. Varro added that he was then at Canusium, attempting to bring together the remnants of that catastrophic defeat. He had about 10,000 men with him, he said, in no order and unassigned to companies, and the Carthaginian—displaying neither the spirit of a victor nor the behaviour of a great leader—was ensconced at Cannae haggling over prisoners' ransoms and other plunder.

Personal losses were then made known from house to house, and so overwhelmed with grief was the whole city that the annual rites of Ceres were suspended. There was a religious interdiction against participation in the ceremony by people in mourning, and at that time there was no married woman left untouched by bereavement. So, to prevent other rites, whether state-sponsored or private, being abandoned for the same reason, a thirty-day limit was imposed on the period of mourning by senatorial decree.

When the unrest settled down in the city, the senators were recalled to the house. A further letter was now delivered, this time from the propraetor Titus Otacilius in Sicily. Otacilius reported that the kingdom of Hiero was being laid waste by a Punic fleet. He wished to respond to Hiero's appeals for help, but he had received a report that a second fleet, equipped and ready for action, was anchored off the Aegates Islands. For, he explained, the Carthaginian plan was to launch an immediate attack on Lilybaeum and other parts of the Roman province, when they became aware that Otacilius had turned to the defence of the Syracusan coastline. A fleet was therefore necessary if the senators wished to protect Sicily and the allied king.

57. The letters from the consul and the praetor were read out, and the senators took the following decision. The praetor Marcus Claudius, commander of the fleet lying off Ostia, was to be sent to the army at Canusium. The consul was then to be given written orders to turn his army over to the praetor, and come to Rome at the earliest possible opportunity that was consistent with the interests of the state.

These terrible disasters aside, the Romans were also alarmed by a number of prodigies, especially the conviction that year of two Vestals, Opimia and Floronia, on charges of sexual misconduct.* One had received the traditional penalty of being buried alive near the Porta

Collina, and the other had committed suicide. The man guilty of the misconduct with Floronia, Lucius Cantilius, was the secretary of a pontiff—one of those officers that are these days called minor pontiffs—and he was so badly flogged in the Comitium, at the orders of the *pontifex maximus*, that he expired under the lash.

Occurring as it did along with all the other misfortunes, this piece of sacrilege was naturally interpreted as a portent, and the decemvirs were therefore instructed to consult the Books. Quintus Fabius Pictor was also sent to the oracle at Delphi to ask what prayers and acts of supplication they could employ to appease the gods, and further enquire when the Romans would see an end to their great disasters.*

Meanwhile a number of outlandish sacrifices were conducted on instructions from the Books of Fate.* These included a Gallic man and woman, and a Greek man and woman, being interred alive in the Forum Boarium, in a spot enclosed with stones which had already been the scene of this very un-Roman practice of human sacrifice.

When, in the opinion of the decemvirs, enough had been done to placate the gods, Marcus Claudius Marcellus sent 1,500 men from Ostia to Rome, for the defence of the city. These were men whom he had under his command as recruits for the fleet. A few days later, he sent ahead to Teanum Sidicinum the naval legion (that is, the third legion) under its military tribunes, and he transferred command of the fleet to his colleague Publius Furius Philus. A few days later Marcellus himself hurried by forced marches to Canusium.

At this point, Marcus Junius, who had been named dictator by the authority of the Senate, and the master of horse, Tiberius Sempronius, held a troop-levy, and recruited younger men who were seventeen or over, and some who were still wearing the *praetexta*. From these were constituted a force of four legions and 1,000 cavalry. The two men also sent instructions to the allies and those of Latin status for troops to be supplied to them, as prescribed by the treaty. They issued orders for the preparation of armour, weaponry, and other equipment, and removed old enemy spoils that had been hanging in the temples and porticoes. There was also a novel form of recruitment occasioned by the shortage of free men, and by the crisis: they bought and armed, at state expense, 8,000 sturdy young men from the slave population, asking them first on an individual basis if they were willing to serve. Such soldiers were preferred even though the Romans had the chance of ransoming their captives at a lower price.

58. Following his enormously successful engagement at Cannae, Hannibal had busied himself with affairs that were more properly the concern of a victor than a soldier still at war. He brought forth the prisoners, and separated them into groups. As earlier at the Trebia and Lake Trasimene, he had kind words for the allies, whom he once again released without ransom. But he also did something he had never done before: he summoned the Romans and addressed them in gentle terms. His war with the Romans was not a fight to the death but a struggle for honour and power, he told them.* As his ancestors had capitulated before the valour of Rome, so his goal now was to see others in turn capitulating before *his* success and valour. Accordingly, he concluded, he was giving the prisoners the opportunity of ransoming themselves: the price would be 500 *quadrigati* per cavalryman, 300 per infantryman, and 100 per slave.

This was a considerable increase in the price for the cavalrymen that they had negotiated on their surrender, but they gladly accepted any condition that would lead to a settlement. It was decided that ten spokesmen should be elected by them to go to the Senate in Rome, and the only guarantee taken from these was their word that they would return. A Carthaginian nobleman, Carthalo, was sent along with them; he was to offer the terms, if the Romans inclined towards a peace.

After leaving the camp one of the spokesmen—a person of truly un-Roman character—pretended he had forgotten something, and returned to it, simply to discharge the oath. He then caught up with his companions before nightfall. When the news reached Rome that the men were on their way, a lictor was sent to meet Carthalo and inform him, in the name of the dictator, that he was to leave Roman territory before dark.

59. The prisoners' spokesmen were granted an audience with the Senate by the dictator. Their leader then spoke as follows:

'Marcus Junius and members of the Senate: None of us is unaware that no community has ever put less value on prisoners of war than ours. Even so, unless we have undue confidence in our cause, no other men have ever been less deserving of your neglect after falling into the hands of the enemy. For we did not surrender our arms from cowardice in the field of battle. No, we carried on the battle till almost nightfall, standing on the mounds of our dead, before we fell back to our camp. For the rest of the day, and the night that followed, we defended our rampart, exhausted though we were from our efforts and our wounds. We were surrounded and cut off from water by a victorious army, with no prospect of breaking through the dense enemy lines; and, after 50,000 men of our army had been slaughtered, we thought it no crime for a few Roman soldiers to survive the battle of Cannae. So, the next day, we finally negotiated a price for our ransom and release, and surrendered to the enemy the weapons that could help us no more.

'We had also been told that our ancestors secured their release from the Gauls by a ransom paid in gold, and that your own fathers, very much opposed to the peace-terms though they were, nevertheless sent representatives to Tarentum to ransom prisoners of war.* And this despite the fact that both battles, at the Allia with the Gauls, and at Heraclea with Pyrrhus, were notorious less for the losses incurred than the cowardly flight of our side. The plains of Cannae are covered with mounds of Roman corpses, and we survived the battle for one reason only: the enemy ran out of weapons and strength in cutting us down.

'Moreover, there are in our number some who were not even involved in the pitched battle. Left to defend the camp, they simply fell into the enemy's hands when the camp was surrendered. Now I begrudge none of my fellow citizens or comrades-in-arms his good fortune or his circumstances, nor would I wish to promote myself by discrediting another. But consider those men—the ones who ran from the field, most of them without weapons, and did not stop until they reached Venusia or Canusium! Unless it is a question of some prize for being fleet of foot and for racing, even they have no right to set themselves above us and pride themselves on being better defenders of the republic. But you will find them good and valiant soldiers, and us, too, you will find even more ready to fight for our country simply because we shall have been ransomed and restored to our fatherland through your generosity.

'You are recruiting troops of all ages and from every level of society—I am told that 8,000 slaves are being put under arms. Our number is no smaller than that, nor is the cost of our ransom greater than their buying-price. Costs I compare—for comparing *ourselves* with those people would mean my insulting the Roman name!

'This point, too, I would think you ought to take into account in considering such a question. Suppose you should lean towards harshness (though we have done nothing to deserve it); think of the kind of enemy to whom you will be abandoning us. Is it to a Pyrrhus, perhaps, who treated his prisoners like guests? Or is it to a barbarian, and a Carthaginian to boot—and whether the man's greed or his callousness is the greater is hard to say! Could you but set eyes on the chains on your fellow citizens, and their squalor and filthy state, that sight would certainly move you no less than the view of your legions strewn over the fields of Cannae. You can see the anxiety and tears of our relatives, as they stand at the entrance to the Senate house awaiting your response. When these feel such anguish and worry for us, and for those who are not here, what do you think are the feelings of the actual men whose lives and freedom now hang in the balance? Suppose—but some chance there is of that, for God's sake!—that Hannibal should, contrary to his nature, show mercy on us. We should none the less think it not worthwhile to have our lives, since in your eyes we were not worth ransoming. Captives released without payment by Pyrrhus once returned to Rome, but they returned with ambassadors, leading men of the state, who had been sent to ransom them. Am I to return to my fatherland a citizen not worth the payment of 300 coins? Everyone has his own opinions, senators. I know that my life and my personal safety are in jeopardy, but the risk to my reputation concerns me more. I fear that we may leave here condemned and rejected—for people will not believe that it was the cost of the ransom that worried you!'

60. When he finished speaking, a tearful wail immediately went up from the crowd in the Comitium. People stretched out their hands to the Senate house begging the senators to restore their children, their brothers and their relatives to them. Fear and the dire situation had also brought women to join the crowd of men in the Forum.

The Senate was cleared of unauthorized personnel and the debate began. Various opinions were put forward. Some advocated ransom of the prisoners at state expense; others wanted no public expenditure, but said that ransoms paid from private sources should not be disallowed (and any currently lacking immediate funds should be given treasury loans, with the state protected by guarantors with collateral). Then Titus Manlius Torquatus, generally regarded as a man who was old-fashioned and too inflexibly austere, was asked his opinion, and he is reported to have spoken as follows:

'If the request of the spokesmen had been limited to the ransom of those who are in the hands of the enemy, I could have presented my view briefly without criticizing any of them. All you would have needed to be told was that you should maintain the tradition, passed on by your fathers, by now providing an example that is vital for military discipline. As matters stand, however, these men have practically boasted about their capitulation to the enemy. They have also expressed the opinion that they should be seen as superior, not only to the men captured in battle by the enemy, but also to those who reached Venusia and Canusium—and even to the consul Gaius Terentius himself! And so, members of the Senate, I shall not allow you to remain unaware of what went on over there.

'I only wish that the comments I shall make before you were actually being made before the army at Canusium, for that army is the best witness to acts of cowardice and bravery by each of its members. Or, at least, I wish that one man were here, Publius Sempronius. If those fellows had followed Sempronius' lead, they would today be soldiers in a Roman camp instead of prisoners of war in enemy hands. But no! The enemy had, on their side, too, mostly retired to their camp, exhausted from fighting, and exulting in their victory. Thus these men had the opportunity provided by the darkness to break out, and it was quite possible for 7,000 men-in-arms to break through even a dense enemy force. But they made no effort to do so themselves, and were unwilling to follow another. Publius Sempronius Tuditanus spent practically the whole night admonishing them, and encouraging them to follow his lead, while enemy numbers were sparse around the camp, while all was still and quiet, and while darkness could provide cover for the operation. He told them that they could reach a safe haven and allied cities before dawn.

'Suppose Sempronius had said what the military tribune Publius Decius said in Samnium in our grandfathers' time, and what in our youth Calpurnius Flamma said to 300 volunteers in the earlier Punic War, when he was leading a charge to take a hill situated in the enemy's midst. "Men! Let us die, and by our deaths raise the siege in which our legions are caught!" was what they said. If those had been Publius Sempronius' words, he would have considered you to be not even men, and certainly not Romans, if none of you had stepped forward to share that act of valour. In fact, it was not the path of glory Sempronius was pointing out to you as much as the one leading to safety; he was bringing you home to your parents, your wives, and your children. You lacked the courage even to save yourselves! What would you have done if you had had to die for your country?

'Fifty thousand of your fellow citizens and allies lay cut to pieces around you that very day. If all those examples of courage make no impression on you, then nothing will. If a disaster of such magnitude did not make you hold life cheap, nothing will.

'You must long for your country while you are still free, with your rights intact, or rather while it is still your country and while you are still its citizens. Your longing for it now comes too late; you have lost your status, forfeited your rights as citizens, become slaves of the Carthaginians. Is payment to be made for you to return to the position you gave up through your scandalous cowardice? Your countryman Publius Sempronius told you to take up your arms and follow him, and you did not listen; but you did listen to Hannibal shortly afterwards, when he told you to betray your camp and surrender your weapons.

'But why am I accusing those people of cowardice, when I can accuse them of a criminal act? Not simply refusing to follow a man who gave them sound advice, they actually tried to impede him and hold him back—only some courageous men drew their swords and pushed the cowards aside. I tell you, Publius Sempronius had to break through a column of his countrymen before breaking through the enemy column! Will our country miss citizens like this? Had the others been like that, she would today have not one citizen of all those who fought at Cannae.

'Of a total of 7,000 soldiers, there were 600 who had the pluck to make a sortie, who returned to their native land free and still under arms; and these 600 met no resistance from the enemy. How safe a passage do you think a column made up of almost two legions would have had? Members of the Senate, you would have in service today at Canusium 20,000 brave and loyal soldiers. As matters stand, though, how can these men be good and loyal citizens (for "brave" is not a word even they would use of themselves!)? Unless one can really believe that they were helping their comrades with the sortie, when in fact they tried to impede them! Or unless one can believe they do not look with jealousy on their comrades' safety, and the renown they earned by their valour, when they know that it was their own fear and cowardice that brought about their own degrading captivity! They preferred to skulk in their tents, awaiting the arrival of dawn and the enemy along with it, though they had the chance to break out when all was quiet at night.

'But perhaps you think that, though they lacked the spirit to make the break, they still had the courage to put up a bold defence of the camp. Perhaps they spent a number of days under siege, protecting their rampart with their arms, and protecting themselves with their rampart. Perhaps it was only after a last-ditch effort and extreme suffering, only after running out of everything that sustains life and after they were no longer able to hold their weapons, their strength sapped by hunger—only then were they overcome, and by the constraints of the human condition rather than by the enemy! But no! At sunrise the enemy approached the rampart. Before the second hour of the day, without risking any engagement, these men surrendered their weapons and themselves.

'This, you see, was the extent of these men's military action over the two-day period. Honour called for them to stand in the battle line and fight; they ran back to camp. They should have fought for their rampart; they surrendered the camp. Neither in the field of battle, nor in the camp, did they show themselves to be of any worth. And we are supposed to ransom you? When you should force your way out of camp, you hang back and stay there. When you are required to stay and defend the camp by force of arms, you surrender camp, weapons, and yourselves to the enemy. For my part, members of the Senate, I do not recommend ransoming those people any more than I would recommend surrendering to Hannibal the men who made the sortie from the camp, through the midst of the enemy, and who, by their supreme courage, restored themselves to their country.'

61. Most of the senators also had relatives amongst the prisoners, but after Manlius' address they were concerned not only about the precedent—from early days the state had shown little regard for prisoners of war—but also about the amount of money involved. They did not wish to see the treasury depleted (for they had already spent a large sum on buying and equipping the slaves for service) and they also did not want any improvement in the finances of Hannibal who, rumour had it, was particularly deficient in this respect. The delegates were given the grim reply that the prisoners were not to be ransomed. Fresh anguish was now added to the old over the sacrifice of so many citizens, and it was with flowing tears and lamentation that the people accompanied the delegates to the gate. One of these went off home, claiming he had fulfilled the obligation of the oath by his ploy of returning to the camp. When this became known, and word of it reached the Senate, the senators unanimously voted that the man be arrested and taken back to Hannibal with an official escort.

There is another version of the story of the prisoners. According to this, the ten men came first, and some doubts were expressed in the Senate over whether or not they should be allowed into the city. They were admitted, but only on condition that they not be granted a senatorial audience. Then, since they were away longer than anyone expected, three further delegates appeared on the scene, Lucius Scribonius, Gaius Calpurnius, and Lucius Manlius. It was at this point that the motion for the ransoming of the prisoners was finally put to the Senate, by a plebeian tribune who was related to Scribonius, and the Senate voted against the ransom. The three recently arrived delegates then returned to Hannibal, but the ten earlier ones remained behind. These had, they claimed, fulfilled their religious obligations because, after starting their journey, they had gone back to Hannibal on the pretext of checking the prisoners' names. The question of surrendering these was discussed with great acrimony in the Senate, and those who favoured surrendering them were defeated by only a few votes. Under the next censors, however, the men were subjected to all manner of criticism and humiliation, so much so that some immediately committed suicide and the others spent the rest of their lives not only avoiding the Forum but virtually avoiding daylight and public areas. One can easily express surprise at the discrepancy between these accounts; less easy is telling where the truth lies.

How much greater this defeat was than earlier ones is indicated by the following. To that day the loyalty of the allies had remained unshaken, but now it began to waver, and the sole reason for that was surely loss of faith in the empire. The following peoples defected to the Carthaginians:* the Atellani, the Calatini, the Hirpini, some of the Apulians, the Samnites apart from the Pentri, all the Bruttii, and the Lucanians. In addition to these there were also the Uzentini, practically all the Greeks on the coast—the peoples of Tarentum, Metapontum, Croton, and Locri—and almost all the Cisalpine Gauls. And yet these defeats and allied defections prompted no talk of peace anywhere amongst the Romans, neither before the consul's arrival in Rome, nor after his return, which brought back to mind the disaster they had suffered. Such was the strength of character of the citizenry at that very time that, on the return of the consul from the debacle for which he was primarily responsible, people of all classes streamed out to meet him, and thanked him for not having lost confidence in the republic. Had he been a Carthaginian leader there is no manner of punishment that he would not have faced.

BOOK TWENTY-THREE

1. After the battle of Cannae, and the capture and sacking of the camps, Hannibal had wasted no time in moving from Apulia into Samnium. He had been invited into the territory of the Hirpini by Statius Trebius, who undertook to deliver Compsa to him.

Trebius was a Compsan who enjoyed some distinction amongst his people, but who faced harassment from the faction of the Mopsii, a family that was powerful because it enjoyed Roman support. When news came of the battle of Cannae, and—thanks to pronouncements from Trebius—word of Hannibal's coming spread abroad, the supporters of the Mopsii left town. The city was then surrendered to the Carthaginian without a fight, and a garrison was installed. Leaving all his spoils and baggage there, Hannibal now divided his army, and gave Mago orders to take over the cities in that area that were defecting from Rome, or to force them to defect if they refused to do so. He himself made for the Tyrrhenian Sea through Campanian territory, his intention being to attack Neapolis so that he would have a coastal city in his possession.*

On entering Neapolitan territory, Hannibal positioned some of his Numidians in ambush wherever he could opportunely do so—and there are many high-banked roads and hidden recesses in the region. Others he instructed to ride up to the town gates, making a show of driving before them the animals taken as booty from the countryside. Since they appeared to be a small and poorly organized group of men, a cavalry squadron charged out against them, but this was drawn into an ambush by the calculated retreat of the Numidians, and surrounded. Not one of the Neapolitans would have escaped but for the proximity of the sea, where some vessels, mostly fishing boats, were sighted not far from the shore-line, and these offered a means of escape to those who could swim. However, a number of young noblemen were captured or killed in the engagement, and these included the cavalry commander Hegeas, who fell as he pursued the retreating Numidians with too little caution. The sight of its walls dissuaded the Carthaginian from an attack on the city, for they were no easy proposition for an assault force.

2. Hannibal then veered towards Capua, which had long been basking in prosperity and the favour of fortune. Of particular significance in the general decadence, however, was the licence of its common people, whose freedom knew no bounds.

One Pacuvius Calavius—a nobleman who was also a supporter of the popular party, but who had gained power by disreputable means—had made the senate of Capua submissive to himself and the commons. He happened to be occupying the most senior magistracy in Capua the year of the defeat at Trasimene, and he believed that, because of their long-standing hatred of the senate, if given the opportunity for a revolution, the commons would be ready to commit a monstrous crime. Should Hannibal arrive in the area with his victorious army, he thought, they would butcher the senate and surrender Capua to the Carthaginians. Pacuvius was a rogue, but not totally unscrupulous.* He preferred to wield power in a republic that was healthy rather than one brought to ruin, and at the same time he believed no republic was healthy if shorn of its deliberative council. He consequently embarked on a scheme to save the senate and also make it subservient to himself and the commons.

Pacuvius convened the senate and, by way of introduction, stated that any plan of seceding from the Romans would find no favour with him, unless it proved essential; he had children by a daughter of Appius Claudius, and had given his daughter's hand to Marcus Livius in Rome. But, he continued, something much greater and more fearful was afoot. The commons did not merely intend to drive the senate from the state by a revolt, he explained; they actually wished to murder the senators and surrender a defenceless republic to Hannibal and the Carthaginians. But, he said, he could free them from that danger, if they left the matter in his hands and trusted him, forgetting all their political differences.

Overcome with panic, the senators all agreed to leave matters to him, and Pacuvius said to them: 'I am going to lock you in the senate house. I shall pretend to go along with the plot they are hatching and, in endorsing plans it would in any case be useless for me to oppose, I shall find a way to rescue you. You can have any pledge you wish on this.'

Pacuvius gave the pledge, went out, and ordered the senate house to be locked. He left a guard at the entrance so that no one could enter or leave the building without his order.

3. He then summoned the commons to a meeting. 'People of Capua,'* he said, 'you now have what you have often wished for, the power to punish an unconscionable and despicable senate. And you have it without danger and freely given to you—with no need for violent attacks, at enormous risk to yourselves, on individuals' homes that are defended by troops of clients and slaves. Take them now—they are all locked in the senate house, alone and unarmed. But take no hasty or random and ill-considered action. I shall give you the authority to decide the fate of every one of them, so they can all receive the punishment they deserve. But in gratifying your resentment you must above all see that your own safety and self-interest come before your anger. For, in my opinion, it is these particular senators that you hate; you do not wish to have no senate whatsoever. Indeed, you must choose between having a king—God forbid!—or a senate, the one deliberative body in a free state. Accordingly, you have to do two things at the same time. You must dissolve the old senate and also select a new one. I shall have the senators summoned one by one, and I shall consult you on what their fate is to be. Whatever action you decide on will be put into effect, but before the guilty party is punished you must select as his replacement a brave and dynamic new senator.'

Pacuvius then took his seat. The names of the senators were placed in an urn, and he gave orders for the first name drawn to be read out, and for that person to be brought from the senate house. When the name was heard, everyone cried out that the man was a rogue and a scoundrel, and that he deserved to be executed.

'I see what your judgement is on this man,' Pacuvius then observed. 'So give me an honest and fairminded senator in place of this rogue and scoundrel'.

At first there was silence; they could find no one better to suggest. Then one man overcame his bashfulness and gave some name or other. The clamour that immediately went up was much louder, some saying they did not know the man, and others uttering derogatory remarks on his disreputable conduct or his lack of breeding, his shabby poverty, and his degrading trade or means of livelihood. The reaction was all the more boisterous with the summoning of the second and third senator, making it abundantly clear that, while the commons had no time for the individual in question, they had no one to put in his place. And, in fact, nominating the same people over again served no purpose, since nomination had merely exposed them to verbal abuse, and any remaining candidates were much more lowly and obscure than those who first came to mind. As a result, men slipped away, proclaiming that the devil one knows best is the easiest to tolerate, and calling for the senators' release from custody.

4. In this way, by the gift of life to its members, Pacuvius made the senate subservient, and more so to himself than to the commons, and he now held supreme power without the need of weapons, since everybody deferred to him.* After this, the senators gave no thought to their position or their independence. They fawned on the commons, greeted them in passing, gave them cordial invitations, and hosted sumptuous meals for them. They took on their lawsuits, and always appeared as advocates for the side, or voted as jurymen for the case, that was closer to the people, and more likely to win favour with the crowd. In fact, all business in the senate was now conducted just as if it were an assembly of the commons that was being held there.

Capua was always a city-state inclined to hedonism. This arose not merely from a flaw in the national character but also because the town afforded an unstinting supply of entertainment, as well as all the exquisite delights that come from land and sea. And at that particular time, too, the sycophancy of the nobles and the licence of the commons led to such profligacy that lust and extravagance knew no bounds. There was disrespect for the laws, the magistrates, and the senate; and to this was now added, following the defeat at Cannae, disdain for the power of Rome, for which there used to be some respect. One thing alone held the Capuans back from immediate secession: the time-honoured right of intermarriage had connected many of their distinguished and powerful families with Roman families. In addition, while a considerable number of Capuans served amongst the Romans, a particularly strong link existed in the 300 cavalrymen—Campanians of the best families—who had been handpicked and sent by the Romans for garrison duty in the Sicilian city-states.

5. It was the parents and kinsmen of these men who, with some difficulty, won assent for delegates to be sent to the Roman consul. The delegates found the consul at Venusia, with a few poorly armed men, before his departure for Canusium. He cut a figure that was as poignant as could be for allies who were loyal, but one that would generate only contempt in those who, like the Capuans, were arrogant and untrustworthy. In fact, by his excessive openness and candour in discussing the defeat, the consul only increased their disdain for him and his plight.* The delegates reported to him the distress of the Capuan senate and people over any misfortune suffered by the Romans, and undertook to supply all the assistance they might require for the war.

'Men of Campania,' Varro replied, 'in telling me to ask of you what we need for the war, you have maintained the usual form of discourse with allies, instead of adopting a manner of address appropriate to our current fortunes. For what do we have left at Cannae to justify our asking allies to make up what we lack—which presupposes that we actually possess something? Are we to levy infantry from you—as though we still have cavalry? Are we to tell you we are lacking in cash, as if that is all we lack? Fortune has left us absolutely nothing that we can even supplement! Legions, cavalry, weapons, standards, horses, men, cash, supplies—all perished, either on the battlefield or in the loss of the two camps the following day. And so, men of Campania, it is not so much a question of your having to help us in the war as of your practically fighting the war for us.

'Think of the time when your ancestors were driven panic-stricken within their fortifications, and it was not just the Samnite enemy they dreaded, but the Sidicinian as well. Remember how we took them under our protection and defended them at Saticula; and how a war with the Samnites, which we started for your sake, we fought for almost a century, with mixed success. Consider these points, too. When you capitulated, we gave you a peace treaty on fair terms, and allowed you your own legal system; and finally—a very great concession, at least until the defeat at Cannae—we gave most of you Roman citizenship, sharing our state with you.

'And so, men of Campania, you should consider that you have a share in this defeat that has been sustained, and should think that you ought to protect the fatherland that we share. Our fight is not with Samnite or Etruscan, which would at least mean that power wrested from us would still remain in Italy. This is a Carthaginian enemy, not even native to Africa, and he brings from the farthest limits of the earth—from the waters of the Ocean and the Pillars of Hercules—soldiers who have no knowledge of human law and civilization, and, one can almost say, of human language. These men are bloodthirsty and brutish in their nature and customs, and their leader has further brutalized them by building bridges and dykes from piles of human bodies and—one shudders even at the mention— by teaching them to feed on human flesh.* It would be a crime even to touch such abominable banquets, but to look upon, and have as masters, men who have fed on them, to have laws imposed from Africa and Carthage, to permit Italy to be a Numidian and Moorish province—one only needs to be born in Italy to find this abhorrent.

'It will be a noble achievement, men of Campania, if the power that was prostrated by a defeat of the Romans should prove to have been sustained and revived by your loyalty and your resources. Thirty thousand infantry and 4,000 cavalry can, I think, be raised from Campania, and you have cash and grain to spare. If you have as much loyalty as you have material assets, then Hannibal will not feel that he has won a victory, and no more will the Romans feel that they are defeated.'

6. Following these words from the consul the delegates were discharged. As they made their way home, one of their number, Vibius Virrius, remarked that the time had arrived when the Campanians could not merely recover the land of which they had once been unjustly divested by the Romans but also gain supreme power in Italy. They would now make a treaty with Hannibal on any terms they wished, he said, and there was no question but that the Campanians would be left with sway over Italy once Hannibal finished off the war, retired in triumph to Africa, and took his army off with him. Virrius' words won the approval of all his colleagues, who so framed the report on their mission as to make everyone think the Roman name had been wiped out.

The immediate result was that the commons of Capua, and most of the senate, began to consider abandoning Rome, but matters were delayed for a few days, thanks to the influence of the older senators. Eventually the majority opinion won the day: the same delegates that had gone to the Roman consul were to be sent to Hannibal. I find in some sources the statement that, before these men went to Hannibal, and the plan to defect became a reality, a deputation was sent to Rome by the Campanians demanding that, as a condition for their assisting the Roman cause, one of the two consuls should be Campanian. There was an angry outburst. The order was given for the delegates to be removed from the Senate house, and a lictor was sent to take them from the city and command them to be out of Roman territory that day. A demand once made by the Latins is too similar for coincidence, and Coelius and other authors have understandably omitted the episode. I therefore feel apprehensive about recording it as a fact.*

7. The envoys came to Hannibal and negotiated a peace treaty with him on the following terms:

No Carthaginian general or magistrate was to have authority over a Capuan citizen, and a Capuan citizen was not to perform any military or other service against his will.

Capua was to have its own legal system and its own magistrates.

The Carthaginian commander was to give 300 of his Roman prisoners of war to the Campanians. The Campanians themselves were to choose these, and use them to effect an exchange for the Campanian cavalry serving in Sicily.

Such were the terms and, in addition to the pact that they made, the people of Capua also committed some atrocities. There were prefects of the allies and other Roman citizens in Capua, some in an official military capacity and others involved in private business affairs. The commons suddenly arrested all of these and, on the pretext of keeping them under guard, had them locked in the baths so they would die a horrible death by asphyxiation in the searing heat.*

Vigorous opposition to such acts, as well as to the sending of the delegation to the Carthaginian, had been voiced by Decius Magius. He was a man who lacked none of the attributes for achieving the highest position—apart from having compatriots in their right mind. Hearing that a garrison was being dispatched to Capua by Hannibal, Decius first of all openly and loudly protested against admitting it, and he cited the examples of Pyrrhus' high-handed despotism, and the wretched subjugation of the people of Tarentum. Then, when the garrison *was* admitted, he declared that it should be driven out. Alternatively, he said, if the people of Capua wished to perform some bold and memorable act to redeem themselves for the terrible crime of abandoning their oldest allies, and their kinsmen, they should murder the Punic garrison and return to their allegiance to Rome.

These recommendations were not made in secret and, when they were reported to Hannibal, he first of all sent people to summon Magius to him in his camp. Magius, in no uncertain terms, refused to go—Hannibal had no authority over a Campanian citizen, he said—whereupon the Carthaginian, beside himself with anger, ordered the man to be seized and dragged before him in irons. He then became afraid that the use of force might precipitate some disturbance, and that there might be some unwise confrontation if passions flared. He therefore sent a message to the Capuan praetor, Marius Blosius,* saying that he would be in Capua the following day. He then set off from camp with a small escort.

Marius convened a popular assembly at which he told the people to go in a crowd, along with their wives and children, to meet Hannibal. His instruction was carried out by the whole population, not only without demur but with enthusiasm, for the proletariat supported Hannibal and were eager to see the general now famous for so many victories. Decius Magius did not go forth to meet him, nor yet did he keep out of the public eye, for that might suggest some fear on his part, arising from a guilty conscience. He took a leisurely stroll in the forum with his son and a few of his clients, while the entire community was agog at the prospect of welcoming, and setting eyes on, the Carthaginian.

Entering the city, Hannibal immediately demanded an audience with the senate. The most prominent Campanians then begged him not to conduct any serious business on that day and to celebrate with joy and a light heart the day his arrival had made into a holiday. Hannibal was irascible by temperament, but he wanted to avoid saying 'no' to anything right at the outset. He therefore spent most of the day touring the city.

8. Hannibal stayed at the home of the two Ninnii Celeres, Sthenius and Pacuvius, men distinguished for their breeding and wealth. To this house Pacuvius Calavius brought his young son (Calavius, mentioned above, was the leader of the party that had mustered support for the Carthaginians). He had dragged the boy from the side of Decius Magius, with whom he had been fervently championing the Roman alliance against the pact with Carthage, deterred neither by the fact that his city-state's sympathies leaned the other way, nor by deference to his father. For this young man the father at that time gained Hannibal's indulgence, more by entreaties than by offering justification for his behaviour. In fact, overwhelmed by the father's tearful pleas, Hannibal even had the boy invited to dinner along with his father, and this was a gathering at which he would be entertaining

no Campanian apart from his hosts and a distinguished soldier, Vibellius Taurea.

They began dining in daylight, and the banquet had nothing in keeping with Carthaginian mores or military discipline. On the contrary, it suited the wealth and extravagance of the city-state and, indeed, of the house, and included all manner of titillating delights. Only one person could not be induced to take a drink, despite invitations to do so from the hosts or, occasionally, from Hannibal himself, and this was Calavius, the son. He himself pleaded an illness, and his father proffered the excuse of an emotional upset, which was quite plausible.

Towards sunset the elder Calavius left the dinner-party, followed by his son. When they reached the seclusion of a garden to the rear of the building, the son spoke. 'Father,' he said, 'I have a plan that will do more than secure us pardon from the Romans for the wrong we did in going over to Hannibal. It will also give us Campanians much greater standing and favour with them than ever before.' The father, taken aback, asked what the plan could be. The boy threw back his toga from his shoulder, revealing a sword strapped to his side. 'I am now going to ratify our treaty with Rome by shedding Hannibal's blood,' he said. 'I wanted you to know about it ahead of time in case you preferred to be absent while the deed is done.'

9. When the old man saw the weapon and heard his words, it was as if he were already witnessing the coup of which he was being told, and he was frightened out of his wits. 'Son,' he said 'I beg and beseech you, in the name of all the rights that bind children to their parents, do not follow through before your father's eyes on this totally unspeakable scenario, and yourself suffer its consequences. Only a few hours have elapsed since we took a solemn oath, swearing by all that was holy, and joining our right hands with Hannibal's. What for? So that we should leave our conversation with him, and immediately put weapons to use against him into the hands bound by that oath? Can you rise from your host's table—to which only you and two other Campanians were Hannibal's invitees—to stain that very table with the blood of your host? I was able to gain Hannibal's indulgence for my son; can I not gain my son's for Hannibal?

'But forget about what is sacred; forget about trust, religion, duty. Dare to do your unspeakable acts—as long as they do not destroy us, as well as making us criminals! Are you going to attack Hannibal single-handed? What about the crowd of men that he has, free and slaves? What about the fact that everyone's eyes will be fixed on you alone? What about all those hands ready to act? They will do nothing at that moment of madness? And will you stand up to the look of Hannibal, which whole armies bearing weapons are unable to face, which makes the Roman people shudder in terror? And suppose he has no other help. Will you have the heart to strike *me*, as I place my own body before his? For, yes, it is right through my breast that you must lunge at him, and stab him. Allow yourself to be deterred from that course of action *here* rather than be overpowered *there*. Let my prayers now carry weight *with* you, as they carried weight *for* you today.'

The father then saw the young man in tears. He put his arms around him and kissed him, not abandoning his entreaties until he convinced him to drop the sword and give his word not to take any such action.

'For my part,' said the young man, 'I shall discharge to my father the duty I owe to my fatherland. But I feel sorry for you. You must face the charge of betraying your fatherland three times: first when you initiated the break with the Romans; secondly when you brokered the peace-treaty with Hannibal; and, thirdly, today when you are responsible for delaying and hindering the restoration of Capua to the Romans. You, my country, take back the sword with which I armed myself to fight for you, when I entered this bastion of the enemy—for my father wrests it from me.' So saying, he flung the sword over the garden wall into the street, and, to avoid suspicion, made his return to the banquet.

10. The next day Hannibal was granted an audience with a packed senate. At first his language was very cordial and affable. He thanked the Campanians for preferring friendship with him to an alliance with Rome, and amongst other extravagant promises was a commitment that Capua would shortly be the capital of all Italy, with the Roman people, and all the other Italian peoples, subject to her laws. One man alone, he continued, was excluded from friendship with Carthage, and the treaty that had been struck with him, a man who did not deserve to be, or to be called, a man of Capua—Decius Magius. He was demanding that Magius be surrendered to him, he said, and that the matter be discussed, and a senatorial decree passed on it, in his presence. There was unanimous support for the proposal,

though most members felt Magius did not deserve such a blow, which they also thought represented no small first step towards the curtailment of their rights and freedoms.

On leaving the senate house, Hannibal took his seat in the area set aside for the magistrates. He gave orders for Decius Magius to be arrested and left alone at his feet to defend himself. Magius' defiant attitude was unchanged, and he declared that he could not, under the terms of the treaty, be compelled to do this. He was thereupon clapped in irons, and orders were issued for him to be taken to Hannibal's camp, a lictor following behind. All the while that he was being shepherded along with his head uncovered, he delivered a walking tirade, shouting out to the crowds milling around him on all sides: 'People of Capua, you have the liberty you sought! I am second to no Capuan, but now I am being taken to my execution in irons— in the midst of the forum, in broad daylight, and before your eyes. What greater outrage could be committed if Capua were captured? Go and meet Hannibal! Deck out your city and make the day of his coming a festival, so that you may come and see his triumph over your fellow citizen!'

The crowd was clearly being moved as Magius bellowed this out, and so a hood was put on his head, and the order given for him to be taken out of the gate at a more rapid pace. He was brought to the camp, and then immediately bundled onto a ship and sent off to Carthage,* for Hannibal feared that his own outrageous behaviour in the affair could lead to civil unrest in Capua, and make the senate regret having surrendered a prominent citizen. If they then sent a delegation to him to demand Magius' return, he would be obliged either to offend his new allies by refusing their very first request or, if he acceded, to keep on in Capua someone who would initiate sedition and rebellion.

A storm drove the vessel off-course to Cyrene, which was then under the rule of the kings of Egypt. There Magius sought protection at the statue of King Ptolemy, and was conveyed under guard to Ptolemy in Alexandria.* Explaining to the king that he had been put in chains by Hannibal, contrary to the terms of the treaty, he was relieved of his fetters and given permission to return, either to Rome or to Capua, as he chose. Magius replied that Capua would not be safe for him and, at a time when a state of war existed between the Romans and the Campanians, he would be residing in Rome more as a deserter than a visitor. He would like to live nowhere more than in the kingdom of the man whom he now regarded as the champion and guarantor of his liberty, he said.

11. In the course of these events, Quintus Fabius Pictor returned to Rome from his mission to Delphi, and read out the text of the oracular response. This listed the gods and goddesses for whom propitiatory rites were to be held, and procedure involved. The document continued: 'If you follow these instructions, men of Rome, your circumstances will improve and become easier. The future of your republic will be more according to your wishes, and victory in the war will go to the Roman people. When your republic's success and safety are won, see that you send to Pythian Apollo a gift from the gains you shall have made, and that you do him honour with the plunder, booty, and spoils. Guard against gloating over your success.'

After he had read this out, translated from the Greek verse, Pictor added that, on emerging from the oracle, he had immediately used offerings of incense and wine to sacrifice to all the deities specified. Also, he had worn a laurel wreath both coming to the temple and while performing the sacrifice there, and he had been told by the temple priest also to wear it to board ship, and not to remove it before reaching Rome. He had been very particular and precise in carrying out all the instructions he had been given, he said, and he had set the wreath on the altar of Apollo in Rome. The Senate decreed that all sacrifices and propitiatory rites that had been indicated should be carefully performed at the earliest possible opportunity.

During the course of these events in Rome and Italy, news of the victory at Cannae had reached Carthage, thanks to Mago, son of Hamilcar. (Mago had been sent by his brother, though not directly from the field of battle—he had been held back a number of days enlisting the Bruttian and <. . .> communities* that were abandoning their allegiance to Rome.) Granted an audience with the senate, Mago recounted his brother's exploits in Italy.* Hannibal had met six commanders on the battlefield, he said, four of them consuls and the two others a dictator and a master of horse, and with them six consular armies; and he had killed upwards of 200,000 of the enemy, and taken more than 50,000 prisoners. Of the four consuls, he had killed two; one of the remaining two was wounded, and the other had fled with barely fifty men after losing his entire army. The master of horse—a position as powerful as that of consul—had been defeated and put to flight, while the dictator was hailed as a peerless general because he had never committed himself to battle! The Bruttii, the Apulians, and a number of the Samnites and Lucanians had defected to the Carthaginians, and Capua had surrendered to Hannibal— Capua, the capital not just of Campania but, after the drubbing the Romans had received at the battle of Cannae, of Italy, too. For these victories, so great and numerous, Mago concluded, the immortal gods should be truly thanked.

12. At that point, to prove how successful the campaign had been, Mago ordered gold rings to be poured out at the entrance to the senate house. The mound they formed was so great that, according to some sources, they amounted to more than three measures (though the story that has prevailed—and this is closer to the truth—is that it was no more than one measure). Mago then added a commentary to make the defeat look even greater: only knights wore this status symbol, he said, and of knights only the most distinguished. The nub of his address was that the closer Hannibal came to realizing his hope of finishing the war, the more he should be assisted in every way. The campaign was being fought a long way from home, in the midst of the country of the enemy, he said. Grain and cash was being used up in large quantities, and all those pitched battles, while they had indeed wiped out so many enemy armies, had also involved some attrition to the victor's forces. Accordingly, Mago concluded, they should send reinforcements, and they should also send grain, and money for their pay, to the soldiers who had served the Carthaginian people so well.

After these comments from Mago everyone was overjoyed, and Himilco,* a member of the Barca faction, thought he had a chance to taunt Hanno. 'Well, Hanno,' he said, 'are you still sorry that war was started with the Romans? Order the surrender of Hannibal now, and tell us not to offer thanks to the immortal gods when things go so well! Let us listen to a Roman senator in the senate house of Carthage!'

'I would normally have remained silent today, members of the senate,' replied Hanno, 'so as not to make you hear what you would consider less happy words in the midst of such universal rejoicing. But now a senator asks me if I am still sorry that war was started with the Romans. Remaining silent would make me appear either supercilious or a lickspittle—a man, in the first case, oblivious to others' independence, or, in the second, oblivious to his own. My reply to Himilco would be that I have not stopped regretting the war, and that I shall not stop criticizing your "invincible" general until I see the war brought to an end on terms that are, at least, acceptable. And nothing other than a new peace will end my longing for the old peace.

'Those boastful remarks that Mago made a moment ago are pleasing to Himilco and the rest of Hannibal's partisans. They are possibly pleasing to me, too—because military successes will give us a more favourable peace if we are prepared to follow up our good fortune. This is an opportune moment at which we can be seen to be offering peace-terms rather than being offered them; let it slip and I fear that this jubilation of ours may be overindulgent and prove illusory.

'But just what is this jubilation all about anyway? "I have wiped out enemy armies—send me soldiers." How would your request be different if you had suffered defeat? "I captured two enemy camps, which were, of course, full of spoils and supplies—give me grain and cash." What else would you be asking for if your own camp had been seized and taken from you? But, so that I not be alone in marvelling at all this, I should like to get some answers either from Himilco—which is only fair and right since *I* have answered *him*—or from Mago. First, since the battle at Cannae has meant the annihilation of Roman power, and since it is an established fact that all of Italy is up in arms, has any people from the Latin league gone over to us? And, secondly, has any individual from the thirty-five Roman tribes deserted to Hannibal?'

When Mago answered 'no' to both questions, Hanno continued: 'So, in fact, as far as enemies are concerned, we still have all too many of them! But those large enemy numbers—I should like to know what their morale is, what hopes they still have.'

13. When Mago said he did not know, Hanno retorted, 'No knowledge is easier to come by. Have the Romans sent Hannibal ambassadors to sue for peace? Have you in fact received any report of peace being talked about in Rome?'

When Mago's reply was once more in the negative, Hanno said: 'So we have a war in which we are no further forward than the day Hannibal crossed into Italy. There are a large number of us still alive who remember how victory shifted back and forth in the earlier

Punic War. Prior to the consulship of Gaius Lutatius and Aulus Postumius we seemed successful as never before in land and sea operations; but when Lutatius and Postumius were consuls we were defeated off the Aegates Islands. Suppose that on this occasion, too (God forbid such a thought!), fortune should shift. When we go down in defeat, do you expect peace-terms such as no one offers now when we are winning?

'I do have an opinion to express, if anyone raises the question of offering peace-terms to the enemy, or accepting them from him. But if it is the matter of Mago's requests that you are raising, I do not think it serves any purpose to send assistance to a force that is already victorious, and much less will I vote for sending it to men who are hoodwinking us with false and groundless hopes.'

Hanno's address impressed few of his hearers. His vendetta with the Barca family diminished his credibility, and hearts filled with the joy of the moment refused to listen to anything that might test the validity of their satisfaction. A little more effort, they thought, and the war would soon be won. Accordingly, by a huge majority, a senatorial decree was passed that authorized the sending of 4,000 Numidians to reinforce Hannibal, and with them forty elephants and <. . .> talents of silver. And a dictator* was also sent to Spain with Mago to raise a mercenary force of 20,000 infantry and 4,000 cavalry, as reinforcements for the armies in Italy and Spain.

14. However, these resolutions were put into effect in a slow and casual manner, a common phenomenon in times of success; but Roman procrastination was ruled out by their circumstances, to say nothing of the inbred energy of the people. The consul was found wanting in no sphere for which he was responsible.* The dictator Marcus Junius Pera completed the religious ceremonies, and then made the usual proposal to the people that he be authorized to mount a horse.* He already had the two city legions that had been mobilized by the consuls at the start of the year, the slave conscripts, and the cohorts gathered from the countryside of Picenum and Gaul, but he now descended to the last resort of a state that was almost desperate, when honour yields to practicality. He issued an edict that he would order the cancellation of the penalty or the debts of men who had been condemned and imprisoned for a capital offence or debt, if they would serve in his army. In this way he recruited 6,000 men, whom he armed with Gallic spoils that had

been carried in Gaius Flaminius' triumph. He then left the city with 25,000 soldiers.

After taking possession of Capua, Hannibal alternated promises and threats in a second attempt to win the support of the Neapolitans, and when this failed he led his army across into the territory of Nola. He did not immediately strike a threatening pose, as he was not without hope of a voluntary surrender, but he was ready to spare its people no suffering or terror if they frustrated his expectations. The town senate—and especially its most important members—was solidly for the alliance with Rome. However, the commons, as usual, were all for change,* and all in favour of Hannibal. They also feared the devastation of their farmlands, and envisioned the many serious and shocking ordeals to be faced in a siege. And men to instigate a revolt were not in short supply.

Gripped by a fear that, if they proceeded openly, the proletariat would rise up and be impossible to resist, the senators found a way of postponing the evil moment by pretending to go along with their wishes. They pretended that they favoured defection to Hannibal, but that there was little agreement amongst them on the terms for transfer to the new treaty and new alliance. In this way they gained a breathing space; and they quickly dispatched delegates to the Roman praetor Marcus Claudius Marcellus, who was at Casilinum with his army, and informed him of the parlous situation in Nola. Their farmlands were in the hands of Hannibal and the Carthaginians, they said, as the city soon would be, if no help were sent. They explained that it was only by agreeing with the commons to defect, at any time the commons chose, that the senate had succeeded in heading off a hasty defection. Marcellus complimented the Nolan representatives. He told them that that same pretence should be continued to drag matters out until his arrival, and that meanwhile their dealings with him and any prospect of Roman assistance should remain a secret. Marcellus himself headed for Caiatia from Casilinum. After that he crossed the River Volturnus and, making his way through the territory of Saticula and Trebia, reached Nola by a route through the mountains above Suessula.

15. With the Roman praetor's arrival, the Carthaginian left the territory of Nola and came down to the coast near Neapolis, for he wanted to occupy a coastal town that would afford his ships a safe crossing from Africa. He then learned that Neapolis was in the hands

of a Roman prefect—this was Junius Silanus, who had been called in by the inhabitants of Neapolis—and so he headed for Nuceria, bypassing Neapolis, as he had done Nola. He blockaded Nuceria for some time, making numerous assaults on it, as well as numerous unsuccessful overtures, to the commons on some occasions and to the leading citizens on others, but eventually starved it into submission. The terms of surrender he dictated were that the inhabitants could leave unarmed and with one item of clothing per person.

From the start, Hannibal had wished to be seen as compassionate to all Italians except the Romans, and he now offered rewards and important positions to any of the people of Nuceria who would remain in the town and were prepared to serve with him. Not even with promises like that did he get any to stay. The Nucerians all slipped away to various Campanian cities, particularly Nola and Neapolis, wherever offers of accommodation or impulse took them. Some thirty senators—and, as it happened, all the leading members— made for Capua, but were refused entry for having shut their gates on Hannibal. They then went to Cumae. The spoils of Nuceria were given to the Carthaginian rank and file, and the city was sacked and put to the torch.*

At Nola, Marcellus' hold on the town rested more on the favour of the leading citizens than any confidence he had in his garrison. The commons were a source of anxiety for him, and a certain Lucius Bantius more than anyone. Bantius' guilt over the attempted defection, and his fear of the Roman praetor, were inciting him to betray his native city or, in the event of fortune failing him, to desert to the enemy. He was an energetic young man, and at that time close to being the most famous knight amongst the allies. Found half-dead amidst a heap of corpses at Cannae, he had been kindly treated by Hannibal, who had even sent him home with gifts.

Feeling gratitude for Hannibal's kindness, Bantius had wanted to put the state of Nola under the authority and control of the Carthaginian, and the praetor could see that he was tense and restless in his desire for change. He had either to be subdued by punishment, or else appeased by kindness, and Marcellus preferred to enlist for himself an ally who was strong and full of energy, rather than simply take such an ally from the enemy. He therefore had him summoned and addressed him with kind words.

There were many amongst Bantius' compatriots who were jealous of him, said Marcellus. This was easily deduced, he explained, from the fact that no citizen of Nola had made any mention to him of Bantius' many outstanding military exploits—and yet his courage could not be a secret to anyone who had served in a Roman camp. Many who had campaigned with Bantius would tell him about the sort of man this Nolan was, and about the dangers he had often faced to preserve the security and honour of the Roman people. And they would talk of how, at the battle of Cannae, Bantius did not quit the field until the point when, well nigh exhausted, he was buried under the men, horses, and arms that came crashing down on him.

'So, my compliments to you on your courage!' continued Marcellus. 'In my camp, every kind of honour and reward will be yours, and the more time you spend with me the more you will find that quality of yours redounding to your prestige and your advantage.' The young man was pleased with the Roman's assurances. Marcellus then presented him with a superb horse and instructed his quaestor to pay him 500 *denarii*.* He also told his lictors to grant Bantius access to him whenever he wished to see him.

16. The truculent young man's temper was so softened by this considerate approach on Marcellus' part that, from that point on, no ally served the Roman cause with greater courage and loyalty.

Hannibal was again at the gates, having once more moved camp from Nuceria to Nola, and the Nolan masses were for a second time contemplating changing sides. On the enemy's arrival, Marcellus withdrew within the walls, not because he feared for his camp, but simply in order not to give an opportunity of betraying the city to the all-too-many people who were seeking one. The battle lines then began to form up on both sides, the Romans before the walls of Nola, and the Carthaginians in front of their camp. Some minor skirmishes ensued in the space between the city and the camp, with varying outcomes. The commanders were unwilling to check the few men who recklessly charged the foe, but they were also unwilling to give the signal for a full-scale engagement.

During this daily stand-off between the two armies, leading Nolan citizens reported to Marcellus that nightly discussions were taking place between the commons and the Carthaginians. At these, they said, a decision had been taken to plunder the Romans' equipment and baggage when their battle line had marched out of the gates. The insurgents would then shut the gates, seize the walls, and, when they were masters of the situation and of the city, they would let in the Carthaginians in place of the Romans. When Marcellus was advised of this, he commended the Nolan senators and decided to risk a battle before there could be any trouble within the city. He marshalled his army in three divisions at each of the three gates facing the enemy, and he gave orders for the baggage to follow behind, and for the attendants, camp-followers, and invalids to carry palisade-stakes. At the centre gate he positioned his strongest legionary troops and the Roman cavalry, and at the two side gates he placed the new recruits, the light infantry, and the allied cavalry. The people of Nola were forbidden to approach the walls and the gates, and the troops designated as reserves were assigned to the baggage to prevent an attack being made on it while the legions were engaged in the battle. Formed up in this way, the Romans now stood within the gates.

Following his practice of the previous few days, Hannibal spent a large portion of the day in battle formation. He was initially sur-prised that the Roman army did not emerge from the gate, and also that there was not a single armed man on the walls. He then assumed that the secret discussions had been divulged to the Romans, and that it was fear that kept them inactive. He therefore sent a number of his men back to camp with orders to bring up to the front line, at the double, all the equipment needed for an assault on the town. He was quite sure that, if he put pressure on the Romans while they wavered, the masses would start some disturbance within the town.

While all were feverishly scurrying to the front ranks to take up their various duties, and as the battle line was approaching the walls, the gate suddenly swung open. Marcellus gave the order to sound the attack and raise the battle-cry, and commanded first the infantry, and then the cavalry, to charge out at the enemy as hard as they could. When these had already caused much panic and commotion in the Carthaginian centre, the legates Publius Valerius Flaccus and Gaius Aurelius burst out against the enemy flanks from the two side gates. The uproar was increased by shouts from the camp-followers, attendants, and numerous other men assigned to guarding the baggage, and the result was that the Carthaginians, who had nothing but contempt for their foes' inferior numbers, suddenly had the impression of a mighty army before them.

I would not presume, as some authors do, to put the number of enemy dead at 2,800, with the loss of no more than 500 Romans.

However, whether the victory was as decisive as that, or whether it was smaller, the achievement of that day was enormous, and possibly the greatest of that war.* For it was more difficult to avoid defeat by Hannibal at that time than it was to defeat him later on.

17. Cheated of his hope of taking Nola, Hannibal fell back on Acerrae. Marcellus immediately shut the gates and posted guards to prevent anyone from leaving, and then, in the forum, publicly interrogated the men who had engaged in the secret talks with the enemy. Upwards of seventy people were found guilty of treason. Marcellus had them beheaded, and declared their belongings the common property of the Roman people. Government of the state was put in the hands of the senate. Marcellus then set off with his entire army and took up a position above Suessula, where he established a camp. The Carthaginians at first tried to coax Acerrae into voluntary surrender, but then, when they saw the people were intransigent, they prepared for a blockade and an assault on the town.

In fact, the people of Acerrae had more determination than strength. Losing hope of defending their city, and seeing their walls being ringed with siege-works, they slipped out in the still of the night before the enemy could complete the circumvallation, passing through gaps in the enemy breastworks and the neglected sentry-posts. Then, taking roads or travelling cross-country, and either following a planned route or drifting aimlessly, they made good their escape to towns of Campania that they were sure had not switched allegiance.

Hannibal sacked Acerrae and put it to the torch. Then, when he was brought a report that the Roman dictator and his new legions were being summoned to Casilinum, he led his army to that town, fearful that there might also be some insurgency at Capua, with the enemy camp in such close proximity. At that time Casilinum was occupied by 500 men from Praeneste, along with a few Romans and Latin allies,* news of the defeat at Cannae having brought them to the same spot. The mobilization at Praeneste had not been completed on schedule, and these men of Praeneste had thus been somewhat late in leaving home, so that they had reached Casilinum before there was any word of the defeat. Others, Romans and allies, had joined them there, and they had set out together from Casilinum in quite a large column when a report of the battle of Cannae brought them back to the town.

They remained there for a number of days, eyed with suspicion by the Campanians whom they themselves feared, and they spent the time guarding against sedition, and in turn fomenting it. On receiving reliable information that negotiations were under way for Capua's defection, and that Hannibal was being welcomed in the city, they massacred the town's population at night* and seized the part of the city north of the Volturnus, a river that cuts the town in two. These were the men who comprised the Roman military presence in Casilinum, and that was augmented by a cohort from Perusia, 460 men who had been driven to Casilinum by the same report that had brought the men of Praeneste a few days earlier. It was a sufficiently large armed force to defend walls of such limited compass, which also received cover from the river on one of its two sides—in fact the shortages of grain made even this group of men seem inordinately large.

18. When Hannibal was already not far from the town, he sent a party of Gaetulians ahead under an officer named Isalca.* He told Isalca to begin with conciliatory words, should he be granted the opportunity to parley, and to try to coax those inside to open the gates and admit a garrison. If they remained defiant, Isalca was to use force and try to break into the city wherever he could.

When the Gaetulians approached the walls, the silence suggested that they were deserted. The barbarians assumed the Romans had been frightened into withdrawal, and so they prepared to force the gates and smash the bolts. Suddenly, the gates opened and two cohorts, formed up inside expressly for the purpose, burst forth with a deafening clamour and wreaked havoc on the enemy. The first wave repulsed in this way, Maharbal was sent in with a stronger force, but he, too, could not stem the counterattack from the cohorts. Finally, Hannibal encamped right before the city walls and prepared to storm this little town, and its little garrison, with an all-out assault and using all of his troops. While he pressed ahead and attacked the enemy, completely surrounding the walls with a ring of troops, he lost a number of men, including his best fighters, to missiles from the wall and turrets. On one occasion, when the enemy took the initiative with a sortie, Hannibal almost cut them off from the town by setting a column of elephants in their way.* He then drove them in panic into the town with comparatively heavy losses, given their numerical weakness. There would have been further casualties had night not broken off the battle.

The following day the hearts of all the Carthaginians were fired up for the attack, especially when the prospect of a golden 'wall-scaling crown' was set before them and after the commander himself delivered some sharp words. These conquerors of Saguntum were mounting a lacklustre assault on a small fortress on level ground, he said, and he reminded them one and all of Cannae, Trasimene, and the Trebia. Then they began moving up the mantlets and making tunnels. And the Roman allies did not lack energy or ingenuity in countering the various designs of the enemy. They set up protective devices against the mantlets, used intercepting ditches to head off the enemy tunnels, and took countermeasures against all their operations, whether open or covert, until eventually humiliation made Hannibal drop his enterprise. He fortified his camp, established a small garrison (to avoid the impression of abandoning the campaign), and withdrew to winter quarters in Capua.

In Capua, Hannibal kept his army in housing for most of the winter. It was a force that many ordeals over a long period had hardened to face all life's discomforts, but which had no experience of, or exposure to, its good things. The result was that men whom the most intense misery had failed to break were now ruined by excessive comfort and unlimited pleasure—and the more thoroughly ruined because, thanks to their inexperience, they had immersed themselves in them all the more eagerly. Sleep, drink, dinner-parties, whores, baths, and inactivity that, from habit, became sweeter every day—all this sapped their physical and moral strength. So much so, in fact, that their protection now came from past victories rather than their current strength, and this came to be regarded by military scientists as a greater blunder on the leader's part than his failure to march on Rome straight from the battle of Cannae. For Hannibal's hesitation on that occasion could have been seen as merely postponing the victory, but this mistake could be seen as having deprived him of the strength needed to win. And so, indeed, when he left Capua, it was as if he were at the head of another army. No trace remained of its former discipline.* Large numbers came back from the city embroiled in relationships with prostitutes and, as soon as they were bivouacked in tents, and were faced with marching and other military chores, their lack of strength and morale was like that of a raw recruit. Then, throughout the summer season, most began to slip away from the standards without leave, and the deserters' hiding-place was always Capua.

19. As the winter began to lose its harshness Hannibal led his men from winter quarters and returned to Casilinum. Though the assault had been suspended, the ongoing blockade had nevertheless brought the townspeople and its garrison to the depths of deprivation. The Roman camp in the area was under the command of Tiberius Sempronius, the dictator having left for Rome to retake the auspices. Marcellus also wanted to bring assistance to the beleaguered townspeople, but he was detained by the flooding of the River Volturnus, and also by the entreaties of the townspeople of Nola and Acerrae, who feared what the Campanians might do if the Roman garrison departed. As for Gracchus, he merely stuck close to Casilinum without making any move, for he was under orders from the dictator to take no initiative during his absence—and yet the news coming from Casilinum was such as would easily try anyone's patience. There were reports of people having hurled themselves from the walls because they could not bear the hunger, and of others standing on them unarmed, offering their unprotected bodies to the missiles that were hurled at them. Gracchus was deeply distressed at this situation. He dared not open hostilities without the dictator's authorization, and yet he could see that a fight was necessary for him to bring wheat into the town in the open—and there was no hope of bringing it in unobserved. His solution was to fill several jars with grain that he brought together from all the surrounding farmland, and then send a message to the magistrates in Casilinum telling them to fish out any jars the river brought down.

The following night the attention of all was focused on the river, with hopes raised by the message from the Romans; and the jars, which had been released midstream, came floating down to them. The grain was then doled out in equal shares amongst the entire population. This was repeated the next day, and the day after that, the containers being released, and also reaching their destination, at night and so escaping the notice of the enemy sentinels. But then, thanks to an unbroken period of rain, the river began to flow faster than usual and it drove the jars in a cross-current towards a section of the bank patrolled by the enemy. There they became caught up in some willows growing from the banks, and were spotted. A report was brought to Hannibal, and after that greater care was taken to prevent anything being sent unobserved down the Volturnus to the city. Even so, some nuts that were thrown from the Roman camp did float down to Casilinum midstream, and were fished out with wicker baskets.

Eventually, those inside faced such extreme privation that they tried chewing straps, and leather stripped from shields, softening it in boiling water. They did not stop short of eating mice and other creatures, either, and they pulled up all kinds of grass and roots from the banks at the base of the city wall. When the enemy then ploughed up all the patches of grass outside the wall, the defenders planted turnip seeds, prompting Hannibal to exclaim 'Am I going to sit before Casilinum until *they* begin to sprout?' And the man who before that had refused to hear any talk of negotiations now finally agreed to discuss the ransoming of free men in the town. A price of seven ounces of gold per person was settled upon and, when they were given Hannibal's solemn assurance on this, the people of Casilinum surrendered. They were kept in irons until the gold was paid in full, but then they were released just as promised.

This version of events is more credible than the other, that the released men were murdered by horsemen sent to attack them as they left. Most of them were men of Praeneste. Of the 570 members of the garrison, fewer than half lost their lives to the sword or starvation, and the rest returned unharmed to Praeneste with their praetor, Marcus Anicius (a former clerk). Proof of this lay in the statue of Anicius that was set up in the forum of Praeneste. He wears a cuirass and a toga, and has his head covered, and there is an inscription on a bronze plate stating that Marcus Anicius had fulfilled his vow for the soldiers who served in the garrison at Casilinum. An identical inscription was placed beneath the three statues set up in the temple of Fortune.*

20. The town of Casilinum was restored to the Campanians, and it was furnished with a garrison of 700 soldiers from Hannibal's army to prevent a Roman attack when the Carthaginians left. The Roman Senate passed a decree granting the Praenestine soldiers double pay and a five-year immunity from military service. They were granted Roman citizenship in recognition of their valour, but declined to make the change. The record is less clear on the lot of the men from Perusia—no light is shed on it by any monument the Perusians set up themselves, or by any Roman decree.

Amongst the Bruttii, only the people of Petelia had remained loyal to the Roman treaty, and at this time they came under attack, not only from the Carthaginians who controlled the region, but also—because of their difference in policy—from the rest of the Bruttii. Unequal to the difficulties facing them, the Petelians sent an embassy to Rome to ask for military assistance. When they were told they must fend for themselves, the ambassadors burst into tearful protestations in the vestibule of the Senate house, and their entreaties and weeping moved the Senate and common people to profound sympathy. The matter was therefore raised for a second time with the senators by the praetor Marcus Aemilius. The senators took stock of all the reserves of the empire and were forced to admit that they had not the resources to assist allies so far removed. They told the Petelians to go home and, when they had taken their loyalty to the limit, to look after their future well-being as circumstances directed.

When the outcome of the mission was reported to the people of Petelia, deep melancholy and dread instantly gripped their senate. A number advocated that they all flee as best they could and abandon the city. Others were for joining the rest of the Bruttii and using them as intermediaries to surrender to Hannibal, now that they had been deserted by their traditional allies. The view that prevailed, however, was that of the men who voted that they should take no hasty or foolhardy action, and that they should consider the matter afresh. The issue was raised again the following day when there was less hysteria, and the most distinguished members successfully upheld their view that they should bring all produce in from the fields and strengthen the city and its walls.

21. At about this same time letters were brought to Rome from Sicily and Sardinia. The one from Sicily, from Titus Otacilius, was the first to be read out in the Senate, and it recounted that the praetor Publius Furius had come to Lilybaeum from Africa with his fleet, but that he had been seriously wounded and his life was hanging by a thread. Soldiers and crews were not being given their pay or grain rations on time, said Otacilius, and there were no resources to make this possible. He was therefore strongly urging that these items be dispatched at the earliest opportunity and, also, if the senators agreed, that they send out one of the new praetors to succeed him. Much the same message concerning pay and grain was contained in the letter from the propraetor Aulus Cornelius Mammula in Sardinia. The answer given to both men was that there were no resources

available, and they were to take personal responsibility for provisions
for their fleets and armies. Titus Otacilius then sent a delegation to
Hiero, a man without peer in his support of the Roman people, and
from him received all the money he needed for his men's pay, plus
six months' supply of grain. In Cornelius' case in Sardinia, the allied
city-states contributed generously to support him.

In Rome, the financial crisis also led to the appointment (on a
proposal from the plebeian tribune Marcus Minucius) of a trium-
virate of treasury officials. These were the former consul and censor
Lucius Aemilius Papus; Marcus Atilius Regulus, former consul on
two occasions; and Lucius Scribonius Libo, currently a plebeian
tribune. Marcus and Gaius Atilius were elected duumvirs, and these
dedicated the temple of Concord that Lucius Manlius had promised
in a vow during his praetorship. Three pontiffs were also elected:
Quintus Caecilius Metellus, Quintus Fabius Maximus, and Quintus
Fulvius Flaccus. These replaced respectively Publius Scantinus, who
had died, and Lucius Aemilius Paulus, the consul, and Quintus
Aelius Paetus, both of whom had fallen in the battle of Cannae.

22. Having now filled—as far as human resourcefulness could—all
the gaps left by the unbroken string of disasters, the senators finally
took account of themselves, specifically of the empty Senate house,
and the paucity of their numbers when meeting to decide public
policy. In fact, there had been no revision of the Senate since the
censorship of Lucius Aemilius and Gaius Flaminius, despite the fact
that, in the intervening five years, so many senators had been carried
off by the defeats as well as by individual misfortunes.

The dictator had finally left the city to join his army after the loss
of Casilinum, and it was the praetor Marcus Aemilius who, in
response to a general demand, raised the matter in the house. Spurius
Carvilius thereupon delivered a long speech deploring not merely
the dearth of senators but the shortage of citizens from whom members could be selected for the Senate. He then declared that he
strongly urged the granting of citizenship to two senators of each of
the Latin peoples, these to be chosen by the members of the Roman
Senate; from this pool, he said, men could be selected for the Senate
to replace deceased members. The proposal, he explained, was
aimed at bringing the number of the Senate up to quota, and also at
forging closer ties between the Latin and Roman peoples.

The senators' reaction to this proposal was no more favourable than when the Latins themselves had earlier made the same request. There was a buzz of indignation all through the house, and Titus Manlius, in particular, observed that there still lived a descendant of the family of that consul who had once, on the Capitol, threatened to kill with his own hands any Latin he saw in the Senate house. At this juncture Quintus Fabius Maximus declared that no subject had ever been raised in the Senate at a more inappropriate time than this one. The allies' feelings were unpredictable, and their loyalty uncertain, he said, and a comment like that could only unsettle them even more. This foolhardy remark coming from a single individual, he continued, should be suppressed by everybody else's silence. If there ever was anything of an intimate or sacred nature that needed to be kept secret in the house, then this was certainly it—something to be covered over, concealed, forgotten, and regarded as unsaid! And so it was that all mention of the proposal was stifled.*

It was decided that a dictator should be appointed for recruiting members to the Senate. He was to be a man who had already been a censor, and was the oldest of all ex-censors still alive, and the Senate ordered that the consul Gaius Terentius be summoned to make the appointment. Terentius returned to Rome from Apulia by forced marches, leaving a military presence in place, and made the appointment the following night, as was customary. In accordance with a senatorial decree, he appointed Marcus Fabius Buteo* dictator for six months, without a master of horse.

23. Fabius climbed the Rostra with his lictors. He did not approve of the unprecedented situation of there being two dictators in office at the one time, he said, and he disapproved of his being a dictator without a master of horse. He likewise disapproved of the censor's power being granted to a single individual—and to one who had already held it, at that—and of a six-month *imperium* being granted to a dictator, unless he had been appointed to conduct military operations. This irregular situation, he continued, was the result of chance, the times, and the exigencies of their situation, but he was going to circumscribe it. He would not remove from the Senate any of the appointees Gaius Flaminius and Lucius Aemilius had as censors selected for the house; he would merely have their names written down and read out. In this way the reputation and character of senators would not be subject to the judgement and ruling of a single individual. Moreover, he would replace deceased members in such a

way as to let it be seen that preference was given to one rank over another, not to one man over another.

After reading out the names of the members of the old Senate, Fabius began by replacing deceased members with men who had held curule offices after the censorship of Lucius Aemilius and Gaius Flaminius, but who had not yet been selected for the Senate; and he prioritized them on the basis of who had been elected first. He then chose former aediles, plebeian tribunes, or quaestors and, after these, men who had not gained magistracies but who had spoils from the enemy affixed to their houses, or who had been awarded the civic crown.* In this way 177 members were inducted into the Senate, and with great approval. Fabius then immediately resigned his office and, telling his lictors to leave, came down from the Rostra a private citizen. He joined the crowds who were occupied with their own private business, deliberately frittering away the time so as not to draw people from the Forum to escort him home. Even with that interlude men's support for him did not flag, and he had a large entourage escorting him to his home. The consul returned to his army the following night, but did not inform the Senate for fear of being detained in the city to oversee the elections.

24. The following day, on a motion from the praetor Marcus Pomponius, the Senate decided that the dictator should be sent written instructions to come to Rome (if he deemed it in the public interest) to oversee the consular elections, bringing with him his master of horse and the praetor Marcus Marcellus. The senators could then learn directly from these men how matters stood for the state, after which they could formulate policy as the situation required. All three individuals summoned did appear, leaving subordinates in command of their legions. The dictator spoke briefly and in modest terms about himself, but passed most of the credit on to his master of horse, Tiberius Sempronius Gracchus. He announced the date for the elections, and at these the consuls elected were Lucius Postumius (elected for the third time and *in absentia*, since his sphere of responsibility at the time was Gaul) and Tiberius Sempronius Gracchus, who was then master of horse and curule aedile. Then the praetors were elected: Marcus Valerius Laevinus (for a second time), Appius Claudius Pulcher, Quintus Fulvius Flaccus, and Quintus Mucius Scaevola. After the election of the magistrates, the dictator returned to his army in its winter quarters at Teanum.

He left in Rome the master of horse, who was going to assume office in a matter of days and could discuss with the senators the enlistment and mobilization of troops for the coming year.

Just at the point when these proceedings were under way, news came of a fresh setback, as fortune piled one disaster on another that year. The consul designate Lucius Postumius and his army had been wiped out in Gaul.

Postumius was going to lead his army through a huge wood called Litana by the Gauls. To the right and left of the road that went through the forest, the Gauls cut the trees in such a way that, with no pressure on them, they would remain standing, but if given a slight push they would topple over. Postumius had under his command two Roman legions, and he had mobilized a contingent of allies from the Adriatic coast so large that he was leading 25,000 troops into enemy territory. The Gauls had surrounded the forest perimeter, and, when the Roman column entered the woods, they pushed at some of the outer trees that they had severed. These fell one on another, each of them unsteady itself and barely keeping upright, and, crashing down on both sides of the road, crushed weapons, men, and horses. The result was that barely ten men made good their escape. Most were killed by the tree-trunks and broken branches, and the Gauls who waited in arms all around the woodland area dispatched the remainder, panic-stricken as they were after this unforeseen calamity. From such a large number few prisoners were taken. These were men who headed for the bridge over the river, only to find themselves cut off since the bridge had already been seized by the enemy.

Postumius fell at the battle site as he fought with all his might to avoid capture. The jubilant Boii carried the spoils from the general's body, and his severed head, to what is their most sacred temple. Then, as is their custom, they scraped out the head and overlaid the skull with gold, and this served them as a holy vessel for the pouring of libations at religious ceremonies, and also as a drinking cup for the high priest and the temple overseers. Indeed, for the Gauls, the spoils were no less important than the victory. It is true that most of the animals were crushed in the collapse of the trees, but everything else was found all along the path of the devastated column, since there had been no flight to disperse it.

25. Such was the alarm in Rome for several days following the

report of the defeat that shops remained closed and a hush like that at the dead of night descended on the city. The Senate therefore assigned the aediles the task of patrolling the town, and issuing orders for shops to be opened and the atmosphere of public gloom dispelled. Tiberius Sempronius then called a meeting of the Senate. There he consoled the senators, and, to encourage them, said that men who had refused to give up after the disaster at Cannae should not lose heart in the face of lesser setbacks. In the case of the war with their Carthaginian foes and Hannibal, he said, he simply prayed that things would go as he hoped. The Gallic war could be shelved and left in abeyance, and it would be for the gods and the people of Rome to avenge later the treachery of the Gauls. What they had to consider and discuss now was the Carthaginian foe, and the armies to be used for the campaign against him. Sempronius himself first briefed them on the numbers of infantry and cavalry, and of citizens and allies, in the dictator's army, and then Marcellus enumerated the troops under his command. Intelligence on forces with the consul Gaius Terentius in Apulia was sought from informed individuals. But no way could be found of forming two consular armies strong enough to cope with such an extensive theatre of war. And so, prodded though they were by righteous indignation, they decided that Gaul be shelved for that year.

The dictator's army was now allocated to the consul. With regard to the army of Marcus Marcellus, it was decided that those soldiers who had been part of the flight from Cannae should be shipped over to Sicily, to serve there for as long as the war lasted in Italy. All the weaker soldiers in the dictator's legions were also to be removed to this destination, but with no period of service defined apart from their regular terms. The two city legions were allocated to the other consul, who would be replacing Lucius Postumius, and he was to be elected as soon as possible, account being taken of the auguries. It was further decided that two legions should be brought from Sicily at the earliest opportunity—from these the consul who was assigned the urban legions was to take all the men he needed. The consul Gaius Terentius would have his *imperium* extended for a year, and there would be no cuts made to the army he was commanding for the defence of Apulia.

26. Such were the activities and preparations in Italy. Meanwhile, in Spain, the war was no less intense, but, to that point, it was more

successful for the Romans. Publius and Gnaeus Scipio had divided their troops, Gnaeus taking charge of land operations, and Publius those at sea. The Carthaginian commander Hasdrubal, however, had little confidence in either branch of his forces and gave his enemy a wide berth, using distance and position to protect himself, until, finally, in response to his urgent and repeated requests, he was sent reinforcements of 4,000 infantry and 500 cavalry from Africa. With that, his hopes finally revived, he moved camp closer to the enemy, and he, too, issued orders for a fleet to be prepared and equipped to protect the islands and the mainland coast. Just as he was thrusting ahead with his renewed operations, he was thrown off balance by the desertion of his naval captains. These had received a serious reprimand from him after they panicked and abandoned the fleet at the Ebro, and since then they had never been completely loyal either to their commander or the Carthaginian cause. The deserters had fomented unrest amongst the Tartesii,* a number of whose cities had, thanks to their efforts, seceded from the Carthaginians—and one they had even taken by storm.

Hasdrubal now directed hostilities against this tribe instead of the Romans, and with an invading army entered the territory of his enemy. He decided to make an attack on Chalbus, a celebrated chieftain of the Tartesii, who was now encamped with a powerful force before the walls of a city that he had captured a few days earlier. Hasdrubal sent forward his light infantry to draw the enemy into battle, and dispatched a section of his cavalry to conduct predatory raids throughout the countryside and to round up stragglers. At one and the same moment there was agitation in the enemy camp, and flight and slaughter throughout the surrounding countryside. Presently, however, the Tartesii returned to camp by various routes from every direction, and fear suddenly vanished from their minds— they now had enough courage not only to defend their fortifications, but even to launch an offensive against their enemy. They burst from their camp in a column, performing their traditional war dance, and this sudden display of bravado struck terror into an enemy that was on the attack shortly before.

Accordingly, Hasdrubal himself withdrew his troops to a hill that was quite steep, and further protected a river flowing before it, and he also pulled back to the same spot the light-armed infantry that he had sent ahead, and the cavalry that were scattered through the countryside. In addition, having little confidence in the protection offered by either hill or river, he strengthened his camp with a palisade. As the panic swung from one side to the other, there were a number of clashes. In these, the Numidian cavalryman proved no match for his Spanish counterpart, nor the Moorish javelin-thrower for the *caetra*-armed soldier. Their enemy's equal in agility, the Spanish troops were considerably superior in determination and physical strength.

27. The Tartesii were unable to draw the Carthaginian into combat by moving up close to his camp, and an assault on the camp was not going to be easy. They therefore stormed the city of Ascua, where Hasdrubal had deposited his grain and other provisions on entering enemy territory, and took possession of all the surrounding countryside. After that the Spaniards could be restrained by no authority, whether on the march or in camp. Hasdrubal took note of this common phenomenon, the carelessness following on the heels of success. He urged his men to launch an attack on the enemy while they were straggling and out of formation, and, descending the hill, he proceeded to march on their camp in battle order.

Word of his approach was brought by messengers, who came running back in panic from lookout stations and sentinel posts, and the call to arms went up. Snatching up weapons as they came to hand, the Tartesii rushed into the fray without orders, without awaiting a signal, and in total disarray and confusion. When the first-comers had already engaged, others were still running up in separate groups, and yet others had not even left the camp. Even so, their bravado alone at first unnerved their enemy. But the Tartesii were coming in small bands against men formed in ranks, and their small numbers gave them no protection. They all began to look for assistance from their comrades and, under pressure from every side, formed a circle. As bodies jostled with bodies and weapons engaged with weapons, they were driven together into a confined space where they had scarcely enough room to wield their arms. Completely encircled by the enemy, they were subjected to wholesale slaughter till late in the day, and only an insignificant number managed to break out and head for the woods and hills. In the same panic, the camp was abandoned, and the following day the entire tribe capitulated.

But the Tartesii did not long abide by the terms of surrender. Shortly after the battle, Hasdrubal received an order from Carthage to lead his army into Italy at the earliest opportunity and, when news of that spread through Spain, it diverted the support of almost all the tribes from the Carthaginians to the Romans. Hasdrubal, therefore, immediately sent a letter to Carthage in which he made it known how much harm rumours of his departure had done. If he did in fact leave, he said, Spain would be in Roman hands before he crossed the Ebro. Apart from the fact that he had no military force or commander to leave in his place, he explained, the quality of the Roman generals was such that opposition would scarcely be possible, even if the two sides had equal strength. Accordingly they should send him a successor with a powerful army, if Spain meant anything to them; but even if all went well for that man, Hasdrubal concluded, he would not find his charge an easy one.

28. The letter at first made a deep impression on the Carthaginian senate. However, Italy was the first and more urgent priority, and no change was made with respect to Hasdrubal and his forces. Instead, Himilco was dispatched with a complete army, and an enlarged fleet, to hold and protect Spain by land and sea. After taking his land and naval forces over to Spain, Himilco established a fortified camp, beached his ships, and surrounded them with a palisade. Then he personally took some of his elite cavalry and made his way to Hasdrubal with all the speed he could muster, equally vigilant as he passed through tribes of dubious loyalty and those that were openly hostile.

Himilco acquainted Hasdrubal with the decrees and instructions of their senate, and was in turn informed of how the war in Spain should be handled. He then returned to his camp, his safety secured by his speed more than anything else, since he got away from each area before its inhabitants could agree on a plan of action.

Before striking camp, Hasdrubal levied funds from all the tribes in his jurisdiction. He was well aware that Hannibal had occasionally used money to secure a passage, that it was only by hire that he had raised his Gallic auxiliary troops, and that he would barely have made it as far as the Alps had he started his immense journey without funds. Hasdrubal therefore hurriedly levied moneys before marching down to the Ebro.

When word of the Carthaginian decrees and Hasdrubal's march reached the Romans, the two commanders dropped everything else, joined forces, and prepared to oppose and thwart their enemy's designs. Hannibal was an enemy that Italy could barely resist when he was operating on his own, they thought, and if he were joined by a general like Hasdrubal, and by an army from Spain, that would spell the end of the power of Rome. Gripped by worries such as this, they brought their forces together at the Ebro. After crossing the river, they long debated whether to bring their camp closer to Hasdrubal's or whether it would suffice for them to delay the enemy's projected march by launching attacks on Carthaginian allies. They finally prepared to attack what was at that time the richest city in the region, Hibera,* which was named after the nearby river. When Hasdrubal heard about this, instead of bringing assistance to his allies, he chose rather to proceed himself with an attack on a town that had recently surrendered to the Romans. The blockade of Hibera, which had already commenced, was therefore abandoned by the Romans, whose operations were now focused directly on Hasdrubal himself.

29. The two sides had their camps five miles apart from each other for a number of days and, while there were some minor skirmishes, they avoided pitched battle. Finally, almost as if by agreement, the signal for battle was hoisted on both sides on the very same day, and they both went down to the plain in full force.

The Roman army stood three lines deep. Some of the skirmishers were positioned amongst the front-line troops, and others behind the standards, while the cavalry covered the flanks. Hasdrubal strengthened his centre with Spanish troops. On the flanks, he placed Carthaginians on the right, and Africans along with mercenary auxiliaries on the left. His cavalry he positioned on the wings, setting the Numidian horse alongside the Carthaginian infantry, and the others beside the Africans. Not all of the Numidians were placed on the right wing, however*—only those whose practice it was to take two horses apiece and, like circus performers, jump fully armed from a weary mount to a fresh one, often when the fighting was at its most fierce. Such is the agility of these horsemen, and so trainable this breed of horse.

As the two sides stood drawn up in this manner, their commanders differed little in terms of confidence. In numbers or quality of men one side was not in the slightest superior to the other; but the morale of the soldiers was very different. Although the Romans were fighting far from home, their officers had found it easy to persuade them that their fight was for Italy and the city of Rome. For them, their return home turned upon the outcome of that battle, and they had resolutely decided to win or to die. The other army consisted of men less resolute. Most were Spaniards, and they preferred to face defeat in Spain rather than win and be dragged into Italy.

The result was that, at the very first clash and when the javelins had barely been thrown, the Carthaginian centre gave ground and, as the Romans came bearing down on them with a powerful charge, they took to their heels. The engagement was no less intense on the wings. Here there was heavy pressure from the Carthaginians on one side, and the Africans on the other; and these, having virtually encircled the Romans, were engaging them on the two fronts. But by then the Roman line had entirely converged on the centre, and so had sufficient strength to push back the wings on either side. Thus there were two separate battles in progress, and in both there was no doubt as to the superiority of the Romans who, after the enemy centre was driven back, had the edge in the numbers, as well as the strength, of their men.

The casualties of the battle were extremely heavy, and very few would have survived from the entire enemy fighting line but for the wild flight of Spaniards when the battle had barely got under way. As for cavalry action, there was hardly any. As soon as the Moors and Numidians saw the centre give way, they immediately took to headlong flight, driving the elephants before them, and left the wings without protection. Hasdrubal waited to see the final outcome of the engagement, and then he too slipped away from the midst of the slaughter with a few companions. The Romans captured and sacked the enemy camp.*

That battle brought over to the Romans any wavering elements that remained in Spain, and left Hasdrubal with no hope, not merely of taking his army across into Italy, but even of remaining in Spain with any kind of security. These events were made known in Rome by a dispatch from the Scipios, and the ensuing rejoicing was less over the victory than the fact that Hasdrubal's passage into Italy had been stopped.

30. While this was going on in Spain, Petelia, the town in Bruttium,* fell to Hannibal's lieutenant Himilco, after a siege that had begun some months earlier. That victory cost the Carthaginians dear in blood and injuries, and the pressure that brought the beleaguered townspeople to their knees was that of hunger more than anything else. After exhausting their supplies of grain, as well as meat from

every kind of quadruped (conventional food or not), they finally kept themselves alive by eating leather, grass, roots, the soft parts of tree-bark, and strips of leaves. It was only when they lacked the strength to man the walls and bear arms that they were finally vanquished.

After taking Petelia, the Carthaginian led his forces over to Consentia, and, as this was defended with less resolve, he accepted its surrender in a matter of days. At about this time a Bruttian army also laid siege to the Greek city of Croton.* This had once been a powerful and populous town, but it had by now been so devastated by many brutal reverses that it was left with fewer than 2,000 citizens all told. As a result the enemy easily took possession of a city devoid of defenders. Only the citadel remained in the citizens' hands: in the confusion following the capture of the town a number fled there from the slaughter surrounding them. In addition, Locri defected to the Bruttii and the Carthaginians, the common people having been betrayed by the aristocrats. In that part of the country only Rhegium maintained its loyalty to the Romans, and its own independence, to the end.

The same backsliding reached Sicily, too, where not even Hiero's family was untouched by defection. Gelo, eldest of Hiero's children, felt only contempt for his father's advanced years and also, following the defeat at Cannae, for the alliance with Rome, and he transferred his allegiance to the Carthaginians. Gelo would, in fact, have fomented rebellion in Sicily had not his timely death—so timely as to taint even the father with suspicion—removed him as he was busy arming the commons and sowing disaffection amongst the Roman allies. Such were that year's events, and their varied outcomes, in Africa, Sicily, and Spain.

At the end of the year Quintus Fabius Maximus asked the Senate's permission to dedicate to Venus Eryx the temple that he had promised in a vow when he was dictator. The Senate decided that the consul designate Tiberius Sempronius should, when he entered office, propose to the people that Quintus Fabius be appointed a duumvir for the dedication of the temple. Also that year, Marcus Aemilius Lepidus, who had been consul and an augur, was honoured by his three sons, Lucius, Marcus, and Quintus, with funeral games lasting three days, including twenty-two pairs of gladiators put on display in the Forum. The curule aediles Gaius Laetorius and Tiberius Sempronius Gracchus (a consul designate who had been master of horse during his aedileship) celebrated the Roman Games, three days of which were repeated. The Plebeian Games put on by Marcus Aurelius Cotta and Marcus Claudius Marcellus were repeated three times.*

The third year of the Punic War was now at an end, and on 15 March Tiberius Sempronius entered office as consul. As their jurisdictions, the praetors gained by lot the following: Quintus Fulvius Flaccus (former consul and censor), urban jurisdiction; Marcus Valerius Laevinus, jurisdiction over foreigners; Appius Claudius Pulcher, Sicily; and Quintus Mucius Scaevola, Sardinia. The people vested Marcus Marcellus with proconsular *imperium* because he alone of Roman commanders had operated successfully in Italy after the defeat at Cannae.

31. On the first day of its session on the Capitol, the Senate decreed double taxation for that year, with the regular taxes levied immediately so that from them a cash payment could be made to all soldiers, apart from those who had served at Cannae. As for disposition of the armies, the senators decided that the consul Tiberius Sempronius should fix a date for the muster of the two urban legions at Cales, from where they were to be marched to the Castra Claudiana* above Suessula. The legions already in place there—principally soldiers from the army at Cannae—were to be transferred to Sicily by the praetor Appius Claudius Pulcher, and those in Sicily would be shipped to Rome. Marcus Claudius Marcellus was sent to the army that was scheduled to muster at Cales, and he was under orders to lead the urban legions to the Castra Claudiana. Tiberius Maecilius Croto was dispatched by Appius Claudius as his legate to take charge of the old army and conduct it from the Castra Claudiana to Sicily.

At first, people had said nothing as they waited for the consul to hold elections for the appointment of his colleague. Then they saw Marcus Marcellus removed from the scene as though on purpose, and he was the man they particularly wanted as consul that year because of his successful record in his praetorship. A murmuring now arose in the Senate. Hearing this, the consul remarked: 'Both decisions were in the interests of the state, members of the Senate. It is beneficial first for Marcus Claudius to leave for Campania to see to the exchange of troops, and secondly for the elections not to be scheduled until he has come home after finishing the business assigned to him. Thus you may have the consul the state needs at the moment, and the one you want most.' And so talk of elections was silenced until Marcellus' return.

Meanwhile, Quintus Fabius Maximus and Titus Otacilius Crassus were appointed duumvirs for the dedication of temples, Otacilius for the temple of Mens, and Fabius for the temple of Venus of Eryx (both of them are on the Capitol, separated by a single drainage channel). In addition, a proposal was put before the people to grant Roman citizenship to 300 Capuan knights who had come to Rome after loyal service in Sicily. It was further proposed that these should enjoy the rights of townspeople of Cumae dating from the day before the people of Capua defected from the Roman people. The prime impetus behind the proposal was the knights' own assertion that they did not know the class to which they belonged. They had abandoned the city that had been their home, but had not yet been granted formal admission to the one to which they had now come on their return to Italy.

On Marcellus' return from the army, notice was given of an election to appoint a single consul as a replacement for Lucius Postumius. Marcellus was elected with an overwhelming majority, and he was to take office immediately. But there was a peal of thunder at the moment of his entering his consulship, and when the augurs were summoned they declared that there appeared to be something amiss with his election. The patricians thereupon spread the word that the gods were displeased at the precedent-setting election of two plebeian consuls at the same time. Marcellus withdrew from office, to be replaced by Quintus Fabius Maximus,* now consul for the third time.

The sea caught fire that year, and in the area of Sinuessa a cow gave birth to a foal. Statues near the temple of Juno Sospita in Lanuvium dripped blood, and around the precinct stones fell as rain. There were the customary nine days of religious observances because of this shower, and expiatory rites were attentively discharged for the other prodigies.

32. The consuls now divided the armies between them. That at Teanum, formerly under the dictator Marcus Junius, fell to Fabius, and to Sempronius, at Rome, fell the slave volunteers stationed there, and 25,000 allied troops. The legions that had returned from Sicily were officially assigned to the praetor Marcus Valerius. Marcus Claudius was sent as a proconsul to the army stationed above

Suessula for the defence of Nola; and the praetors went off to Sicily and Sardinia.

The consuls issued a proclamation that, whenever they convened the Senate, senators and all having the right to express an opinion in the house should come together at the Porta Capena.* The praetors charged with administration of justice established their tribunals at the Piscina Publica. It was here, they ordered, that litigants had to undertake to make their court appearance, and it was the city's legal centre during that year.

Meanwhile, at Carthage, Hannibal's brother Mago was on the point of shipping to Italy 12,000 infantry, 1,500 cavalry, twenty elephants, and 1,000 talents of silver, with an escort of sixty warships.* Then news reached the city of the reverse in Spain and of the almost complete defection to the Romans of the tribes in the province. There was some suggestion that they should forget Italy and redirect Mago with that fleet and armament to Spain, but then came a sudden flicker of hope that Sardinia could be recovered. It was reported that the Roman army in Sardinia was small, and that the old praetor, Aulus Cornelius, who knew the province well, was leaving and a fresh replacement was expected. In addition to this, the Sardinians were tired of Roman dominion, which had gone on for so long; during the past year they had found the administration harsh and rapacious; and they were also burdened with an oppressive tribute and an unfair grain-levy. All that was needed was a leader to whom they could defect. This information had been covertly transmitted to Carthage by some leading Sardinian citizens, the prime mover in the affair being Hampsicora who at that time far surpassed the others in influence and wealth.

These two reports brought anxiety and elation to the Carthaginians, almost at the same time. They dispatched Mago to Spain with his fleet and his troops, but they also selected Hasdrubal as commander for Sardinia, and assigned to him a force of roughly the same proportions as the one they had assigned to Mago.

At Rome, too, where all necessary dispositions within the city had been made, the consuls were now preparing for the campaign. Tiberius Sempronius officially gave his soldiers a date for muster at Sinuessa and, after first consulting the Senate, Quintus Fabius ordered the general transportation of grain from the countryside into fortified towns before the coming 1 June. In the case of anyone failing to effect the transportation, he said, he would lay waste the man's land, auction off his slaves and burn his farm buildings. Not even the praetors voted into office for legal duties were granted exemption from military administration. The praetor Valerius, it was decided, should proceed to Apulia to assume command of the army of Terentius. When the legions from Sicily arrived, Valerius was to rely mainly on them for the defence of that region, and the army of Terentius was to be sent to Tarentum under one of his lieutenants. He was also assigned twenty-five ships to enable him to give protection to the coastline between Brundisium and Tarentum. The same number of ships was allocated to the urban praetor Quintus Fulvius for the protection of the shores close to the city. The proconsul Gaius Terentius was given the duty of levying troops in the territory of Picenum and of defending that area. Finally, after his dedication of the temple of Mens on the Capitol, Titus Otacilius Crassus was dispatched to Sicily with *imperium* to assume command of the fleet.

33. This was a struggle between the two most prosperous nations in the world, and all rulers and nations had their attention focused on it. These included King Philip of Macedon, who was all the more concerned for being closer to Italy, with only the Ionian Sea separating him from it. As soon as he got wind of Hannibal's crossing of the Alps, he had been overjoyed at the outbreak of war between Rome and Carthage, but he had also been unsure, their relative strengths being still unknown, which of the two peoples he wished to see prevail. Now, after the third battle had been fought, and the third victory had gone to Carthage, he leaned towards success and sent emissaries to Hannibal.

The emissaries avoided the ports of Brundisium and Tarentum, since they were occupied and guarded by Roman ships, and disembarked instead near the temple of Juno Lacinia. From there they headed through Apulia towards Capua, only to fall in with some Roman patrols, by whom they were escorted to the praetor Valerius Laevinus, then encamped in the neighbourhood of Luceria. There the leader of the delegation, Xenophanes, boldly stated that he was on a mission from King Philip, the aim of which was to establish a treaty of friendship with the Roman people. He added that he had dispatches to convey to the consuls, and to the Senate and People of Rome. With old allies seceding from Rome, the praetor was delighted at the prospect of a new alliance with such an illustrious king, and he gave his enemies the warm welcome accorded to guests. He provided them with an escort, and supplied detailed information about their itinerary, indicating the areas and passes held by either the Romans or the enemy.

Xenophanes came through the Roman posts into Campania, and from there reached Hannibal's camp by the shortest route. Here he struck a treaty of friendship with the Carthaginian,* the terms of which were as follows. King Philip was to cross to Italy with the largest fleet he could possibly muster—it seemed likely that he would put together two hundred ships—and there lay waste the coast, and conduct land and sea operations to the best of his ability. At the war's end, all Italy, together with the actual city of Rome, was to be the possession of the Carthaginians and Hannibal, and all the plunder was to go to Hannibal. With Italy conquered, the allies were to sail to Greece and open hostilities against any peoples the king might choose. City-states on the mainland, and islands off Macedonia, would belong to Philip and his realm.

34. Such, in essence, were the terms of the treaty struck between the Carthaginian leader and the Macedonian delegates, and Carthaginian spokesmen, Gisgo, Bostar, and Mago, were then sent along with the delegates to have the agreement ratified by the king himself. They came to that same spot near the temple of Juno Lacinia, where a ship lay at anchor hidden from view. They cast off, but while they were heading out to sea they were sighted by the Roman fleet that was patrolling the coastal areas of Calabria, and Valerius Flaccus then sent some skiffs to give chase to the ship and bring it back. At first the king's representatives attempted to run, but when they saw they were being overtaken, they surrendered to the Romans and were brought before the admiral of the fleet. Flaccus asked their identity, where they had come from, and where they were headed. Xenophanes at first proceeded with the fiction that had already served him well on one occasion. He was on a mission from Philip to the Romans, he said, and had made it as far as Marcus Valerius, the only person he could reach in safety. He had been unable to get across Campania because it was blocked by enemy guard-posts. Then the Carthaginian dress and appearance raised suspicions about Hannibal's emissaries, and when these were interrogated their accent gave them away. After this, their attendants were taken aside and

subjected to intimidating threats, and a letter from Hannibal to Philip also came to light along with a text of the agreements made between the Macedonian king and the Carthaginian leader.

The facts being sufficiently established, it seemed best to send the prisoners and their attendants to the Senate in Rome as soon as possible, or, alternatively, to the consuls, wherever they happened to be. Five swift ships were picked out for this mission, and Lucius Valerius Antias was sent to take command. Antias was instructed to distribute the emissaries amongst all his vessels, have them guarded separately and generally do what he could to prevent any conversation or exchange of ideas amongst them.

It was at this same time that Aulus Cornelius Mammula, who was retiring from his province of Sardinia, made his report in Rome about the state of affairs on the island. The entire population had its mind set on war and rebellion, he said. His successor, Quintus Mucius, had on his arrival fallen prey to the oppressive climate and bad water, and had contracted a sickness which, while not life-threatening, would be of long duration. This, said Mammula, would put him out of action for military duties for quite some time; and, in addition, the army on the island, while strong enough to police a province that was at peace, was too small for the war that seemed likely to break out. The senators therefore decided that Fulvius Flaccus should levy 5,000 infantry and 400 cavalry, and have this legion shipped to Sardinia as soon as possible. Flaccus was also to send a man of his own choosing, furnished with *imperium*, to take command until Mucius recovered. The man sent on this assignment was Titus Manlius Torquatus. Twice consul, Torquatus had also been a censor, and had crushed the Sardinians during one of his consulships.

At about the same time a fleet had also been dispatched to Sardinia from Carthage. Commanded by Hasdrubal, surnamed Calvus,* this had been overtaken by bad weather and driven off-course towards the Balearic Islands. The ships' hulls as well as the rigging had received extensive damage, and so the ships were hauled ashore and the repairs entailed a considerable loss of time.

35. In Italy the war was flagging after the battle of Cannae: one side's strength was shattered, and the other's morale had been sapped. At this juncture the people of Capua made an independent effort to bring Cumae under their control. First, they invited the people of

Cumae to secede from Rome and, when little came of that, they devised a scheme for trapping them. There was at regular intervals a Pan-Campanian festival at Hamae. The Capuans informed the people of Cumae that the Capuan senate would be in attendance, and they invited the Cumaean senate to attend as well, so they could hold joint discussions on how the two peoples could have the same allies and the same enemies. They added that they would have a military presence there to meet any threat from the Romans or the Carthaginians. The Cumaeans suspected that treachery was afoot, but made no objection, thinking that in this way they would have cover for a ruse of their own.

Meanwhile, the Roman consul Tiberius Sempronius had conducted a review of his army at Sinuessa, where he had scheduled the muster of his troops. He then crossed the River Volturnus and encamped near Liternum. There was too much free time in camp, and Sempronius insisted on frequent drills for his men so that the new recruits, most of them slave volunteers, could gain experience in following the standards and recognizing their place in the ranks in battle. During the drills the leader was particularly concerned—and the orders he had given the legates and tribunes were to this effect— that no uncomplimentary remarks about anyone's erstwhile status should sow discord in the ranks. The veteran should allow himself to be put on the same level as the new recruit, the free man on the same level as the slave volunteer, he said. They should regard all men to whom the Roman people had entrusted its arms and standards as having rank and pedigree enough, and the same unfortunate circumstances that had made such measures necessary compelled them to respect them now they were in place. The men were as punctilious in observing these rules as the officers were in enforcing them, and in a short while such harmony had been established amongst the entire force that what each man's background had been upon his becoming a soldier was well-nigh forgotten.

While Gracchus was thus engaged, he received from Cumaean envoys a report on the delegation that had come from the Capuans a few days earlier, and of the reply that the Cumaeans had given. The festival was three days away, they said, and not only would their entire senate be present, but there would also be a Capuan army encamped there. Gracchus instructed the Cumaeans to bring everything into the city from the fields, and to remain inside their walls;

and, on the day before that fixed for the Campanian rite, he himself moved his camp to Cumae.

Hamae lies some three miles from Cumae. As agreed, the Capuans had gathered there in large numbers, but not far away Marius Alfius, their *medix tuticus* (the chief Capuan magistrate), was secretly encamped with 14,000 soldiers. But Alfius was considerably more focused on preparations for the rite, and on setting the trap during the preparations, than he was with fortifying the camp or any other military employment.

It was a nocturnal rite, but one that was to be completed before the middle of the night. That, thought Gracchus, was the point at which to bring off his coup. He set guards at the camp gates to prevent anyone from leaking information on his design, and after the tenth hour of daylight brought his men together. He told them to take refreshment and see to it that they got some sleep, so that they could assemble when the signal was given at dusk. Then, at about the first watch, he ordered the standards raised, and set off, his column maintaining silence. Reaching Hamae in the middle of the night, he made an attack on the Capuan camp through all its gates at the same moment—it was poorly guarded, as one might expect during a festival celebrated at night. Some he slaughtered as they lay sleeping, others as they were returning unarmed from the completed rite. The death toll from that nocturnal mêlée surpassed 2,000 and included the commander, Marius Alfius, himself <. . .> and thirty-four military standards <. . .> were captured.*

36. Gracchus took the enemy camp with the loss of fewer than a hundred men and then beat a hasty retreat to Cumae, for he felt uneasy about Hannibal who was encamped in the Tifata Mountains above Capua. His premonition did not prove incorrect. As soon as news of the debacle reached Capua, Hannibal surmised that he would find at Hamae an army of fresh recruits, slaves for the most part, gloating over their success and busy stripping the bodies of the vanquished and driving off the captured animals. He therefore took his army at a rapid pace past Capua, issuing orders for Campanian fugitives that he met en route to be taken to Capua with an escort, and the wounded transported to the town on wagons. Hannibal himself then came to Hamae, where he found the camp abandoned by the enemy, and nothing more than vestiges of the recent massacre, the corpses of his allies strewn everywhere.

There were some who recommended that he march directly to Cumae and attack the town. This Hannibal passionately wished to do: with Cumae he would at least have a coastal city at his disposition, something he had not been able to manage with Neapolis. However, because of the rapid pace of the march, his men had brought with them nothing but their weapons, and so he withdrew once more to his camp on Tifata. Then, the next day, overwhelmed by the pleas of the Campanians, he returned from the camp to Cumae bringing with him all the equipment necessary for attacking a city. He laid waste the Cumaean farmlands and pitched camp a mile from the city. Gracchus, meanwhile, remained in Cumae, and this was more because he was ashamed to leave his allies in such a desperate plight—allies who were begging for his protection and that of the Roman people—than because he had any great confidence in his army. The other consul, Fabius, who was encamped at Cales, would not risk taking his army across the River Volturnus, either; he was preoccupied with retaking the auspices, in the first place, but then also with prodigies, reports of which were streaming in one after the other. As Fabius performed the expiatory sacrifices for these, the soothsayers kept reporting that favourable signs were not easy to obtain.*

37. Such were the circumstances that kept Fabius in place, and meanwhile Sempronius was facing a blockade and siege-works that were now proceeding against him. A massive wooden tower had been brought up to the city, and to fend this off the Roman consul erected another tower on the wall itself. This was somewhat higher than the enemy's: the wall was quite high in itself, and Sempronius had used it as a base, bracing it with strong wooden piles. From this structure the defenders at first defended the walls and the city by hurling down stones, stakes, and other projectiles. Eventually, they saw that their enemy, by pushing forward their tower, had brought it into contact with the wall, and they now set it on fire at several points simultaneously by hurling flaming torches at it.

The blaze spread panic amongst the crowd of soldiers on the enemy tower, who flung themselves down from it. At this point, too, there was a counterattack launched from the two gates of the town at the same time. This scattered the forward posts of the enemy and sent them fleeing back to camp, so that on that day the Carthaginians appeared more like the besieged than the besiegers. The Carthaginian death toll was around 1,300, and 59 were taken alive (these were men who had been taken by surprise, when they were at ease and off guard close to the walls and at their posts, and fearing anything but a counterattack). Before the enemy had time to recover from their sudden panic, Gracchus signalled the retreat and brought his men back within the walls.

The following day Hannibal assumed that the consul's success would lead him to fight a pitched battle, and so he marshalled his line between the camp and the city. However, when he saw no movement from their usual defensive position and nothing being staked on foolhardy hopes, he returned to the Tifata Mountains with nothing achieved.

During the very same time that the siege of Cumae was raised, Tiberius Sempronius, who was surnamed Longus, also fought a successful engagement against the Carthaginian Hanno near Grumentum in Lucania.* Sempronius killed upwards of 2,000 men, losing 280 of his soldiers in the process, and captured about forty-one military standards. Driven out of Lucanian territory, Hanno retired into that of the Bruttii.

Three towns of the Hirpini that had revolted from the Roman people—Vercellium, Vescellium, and Sicilinum*—were also recaptured, and the ringleaders of the revolt were beheaded. More than 5,000 prisoners of war were auctioned off. The rest of the booty was left to the rank and file, and the army was marched back to Luceria.

38. In the course of these operations amongst the Lucanians and the Hirpini, the five ships that were taking the captured Macedonian and Carthaginian emissaries to Rome had skirted practically the whole of the Italian coastline on their journey from the Adriatic to the Tyrrhenian Sea. As they passed Cumae under sail, one could not tell for sure whether they were enemy or allied vessels, and Gracchus sent some ships from his fleet to intercept them. In the course of the questions that each party put to the other, it was established that the consul was at Cumae. The ships accordingly put in at Cumae, and the prisoners were escorted to the consul, who was also given the documents they had been carrying. After reading the correspondence between Philip and Hannibal, the consul sent all the documents overland to the Senate under seal, but ordered the emissaries to be transported by sea.

The letters and emissaries reached Rome almost on the same day, and an interrogation found the men's statements to be in line with the documents. At first, the senators were seriously worried: they could see on the horizon a war of massive proportions with Macedon, at a time when they could barely cope with the Punic War. But they certainly did not knuckle under, and in fact their immediate topic for discussion was how they could deflect the enemy from Italy by actually taking the offensive.

The senators ordered the prisoners to be clapped in irons, and they sold off their attendants at auction. They next issued a decree ordering that a further twenty-five ships be equipped to add to the twenty-five under the command of the prefect Publius Valerius Flaccus. The new vessels were brought together and launched, and to them were added the five that had brought the captured emissaries. The thirty ships then set sail from Ostia for Tarentum. There Publius Valerius was instructed to take on board the troops of Varro, who were stationed at Tarentum under the command of the legate Lucius Apustius, and with this combined fleet of fifty-five ships to patrol the Italian coastline, and also gather intelligence on the possibility of war with Macedon. If Philip's projects squared with the letters and the data supplied by the emissaries, Publius Valerius was to impart this information by letter to the praetor Marcus Valerius. Valerius was then to leave the legate Lucius Apustius in command of the army, proceed to the fleet at Tarentum, and, at the earliest opportunity, cross to Macedonia where he was to do all he could to keep Philip within the confines of his realm. Moneys had been sent to Appius Claudius in Sicily to be repaid to King Hiero, but these were now transferred by decree to the maintenance of the fleet and to the war with Macedon. The cash was transported to Tarentum by the legate Lucius Antistius, and at the same time 200,000 measures of wheat and 100,000 measures of barley were sent by Hiero.

39. While the Romans were taking these preparatory measures, one of the captured Carthaginian vessels that had been sent to Rome with the other ships slipped away from its course and fled to Philip, who was thus made aware of the capture of his emissaries and the letters. The king did not know what understanding had been reached between his own emissaries and Hannibal, or what proposals Hannibal's emissaries had been going to bring to him, and so he sent off a second deputation with the same instructions as before. The

emissaries sent to Hannibal were Heraclitus, who was nicknamed Scotinus, the Boeotian Crito, and the Magnesian Sositheus. They were actually successful in taking and bringing back their messages, but the summer came to an end before the king could react or take any initiative. So crucial was the capture of one vessel carrying diplomats for postponing a war that threatened the Romans!

Around Capua, meanwhile, Fabius had crossed the Volturnus after finally completing the expiatory rites for the prodigies, and the two consuls were now acting in concert. Fabius forced into submission the towns of Combulteria, Trebula, and Austicula, which had gone over to the Carthaginians, and members of Hannibal's garrisons and large numbers of Campanians were taken prisoner in them.

At Nola, the senate was pro-Roman and the commons pro-Hannibal, as the year before, and there were covert plots to murder the leading citizens and betray the city. To forestall such plans, Fabius took his army on a course between Capua and Hannibal's camp on the Tifata Mountains, and ensconced himself above Suessula in the Castra Claudiana. From there he dispatched to Nola the propraetor Marcus Marcellus, together with the forces under Marcellus' command, to garrison the town.

40. In Sardinia, military operations had been suspended after the praetor Quintus Mucius succumbed to his serious disease, but these were now reopened under the command of the praetor Titus Manlius. Manlius hauled his warships ashore at Carales, and furnished the crews with arms so he could fight on land. With these and the army that he received from the praetor Mucius he made up a force of 22,000 foot and 1,200 horse. At the head of such cavalry and infantry troops he set out into enemy territory, pitching his camp a short distance from Hampsicora's. It so happened that Hampsicora had at that point left on a journey to the Pelliti-Sardinians,* intending to arm their young men and thereby augment his forces; and his son, who was called Hostus, was in command of the camp. Youthfully headstrong, Hostus recklessly committed to battle, and was defeated and routed. Some 3,000 Sardinians were killed in the battle, and about 800 taken alive. The rest of the army at first dispersed in flight through the fields and forests, but then sought refuge in the regional capital, a city called Cornus, to which it was rumoured their leader had made his escape. That battle might have marked the end of the war in Sardinia, but for the timely arrival of the Carthaginian fleet under Hasdrubal's command. This had been driven off course to the Balearic Islands by bad weather, but now arrived at a good time to raise hopes of recommencing hostilities.

On receiving word of the docking of the Punic fleet, Manlius withdrew to Carales, thus giving Hampsicora the opportunity of joining up with the Carthaginians. Hasdrubal disembarked his troops, sent the fleet back to Carthage, and set off, guided by Hampsicora, to plunder the farmlands of allies of the Roman people. He would have reached Carales had not Manlius confronted him with his army and put a stop to his widespread pillaging. Initially, the two camps simply faced each other, a short distance apart, and then there were some sudden charges that provoked minor skirmishes, with varying results. Finally they took to the field. Clashing in pitched battle, they fought for four hours. The Sardinians were accustomed to being easily defeated, but the Carthaginians long kept it an indecisive battle. Finally, when all that was to be seen was Sardinians being slaughtered or in flight, the Carthaginians, too, were routed; but, as they turned to run, the Romans cut them off by wheeling round the wing with which they had driven back the Sardinians. After that it was more a bloodbath than a battle. Twelve thousand of the enemy, Sardinians and Carthaginians alike, were cut down, and some 3,700 taken prisoner, with the capture of twenty-seven military standards.

41. What more than anything made the battle famous and memorable was the capture of the commander, Hasdrubal, and of the Carthaginian nobles Hanno and Mago. Mago belonged to the Barca clan, and was closely related to Hannibal, while Hanno had been responsible for the Sardinian defection and was unquestionably the man who had fomented that war. But the fates that overtook the Sardinian leaders contributed no less to the fame of that particular engagement. Hampsicora's son Hostus died on the field of battle. Hampsicora made off with a few horsemen but, when he received the news that, in addition to the defeat, his son was also dead, he committed suicide—and at night so no one would intervene and thwart his plan. For the others, the town of Cornus again provided shelter in their flight, as it had done before, but Manlius attacked it with his victorious army and reduced it in a few days. After that other city-states that had gone over to Hampsicora and the Carthaginians also gave hostages and capitulated. Manlius imposed payments of tribute

and grain on them, assessed according to their strength or the extent of their transgressions, and then led his army back to Carales. At Carales he launched his warships and embarked on them the soldiers he had brought with him, after which he sailed to Rome and announced to the Senate that Sardinia had been completely subdued. He also delivered the tribute to the quaestors, the grain to the aediles, and the prisoners of war to the praetor Quintus Fulvius.

In this same period the praetor Titus Otacilius sailed across to Africa from Lilybaeum and pillaged the farmland of Carthage. Heading from there to Sardinia—there were reports of Hasdrubal's recent crossing to the island from the Balearics—he encountered the fleet of Hasdrubal as it was returning to Africa. There was a minor engagement on the open sea in which Otacilius captured seven ships with their crews, and panic scattered the other enemy vessels far and wide just like a storm.

It so happened that during that time, too, Bomilcar arrived in Locri with troops, elephants, and provisions sent as reinforcements from Carthage. To take him by surprise, Appius Claudius swiftly led his army to Messana, on the pretence of doing the rounds of his province, and then, wind and tide being with him, crossed to Locri. Bomilcar, however, had already left to join Hanno in Bruttium, and the Locrians closed their gates on the Romans. Appius headed back to Messana with nothing to show for his great effort.

That same summer Marcellus made repeated forays out of Nola, which he was occupying with a garrison, into the farmlands of the Hirpini and against the Samnites of Caudium. Such was the havoc he wreaked everywhere with fire and the sword that he revived in Samnium memories of its disasters of old.

42. As a result, representatives from both tribes were immediately sent to Hannibal, and they made the following address to the Carthaginian:*

'Hannibal, we at first stood on our own as enemies of the Roman people, for as long as our own arms and resources were sufficient to give us protection. When we came to have little confidence in these, we made an alliance with King Pyrrhus. Abandoned by him, we accepted a peace treaty that was forced upon us, and we stuck to that for well-nigh fifty years, up to the time when you came to Italy. Your courage and success won our hearts, but no less so did your singular courtesy and graciousness towards our citizens, whom you returned to us after capturing them. So much so, in fact, that if you, our friend, were safe and sound, we had no fear, not merely of the Roman people but even of the wrath of the gods (if I may say so without offending them). But now you have actually been not only safe and victorious, but you have been present with us, able almost to hear the weeping of our wives and children and to see our homes ablaze. And yet—for heaven's sake!—we have at times this summer suffered such devastation that one would think that it was Marcus Marcellus who prevailed at Cannae, not Hannibal; and the Romans are now boasting that you had strength only to strike one blow and that your sting is spent and you are powerless.

'We waged a war with the Romans for a century, receiving no assistance from any foreign general or army—except for a two-year period, when it was a case of Pyrrhus using *our* soldiers to augment *his* forces rather than using *his* forces to defend *us*. I shall not boast of our triumphs, of the two consuls and two consular armies that we sent beneath the yoke, and of all our other successes and accomplishments. As for the difficulties and adversities that befell us then, we can speak of those now with less resentment than we can of what is happening to us today. Great dictators would invade our territory with their masters of horse, the two consuls with their consular armies. They would conduct reconnaissance and post reserve troops, and then lead their men in regular order to plunder our land. But now we are the prey of a single praetor, and of a tiny garrison left to defend Nola! They come not even grouped in companies but like bandits, overrunning our territory from end to end as nonchalantly as if they were roaming through the farmlands of Rome. And this is the explanation. *You* are not protecting us, and our own young men, who would be defending us if they were at home, are all serving in *your* forces.

'I would be showing ignorance of you and your army if I did not say that it would be easy for you to crush these itinerant marauders— these men wandering around in disorder, each drawn by hope, no matter how illusory, of gaining plunder. For I know about all the Roman armies that have been defeated and routed by you. Those men will fall prey to a few Numidians, and you will have sent us support, and simultaneously taken it from Nola—but only if you consider those people whom you thought worthy to be your allies to be also not unworthy of your defence and protection.'

43. Hannibal's response to these remarks was that the Hirpini and Samnites* were doing everything at the same time—apprising him of their losses, asking for military assistance, and complaining of being undefended and neglected. What they should have done was to apprise him of the losses first, then taken the step of requesting aid, and only in the event of their request going nowhere should they finally have complained that their appeals for help had been in vain. He was not going to lead his army into the land of the Hirpini and Samnites, he said, for fear of making himself a burden on those peoples, but he would take it into the closest areas belonging to allies of the Roman people. By pillaging these lands he would satisfy his own men's hunger for spoils, and also create fear such as would keep the enemy at a distance from his allies. As for the war with Rome, if the battle of Trasimene outshone the Trebia, and if Cannae outshone Trasimene, he was going to win a greater and more brilliant victory that would eclipse even the memory of Cannae.

He sent the envoys off with this answer and some splendid gifts. Then, leaving a small garrison on the Tifata Mountains, he set off in person with the rest of his army and advanced to Nola. Leaving Bruttium, Hanno also came to Nola, bringing reinforcements that had been shipped from Carthage, and a number of elephants.* Establishing his camp not far from the town, Hannibal investigated the situation and discovered everything to be very different from the reports he had received from the representatives of his allies. Marcellus' conduct had been such that he could not be said to have left anything to chance, or recklessly to have given the enemy any leeway. His raids had come after careful reconnoitring, and were conducted with strong supporting troops; and he always had his retreat assured. All precautionary measures had been carefully taken as if he had been facing Hannibal in person.

At that time, aware of the enemy's approach, Marcellus kept his forces within the fortifications, and he instructed the senators of Nola to walk along the walls and examine all enemy activity in the neighbourhood. Hanno now approached the city wall and invited two of these senators, Herennius Bassus and Herius Pettius, to parley. When they came forth, with Marcellus' permission, Hanno addressed them through an interpreter. He praised Hannibal for his bravery and good fortune in war, and denigrated the greatness of Rome, which he said was on the decline, along with her strength. And even if that former equality between the two powers were still there, he continued, the allies had nevertheless discovered how oppressive Roman dominion was, and how lenient Hannibal had been even to all his prisoners of war of Italian birth. They should therefore choose to have a friendship and alliance with Carthage rather than with Rome. Even if the two consuls were at Nola with their armies, he continued, they would still be no more a match for Hannibal than they had been at Cannae—and much less would a single praetor be able to defend Nola with a few raw recruits! It made more difference to the people of Nola than it did to Hannibal whether the Carthaginian took their town by force or by surrender—for take it he would, just as he had taken Capua and Nuceria. But the difference between the fate of Capua and that of Nuceria they, as Nolans, well knew for themselves, being more or less placed between the two. He did not wish to predict what would befall their city if it were captured. Rather, he was making a commitment to them that, if they surrendered Marcellus and his garrison, along with Nola, they, and no one else, would dictate the terms on which they would enter into an alliance and compact of friendship with Hannibal.

44. In reply, Herennius Bassus observed that the bond of friendship between the peoples of Rome and Nola had existed for many years, and that to that day neither party had reason to regret it. If the people of Nola ought to have changed their loyalties as fortunes changed, he added, it was now simply too late for the change. And if they were going to surrender to Hannibal, why would they have bothered sending for a Roman garrison? They had fully thrown in their lot with those who had come to defend them, and that is how it would be to the end.

The parley removed any hope Hannibal might have had of taking Nola through betrayal, and he surrounded the town with a cordon of troops for a simultaneous attack on the walls from all directions. When Marcellus saw that Hannibal had moved up close to the walls, he drew up his fighting line within the gate, and launched a deafening counterattack from the town. A number of the enemy were taken by surprise and killed at the first onset. Then there was a rush to the scene of the fighting and, when both sides' forces evened up, it began to turn into a ferocious struggle, one that would have been memorable as few others had been, had not torrential rain arrived with gale-force winds to part the combatants. In fact, however, the day saw the

Romans return to the city, and the Carthaginians to their camp, after only a minor tussle, which merely served to stimulate both sides. Even so there were losses, no more than thirty on the Carthaginian side—those taken by surprise in the initial counterattack—and fifty on that of the Romans. The rain persisted without a break throughout the night, until the third hour of the following day, and so although both sides were eager for the fight they nevertheless kept within their fortifications that day.

The following day Hannibal sent a section of his troops out to conduct predatory raids on Nolan farmland. Observing this, Marcellus straight away led out his troops to form a battle line, and Hannibal did not decline the offer of combat. There was a distance of about a mile between the city and the camp, and it was in this space (Nola is completely surrounded by flat land) that they engaged. The shout that arose from both sides brought back those who were closest to the fighting in the cohorts that had gone out to raid the fields, and they joined the battle that was already in progress. The men of Nola also came to reinforce the Roman line. After applauding their action, Marcellus instructed them to remain in reserve, and bear the wounded from the field, but to keep out of the fighting, unless they received a signal from him.

45. The battle hung in the balance, with the generals spurring on their men, and the soldiers fighting, with all their might. Marcellus told the Romans to put pressure on men they had defeated two days before and chased from Cumae a few days earlier, men whom he had himself, with other troops, driven from Nola the previous year. Not all the enemy were on the battlefield, he told them. Some were roaming the fields in raiding parties, but those in the battle were drained of their strength by excesses in Campania, exhausted from a whole winter of drinking, womanizing, and all manner of depravity. Gone was their renowned ferocity and vitality, he said, and lost that physical and mental toughness that enabled them to scale the heights of the Pyrenees and the Alps. These were the remnants of that band of men, and they were having difficulty holding their weapons and standing up to fight. Capua had been Hannibal's Cannae, he declared. It was there that the Carthaginians' military prowess had been snuffed out, along with their military discipline, their fame of old, and their hopes for the future.

While Marcellus was trying to boost his men's morale with these disparaging comments on the enemy, Hannibal was using much harsher language to chasten his men. He recognized his soldiers' arms and standards, he said—they were the same that he had seen, and put into use, at the Trebia, at Trasimene, and finally at Cannae. But, he added, it was one army that he had taken into winter quarters at Capua, and another that he had taken out.

'You are men whom two consular armies could never withstand,' he told them. 'Are you finding it hard, despite all your efforts, to face up to a Roman lieutenant, and to do battle with a single legion and a cavalry squadron? Is Marcellus getting away with attacking us yet again, and with recruits and Nolan reservists? Where is that soldier of mine who dragged the consul Gaius Flaminius from his mount, and walked off with his head? Where is the man who killed Lucius Paulus at Cannae? Are your swords now blunted? Are your sword hands grown weak? Or is this some other strange phenomenon? You were a handful of men used to defeating superior numbers; now that you have the greater numbers, are you unable to take on a handful? You used to boast that you would take Rome by storm if someone led you there—you were brave in your language! But, look, this is a lesser task in which I want to test your drive and your courage. Storm Nola! It is a city on the plains, with no protection from a river or the sea. I shall take you from here—or—I will follow you wherever you want, once you are loaded with the plunder and spoils from this affluent town.'

46. No words of encouragement or reproach could re-establish the morale of the Carthaginians. They were driven back in every quarter, and Roman confidence rose, thanks partly to their commander's encouragement, but thanks also to the citizens of Nola, who spurred them to fight with shouts of support. The Carthaginians turned tail, and were driven back into their camp. The Roman soldiers were eager to assault the camp, but Marcellus led them back to Nola, to the sound of rejoicing and applause, which came from the commons who had earlier favoured the Carthaginians.

More than 5,000 of the enemy were killed that day, and 600 were taken alive. Nineteen military standards were also captured, and two elephants, four having fallen in the battle. Roman losses were fewer than a thousand.* The two sides spent the following day observing an undeclared truce and burying comrades who were killed in the field. Marcellus burned the enemy spoils in fulfilment of a vow to

Vulcan. Two days later, disgruntled over something, presumably, or else hoping for better pay for their service, 272 cavalrymen, a mixture of Numidians and Spaniards, deserted to Marcellus. The Romans subsequently made frequent use of their staunch and loyal support in that war, and after the war, in recognition of their valour, these men were awarded grants of land, the Spaniards in Spain and the Numidians in Africa.

Hannibal then sent Hanno back from Nola to Bruttium with the troops with which he had come, and he himself headed for winter quarters in Apulia, where he encamped close to Arpi. On hearing that Hannibal had left for Apulia, Quintus Fabius transported grain from Nola and Neapolis to the camp above Suessula. He strengthened the camp's fortifications, left a force sufficient to hold the position through the winter, and moved his camp closer to Capua. He now wreaked destruction on the farmlands of Capua with fire and the sword until the Capuans, despite an almost total lack of confidence in their strength, were forced to come forth from their gates and establish a fortified camp on open terrain before their city. The Capuans had 6,000 men under arms. Their infantry was ineffectual, and they had more strength in their cavalry; and so it was by initiating cavalry engagements that they challenged their enemy.

Amongst the many noted Campanian horsemen was one Cerrinus Vibellius, whose surname was Taurea. He was a citizen of Capua, and was by far the strongest horseman of the Campanians, so much so that, when he was serving with the Romans, only a single Roman, Claudius Asellus, had been able to match his reputation for horsemanship. This Taurea now spent a long time riding up to the enemy cavalry squadrons and running his eyes over them. Finally, when silence fell, he asked where Claudius Asellus was. The two of them had been in the habit of arguing about their abilities in the field, he explained, and he wondered why Asellus would not now let the sword decide the issue, conceding the *spolia opima** if he were defeated and taking them if he won.

47. When this was reported to Asellus in camp, he waited only long enough to ask the consul's permission to leave the ranks to fight the foe who was issuing the challenge. Then, with the consul's approval, he immediately seized his weapons, rode forward in front of the enemy guard-posts and called on Taurea by name, telling him to

come and face him wherever he wished. By now the Romans had come crowding out to view the fight, and the people of Capua had filled all the space not just on the earthworks of their camp, but even on the walls of the city, to see it. The combatants' earlier boasts had provided great publicity for the event, and now, spears poised, they spurred on their mounts. But as they weaved and dodged in the open space, they were only dragging out the fight without injury.

'This is going to be a test of horses not of horsemen,' the Campanian then said to the Roman, 'unless we take the horses from the level ground and head them down into the sunken road just here. There we shall have no room for avoiding each other, and we shall come to grips.'

Almost before the words were out, Claudius galloped his horse down into the road. But Taurea's words were braver than his actions. 'No thanks, nag and ditch don't mix,' he said, an expression that was thereafter passed down as a country proverb.* Claudius covered a great distance on the sunken road and, failing to encounter any enemy, rode up again to the level ground, uttering words of reproach for his enemy's cowardice. He then returned triumphant to camp amid jubilant cheering and shouts of congratulation. To this equestrian duel there is added in some accounts a detail that is, to say the least, amazing, though how true it is we must all judge for ourselves. Taurea, these claim, fled back to the city with Claudius in pursuit. Claudius rode in through one of the enemy's gates, which was open, and exited unhurt by a second gate, leaving the enemy speechless at the astonishing event.

48. After that the camp remained at peace. The consul even withdrew his force to let the Campanians get on with their crop-planting, and did not harm their land again until the grain in the fields was high and able to provide him with fodder. He then transported that fodder to the Castra Claudiana above Suessula, where he constructed winter quarters. He gave the order to the proconsul Marcus Claudius to keep at Nola only the force essential for the city's protection, and to send his other troops back to Rome so they would not burden the allies and be an expense for the state. In addition, Tiberius Gracchus led his legions from Cumae to Luceria in Apulia, and from there dispatched to Brundisium the praetor Marcus Valerius at the head of the army that he had commanded at Luceria. Valerius' orders were to patrol the coastline of Sallentine territory, and take such precautionary measures as were necessary in regard to Philip and a Macedonian war.

As the summer of the events I have just narrated came to an end, a dispatch arrived from Publius and Gnaeus Scipio with news of their very important and very successful campaigns in Spain. But, the letter continued, there was need of cash for their men's pay, and the army stood in need of clothing and food rations, and the naval crews in need of everything. In the matter of pay, they said, they would find some way of extracting it from the Spaniards, if the treasury were depleted; but everything else certainly had to be sent from Rome and, without it, maintaining either the army or the province was an impossibility.

When the dispatch was read out there was not a single senator who did not accept the veracity of the report, and the fairness of the requests. But they were aware, too, of the large number of land and naval forces they were keeping in service, and of the size of the new fleet they had to equip in the near future, should there be war with Macedon. They realized that Sicily and Sardinia had, before the war, paid tribute into the treasury, and that now they could barely afford the upkeep of the armies patrolling those provinces. The war tax had helped defray expenses, but the number contributing that tax had been reduced by the enormous losses at both Lake Trasimene and Cannae. If the few survivors of those battles were burdened with an exponential increase in payment, they would be claimed by another kind of ruin! The republic could not survive on its resources, they concluded—it would have to survive on credit. They decided that the praetor Fulvius should go to the public assembly and make clear to the people the needs of the state. Fulvius was then to urge those people who had increased their personal wealth through public contracts to grant the state extra time for repayment—since the state was responsible for their increased wealth—and to take on contracts for supplying all essential materials for the army in Spain. The contracts would be issued on the understanding that the contractors would be the first to be paid when there was money in the treasury.

The praetor delivered his speech in the assembly, and specified a date on which he would put out contracts for furnishing the Spanish army with clothes and grain, and meeting all the other needs of the naval crews.

49. When that day arrived, three companies, each made up of nineteen individuals, showed up to bid for the contracts. They had two requests: first, that they be exempted from military service while they were engaged in this public service; and, secondly, that the cargoes they shipped be insured by the commonwealth against risks from enemy attack and bad weather. When both requests were granted, the companies accepted the contracts, and state business was conducted with private funding. Such was the character and such the patriotism that obtained, more or less uniformly, throughout the city's classes. The scrupulousness with which the contracts were fulfilled* matched the magnanimity with which they were taken on, and the soldiers were as well provisioned in every respect as if their support came from a well-stocked treasury, as in the past.

At the time that these supplies arrived, the town of Iliturgi was under attack from Hasdrubal, from Mago, and from Hannibal son of Bomilcar, because it had gone over to the Romans. Making their way between these three enemy camps, the Scipios put up a great fight to reach their allies' city, inflicting heavy losses on those standing in their way. They brought grain, which was in short supply in the town, and they urged the inhabitants, in defending their walls, to show the same spirit as they had seen in the Roman army that had been fighting on their behalf. They then advanced to launch an attack on the largest of the three camps, the one under Hasdrubal's command. The two other Carthaginian leaders, and their two armies, also converged on the same spot, for they perceived it to be where the whole issue was being decided.

The engagement began with a charge from the camp. The enemy had 60,000 in the battle that day, while there were about 16,000 on the Roman side. And yet the victory was far from indecisive. The Romans cut down the enemy in numbers greater than they were actually fielding themselves; they took more than 3,000 prisoners and captured slightly fewer than 1,000 horses. Also taken were fifty-nine military standards and seven elephants (five having been killed in the engagement), and that day the Romans took possession of the three enemy camps.

With the siege of Iliturgi raised, the Carthaginian armies were marched overland to assault Intibili. Supplementary troops had been raised from the province, for it had a greater appetite for war than any other, provided that plunder or payment were in the offing, and it then had an abundance of men of serviceable age. Once more there was a pitched battle, which again yielded the same result for the two sides. More than 13,000 of the enemy were killed and more than 2,000 taken prisoner, with forty-two standards and nine elephants captured. At that point nearly all the tribes of Spain went over to the Romans, and the operations in Spain that summer were far more impressive than those in Italy.*

BOOK TWENTY-FOUR

1. After his return from Campania to Bruttium, Hanno took the offensive against the Greek cities in the area, and the Bruttii aided him and acted as his guides. These cities had found it easier to maintain their alliance with Rome after seeing that the Bruttii, whom they both loathed and feared, had espoused the Carthaginian cause. Rhegium was the first city targeted, and a number of days were spent there, but without success. Meanwhile the people of Locri hurriedly gathered grain, wood, and all other vital supplies into their city from their fields (which served the added purpose of leaving the enemy nothing to plunder), and each day the crowds issuing from the gates increased in size. Eventually, the only people left in town were those who had to effect repairs to the walls and gates, and to stock-pile weapons on the battlements. As the motley crowd, made up of people of all ages and classes, roamed through the countryside, most of them unarmed, the Carthaginian Hamilcar* unleashed his cavalry against them. Under orders not to inflict injury, the cavalry merely used some squadrons as a barrier to cut off from the city those who scattered in flight.

The commander himself took up a position on rising ground so as to have a view of the countryside and the city, and ordered a cohort of the Bruttii to approach the walls. The Bruttii were to invite the leading Locrians to parley, and to urge them, with a promise of Hannibal's friendship, to surrender the city. In this exchange, the Bruttii at first failed to persuade the Locrians with anything they said. Then the Carthaginians appeared on the hills, and the few escapees reported that the rest of the crowd in the fields was entirely in enemy hands. At this point the Locrians caved in from fear, and replied that they would consult the people. A popular assembly was immediately convened, at which all the most feckless individuals opted for a change of policy and a change of alliance. In addition, those whose kinsmen had been cut off outside the city felt their loyalties just as compromised as if they had given hostages, and the few others simply gave unspoken support for staying true to their allegiance, without daring to express their preference. The result was capitulation to Carthage with what looked like clear unanimity.*

The garrison commander, Lucius Atilius, and the Roman soldiers under him, were surreptitiously escorted to the harbour and put on board ships for passage to Rhegium. The townspeople then admitted Hamilcar and the Carthaginians, on condition that a treaty be immediately established on equitable terms. This condition came close to being violated when the Carthaginians charged the Locrians with duplicity for letting the Romans go free, while the Locrians claimed that they had escaped unaided. There was even a cavalry pursuit on the off-chance that the current might hold the ships in the strait or sweep them to shore. In fact, the cavalry failed to overtake the men they were chasing, but they did catch sight of other vessels heading across the strait from Messana to Rhegium. These were the Roman soldiers who had been dispatched by the praetor Claudius to hold the city with a garrison. As a result, the Carthaginians immediately abandoned the siege of Rhegium.

On Hannibal's orders the Locrians were granted peace, with liberty under their own constitution assured them. The city was to be open to the Carthaginians, but with the port under Locrian control, and the basis of the treaty was that, in peace and war, Carthage would aid Locri and Locri Carthage.*

2. Thus it was that the Carthaginians were withdrawn from the strait, much to the chagrin of the Bruttii—their allies had now left Rhegium and Locri intact, cities the Bruttii had had their hearts set on plundering. They therefore took action themselves, enlisting and arming 15,000 of their young men, and setting off to launch an attack on Croton. This, too, was a Greek city and it was also on the coast, and the Bruttii reckoned that possession of a well-fortified coastal city with a port and defensive walls would greatly increase their strength.

One thing, however, caused the Bruttii grave concern. They could hardly omit a request for the Carthaginians to come to their aid—such conduct would appear inappropriate for allies. And yet, if the Carthaginian again turned out to be a peace-broker, rather than a collaborator in the war, fighting for Croton's liberation from Rome would be a waste of time, as had been the case earlier with the Locrians. The best solution seemed to be to send a deputation to Hannibal and secure a guarantee from him that when Croton was taken it would be a Bruttian possession. Hannibal's reply was that this had to be decided by those on the spot, and he referred them to

Hanno, but no clear answer came back from Hanno, either. He was loath to see a famous and wealthy city pillaged, and he was also hoping that, when the Bruttii attacked, and it became clear that the assault had neither the approval nor the support of the Carthaginians, the people of Croton would defect to him all the more promptly.

In Croton there was no solidarity of purpose or sentiment amongst the people. It was as if a single disease had infected all the city-states of Italy:* the commons were always in disagreement with the aristo-crats, the senate favouring the Romans and the commons advocating a pro-Carthaginian policy. A deserter reported to the Bruttii such a conflict in the city of Croton. He informed them that the leader of the common people was one Aristomachus, and that he favoured surrendering the city. He also said that in this desolate city, with its widely scattered fortifications, the senators' sentry-posts were few and far between, and where men from the common people were on guard, the Bruttii had easy access.

Accepting the deserter's information and guidance, the Bruttii surrounded the city with a military cordon, and at the first attack they were admitted by the commons. After that they went on to take the whole town, apart from the citadel. The nobles held on to the citadel, which they had earlier prepared as a place of refuge, to meet just this sort of eventuality. Aristomachus also fled to the same place, claiming that he had recommended delivering the city to the Carthaginians, not the Bruttii.

3. Before Pyrrhus' arrival in Italy, the city of Croton had walls with a twelve-mile circumference, but after the destruction brought about by that war barely half the space within them was occupied. The river that had run through what had been the centre of town now flowed beyond the built-up sections, and the citadel was some distance from the inhabited area. Six miles away from the city lay a famous temple which was even more famous than the town itself—the temple of Juno Lacinia,* which is venerated by all peoples in the area. Here there was a grove ringed by thick woods of towering fir-trees, and in its midst was lush pasture where all manner of livestock, sacred to the goddess, would graze, unsupervised by any herdsman. At night the herds would make their way back to their folds, each species separate from the others, never coming to harm from crea-tures on the prowl or traps laid by men. As a result, large profits were derived from these animals, and from these profits a pillar of solid

gold was cast and consecrated to the goddess. In fact, the temple was famed for its riches as well as its sanctity. Indeed, as usually happens with famous places, people also credit it with paranormal attributes, and it is said that there is an altar in the forecourt of the temple on which the ashes are never moved by the wind.

The citadel of Croton looks out over the sea on one side, while the other side faces its farmlands. At one time its defences lay entirely in its natural position, but later a protective wall was added at the sequestered bluff where it had been captured by the stratagem of Dionysius, tyrant of Sicily.* It was in this citadel—which seemed secure enough—that the aristocrats of Croton were holding out, while their own proletariat and the Bruttii lay siege to them.

Eventually the Bruttii saw that taking the citadel was beyond their capabilities, and they were compelled by their difficulties to beg Hanno for assistance. Hanno tried to pressure the aristocrats into a surrender that was conditional upon their accepting the establishment of a colony of the Bruttii, which would allow the city, depopulated and rendered desolate by war, to recover its earlier numbers. This impressed none but Aristomachus. The aristocrats said they would sooner die than merge with the Bruttii, and switch to the religion, customs, and laws, and eventually even to the language of foreigners. Unable to bring them to surrender by persuasion, and finding no opportunity to betray the citadel as he had the city, Aristomachus deserted to Hanno, on his own. Shortly afterwards, with Hanno's permission, ambassadors from Locri entered the citadel and convinced the aristocrats to accept a transfer to Locri rather than hold on to the bitter end. The Locrians had already gained clearance for this from Hannibal through a deputation they sent to him. Croton was therefore abandoned, and the citizens were escorted down to the sea where they boarded some ships. The whole population then departed for Locri.

In Apulia, even the winter did not pass without incident for the Romans and Hannibal. The consul Sempronius spent it at Luceria, and Hannibal not far from Arpi. Between them there were intermittent skirmishes as the occasion offered or as one or the other side saw some opportunity. Thanks to these, the Romans improved as soldiers, and each day became more vigilant and more secure against the wiles of the enemy.

4. In Sicily, Hiero's death had changed the entire situation. The

throne had passed to Hiero's grandson Hieronymus,* a boy who was not likely yet to assume adult independence, and much less unlimited power, with any restraint. The boy's guardians took advantage of his years and character to plunge him into all manner of depravity. Hiero, it is said, had foreseen such an eventuality, and in the last years of his long life had wanted to leave Syracuse free. He did not wish a throne that had been acquired and strengthened by honourable means to become a mockery and go to ruin under a boy's tyrannical rule. Hiero's daughters did all they could to oppose this plan of his, for they thought that, while the royal title would remain with the boy, control of everything would rest with them and their husbands, Adranodorus and Zoippus, who were being left as Hieronymus' chief guardians. For Hiero, now in his ninetieth year, and surrounded day and night by these women's cajoling, it was not easy to take his mind off other things, and focus on public rather than private concerns. All he did, therefore, was to leave the boy fifteen guardians, and on his deathbed he implored them to keep intact the loyalty that he had shown the Roman people over fifty years, and, in particular, to see that the young man followed in his footsteps, and maintained the principles with which he had been reared.

Such were Hiero's instructions. On his death, the guardians produced his will and brought the boy, then about fifteen years old, before a meeting of the people. A few men had been planted at various points in the assembly to raise, and these voiced their approval of the will, but the rest felt only fear—it was as though they had lost a father and their state was orphaned. And so the guardians took up their duties. The royal funeral followed, marked more by the love and affection shown by the citizens than any emotion on the part of the family. In a short while, Adranodorus removed the other guardians, claiming that Hieronymus was now a young man and capable of assuming the throne. In fact, he renounced his own guardianship, which he had held along with several others, but then channelled into his own hands the power of them all.

5. It would not have been easy even for a good and considerate king to win support amongst the Syracusans, succeeding, as he was, someone as much loved as Hiero. But in Hieronymus' case it was as though he wanted his own failings to make his grandfather's loss truly felt, and on his first appearance he immediately demonstrated how much everything had changed. These people had, over so many

years, seen Hiero and his son Gelo dressed no differently from the other citizens, and wearing no special regalia. Now they looked upon a purple robe, a diadem, and an armed bodyguard—and sometimes they even saw their ruler leaving the palace in a chariot drawn by four white horses, like the tyrant Dionysius. This swaggering pomp and posturing was matched by his behaviour: contempt for all people; disdain for those in audience with him; insulting language; access rarely granted not only to outsiders but even to his guardians; bizarre depravities; and inhuman cruelty. Such was the terror that seized everybody as a result of this that a number of the guardians forestalled the executions they feared by suicide or flight.

Only three of the guardians could enter the palace on some basis of familiarity: Hiero's sons-in-law Adranodorus and Zoippus, and a certain Thraso. These did not receive much attention generally; but as two of them were promoting the Carthaginian cause, and Thraso the alliance with Rome, they roused the young man's interest with their antagonism and partisan disputes. And, during this time, information about a conspiracy against the king's life was brought by a certain Callo, a contemporary of Hieronymus, who had from boyhood enjoyed all the familiarity with him a friend might expect.

The informer could name only one of the conspirators— Theodotus, the man by whom he had been approached. Theodotus was immediately arrested, and delivered to Adranodorus for torture, but while he did not hesitate to confess his own guilt, he concealed the identity of his accomplices. Finally, afflicted with torments beyond human endurance, he pretended to be broken by his agonies and supplied information, which he directed against innocent men rather than his fellow conspirators. He falsely claimed that Thraso was the ringleader of the plot. The conspirators would not have risked such a coup but for their confidence in so powerful a leader, he said. He added the names of supporters of Hieronymus who were always at the tyrant's side, creatures of the slightest worth who popped into his head while he concocted his story between his screams of pain.

To the tyrant's way of thinking it was the naming of Thraso that gave the charges the most credibility. The man was immediately handed over for execution, and all the others, men as innocent as he, shared his punishment. Despite the prolonged torture of their collaborator in the plot, not one of Theodotus' associates either went into hiding, or ran away. Such was their confidence in Theodotus' courage and loyalty, and such was Theodotus' own capacity to keep his secret.

6. With Thraso out of the way—the one remaining link with the Roman alliance—things were clearly moving towards a change of allegiance. Ambassadors were dispatched to Hannibal, and Hannibal sent back, in the company of a young nobleman, who was also called Hannibal,* Hippocrates and Epicydes. These two had been born in Carthage,* and were themselves Carthaginian on their mother's side, but they traced their origins back to Syracuse where their grandfather had been in exile. Through their agency a treaty was forged between Hannibal and the Syracusan tyrant, and the two remained at the tyrant's court, an arrangement to which Hannibal did not object.

Appius Claudius was the praetor with responsibility for Sicily, and when he got word of this development he immediately sent envoys to Hieronymus. They informed the tyrant that they had come to renew the alliance that had existed with his grandfather, but their words met with derision, and they were dismissed by Hieronymus, who, to poke fun at them, asked how the battle at Cannae had gone for them. The account Hannibal's envoys gave of it was scarcely credible, he said, and he wanted to know the truth of the matter, so that he could then make a decision on which side to pin his hopes. The Romans withdrew from the tyrant, saying that they would return when he started to give serious attention to embassies, and left him with a warning, rather than a request, not to be too hasty in switching his allegiance.

Hieronymus now sent a delegation to Carthage to establish a treaty on the terms negotiated with Hannibal. The agreement reached by the parties was that when they had both driven the Romans from Sicily—which would be soon, if the Carthaginians sent ships and an army—the boundary between the kingdom of Syracuse and the Carthaginian empire would be the River Himera, which virtually divides the island in two. But Hieronymus had become very overbearing from the flattery of men who told him to remember not just Hiero, but King Pyrrhus, too, his grandfather on his mother's side, and he subsequently sent a second delegation. This time he expressed his opinion that it was only fair that all Sicily should be ceded to him, and that the Carthaginian people should claim as *their* right dominion over Italy. The Carthaginians expressed no surprise at the young madman's fickleness and bluster, and would not criticize him—provided they could sever his ties with Rome.

7. But everything was conspiring to hurl Hieronymus to his destruction. He had sent Hippocrates and Epicydes ahead, each with 2,000 men, to assault the cities occupied by Roman garrisons, and he had then set off himself for Leontini with the rest of his forces, which totalled about 15,000 foot and horse. In Leontini, the conspirators, who all happened to be in the armed forces, took over a vacant building overlooking the narrow road by which the king usually went down to the forum. There, with a single exception, they all stood armed and at the ready, waiting for the king to pass. The one other, whose name was Dinomenes, was a bodyguard of Hieronymus, and the role he was assigned was to find some way of halting the crowd of people behind him in the narrow street, at the moment when the king was approaching the door of the house.

All went as arranged. Dinomenes lifted his foot, pretending to loosen a lace that was too tight, and held up the crowd. He created such a gap that the king, attacked as he passed the house without his armed guards, received several stab wounds before help could be brought.* When the shouting and uproar were heard, spears were hurled at Dinomenes, who was obviously creating an obstruction, but he escaped from under them with only two wounds. When they saw the king on the ground, Hieronymus' attendants took to their heels. Some of the assassins marched to the forum to join the crowds who were revelling in their liberation, and others went to Syracuse to nip in the bud any plans that Adranodorus and other supporters of the king might have.

In this precarious situation, Appius Claudius could see a war looming on his doorstep, and he informed the Senate by letter that Sicily's allegiance was being enticed away from Rome to the Carthaginian people and Hannibal. To counter any plans being hatched by the Syracusans, Claudius himself massed all his forces on the boundary between his province and the Syracusan kingdom.

At the end of that year, with the authorization of the Senate, Quintus Fabius fortified and garrisoned Puteoli, which in the course of the war had started to become a busy trading centre. En route from Puteoli to Rome to oversee elections, he gave notice that these would be held on the first available election day. Then, immediately

on his arrival, he bypassed the city and went down to the Campus
Martius. On that day the younger century of the tribe of Anio was
allotted the right to vote first,* and its vote was for Titus Otacilius and
Marcus Aemilius Regillus as consuls. At this point Quintus Fabius
called for silence, and delivered a speech much as follows:

8. 'If we now had peace in Italy, or a war and an enemy that would
grant us some latitude for sloppiness, then anyone attempting to
curb the enthusiasm you bring to the Campus to bestow office upon
men of your choosing—I would think such a man had too little
consideration for your liberties. But, in the case of this war and this
enemy, no mistake made by any commander has yet failed to precipitate disaster on a massive scale. You must therefore proceed to the
vote for electing your consuls with the same caution that you exercise when you go in armour to the battlefield, and every man should
say to himself: "I propose a consul who can match Hannibal as a
commander."

'This year, at Capua, the top Campanian horseman, Vibellius
Taurea, challenged, and was faced by, the top Roman horseman,
Asellus Claudius. When a Gaul once issued a challenge on a bridge
over the Anio, our ancestors sent against him Titus Manlius, a man
confident in his courage and strength. I would not deny, either, that
the same factors were involved a few years later in the confidence
placed in Marcus Valerius when he faced a similar challenge and
took up arms to fight a Gaul. We wish to have infantry and cavalry
that are stronger or, at least, as strong as the enemy's. We should
likewise seek out a commander who is a match for the enemy leader.
When we have designated the man who is the greatest commander in
the state, he will still have been chosen quickly, and been elected only
for a year. And he will be pitted against a veteran general with
unlimited command, one hindered by no time or jurisdictional limitations from fulfilling all the operational and administrative duties
the war might impose on him at any moment. In our case, by contrast, a year goes by while we are in the actual preparation stage and
merely getting started.

'Enough has been said about the qualities needed in the men you
elect as consuls; it now remains for me to say a few words about those
men most favoured by the century with the prerogative of voting
first. Marcus Aemilius Regillus is the Flamen of Quirinus.* We cannot
send him away from his religious duties, or keep him at home, without

abandoning either our obligations to the gods, or our obligations to the war effort. Titus Otacilius is married to my sister's daughter and has children by her. Even so, such are the benefits that you have conferred on my ancestors and me that I must hold the interests of state more important than personal ties. When the sea is calm, any one of the crew or passengers can steer the ship; when a raging tempest has arisen, and the ship is driven by the wind over a turbulent sea, what is needed then is a man of action, a helmsman. We are not sailing a calm sea; we have already been almost sunk by a number of storms. As a result, it is imperative that you exercise the greatest care and foresight in selecting the man who is to sit at the helm.

'Titus Otacilius, we have used your services in a less urgent matter, and you have certainly not given us any grounds for placing our confidence in you for greater ones. This year we fitted out a fleet, which was under your command, with three aims. First, it was to conduct raids on the coastline of Africa. Secondly, it was to maintain for us the safety of the Italian seaboard. Thirdly, and most important of all, it was to prevent the transport of reinforcements for Hannibal, along with cash and provisions, from Carthage. Elect Titus Otacilius as your consul if he managed to accomplish for the state . . . I shall not say all of these aims, but at least one of them. But if, while you commanded the fleet, supplies that Hannibal needed often reached him from home safe and sound, as if there were no war at sea; if the coast of Italy has this year been more threatened than the coast of Africa, what reason can you give for us to put you, of all people, in command against an enemy like Hannibal? If you were consul, I would follow the example of our ancestors and vote for the appointment of a dictator, and you could not be angry over another man in the Roman nation being considered your superior in warfare. It is to your advantage, more than anyone else's, Titus Otacilius, that a burden under which you would collapse not be put on your shoulders.

'Suppose, my fellow citizens, that you were standing under arms in the field of battle, and were obliged to pick two generals under whose leadership and auspices you were to fight. The considerations you would bring to that choice I now earnestly beg and urge you to apply today, when you elect the consuls to whom your children are to swear their oath, at whose order they are to muster, and under whose guardianship and care they are to fight. Lake Trasimene and Cannae—they are depressing cases to recall, but they do serve as a warning to us to be on our guard against such disasters. Herald, call the younger tribe of Anio to retake the vote!'

9. Titus Otacilius stridently cried out in protest that Fabius only wanted to extend his own period as consul, and Fabius then ordered the lictors to approach Otacilius. Through them he advised him that his *fasces* still had their axes when they were carried ahead of him, because in coming straight to the Campus after his journey he had not entered the city. Meanwhile, the first century proceeded to take the vote, and its decision was to elect Quintus Fabius Maximus consul for the fourth time, and Marcus Marcellus for the third.* The same men were unanimously declared consul by all the other centuries. One of the praetors, Quintus Fulvius Flaccus, was also re-elected, while the others were new appointments: Titus Otacilius Crassus (for his second praetorship), Quintus Fabius (the consul's son, at that time curule aedile) and Publius Cornelius Lentulus. On the termination of the praetorian elections, a senatorial decree was issued giving Quintus Fulvius the city jurisdiction by special appointment, and vesting in him above all others authority over the city when the consuls should leave for the war.

There was flooding on two occasions that year; the Tiber inundated farms, and caused widespread destruction of buildings and animals, and much loss of life.

It was the fifth year of the Second Punic War, and Quintus Fabius Maximus' and Marcus Claudius Marcellus' entry into the consulship (Fabius for the fourth time, Claudius for the third) attracted more than usual attention from the citizen body. It had been many a year since a pair of consuls like that had been seen. Old men recalled the similar circumstances in which Maximus Rullus* had been declared consul for the Gallic War, with Publius Decius as his colleague, and later Papirius and Carvilius for operations against the Samnites, the Bruttii, and against the Lucanian and Tarentine peoples. Marcellus was elected consul *in absentia*, since he was with the army, and Fabius had his consulship prolonged while he was present and actually supervising the elections. The time, the demands of the war, and the critical situation facing the state deterred anyone from looking for a precedent, or from suspecting lust for power on the part of the consul. In fact, people actually praised his magnanimity. He knew that what the republic needed was a first-rate commander, and that he was unquestionably that; and he was less concerned about any unpopularity that might arise from this affair than he was about the public good.

10. On the day of the consuls' entry into office there was a meeting of the Senate on the Capitol. Its very first decree stipulated that the consuls should decide by lot, or arrange between themselves, which, before he left to join his army, was to supervise the elections for appointing the censors. After that, all commanders who were with their armies had their *imperium* extended, and were ordered to retain their current responsibilities. Tiberius Gracchus was to remain in Luceria, where he was serving with an army of slave volunteers, Gaius Terentius Varro in Picenum, and Marcus Pomponius in Gallic territory. The praetors of the previous year were to function as propraetors, Quintus Marcus assuming responsibility for Sardinia, and Marcus Valerius taking charge of the coastal region at Brundisium. Valerius was also to keep a watchful eye on all the movements of King Philip of Macedon. The praetor Publius Cornelius Lentulus was assigned Sicily as his area of responsibility, and Titus Otacilius was charged with the fleet that he had commanded against the Carthaginians the previous year.

There were many reports of prodigies that year, the number increasing as naive and superstitious people became more inclined to accept their validity. At Lanuvium ravens were said to have nested in the inner part of the temple of Juno Sospita. It was claimed that in Apulia a green palm tree had caught fire, and that in Mantua a pond formed by an overflow of the River Mincius appeared bloody. At Cales, a shower of chalk was reported and, in the Forum Boarium in Rome, one of blood. In the Vicus Insteius* a subterranean spring was said to have flowed with such violence that, almost like a torrent-stream, it knocked over and swept away jars and large storage casks in the area. Lightning was said to have struck the public hall on the Capitol, the temple of Vulcan in the Campus Martius, a citadel and a public road in Sabine territory, and the city wall and a gate at Gabii. Soon talk spread of other supernatural phenomena. At Praeneste, a spear of Mars purportedly moved forward of its own accord; a cow talked in Sicily; and amongst the Marrucini a baby still in its mother's womb cried out 'Io, triumphe!' At Spoletum, a woman turned into a man and, at Hadria, an altar was seen in the sky, with the forms of men dressed in white around it. Indeed, right in the city of Rome a swarm of bees was sighted, and afterwards some men called the citizens to arms claiming that they could see armed legions on the Janiculum, although the people on the Janiculum declared that no one had appeared there besides the hill's usual residents. There were atonement ceremonies for these prodigies, with full-sized victims in accordance with the seers' pronouncements, and an official order was given for a period of public prayer to be held for all the deities having couches in Rome.

11. When all had been done to conciliate the gods, the consuls raised with the Senate questions relating to the state, the conduct of the war, and the number and disposition of troops. A decision was taken that the war be waged with eighteen legions.* The consuls were each to take two for themselves, and Gaul, Sicily, and Sardinia were each to be secured with two. The praetor Quintus Fabius was to take charge of Apulia with two, and Tiberius Gracchus was to command his two of slave volunteers in the area of Luceria. Gaius Terentius, the proconsul, and Marcus Valerius were each to be left one legion, in the former case for Picenum, in the latter for naval operations in the area of Brundisium; and there were to be two legions for the defence of the city. To reach this number of legions, six new ones had to be raised. The consuls were instructed to raise these at the earliest possible moment, and also to assemble a fleet such that, with the vessels then at anchor defending the coastline of Calabria, the naval complement for the year would be a hundred and fifty warships. The mobilization completed, and a hundred new vessels launched, Quintus Fabius proceeded with the elections for the censorship. In these, Marcus Atilius Regulus and Publius Furius Philus were elected.

Rumours of war in Sicily were now on the increase, and Titus Otacilius was ordered to proceed there with his fleet. There was a shortage of sailors, however, and, in response to a senatorial decree, the consuls issued an edict on the matter. Any man who, in the censorship of Lucius Aemilius and Gaius Flaminius, had his own property, or that of his father, assessed at between 50,000 and 100,000 *asses* (or if it subsequently reached that level) was required to supply a single sailor, along with six months' pay. Anyone assessed above 100,000 and up to 300,000 was to supply three sailors, along with a year's pay. For assessment above 300,000 and up to a million, it was five sailors, and above a million it was seven. Senators were to supply eight sailors, with a year's pay. The sailors who were supplied in accordance with this edict were armed and equipped by their masters, and they boarded their ships with a thirty days' supply of cooked rations. That was the first occasion on which a Roman fleet was manned with crews raised from private funds.

12. Such extraordinary preparations particularly alarmed the Campanians, who feared that the Romans might commence the year's campaign by blockading Capua. Accordingly they sent a delegation to Hannibal to plead with him to move his army up to Capua. Fresh armies were being raised at Rome for the purpose of attacking the city, the delegates told him, and no city's defection had angered the Romans more than theirs. The panic with which they delivered the message made Hannibal think he should lose no time in case the Romans reached the city first. He set out from Arpi and moved into his old camp at Tifata, overlooking Capua. Leaving here his Numidians and Spaniards as protection for the camp, and at the same time for Capua, he went down with the rest of his army to Lake Avernus, ostensibly to offer sacrifice,* but really to launch an attack on Puteoli and whatever garrison was stationed there. Brought the report that Hannibal had left Arpi and was on his way back to Campania, Maximus returned to his army without stopping either by day or night. He then ordered Tiberius Gracchus to move his troops forward to Beneventum from Luceria, and instructed the praetor Quintus Fabius (son of the consul) to take over from Gracchus at Luceria.

Two praetors left for Sicily at the same time, Publius Cornelius to join the army, and Titus Otacilius to assume command of the littoral, and of naval operations. The other magistrates also left for their various spheres of command, and the men whose *imperium* was extended kept the same regions as they had the previous year.

13. When Hannibal was at Lake Avernus, five young nobles came to him from Tarentum. Some had been taken prisoner at Lake Trasimene, and some at Cannae, and they had been sent back to their homes with the usual courtesy that the Carthaginian had accorded all the allies of Rome. Remembering his kind treatment of them, they now reported to him that they had convinced most of the younger men of Tarentum to choose an alliance of friendship with Hannibal over one with the Roman people. They had been sent by their people as official representatives with a request to Hannibal that he move his army closer to Tarentum, they said. If his standards and his camp were sighted from Tarentum, the city would be put in

his hands without a moment's delay—the masses were controlled by the younger men of the town, and political power in Tarentum lay in the hands of the masses. Hannibal commended the young men, and showered them with lavish promises, telling them to return home to finalize their plans, and agreeing to come at the appropriate moment. Such were the hopes with which the Tarentines were sent on their way.

Hannibal had himself been overtaken by a keen desire to take possession of Tarentum. He could see that it was a rich and famous city, and also that it was on the coast and, conveniently, faced Macedonia. King Philip would head for this port if the Romans were in control of Brundisium when he crossed to Italy. Hannibal now performed the sacrifice for which he had come, and took advantage of his time in the area to pillage the territory of Cumae as far as the promontory of Misenum. He then abruptly turned his column towards Puteoli, his aim being to catch the Roman garrison off guard. The garrison comprised 6,000 men, their position strengthened by fortifications as well as natural defences. The Carthaginian spent three days at Puteoli, striking at the garrison from every side, but, achieving no success, he went forward to plunder the farmlands of Neapolis, more from rage than hope of taking the city.*

Hannibal's arrival in territory neighbouring theirs brought excitement to the common people of Nola, who had long been ill-disposed towards the Romans, and at odds with their own senate. So it was that an embassy came to Hannibal to invite him to the city, and giving him an explicit promise to surrender it. Their initiative was pre-empted by the consul Marcellus, who had been invited to Nola by its leading citizens. Marcellus had made the journey from Cales to Suessula in a single day, despite the delay occasioned by the crossing of the River Volturnus, and the following night had sent 6,000 infantry and 500 cavalry from Suessula into Nola for the senate's protection. And while all the measures for securing Nola ahead of his enemy were energetically carried out by the consul, Hannibal merely frittered away the time. After two prior attempts had come to nothing, he was less inclined to feel confidence in the people of Nola.

14. At the same time as this, the consul Quintus Fabius took the offensive against Casilinum, which was held by a Punic garrison. Also at this time, and almost as if they had arranged it, Hanno—he was at the head of a large infantry and cavalry force, and coming

from the Bruttii—advanced on Beneventum from one side, while Tiberius Gracchus approached it from the opposite direction, from Luceria. Gracchus entered the town first. He was then told that Hanno had encamped some three miles from the city at the River Calor, from which position he was raiding the farmlands. Gracchus, therefore, also left the city and pitched camp about a mile from the enemy. There he held an assembly of his men.

Gracchus had under his command legions for the most part made up of slave volunteers who, now in their second year, had preferred to earn their freedom quietly rather than openly demand it. Even so, on leaving winter quarters, he had noticed murmuring in the column, with some of these soldiers asking if the time would ever come when they would serve as free men. He had then written to the Senate to report not what the men wanted so much as what they had merited. To that day, he said, he had received loyal and stalwart service from them, and all they lacked to be exemplary regular soldiers was their freedom. Gracchus had then been given carte blanche by the Senate to take whatever action in the matter he deemed in the public interest. He therefore made a proclamation before he engaged the enemy, telling the men that the time had come for them to have the freedom for which they had long been hoping. The following day they would meet the enemy in pitched battle, he said, on a field that was clear and open, where the encounter could be decided on pure courage, with no fear of ambush. Any of them bringing back the head of an enemy he would immediately declare a free man, but anyone who gave ground he would punish as a slave—so each man's fate was in his own hands. He added that it was not only he who would be responsible for their liberation; the consul Marcus Marcellus and all the senators would be as well, inasmuch as he had consulted them, and they had granted him discretion regarding their freedom.

Gracchus then read aloud the consul's letter and the senatorial decree, which met with loud cheers of approval. The men demanded combat, vehemently insisting that Gracchus give the signal immediately. He proclaimed that the battle would take place the next day, and then broke up the assembly. The men were delighted, above all those who were going to have freedom as the pay of a single day's efforts, and they spent the remains of the day preparing their equipment.

15. These men, all ready and formed up, were the very first to

muster at the general's tent when the signals began to ring out the following day. At sunrise Gracchus led his forces into the line, and the enemy did not hesitate to take the field, either. The Punic force comprised 17,000 infantry, for the most part Bruttii and Lucanians, and 1,200 cavalry, which included a very small number of Italians, the rest being almost exclusively Numidians and Moors.

The fighting was long and fierce, and for four hours neither side had the upper hand. And nothing more impeded the Romans than the fact that the heads of the enemy had been made the price of liberty. The men all showed great spirit in dispatching an enemy, but the first thing they did after that was to waste time in the difficult task of severing the head in the confused mêlée. Then, their right hands fully employed holding the head, all the most intrepid gave up the fight, leaving the battle to the laggards and the faint-hearted. The military tribunes brought this news to Gracchus. The enemy, he was told, was no longer being dealt wounds while standing up, but was being butchered on the ground, and in his men's right hands there were human heads rather than swords. Gracchus promptly had the signal given for the men to throw down the heads and attack the enemy, saying that their courage was sufficiently clear and easy to see, and that these stouthearted men's freedom was not in doubt.

With that the fighting was renewed, and the cavalry were also unleashed against the enemy. These were stoutly opposed by the Numidians, and the cavalry engagement was no less fierce than that of the infantry, so that the issue was brought into doubt once more. On both sides the commanders were hurling abuse, the Roman at the Bruttii and Lucanians who, he said, had so often been defeated and crushed by his ancestors, and the Carthaginian at what he called 'Roman slaves' and 'chain-gang soldiers'. Finally Gracchus proclaimed that his men had absolutely no hope of freedom unless the enemy were on that day scattered and put to flight.

16. It was this pronouncement that finally fired their hearts to raise the war cry again and, suddenly transformed into new men, to charge the enemy with such force that there was no longer any question of resistance. First the Carthaginians before the standards were thrown into confusion, and then those at the standards; and finally the whole army was driven back. At that point they quite clearly gave up the fight. In full flight they rushed back into their camp in such panic and alarm that there was no stopping even at the

gates or the rampart. The Romans followed, almost making a single column with them, and started a fresh engagement within the confines of the enemy rampart. There, with the fighting restricted within the cramped space, the slaughter was all the more horrific.

There was help from the prisoners in the camp, too. They seized weapons in the pandemonium, and massed together, slashing at the Carthaginians from behind and impeding their escape. The result was that, from such a massive army, fewer than 2,000 men succeeded in escaping (and most of these were cavalry), the leader himself being one. All the others were either killed or taken prisoner, and thirty-eight military standards were captured. Of the victors some 2,000 fell in the battle. All the booty, apart from the prisoners, was turned over to the men, and an exception was also made of livestock identified by their owners within thirty days of the battle.

The Romans returned to camp weighed down with booty. Then, fearing punishment, some 4,000 slave volunteers who had fought half-heartedly, and not charged the enemy camp with the others, seized a hill adjacent to their camp. The next day they were brought down by military tribunes, and they appeared at a meeting of the troops convened by Gracchus. Here the proconsul first of all presented the veterans with military rewards, according to the valour each had shown, and the part he had played in the battle. Then he declared that, in the case of the slave volunteers, he preferred all to receive commendations from him, whether they deserved it or not, rather than that any individual be punished that day, and, with a prayer that the act prove to be auspicious, fortunate, and advantageous for the state, as well as the recipients, he declared them all free men. The pronouncement was met with enthusiastic cheers, and at one moment the men hugged and congratulated each other, and at the next raised their hands to the sky and prayed that all manner of blessings befall the Roman people and Gracchus himself.

'Before I made you all equals by conferring on you the right of liberty,' Gracchus then said, 'I did not want to brand any individual either as a valiant or as a cowardly soldier. Now my official oath to you has been fulfilled, and I do not wish to see the distinction between courage and cowardice entirely lost. I shall therefore have brought to me the names of those men who, conscious of shirking the fight, recently parted company with us. I shall summon them individually, and make them swear an oath that, those with the plea of ill-health excepted, they will take their food and drink in a standing position only, for as long as their service shall last. This penalty you will accept with equanimity if you take into account that no mark of disgrace imposed on you for your cowardice could have been slighter.'

Gracchus then gave the signal to pack up, and the soldiers, carrying or driving along their booty, returned with jokes and merriment to Beneventum. So high were their spirits that they gave the impression of returning not from the battlefield, but from a banquet on some great festal day. The people of Beneventum all came streaming out in a crowd to meet them at the gates. They hugged the soldiers, congratulated them, and offered them hospitality. Dinners had been made ready in the forecourts of their houses by all the citizens; and to these they invited the soldiers, begging Gracchus to give his men permission to join the feast. Gracchus did indeed grant his permission, but on condition that everyone eat in public, all the hosts before their own doors. Everything was then brought out. The slave volunteers dined wearing caps, or had fillets of white wool on their heads. Some were reclining and others standing, the latter serving food and eating at the same time. The event seemed worthy of a picture, and so on his return to Rome Gracchus had a painting of that festive day* made in the temple of Liberty which his father had had constructed and had dedicated on the Aventine.

17. While this was taking place at Beneventum, Hannibal, after his depredations in the countryside of Neapolis, moved his camp to Nola. When he discovered that Hannibal was approaching, the consul sent for the propraetor Pomponius* and the army that was encamped above Suessula, and prepared to meet the enemy and engage him without delay. In the dead of night, and by the gate situated at the furthest point from the enemy, he sent out Gaius Claudius Nero with the pick of his cavalry. Nero was ordered to make a furtive detour around the enemy, cautiously follow his column, and, when he saw the battle had begun, attack him from the rear. He was unable to carry out this order; whether he lost his way or was short of time is unclear.

Battle was joined in Nero's absence, and the Romans quite clearly were on top. But because the cavalry were not there on time, the strategy for the operation was thwarted. Marcellus had not the nerve to pursue the retreating Carthaginians, and he gave his men, triumphant though they were, the signal to fall back. Even so the enemy reportedly suffered more than 2,000 casualties that day, and the Romans fewer than 400. It was about sunset that Nero returned, without having even caught sight of the enemy, his horses and men uselessly exhausted after a march that lasted a day and a night. He was given a severe reprimand by the consul;* it was thanks to him, said Marcellus, that the enemy were not being repaid with a defeat such as the Romans had suffered at Cannae.

The next day the Romans went out to battle stations, and the Carthaginians, with a tacit admission of defeat, stuck to their camp. On the third day, abandoning all hope of taking Nola, where he had never had success, Hannibal set off in the dead of night for Tarentum, which offered better prospects of a treacherous surrender.

18. The workings of government were as vigorous at home as they were in the field. Because of the insolvency of the treasury, the censors were freed from the contracting out of public works, and they turned their attention to regulating morality and chastening the vices that had arisen from that war, like the maladies ailing bodies produce as the result of chronic sickness. The first people they arraigned were those who were said <to have planned to desert the republic after the battle of > Cannae. Their leader, Marcus Caecilius Metellus, happened to be a quaestor at that particular time. He and the other people accused of the same offence were ordered to present their case, but were unable to clear themselves. The censors declared them guilty of making statements and holding conversations injurious to the state, with the intention of forming a conspiracy to abandon Italy. The men brought up after these were those who had been too clever in judging their oath fulfilled—those Roman prisoners who had secretly gone back to Hannibal's camp after leaving it, and thought they had thus discharged their sworn undertaking to return. Members of this and the former group who possessed public horses had them confiscated, and they were also removed from their tribe and given the status of poll-tax payers.

The attention of the censors was not limited to measures for the Senate or equestrian order, either. They extracted from the registers of military-aged men the names of all those who had not served in four years but had no official exemption from service or plea of ill-health. More than 2,000 such names were found;* the men were reduced to the status of poll-tax payers and all banished from their tribes. To this harsh demotion inflicted by the censors was added a stern decree of the Senate to the effect that all whom the censors had dishonoured must do military service on foot and be sent to Sicily to join the remnants of the army that had fought at Cannae. This class of soldier's period of service was not to end until the enemy had been driven from Italy.

Because of the shortages in the treasury, the censors were now holding back from contracting out the upkeep of temples, the provision of horses for ceremonial occasions, and other such services, and they were approached by large numbers of people who had routinely tendered for such contracts. They urged the censors to carry on and put out the contracts, just as if there were money in the treasury. None of them would seek payment from the public purse until the war was brought to an end, they said. Next to approach the censors were the owners of the slaves whom Tiberius Sempronius had freed at Beneventum. These said that they had been summoned by the three directors of the exchequer to be compensated for the slaves, but that they would not take the compensation until the war was over. In this atmosphere of public willingness to sustain the insolvent treasury, the moneys held in trust first for orphans, and then for husbandless women, also began to be deposited there. Those making the deposits felt that their money would nowhere be more securely deposited, or for a nobler cause, than under state warranty. After that any purchase or provision made for orphans or husbandless women was made by a requisition from a quaestor. This generosity shown by private individuals also spread from the civil to the military sector. No cavalryman and no centurion would accept his pay, and anyone who did accept was insultingly dubbed a mercenary.

19. The consul Quintus Fabius was encamped at Casilinum, which was garrisoned by a force of 2,000 Campanians and 700 of Hannibal's soldiers. The garrison commander was Statius Mettius, who had been sent to the town by that year's *medix tuticus*, Gnaeus Magius Atellanus. Mettius had been indiscriminately arming slaves and the common people in order to launch an attack on the Roman camp while the consul was absorbed with blockading the town.

None of this eluded Fabius. He sent a message to his colleague at Nola to tell him that he needed a second army to face the Campanians, while Casilinum was under siege. He suggested that Marcellus leave a small garrison at Nola and come himself; otherwise, if the situation at Nola required the consul's presence and Hannibal still posed a threat, he would ask the proconsul Tiberius Gracchus to come from Beneventum. On receiving this message, Marcellus left 2,000 men to defend Nola, and came to Casilinum with the rest of his army. The Campanians were already mobilizing, but on his arrival they stopped, and the siege of Casilinum began under two consuls.

Incautiously approaching the walls, the Roman soldiers began to sustain injuries on a large scale, and the effort was not going well. Fabius therefore suggested that they drop the operation—it was a minor one, he said, but just as difficult as important ones—and leave the area. For, he declared, there were greater challenges around the corner. Marcellus replied that there were, indeed, many operations that great commanders should not undertake, but, once they had been undertaken, they should not be abandoned, since they became very important for one's reputation, whichever way they went. With this argument Marcellus won Fabius' agreement not to abandon the attempt and leave.

Siege-sheds and all other sorts of structures and equipment were then moved into place, and the Campanians proceeded to implore Fabius to let them leave for Capua in safety. A few had come out when Marcellus seized the gate by which they were leaving, and indiscriminate slaughter began—of all in the vicinity of the gate in the first place, and then, after Marcellus' men burst in, of those within the city as well. About fifty of the Campanians who had been the first to come out sought refuge with Fabius and reached Capua with an escort provided by him. During the parleying, and time spent in appeals for protection, an opportunity appeared, and Casilinum was taken. Prisoners who were Campanians, or soldiers of Hannibal, were transferred to Rome and incarcerated; the majority of the townspeople were distributed amongst the neighbouring peoples to be kept under guard.

20. At the time of the withdrawal from Casilinum after this successful operation, Gracchus was in Lucania. There he sent out a number of locally conscripted cohorts, under the command of an allied prefect, to conduct raids on the enemy's farmland. Hanno fell on these as they wandered about in disorder, and repaid his enemy with a defeat not much less serious than he had himself received at Beneventum. He then fell back quickly to Bruttium so that Gracchus would not overtake him. As for the consuls, Marcellus returned to Nola, whence he had come, and Fabius pushed ahead into Samnite territory to plunder farmland and to recover by force of arms the cities that had defected. The Samnites of Caudium especially suffered in the raids, with fields burned far and wide, and livestock and people driven off as plunder. Towns taken by force in the area were Conpulteria, Telesia, and Compsa, as well as Fugifulae and Orbitanium in Lucania; and Blanda and the Apulian town of Aecae were also blockaded. Twenty-five thousand of the enemy in these cities were taken prisoner or killed, and 370 deserters were recovered. The consul despatched the deserters to Rome, and there they were all flogged in the Comitium, and hurled down from the rock.*

Such were Fabius' achievements in just a few days. Marcellus, however, was detained at Nola by an illness that kept him out of action. During that period, too, the town of Acuca was taken by storm, and a permanent camp established at Ardaneae, by the praetor Quintus Fabius, who was responsible for the area around Luceria.

While these Roman operations were under way in various locations, Hannibal had reached Tarentum, causing enormous devastation wherever his path had taken him. Only on reaching Tarentine territory did his column begin to move forward in a peaceable manner. No damage was done in the area, and there was no leaving the line of march; and this was evidently not restraint on the part of the men or their leader, but an attempt to win the support of the people of Tarentum. When Hannibal approached the city walls, however, the initial sight of his column did not, to his surprise, bring any reaction, and he encamped about a mile from the city. In fact, Marcus Livius had earlier been sent to Tarentum by the propraetor Marcus Valerius, commander of the fleet at Brundisium. Three days before Hannibal approached the walls, Livius had taken great pains to draft young men and deploy guards at all the gates, as circumstances required. Equally vigilant by night and by day, he gave neither the enemy nor unreliable allies any opportunity to make a move.

Hannibal consequently spent a number of days at Tarentum to no purpose. Then, when none of the people who had come to him at Lake Avernus appeared in person, or sent him any communiqué or letter, he became aware that he had wasted his time following up idle promises, and he struck camp. Even at that point he left the lands of Tarentum intact; although his fake clemency had, as yet, gained him nothing, he still did not abandon hope of undermining Tarentine loyalty. On reaching Salapia, he gathered in grain from the surrounding areas of Metapontum and Heraclea, for summer was now finished, and he fancied the area as a location for winter quarters. From there, Numidians and Moors were sent on predatory raids throughout the territory of the Sallentini and the grazing lands bordering Apulia. Herds of horses were driven off—and not much else in the way of plunder—and of these some 4,000 were distributed amongst the cavalry to be broken in.

21. A war not to be ignored was now on the horizon in Sicily, where the upshot of the tyrant's death had been to provide the Sicilians with enterprising commanders rather than to change their circumstances or their sentiments. The Romans therefore assigned this sphere of responsibility to one of the consuls, Marcus Marcellus.

The assassination of Hieronymus had been immediately followed by unrest amongst the troops in Leontini, and there had been furious demands for the blood of the conspirators in atonement for their king's death. Then the sweet-sounding expression 'liberty restored' came into circulation; hopes arose of largesse from the tyrant's money and of military service under more able officers; and there were reports of the tyrant's repulsive crimes, and even more repulsive sexual practices. This so transformed sentiments that they left the corpse of their recently regretted monarch to lie unburied.

While the other conspirators stayed behind to keep the army in check, Theodotus and Sosis took the king's horses and hurried to Syracuse with all the speed they could muster. They hoped to catch the tyrant's supporters while they were unaware of all that had transpired. But they had been outrun not only by rumour, whose speed is unbeatable in such situations, but also by one of the palace slaves, who had arrived with the news. As a result, Adranodorus had secured the Island with armed guards,* and the citadel, too, and any other points that he could strengthen and which seemed likely targets. The sun had set and dusk already fallen when Theodotus and Sosis rode into the city by way of the Hexapylon. They produced the monarch's bloodstained robe and diadem, rode through Tycha, and, summoning the people to seize their liberty and weapons at the same time, called for an assembly in Achradina.

Some of the people now rushed out into the streets; some stood in their doorways; others looked from roofs or windows, asking what was going on. Everywhere there was a blaze of lights and a confused and noisy uproar. Armed men grouped together in the open spaces; those without arms took down from the temple of Olympian Jupiter the spoils of the Gauls and Illyrians, gifts made to Hiero by the Roman people and hung there by the king. They asked Jupiter in prayer to lend his sacred arms with his grace and favour to men arming themselves to defend their country, the shrines of the gods and their freedom. This whole crowd then joined the guards deployed at the key points of the city.

On the Island, Adranodorus had secured numerous points, including the public granaries. The area, which was surrounded by a wall of dressed stones and fortified like a citadel, was seized by some soldiers who were posted there to defend it. These then sent messengers into Achradina to report that the granaries, and the grain in them, were now under senatorial control.

22. At dawn the whole people, armed and unarmed alike, gathered at the senate house in Achradina. There, in front of the altar of Concord situated in the locality, one of the leading citizens, whose name was Polyaenus, gave a speech that was at once forthright and yet restrained in tone.

Men, he said, had been provoked to oppose a curse that, from their own experience of the degradation and humiliation of slavery, they knew very well—but the disastrous consequences of civil conflict Syracusans had heard about from their fathers, rather than seen themselves. He commended them for their alacrity in taking up arms, he continued, but would commend them even more if they used them only as a last resort. For the moment he was of the view that spokesmen should be sent to Adranodorus to order him to accept the authority of the senate and people, to open the gates of the Island, and surrender his garrison. Adranodorus was holding a throne in keeping for another, he concluded, and if his aim was to turn that into a throne for himself, then he, Polyaenus, also thought that they should reclaim their freedom from Adranodorus with much greater vigour than they had from Hieronymus.

After this harangue the spokesmen were sent on their mission, and a meeting of the senate began. The senate had remained the deliberative body of the people during Hiero's reign, but after his death had not, until that day, been convened or consulted on any matter whatsoever. When the spokesmen came to Adranodorus, he was indeed impressed by the harmony amongst his fellow citizens, and also by the fact that various parts of the city, including the most strongly fortified section of the Island, had been betrayed and taken out of his hands. But his wife Damarata, a daughter of Hiero, had still the pride of royalty combined with the wilfulness of a woman, and she called him away from the spokesmen and reminded him of the words often uttered by the tyrant Dionysius. A man should leave the tyranny, Dionysius had said, dragged by the heels, not mounted on a horse. It was easy to renounce, whenever one chose, a great fortune within one's possession, said Damarata; creating and acquiring it was the difficult and arduous task. Adranodorus should gain time from the spokesmen to think things over, she said, and use that time to bring in soldiers from Leontini. If he promised these men the money left by the tyrant, he would have everything under his control.

Such was the woman's advice, and Adranodorus did not reject it outright, nor did he immediately accept it, for he felt the more secure road to power lay in accepting circumstances for the time being. He therefore told the spokesmen to report that he would accept the authority of the senate and people.

At dawn the next day, Adranodorus threw open the gates of the Island and came into the forum of Achradina. There he went up to the altar of Concord, from which Polyaenus had delivered his address the day before, and proceeded to deliver a speech, which he began by requesting forgiveness for his hesitation. He had kept the gates closed, he explained, not to separate his private interests from those of the state, but because he was afraid of where the killing would end, once swords had been drawn. He had been wondering whether they would be satisfied with the tyrant's death, which sufficed to give them liberty, or whether all connected to the palace by ties of blood or marriage, or any administrative posts within it, would also be slaughtered, being blamed for the guilt of another. But he then realized that those who had freed their country also wanted to keep her free, and that it was the common good that was in the minds of all. At that point, he said, he had not hesitated to restore to the fatherland his own person, and everything in his care and protection, since the man who had entrusted them to him had been destroyed by his own lunacy. Adranodorus then turned to the tyrant's killers and, calling on Theodotus and Sosis by name, said: 'Yours was a memorable exploit but, believe me, your days of glory have just begun—they are not yet over! There remains a great danger that we may see the burial of this newly liberated state, unless you take steps to ensure peace and concord.'

23. After this speech Adranodorus set the keys of the gates and the tyrant's treasury at their feet, and, on that day at least, at the conclusion of the assembly, the people happily visited all the temples of the gods with their wives and children to give thanks. The next day elections were held for the appointment of praetors.* Amongst the first elected was Adranodorus, and the others were mostly men who had been responsible for the tyrant's assassination. Two— Sopater and Dinomenes—they even elected *in absentia*. When these two heard of the developments in Syracuse, they brought to the city the money in Leontini that had belonged to the tyrant, and turned it over to quaestors expressly appointed to handle it. The money in the Island was also transferred to Achradina. Further, with everyone's agreement, that section of the wall that provided too great a barrier between the Island and the rest of the city was demolished. The other measures taken were also in accord with this general tendency towards liberty.

When word of the tyrant's death got out, notwithstanding Hippocrates' attempts to conceal it (he had gone so far as to kill the messenger), Hippocrates and Epicydes were deserted by their men. They then took what seemed to be the safest course in the circumstances, and returned to Syracuse. But they did not want their presence there to be seen as an attempt to destabilize the situation, and so they first approached the praetors and then, through them, the senate. They declared that they had been sent by Hannibal to Hieronymus, who was Hannibal's friend and ally; and they had simply obeyed the man whom their own commander wanted them to obey. They wished now to return to Hannibal, they said, but the way was not safe, as there were Romans circulating throughout Sicily. They were therefore requesting an escort of some kind, so they could be conducted to Locri in Italy; for this small service, the Syracusans would find Hannibal very appreciative.

The request was willingly granted. The authorities wanted them gone, for they had been officers of the tyrant, and they were also accomplished soldiers, and at the same time needy and reckless men. But the senators failed to put their wishes into effect as promptly as they should have. The young men had military backgrounds and

were used to soldiers, and in the meantime they talked—sometimes
to the soldiers themselves, at other times to the deserters (most of
them from the Roman naval crews), and then even to the dregs of the
common people—denouncing the senate and the nobility. There was
a secret agenda, they claimed, a plan to have Syracuse under Roman
domination under the pretext of re-establishing the alliance. Then a
faction would take power, they said, one made up of a few supporters
of the renewed treaty.

24. People ready to hear and believe such charges began to flood
into Syracuse in greater numbers every day, raising hopes of a coup
not only in Epicydes, but in Adranodorus as well. Adranodorus had
finally bowed to his wife's admonitions. The time was now ripe for
seizing power, she told him, while the total chaos of the new and
unregulated freedom still reigned, while the soldiers were going
about fattened on the tyrant's money, and while the officers sent by
Hannibal, who were used to soldiers, could help the enterprise.
Adranodorus therefore entered into partnership with Themistus,
who was married to a daughter of Gelo. A few days later, however, he
indiscreetly revealed the plot to a certain Aristo, a tragic actor to
whom he had regularly entrusted other confidences. Aristo's family
and social standing were respectable, and not tarnished by his profession, as that sort of employment is not dishonourable in Greek
society.* Thinking the loyalty he owed his country had priority,
Aristo brought his information before the praetors; and they discovered, on the basis of incontrovertible evidence, that it was no idle
tale he was telling. They therefore consulted the elder senators and,
on their authority, posted a guard at the doors of the senate house,
and had Themistus and Adranodorus killed when they entered.

Uproar followed this act which, since the others present were
ignorant of the facts, appeared particularly monstrous, but when
silence was obtained the praetors brought the informer into the
senate. Aristo gave a step-by-step account of the whole affair.
The conspiracy originated with the marriage of Gelo's daughter
Harmonia to Themistus, he said. Then African and Spanish auxiliaries were mobilized to kill the praetors and other leaders of the
community, the assassins being promised the property of the victims
as their reward. A band of mercenaries who were normally under
Adranodorus' orders had been poised to retake the Island. Aristo
then gave a detailed picture of what was to be done, and by whom,

and of a conspiracy planned to the last detail in terms of manpower and weapons. To the senate it did indeed seem that the men deserved their death as much as Hieronymus. In front of the senate house, however, shouts were rising from a crowd with divided loyalties, and little grasp of the facts. These people were uttering strident threats, but the bodies of the conspirators at the entrance of the house checked them, and frightened them so much that they silently followed the more sober members of the commons to the assembly. Sopater was given the task of addressing them by the senate, and by his colleagues.

25. Sopater launched into what seemed like a formal prosecution, beginning with Adranodorus', and Themistus' past record, and then attributing to them every heinous and wanton act that had followed the death of Hiero. For what could Hieronymus have done on his own, he asked—he was just a boy, barely a teenager! It was his guardians and teachers who had been ruling, while another faced the unpopularity! And so it was right for them to die—either before Hieronymus or at least with him. But, destined then to die a death they richly deserved, they had actually gone on to plot new crimes after the tyrant was killed! They had done it openly at first, he said; Adranodorus had closed the gates of the Island, and taken the kingdom as his inheritance, assuming the ownership of what he had held in trust. But then he had been let down by the men who were in the Island, and found himself blockaded by all the citizens holding Achradina. His open and undisguised attempt to acquire the throne a failure, he now tried to gain it by stealth and trickery. Even when he was elected praetor along with the country's liberators, though himself a traitor to the cause of freedom—even this promotion and honour could not hold him back! In fact, Sopater explained, these men's tyrannical disposition came from having wives from tyrant families, one being married to Hiero's daughter, the other to Gelo's.

At these words the cry arose from all parts of the meeting that neither of the women should live, and nobody of the tyrants' line should survive. Such is the nature of the crowd—it is either abjectly submissive or ruthlessly domineering. The independence that lies between these two extremes it cannot assume, or wield, with moderation and, when men have an inordinate lust for punishment, rarely are there lacking others to indulge and feed their anger and incite them to bloodshed and murder. So it was on that occasion. The praetors immediately proposed a motion—and it was approved almost before it was proposed—that all of royal descent be executed. Agents sent by the praetors then put to death Damarata, daughter of Hiero, and Harmonia, daughter of Gelo, the wives of Adranodorus and Themistus.

26. Heraclia was also a daughter of Hiero. She was the wife of Zoippus who had been sent by Hieronymus as an ambassador to King Ptolemy, and had decided on voluntary exile for himself. When Heraclia learned in advance that men were coming for her, too, she took her two unmarried daughters with her and sought refuge in a shrine before her tutelary gods, her hair dishevelled, and her appearance generally pitiful. She further added her entreaties, invoking the gods one moment and the memory of her father Hiero, and brother Gelo, the next. She was innocent, she declared, and the men should not let her burn in flames of hatred felt for Hieronymus. She had gained nothing but her husband's exile from Hieronymus' reign; she had not enjoyed the same fortune as her sister in Hieronymus' lifetime, and her case was not the same as hers now that he was dead, either. If Adranodorus' plans had come off, she said, then her sister would have shared the rule with her husband, and she, like everyone else, would have had to obey them. If someone should report to Zoippus that Hieronymus had been killed, and Syracuse liberated, she added, it was perfectly clear that he would immediately board ship, and return home. How human hopes are frustrated, she exclaimed! Zoippus' native land had now been liberated, and yet, within it, his wife and children were fighting for their lives—and what kind of obstruction to liberty and the rule of law were they? What risk was she to anyone, a woman alone and virtually a widow, or her girls, who were living as orphans? Ah, but perhaps it would be said that, while there was no danger to be feared from her, the line of the tyrants was nevertheless hated. In that case, she said, they should banish her and her daughters far from Syracuse and Sicily—order them transported to Alexandria, the wife to her husband, the daughters to their father!

Ears and hearts were turned from her.† The men shouted to her not to waste their time† and she saw some of them drawing their swords. She gave up entreaties for herself and started begging them at least to spare the girls—they were of an age even a furious enemy would not touch, she said, and in taking their revenge on tyrants

they should not repeat the crimes they themselves found abominable. As she said this, they dragged her from the sanctuary and slit
her throat. They then turned on the girls, now spattered with their
mother's blood. Hysterical with grief and terror, the girls dashed
from the shrine as though gripped by frenzy, and with such speed
that, had it been possible for them to get out into the street, they
would have raised pandemonium throughout the city. Even as it was,
within the narrow confines of the house, and with armed men all
around, they more than once escaped unharmed and, despite con-
tending with hands so many and so strong, tore themselves from the
assassins' clutches. Finally, exhausted from wounds and having
covered everything with their blood, they fell lifeless to the ground.*

The killing was tragic in itself but was rendered more tragic by
the arrival of a message, shortly afterwards, cancelling the execution—there had been a sudden change of heart and softening of
feelings. Then, after pity, came anger over their haste to inflict punishment, without leaving themselves any leeway to reconsider or let
passions cool. And so the crowd grumbled, and demanded an election to replace Adranodorus and Themistus (for both had been praetors), an election that was certainly not going to be to the praetors'
liking.

27. An election day was scheduled. On that day, to everyone's
surprise, one individual right at the back of the crowd nominated
Epicydes, and then another nominated Hippocrates. After that,
voices supporting these men increased, clearly with the approval of
the crowd. The gathering was, in fact, made up of diverse elements,
comprising not only citizens but soldiers as well, many of them
deserters with an agenda for radical change. The praetors at first
pretended not to notice, and tried to drag out the proceedings, but
finally, overwhelmed by the solidarity of feeling and fearing a riot,
they declared the two men praetors.

The two did not disclose their intentions as soon as they were
elected, unhappy though they were that delegates had gone to Appius
Claudius to request a ten-day truce, and that, when the truce was
granted, others had been sent to discuss renewing the old treaty. At
the time, the Romans had a fleet of a hundred vessels off Murgantia,
and there they waited to see how the unrest in Syracuse following the
assassination of the ruling family would turn out, and where the
people would be taken by their new and unfamiliar freedom.

In the meantime, the Syracusan delegates had been sent on to Marcellus, on his landing in Sicily, by Appius. After hearing their peace proposals, Marcellus felt some agreement was possible, and he dispatched his own delegates to Syracuse to discuss the renewal of the treaty face-to-face with the praetors. And by this time there was nothing like the earlier calm and tranquillity in the city. A report of the arrival of a Carthaginian fleet off Pachynum relieved Hippocrates and Epicydes of their fears, and they had been making allegations to the mercenaries, and then the deserters, that Syracuse was being betrayed to the Romans. And indeed when Appius began to keep some ships stationed at the harbour mouth, in order to raise the morale of the supporters of the faction he favoured, these groundless charges had apparently been given weighty corroboration. At first, in fact, a crowd had rushed wildly down to the shore to check the Romans if they tried to land.

28. In the midst of this chaos it was decided that a popular assembly should be held. Here there was some difference of opinion, and a riot was imminent, when one of the leading citizens, Apollonides, made what was, in the circumstances, a salutary address. No state, he said, had ever come closer either to realizing its hope for security or to being destroyed. For, he explained, if they were all in agreement in favouring *either* the Romans *or* the Carthaginians, then no state would be in a more fortunate or favourable position. If, however, they pulled in different directions, then the war between Carthage and Rome would be no more bloody than the war the Syracusans would fight amongst themselves, since, in this war, each side would have its own armies, its own weapons, and its own commanders within the very same walls. Accordingly, said Apollonides, they must do their utmost to achieve unanimity. The issue of which alliance was more advantageous to them was secondary, and of much less significance. However, he added, in choosing allies, one would do better to follow the judgement of Hiero rather than that of Hieronymus—or, rather, to prefer a friendship with which they had been happy over fifty years to one that was now unfamiliar to them, and which in the past had been unreliable. There was also another factor of some importance to their deliberations, he said. The Carthaginians could be refused a peace treaty without that necessarily entailing immediate war with them; with the Romans they must immediately have either war or peace.

The speech carried all the more weight for its apparent lack of self-interest and partisanship. The praetors and a select body of senators were joined by a committee of military advisers, and the commanders of army units and prefects of the auxiliaries were also instructed to take part in their discussions. The issue was frequently and hotly debated. As it became clear that there was no way in which they could conduct a war against the Romans, they finally decided that peace should be made with them, and that an embassy be sent to conclude it.

29. Not many days passed before ambassadors from Leontini came with a plea for help in defending their territory, and this embassy seemed to provide a welcome opportunity to unburden the city of a crowd of unruly subversives and remove their leaders. The praetor Hippocrates was instructed to take the deserters to Leontini, and a large contingent of mercenary auxiliaries went with them, bringing the number of soldiers to 4,000. Those doing the sending and those being sent were both well pleased with the mission, one group having been granted its long-desired opportunity of fomenting revolution, and the other being delighted with the siphoning off of what it perceived as the scum of the city. But it was only temporary relief that they brought to this sick body, which would soon relapse into a more severe disease.

This was because Hippocrates began to plunder lands lying next to the area of Roman control. He did so with stealthy raids at first, but later, when military aid was sent by Appius to defend the fields of the Roman allies, he launched a full-scale attack on a guard-post that opposed him, causing heavy casualties.

When this was reported to Marcellus, he immediately sent delegates to Syracuse to say that the peace guaranteed by the Syracusans had been broken, and that a motive for war would never be lacking unless Hippocrates and Epicydes were sent far away, not just from Syracuse, but from the whole of Sicily. Epicydes feared that, while he remained in Syracuse, he might be charged with his absent brother's crime, or that he might fail there to do his part in fomenting the war, and so he, too, left for Leontini. He could see that the citizens of Leontini were already sufficiently incensed with the Roman people, and he began trying to detach them from the Syracusans, as well. The basis of the peace treaty that the Syracusans had struck with the Romans, he told them, was that the peoples formerly ruled by the tyrants would now also be under Syracusan authority. The

Syracusans were no longer satisfied with their own freedom unless they also had power and dominion over others, he said. So they should be formally notified that the people of Leontini felt that they, too, should be free—whether because it was on the soil of their city that the tyrant was killed, or because it was there that the call for liberty first went up, when people deserted the tyrant's captains and came running to Syracuse. And so, concluded Epicydes, that clause had to be removed from the treaty, or else the people of Leontini should reject a treaty that was so worded.

The masses were easily persuaded, and when the Syracusan delegates protested over the killing of the Roman guards, and demanded that Hippocrates and Epicydes leave for Locri—or for any other location more to their liking, provided they left Sicily—they received a truculent reply. They had not entrusted to the Syracusans the responsibility of making peace with the Romans on their behalf, the people of Leontini told them, and they were not bound by treaties that others had made. The Syracusans reported this to the Romans, adding that Leontini was not under their control. Accordingly, they said, the Romans could go to war with that city without breaking their treaty with Syracuse, and the Syracusans would not stay out of the war, either, provided that the people of Leontini became subject to them once more when they were defeated, as the peace treaty provided.

30. Marcellus set out for Leontini with his entire army, summoning Appius to attack the town from the other direction. Such was the fervour that he found in his men, who were incensed at the killing of the guards during peace negotiations, that they took the city at the first assault. When Hippocrates and Epicydes saw the walls being taken, and the gates smashed in, they retreated to the citadel with a few men, and then secretly made good their escape to Herbesus under cover of night.

The Syracusans had now left home in a column of 8,000 men, and at the River Mylas a messenger met them with the news of the city's capture. The rest of the report, however, was a tissue of lies containing strands of truth. There had been an indiscriminate massacre of soldiers and townspeople, said the messenger, and he thought no adult had survived; and the town had been sacked, the property of the wealthy being given to the troops. The appalling news brought the column to a halt. There was alarm throughout the ranks, and the leaders (they were Sosis and Dinomenes) discussed what action they should take. The fact that deserters—some 2,000 men—had been flogged and decapitated bolstered the lies, adding plausible grounds for fear. In fact, however, none of the people of Leontini, and none of the other soldiers, had been harmed after the city was captured; and property had been returned in full, apart from what was lost in the initial chaos immediately following the capture. The Syracusan soldiers protested that their comrades had been betrayed and put to death, and they could not be constrained either to continue to Leontini or to wait on the spot for more reliable information. The praetors could see they were verging on mutiny, but saw, too, that the agitation would be short-lived if the men responsible for such idiocy were removed, and so they led the army to Megara. They then set off themselves to Herbesus with a few cavalrymen, hoping that, in the general panic, they could take possession of the town through treachery.

This proved a fruitless undertaking, and they felt they should use force. The following day they moved camp from Megara, intending to mount an all-out attack on Herbesus. Hippocrates and Epicydes now decided to put themselves in the hands of their soldiers, who for the most part knew them well and were, at that moment, incensed over the report of the massacre of their comrades. At first sight this course did not seem very safe, but with hopes dashed on every side they thought it was the only one possible, and so they went out to meet the column. As it happened, at the head of the column were 600 Cretans who had served under the two men in Hieronymus' army, and who were obliged to Hannibal for releasing them after they were taken prisoner, along with other Roman auxiliary troops, at Trasimene. When Hippocrates and Epicydes recognized them by their standards and the style of their armour, they held out olive branches and other symbols of supplication, begging them to receive and protect them, and not surrender them to the Syracusans. For, they said, the latter would soon deliver them to the Roman people to be put to the sword.

31. The Cretans, in fact, loudly encouraged them to take heart; they would share with them whatever fortune had in store, they said. During this exchange, the standards had come to a halt and the column was held up, but the reason for the delay had not yet reached the commanders. Word then spread through the ranks

that Hippocrates and Epicydes were there, and there was a buzz of evident approval over their arrival throughout the column, prompting the praetors to gallop immediately to the head of line. What sort of conduct was this, they asked. What was this slipshod behaviour of the Cretans—engaging the enemy in conversation, and bringing them into the column without an order from their praetors! They then ordered Hippocrates arrested and clapped in irons. When the order was given, there was such a deafening outcry—initially from the Cretans, but then taken up by others—that it was quite clear that, if the praetors took the matter any further, they would have to fear for their own safety. Perturbed and unsure how to handle the situation, they ordered a withdrawal to Megara, their point of departure, and sent messengers to Syracuse to report their current plight.

At this moment, when everything was regarded with suspicion, Hippocrates also came up with a piece of trickery. He sent a number of Cretans to keep watch on the roads, and then read out a letter that he claimed to have intercepted, but which was really his own composition. Headed 'From the praetors of Syracuse to the consul Marcellus', it declared, after the formula of salutation, that the consul's action in sparing nobody in Leontini had been right and proper. But, the letter continued, the case was the same for all the mercenary troops, and there would never be peace in Syracuse as long as any foreign auxiliaries remained in either the city or the army. Marcellus should therefore take steps to bring under his authority the men encamped with the praetors at Megara, and he should free Syracuse once and for all by executing them.

After the letter was read out, there was a rush to arms with such an uproar that the praetors, panic-stricken, took advantage of the confusion and rode off to Syracuse. Even their flight failed to stem the mutiny, however, and attacks began to be made on the Syracusan soldiers, none of whom would have been spared had not Epicydes and Hippocrates stood up to the furious mob. (Not that they felt any compassion or pity for them; it was simply not to curtail their own hopes of return. For they could gain the soldiers' loyalty while they also kept them as hostages, and they could, furthermore, secure the support of their relatives and friends, first by the service they had rendered, and then by using the men as security.) Experience had also shown them how the crowd could be swayed by a breeze ever so slight and insubstantial. They therefore acquired the services of one of the soldiers who had been under siege at Leontini, and bribed him to take to Syracuse information consistent with the false reports made at the River Mylas. The aim was for the man to stir the people to fury by presenting himself as an authority on the incident, and giving an account of the unsubstantiated events as if he were an eyewitness,

32. The fellow not only gained credence with the common people, but, when he was brought into the senate house, he also impressed the senators. Some men who were not without influence openly proclaimed that it was just as well that the greed and brutality of the Romans had been brought to light at Leontini; they would have done the same, or even worse, had they entered Syracuse, the reward for their avarice being so much the greater there. The result was that the Syracusans voted unanimously to close their gates and put the city on a defensive footing.

However, the fears and animosities of the Syracusans were not all centred on the same people. In the case of all the soldiers and most of the commons their hostilities centred on the Romans; but the praetors, and a few of the nobility, excited though they were by the fraudulent report, were more wary of the closer and more immediate threat. And, in fact, Hippocrates and Epicydes were already at the Hexapylon. There, by means of relatives of citizens who were in the army, they were initiating discussions in which they urged the people to throw open the gates to them, and to allow the country which they shared to be defended against a Roman attack.

One of the gates of the Hexapylon had actually been opened, and men had begun to be let in, when the praetors arrived on the scene. They tried to stop this, first by orders and threats, and then by using their personal authority. When all their attempts failed, they finally forgot their dignity and pleaded with the people not to betray their native land to men who were former henchmen of the tyrant, and who were now corrupting the army. But the crowd had been stirred up, and their ears were deaf to all this; and the doors were being battered as violently on the inside as on the outside. When all of them were broken down, the army was let in at all points of the Hexapylon.

The praetors sought refuge with the younger members of the population in Achradina; and the mercenaries, deserters, and all the tyrant's soldiers still left in Syracuse swelled the numbers of the enemy. So it was that Achradina was taken at the first assault, and all the praetors (apart from those who slipped away during the turmoil) were put to death. Nightfall brought an end to the killing. The next day slaves were invited to assume the cap of freedom, and convicts were released from prison. This motley crowd of people unanimously elected Hippocrates and Epicydes praetors, and after a fleeting gleam of liberty Syracuse had relapsed into its servitude of old.

33. When this was reported to the Romans, the camp was promptly moved from Leontini to Syracuse. Also, it so happened that some emissaries had been sent through the harbour, in a quinquereme, by Appius. A quadrireme that had been sent ahead of them was captured when it entered the harbour mouth, and the emissaries had a narrow escape. So, by now, not even the rules of peace, much less those of war, had been left inviolate, and at this point the Roman army pitched camp a mile and a half from the city, at the Olympium, a temple of Jupiter.* It was decided that envoys should be sent from there, but, to prevent them entering the city, Hippocrates and Epicydes came to meet them outside the gate with their supporters.

The spokesman for the Romans said it was not war, but support and aid, that they were bringing to the Syracusans, both to those who had sought refuge with his people after escaping from the midst of the carnage, and to those who, from fear, were enduring a servitude worse than exile, worse even than death. The Romans would not, he said, allow the barbaric slaughter of their allies to go unpunished. So, if those who had sought refuge with the Romans were granted a safe return home, if those responsible for the slaughter were surrendered, and if the Syracusans had their freedom and constitution restored to them, there was no need for war. But if these conditions were not met, he warned, the Romans would open hostilities against any who opposed them.

Epicydes replied that if the envoys' demands had been addressed to him and his colleague, they would have had an answer for them. Now they should come back at a time when the people to whom they had actually come were in power in Syracuse. If the Romans opened hostilities, he added, they would discover from the results that attacking Syracuse was not at all the same as attacking Leontini. With that, Epicydes left the envoys and closed the gates.

After that Syracuse came under attack on land and by sea simultaneously, on land at the Hexapylon, and by sea at Achradina, the wall of which is at the water's edge. The Romans had taken Leontini by the panic they inspired with their first assault, and so they were now quite confident that they would find some way of breaking into a vast city that sprawled over a wide area. They therefore moved up to the walls all the machinery they had for conducting assaults on cities.

34. In fact an operation that commenced with such vigour would have been successful, but for the presence in Syracuse at that time of one man. This was Archimedes.* A peerless observer of the sky and heavenly bodies, he was an even greater marvel when it came to inventing and constructing artillery and war engines with which he would, with very little effort, frustrate any large-scale enemy operation.

The city wall ran over rising terrain of uneven elevation, with sections that were high and difficult of access, but with others, too, that were low and approachable from the flat ground in the depressions. These Archimedes furnished with all manner of artillery, as he thought appropriate to each location.

With sixty quinqueremes, Marcellus proceeded with an assault on the wall of Achradina which, as was observed above, stands at the water's edge. The ships were, for the most part, manned with archers and slingers and even with skirmishers equipped with javelins difficult for any lacking the proper experience to throw back, and these men made sure that hardly anyone could stand on the wall without receiving a wound. Because they needed space for their missiles to be effective, the crews kept the vessels at a distance from the wall. The remaining quinqueremes were lashed in pairs, and the inner rows of oars were removed so that the sides of the vessels were touching, and they could be rowed along like a single ship by the outer banks of oars. They carried towers that were built up in storeys, and other apparatus for pounding the walls.

To meet this armada, Archimedes deployed along the walls catapults of varying dimensions. Against ships in the distance he would launch rocks of massive proportions, but at the closer ones he would aim projectiles that were light, and therefore able to be shot with greater frequency. Finally, to give his own soldiers protection as they showered weapons on the enemy, he pierced the wall from bottom to top with numerous slits, about a cubit long, through which they would target the enemy without being seen, some shooting arrows and others using small 'scorpions'. Some ships came in closer so as to be beneath the range of the artillery. To combat these Archimedes had a swing beam projecting over the wall, and from it a grappling hook attached to a sturdy chain would be dropped onto the prow of the ship. The beam would then be brought to the ground by a heavy lead counterweight, standing the ship on its stern by raising its prow in the air. Then, suddenly released, it would send the ship crashing down into the water, as though it were actually falling from the wall. This caused sheer panic amongst the crew, and it fell with such force that, even coming down upright, it still shipped a considerable amount of water. In this way the sea-offensive was foiled, and all hope was now focused instead on a full-scale attack by land.

But on that front, too, thanks to Hiero's expenditure and vigilance over many years, and thanks to Archimedes' incomparable engineering, a whole panoply of catapults had been deployed. The natural features of the location also helped. The rocky outcrop on which the walls' foundations had been set was, for the most part, so sheer that not only missiles from a catapult, but even objects rolling under their own weight, came crashing down heavily on the enemy. The same factor made approaching the wall difficult, and the men's footing unsteady.

The Romans therefore held a meeting, and it was decided that, since they were foiled at every turn, they should abandon the direct offensive, and limit themselves to a blockade to cut the enemy off from supplies by land and sea.

35. In the meantime, Marcellus set out with about a third of his army to recover the cities which, in the general upheaval, had defected to the Carthaginians. Helorus and Herbesus he recovered when their populations surrendered, but Megara he took by armed force, and then destroyed and pillaged it to inspire terror in the other cities, especially Syracuse.

Himilco* had long been keeping his fleet at anchor off the promontory of Pachynum, and at about this time he disembarked at Heraclea (also called Minoa) 25,000 infantry, 3,000 cavalry, and twelve elephants. In fact, the troops with which he had earlier held his fleet at Pachynum were far fewer. After the seizure of Syracuse by Hippocrates, however, Himilco had left for Carthage, where he had been supported by ambassadors from Hippocrates, and also by a letter from Hannibal, who asserted that the time had arrived for a glorious venture to recover Sicily. And being there in person, an adviser not without influence, he had easily convinced the Carthaginians to ship to Sicily as strong a force of infantry and cavalry as they possibly could.

Within days of his arrival at Heraclea, Himilco retook Agrigentum; and he so inspired other states supporting Carthage to hopes of driving the Romans from Sicily that eventually even those under siege in Syracuse took heart. In fact, the Syracusans now felt that the defence of their city required only a part of their troops, and they divided military duties: Epicydes was to take charge of the city's protection, and Hippocrates was to join Himilco in operations against the Roman consul. Hippocrates set off at night with 10,000 infantry and 500 cavalry, choosing a path through spots free of Roman sentries, and proceeded to pitch his camp in the environs of Acrillae. While the men were digging in, Marcellus stumbled on them on his way from Agrigentum, which was now in enemy hands. Marcellus had failed to beat the enemy in the race for Agrigentum, and he was now on his way back, expecting least of all to encounter a Syracusan army at that time and in that location. However, his fear of Himilco and the Carthaginians, for whom he was certainly no match with the forces that he had, meant that he was advancing with all possible caution, and with his column arranged so as to meet any eventuality.*

36. The precautions taken for meeting the Carthaginians now proved effective against the Sicilians. Finding them disordered, and out of formation, as they established their camp, most of them without their weapons, Marcellus surrounded their entire infantry force, though the cavalry, after a slight skirmish, fled to Acrae with Hippocrates.

With that battle Marcellus kept in line the Sicilians who were defecting from the Romans, and he now returned to Syracuse. A few days later, Himilco joined up with Hippocrates and pitched camp at the River Anapus, about eight miles distant from the city. In this same period fifty-five Carthaginian warships under Bomilcar, admiral of the fleet, happened to sail from the open sea into the great harbour of Syracuse, while a Roman fleet of thirty quinqueremes also put ashore the first legion at Panormus.* One might well have thought that the theatre of war had shifted from Italy, so focused on Sicily were the two peoples.

Himilco believed that the Roman legion that had been landed at

Panormus and was now en route for Syracuse, would certainly fall to him as a prize, but he was cheated out of it by the route he took. The Carthaginian led his men along an inland path, whereas the Roman legion, with the fleet escorting it, came through the coastal areas to Appius Claudius, who had advanced to Pachynum with some of his troops in order to meet it.

The Carthaginians now waited no longer at Syracuse. Bomilcar had little confidence in his navy, for the Romans possessed a fleet that was twice the size of his, and at the same time he was aware that the only outcome of his pointless delay was seeing his allies' shortage of provisions aggravated by his men's presence. He therefore put to sea and crossed to Africa. As for Himilco, he had wasted his time following Marcellus to Syracuse in the hope of engaging him before the Roman could be joined by larger forces. The hope had not materialized, and he could see that his enemy, well fortified and numerically strong, was safely ensconced around Syracuse. And so, not to fritter away time uselessly sitting there and watching the blockade of his allies, Himilco struck camp. His plan was to bring his army to whatever areas the prospect of defections from the Roman might call him, and there, by his presence, raise the spirits of those espousing his cause. Murgantia was the town that he first recovered, the Roman garrison betrayed by the townspeople, and here large quantities of grain and all manner of provisions had been stockpiled for the use of the Romans.

37. This defection also gave encouragement to other city-states, and Roman garrisons now began to be expelled from the citadels, or crushed after being treacherously betrayed. Henna, however, enjoyed an impregnable position, located as it was on a high bluff, sheer on all sides; it also had a strong garrison in its citadel, and a garrison commander by no means susceptible to duplicity. This was Lucius Pinarius. He was an intrepid soldier, and a man who would rely more on making betrayal impossible than he would on the loyalty of the Sicilians. Furthermore, at that particular time, Pinarius had been prompted to take every possible precaution by the news of all the treacherous defections in the various cities and the annihilation of their garrisons. And so, day and night alike, everything was prepared and ready, with guards and sentries in position, and no soldier setting down his arms or quitting his post.

Now the leading citizens of Henna had already made a pact with

Himilco to betray the garrison, but when they became aware of the situation and saw the Roman was leaving no room for treachery, they thought they had to act openly. They declared that the city and its citadel should be in their hands, if they had entered an alliance with the Romans as free men and had not simply been delivered to them for imprisonment like slaves. They then voiced the opinion that it was only fair for the keys of the city to be returned to them. The strongest bond between good allies was mutual trust, they said, and the only way the people of Henna could have the gratitude of the Roman people and the Senate would be by remaining on terms of friendship with them of their own volition, and not under duress.

The Roman's answer to this was that he had been installed in his position by his commanding officer, from whom he had also received the keys of the gates and the task of defending the citadel. It was not by his own authority, or that of the people of Henna, that he held these responsibilities, he said, but by the authority of the man who had put them in his hands. Leaving one's post was a capital offence for Romans, Pinarius continued, and fathers had even put their own children to death in punishment for such an act. The consul Marcellus was not far off, he said in conclusion, and they should send a delegation to him, since he had the right and authority to decide on the matter.

The people of Henna replied that they would certainly not do that, and declared that if talk got them nowhere they would seek some way of asserting their liberty. Pinarius then said that, if they objected to a deputation to the consul, he himself should be admitted to their popular assembly, so he could ascertain whether the declaration they were making came from a few, or from the entire citizen-body. It was agreed that an assembly be called the following day.

38. Leaving that meeting, Pinarius went back to the citadel. He brought his soldiers together and said:

'I think you have heard, men, of how Roman garrisons have been set upon and overpowered by Sicilians in recent days. Such treachery *you* have avoided, first of all thanks to the goodwill of heaven, and then thanks to your own courage, standing vigilantly on guard, day and night, under arms. I only wish that the rest of our time here could be passed without our suffering, or initiating, barbaric acts! The precautions we have so far taken have worked in the case of covert treachery; since treachery has achieved little success, there is now a clear and explicit demand being made for the keys to the city gates. The moment we surrender these, Henna will immediately be in the hands of the Carthaginians, and we shall be butchered here with greater savagery than that with which the garrison at Murgantia was murdered. I have only with difficulty managed to gain this one night for a discussion in which to inform you of the peril that lies ahead. At dawn they are going to hold an assembly; at this their purpose is to incriminate me, and incite the populace against you. As a result, Henna will tomorrow run either with your blood or with the blood of its people. Pre-empted by them, you will have no hope; anticipate them, and you will face no danger. Victory will go to the man who first draws the sword. So you must all await the signal, alert and under arms. As for me, I shall be at the assembly, and there I shall spin out the time with talk and argumentation until all is prepared. When I give the signal by moving my toga, I want you at that point to raise a cry in every quarter, fall on the crowd, and bring down everything with your swords. See to it that nothing survives whose brute force or treachery could possibly be cause for fear in future.

'I pray to you, mother Ceres and Proserpina, and all the other deities above and beneath the earth who dwell in this city and these holy lakes and groves: help us with your favour and goodwill, if truly we have adopted such a plan only to avoid, and not ourselves commit, a treacherous act.

'I would address you with a longer speech of encouragement, men, were the fight ahead with an armed foe. They are unarmed and unprepared, and you will slaughter them till you tire of it. And, to relieve you of any possible fear with regard to Himilco and the Carthaginians, the consul's camp is in the vicinity.'

39. Following this exhortation the men were sent off to take food and rest. The next day they were assigned to various locations for blockading roads and shutting off escape routes. Most of them, since they had also in the past been regular observers of the assemblies, took up positions above and around the theatre.

The Roman commander was introduced to the people by the magistrates. He declared that it was the consul, not he, who had jurisdiction and authority in the matter, and then added much the same remarks as he had made the day before. At first there were only hesitant calls from a section of the crowd for the surrender of the keys, but soon they were all clamouring with a single voice. When

Pinarius became hesitant and evasive, they burst into fierce threats, and were evidently not going to refrain any longer from extremes of violence. At that point the commander gave the pre-arranged signal with his toga. His soldiers, who had for some time been ready and waiting for action, then raised the shout, and came rushing down upon the rear of the assembly from the higher ground, while others massed together and blocked the exits from the theatre.

Enclosed in the seating area, the people of Henna faced a massacre. The piles of bodies grew, not just from the killing but also from the stampede, as they charged down over each other's heads and ended in heaps, the uninjured falling on the wounded, the living on the dead. Then the Romans took off in all directions, and the entire scene was one of flight and panic, as in a city taken by storm. And the fact that they were butchering an unarmed crowd did not diminish the fury of the soldiers—danger shared by both sides, and the heat of battle, would not have excited them more. Henna was thus retained by an act that was heinous, or necessary.*

Marcellus did not object to what had happened, and in fact ceded the spoils of Henna to the rank and file—he believed that the Sicilians would, in future, be deterred by fear from betraying the garrisons. However, this was a city in the heart of Sicily, famed equally for its natural defences and for the veneration the whole area received from having been trodden by Proserpina, who was abducted there; news of the tragic episode naturally spread throughout the island almost in a single day. People felt that, by this unspeakable butchery, a dwelling of the gods, and not simply of men, had been violated; and, with that, even those who had been vacillating earlier now went over to the Carthaginians.

Hippocrates then withdrew to Murgantia, and Himilco to Agrigentum, for bringing the army to Henna at the invitation of the traitors had proved a waste of time. Marcellus went back to Leontini, where he stockpiled grain and other provisions in the camp. He then left a small garrison in place, and came to Syracuse to continue the siege. From Syracuse he sent Appius Claudius to Rome to stand for the consulship, and in his place he put Titus Quinctius Crispinus in command of the fleet and the old camp. Marcellus himself constructed fortified winter quarters five miles from the Hexapylon, at a place called Leon. Such were operations in Sicily up to the start of winter.

40. That same summer the long-expected war with King Philip also broke out.* Ambassadors came from Oricum to the praetor Marcus Valerius, who was standing guard with his fleet over Brundisium and the nearby Calabrian coastline. They informed Valerius that Philip had initially sailed upriver with a hundred and twenty light biremes, and had attacked Apollonia. However, when the operation dragged on longer than he had expected, Philip had, under cover of night, secretly moved his army to Oricum, and, since the city stood on a plain, and had no strength in terms of fortifications, manpower, or armaments, it had been taken at the first assault. As the ambassadors reported this, they begged Marcellus to bring them aid and, by land and sea operations, to keep a man who was undeniably an enemy of Rome away from the coastal towns, which were under attack for no other reason than that they faced Italy.

Leaving behind a garrison of 2,000, which he put under the command of his legate, Publius Valerius, Marcus Valerius set off with his fleet drawn up and ready for action, and with the men for whom there was insufficient room on the warships boarded on freighters, he reached Oricum the next day. Holding the town was a feeble garrison that the king had left in place on his departure, and Valerius took it without much of a fight. Envoys from Apollonia came to the town bringing a report that their people were under siege because they refused to break with the Romans, and that they could no longer withstand the pressure being applied by the Macedonians, unless they were sent Roman aid. Valerius promised to comply with their wishes, and dispatched 2,000 elite troops to the river-mouth in warships. The force was under the command of a prefect of the allies, Quintus Naevius Crista, a man of energy and an experienced soldier.

Crista set his men ashore, and sent the ships back to rejoin the rest of the fleet at Oricum, his point of departure. Then, keeping his distance from the river, he led his men along a path that was little patrolled by the king's troops, and slipped into the city at night, unnoticed by any of the enemy. The following day the force remained inactive to give the prefect the time to review the men of fighting age in Apollonia, as well as the town's armaments and other strengths. An inspection and review of these gave Crista considerable reassurance, and at the same time he learned from his scouts the extent of the enemy's slackness and negligence. He therefore slipped noiselessly from the city at the dead of night, and made his way into the enemy camp. Security here was so slipshod and slack that it was reliably recorded that more than a thousand men passed over the rampart before anyone became aware of it, and that, had they avoided bloodshed, they could have reached the king's tent. It was the killing of the Macedonians closest to the gate that awoke the enemy. With that, sheer panic and trepidation seized them all, so that no one else took up arms, or tried to drive the foe from the camp. In addition, the king himself took to his heels, in the almost half-naked state in which he had been awakened from his sleep, and he fled to his ships on the river, dressed in a manner that was unbecoming for a common soldier, much less a king. The other Macedonians poured out in a crowd after him.

Slightly fewer than 3,000 men were either taken prisoner or cut down within the camp, but considerably more were taken prisoner than were killed. After the camp had been pillaged, the Apollonians hauled off to Apollonia catapults, ballistas, and other artillery that had been concentrated there to lay siege to the city. These they would use to defend their walls in the event of such a situation arising in future. All the other plunder from the camp was ceded to the Romans.

When news of the action was brought to Oricum, Marcus Valerius immediately brought the fleet to the river-mouth to prevent the king making good his escape by ship. And so Philip began to lose confidence in his ability to match his foe in battle, whether on land or sea. He beached and burned his ships, and then headed for Macedonia overland, his army for the most part stripped of its arms and belongings. The Roman fleet, under Marcus Valerius' command, wintered at Oricum.

41. The same year's operations in Spain met with mixed success. Before the Romans could cross the River Ebro, Mago and Hasdrubal routed huge forces of the Spaniards.* In fact, Further Spain would have defected from Rome but for Publius Cornelius, who swiftly took his army across the Ebro and arrived in the nick of time when the allies were still wavering. The Romans first encamped at Castrum Album, which is famed as the spot where the great Hamilcar was killed. Here the citadel had been fortified, and they had stockpiled grain in advance. However, the surrounding areas were completely occupied by hostile forces, and a Roman column had been attacked by enemy cavalry without being able to retaliate—some 2,000 of

them had been killed when they failed to keep up, or were scattered through the countryside. The Romans therefore withdrew to a location closer to more peaceful areas, and established a fortified camp at Mt. Victory.* To this spot Gnaeus Scipio came with his entire force; and so, too, did Hasdrubal, son of Gisgo—he was now the third Carthaginian general—at the head of an army with its full quota of men. All three Carthaginian generals then took up a position across the river from the Roman camp.

Taking some light-armed troops, Publius Scipio set off stealthily to reconnoitre the surrounding area, but he failed to escape the attention of the enemy, who would have crushed him on the open plains, had he not taken over a nearby hillock. Even there he was surrounded, and was only rescued from a siege by his brother's arrival.

Castulo* then went over to the Romans. This was a powerful and famous city, so well connected with Carthage that Hannibal's wife actually came from there. The Carthaginians now proceeded to attack Iliturgi: there was a Roman garrison in the town and, mostly because of food-shortages there, it also seemed likely that they would take the place. To assist the allies, as well as the garrison, Gnaeus Scipio set off with a lightly equipped legion, passed between the two Carthaginian camps, causing heavy enemy casualties in the process, and entered the city. The next day he fought again, making a charge from the city which was equally successful. Upwards of 12,000 men were killed in the two engagements, and more than a thousand taken prisoner, with the capture of thirty-six military standards. The Carthaginians accordingly withdrew from Iliturgi. It was then the turn of the city of Bigerra to come under attack from them—its people were also Roman allies—but Gnaeus Scipio's arrival raised the siege without a fight.

42. The Punic camp was then moved to Munda,* and the Romans immediately followed. At Munda there was a pitched battle that lasted almost four hours. The Romans were winning a brilliant victory when the signal was given to retreat: Gnaeus Scipio had taken a javelin through the thigh and fear had seized the men around him that the wound might be fatal. There was no doubt that, but for this interruption, the Punic camp could have been taken that day. By that stage, elephants as well as soldiers had been driven right back to the rampart, and thirty-nine elephants had also been transfixed with javelins. In this battle, too, it is said, some 12,000 men

were killed, and almost 3,000 captured, along with fifty-seven military standards.

The Carthaginians then fell back to the city of Auringis,* and the Romans followed in order to press their advantage on a demoralized foe. There Scipio fought a second battle, being carried into the fighting line on a stretcher. The victory was not in doubt, but enemy casualties were less than half what they were earlier—because fewer had survived to fight the engagement! But the Spanish people* are naturally adept at repairing, and making good, the losses of war, and when Mago was sent by his brother to recruit soldiers, they soon brought the army up to its complement, and gave it the spirit to enter the fray once more. The soldiers were mostly new recruits but, being now on a side beaten so many times in a matter of days, they fought with the same spirit as those who had gone before them, and achieved the same result. More than 8,000 men were killed, and little short of 1,000 taken prisoner, with fifty-eight military standards captured. The spoils were mostly of Gallic origin—golden necklaces and armbands, and large numbers of them. Two famous Gallic chieftains, called Moeniacoeptus and Vismarus, also fell in the battle. Eight elephants were captured and three were killed.

As things were going so well in Spain, shame finally overtook the Romans that the town of Saguntum, the grounds for the war, had now been seven years in enemy hands.* And so they forcefully ejected the Carthaginian garrison, and recovered the town, restoring it to those of its former residents who had survived the ravages of the war. In addition, the Romans brought under their control the Turdetani,* who had brought about the conflict between the Saguntines and the Carthaginians, and then sold them into slavery and destroyed their city.

43. Such were operations in Spain during the consulship of Quintus Fabius and Marcus Claudius. At Rome, no sooner had the new tribunes of the plebs entered office than an indictment to appear before the people was issued by one of these tribunes, Marcus Metellus, to the censors Publius Furius and Marcus Atilius. The previous year, when Metellus was quaestor, these men had deprived him of his horse, expelled him from his tribe, and degraded him to the poll-tax paying class because of his participation in the conspiracy to abandon Italy that had been hatched at Cannae. However, the censors were aided by nine of the tribunes, who ruled against their being tried

while in office, and the men were released. They were prevented from performing the ceremony* at the end of their term because Publius Furius died. Marcus Atilius resigned his office.

The consular elections were presided over by the consul Quintus Fabius Maximus, and the men elected to the office—both of them in their absence—were Quintus Fabius Maximus, son of the consul, and Tiberius Sempronius Gracchus (who was elected for the second time). Two men who were curule aediles at the time, Publius Sempronius Tuditanus and Gnaeus Fulvius Centumalus, were elected praetors, along with Marcus Atilius and Marcus Aemilius Lepidus. It is on record that this was the first year in which theatrical competitions lasting four days were staged by the curule aediles. The aedile Tuditanus was the man who, at Cannae, led his men through the middle of the enemy, when others caught in that great disaster were paralysed with fear.

The elections finished, the consuls elect were, on a proposal made by the consul Quintus Fabius, summoned to Rome, where they took up their office. They then consulted the Senate on the conduct of the war, on the assignment of areas of responsibility—their own and those of the praetors—and on the armies to be employed and their commanders

44. The distribution of responsibilities and armies was accordingly made as follows:

The war with Hannibal was assigned to the consuls. They were to have two armies, one that had been under the command of Sempronius himself, the other under Fabius, the retiring consul. The armies comprised two legions each.

The praetor Marcus Aemilius, who had drawn the foreigners' jurisdiction in the sortition, was to have Luceria as his province, his judicial responsibilities being reassigned to his colleague Marcus Atilius, the urban praetor. Aemilius was to have the two legions which Quintus Fabius, who was now consul, had commanded as praetor.

Publius Sempronius (Tuditanus) was allotted Ariminum as his responsibility, Gnaeus Fulvius Suessula. Each was to have two legions, Fulvius taking the urban legions and Tuditanus receiving those of Marcus Pomponius.

Extensions of commands and responsibilities were given as follows:

Marcus Claudius: Sicily, within the confines of what had constituted the kingdom of Hiero, with Publius Lentulus taking over the old province as propraetor.

Titus Otacilius: the fleet.

(There was no assignment of fresh troops for these three officers.)

Marcus Valerius: Greece and Macedonia, with the legion and fleet then under his command.

Quintus Mucius: Sardinia, along with its former army, which comprised two legions.

Gaius Terentius: Picenum, with the one legion that was already under his command.

In addition, orders were issued for the mobilization of two city legions, and 20,000 allies.

Such were the commanders and forces with which the Romans, facing multiple wars at the same time, either in progress or thought to be coming, defended their empire.

The consuls mobilized the two city legions, and raised supplementary troops for other legions; then, before leaving the city, they saw to the expiation of prodigies that had been reported. The town wall and a gate had been struck by lightning at Caieta, as had the temple of Jupiter at Aricia. In addition, there were tricks played on eyes and ears that were accepted as real. There was the sighting of non-existent warships on the river at Tarracina; the sound of arms clashing in the temple of Jupiter Vicilinus, in the area of Compsa; and the river at Amiternum running with blood. These portents were expiated in accordance with a decree of the pontiffs, and the consuls left Rome, Sempronius for Lucania, and Fabius for Apulia.

Fabius the elder came to his son's encampment in Apulia to serve as his legate. The son went forward to meet him and (out of respect for the father's eminence) his lictors were silent as they went ahead of him. The old man had ridden past eleven sets of *fasces* when the consul told the lictor closest to him to pay attention. The lictor then called to the elder Fabius to dismount, and at this the father finally jumped from his mount, saying: 'My son, I wanted to see if you were fully aware that you are a consul.'

45. Dasius Altinius, a native of Arpi, came to that camp furtively during the night with three slaves, and promised to betray Arpi for a price. When Fabius raised the matter with his council, all except his father were for having the man flogged and put to death as a deserter. Altinius was a man of dubious loyalty, they said, and an enemy

to both sides. After the debacle at Cannae, he had gone over to Hannibal, and brought Arpi to defect—for him, it seemed, loyalty belonged only with success. Now, contrary to his hopes and wishes, the fortunes of Rome appeared to be radically changing, and experiencing a virtual renaissance, and he was therefore undertaking to compensate those whom he had already betrayed with a new act of treachery! He was always standing on one side, with his sympathies on the other, a perfidious ally and ineffectual enemy. He should join the men who betrayed the Falerii and Pyrrhus as a third object lesson for deserters.

The elder Fabius disagreed. Men, he said, are forgetting their own situation if, when war is raging hot about them, they give free rein to their ideas on any matter as if they were at peace. Instead, their actions and deliberations should have one goal, namely to prevent, if it can be done by any means, the defection from the Roman people of any of its allies. This, Fabius continued, they were not considering; they were saying instead that an example should be made of anyone coming to his senses, and looking back wistfully on a former alliance. If, however, one is allowed to abandon the Romans, but not return to them, it was perfectly obvious that the Roman cause would soon entirely lose the support of its allies, and they would see everything in Italy unified under treaties with Carthage. Now, he was not a man who would advocate putting the slightest trust in Altinius, he said, but he would follow a strategy that represented a middle course. His opinion was that, for the moment, Altinius should be considered neither an enemy nor a friend; he should be held for the duration of the war in open custody, not far from the camp, in some community loyal to them. The war over, they should then consider whether his earlier defection was more deserving of punishment than his present return was of pardon.

Fabius won assent. Altinius himself was handed over to some officials from Cales, along with his companions, and instructions were given for the large quantity of gold that he had brought with him to be held in safekeeping. At Cales, he was at liberty all day, but guards attended him, and at night they kept him confined.

At Arpi it was in his home that Altinius' absence was first noticed and a search for him was initiated. Then word of his disappearance spread throughout the city, causing the commotion one might expect at the loss of a leader, and fear of a coup prompted them to send off messengers to Hannibal at the double. The Carthaginian leader was by no means upset at the news. He, too, had long suspected Altinius to be of dubious loyalty, and he had now gained a pretext for confiscating and selling off the property of a man of considerable means. But to make people think he was motivated by anger rather than greed, he added to his avarice an act of cruelty as well. He summoned Altinius' wife and children to the camp, and interrogated them first about the man's flight, and then about the amount of gold and silver that had been left in his house. When he had satisfactory answers to all his questions, he burned them alive.*

46. Leaving Suessula, Fabius proceeded first with an attack on Arpi. Encamping about half a mile away, he took a close look at the lie of the city, and its walls. He then decided to make his assault right at the point where it was best protected by the walls, because he saw that that was the spot least attentively guarded. He brought together all the equipment used for assaults on cities, and then picked out from his entire army the very best of his centurions, whom he put under the command of some courageous tribunes. He assigned to this group a force of 600 soldiers, enough, he thought, for the job in hand, and ordered them to carry ladders to the appropriate spot at the sound of the signal for the fourth watch.

In that sector was a gate that was low and narrow: the road there was not much used as it passed through a sparsely populated section of the city. Fabius ordered the men first to scale the wall with their ladders, and then open the gate from the inside, or break its bars. When they had secured that part of town, they were to give a signal on a bugle for the rest of the troops to move up—Fabius would have everything ready and prepared.

The orders were briskly carried out, and what seemed likely to impede their effort proved of the greatest assistance in tricking the enemy. A rainstorm started at midnight, forcing the guards and sentries to slip away from their posts, and run for shelter in the buildings. Then, because of the beating of the rain, which was heavier at first, the downpour also prevented the din of the men working on the gate from being heard. Later, as the defenders heard the rain falling more gently and steadily, it lulled most of them to sleep. Taking possession of the gate, the Romans ordered their trumpeters, placed at equal intervals along the street, to give the signal for calling the consul. This was done in the manner agreed upon, the consul ordered the advance and, shortly before daybreak, he entered the city through the gate that had been forced open.

47. It was at this point that the enemy finally woke up, when the rain was tailing off and dawn was near. Within the city, Hannibal had a garrison of about 5,000 soldiers, and the people of Arpi had themselves put 3,000 men under arms. It was the latter that the Carthaginians put in the front line to face the enemy, so that they would have no treachery behind them. The fighting started in the dark in the narrow streets. The Romans seized not only the streets, but the buildings next to the gate, as well, to remove any possibility of their being targeted and wounded from the rooftops. Some of the inhabitants of Arpi and some Romans then recognized each other, and conversations started up between them. The Romans asked what the people of Arpi thought they were doing, what misdeed of the Romans, or what benefit from the Carthaginians, was leading them to wage war against their old Roman allies, in support of foreigners and barbarians, and to turn Italy into a tax-paying subject of Africa. The excuse of the people of Arpi was that, unbeknownst to them, they had been sold out to the Carthaginians by their leaders, that they had been overpowered and oppressed by a handful of men. Once a start had been made, the conversations became more widespread, and eventually the chief magistrate of Arpi was brought before the consul by his compatriots. Amidst the standards and battle lines, assurances were given, and suddenly the citizens of Arpi turned their weapons on the Carthaginians, and fought for the Romans. The Spaniards, too, transferred their allegiance to the consul. They numbered slightly fewer than 1,000, and the pact they made with the consul promised no more than the release, with impunity, of the Punic garrison. The doors were opened for the Carthaginians who, released with a guarantee of safe conduct, came unharmed to Hannibal at Salapia. Arpi was then returned to the Romans without any loss of life, with the sole exception of a long-time traitor who had recently deserted. Orders were issued for the Spaniards to be given double rations, and the republic thereafter frequently made use of their courageous and loyal service.

One of the consuls was in Apulia, and the other in Lucania, when 112 Campanian knights of noble birth left Capua with their magistrates' permission, ostensibly to take plunder from enemy territory. They came to the Roman camp above Suessula. They gave their identity to the guards on duty, and said they wanted a word with the praetor. The camp was under the command of Gnaeus Fulvius, who, when the message was brought to him, ordered ten of the group to be brought to him unarmed. On hearing their request—they sought nothing more than the return of their property when Capua was retaken—he accepted them all under his protection.

The town of Atrinum was stormed by the other praetor, Sempronius Tuditanus, with more than 7,000 prisoners taken, along with a quantity of bronze and silver coin.

At Rome there was a terrible fire that went on for two nights and a day. Everything between the Salinae and the Porta Carmentalis was razed to the ground,* including the Aequimaelium, the Vicus Iugarius, and the temples of Fortuna and Mater Matuta. The fire also spread outside the gate, destroying many buildings, religious and secular.

48. Since things were going well in Spain, and they were enlisting new allies as well as recovering many of the old ones, Publius and Gnaeus Cornelius that same year expanded their ambitions to include Africa as well.* The Numidian king Syphax had been suddenly turned into an enemy of the Carthaginians, and to him the Cornelii sent a delegation of three centurions. These were to conclude a treaty of friendship with the king, and promise the gratitude of the Senate and People of Rome if he continued to put military pressure on the Carthaginians, adding that the Romans would, at the appropriate moment, discharge their obligation to him with handsome interest.

The barbarian was delighted with the delegation, and he discussed tactics for the war with the delegates. But when he listened to the words of these seasoned fighters, and compared their well-disciplined organization with his own, he realized just how much he did not know. His first request of them, as good and loyal allies, was for two of the centurions to carry back to their commanders the results of their mission while one remained behind as his instructor in military matters. The Numidian people, he explained, had no experience in infantry fighting, their expertise being confined to horses.* This was how his ancestors had conducted their wars since the earliest days of their nation, he said, and it was in this that his people had been trained from childhood. But, Syphax added, he had an enemy who relied on fighting on foot, and, if he wanted to be that man's equal in military strength, he too had to acquire infantry. In fact, his kingdom had a large population well suited for that, but he had no idea how to arm, equip, and train it. In fact it was a complete and utter shambles, like a randomly assembled crowd of people, he said.

The delegates replied that they would do what he wanted for the time being, on condition that he solemnly undertook to send the man back immediately, if their commanders did not give approval to their action. The man who remained at the king's court was called Quintus Statorius.

The king selected and sent a number of Numidians to Spain along with the two Romans. These were to act as his representatives, and gain approval for the treaty from the Roman commanders. But he also instructed them to lose no time in inciting the Numidian auxiliaries, who were serving with the Carthaginian troops, to desert.

Meanwhile, Statorius conscripted an infantry force for the king from amongst the large numbers of Numidian men of fighting age. He formed them up pretty well after the Roman manner, and, by putting them through manœuvres and military drill, taught them to follow their standards and keep their ranks. He also familiarized them with siege-work construction and the other regular duties of the soldier. So thorough was he that, in a short while, the king had no greater confidence in his cavalry than he did in his infantry, and, in an engagement fought on level ground, he defeated the Carthaginian enemy in pitched battle. Moreover, the Romans in Spain derived great benefit from the arrival of the king's representatives—at the news of their coming, cases of desertion by the Numidians began to be commonplace.

So began the friendly relations of the Romans with Syphax. When the Carthaginians learned of it, they immediately sent a delegation to Gala,* who was king in another area of Numidia. His people are called the Maesuli.

49. Gala had a son, Masinissa. He was only seventeen years old,* but was a young man of such qualities that it was already apparent that he was going to make the kingdom greater and richer than what he inherited. The Carthaginian delegates explained that Syphax had joined the Romans to strengthen himself, by that alliance, against the kings and peoples of Africa. It would also be better for Gala to join the Carthaginians as soon as possible, they said, before Syphax

crossed to Spain, or the Romans to Africa—Syphax could be caught off guard before he had derived anything more than nominal benefit from the alliance.

Persuading Gala to send an army was easy, since his son insisted on the war, and, when Masinissa joined up with the Carthaginian legions,* he defeated Syphax in a great battle. In that battle, it is said, 30,000 men were killed. Syphax fled the field with a few horsemen, and came to the Maurusian Numidians, who live near the Ocean in the far reaches of the country, opposite Gades. At the news of his arrival, barbarians flocked to him from all quarters, enabling him, in a short time, to put under arms huge forces with which he intended to cross to Spain, separated from him by only a narrow strait. But Masinissa then arrived with his triumphant army, and there, on his own and without any assistance from the Carthaginians, he covered himself with fame, fighting a war with Syphax.

There were no notable events in Spain, apart from the Roman commanders' success in enticing the young Celtiberian soldiers to their side, with the same level of pay these had settled on with the Carthaginians. The Romans also sent more than 300 Spaniards of the highest rank to Italy, to encourage disaffection amongst their countrymen who were serving in the auxiliary troops of Hannibal. This is all that is worth recording in Spain for that year. Its significance lies in the fact that, prior to the hiring of the Celtiberians at that time, the Romans had never had mercenary soldiers in their service.

BOOK TWENTY-FIVE

1. While these events were taking place in Africa and Spain, Hannibal spent the summer in the territory of the Sallentini, where he hoped to take control of the city of Tarentum by means of treachery. During that time, some insignificant cities of the Sallentini went over to him,* but in the same period, in Bruttium, two of the twelve peoples who had defected to the Carthaginians the year before, namely the Consentini and the Tauriani, returned to their allegiance to the Roman people. In fact, more would have returned had it not been for Titus Pomponius Veientanus, an officer of the allies. After a number of successful plundering expeditions in Bruttian territory, Veientanus had acquired the stature of a regularly appointed commander, and he had come up against Hanno with a makeshift army that he had raised. Large numbers of men—though they were really just an ill-organized assortment of peasants and slaves—were killed or taken prisoner. The least significant loss was the commander, who was one of the men taken prisoner. Veientanus was responsible for the foolhardy encounter on that particular occasion, and earlier, as a tax-gatherer, he had been guilty of all manner of corrupt practices, and had swindled both the state and private companies, and cost them dear. The consul Sempronius fought many minor engagements in Lucania, none worth recording, and took a few insignificant Lucanian towns.

The war dragged on, with success and failure changing the mentality of people as much as it did their material circumstances, and the longer it did so the more superstition—and mostly foreign superstition—permeated the citizen body.* So much so, in fact, that it seemed that either human beings or the gods had undergone a sudden transformation! Roman ritual was falling into disuse, and not just in private, and within the home. In public, too—in the Forum and on the Capitol—there were crowds of women whose sacrifices and prayers to the gods did not follow traditional practice. Priests and oracle-mongers had taken possession of the minds of the public, and the numbers of such people were swollen by the rustic proletariat, who had been forced into the city, by poverty and fear, from fields that long years of war had left untilled and insecure. There was also easy money to be gained from the superstition of others, through an occupation its practitioners conducted as though it were legitimate.

At first, there were angry comments made in private by reputable people, but then the matter also came to the notice of the senators and became the subject of official complaint. The aediles and *triumviri capitales* were severely criticized by the Senate for their failure to suppress these practices, but when these magistrates attempted to remove the crowd from the Forum, and dismantle their ceremonial apparatus, they were almost physically assaulted. The malaise now seemed too great to be effectively checked by junior officials, and the city praetor Marcus Aemilius was given the task by the Senate of freeing the people of such superstitions. Aemilius read the senatorial decree aloud at an assembly of the people, and also issued an edict that anyone in possession of books of oracles, prayer formulae, or a documented procedure for sacrifice should bring all such records and literature to him before 1 April. He also forbade anyone to offer sacrifice, in a public or sacred location, using any unfamiliar or foreign ritual.

2. There were a number of deaths in the state priesthood that year: Lucius Cornelius Lentulus, *pontifex maximus*; Gaius Papirius Maso, son of Gaius, pontiff; Publius Furius Philus, augur; and Gaius Papirius Maso, son of Lucius, decemvir for sacrifices. Marcus Cornelius Cethegus and Gnaeus Servilius Caepio were appointed pontiffs to replace Lentulus and Papirius respectively; Lucius Quinctius Flamininus was elected augur, and Lucius Cornelius Lentulus decemvir for sacrifices.

The date of the consular elections was now approaching, but the consuls were focused on the war, and it was decided not to call them away from it. Instead, the consul Tiberius Sempronius appointed Gaius Claudius Cento dictator for the holding of the elections, and Cento appointed Quintus Fulvius Flaccus his master of horse.

On the first available election day the dictator returned as consuls his master of horse, Quintus Fulvius Flaccus, and Appius Claudius Pulcher, who had had Sicily as his province during his praetorship. After that the following praetors were elected: Gnaeus Fulvius Flaccus, Gaius Claudius Nero, Marcus Iunius Silanus and Publius

Cornelius Sulla. The elections completed, the dictator resigned his position.

Publius Cornelius Scipio, the man who later bore the cognomen Africanus, was curule aedile that year, with Marcus Cornelius Cethegus as his colleague. When Scipio stood for election to the aedileship, the plebeian tribunes attempted to block his candidacy, claiming that he did not have the right to stand because he was not yet of legal age to seek office.*

'If all the citizens of Rome want to make me an aedile,' Scipio declared, 'then I am old enough.' After that, when the people divided into tribes for the vote, the support for Scipio was so strong that the tribunes promptly abandoned their efforts. The largesse of the aediles that year lay in the staging of the Roman Games on what was, for the resources of the day, a lavish scale (and with a single day's repetition*), and gifts of measures of oil being made to each locality.

The plebeian aediles Lucius Villius Tappulus and Marcus Fundanius Fundulus brought before the people charges of immoral conduct against a number of married women, and some were found guilty and sent into exile. The Plebeian Games were repeated for a period of two days, and there was a banquet for Jupiter in honour of the games.

3. Quintus Fulvius Flaccus and Appius Claudius now entered their consulship, Flaccus for the third time. The praetorian sortition of duties was as follows:

Publius Cornelius Sulla	Urban and Foreigners' Jurisdiction (formerly these had been separate portfolios*)
Gnaeus Fulvius Flaccus	Apulia
Gaius Claudius Nero	Suessula
Marcus Iunius Silanus	Etruria

The consuls were assigned the conduct of the war with Hannibal, for which they were to have two legions each; one was to take over the troops of the previous year's consul, Quintus Fabius, and the other those of Fulvius Centumalus. In the case of the praetors, Fulvius Flaccus was to have the legions that were currently under the command of the praetor Aemilius in Luceria, Claudius Nero those under Gaius Terentius in Picenum. Both were to supplement these troops with levies of their own. Marcus Iunius was assigned the urban legions of the previous year for service in Etruria. Tiberius Sempronius Gracchus and Publius Sempronius Tuditanus saw their commands extended in their provinces of Lucania and Gaul respectively, where they also retained their armies. The same applied to Publius Lentulus within the old province of Sicily, and to Marcus Marcellus in Syracuse, and what had been Hiero's kingdom. Titus Otacilius was allocated the fleet, Marcus Valerius Greece, Quintus Mucius Scaevola Sardinia, and Publius and Gnaeus Cornelius the Spanish provinces. To supplement the old armies, two urban legions were mobilized by the consuls, and the total number of legions for that year was twenty-three.*

The consuls' troop-levy was hindered by the actions of Marcus Postumius of Pyrgi,* which almost led to a riot. Postumius was a tax-collector who, in many years, had had no equal in the state for corruption and avarice, with the exception of Titus Pomponius Veientanus (the man whom the Carthaginians, under Hanno, had captured the year before, as he recklessly plundered farmland in Lucania). Because, in the case of goods shipped to the troops, risks from violent storms were assumed by the state, these two men had invented stories of shipwrecks, and even the real ones that they had reported had been due not to accident, but to their dishonesty. They would put small quantities of goods of little worth on old ships in poor repair. They would then sink the ships on the open sea, picking up the crews in boats kept ready for the purpose, and falsely report the cargoes to have been many times more valuable than they really were.*

This swindle had been brought to the notice of the praetor Marcus Aemilius the previous year, and by him it had been brought before the Senate. It had not, however, been censured by any senatorial decree because the senators were reluctant to upset the league of tax-gatherers at such a critical time. The people proved to be stricter punishers of embezzlement. Two of the plebeian tribunes, Spurius Carvilius and Lucius Carvilius, were prompted to take action when they saw the indignation roused by the scandalous affair, and they fined Marcus Postumius 200,000 *asses*. The day arrived for Postumius to challenge the ruling, and the plebeian assembly was so packed that the space before the Capitol could barely hold the crowds. After the trial wound up, the last resort for Postumius seemed to be the possibility of Gaius Servilius Casca, a plebeian tribune, who was a close relative of his, interposing his veto before the tribes could be called to vote.

The tribunes furnished their witnesses, and pushed back the crowd, and the urn was brought so that they could decide by lot the tribe in which the Latins would vote. Meanwhile, the tax-collectors were putting pressure on Casca to suspend the day's proceedings in the assembly. The people objected to this. As it happened, Casca was sitting in front, in a seat right at the end, fear and shame simultaneously preying on his mind. When there was apparently little help forthcoming from Casca, the tax-collectors, in order to disrupt the proceedings, formed a phalanx and, hurling abuse at both the people and the tribunes, charged into the area that had been cleared. It had almost reached the point of open warfare, when the consul Fulvius said to the tribunes: 'Do you not see that your authority has been slighted, and that a riot is coming unless you quickly dissolve the assembly of the people?'

4. The people were dismissed, and the Senate was convened. Here the consuls brought before the meeting the matter of the assembly of the people that had been disrupted by the tax-gatherers' shameless display of force. They cited the example of Marcus Furius Camillus, whose exile was likely to be followed by the city's downfall—he had accepted the sentence that was passed on him by his ungrateful compatriots. And before Camillus there were the decemvirs, under whose legislation the Romans were living till that very day, and many other leaders of the community after them who had also accepted the judgement passed on them by the people. But Postumius of Pyrgi had torn the vote from the hands of the Roman people. He had disrupted an assembly of the plebs, undermined the authority of the tribunes, formed a line of battle against the Roman people, and seized a position where he could keep the tribunes away from the people, and prevent the tribes from being called to vote. The only thing that had stopped men from killing and fighting each other had been the understanding shown by the magistrates. They had for the moment yielded to the rage and recklessness of a few. They had permitted themselves, and the Roman people, to be overpowered, and they had, of their own accord, adjourned the assembly that the defendant intended to obstruct by armed violence. They did not want a reason for a fight being given to men who were looking for one.

These words were accepted by all the more fair-minded senators as an appropriate response to the scandalous performance, and the Senate decreed that the act constituted violence against the state and set a deadly precedent. The Carvilii, the plebeian tribunes, thereupon abandoned the legal contest for the fine and instead arraigned Postumius on a capital charge, giving orders for him to be arrested by an officer of the court, and imprisoned, if he failed to provide a bond. Postumius provided the bond, but did not appear. The tribunes then put a motion to the plebs, which the plebs ratified, that if Marcus Postumius failed to appear before 1 May, and if he did not respond to his summons on that day, and had not been excused, then he should be deemed to be in exile. His goods were to be sold, and he himself was to be refused water and fire as an outlaw.

After that the tribunes proceeded to arraign on a capital charge all the individuals who had been agitators in the violent disorder, and to demand bonds from them. At first they imprisoned those failing to provide a bond, and later even those who were able to provide one. Most simply went into exile,* thereby avoiding the danger of this.

5. So ended the episode of the tax-collectors' fraud and its brazen cover-up. Elections for the post of *pontifex maximus* were then held, and they were run by Marcus Cornelius Cethegus, a new pontiff. Three men hotly contested the position: Quintus Fulvius Flaccus, the consul, who had twice been consul and who had also been a censor; Titus Manlius Torquatus, who was likewise well known for two consulships and a censorship; and Publius Licinius Crassus, who was about to run for the curule aedileship. In that contest the young man defeated the senior men who had already held office. Before Crassus, no one had, over a period of a hundred and twenty years, been elected *pontifex maximus* without his first having held a curule chair, the one exception being Publius Cornelius Calussa.*

The consuls had problems completing their troop-levy. The shortage of younger men made it difficult for them to attain their twin objectives of enrolling fresh city legions and supplementing the old ones. The Senate instructed them not to abandon their efforts, and also gave orders for the establishment of two boards of triumvirs. These were to inspect the entire range of free men in the country areas, rural towns, and administrative centres, and recruit as soldiers any who seemed to have the strength to bear arms, even if they were not yet of military age. One board was to take the area within a fifty-mile radius of the city, the other the countryside beyond that point.

The tribunes of the plebs, if they saw fit, were to bring before the people a proposal that the service of any who took the oath before the age of seventeen should be regarded as the same as if they had entered service at seventeen or older. Following this decree of the Senate, two triumviral boards were established,* and these conducted troop-levies of freeborn men throughout the countryside.

In this same period a letter from Marcus Marcellus in Sicily was read out in the Senate. It dealt with demands made by soldiers serving under Publius Lentulus. This force—all that remained from the disaster at Cannae—had been sent off to Sicily, as noted above, and was not to be brought back to Italy before the end of the Punic War.

6. With Lentulus' permission, these men had sent their leading cavalrymen and centurions, and the cream of the legionary infantry, to Marcus Marcellus in his winter quarters, to act as their representatives. One of them, given permission to make a statement, spoke as follows:

'Marcus Marcellus: We wanted to come to you in Italy, during your consulship, at the time of the passing of this decree of the Senate which was certainly harsh, if not unfair. What held us back was wishful thinking. We thought we were being sent into a province that was in chaos after the death of its rulers, to take on a serious war against the Sicilians and Carthaginians at the same time. We felt that by shedding our blood, and accepting our wounds, we would make amends to the Senate, just as, in our fathers' time, those captured by Pyrrhus at Heraclea made amends by fighting against Pyrrhus himself. And yet what did we do to deserve your anger at us in the past, or now, members of the Senate?* (For when I look at you, Marcus Marcellus, I feel that I am looking at the two consuls along with the entire Senate; and if we had had you as our consul at Cannae, both the republic and we ourselves would now be in a better condition.)

'Before I start an appeal against our treatment, please allow me to clear us of the transgression with which we are charged. If the catastrophe we suffered at Cannae is attributable to human error, and not to divine wrath or fate, by whose law all human events are immutably linked together—then whose error was it, for heaven's sake? The enlisted men's or their commanders'? Now I am an enlisted man, and I would never say anything about my commander. Especially when I know that he received thanks from the Senate for not having lost confidence in the republic, and when he has seen his *imperium* extended every year since the rout at Cannae. It is the same for those other men who survived that disaster, men whom we had as our military tribunes. We have been told that they are running for office, holding office, and being given tours of duty. Can it be, members of the Senate, that you find it easy to pardon yourselves and your sons, and yet you vent your rage on us poor creatures? And though it was no disgrace for a consul, and other leaders of the community, to escape when there was no hope left, did the common soldiers have to die, come what may, when you sent them into battle?

'At the Allia almost the entire army took to flight, and at the Caudine Forks* the army surrendered its weapons to the enemy without so much as tasting battle—I make no mention of other shameful defeats of our armies, but there was no question of those armies earning any disgrace. No, the city of Rome was actually retaken by the army that had fled from the Allia over to Veii. And the legions from Caudium, which had returned to Rome without their weapons, were rearmed and sent back to Samnium, where they sent under the yoke the very same enemy that had earlier taken pleasure in inflicting that humiliation on them.

'But can anyone accuse the army at Cannae of flight or panic? More than 50,000 men lost their lives there; the consul fled with a mere seventy cavalrymen; and there were no survivors except those left by an enemy physically exhausted from killing. When the prisoners were refused ransom, we were praised in all quarters for having preserved ourselves for the good of the state, and for having returned to the consul at Venusia and presented the general appearance of a regular army. But now we are treated worse than prisoners were treated in our forefathers' time. For them, all that changed was their weapons, their military rank, and the location in which they pitched their tent in the camp—and this they remedied by one act of service to the state, by fighting one successful battle. None of them was sent into exile, none robbed of his hopes of serving out his time. They were, in short, granted an enemy, fighting whom would once and for all put an end either to their lives or to their disgrace. In our case, we can be reproached with nothing, apart from seeing to it that *some* Roman soldiers survived the battle of Cannae. And for that we are banished far away, not only from our home, but even from the enemy, there to grow old in exile, with no hope or opportunity of removing our disgrace, allaying the anger of our fellow citizens or of even dying an honourable death.

'We do not ask for an end to our disgrace or a reward for our valour. Just allow us to put our spirit to the test and our courage into action. It is hardship and danger that we ask for, so that we may fulfil our role as men and soldiers. The war in Sicily is now in its second year, its ferocity intense. The Carthaginians are assaulting some cities, the Romans others; infantry and cavalry are clashing on the field; at Syracuse the war proceeds on land and sea. The shouting of the combatants and the clash of arms we hear as we idly fritter away our time, seemingly without weapons and the hands to use them. The consul Tiberius Sempronius has on many occasions used legions composed of slaves to engage the enemy in pitched battle; they have their liberty, and the grant of citizenship, as a reward for their efforts. Let us at least be regarded as your slaves, bought for this war; give us the right to engage the enemy and seek our liberty through battle. Do you want to test our mettle on sea, on land, in the field of battle, in assaulting cities? We ask for all the harshest tasks and dangers, so that what should have been done at Cannae can be done as soon as possible. For our life since then has all been doomed to ignominy.'

7. Saying this, the men fell at Marcellus' knees. Marcellus replied that he had neither the right nor the power to grant their request, but that he would write to the Senate, and follow the ruling of the members to the letter. The letter was brought to the new consuls, by whom it was read out in the Senate. When asked for its ruling, the Senate decided that it saw no reason to entrust state security to men who had abandoned their colleagues in the battle at Cannae. If the proconsul Marcus Claudius thought differently, the senators added, he could take measures that were in accord with the interests of state and his own conscience. But none of the men were to be excused any duty, receive any military recognition for his courage, or be taken back to Italy for as long as the enemy remained on Italian soil.

After that elections were held by the urban praetor, following a decree of the Senate which was ratified by the people. In these a board of quinquevirs was elected for the repair of the city's walls and towers. Two boards of triumvirs were also appointed, one to search out sacred objects and make an inventory of temple gifts, and the other to rebuild the temples of Fortune and Mater Matuta inside the Porta Carmentalis, and that of Hope outside the gate. The temples had been destroyed in the fire of the previous year.*

There were some severe storms, and on the Alban Mount it rained stones continuously for two days. There were many places struck by lightning: two temples on the Capitol, and many points on the rampart in the camp above Suessula, where two sentinels were also killed. The wall and a number of towers at Cumae were not merely struck by bolts of lightning but actually knocked down. At Reate, a huge rock seemed to be in flight, and the sun was redder than usual, taking on a bloody hue. In view of these portents, there was a one-day period of public prayer, and the consuls devoted themselves to religious observances for a number of days, which included a nine-day ceremony during that time.

The defection of Tarentum was something that Hannibal had long hoped for, and that the Romans had long suspected to be coming; and, as it happened, a reason for advancing its timing came up from outside. Phileas of Tarentum had already been in Rome for some time, ostensibly on an embassy. A man of restless character, he had little patience with his long inactivity, in which he simply felt he was now growing old. Phileas found a way of gaining access to the hostages of Tarentum and Thurii. They were under guard in the Hall of Liberty,* but security was quite lax, because playing the Romans false served the interests neither of the hostages nor their states. In the course of numerous meetings Phileas won them over, and, after bribing the sacristans and temple guards, he brought them out of their prison, just as darkness fell. He then joined them on their secret journey, and became a fugitive himself. At daybreak, news of the escape spread through the city. Men were sent in pursuit; and they caught them at Tarracina and brought them all back to the city. The fugitives were ushered into the Comitium and, with the approval of the people, they were flogged and hurled down from the rock.

8. The brutality of this punishment caused ill-feeling in the two most famous Greek city-states in Italy, and on a personal as well as national level, in so far as individuals were connected by family or friendship with the men who had faced such horrible deaths. Some thirteen such people, young noblemen of Tarentum, formed a conspiracy, its leaders being Nico and Philemenus. The conspirators felt they should discuss matters with Hannibal before making any move, and so, leaving the city on the pretence of going hunting, they set off at night to see him.

When they were not far from the Carthaginian camp, the others hid in a wood close to the road while Nico and Philemenus went ahead to the guard-posts. They were arrested, and, at their own request, brought to Hannibal. They told him the reasons for their plot, and what they planned on doing, and for this they received high praise from Hannibal, who showered them with promises. They were then instructed to drive back to the city some cattle of the Carthaginians that had been turned out to graze, in order to convince their compatriots that they had left the city on a plundering expedition. They were assured that they would be safe doing this, and would encounter no opposition.

The plunder of the young men received some attention, and their second and subsequent forays caused less surprise. Meeting Hannibal again, they secured an assurance from him that, after their liberation, the people of Tarentum would retain their own laws and keep their possessions, and would not pay any tax to the Carthaginians or have a garrison installed against their wishes. After its betrayal, the Roman garrison was to be in the hands of the Carthaginians. After they reached this agreement, Philemenus made a more regular practice of leaving and returning to the city at night. He did, in fact, have a reputation for his passion for hunting, and he always had his dogs and other hunting equipment with him. He would usually bag something, or he was brought something by the enemy by previous arrangement. This he would carry back, and present to the commander, or the guards at the gates, as a gift. His choice of the night as the time for his comings and goings was, they believed, prompted by fear of the enemy.

By now Philemenus' practice had become so routine that, when he gave his signal with a whistle, no matter what the time of night, the gate would be opened for him, and Hannibal decided the time for action had come. He was three days' march from the town and, to lessen surprise at his remaining encamped in the same spot for so long, he feigned illness. Even the Romans in the garrison at Tarentum had by now ceased to be suspicious at his prolonged inactivity.

9. After deciding to march to Tarentum, Hannibal picked out 10,000 infantry and cavalry, men whom he thought best suited for the mission by virtue of their speed and light armour, and moved out at the fourth watch of the night,* He sent ahead a force of about eighty Numidian horsemen with orders to ride through the area surrounding the roads and conduct a thorough reconnaissance, to

ensure that no peasant spotted his column from a distance unbeknownst to them. Any peasants who were ahead of them they were to turn back, and they were to kill any they met, so that the local people would have the impression they were raiders rather than a regular army. Hannibal himself marched the army forward at a swift pace, pitching camp some fifteen miles from Tarentum. Not even at that point did he announce their objective. He merely summoned the men and told them to keep to the road and not let anyone stray from it or break ranks as they marched. Above all, they were to stay alert to catch their orders, and not do anything unless commanded to do so by their officers—Hannibal would let them know at the appropriate moment what he wanted done.

It was at about that same hour of the day that a rumour had reached Tarentum that a few Numidian horsemen were raiding the fields and had struck panic into the country people far and wide. The Roman commander's reaction* to the news was no more than to issue orders for some of his cavalry to go out at dawn the following day to keep the enemy from plundering. So negligible was his vigilance in all other respects that he even accepted the Numidians' raid as evidence that Hannibal and his army had not broken camp.

Hannibal moved forward in the early hours of darkness. His guide was Philemenus, who had with him his customary load of game; the rest of the traitors were waiting to make their contribution to the pact. It had been agreed that Philemenus would take his game in by the small entranceway he normally used, and bring some armed men in with him, while Hannibal would approach the Temenid gate from another direction. That area of town is on the landward side, facing east, and tombs take up a considerable space inside the walls. As Hannibal approached the gate, he lit a torch, the pre-arranged signal, and the same signal gleamed back from Nico. Then both lights were extinguished. Hannibal led his men to the gate in silence, and Nico made a surprise attack on the sleeping guards, killed them in their beds, and threw open the gate. Hannibal entered the town with his infantry column, but instructed his cavalry to remain behind so they would be free to charge over the open plain to wherever they might be needed.

On the other side of town, Philemenus, too, was now approaching the little entranceway through which he had been regularly coming and going. His familiar voice and the well-known signal woke the sentry, and, just as Philemenus was commenting that a beast of that size was almost too heavy to carry, the gate was opened. Two young men brought in a wild boar, and Philemenus and a hunter who was carrying little equipment came in after them. The sentry turned to the bearers with too little caution, amazed at the animal's size, and Philemenus ran him through with a hunting-spear. Then some thirty armed men entered, cut down the other sentries, and smashed in the gate next to the entranceway; and with that a column immediately burst into the town, in regular formation. From there they marched in silence into the forum, where they joined Hannibal. The Carthaginian formed up 2,000 Gauls in three divisions, and sent them off through the city, giving each division two men of Tarentum as guides. He gave orders for the busiest thoroughfares to be secured and, when the uproar started, for the Romans to be indiscriminately massacred, but the Tarentines spared. To make that possible, he issued instructions to his young Tarentine supporters to tell any of their townspeople that they saw in the distance to remain calm, stay silent, and keep their hopes up.

10. By now there was the uproar and shouting that occurs when a city is captured, but what was happening nobody really knew. The people of Tarentum thought the Romans had risen up to pillage their city; to the Romans it seemed to be some kind of treacherous uprising by the townspeople. The garrison commander, awakened by the initial commotion, slipped away to the harbour, where he was taken aboard a boat and ferried around to the citadel. Uncertainty was compounded by a bugle-call heard coming from the theatre. It was a Roman bugle, acquired ahead of time by the conspirators for this very purpose, but it was also blown ineptly by a Greek, making it unclear who was giving the signal, and to whom it was being given.

When daylight came, the Romans recognized the Carthaginian and Gallic armour, and this removed all doubt from their minds; and the sight of butchered Romans lying everywhere made the Greeks aware, too, that the city had been captured by Hannibal.

The light grew stronger; the Romans who had survived the massacre had taken refuge in the citadel; and the uproar gradually began to die down. At this point, Hannibal had the people of Tarentum summoned, without weapons. They all assembled, apart from those who had followed the Romans when they retreated to the citadel, ready to share with them whatever fortune had in store. At the meeting, Hannibal made a conciliatory address to the Tarentines, reminding them of his kind treatment of their fellow citizens whom he had taken prisoner at Trasimene and Cannae, and at the same time berating the Romans for their high-handed governance. He then told them to return to their homes, and write their names on their doors. He said that he would immediately give a signal for houses that were not so marked to be looted, and that he would regard as an enemy anyone who wrote his name on a dwelling inhabited by a Roman citizen (for the Romans were occupying vacant houses). The meeting was then adjourned. When the doors had been marked with names, distinguishing a friendly habitation from that of a foe, a signal was given, and men rushed off in all directions to loot the Romans' living-quarters. And a substantial quantity of plunder was taken.

11. The next day Hannibal led his men to launch an attack on the citadel. He could see, however, that it could not be taken by storm or by siege-works, since the section facing the sea—and it is mostly surrounded by the sea, like a peninsula—was protected by towering cliffs; and, on the side of the city, its defences were a wall and a huge moat. He was, however, concerned that the effort of safeguarding the Tarentines would hold him back from more significant operations, whereas, if these were left without a strong defensive force, the Romans could attack them from the citadel whenever they liked. He decided, therefore, to isolate the city from the citadel by means of earthworks. He was not without hope, too, that the Romans would try to block the work, and could be drawn into an engagement. In fact, if their attack were too confident, he hoped that the strength of their garrison would be reduced by heavy casualties, to the point where the Tarentines might easily be able to defend the city against them on their own.

When the construction had got under way, the gate was suddenly flung open, and the Romans attacked the working parties. The guards in the post in front of the works allowed themselves to be driven back so that the Romans, their recklessness growing with success, would chase their defeated foe in greater numbers, and over a greater distance. Then a signal was given and the Carthaginians— whom Hannibal had kept formed up just for this purpose—rose to the attack on every side. The Romans could not withstand the assault, but the restricted space, and the obstacles they faced in the works already under construction, and the building materials for the others, impeded their headlong flight. Large numbers threw themselves into the moat, and the loss of life was greater in the retreat than in the fighting. After that there was no obstruction when work recommenced. A huge ditch was dug, an earthwork was erected behind it,* and, a short distance away, Hannibal was also preparing a wall running parallel to them, to give the Tarentines the capability to defend themselves against the Romans even without a garrison. He did, nevertheless, leave behind a garrison of modest proportions, which would also be able to help with the completion of the wall; and he then set off with the rest of his troops and encamped at the River Galaesus, which is five miles from the city.

When Hannibal returned from this camp to inspect the work, it had progressed with considerably greater speed than he had expected, and he conceived the hope that the citadel could even be taken by assault. In fact, its security does not lie in its height, as with other citadels; it is situated on level ground, and is cut off from the city only by a wall and a moat. The attack was going ahead, with all kinds of assault machinery and siege-works, when the Romans received armed assistance from Metapontum,* giving them the courage to launch a surprise attack by night on the enemy works. They smashed some, and others they destroyed by fire—and that spelled the end of Hannibal's assault on the citadel from that direction.

The only remaining hope was a blockade. That was unlikely to be very effective, however, because the citadel was on a peninsula, and overlooking the harbour-mouth, giving those holding it free access to the sea. The city, by contrast, was cut off from seaborne supplies, and a besieging force was more likely to starve than the besieged.

Hannibal called the leading Tarentines together and explained all the problems they faced. He could see no way of taking such a well-protected citadel by assault, and he had no confidence in a blockade, either, as long as the enemy controlled the sea. But if he had ships with which he could head off the conveyance of supplies, he added, the enemy would either immediately leave the citadel or surrender. The Tarentines agreed, but said they thought that the man responsible for the idea should also be responsible for providing the means to carry it out. Punic ships brought from Sicily could achieve his end, they said, but their own ships were confined within a narrow bay, with the enemy in control of the harbour entrance—how could they possibly make it out to the open sea?

'They will make it out,' said Hannibal. 'Many problems that nature puts in one's way are solved by thinking them through. You have a city that lies on a plain; you have streets that are level, and very broad, running in all directions. I shall transport the ships on wagons along the street that runs through the city centre from the harbour to the sea. It will not take much effort, and the sea that the enemy now controls will be ours. Then we shall blockade the citadel by sea, on the one side, and by land, on the other. No, rather, we shall soon capture it, either abandoned by its defenders or along with its defenders!'

These comments aroused not only hopes for success but admiration for the commander. Wagons were immediately assembled from all quarters and lashed together; cranes were brought up for hauling the ships ashore; and improvements made to the road to ease the passage of the carts and lighten the effort of moving them. Then pack animals and workmen were brought together, and the work started with gusto. And so, a few days later, a fleet that was equipped and ready for action sailed around the citadel, and dropped anchor right before the harbour mouth. This was how Hannibal left matters at Tarentum when he returned to his winter quarters. Whether the defection of the Tarentines occurred in the previous year or in this year is, however, disputed by historians, though most, including those living closer to the time when the facts were still remembered, place it in this year.*

12. Back in Rome, the Latin Festival kept the consuls and praetors in the city until 27 April. On that day they performed the sacrifice on the Alban Mount, and then set off for their various provinces.

After that, fresh religious impediments arose as a result of the prophecies of Marcius.* This Marcius had been a famous prophet, and, during the Senate-authorized hunt for documents of this kind the previous year, his prophetic verses had fallen into the hands of Marcus Aemilius, the urban praetor, who was conducting the search. Aemilius had immediately passed them on to the new praetor, Sulla. There were two predictions made by this Marcius. One of them was made public only after the relevant event, but the authority it acquired by its fulfilment added credibility to the other, the time for which had not arrived.

In the first prophecy the disaster at Cannae had been predicted in words much as follows:

'Child of Troy, flee the River Canna,* lest men from abroad force you to do battle on Diomede's plain. But you will not believe me until you have filled the plain with blood, and the river bears your dead in many thousands from fertile land to the great sea. For fish and birds and beasts that dwell on the land let your flesh be food. For this has Jupiter said to me.'

And, indeed, those who had fought in the area recognized in the prophecy the plains of the Argive Diomedes and the River Canna, as well as the defeat itself.

The second prophecy was then read out. This was not only more difficult to fathom because the future is less clear than the past, but was also more cryptic in the way it was written:

'Romans: If you wish to drive out the enemy, the tumour* that comes from afar, my advice is to dedicate games to Apollo, annual games to be held with good cheer in Apollo's honour. When the people have given part from the public purse, then let private individuals contribute for themselves and their relatives. The praetor who will be dispensing supreme justice to the people and plebeians shall be in charge of the conduct of such games. The decemvirs should offer sacrifice after the Greek manner.* If you do this correctly, you shall rejoice for ever, and your circumstances shall improve. For he will wipe out your enemies, that one of the gods who gently nourishes your fields.'

The authorities spent one day deciphering the prophetic verse, and on the next came a decree of the Senate bidding the decemvirs to consult the Sibylline Books about games in Apollo's honour, and sacrificial offerings to him. After these had consulted the Books, and reported their findings to the Senate, the senators decided that games be offered in a vow to Apollo, and held in his honour. After the holding of the games, twelve thousand *asses* and two full-grown sacrificial victims were to be given to the praetor for the religious ceremony. A second senatorial decree stipulated that the decemvirs were to conduct the ceremony after the Greek manner, and with the following sacrificial victims: for Apollo, an ox with gilded horns and two white she-goats with gilded horns; for Latona, a cow with gilded horns.

When the praetor was about to open the games in the Circus

Maximus, he made a proclamation that, during the period of the games, the people should make an offering of money to Apollo that they could comfortably afford.

Such is the origin of the Apollinine Games, which were vowed and instituted to secure victory, and not good health, as most people think. The people watched the events wearing garlands, and matrons offered prayers. All over the city, dinners were held in the forecourts of houses, with doors left open, and the day was solemnized with all manner of ceremonies.

13. Hannibal was now in the neighbourhood of Tarentum, and both the consuls, though both were in Samnium, clearly intended to blockade Capua. The people of Capua were, in fact, already experiencing hunger, the usual cruel result of a protracted siege, because the Roman armies had prevented them from seeding their fields.* They therefore sent spokesmen to Hannibal and begged him to have grain transported to Capua from the neighbouring districts before the consuls could bring their legions into the Capuan countryside and there were enemy roadblocks everywhere. Hannibal instructed Hanno to cross over with his army from Bruttium into Campania, and make every effort to have the Campanians provisioned with grain.

Hanno left Bruttium with his army and, taking care to avoid the enemy camp and the consuls in Samnium, approached Beneventum, encamping on some elevated ground three miles from the actual city. He gave orders for grain to be carted into his camp from the allied peoples round about, with whom it had been stockpiled in the summer, and he provided an armed escort for the consignments. He next sent a message to Capua indicating the date on which people should be present in the camp to accept the grain, and telling them to come with all manner of carts and pack animals, which they should gather in from the countryside. Hanno's instructions were followed by the Capuans with their typical lethargy and carelessness, and not many more than four hundred carts and a few pack animals were actually sent along. For this they were reproached by Hanno, who told them that even the hunger that provoked dumb animals to action could not stimulate them to make an effort, and another date was fixed for them to come with more equipment to collect their grain.

All these developments were reported, as they happened, to the people of Beneventum and the Beneventans lost no time in sending ten envoys to the consuls—the Roman camp was close to Bovianum. When the consuls heard what was happening at Capua, they came to an agreement that one of them should take his army into Campania. Fulvius, to whom this area of responsibility had fallen by sortition,* then set off and entered the fortifications of Beneventum during the night. Now close to the action, Fulvius learned that Hanno had left on a foraging expedition with a section of his army; that the Capuans had been supplied with grain by Hanno's quaestor;* and that 2,000 wagons and a motley crowd of unarmed men had arrived. Confusion and panic reigned everywhere, he was told, and camp organization and military routine had been undermined by peasants and slaves who had also come on the scene.

After having this confirmed, the consul instructed his men to get ready only their standards and weapons for the oncoming night— they had to attack the Punic camp. Leaving all their kit and baggage at Beneventum, they set out at the fourth watch, and reached the camp shortly before dawn. Such was the panic they struck in the enemy that there was no doubt that the camp could have been taken at the first assault, had it lain on level ground. It was its elevation and fortifications—unreachable on any side, except by a steep and difficult slope—that protected it. At daybreak a fierce battle broke out, and the Carthaginians not only defended their rampart but also, having the territorial advantage, flung down their enemies as they struggled up the heights.

14. Unflagging courage, however, conquers all, and the Romans reached the rampart and ditches at several places at the same time, though at a heavy cost in wounds and soldiers' lives. The consul therefore summoned his legates and military tribunes, and told them they had to abandon this reckless venture. It seemed to him safer to take the army back to Beneventum that day, he said, and then, on the following, to pitch their camp close to the camp of the enemy, in order to prevent the Campanians from leaving, or Hanno from coming back. To make that easier, he would also send for his colleague and his forces, and together they would bring all their military resources to bear on this one objective.

Such was the commander's plan of campaign, but it was scattered to the winds, just as he was sounding the retreat, by the shouts of soldiers indignantly rejecting the spineless order. The unit closest to the enemy happened to be a Paelignian cohort.* Its prefect, Vibius

Accaus, grabbed the cohort's banner and hurled it over the enemy rampart. He then called down curses on himself and on the cohort if the enemy got their hands on the banner, and, forging ahead of the others over ditch and rampart, he burst into the Carthaginian camp.

The Paeligni were now fighting within the enemy rampart while, on the other side of the camp, Valerius Flaccus, military tribune of the third legion, was severely reprimanding the Romans for their cowardice in ceding to allies the distinction of taking the camp. Then Titus Pedanius, the first centurion of the *principes*,* took the standard from the bearer and declared: 'This standard and this centurion are soon going to be inside the enemy rampart. Those who are going to prevent its capture by the enemy, follow me!' As he crossed the ditch, his comrades from his maniple were the first to follow him, and then the whole legion came after them.

The sight of the men crossing the ditch changed the consul's mind. Now he turned from recalling them, and trying to bring them back, to urging them on and giving encouragement, and he pointed out the dangerous predicament in which the bravest of the allied cohorts, and a legion of their fellow citizens, now found themselves. And so, with each man making an effort, they clambered over ground easy and difficult, under showers of missiles hurled from every direction, and with the enemy blocking them with their weapons and their bodies, and burst into the camp. Many of the wounded, even as strength and blood drained from them, strained to fall within the enemy rampart. And so, in an instant, the camp was taken, as if it had been sitting in the plain without fortifications. Then, as the two sides swarmed together within the rampart, it was a bloodbath, and no longer a battle.

More than 6,000 of the enemy were killed. More than 7,000 men were taken prisoner, and captured along with them were the Capuans who had come for the grain, and the whole array of wagons and pack animals. There was also a huge store of plunder that Hanno had hauled from the fields of Roman allies, at the time when he had gone off on his widespread raids. After that, the Romans destroyed the enemy camp and returned to Beneventum. There the two consuls— for Appius Claudius also arrived a few days later—sold the booty and divided the proceeds. In addition, the men whose efforts had resulted in the capture of the enemy camp were rewarded, especially

Accaus the Paelignian and Titus Pedanius, the first centurion of the third legion.

News of the loss of the camp reached Hanno at Cominium Ocritum. He left the town along with a few foragers that he had happened to have with him, and his return to Bruttium was more like a flight than a march.

15. When they heard about the disaster that had struck both them and their allies, the Capuans sent envoys to Hannibal to report that the two consuls were at Beneventum, a mere day's march from Capua, which meant that the war was practically at their gates and walls. If Hannibal did not come swiftly with aid, then Capua would fall into the hands of the enemy more quickly than Arpi had done. The envoys were to impress on him that he should not set such great store by Tarentum, and much less by just its citadel, as to deliver Capua, which he had habitually compared with Carthage, to the Roman people abandoned and undefended.

Hannibal promised to take care of the situation in Campania, and, as a temporary measure, sent 2,000 cavalry with the envoys so the Campanians could use this force to protect their farms from enemy depredations.

The Romans, meanwhile, were preoccupied with a number of things, including the citadel of Tarentum, and the garrison under siege within it. On senatorial authority, the legate Gaius Servilius had been despatched to Etruria to purchase grain by the praetor Publius Cornelius, and he made it into the harbour of Tarentum with a number of loaded ships, slipping between the enemy patrols. Thanks to his arrival, the people who, as hope faded, had been invited to change sides at various meetings with the enemy now themselves began to invite and coax the enemy to change sides! And, in fact, the garrison was now of sufficient strength since men who had earlier been stationed in Metapontum had been reassigned to the defence of the citadel of Tarentum. The result of that was that the people of Metapontum, suddenly unburdened of the fear by which they had been held in check, went over to Hannibal.

The same thing also happened with the people of Thurii, on the same coastline. What motivated these was not so much the defection of the peoples of Tarentum and of Metapontum (with whom they actually shared a bond of kinship, the two having the same land of origin, Achaea) as their anger with the Romans over the recent execution of their hostages. The friends and relatives of the victims sent letters and messages to Hanno and Mago,* who were close by in Bruttium, informing them that, if the two generals brought an army up to their walls, they would deliver the city into their hands. The Roman commander at Thurii was Marcus Atinius, who had only a small garrison, and the conspirators thought he could easily be enticed into recklessly engaging in battle through confidence, not in his men, whose numbers were very small, but in the young men of Thurii. Atinius had made a point of forming these up in centuries, and equipping them with weapons, to meet such emergencies.

The Carthaginian commanders divided their forces and marched into the territory of Thurii. Hanno proceeded to the city with the infantry column drawn up ready for action, and Mago, with the cavalry, took up a position under the cover of some hills that were conveniently situated for concealing an ambush. From his scouts, Atinius had learned only about the infantry column, and he led out his troops for battle, unaware of the conspiracy within the city, and the ambush set by the enemy. The infantry engagement was sluggish: there were few Romans in the front line, and the Thurians were waiting for, rather than helping to achieve, an outcome. The Carthaginian line now began deliberately to fall back, to draw the unsuspecting enemy behind the hill occupied by their cavalry. When they reached that point, the Carthaginian cavalry charged to the attack with a shout, swiftly driving off the mass of Thurians, who were almost in chaos, and had little loyalty to the side on which they stood. The Romans, surrounded and under pressure from the infantry on one front, and from the cavalry on the other, still managed to keep up the fight for a time. Eventually they, too, turned and fled to the city.

In town the conspirators had banded together and, with the gates wide open, they let in the body of their compatriots. But when they saw the defeated Romans surging towards the city, they cried out that the Carthaginians were hard on their heels, and that the enemy would also come into the city mixed with the fugitives, if the Thurians did not swiftly close the gates. And so they shut out the Romans, offering them up to the enemy for slaughter, though Atinius and a few others were admitted. Discord followed for a time, as some advocated remaining true to Rome, and others felt they should accept what fortune brought, and surrender the city to the victors. As usual, however, fortune and bad advice carried the day. Atinius and his entourage were taken to some ships on the shore,* more because the Thurians were concerned for him personally, because of his clement and fair jurisdiction over them, than from any regard for the Romans. They then admitted the Carthaginians into the city.

The consuls marched their legions from Beneventum into Campanian territory, intending not only to destroy the grain that was already sprouting, but also to make an attack on Capua. They thought that destroying such a wealthy city would add lustre to their consulship, and that they would, at the same time, be removing from the empire the deep disgrace of leaving the secession of a nearby city unpunished for more than two years. But they did not want Beneventum left without a garrison, and they also wanted to have the ability to face military emergencies, and stem the violence of Hannibal's cavalry, should he come to Capua to assist his allies, as they were sure he would. Accordingly, they instructed Tiberius Gracchus to come from Lucania to Beneventum with his cavalry and light infantry, and told him to put someone in command of the legions and camp in Lucania, in order to retain control of the region.

16. Before moving out of Lucania, Gracchus conducted a sacrifice, and there was a grim portent. The sacrificial act completed, two snakes slithered unobtrusively up to the entrails, and ate part of the liver; and then, when they were spotted, they suddenly disappeared. Therefore, on the advice of the seers, the sacrifice was repeated, and greater care was taken with the entrails, but tradition has it that the snakes slithered up on a second and third occasion, tasted the liver, and left unharmed. The seers gave advance warning that the focus of the omen was on the commander, and that he should be on his guard against men working and planning against him in secret. However, his impending doom could be averted by no clairvoyance.

The Lucanian Flavus was leader of the faction of Lucanians that remained pro-Roman when some of the people defected to Hannibal. He had been elected praetor by the members of his faction, and was already in his second year of office. He suddenly changed his sympathies and looked for an opportunity to ingratiate himself with the Carthaginians. He did not feel that simply deserting and drawing the Lucanians into defection was enough—he had to endorse his pact with the enemy by betraying his commander, who was also a personal friend, and taking the man's life.

Flavus came to talk in secret with Mago, the Carthaginian commander in Bruttium, and was given an assurance that the Lucanians should live as free men under their own constitution, and enjoy the friendship of the Carthaginians, if he delivered the Roman commander to them. He then took the Carthaginian to a place to which he said he would bring Gracchus, along with a small escort. He told Mago to hide some armed infantry and cavalry there, noting that the hiding-place could hold a large number of men. When they had thoroughly inspected and patrolled the location, a date was set for executing the plan.

Flavus came next to the Roman commander. He had embarked on an important project, he told him, but he needed Gracchus' personal assistance to put the final touches to it. He had convinced the praetors of all those peoples who had defected to the Carthaginian, during the general unrest in Italy, to return to their treaties of friendship with Rome. He had impressed on them that the situation of Rome, which had come close to ruin with the disaster at Cannae, was becoming better and stronger each day, while Hannibal's power was weakening and had almost vanished. As for their past offence, the Romans would not be unforgiving, he had told them; no people had ever shown themselves more clement, or ready to forgive—witness the number of times even the Lucanians' ancestors had been forgiven for their insurrections! These points he had himself made to the praetors, said Flavus, but they preferred to hear the same things directly from Gracchus, and to have him present so they could grasp his right hand, and take away with them this assurance of his good faith. He had fixed a venue for their meeting, he said, one that was secluded and not far from the Roman camp, and there it would take only a few words to have all the Lucanian people under the protection of Rome, and allied with her.

Gracchus suspected no treachery in the man's words or the project, and he was taken in by the plausible scenario. Leaving camp with his lictors and a cavalry squadron, and guided by his 'personal friend', he fell right into the trap. The enemy suddenly rose up and, to leave no doubt about the betrayal, Flavus joined them. Missiles were hurled at Gracchus and his horsemen from every direction. He dismounted, ordering the others to do the same, and exhorting them to embellish with their valour the one option that fortune had left them. They were few in number, surrounded by a host of men in a valley enclosed by forest and hills—what was left to them but death, he asked. What mattered now was whether they were going to be butchered without retaliation, offering up their bodies like cattle, or whether they would, instead, reject completely the idea of submissively awaiting the outcome, and launch a furious attack on the enemy. Would they take action and show defiance, and fall covered with the blood of their foe amidst the mounds of their dying enemies' weapons and bodies? They must all make their target the Lucanian who betrayed and deserted them, said Gracchus. The man who sent that victim down to the underworld ahead of himself, would win outstanding honour, and singular consolation for his own death.

So saying, Gracchus wrapped his general's cloak around his left arm—they had not even brought their shields with them—and rushed at the enemy. The ensuing fight was fiercer than the numbers involved would have led one to expect. It was to the javelins that the Romans were most exposed; and by these they were being transfixed, as the enemy could hurl them down, from their higher positions, into the sunken hollow. Gracchus was by now stripped of his escort, and the Carthaginians were attempting to take him alive. But he caught sight of his Lucanian 'friend' in the enemy's midst, and made such a furious charge into the closely packed group that sparing his life was impossible without the loss of many men. Mago immediately sent the dead body to Hannibal, with instructions for it to be set before the general's tribunal together with the *fasces* that had been taken. If this is the correct version, Gracchus fell at the so-called 'Old Fields' in Lucania.

17. There are some who place Gracchus' death near the River Calor in the area of Beneventum. He had left his camp with his lictors and three slaves to wash himself down, these people claim, and some of the enemy happened to be hiding among the willows growing on the river-bank. He was killed, naked and unarmed, as he fought back with the stones that the river rolled along. There are others whose accounts have him going a half-mile from the camp, on the advice of his seers, to expiate on pure soil the portents mentioned above, and being surrounded by two squadrons of Numidians who chanced to be lying in ambush there. Such is the uncertainty surrounding where and how such a famous and distinguished man met his end.*

Accounts of Gracchus' funeral also vary. Some report that he was buried by his own men in the Roman camp. Others—and this is the more widespread version—claim that a pyre was erected for him, on Hannibal's orders, in the area before the Carthaginian camp. Then the army paraded in battledress, with the Spaniards performing dances, and all the tribes using their bodies and weapons to execute their traditional movements, and Hannibal himself did and said whatever he could to honour the man's funeral. Such is the account of authors who locate the events in Lucania. If one prefers to accept the version of those who put his death at the River Calor, then Gracchus' enemies took possession of his head only. The head was brought to Hannibal, who immediately despatched Carthalo to take it to the quaestor Gnaeus Cornelius in the Roman camp. Cornelius held the commander's funeral in the camp, and the people of Beneventum joined the army in the ceremonies.

18. After entering the farmlands of Campania, the consuls were conducting widespread raids when a counterattack from the towns-people, and from Mago and his cavalry, filled them with alarm. Panicking, they called their widely scattered men back to the stand-ards, but they were routed after barely forming a battle line, with the loss of more than 1,500 soldiers. The Campanians were a tempera-mentally arrogant people, and after this incident their belligerence increased enormously. They began to harass the Romans with numerous engagements; but the single battle that they had incau-tiously and unwisely joined had made the consuls more prone to caution. Nevertheless, one minor event came to restore the confidence of the one side, and curtail the recklessness of the other—and yet, in warfare, nothing is so insignificant that it cannot at times have important consequences.

Titus Quinctius Crispinus had a personal friend from Capua called Badius, with whom he had very strong ties of hospitality.* Their friendship had intensified because, before the defection of the Capuans, Badius had fallen sick in Rome, and had received generous and obliging treatment at Crispinus' house.

This Badius now advanced beyond the Roman guard-posts in front of the camp gate and asked for Crispinus to be summoned. When Crispinus was given the message, he assumed that the point of the summons was a friendly, personal conversation, and that, despite the breakdown of the treaties between their peoples, there still remained the memory of their private relationship. He therefore went towards Badius slightly ahead of his comrades. When the two came in sight of each other, Badius said: 'Crispinus, I challenge you to a duel. Let us mount our horses, move others aside, and see which of the two of us is superior in combat.'

Crispinus' reply was that neither he nor Badius was short of people on whom to demonstrate their prowess. Even if he met Badius in battle, he would refuse to fight him, he said, for fear of sullying his right hand with the blood of a man with whom he had ties of mutual hospitality. With that, he turned and left. At this point the Campanian became even more truculent, taunting Crispinus with being a spineless coward, and showering on the innocent man insults that he himself deserved. He called Crispinus his 'social enemy', and said that he was simply making a pretence of showing mercy to a man for whom he knew he was no match. If Crispinus did not think that their personal relationship was not also shattered with the rupture of their peoples' treaties, then he, Badius of Campania, now publicly declared, in the hearing of the two armies, that he was renouncing his social ties with the Roman Titus Quinctius Crispinus. He was Crispinus' enemy, and had no relationship, no bond with this enemy who had come to attack his homeland, and the gods of his people and of his own house. If Crispinus were a man, Badius concluded, he should face him in battle!

Crispinus hesitated for some time, but his comrades in his squadron pushed him not to let the Campanian get away with his insults. He waited only long enough to ask his commanders' permission to leave the ranks to fight an enemy who was challenging him. Then, with their leave, he seized his weapons, mounted his horse, and, calling on Badius by name, summoned him to combat. There was no hesitation on the Campanian's part, and the two clashed on charging steeds. Crispinus thrust his spear into Badius' left arm, above his shield, and, when the wound unseated the Campanian, he jumped onto him from his horse to finish him off, on foot, as he lay on the ground. Before he could be caught, Badius ran back to his own side, leaving his shield and his horse behind. Proudly displaying the horse and the arms that he had taken, and his bloody lance, Crispinus was conducted to the consuls, resplendent with his trophies, while the men loudly cheered and congratulated him. There he was given a magnificent commendation, and presented with gifts.

19. Hannibal now moved camp from the area of Beneventum

towards Capua, and two days after his arrival he led his troops into combat. He had no doubt that, after the Campanians' successful engagement during his absence a few days earlier, the Romans would be much less capable of resisting him and his army, which had won so many victories. From the start of the battle the Roman line was under pressure, mostly because of a cavalry charge that subjected it to a hail of javelins, until the signal was given to the Roman cavalry to charge the enemy. It thus became a cavalry engagement, but then Sempronius' army, now commanded by the quaestor Gnaeus Cornelius, was spotted in the distance, and this struck fear in both sides alike that fresh forces of the enemy were arriving. On both sides, as though by agreement, the signal for retreat was given, and the men were led back to their camps, parting on almost equal terms (though losses were heavier on the Roman side, thanks to the initial cavalry attack).* In an attempt to divert Hannibal from Capua, the consuls left there the following night, moving in opposite directions, Fulvius heading into the countryside of Cumae, and Claudius into Lucania. The following day Hannibal was brought word that the Roman camp was deserted, and that the enemy had gone off as two columns in opposite directions. Unsure at first which one to follow, he eventually set off in pursuit of Appius. After leading his enemy where his fancy took him, Appius returned to Capua by another road.

Hannibal was offered a second chance of success in the area. There was one Marcus Centenius, surnamed Paenula, who stood out amongst the leading Roman centurions for his large build and courage. The man, who had completed his term of service, was brought before the Senate by the praetor Publius Cornelius Sulla, and there he requested of the senators that he be assigned 5,000 men. He knew both the enemy and the country, he explained, and he would soon make the investment worthwhile; he would turn against their originator those very tactics by which both our commanders and our armies had been taken by surprise. The promise was foolish, but just as foolish was the credence it received—as though the skills of a soldier were the same as those of a commander.

Centenius was assigned not 5,000 but 8,000 men, half of them citizens, half allies. In addition, he personally raised a number of volunteers in the countryside en route, and he arrived in Lucania, where Hannibal had come to a halt after an unsuccessful pursuit of Claudius, with an army that had almost doubled in size. There was no doubt about the outcome of a battle between a commander like Hannibal and a centurion, and between an army seasoned from victory and one completely new that was, for the most part, an assortment of poorly equipped men. The columns caught sight of each other; neither side declined battle; the lines were immediately drawn up. But the battle reflected the inequality of the situation, though hope sustained the Roman line for more than two hours, as long as the leader stood his ground. But to protect his reputation of old, and fearing also the disgrace of surviving a disaster brought on by his own recklessness, Centenius deliberately exposed himself to the enemy's weapons, and met his end. After that the Roman line was immediately driven back. But all the roads were blocked by cavalry, and so restricted was their avenue of escape that, from such a huge force, scarcely 1,000 managed to get away, while the others perished, right and left, by one means or another.*

20. The consuls now recommenced an all-out blockade of Capua, and all the materials for the operation were being brought together and made ready for action. Grain was stockpiled at Casilinum, and a fortress was built at the mouth of the Volturnus, where a city stands today. A garrison was established in the fort, and also at Puteoli, which Fabius Maximus had already fortified, so the Romans would have the river, and the sea nearby, in their power. Grain had recently been sent from Sardinia, and the praetor Marcus Iunius had bought more from Etruria. This was now transported from Ostia to these two maritime strongholds so that the army would be provisioned through the winter.

To add to the defeat suffered in Lucania, however, the army of volunteer slaves deserted its standards. It had served with unswerving loyalty while Gracchus was alive, but felt that the leader's death released it from its obligations.

Hannibal was reluctant to leave Capua neglected, and his allies deserted, at such a critical moment, but, after the success that came his way from the recklessness of one Roman leader, he was on the lookout for an opportunity to surprise a second leader and a second army. Apulian envoys now kept bringing him reports on the praetor Gnaeus Fulvius. They told him that, at first, while he was attacking some Apulian cities that had gone over to Hannibal, Fulvius had done his job with considerable diligence, but that subsequently too much success had made him and his booty-laden soldiers so neglectful and apathetic that military discipline was non-existent. Hannibal, who had on many other occasions, and particularly in the past few days, seen what an army could be like under an inept commander, moved his camp into Apulia.

21. The Roman legions, and the praetor Fulvius, were in the neighbourhood of Herdonea and, when news reached them of the enemy's approach, they all but broke camp and went into battle without the praetor's order. What held them back more than anything was the certainty they felt that they could do this, whenever they wished, at a moment convenient to them. Knowing that there had been a disturbance in the camp, with several people raising the call to arms and aggressively pushing the general to give the signal, Hannibal had no doubt that he was being offered the chance of a successful engagement. And so, that night, he stationed 3,000 light-armed men in nearby farms, and in undergrowth and woods, with orders to emerge all together from their cover, when given the sign. He also instructed Mago and some 2,000 horsemen to secure all the roads at the points where he thought the enemy would flee.

After making these preparations during the night, Hannibal led his troops out for battle at dawn. Fulvius showed no hesitation either, drawn into action less by his own hopes than by the impulsive reaction of his men. They formed up with the same lack of caution with which they had proceeded to the engagement, and at the whim of the common soldiers, who ran forward haphazardly to take any position they fancied, and then abandoned it on impulse or from fear. The first legion and the left allied wing were drawn up at the front, and the line was disproportionately long. The tribunes cried out that there was no firmness or strength within the battle line, and that the enemy would break through wherever they attacked; but the men refused to hear, much less accept, any salutary advice. And there, on the field, was Hannibal, a general not like their own, and with an army that was not like theirs, or drawn up after their manner.

The result was that the Romans failed to resist even their war cry and initial charge. Their leader was Centenius' equal in stupidity and recklessness, but was not in his class for courage. When he saw things go against him, and his men in panic, he grabbed a horse, and made off with about 200 cavalrymen. The rest of the force, driven back at the front, and then encircled to the rear and on the flanks, was cut to ribbons—so much so that from 18,000 men not more than 2,000 got away.* The enemy took possession of the camp.

22. When news of these successive defeats reached Rome, deep anxiety and alarm did, indeed, seize the community; but because supreme conduct of the war lay with the consuls, and to that point they had been successful, the defeats excited less emotion than they might have otherwise. Gaius Laetorius and Marcus Metilius were sent as envoys to the consuls. They were to instruct them to gather carefully together what remained of the two armies, and see that fear and despair did not lead the men to surrender to the enemy, as had happened after the debacle at Cannae. The consuls were also ordered to hunt down deserters from the army of slave volunteers. The same assignment was given to Publius Cornelius, who also had the responsibility of raising fresh troops. Cornelius made a proclamation throughout the country towns and administrative centres that the slave volunteers should be hunted down and brought back into service. All these instructions were attentively carried out.

The consul Appius Claudius put Decimus Junius in command at the mouth of the Volturnus, and Marcus Aurelius Cotta at Puteoli; these were to dispatch grain to the camp the moment ships arrived from Etruria and Sardinia. Claudius himself returned to Capua where he found his colleague Quintus Fulvius in the process of transporting everything from Casilinum, and actively preparing for the blockade of Capua. The two then proceeded with the investment of the city, and they also called to their assistance the praetor Claudius Nero from the Castra Claudiana at Suessula. Claudius left a small garrison at Suessula to hold the position, and came down to Capua with the rest of his troops. Thus three generals' headquarters were set up around Capua, and three armies got down to work at different points, making ready to invest the city with a ditch and rampart, and erecting fortresses at fairly narrow intervals. At the same time they clashed at many points with the Capuans, who were trying to block the siege operations, and did so with such success that eventually the townspeople kept within their gates and fortifications.

Before these different works could be joined up, however, spokesmen were sent to Hannibal to protest against his abandonment of Capua, which, they said, had been practically returned to the Romans, and to appeal to him to finally bring assistance, now that they were not just under siege but actually surrounded by entrenchments. The consuls also received written orders from the praetor Publius Cornelius* to permit any of the Capuans who so wished to leave, and take with them all their possessions before they completely cut off the city with their siege-works. Those leaving before 15 March* would remain free, and retain possession of all their property, but any leaving after that date, or remaining in the town, would be counted as enemies. This offer was communicated to the Capuans, who treated it with such contempt as to respond with insults and threats.

Hannibal had brought his legions to Tarentum from Herdonea, hoping to take the citadel of Tarentum, either by force or through intrigue. When that met with little success, he turned instead towards Brundisium, expecting that town to be betrayed to him. Here, too, he found that he was simply wasting his time, and it was at this point that the Capuan spokesmen reached him with their protests and appeals. Hannibal had a boastful reply for them. He had raised their siege before, he said, and on this occasion, too, the consuls would not withstand him when he arrived. Such were the hopes with which the spokesmen were sent off, and they were barely able to get back to Capua, which was now surrounded with a double trench and a double rampart.

23. At precisely the time that Capua was being encircled with siege-works, the assault on Syracuse came to an end. This was achieved by the aggressiveness and courage of the general and his army, but it was facilitated, too, by internal treachery. At the start of spring, Marcellus had been unsure whether to redirect the war effort towards Himilco and Hippocrates in Agrigentum, or to intensify the siege of Syracuse. He could see that taking the city by assault was impossible since its topography made it impregnable both by land and sea; and, alimented by supplies arriving almost freely from Carthage, she could not be starved into submission. But he would leave no avenue unexplored. There were amongst the Romans some prominent Syracusan nobles who had been driven out, at the time of the break with Rome, for disagreeing with the new policy. Marcellus instructed these refugees to meet, and probe the sympathies of, the men of their party in the city, and to assure them that they would have their freedom, and live under their own constitution, if Syracuse were delivered to the Romans.

No opportunity of arranging a meeting materialized: the loyalty of many people was suspect, and this had made everybody wary, and put them on guard against such activities taking place undetected. But then one slave belonging to the exiles was accepted in the city posing as a deserter, and he met a handful of people and initiated discussions on the subject. Subsequently a number of men were transported around to the Roman camp, concealed under some nets in a fishing boat, and they held discussions with the refugees. The same men repeated the procedure on a number of occasions, and were joined by others, and others again, until their total number eventually reached eighty. Then, just when preparations for the betrayal were complete, the plot was betrayed to Epicydes by a certain Attalus, who was incensed at not having been made party to it, and all the conspirators were tortured to death.

This hope had proved illusory, but another immediately arose in its place. A Spartan named Damippus had been sent to King Philip from Syracuse, and had been captured by some Roman ships. Epicydes was anxious to ransom him at any price; and Marcellus did not object, because at that moment the Romans were courting the friendship of the Aetolians,* with whom the Spartans were allied. The men sent to discuss the ransom thought that the most central location for their meeting, and the one most convenient for both parties, was at the Trogili port, close to the tower they call Galeagra.* Their comings and goings to this spot became quite frequent, and, in the course of them, one of the Romans took a close look at the wall. By counting the stones, and judging for himself the dimensions of each of their faces, he calculated the wall's height as well as one could by guesswork. He decided that it was considerably lower than he and everyone else had earlier supposed, and that it could be scaled with even quite short ladders, and he reported this to Marcellus. The idea seemed one not to be rejected out of hand. However, access to that spot was impossible, since it was more carefully guarded for the very reason just mentioned, and they needed some window of opportunity. This a deserter provided when he reported that a three-day festival of Diana* was being held in town, and that, because of the shortage of other goods during the siege, the feasting involved more copious quantities of wine than usual. The wine had been supplied to all the people by Epicydes and distributed amongst the tribes by the leading citizens.

When Marcellus received the news, he had a word with a few of his military tribunes. Through them, centurions and ordinary soldiers who were up to taking on and braving the dangers of such a bold venture were singled out, and ladders were secretly prepared. Marcellus ordered the other men to be given the signal to take refreshment and rest in good time, as they had a night operation ahead of them. Then, when he felt the point had come at which people who had been feasting during the day would have had enough wine and would be falling asleep, he ordered the soldiers of a single maniple to take up the ladders, and about 1,000 armed men were led silently to the appropriate point in a narrow column. When the first men had scaled the wall noiselessly and calmly, the others followed them up in rows, for the daring of those ahead of them encouraged even the hesitant.

24. When the 1,000 soldiers had taken possession of a section of the wall, the rest of the troops were brought forward and they began to scale it with a greater number of ladders. They had already been given a signal from the Hexapylon, which the advance party had reached after coming through a district that was thoroughly deserted, for most of the sentries had feasted in the towers, and had either fallen asleep over their cups or were still drinking in a semi-inebriated state. A few they surprised and killed in their beds.

Near the Hexapylon is a small gate. Work had begun on smashing this in with extreme force; the agreed trumpet-signal had been given from the Hexapylon; and by this point the secret operation was everywhere turning into open violence. For they had reached Epipolae, which they found strongly guarded; and it was now a question of frightening the enemy rather than eluding them—and frighten them they did. As soon as the blasts of the trumpets were heard, and the shouting of the Romans who were now in control of the walls and a section of the city, the sentinels thought the whole town was occupied, and ran off. Some fled along the wall, others jumped from it, or were pushed off by the frenzied crowds. Most, however, were unaware of the cataclysmic event. They were all heavy with drink and sleep and, in a town of such vast dimensions, news of what was going on in one quarter did not become known to the whole. At dawn, after breaking into the Hexapylon, Marcellus entered the city with all his troops, waking everybody and sending them all scurrying for their weapons, to bring whatever help they could to their almost-captured city.

Epicydes came at a quick march from the Island (which the Syracusans themselves call the Nassos*), quite certain that it was only a case of a few men having taken advantage of the sentinels' negligence to slip over the wall, and that he would soon drive them out. When he was confronted with people running in terror, he would tell them they were only increasing the panic, and that their reports were exaggerated and alarmist. But when he saw the whole area around Epipolae filled with armed men, he merely assailed his enemy with a few javelins and then marched his column back to Achradina. He was, however, less afraid of the strength and superior numbers of his enemy than he was of the opportunity that might be given for internal treachery, which, he thought, could result in his finding the gates of Achradina and the Island closed to him in the upheaval.

When Marcellus came over the fortifications, and from the higher ground saw what was probably at the time the world's most beautiful city stretched out before his eyes, they say he shed tears, partly from joy over the greatness of his achievement, but partly, too, because of the city's glories of old. He was reminded of the Athenian fleets that had been sunk there, of the two mighty armies that had been destroyed along with their leaders, of all the critical wars fought with the Carthaginians. He thought of all the city's wealthy tyrants and kings, and of Hiero above all, a king whose memory was still fresh and who—a fact more important than everything that his courage and success had brought him—was remarkable for his services to Rome. All this came to mind, and it occurred to him that in the space of an hour it would all be ablaze and reduced to ashes.* Before advancing his troops to Achradina, he sent ahead some Syracusans who, as was noted above, were serving with the Roman troops, to see if they could, with conciliatory language, induce the enemy to surrender their city.

25. The gates and walls of Achradina were, for the most part, held by deserters who, having no hope of pardon under terms of surrender, permitted no one to approach the walls, or to parley. After the failure of this approach, Marcellus ordered a retreat to the Euryalus. This is a hill on the outskirts of the city, away from the sea, overlooking the road leading into the countryside and to the interior of the island, and therefore very conveniently situated for receiving supplies. The man who had been put in command of this vantage-point by Epicydes was an Argive called Philodemus, and to him

Sosis, one of the tyrant's assassins, was sent by Marcellus. The two had a long conversation in which Sosis was stalled by the other's evasive language, and he reported to Marcellus that Philodemus had taken time to reflect on the matter. Philodemus then proceeded to put things off from day to day, waiting for Hippocrates and Himilco to move up their camp and their legions, for he was certain that, if he took these into his stronghold, the Roman army could be boxed in within the city walls and destroyed. Marcellus saw no possibility of the Euryalus being either surrendered or captured, and he established a camp between Neapolis and Tycha (these are the names of areas in the city which are themselves the size of cities!), for he feared that, if he entered heavily populated districts, his plunder-hungry men simply could not be held in check. Spokesmen from Tycha and Neapolis came to him there wearing woollen fillets and carrying suppliant branches, and begged him to refrain from slaughter and burning. Marcellus held a meeting to discuss what constituted entreaties rather than demands on their part, and, with the agreement of all present, he issued orders to the men that no one should do harm to any free person. All else, he said, would be regarded as booty.

The camp was enclosed by a series of interconnected house-walls.* Marcellus placed sentry-posts and pickets at its gates, where they opened to the streets, to prevent an attack on the camp while the men were scattered in the town. He then gave the signal and the soldiers ran hither and thither, smashing in doors, and making the whole city ring with panic and confusion. But of bloodshed there was none. There was no end to the looting until the men had carried off the whole mass of goods that years of prosperity had built up. In the meantime, Philodemus lost all hope of receiving assistance. He accepted a guarantee of a safe conduct to return to Epicydes, led out his garrison, and surrendered the hill to the Romans.

While everyone's attention was focused on the confusion in the captured section of the city, Bomilcar seized on a night when a violent storm made it impossible for the Roman fleet to ride at anchor on the open sea, and left the harbour of Syracuse through unpatrolled waters. He headed out to sea with thirty-five ships (leaving fifty-five for Epicydes and the Syracusans), and, after giving the Carthaginians a full account of the critical situation in Syracuse, returned a few days later with a fleet of a hundred. He was rewarded by Epicydes, it is said, with numerous gifts from Hiero's treasure.

26. After taking control of the Euryalus, Marcellus posted a garrison there, and thus freed himself of one particular concern. Now he need have no fear of an enemy force being taken into the citadel to his rear, and creating havoc amongst his troops who were enclosed within the confines of the city walls. He thereupon proceeded to blockade Achradina, establishing three camps at strategic points, in the hope of bringing the enemy who were under siege there to the point of complete privation.

The forward posts of both sides had seen no action for a number of days when, suddenly, the arrival of Hippocrates and Himilco actually put the Romans under attack on every side. Hippocrates established a fortified camp at the great harbour; and then, giving a signal to the men who were occupying Achradina, he launched an assault on the old camp of the Romans, which was under Crispinus' command. Meanwhile, Epicydes made a counterattack on the forward posts of Marcellus, and the Punic fleet also landed on the shoreline between the city and the Roman camp, in order to make it impossible for Crispinus to be sent assistance by Marcellus. Even so, the enemy produced more of a disturbance than a battle. Crispinus not only flung Hippocrates back from his fortifications, but even chased him as he fled in panic, and, moreover, Marcellus forced Epicydes back into the city. In fact, it seemed that enough had been done to ward off any danger in future from surprise attacks by the enemy.

Both sides now faced the further problem of a plague, which was such as to easily distract attention from strategic planning for the war. It was autumn, and the area was naturally insalubrious, though much more so outside the city than within; and an unbearable heat severely affected the health of almost everybody in the two camps. At first, the instances of sickness and death were the result of the season and unhealthy locale. Later on, simply nursing the sick, and physical contact with them, spread the disease, so that those who fell ill died neglected and alone; or else they infected with the same violent disease those who visited their bedside and attended to their needs, and took them off to the grave with them. Funerals and death were every day before men's eyes, and cries of lamentation were to be heard everywhere, day and night. Eventually, familiarity with the affliction had so desensitized them that they not only ceased to hold processions for the dead, with tears and the appropriate cries of grief, but they did not even bear them out to the pyre, and bury their remains. The result was that corpses lay strewn around before the eyes of people who were anticipating such a death themselves, and, thanks to this fear, along with the rotting and noxious stench of the cadavers, the dead were wreaking havoc on the sick, and the sick on the healthy. Preferring death by the sword, a number charged alone into the enemy outposts.

The plague had attacked the Carthaginian camp much more fiercely than it had the Roman, however, since the Romans had, from their long blockade of Syracuse, become more habituated to the climate and the water. The Sicilians in the enemy army slipped away to their various cities nearby as soon as they saw the noxious environment turning the disease into an epidemic; and, with nowhere to go themselves, the Carthaginians perished to a man, their generals Hippocrates and Himilco with them. When the plague began to develop that level of intensity, Marcellus had brought his men into the city, where shelter and shade had restored their weakening physical condition. Even so, many in the Roman army lost their lives to that same disease.

27. After the land force of the Carthaginians was wiped out, the Sicilians who had fought under Hippocrates had taken over <. . .>* These are not large towns, but they are protected by their position and defences. One of them is three, the other five, miles from Syracuse. To these towns they proceeded to bring provisions from their own communities, and they also sent out for military support. Meanwhile Bomilcar once more set off for Carthage with his fleet. There he presented the situation of the Carthaginian allies in such a way as to raise hopes not only that these could be brought salutary assistance, but also that the Romans could be taken, along with the city which they had themselves virtually taken. Bomilcar thus induced the Carthaginians to send back with him as many cargo ships as they could, laden with supplies of all kinds, and also to increase the numbers in his fleet. So it was that he set off from Carthage with a hundred and thirty warships and seven hundred freighters.* He met with winds favourable enough for the crossing to Italy, but those same winds prevented him from rounding Pachynum.

The news of Bomilcar's coming, and then of his unexpected delay, brought alternating joy and trepidation to Romans and Syracusans alike. Epicydes was afraid that if the easterly winds, which were holding at the time, continued for several days, the Punic fleet would head back to Africa, and so he put Achradina in the hands of the leaders of the mercenaries, and sailed out to Bomilcar. Bomilcar had his fleet at anchor facing Africa, and was dreading a naval engagement. It was not that he was no match for the enemy in strength, or the number of his ships—in fact, he outnumbered him—but the winds favoured the Roman fleet more than his. Even so, Epicydes convinced him to risk a battle at sea. And when Marcellus saw a Sicilian army being drawn together from all over the island, and a Punic fleet also approaching with copious supplies, he too decided, despite being outnumbered in ships, to stop Bomilcar from approaching Syracuse. He feared that he might be under pressure in an enemy city, cut off by both land and sea.

The two fleets faced off against each other around the promontory of Pachynum, ready to engage as soon as the sea was calm enough for them to make for the deep water. When the south-easterly wind that had been at gale force for several days subsided, Bomilcar made the first move. His fleet seemed at first to be heading out to deep water simply to make it easier to sail around the promontory, but when he saw the Roman ships bearing down on him, he took off out to sea, though what caused his sudden panic is uncertain. He sent messengers to Heraclea to order the freighters to return to Africa, and he himself skirted the coast of Sicily and headed for Tarentum. Suddenly robbed of his high hopes, Epicydes sailed for Agrigentum, unwilling to return to a city that had been mostly captured, and where he would be under siege. There he would now await the outcome, rather than take any initiative.

28. When news now reached the Sicilian camp* that Epicydes had left Syracuse, and that the island had been abandoned by the Carthaginians, and, for a second time, virtually delivered to the Romans, the Sicilians first held meetings to sound out the feelings of those under siege and then sent spokesmen to Marcellus to negotiate terms for surrendering the city. There was very little disagreement between the parties on a settlement that would have the Romans take control of what had anywhere been under the tyrants, with the Sicilians keeping everything else, along with their liberty and laws. Then, calling a meeting of the men who had been left in charge by Epicydes, the spokesmen told them that they had been sent by the Sicilian army on a joint mission to them and to Marcellus. The

purpose of this was to ensure that those under siege, and those who were not, might all share the same fortunes, they said, and that one group could not negotiate a special deal for itself.

The spokesmen were then welcomed into the city by them so they could speak with relatives and friends. They described to them the understanding they had already reached with Marcellus, and, by offering hope of safety, persuaded them to join them in an attack on Epicydes' lieutenants, Polyclitus, Philistio, and another Epicydes (who had the surname Sindon). The three were murdered, and the citizen body was summoned to an assembly. Here the spokesmen deplored the food-shortages and the other things that the inhabitants had often been complaining about in secret amongst themselves, but they added that, despite all these afflictions, the townspeople could not blame Fortune, since it was for them to decide how long they were going to suffer them. What had caused the Romans to mount their attack on Syracuse had been their affection for the Syracusans, not hatred, they said. It was only when they heard of power being seized by Hippocrates and Epicydes—who were lackeys of Hannibal, and later of Hieronymus—that they had opened hostilities, and proceeded to blockade the city, their intention being to crush not the city itself, but its cruel oppressors. Now, however, Hippocrates had been killed, Epicydes had been cut off from Syracuse and his officers killed, and the Carthaginians had been repulsed on land and sea and deprived of any hold over Sicily. So what reason was there left for the Romans *not* to wish to see Syracuse out of harm's way, as much as if Hiero himself were still alive, that supreme promoter of friendship with Rome? And so, they concluded, the only danger facing the city and its inhabitants came from themselves, from their possibly letting slip the opportunity of settling matters with the Romans. And an opportunity such as they had at that very moment would never come again, if it appeared that <Syracuse> had been freed from a high-handed tyranny <. . .>*

29. The speech received unanimous and enthusiastic support, but it was decided that praetors should be elected before representatives were chosen. Then spokesmen, selected from the praetors, were sent to Marcellus. Their leader spoke as follows:

'It was not we, the Syracusan people, who originally abandoned you, but Hieronymus, who was actually far less a blackguard in his dealings with you than he was with us. Later, too, when peace was concluded at the time of the tyrant's assassination, it was no Syracusan who broke it, but the tyrant's lackeys, Hippocrates and Epicydes, who used both intimidation and treachery to keep us in check. Nor can anyone say that we ever had a period of liberty that was not also a time of peace with you. At all events, the first thing we have now done, after gaining our independence by assassinating the men oppressing Syracuse, is to come to you to surrender our arms, to deliver to you our persons, our city, and our fortifications, and to refuse no conditions that might be imposed on us by you.

'Marcellus, the gods have bestowed on you the glory of capturing the most famous and beautiful city in the Greek world. All our memorable achievements on land and sea—those are added to the record of your triumph. Would you wish the greatness of the city you took as your prize to be entrusted only to word of mouth? Or would you prefer to have it on view for posterity, exhibiting to anyone arriving here, by land or by sea, the trophies *we* won from the Athenians and Carthaginians, and those you have now won from us, and permitting you to pass on to your household a Syracuse unscathed, to be kept under the patronage and protection of the Marcellus family? Do not let the memory of Hieronymus count more for you than the memory of Hiero. Hiero was your friend far longer than Hieronymus was your enemy, and, while you have had tangible evidence of Hiero's benefactions, Hieronymus' madness served only to destroy him.'

As far as the Romans were concerned, all their requests could be granted, and their safety assured; it was with the Sicilians themselves that the prospect of war and danger lay. For the deserters felt they were being surrendered to the Romans, and they saw to it that the mercenary auxiliary troops had the same fear. The mercenaries then seized their weapons and first of all killed the praetors, after which they scattered to massacre Sicilian citizens, murdering in their rage any that chance put in their way, and pillaging whatever came to hand. Then, not to be without leaders, they elected six prefects, three to take charge of Achradina, and three the Nassos. When the uproar finally died down, and the mercenaries made persistent enquiries into the arrangements made with the Romans, the truth of the matter began to become clear, namely that their situation differed from that of the deserters.

30. The spokesmen returned from Marcellus at a timely moment.

They told the mercenaries that the suspicions that had inflamed them were groundless, and that the Romans had no reason to want to punish them.

One of the three prefects in Achradina was a Spaniard called Moericus, and a member of the Spanish auxiliary troops was purposely sent to him as a member of the retinue attending the spokesmen. This man took Moericus aside, and explained to him the conditions prevailing in Spain when he left—he had just come from there. Everything, he told him, was under armed occupation by Rome. Moericus could be a leader of his people, he said, if he made some valuable contribution, whether he chose subsequently to serve with the Romans, or go back to his country. If, on the other hand, he persevered with his choice of remaining under siege, he would be under blockade from land and sea—and what hope would he have then? Moericus felt the force of these arguments. When the decision was made to send representatives to Marcellus, he had his brother included among them. The brother was brought to Marcellus, apart from the others, by the same Spanish auxiliary. After receiving a formal assurance from the commander, and arranging with him how the deed was to be done, he then went back to Achradina.

At that point, to avert any suspicion on anyone's part that treachery was afoot, Moericus declared that he was against the idea of envoys going back and forth. No one, he said, should be either received or sent out and, to tighten up security, appropriate areas should be separately assigned to the prefects, with each one responsible for the defence of his particular sector. Agreement was unanimous. When it came to parcelling out the assignments, Moericus himself received the area from the Arethusa fountain* to the mouth of the great harbour, and he made sure the Romans were aware of it.

And so Marcellus gave orders for a transport ship, manned with troops, to be towed by a quadrireme to Achradina at night, and for the troops to disembark in the area of the gate near the Arethusa fountain. This was done at the time of the fourth watch, and Moericus, as had been agreed, took in through the gate the men who had been set ashore. At dawn, Marcellus launched a full-scale attack on the walls of Achradina. This had the effect not only of focusing on him the attention of the men holding Achradina, but also of making companies of armed men in the Nassus quit their posts, and come running to stem the furious Roman assault. In the mêlée, some skiffs, which had been made ready ahead of time and brought around to the Nassus, landed some armed men, who then made a surprise attack on the half-empty guard-posts and the gate, which was still open after the earlier exodus of troops. They took the Nassus, encountering little resistance since it was abandoned by the guards, who ran off in alarm. None put up a less effective opposition, or showed less determination to remain at their posts, than the deserters; having little trust even in their own side, they fled in the midst of the action. When Marcellus discovered that the Nassus had been taken, that one sector of Achradina was in his hands, and that Moericus and his company had joined up with his men, he sounded the retreat. He wanted to prevent the pillaging of the royal treasures, which were rumoured to be greater than they actually were.

31. The momentum of the Roman troops was thus checked, and the deserters in Achradina were given the time and opportunity to make good their escape. The Syracusans, finally relieved of their fear, opened the gates of Achradina, and sent spokesmen to Marcellus, requesting only that he spare their and their children's lives. Marcellus called a meeting, to which he also invited the Syracusan citizens who had been expelled from their homes during the civil unrest, and had served with the Roman forces. Here, in response to the Syracusan request, he said that the good deeds of Hiero over fifty years did not outnumber the criminal acts committed against the Roman people, during the past few, by those in power in Syracuse. But, he added, most of those acts had fittingly recoiled on their perpetrators, and the guilty parties had punished themselves for breaking the treaties more harshly than the Roman people would have wished. His blockade of Syracuse was now in its third year, he said, and its aim was not to let the Roman people make the city-state its slave, but to prevent leaders of deserters from keeping it in captivity and oppression. An example of what the Syracusans could have done was provided by those citizens of Syracuse serving among the Roman troops, or by the Spanish leader Moericus, who surrendered his garrison, or, finally, by the courageous decision now taken by the Syracusans themselves, late though it was in coming. For himself, he said, being able to capture Syracuse was quite insufficient as a reward for all the hardships and dangers on land and sea that, over such a long period, he had experienced around the Syracusan walls.

A quaestor was then dispatched to the Nassus with a body of soldiers to take charge of the royal treasury, and keep it under guard. The city was handed over to the common soldiers for looting, but guards were posted at the homes of those who had served with the Roman troops. There were many instances of atrocities committed from anger and from greed. Tradition has it that amidst the uproar, such as the fear reigning in a captured city might arouse, with soldiers running on the rampage everywhere, Archimedes was still concentrating intensely on some figures that he had drawn in the dust, and was killed by a soldier who did not know who he was. Marcellus, it is said, was upset by this. He made careful arrangements for his funeral, and also conducted a search for Archimedes' relatives, who then received honour and protection, thanks to the man's reputation and memory.

Such, by and large, was the capture of Syracuse, and the quantity of booty taken was so great that more would hardly have been forthcoming if it were Carthage that had been captured, at a time when the war was being fought on equal terms.

A few days prior to the capture of Syracuse, Titus Otacilius crossed from Lilybaeum to Utica with eighty quinqueremes. He entered the harbour of Utica before dawn, and captured some transport ships with their cargoes of grain. He then disembarked, and conducted raids on quite a large area around Utica, taking back to his ships all manner of plunder. He returned to Lilybaeum two days after setting sail from the town, and brought with him a hundred and thirty freighters loaded with grain and booty. The grain he immediately despatched to Syracuse, where, but for its timely arrival on the scene, conquerors and conquered alike were facing a deadly famine.

32. In Spain there had been no significant development over the previous two years, and it had been a war of diplomatic manœuvring rather than armed conflict, but that summer the Roman commanders joined forces after leaving their winter quarters.* A meeting was called, and opinions were unanimous on one point: since their only achievement to date was to hold back Hasdrubal's advance into Italy, it was time for action to bring the war in Spain to an end. They believed that the 20,000 Celtiberians that had been raised over the winter were a sufficient addition to their strength to achieve this purpose. There were three enemy armies. Hasdrubal, son of Gisgo, and Mago had united their camps, and were about five days' march

from the Romans. Closer to them was a veteran commander in the Spanish campaign, Hasdrubal, son of Hamilcar, who had his army near a city called Amtorgis.*

It was Hasdrubal whom the Roman generals wanted to put out of action first, and they were confident that their forces were more than sufficient for the task. The one thing that disquieted them was the possibility that, if Hasdrubal were defeated, the other Hasdrubal and Mago might withdraw in dismay into the desolate forests and mountains, and so prolong hostilities. They felt the best plan was to split their forces in two, and carry on simultaneous operations throughout the whole of Spain. They therefore made a division that gave Publius Cornelius Scipio command of two-thirds of the combined Roman and allied troops, for operations against Mago and Hasdrubal, while Gnaeus Cornelius Scipio took a third of the original army, plus the Celtiberians, to engage Hasdrubal Barca. The two commanders and their armies set off together, the Celtiberians in front, and they pitched camp at the city of Amtorgis, in sight of the enemy but with a river separating them. There Gnaeus Scipio dug in with the troops mentioned above, while Publius Scipio set off to undertake the share of the campaign that had been assigned to him.

33. Hasdrubal noticed that the Roman force in the camp was small, and that all their hope lay in the Celtiberian auxiliaries. He was thoroughly acquainted with barbarian perfidy, especially that of all the tribes amongst whom he had been campaigning over the years, and communicating with them by language was easy, since both camps were full of Spaniards. He accordingly held covert meetings with the Celtiberian chieftains, and, for a large sum of money, got them to agree to remove their troops from the area. This did not strike the Celtiberians as a serious transgression on their part. It was not a question of turning their weapons on the Romans, and they were being given remuneration large enough for fighting a war for *not* fighting one. Then there was the repose itself, the return to their homes, the pleasure of seeing their own people and their own possessions—all this was very appealing to the common soldier. As a result, the rank and file were as easily persuaded as their leaders, and, at the same time, there was not even any fear of the Romans—given their small numbers—forcibly holding them back. (Roman commanders will always have to be circumspect in this regard,* and instances of this kind should truly be taken as object lessons. They must not put

such reliance on foreign auxiliaries as to fail to keep Roman strength and Roman forces predominant in their camp.)

The Celtiberians abruptly pulled up their standards and left. When the Romans asked why they were going, and pleaded with them to stay, their only reply was that they were called away by war at home. When his allies could be detained neither by entreaty nor by force, and when he saw that he was no match for the enemy without them, that joining up with his brother again was impossible, and that there was no other safe course of action available, Scipio decided to withdraw as far as he could. His one concern in doing so was to avoid engaging the enemy on level ground at any point, and the enemy had now crossed the river and was hard on the heels of the retreating Romans.

34. During this same period Publius Scipio was prey to a fear equally great, and faced a danger that was even greater, from a new enemy. This was the young Masinissa, at that time an ally of the Carthaginians, but whose fame and power came, later, from his friendship with Rome.

Now Masinissa and his Numidian cavalry confronted Publius Scipio while he was on the move, and then kept constant pressure on him day and night. Not only would he capture Romans who wandered too far from camp to gather wood and fodder, but he would ride right up to the camp and, often charging into the midst of the sentry-posts, he would cause terrible confusion everywhere. During the nights, too, there was often panic at the gates, and on the rampart, from his surprise attacks. There was no time and no place that the Romans could be free from fear and worry, and they were pinned down within their fortifications, deprived of access to all essentials. They were now virtually under siege, and one that threatened to become even tighter if Indibilis, who was rumoured to be approaching with 7,500 Suessetani,* joined up with the Carthaginians. Scipio was a careful and prudent leader, but his dire situation obliged him to adopt an audacious plan. He would proceed at night to meet Indibilis, and engage him wherever he found him.

Leaving a small contingent of men in camp under his legate Tiberius Fonteius, Scipio set off in the middle of the night, and engaged the enemy when he encountered him. It was a fight between marching columns rather than battle lines, but the Romans had the upper hand as far as could be told from such a scrappy encounter.

But suddenly the Numidian cavalry, whom the Roman commander thought he had evaded, surrounded their flanks, and struck great panic into them. In addition, after beginning their new fight with the Numidians, the Romans were confronted by a third enemy, the Carthaginian generals who came upon them from behind, when they were already engaged. The battle was now on two fronts for the Romans, who did not know against which enemy, or in which direction, they should close ranks and charge. As their commander fought, gave encouragement and placed himself where the pressure was greatest, his right side was run through by a lance. A group of the enemy had formed a wedge and attacked the men standing close to the commander, and these now saw Scipio slipping lifeless from his horse. Wild with joy, they ran the length of the battle line shouting out the news that the Roman commander had fallen. The report spread far and wide, making it clear that the enemy were victorious, and the Romans beaten. The commander lost, flight from the field began immediately. Breaking through the Numidians, and the other light-armed auxiliaries, did not prove difficult, but they could hardly make good their escape from the large numbers of cavalry, and of infantrymen who were fast enough to keep pace with the horses. There were almost more cut down in the flight than in the fighting, and none would have survived but for the arrival of darkness, the day by now coming quickly to a close.

35. The Carthaginian generals were not slow in exploiting their success. Barely allowing their soldiers their much-needed rest, they hastily marched their column to Hasdrubal, son of Hamilcar, immediately after the battle, quite confident that the war could be wound up if they joined up with him. When they arrived, exuberant congratulations were exchanged between the armies and their generals, elated as they were with their recent victory: a great commander and his entire army had been wiped out, and they took it to be a certainty that another such victory lay ahead.

Word of the crushing defeat had not yet reached the Romans, but there was a dismal silence and the silent foreboding usually present in men's minds when they have a premonition of imminent disaster. The general himself realized that he had been abandoned by his allies, and that the enemy's forces had been enormously increased, and, in addition, deduction and reason led him to suspect that a defeat had been sustained rather than to entertain any sanguine hopes. For, he asked himself, how could Hasdrubal and Mago have brought their army to the spot without a fight, unless they had first wrapped up their own military operations? Or how had his brother not taken a stand against them, or dogged their footsteps? That would at least have enabled him to join forces with his brother, if he could not prevent the enemy armies and generals from joining up.

Tormented by such disturbing questions, Scipio believed the one safe course for the moment was to retreat as far as he could, and in a single night, with the enemy unaware of his departure, and accordingly taking no action, he covered a considerable amount of ground.

At dawn, the enemy realized the Romans had gone and, sending the Numidians ahead, they set off in pursuit with all the speed they could muster. The Numidians caught up with them before nightfall; and by directing attacks on their rear, as well as their flanks, they forced them to halt and defend the column. Scipio, however, repeatedly encouraged the men to fight and keep advancing, as far as they could in safety, before the enemy infantry overtook them.

36. For quite some time, because Scipio kept driving on, and then halting, the column, little headway was made, and now night was coming on. Scipio therefore called his men back from the fight, gathered them in a body, and led them up a hillock, which, while not affording much security—especially for demoralized troops—was nevertheless higher than all the surrounding terrain.

Here baggage and cavalry were placed in the centre, and the infantry posted around them initially had no difficulty in fighting off the attacks of the Numidians. Then the three generals came on the scene with their entire column, comprising three armies with their full complement of troops, and it became clear that the Romans would not have the strength to defend the position just with their weapons and without some means of fortification. Their commander then began to look around and consider if there were some possible means of throwing a palisade around the spot. But the hillock was so bare and composed of such stony soil that there was no brushwood to be found for cutting stakes, and no earth, either, that would enable them to make a rampart of turf, dig a ditch, or construct any other defensive structure. And yet no part of the hill was high or steep enough to make it difficult for the enemy to advance or climb up to them. Everywhere the ground sloped gently. But to put in the enemy's path something that looked like a palisade, they began to encircle themselves with pack-saddles, with the loads still attached, building them up, like a wall, to the usual height of a defence-work. When they ran out of pack-saddles for the barricade, they tossed baggage of all kinds on top.

When the Carthaginian armies arrived, they marched the column up the hillock very easily. Then the novel appearance of the barrier—a remarkable sight—stopped them in their tracks, and shouts from their officers started to go up on every side. Why were they stopped, they asked, and why were they not tearing down and ripping apart this ludicrous object that was barely strong enough to hold back women and children? The enemy was captured and in their hands, lurking behind their baggage! Such were contemptuous reproaches of the officers; but jumping over or clearing away the piles of baggage in their path was no easy matter, nor was cutting a path through the massed pack-saddles buried beneath them. But once they had removed this barrier of packs by means of poles, thus affording the soldiers passage, and this was done at several points, the camp was stormed from every side. The Romans were cut down everywhere; they were few, the enemy many, they were demoralized and the enemy triumphant. Even so, a large number of men managed to flee to the nearby woods and then make good their escape to the camp of Publius Scipio, which was now under the command of Scipio's lieutenant Tiberius Fonteius. Some authorities have it that Gnaeus Scipio was killed on the hillock in the initial charge of the enemy. Others claim that he slipped away with a few men to a tower near the camp. According to this version, a fire was lit around the tower, and it was captured after the door was burned down, the enemy having been completely unable to force it open. All inside were then killed, including the general himself.

Gnaeus Scipio was killed in the eighth year after his arrival in Spain, and on the twenty-ninth day after his brother's death.* Sorrow over the deaths of the men was not more intense in Rome than it was throughout Spain. Indeed, the grief of the citizens of Rome was partly over the destruction of the armies, the loss of a province, and a national catastrophe, whereas in Spain it was the loss of generals themselves that people felt and regretted, and the more so in the case of Gnaeus. For he had been commander for a longer period, had won their esteem earlier than his brother, and, in addition, he had been for them the first example of Roman justice and moderation.

37. It seemed that the armies had been destroyed and Spain had been lost, when a single individual remedied that desperate situation. There was in Gnaeus' army a Roman knight, Lucius Marcius, the son of Septimus Marcius. He was a dynamic young man, whose courage and intelligence were considerably greater than one might expect from the station in which he was born. To complement his natural qualities, he had also had the advantage of Gnaeus Scipio's training, which had, over the course of many years, given him a thorough education in the whole range of military science.

This man brought the soldiers together after their flight, and he also withdrew a number from the town-garrisons.* Out of these he had created an army that was by no means contemptible, and he had joined forces with Tiberius Fonteius, Publius Scipio's lieutenant. The Roman knight, however, stood out for the authority and respect he enjoyed amongst the men. This was made clear when, after a fortified camp was built north of the Ebro,* the decision was taken for the commander of the army to be elected by the vote of the common soldiers. The men then stood in for each other in guard-duty on the rampart and at the sentry-posts until everyone's vote was cast, and with complete unanimity they conferred supreme command on Lucius Marcius.

The time following that (and it was short) Marcius devoted entirely to fortifying the camp, and amassing supplies, and the men followed all his orders energetically and, in addition, with no hint of discouragement. But then word came that Hasdrubal son of Gisgo was coming to finish off what remained of war, that he had crossed the Ebro and was closing in on them; and the men also saw the signal for battle that had been put up by their new commander. At that point they recalled the commanders they had recently had, and the officers and troops they had come to rely on when they went into battle. They all suddenly burst into tears and beat their heads, some of them raising their hands to heaven to reproach the gods, others lying on the ground and calling upon their former commander by name. Quelling the weeping and wailing was impossible, for all the centurions' efforts to restore the morale of men in their companies, and Marcius' own attempts to calm or chasten them. He scolded them for abandoning themselves to useless tears like women, rather than summoning up the courage to defend themselves, and their state along with them, and he asked them not to let their commanders lie unavenged in their graves. Then, suddenly, shouts were heard, and the blare of trumpets; for the enemy were already close to their defence-works.

With that, distress suddenly turned to anger, and the men rushed to arms. They seemed to burn with fury as they converged swiftly on the gates, and flew at the enemy who were advancing towards them in careless disorder. The unexpected occurrence immediately unnerved the Carthaginians. Where, they wondered, could so many enemy soldiers have sprung from, when their army had been practically wiped out? Where had men who were defeated and routed found such spirit, and such self-confidence? Who had emerged as commander after the two Scipios were killed? Who was in command of the camp, and who had given the signal for battle? Faced with so much that they had not expected, they first gave ground, totally baffled and bewildered; then, pushed back by a determined assault, they turned and ran. There would now have followed either horrific slaughter of the fleeing enemy, or an incautious and perilous charge by the pursuers, had not Marcius swiftly signalled recall. Standing before his men at the foremost standards, and grabbing some with his own hands, he checked the over-excited troops. He then led them back to camp still craving slaughter and bloodshed. As for the Carthaginians, after being initially driven in chaos from the enemy rampart, they saw nobody in pursuit, and they returned to camp nonchalantly and at a leisurely pace, thinking their enemy had stopped from fear.

There was the same insouciance with regard to the camp's security. Although the enemy was close at hand, they reflected that they were merely the remnants of the two armies that had been destroyed a few days earlier. As a result, there was neglect of everything on the side of the enemy, and, when he had established this, Marcius turned his thoughts to a plan that was, at first sight, foolhardy rather than simply daring. He would make a pre-emptive attack on the enemy camp, for he thought that storming the camp of a single Hasdrubal would be easier than defending his own would be if the three armies and the three generals linked up again. At the same time he reflected that, if his endeavour were successful, he would restore the battered Roman fortunes; and if he were defeated he would, at least, by taking the offensive, put an end to the enemy's disdain for him.

38. But such an impetuous deed, the panic darkness can cause, and

a plan seemingly at odds with his present circumstances could alarm the men, and to prevent that he felt he should address them with some words of encouragement. He therefore called a meeting, and spoke as follows:

'Men: My respect for our commanders, living and dead, combined with the circumstances in which we all now find ourselves, could make anyone see that this command of mine, though a distinction conferred at your discretion, is really a heavy and worrisome burden. Were fear not deadening my distress, I should scarcely now have the composure to find any solace for my grief-stricken heart, and this is the very time when I must do what is the most difficult thing in times of sorrow, to make plans, alone, on behalf of you all. And yet at a time when I am obliged to think of some way of protecting for our fatherland these remnants of two armies, I cannot take my thoughts away from my constant sorrow. For that bitter memory is ever there, and the two Scipios are on my mind day and night, bringing me worry and sleeplessness. They often wake me from sleep, telling me not to let them remain unavenged—not themselves, not their soldiers (your comrades, who, for eight years, were unconquered in these lands), and not the republic. And they bid me follow their training and principles and, just as no one was more obedient to their commands while they lived than I was, now, after their deaths, they order to me to accept as the best course of action in any situation the one that I think they would have followed.

'In your case, too, men, I would not have you show your respect for them with lamentation and tears as though they were dead—they live on and flourish, thanks to their glorious achievements. No, whenever you call them to mind, I want you to go into battle just as if you can see them encouraging you and giving you the signal. That was certainly the sight that came to your eyes and hearts yesterday. That, and no other, brought off that remarkable battle, a battle with which you proved to the enemy that the Roman name did not die with the Scipios, and that a people whose might and valour were not buried at Cannae would surely rise above every cruel stroke of fortune.

'Because you, of your own accord, showed such remarkable grit, I would now like to see how much you would show when your commander asks for it. Yesterday I gave you the signal for retreat when you were engaged in a disordered pursuit of a routed enemy. My wish was not to curb your valour, only to hold it in reserve for greater glory, and for a greater occasion when you might, given the chance, make an attack as a well-prepared force on an enemy off guard, and as armed men on men unarmed, or even asleep. And the hope of such an opportunity is not one I have idly or fancifully conceived, but is in accord with the facts. Suppose someone were to ask you, in fact, how you managed to protect your camp when you were but a few, and the enemy many, when you had been conquered and they were the conquerors. Your reply would be only that it was from fear of that very imbalance that you fortified all sectors with defence-works, and kept yourselves on guard and at the ready.

'That is how things go, in fact. Men are least safe in the face of what fortune leads them not to fear; for one does not guard or protect oneself against what one does not care about. At the moment there is nothing in the world that the enemy fears less than our attacking *their* camp, not when we were just now under pressure, and being attacked ourselves. Let us dare a deed of incredible daring—it will be easier for the very reason that it seems too difficult. At the third watch of the night, I shall lead you out in silence. I have intelligence to the effect that the enemy has no regular shifts of guards, no regular sentry-posts. Our shout at the gates, and our first attack, will suffice to take the camp. Then, amongst men drowsy with sleep, disoriented by the sudden uproar, and caught unarmed in their beds—that is the time for that massacre from which, much to your annoyance, you were held back yesterday.

'I know it seems a reckless plan, but when the situation is dire, and hopes are dim, the boldest moves are the safest. An opportunity is soon gone; hesitate a little at the instant when it is offered, and you can look for it in vain later, for you have missed it. One army is in the vicinity, two others not far away. Attack now and we have some chance; and you have already put your might and theirs to the test. If we put matters off, and if, when word spreads of yesterday's counter-attack, we cease to be an object of disdain, there is a danger of all their commanders and all their armies linking up. Will we then be able to cope with three commanders of the enemy, and three armies, which Gnaeus Scipio failed to cope with when his army was intact? It was through splitting up their troops that our own commanders perished; and the enemy likewise can be crushed one by one while they are divided. There is no other way to fight the war, so let us wait only for the opportunity the oncoming night will give us. Go now, with the gods' favour, and take your food and rest so that you can, fresh and strong, burst into the enemy camp with the same spirit with which you defended your own.'

The men were overjoyed to hear this new plan from their new leader, and its daring made them like it all the more. The rest of the day was spent seeing to their weapons and preparing themselves physically, and most of the night was given over to sleep. At the fourth watch they moved out.

39. Beyond the closest camp, and separated from it by six miles, was another division of Carthaginian troops. Between the two lay a sunken hollow that was thick with trees. Somewhere towards the middle of the wood a company of Roman infantry and some cavalry were set in hiding, the usual Carthaginian trick. The path between the two forces was thus cut off at the midway point, and the rest of the Roman troops were marched silently to the enemy closest to them. There, since there was no sentry-post before the gates, and no guards on the rampart, they met no resistance, and they marched into the camp as if it were their own. It was then that the trumpets blared, and the battle-cry went up. Some proceeded to massacre an enemy half-asleep; others hurled blazing torches on the huts, which were thatched with dry straw; yet others seized the gates to cut off any escape. The fire, shouting, and killing all together gave the enemy, who were in a daze, no chance to hear anything or take any preventive measures. Unarmed, they wandered amongst groups of armed soldiers. Some ran to the gates; others leaped over the rampart when they found the roadways blocked; and as they all got out, they ran immediately towards the other camp, only to be cut off by the Roman infantry company and cavalry that charged from their hiding-place, killing every last one of them. In fact, even if anyone had managed to escape from the carnage, so speedy was the Roman dash from the captured nearer camp to the other that no one could have reached there before them to report the debacle.

At that camp, in fact, thanks to its greater distance from the enemy, and the fact that a number of men had slipped away before dawn to gather fodder, firewood, and plunder, the Romans found everything in a state of even greater neglect and disarray. In the sentry-posts there were only weapons that had been laid aside, and unarmed men were either sitting or lying around, or walking about before the rampart and the gates. Such were the men, carefree and relaxed, with whom the Romans, still fired up from their recent engagement and flushed with victory, now went into battle. Stopping them at the gates was absolutely impossible. Within the gates there was a rush from all quarters of the camp, when the shouting and uproar started, and a bloody battle ensued. This would have lasted a long time but for the sight of the blood on the Roman shields, which gave the Carthaginians a clue that there had been another defeat, and that filled them with alarm. The terror turned them all to flight; they poured out—at least, those not victims of the slaughter—wherever there was an exit, and lost the camp. So, in a night and a day, two enemy camps were attacked,* under the leadership of Lucius Marcius.

Claudius,* who translated the annals of Acilius into Latin from the Greek, puts the number of enemy dead at about 37,000, with some 1,830 taken prisoner and massive amounts of plunder also won. The plunder, Claudius claims, included a 137-pound silver shield bearing a portrait of Hasdrubal Barca. In Valerius Antias' account, only one camp was taken, that of Mago, and 7,000 of the enemy were killed; but there was, he says, a second engagement, with Hasdrubal, who counterattacked from his camp,* in which 10,000 were killed and 4,330 taken prisoner. Piso* records that 5,000 were killed in an ambush, when Mago was in a disordered pursuit of our retreating soldiers. In all the accounts Marcius, the commander, is well celebrated, and to the praises that genuinely belong to him people also add the supernatural, saying that, as he was making an address, a flame arose from his head, without his realizing it, to the great consternation of his men who stood around him. They also say that, to commemorate his victory over the Carthaginians, a shield bearing the portrait of Hasdrubal and called 'the shield of Marcius' hung in the Capitoline temple right down to the time when the temple burned down.

There followed a period of inactivity in Spain. After receiving and inflicting in turn such monumental defeats, both sides were loath to take a risk on a decisive engagement.

40. Such were events in Spain. Marcellus, meanwhile, had been so scrupulous and honest in all his dealings in Sicily following the capture of Syracuse as to increase not only his own reputation but the majesty of the Roman people, as well. The artwork of the city, however, the sculptures and paintings with which Syracuse was

richly endowed, he shipped off to Rome. True, they were enemy spoils, won under the rules of warfare, but this was what first started the appreciation for Greek works of art, and the licence we now see in the widespread looting of all manner of things sacred and profane.* This eventually recoiled on the Roman gods, and did so first of all on the very temple that was superbly furbished by Marcellus. Temples dedicated by Marcellus close to the Porta Capena used to be visited by foreigners because of their outstanding art works of this kind, but only a tiny fraction of these works now remain.

Deputations were now coming to Marcellus from almost all the communities of Sicily, and the treatment they received differed according to the case they made. Those that had not defected, or which had re-established their alliance, before Syracuse was taken, were regarded, and treated, as faithful allies. Those whom fear had forced to capitulate after the capture of Syracuse were given terms as a vanquished people by the victor.

The Romans, however, still had a considerable amount of residual fighting around Agrigentum. Epicydes and Hanno, commanders of the earlier war, were still active, and there was a third, a new man sent out by Hannibal to replace Hippocrates. He was from Hippacra, and of Libyphoenician nationality.* Called Muttines by his own people, he was an enterprising individual who had gained a thorough mastery of the arts of war under Hannibal's instruction. This Muttines was given some Numidian auxiliaries by Epicydes and Hanno, and with them he made a broad sweep of enemy territory, and kept Carthaginian allies loyal by bringing all of them timely assistance. So successful was he in this that he soon made a name for himself throughout Sicily, and he represented the greatest hope for those espousing the Carthaginian cause. The two other commanders, the Carthaginian and the Syracusan, had until then been pinned down within the fortifications of Agrigentum, but on Muttines' advice, and more because of their confidence in him, they now ventured forth beyond the walls to encamp at the River Himera.

When this was reported to Marcellus, he immediately moved his troops forward, and took up a position about four miles from the enemy, intending to wait and see what they were doing, or preparing to do. Muttines, however, gave him no room to move, and no time to pause or plan; he crossed the river and attacked his enemy's out-posts, causing enormous fright and consternation. The following day he engaged in what was almost a regular battle, and drove the Romans back inside their fortifications. But he was then called away from the front by a mutiny of the Numidians in the camp—some 300 of them had withdrawn to Heraclea Minoa. He set off to calm these men down, and bring them back to service, and it is said that, as he left, he gave the commanders an emphatic warning not to engage the enemy in his absence. This angered the two commanders, Hanno more than his colleague, because he had already been troubled over Muttines' celebrity. He resented the fact that Muttines should be setting limits on his actions—a low-born African limiting a Carthaginian general on assignment from his senate and people! Hanno then convinced the wavering Epicydes that they should cross the river and offer battle. If they waited for Muttines, he explained, and the battle turned out successfully, there was no doubt that the glory would go to Muttines.

41. Now Marcellus felt it would be humiliating for him—the man who had driven Hannibal from Nola, when the Carthaginian was still elated with his victory at Cannae—to give way before this enemy that he had already defeated on land and sea. He therefore issued orders for his men to take up their weapons immediately, and for the standards to be carried out. He was deploying his troops when ten Numidians broke away from the enemy line, and came galloping up. They reported to him that their compatriots would not take part in the battle. First, they said, they sympathized with the mutiny involving the 300 of their number who had withdrawn to Heraclea, but then they were also concerned that their own officer had been removed, just before the battle, by generals trying to belittle his reputation. A duplicitous people, the Numidians were nevertheless true to their word. As a result, when word passed swiftly through the ranks that the enemy had been abandoned by his cavalry, which the Romans had feared most, Roman morale rose. In addition, the enemy were terrified; apart from losing the support of the strongest section of their forces, they were also filled with fear that they might be attacked by their own cavalry. And so it was not much of a fight, and the first battle-cry and the first onslaught decided the outcome. The Numidians stood inactive on the wings during the encounter, and, when they saw their side turn to run, they briefly joined them in their flight. Then they saw that they were all heading in panic for Agrigentum and, fearing to be under siege there, they slipped away in all directions to the nearest communities. Many thousands of men were killed, and 6,000* were captured, along with eight elephants. This was Marcellus' final battle in Sicily, and after it he returned triumphant to Syracuse.

The year was now practically at an end, and so, in Rome, the Senate passed a decree instructing the praetor Publius Cornelius to write to the consuls in Capua to inform them that, while Hannibal was far off, and nothing of any significance was going on around Capua, one of the consuls—if he saw fit*—should come to Rome to supervise the election of the next magistrates. On receiving the dispatch, the consuls agreed between them that Claudius should conduct the elections and Fulvius remain at Capua. The consuls elected under Claudius' supervision were Gnaeus Fulvius Centumalus and Publius Sulpicius Galba, son of Servius Galba. Sulpicius had held no prior curule office. The praetors elected after that were: Lucius Cornelius Lentulus, Marcus Cornelius Cethegus, Gaius Sulpicius, and Gaius Calpurnius Piso. City jurisdiction was allotted to Piso, Sicily to Sulpicius, Apulia to Cethegus, and Sardinia to Lentulus. The consuls saw their *imperium* extended for a year.

BOOK TWENTY-SIX

1. When, on 15 March, the consuls Gnaeus Fulvius Centumalus and Publius Sulpicius Galba began their terms of office, they convened the Senate on the Capitol and sought members' opinions on matters of state, the management of the war, and the question of the provinces and armies. Quintus Fulvius and Appius Claudius, the previous year's consuls, had their *imperium* extended, and were assigned the armies already under their command. They were also instructed not to break off the blockade of Capua until they had captured the city. This was the matter that most preoccupied the Romans at that time. It was not so much because of the resentment they felt towards Capua—though this was more justified in her case than with any city-state in the past—but rather because a city of such renown, and such power, had drawn a number of different peoples with her when she defected, and it seemed likely that recovering her would again bring these peoples to respect their former master. The previous year's praetors, Marcus Junius and Publius Sempronius, also had their *imperium* extended, Junius in Etruria and Sempronius in Gaul, and they retained the two legions they had each had under their command.

Marcus Marcellus' *imperium* was likewise extended to enable him to finish off, as proconsul, what remained of the war in Sicily, with the army then under his command. If he needed that army supplemented, Marcellus was to make up the shortfall from the legions in Sicily under the command of the propraetor Publius Cornelius. He was not, however, to select any member in that group of men to whom the Senate had refused to grant discharge,* or permission to return home, before the war's end. Gaius Sulpicius, who had been allotted Sicily, was assigned the two legions that Publius Cornelius had commanded, and reinforcements from the army of Gnaeus Fulvius. (Fulvius' army had incurred disgrace the year before, when it was cut to pieces and routed in Apulia, and for soldiers in this category the Senate had fixed the same term of service as for the men who had been at Cannae. A further mark of censure for the two groups was a prohibition against their wintering in towns, or building winter quarters closer than ten miles from any city.) In Sardinia, Lucius

Cornelius was given the two legions that had been under Quintus Mucius' command, and the consuls were under orders to raise such reinforcements as were necessary. The coastlines of Sicily and Greece were assigned to Titus Otacilius and Marcus Valerius, along with the legions and fleets that were already under their command (Greece having fifty ships and one legion, Sicily a hundred ships and two legions). Land and sea operations were that year conducted with twenty-three Roman legions.*

2. At the beginning of the year,* the letter of Lucius Marcius was brought up in the Senate. The Senate found his achievements outstanding; but how he styled himself caused widespread offence amongst the members, because he had written 'From the propraetor to the Senate'* when his command had been neither mandated by the people, nor authorized by the Senate. It was felt that a bad precedent was being set—generals being chosen by armies, and the solemn electoral process, with its obligatory auspices, being transferred to unruly soldiers in camps in the provinces, far from the law and magistrates. Some proposed that the matter be formally raised for debate in the house, but it was deemed better that such a discussion be postponed until a time after the departure of the knights who had delivered the letter from Marcius. On the provision of grain and clothing for Marcius' army, it was decided that he should be given the reply, in writing, that the Senate would give its attention to both items. However, it was decided that the reply should not be addressed to 'Lucius Marcius Propraetor' for fear of Marcius thereby attaining, as though it were already decided, the very thing they had shelved for later consideration.

When the knights had been sent on their way, this was the matter that the consuls raised for debate before anything else. There was unanimous agreement that they should discuss with the tribunes of the plebs their putting before the people, at the earliest opportunity, the question of who the people wanted to be sent to Spain, with *imperium*, to take over the army that Gnaeus Scipio had led as commander-in-chief. The matter was discussed with the tribunes, and public notice of the question was given; but now another dispute had seized public attention.

Gaius Sempronius Blaesus had arraigned Gnaeus Fulvius on a charge of losing his army in Apulia,* and he was now harassing him on the subject in public meetings. Many commanders had, through

foolhardiness and experience, taken their army into dangerous terrain, Blaesus would say, but Gnaeus Fulvius stood alone in having
corrupted his legions with all conceivable manner of vice before
betraying them to the enemy. Thus it could be rightly maintained, he
would say, that his men were done for before they set eyes on the foe,
and that their defeat had come not at the hands of Hannibal but
those of their own general.

No one proceeding to the vote, said Blaesus, had much idea of the
person to whom he was actually confiding a command, and confiding
an army—as could be seen in the difference between Tiberius Sempronius and Gnaeus Fulvius! Tiberius Sempronius was given an
army of slaves, but he soon ensured, by his discipline and authority,
that none of those slaves gave any thought to lineage and bloodline
when in battle, and that they served to defend their allies, and strike
terror into their enemies. Cumae, Beneventum, and other cities—
these men had virtually snatched them from Hannibal's jaws and
restored them to the people of Rome. Now Gnaeus Fulvius, he
would say, had an army made up of Roman citizens, men from good
families who had been brought up as free men, and in these he had
instilled the vices of slaves. As a result all *he* ensured was that
they would be hot-headed ruffians with the allies, and spineless cowards with the enemy—unable to withstand even their war-cry, and
much less their charge. Indeed, that his men gave way in battle was
not a surprise, not when their commander was the very first to flee!
He was more surprised, he said, that some had actually made a stand
to the death, and that they had not all shared Gnaeus Fulvius' panic-
stricken flight. Gaius Flaminius, Lucius Paulus, Lucius Postumius,
Gnaeus and Publius Scipio—these had preferred to fall in the line of
combat sooner than desert their encircled armies. Gnaeus Fulvius
had returned to Rome, virtually the only man left to tell of his
army's annihilation! The army that served at Cannae had been
shipped off to Sicily for having fled the battle, he said, and the men
were not to be released from there until the enemy had left Italy; and
now the same conditions had been recently decreed for Gnaeus
Fulvius' army. But it was a shameful crime that Gnaeus Fulvius'
flight—from a battle that he had himself irresponsibly begun—
should go unpunished, and that he would pass his old age in the
same dives and brothels that he had passed his younger days! It was a
crime that his men, whose only wrong was to have imitated their

commander, should be virtually sent into exile and made to submit to dishonourable service! So different at Rome was freedom for the rich, and freedom for the poor, so different for a man who had held office and a man who had not!

3. Fulvius proceeded to defend himself by shifting the blame to his men. They had been aggressively demanding action, he said, but they had nevertheless not been led out into the field on the day they wanted—for it was too late in the day—but on the one that followed, and the timing and the location of their deployment were both favourable. Even so, he said, they had still found themselves no match for the enemy's reputation, or his violent attack. When his men were all in disordered flight, he too was swept away in the crowd, like Varro in the battle of Cannae, and like many other commanders. But how could he have helped the republic by holding his ground on his own, he asked—it was not as if his own death could be a remedy for national disasters! He had not been brought down through running short of provisions; he had not been led into unfavourable terrain through lack of caution; and he had not been ambushed as he proceeded along a path he had failed to reconnoitre. He had been defeated with an open attack on the field of battle. His own men's courage was no more under his control than his enemy's; it was the individual's own make-up that gave him bravery or cowardice.

Fulvius was twice accused, with a fine sought both times. On the third occasion, witnesses were produced and, in addition to the defendant being subjected to all manner of insults, many swore under oath that the panic-stricken flight had actually started with the praetor. The soldiers had been abandoned by him, they said, and had turned to flee because they believed their leader must have had good reason for his fear. Such was the anger this testimony produced that the assembly noisily demanded that Fulvius be arraigned on a capital charge. And that gave rise to a new squabble. When the plaintiff, having twice asked for fines, said on the third occasion that he was now seeking capital punishment, the defendant appealed to the tribunes of the plebs. The tribunes said they would not obstruct their colleague's efforts to press either for capital punishment or a fine against the defendant, as was his right by their ancestral traditions, whether he availed himself of the laws or customary practice. Sempronius then declared that he was seeking Gnaeus Fulvius' condemnation for treason, and he requested of the praetor, Gaius Calpurnius, a date for the assembly of the people.

The defendant then took another promising line: perhaps his brother Quintus Fulvius could attend the trial. Quintus wielded influence at the time because of the fame of his exploits, and because of the prospect, now close to realization, of his taking Capua. In a highly emotional letter in defence of his brother's life, Quintus Fulvius then made the request to attend, but the senators replied that it was not in the interests of the state for him to leave Capua. When the day of the assembly was at hand, Gnaeus Fulvius went in exile at Tarquinii, and the plebs confirmed that the exile was justified.

4. In the meantime, the full force of the war had been brought to bear on Capua. The blockade, however, was having a more severe effect than direct assaults; the slaves and the masses were finding the food deprivation intolerable and, because the guard-posts were so closely spaced, sending messengers to Hannibal was impossible. A Numidian was found who undertook to get through with a letter and proved capable of fulfilling his commitment. He made his way at night through the midst of the Roman camp, and fired the people of Capua with hopes of mounting a counterattack at all points, while they had some strength left for it. In fact, in the numerous engagements that followed, the Capuans were actually successful in most cavalry battles, but their infantry suffered defeat. For the Romans, however, elation over the infantry victories was nothing like as great as the dejection they felt at suffering defeat in any area at the hands of a besieged and practically defeated foe. Eventually, a new tactic was adopted whereby they could use ingenuity to compensate for their inadequate strength.

Throughout the legions young men were picked who were possessed of exceptional speed thanks to their strength and lightness. They were each equipped with shields smaller than those used by the cavalry, and with seven javelins, all four feet long and tipped with iron, like the spears of the light infantry. The cavalrymen would each take one of these men on their horses, and train them to ride behind them and to dismount briskly at a given signal. When daily training seemed to have enabled them to do this with some confidence, they advanced into the plain between the camp and the city wall, to face the Capuan cavalry who were drawn up for battle. Coming within javelin-range, the light infantry dismounted when they were given the signal. The result was a line of infantry suddenly emerging from the cavalry formation to attack the enemy horsemen, unleashing javelin after javelin as they charged. Hurling these weapons in large numbers at horses and riders in every quarter, they inflicted heavy casualties. However, even greater panic was struck in the Capuans by the novel and unexpected manœuvre, and the cavalry then bore down on their frightened enemy, chasing them in bloody flight all the way to the gates. After that the Romans enjoyed cavalry superiority as well. This was the origin of the practice of keeping light infantry amongst the legions;* and the man responsible for the idea of combining infantry with the cavalry was, they say, Quintus Navius, a centurion, and he was given special recognition for it by the general.

5. Such was the situation at Capua, and Hannibal was torn between two conflicting priorities—taking the citadel of Tarentum, and holding on to Capua. But it was his concern for Capua that prevailed. He could see that everyone's attention was focused on the town, his allies' as well as his enemy's, and how Capua's defection from Rome turned out would be seen as setting an example for the future. Accordingly, Hannibal left most of his baggage, and all his more heavily armed forces, in Bruttium, and hastened into Campania at the head of some elite infantry and cavalry troops, equipped as well as they could be for a speedy march. Despite his swift pace thirty-three elephants* came along with him.

Hannibal took up a position in a secluded valley behind Tifata, the mountain overlooking Capua. On his arrival, he took the stronghold of Calatia,* expelling its garrison, and then marched on the force blockading Capua. He sent messengers ahead to the town to announce the time at which he would assault the Roman camp—he wanted the townspeople to be ready for a sortie, and to synchronize the charge from all the gates with his attack—and, in fact, he struck great fear into the Romans. For Hannibal himself attacked on one side while, on the other, the Capuan cavalry and infantry came charging out in full force, and along with them the Carthaginian garrison that was under the command of Bostar and Hanno.

It was an alarming situation for the Romans and, not to leave any point undefended by a simultaneous rush in one direction, they divided their forces. Appius Claudius faced the Capuans, and Quintus Fulvius faced Hannibal; the propraetor Gaius Nero was stationed with the cavalry of six legions on the road leading to Suessa; and the legate Gaius Fulvius Flaccus, with the allied cavalry, was close to the River Volturnus.

It was not just the customary battle-cry and clamour that marked the start of this particular engagement. In addition to the noise of the combatants, horses, and weapons, there was that coming from the crowd of Capuans on the walls, non-participants in the fighting. So loud were their cries, which were accompanied by the clattering of bronze instruments—like that usually raised in the dead of night during a lunar eclipse—that they distracted even the men engaged in the battle. Appius easily kept the Capuans away from the rampart; but the pressure was greater on the other side, where Fulvius faced Hannibal and the Carthaginians. In that sector the sixth legion gave ground, and in giving way permitted a Spanish unit with three elephants to reach the rampart. This unit had broken through the Roman centre, and was now weighing up its hopes against the possible danger—hopes of breaking into the camp, on the one hand, and the danger of being cut off from its own side, on the other.

Seeing the fright this instilled in the legion, and the danger the camp was facing, Fulvius urged Quintus Navius and other first centurions to attack the enemy unit that was in combat beneath the rampart. It was a critical situation, Fulvius told them: they faced the alternatives of letting through the enemy—and these would find it less of a challenge to break into the camp than they had found breaking through the compact Roman line—or else finishing them off beneath the rampart. That, he said, would not involve a great fight: the enemy were few in number, and were cut off from their own men. In addition, while the Romans panicked, their own line had apparently been broken; and if the two parts of it now turned to face the enemy on either side, they would catch him in a pincer movement.

When Navius heard his commander's words, he grabbed the standard of the second maniple of the *hastati* from the standard-bearer, and carried it towards the enemy, threatening to hurl it into their midst if his men did not swiftly follow him and join the fight. He was a mountain of a man, and his weapons made him all the more impressive. In addition, the standard that he held high in the air had attracted the attention of citizen and enemy alike. When he reached the ranks of the Spaniards, however, Navius became the target of spears hurled from every direction, and practically the whole of the enemy line converged on him alone. Even so, neither enemy numbers nor the barrage of weapons could stem the man's charge.

6. The legate Marcus Atilius now proceeded to carry towards the Spanish unit the standard of the first maniple of that same legion. Meanwhile, the legates in charge of the camp, Lucius Porcius Licinus and Titus Popillius, were putting up a spirited defence before the rampart, and they dispatched some of the elephants right on the rampart as these were crossing over. The ditch was now filled with the animals' carcasses, offering the enemy a passageway, as though a mole or bridge had been laid down for them; and there, over the supine bodies of the slaughtered elephants, a furious and bloody struggle broke out.

On the other side of the camp, the Capuans and the Punic garrison had already been pushed back, and fighting was going on right up to the Capuan gate that faced the River Volturnus. The armed resistance the Romans met as they tried to break into the town was less of a problem than the fact that the gate was equipped with ballistas and 'scorpions', which kept the enemy at bay with their projectiles. The Roman thrust was further obstructed when the general Appius Claudius was wounded: urging on his men at the front, he was struck by a Gallic javelin in the upper chest, below the left shoulder. Even so, large numbers of the enemy were killed before the gate, and the remainder were driven panic-stricken into the city. And when Hannibal saw his Spanish unit being cut to pieces and the enemy camp defended with the maximum effort, he abandoned his attack. He proceeded to recall his forces, and turn his infantry back, setting cavalry to their rear to prevent enemy pressure on them as they withdrew.

The legions were all for pursuing the foe, but Flaccus ordered the retreat to be sounded. He thought two ends had been sufficiently achieved: making the Capuans aware of how little support was to be had from Hannibal, and making Hannibal aware of it, too.

Authors who cover this battle list the enemy casualties on that day as 8,000 from Hannibal's army, and 3,000 Capuans, with fifteen standards taken from the Carthaginians and eighteen from the Capuans. In other authors I have found the battle to be nothing like as momentous.* They claim that it was more of a scare than real fighting, and it was occasioned by the Numidians and Spaniards unexpectedly breaking into the Roman camp with elephants. The elephants, trumpeting loudly, trampled down the tents as they passed through the centre of the camp, and stampeded the beasts of burden, which broke their tethers. These sources also claim that, in addition to the confusion, there was some trickery afoot. Men dressed as Italians, and familiar with the Latin language, were sent amongst the Romans by Hannibal to tell them, in the name of the consuls, to look out for their own safety and run for the nearest hills, since the camp had been lost. However, the trick was quickly discovered and foiled, with heavy enemy losses, and the elephants were driven from the camp by fire.

Whatever the details of its beginning and end, this was the final battle before the capitulation of Capua. That year the *medix tuticus*, the supreme magistrate amongst the Capuans, was Seppius Loesius, a man of low birth and slender means. The story goes that his mother was once performing expiatory sacrifice on his behalf, Loesius then being a minor,* in connection with an omen affecting the family. The priest, in delivering his response, stated that the highest power in Capua would come to the boy. At this, the mother, who saw no reason to entertain such hopes, remarked: 'You must be saying that the people of Capua will be in a sorry state at the time when their top office comes to my son!' This snide interpretation of a prophecy that came true turned out to be true itself. When the Capuans were hard pressed by starvation and the sword, and no hope of resistance remained, all those born to the expectation of public offices were turning them down. Complaining that Capua had been abandoned and betrayed by its dignitaries, Loesius became the very last citizen of Capua to gain the city's highest office.

7. Hannibal saw that it was no longer possible to lure the enemy into an engagement, or break through their lines to reach Capua, and, fearing the new consuls might cut off his supplies, he decided to abandon his failed venture and move camp away from the city. He thought long and hard about where to go from there, and the urge took him to head for Rome, the very epicentre of the war. This had ever been his wish, but he had let the opportunity slip after the battle of Cannae—a criticism that others levelled at him, the truth of which he did not himself conceal. He felt that, if there were a sudden outbreak of panic and public disorder, seizing some section of the city was not beyond his hopes; and, if Rome were threatened, then

both Roman commanders, or one, at least, would immediately abandon Capua. And, if they split their troops, they would, by weakening both parts, give him or the Capuans some chance of success. Only one matter was causing him some anxiety: the Capuans might immediately capitulate when he withdrew.

Hannibal bribed a Numidian, who was prepared to undertake any risky venture, to take a letter, enter the Roman camp posing as a deserter, and then slip furtively away on the other side of the camp to Capua. The letter was full of encouragement. His leaving would prove their salvation, Hannibal told the citizens: it would divert the Roman leaders and their armies from the siege of Capua to the defence of Rome. He told them not to be dismayed—by just holding out for a few days they would raise the entire siege. He then ordered ships to be commandeered on the River Volturnus, and brought up to a fort that he had built earlier as a guard-post. Informed that these vessels were so numerous that his army could be ferried over in a single night, he had ten days' worth of rations prepared and, leading his legions to the river by night, shipped them over before dawn.

8. Fulvius Flaccus had received intelligence on this operation from deserters before it took place, and had then reported it in a dispatch to the Senate in Rome,* where reactions to the news varied according to people's temperaments. This being a serious crisis, the Senate was naturally convened immediately; and at the meeting Publius Cornelius, whose surname was Asina, with no thought for Capua or anything else, simply advocated the recall of all generals and armies from everywhere in Italy for the defence of Rome. Fabius Maximus felt a withdrawal from Capua, and allowing themselves to be intimidated by Hannibal, and led around at his beck and call, was disgraceful. Hannibal had not had the nerve to march on the city even after his victory at Cannae, he said, and now he had conceived the hope of taking the city of Rome after being driven from Capua! No, the goal of his march was not to lay siege to Rome, but to raise the siege of Capua, he said. As for Rome, Jupiter was witness to the treaties broken by Hannibal, and he and the other gods would defend her with the army already in place in the city.

In this clash of opinions it was the compromise position of Publius Valerius Flaccus that prevailed. Flaccus remained focused on the two situations, and proposed sending a letter to the generals at Capua. This would apprise them of the resources available for the defence of

Rome, but then say that the generals themselves best knew the size
of the force Hannibal was bringing, and also how great an army was
needed to invest Capua. Perhaps one of them, and some of the
troops, could be sent to Rome without compromising the siege of
Capua, which would be conducted by the general and troops that
remained. If so, then Claudius and Fulvius should agree on who
should continue the siege, and who should come to Rome to prevent
a blockade of their native city.

This decree of the Senate was brought to Capua, and it was the
proconsul Quintus Fulvius who was obliged to return to Rome, his
colleague being incapacitated with a wound. Fulvius selected men
from the three armies, and crossed the Volturnus with about 15,000
infantry and 1,000 cavalry.* Reliably informed that Hannibal would
proceed from there along the Latin Way, he sent messengers ahead
through the townships on the Appian Way, and those in its vicinity
—Setia, Cora, and Lanuvium—ordering the people to have provisions stockpiled in the towns, and, in the case of the more remote
farms, to bring them to the road. The inhabitants were also to muster
troops for the towns, so that each community could look after itself.

9. On the day he crossed the Volturnus, Hannibal pitched camp
not far from the river, and the next day he came past Cales into the
territory of the Sidicini. He spent a day plundering the countryside,
and then took his army along the Latin Way through the country of
Suessa, Allifae, and Casinum. He remained encamped for two days
before the walls of Casinum and conducted widespread raids.
He next came past Interamna and Aquinum to the River Liris, in the
territory of Fregellae, where he found that the bridge had been
broken down by the people of Fregellae to retard his progress.*

Fulvius, too, had been held up by a river, he by the Volturnus:
the boats here had been burned by Hannibal, and because of the dire
shortage of timber Fulvius had problems putting together rafts to
ferry over his army. Once the army was taken across on the rafts,
however, the rest of Fulvius' march went off without a hitch. For
generous quantities of supplies had been left out for him along the
road, as well as in the towns, and the men, remembering that they
were marching to the defence of the fatherland, enthusiastically
urged each other to pick up the pace.

At Rome, meanwhile, a messenger from Fregellae, who had made
a non-stop journey of a day and a night, brought sheer panic to the

city. But people †running about†, adding pure fiction to what they had heard, threw the entire city into even greater turmoil than had the initial report of danger. It was now not just a matter of women's lamentations being heard coming from private homes: all over the city married ladies poured into the streets, and ran around the shrines of the gods. They swept the altars with their dishevelled hair; they fell to their knees with hands held palm-up to heaven and the gods; and they begged the gods to rescue the city of Rome from the hands of the enemy, and save Roman mothers and little children from abuse. The Senate put itself at the disposal of the magistrates in the Forum, in case they wanted to bring up any business. Some were given military assignments, and went off to discharge their various duties; others volunteered themselves for any service they could usefully perform. Defensive units were posted on the citadel, the Capitol, the walls, and around the city, even on the Alban Mount and the citadel of Aefula. In the midst of all this upheaval news was brought that the proconsul Quintus Fulvius had left Capua with an army. To ensure that his *imperium* would not be invalidated by his entry into the city, the Senate decreed that Quintus Fulvius' *imperium* be on a par with that of the consuls.*

The destruction of the bridges led Hannibal to lay waste the agricultural lands of Fregellae with even greater ferocity. After that he passed through the territory of Frusino, Ferentinum, and Anagnia into that of the Labici. He then headed for Tusculum by way of Mt. Algidus; but he was refused entry to the town, and so he veered to the right below Tusculum and went down to Gabii. From there he brought the army down into the area of Pupinia, and encamped eight miles from Rome. The closer the enemy came, the more the fatalities mounted amongst those fleeing to the city—thanks to the Numidians riding in advance of the army—and the greater became the number of prisoners taken, of all classes and all ages.

10. Amidst the chaos Fulvius Flaccus marched into Rome with his army by way of the Porta Capena. He came swiftly through the city centre to the Esquiline, passing through the Carinae, and then, leaving the city once more, pitched his camp between the Porta Esquilina and the Porta Collina.* Here the plebeian aediles brought him supplies. The consuls and Senate also came to his camp, and the crisis facing the state was discussed. It was determined that the consuls should also pitch their camp in the environs of the Porta Collina and

Porta Esquilina, and that Gaius Calpurnius, the city praetor, should take charge of the Capitol and the citadel. The Senate was to maintain a quorum, with meetings held in the Forum, in case consultation were needed in this time of crisis.

Hannibal, meanwhile, moved his camp up to the River Anio, three miles from the city. He established a base there and, taking 2,000 cavalry, he went ahead as far as the temple of Hercules, near the Porta Collina. Here he rode up to the walls and proceeded to examine them, and the lie of the city, from as close a point as he could. To Flaccus it seemed outrageous that Hannibal should be doing this so brazenly and so nonchalantly, and so he unleashed some cavalry against him, with orders to push back the enemy cavalry from the city and drive them back to their camp.

After battle was joined, the consuls ordered some Numidian deserters, of whom there were at that stage about 1,200 on the Aventine, to go through the city centre and cross the Esquiline. None, they thought, would be better suited for fighting on land consisting of hollows, of buildings set in the midst of gardens, and of sepulchres and roads high-banked at every point. But some people in the citadel and the Capitol spotted the men coming swiftly on horseback down the Clivus Publicius,* and they yelled out that the Aventine had been captured. That of itself precipitated such a headlong stampede that, but for the presence of a Punic camp outside the city, the panic-stricken crowd would all have gone pouring out of town. Instead, they sought refuge in their homes and other buildings and, assuming their compatriots who were wandering the streets to be the enemy, they began to pelt them with stones and missiles. And there was no way of suppressing the uproar, or making people see their mistake, because the roads were choked with crowds of peasants and farm animals that the sudden panic had driven into the city.

The cavalry engagement proved successful, and the enemy were pushed back. It was now necessary to suppress the disturbances that had been breaking out at many points in town for no apparent reason, and it was decided that all former dictators, consuls, and censors should hold *imperium* until the enemy left their walls. In fact, during the rest of that day, and the night following it, there were many such disturbances that broke out sporadically and were then suppressed.

11. The next day Hannibal crossed the Anio and led out all his troops for battle; and Flaccus and the consuls did not decline the

fight. The two armies were now deployed for an engagement in which the city of Rome would be the victor's prize. At that point, there was a heavy shower of rain, intermixed with hail, and this caused such havoc in both battle lines that the combatants retired to their camps barely able to hold their weapons, the enemy now the least of their fears. The next day the lines were again drawn up in the same spot, and a storm of similar intensity separated them once more. And yet their return to camp was on both occasions followed by amazingly bright and tranquil weather.* On the Carthaginian side the phenomenon was given a religious significance, and it is said that Hannibal was heard to remark that on one occasion he had been denied the will, and on the other the opportunity, to take Rome. Two other events also dashed his hopes, one of lesser and one of greater significance. The greater one was to be told that, although he was himself ensconced before the walls of Rome with an army, Roman soldiers had set off under their banners as reinforcements for the Spanish campaign. The lesser one was learning from a prisoner of war that, at about that time, the land on which he was encamped had, by chance, been sold, but that, despite the circumstances, there was no diminution in its price. That a buyer should have been found in Rome for land that he had taken in war, land that was firmly in his possession, struck him as so outrageously presumptuous that he immediately summoned an auctioneer and ordered the bankers' shops around the Forum to be put up for sale.

All this prompted Hannibal to pull back his camp to the River Tutia, six miles from the city. From there he marched to the Grove of Feronia, whose temple at that period was famous for its wealth. The people of Capena, and others in the neighbourhood of the shrine, used to bring to the temple their first-fruits, and other gifts, according to their resources, and they kept it well endowed with gold and silver. At that time the temple was stripped of all those offerings. After Hannibal's departure large heaps of bronze were found, since his soldiers were drawn by a pious contrition to lay down pieces of the metal. There is no disagreement in our sources over the actual pillaging of the temple. Coelius records that Hannibal stopped off there on his way to Rome from Eretum; and he has him coming by way of Amiternum, Cutiliae, and Reate. According to Coelius, Hannibal came to Samnium from Campania, and from Samnium into Paelignian territory. He then went past the town of Sulmo into the land of the Marrucini, and from there, by way of Alban territory, into that of the Marsi, after which he reached Amiternum and the village of Foruli.

There can, in fact, be no uncertainty over the route, either, because the passage of such a great leader, and such a great army, could not have become confused in men's minds after so short an interval. And, in fact, there *is* agreement on his itinerary. The only point of disagreement is whether this was the path he took when he was coming *to* the city, or when he was returning to Campania *from* the city.*

12. Hannibal was not as determined to defend Capua as the Romans were to tighten their blockade. Instead, he moved speedily through <Samnium, Apulia>, and the land of the Lucanians into Bruttian territory, reaching the straits and the town of Rhegium, and this he did with such speed that he took its people by surprise, and almost overwhelmed them by the suddenness of his appearance.* The siege of Capua had lost none of its intensity in that period, but the people were aware of Flaccus' arrival, and there was some surprise that Hannibal had not come back at the same time. Then, through talks held with the enemy, they discovered that they had been left in the lurch, and that the Carthaginians had lost hope of holding Capua. In addition, an edict of the proconsuls had been posted in accordance with a decree of the Senate, and had been made known to the enemy, that any Capuan citizen going over to the Romans before a certain date would suffer no harm. Despite this, there was no defection to the Romans, though it was fear that kept the Capuans on side rather than loyalty to Carthage, because the atrocities they had committed in seceding from Rome were, they thought, too great to pardon. But while nobody made an independent decision to go over to the enemy, there was no discussion of measures to be taken for their collective safety, either. The aristocrats had left the government and could not be brought together for a senate meeting; and in the top magistracy was a man who had brought no distinction upon himself—by his own unfitness for office, in fact, he had diminished the effectiveness and authority of the position he held. By now none of the leading people made an appearance even in the forum, or any other public place; they shut themselves away in their houses and every day awaited the downfall of their native city, along with their own destruction.

Overall responsibility for operations had devolved upon Bostar and Hanno, the commanders of the Carthaginian garrison, and what concerned them was their own danger, not that of their allies. The two wrote a letter to Hannibal that was not just outspoken but sharply critical, reproaching him not only with handing Capua to the enemy, but also with leaving them and their garrison to face all manner of torture. In going off into Bruttium, Hannibal was virtually turning his back on them, they said, so as not to have the capture of Capua before his eyes. And, they added, it had still proved impossible to divert the Romans from the siege of Capua even by an assault on the city of Rome—the Roman was far more dedicated an enemy than the Carthaginian was a friend! If Hannibal returned to Capua, and made it the focus of the whole war, they assured him that they, along with the Capuans, would be ready to counterattack. It was not to fight people from Rhegium or Tarentum that they had crossed the Alps, they added; where there were Roman legions—*that* was where the Carthaginian armies ought to be! This was what had given them success at Cannae, and at Trasimene, too—tackling the enemy head-on, setting one's camp down next to his, and putting fortune to the test.

The letter, written in these terms, was entrusted to some Numidians, who, on the promise of a reward, undertook the mission to deliver it. The Numidians came to Flaccus, in his camp, posing as deserters (and the food-shortages that had lasted so long in Capua meant that no one lacked a credible pretext for deserting), their plan being to wait for the right moment, and then slip away. Suddenly, however, a Capuan woman came into the camp. She had been the mistress of one of the 'deserters', and she informed the Roman commander that the Numidians' desertion was a trick, and that they were carrying a letter to Hannibal. She was, she said, ready to offer proof of the charge in the case of one of the Numidians, who had disclosed the affair to her.

The man was brought, and at first he steadfastly claimed not to know the woman. Then, gradually, his case fell apart before the facts and, when he saw instruments of torture being called for, and then being prepared for use, he admitted the truth and the letter was produced. A further piece of information, which had remained a secret, also came to light: there were other Numidians at large in the Roman camp posing as deserters. These men were arrested, more than seventy in all, and, along with the new 'deserters', they were returned to Capua, after being flogged and having their hands cut off.

13. The sight of such a savage punishment broke the Capuans' spirit. People converged on the senate house, forcing Loesius to convene the senate. They also made open threats to the leading citizens, who had long been absenting themselves from public meetings: if these men failed to appear in the senate, they said, they would make the rounds of their homes and drag them all out into the streets. Fear of this happening ensured the magistrate a senate with a full quorum. At the meeting, they were all discussing the idea of sending a deputation to the Roman commanders—all but Vibius Virrius, the man responsible for the Capuan abandonment of the Roman cause. When Vibius was asked his opinion, he declared that those talking about a deputation, and about peace and surrender, did not remember either what they themselves would have done if they had had the Romans at their mercy, or the treatment they themselves were bound to face now.

'Well,' he continued, 'do you think surrender is now going to be the same as on that occasion when we surrendered ourselves, and all that we owned, to the Romans in order to gain their help against the Samnites? Have you already forgotten just when it was that we rebelled from the Roman people and in what circumstances? Have you forgotten how, when we defected, we could have released the garrison, but instead put it to death with torture and shameful abuse? Have you forgotten how often, and how fiercely, we conducted sorties against the blockading forces, attacked their camps, and called on Hannibal to come and crush them? And, the most recent thing, have you forgotten that we sent him from here to attack Rome?

'On the other hand, think back now on their hostile acts against us, so that you can judge from them what to expect. There was an enemy from abroad in Italy; that enemy was Hannibal; and the whole country was engulfed in the flames of war. The Romans still forgot everything else, forgot even Hannibal, and sent two consuls and two consular armies to blockade Capua. This is the second year that they have us walled in and bottled up with their siege, as they grind us down with hunger. And they, too, like us, have faced the most severe of dangers, the most punishing of hardships; often they have been massacred around their rampart and ditches, and finally they were almost driven from their camp.

'But I say nothing of such things—there is nothing new or unusual about hardships and dangers faced in the blockade of an enemy city. The following, however, is real evidence of their rage, and of a hatred that is implacable and deadly. At the head of massive infantry and cavalry forces, Hannibal attacked their camp and took part of it; not even by danger on that scale could they be dislodged from their blockade. He then proceeded across the Volturnus, and put the land of Cales to the torch; not even by such a catastrophe to their allies could they be deflected from their goal. Hannibal then gave orders for an offensive against the city of Rome itself; even to that gathering storm they paid no heed. He crossed the River Anio, encamped three miles from the city, and finally came right up to its walls and gates, making it clear that he would take Rome from them unless they abandoned Capua. They did not abandon it. Even when wild beasts are in the grip of blind and furious rage, you can still make them turn aside to help their own by approaching their lairs and their young. Not the Romans! Rome under siege could not make *them* turn aside from Capua, nor could their wives and children— whose weeping and wailing could be heard almost from here—or their altars, their hearths, the shrines of their gods, or the desecration and violation of their ancestors' tombs. So great is their hunger to exact punishment, so deep their thirst for our blood! And with good reason—perhaps, given the chance, we would have done the same.

'However, the gods have decided otherwise, and I must not even balk at the prospect of death. But the tortures and indignities the enemy is preparing, these I can escape, while I am free and my own master, by choosing a death that is honourable and even merciful. I shall not see Appius Claudius and Quintus Fulvius high and mighty in insolent victory. I shall not be dragged in chains through the city of Rome as an exhibit in their triumph—†then† to be sent down into prison or tied to a post, to have my back lacerated by the whip and place my neck beneath a Roman axe. I shall not see my home city being destroyed and burned, or the rape of Capuan mothers, girls, and free-born boys. Alba, from which they trace their descent, the Romans razed to its foundations,* to leave no memory of their lineage and origins. So I shall certainly not believe they will spare Capua, which they hate more than Carthage.

'And so, for all those of you who intend to let death take them before they witness so many painful sights, a dinner has today been arranged and made ready at my house. When you have had your fill of wine and food, the cup that will have been given first to me will also pass around the company. That is a drink that will rescue your body from torment, your spirit from humiliation, your eyes and ears from all the painful and degrading sights and sounds that await the conquered. Men will be at hand to hurl our lifeless bodies on a pyre that will be lit in the courtyard of the house. This is the only path to death that is honourable and befitting a free man. Our enemies will marvel at our courage, and Hannibal, too, will recognize the fortitude of the allies he forsook and betrayed.'

14. Of Virrius' listeners, more agreed with what he said than had the courage to carry out the plan of which they approved. Most of the senate had little doubt that the clemency of the Roman people, which had been witnessed in so many past wars, would also serve them well; and they decided to send, and then they sent, a delegation to surrender Capua to the Romans. Some twenty-seven senators went home with Vibius Virrius. They had dinner with him and, after doing their best to deaden their minds with wine to the prospect of the horror before them, they all took the poison. The banquet then broke up, and they clasped each other's right hands and embraced for the last time, shedding tears for their own lot and that of their country. Some then stayed so they could be burned on the same pyre; others went home. The fact that their veins were replete with food and wine diminished the efficacy of the poison to bring on a swift death. The result was that most of them were in their death throes throughout the night and part of the next day; but they all breathed their last before the gates were opened to the enemy.

The following day, on the order of the proconsuls, the Porta Iovis, which faced the Roman camp, was thrown open, and a single legion and two cavalry squadrons were sent in, under the command of the legate Gaius Fulvius. Fulvius' very first move was to have all the arms in Capua, projectile and other, brought to him. He then stationed sentries at all the gates to prevent anyone from leaving or being let out; he arrested the Punic garrison; and he ordered the Capuan senate to proceed to the Roman commanders in their camp. On reaching the camp, the senators were all immediately clapped in irons and ordered to bring all the gold and silver they owned out to the quaestors. That amounted to 2,070 pounds of gold, and 31,200 pounds of silver. Of the senators whose views were chiefly responsible for the defection from Rome, twenty-five were sent to Cales for imprisonment, and twenty-eight to Teanum.

15. On the punishment of the Capuan senate there was no agreement at all between Fulvius and Claudius. Claudius was amenable to the idea of a pardon, but Fulvius was more obdurate. Appius therefore began to suggest referring the whole matter back to the Senate for adjudication, adding that he thought it was correct for the senators to be given the opportunity to question the prisoners on whether they had communicated their plans to any of the Latin allies, and whether they had received any assistance from them during the hostilities. Fulvius, however, argued that they must at all costs avoid a situation in which the loyalty of faithful allies could be put at risk through vague insinuations, and in which such allies would be at the mercy of informers who did not care at all about what they said or did. Accordingly, he said, he would overrule and quash questioning of that kind.

When they parted after this conversation, Appius was convinced that his colleague, for all his defiant words, would still await written orders from Rome on a matter of such importance. Fulvius, however, fearing that these orders would interfere with what he proposed to do, dismissed his council, and instructed his military tribunes and allied officers to pick out 2,000 cavalry and order them to be ready when the bugle sounded the third watch.

With this cavalry support, Fulvius left for Teanum at night, and at dawn he passed through the gate of the town and headed straight for the forum. People gathered around when the cavalry first entered; and Fulvius then ordered the chief magistrate* to be summoned, and commanded him to bring out the Capuan citizens that he had in custody. They were all brought out, flogged, and beheaded. Then Fulvius rode at a gallop to Cales. There he took his seat on the podium, and the Capuans were brought out. They were actually being tied to the stake when a horseman arrived post-haste from Rome and delivered to Fulvius a dispatch from the praetor Gaius Calpurnius, along with a decree of the Senate. A murmur then spread from the podium throughout the gathering that the entire case of the Capuan prisoners was being deferred for senatorial adjudication. This was also what Fulvius felt was the case. And so he took the letter, placed it unopened in the breast fold of his robe,* and instructed the herald to give the order for the lictor to carry out the lawful sentence.

So it was that the execution of the prisoners at Cales was also carried out. Only then were the letter and the senatorial decree actually read, too late to prevent something that had been speeded up by all possible means just to make preventing it impossible.

Fulvius was now rising to his feet when Taurea Vibellius, a Capuan citizen,* strode through the midst of the crowd and called on him by name. Wondering what the man wanted of him, Flaccus sat down again.

'Have me executed, too,' said Vibellius. 'You could then boast of having executed a man much braver than you are yourself.' Flaccus declared the man was clearly out of his mind and that, anyway, he was prevented from doing what he asked, even if he wished to, by the decree of the Senate.

'My native city has been captured,' replied Vibellius, 'and my relatives and friends are gone—with my own hand I killed my wife and children to prevent their being subjected to any outrage. But I do not have the same opportunity to die as did these fellow citizens of mine, so let my release from this life that I hate come from my courage.' With that he took the sword that he had hidden under his clothes and plunged it straight through his breast, falling dead before the general's feet.

16. Because the execution of the Capuans, and several other things, resulted from a decision unilaterally taken by Flaccus, some authors record that Appius Claudius was dead before the surrender of Capua. They add that this man Taurea did not come to Cales of his own volition, and did not die by his own hand, but that he had been tied to a stake along with the others, and that Flaccus had called for silence because what the man was shouting could not be heard amidst the clamour. Then Taurea reportedly made the declaration recorded above, that he was a very brave man who was being put to death by one who was nowhere near his equal in courage. At this the herald, on the proconsul's instructions, called out: 'Lictor, apply the lash to the brave man, and carry out the lawful sentence on him first!'

Some sources also record that Fulvius read the senatorial decree before he conducted the execution. But the decree contained the rider 'if the proconsul sees fit,* he should refer the whole matter back to the Senate for adjudication', and he interpreted that as meaning that it had been left to him to decide what was now in the best interests of the state.

From Cales, Fulvius returned to Capua, and accepted the surrender of Atella and Calatia. There, too, punishment was meted out to the ringleaders of the secession. About seventy leading members of the senate were executed. Some 300 Campanian nobles were imprisoned in Rome, and others, who were kept in custody throughout the cities of the Latin allies, met their end in various ways. The rest of the citizens of Capua were sold into slavery.

The question of the city and its lands remained to be discussed, and some people were advocating the destruction of a particularly strong city that was close by and hostile to Rome. But immediate utilitarian considerations prevailed, and it owed its salvation to its agricultural land, which was widely recognized as the foremost in Italy for its overall productivity—the city would be a home to the people farming that land. To keep the city inhabited, its population of resident foreigners, freedmen, traders, and craftsmen was kept on, and all the farmlands and buildings became the public property of the Roman people. But it was decided that Capua should only be inhabited and populated like a city, but that there should be no political structure—no senate, no plebeian council, no magistrates. The idea was that without a public deliberative body and without real authority, the population would be incapable of any uniform policy, having no shared interest in anything. The Romans would send a prefect each year to conduct judicial proceedings.

Thus the matter of Capua was settled by implementing a programme that was laudable in every respect.* The punishment of the most blameworthy was harsh and swift, and the bulk of the citizen body was dispersed, with no prospect of return. But there was no fire and destruction wreaking havoc on inoffensive buildings and walls and, in addition to gaining economic advantage, the Romans also managed to provide their allies with a demonstration of their clemency. For they were leaving untouched a city of great fame and great wealth, whose destruction would have caused tears to flow throughout Campania, and throughout all the peoples living around Campania. The enemy was obliged to admit the magnitude of Roman power when it came to punishing disloyal allies, and the complete inadequacy of Hannibal's assistance for those whom he had taken under his protection.

17. After fulfilling their duties in regard to Capua, the Roman senators issued a decree assigning troops to Gaius Nero.* From the two legions that he had commanded at Capua, Nero was to have 6,000 infantry and 300 cavalry, which he could choose for himself; he was also to have the same number of infantry, and 800 cavalry, from the allies and those of Latin status. Nero put this army aboard ships at Puteoli and transported it to Spain. On reaching Tarraco with the fleet, he disembarked the troops, hauled the ships ashore, and, to increase his numbers, armed his crews as well. He then left for the River Ebro where he took over command of their army from Tiberius Fonteius and Lucius Marcius. From the Ebro he advanced on the enemy. Hasdrubal son of Hamilcar was encamped at the Black Rocks, an area in the land of the Ausetani between the towns of Iliturgi and Mentisa.* This lay in a pass, and Nero seized the entrance to it.

Fearful of being penned in, Hasdrubal sent a herald to Nero with a promise that, if he were allowed out, he would remove his entire army from Spain. The Roman gladly accepted his offer. Hasdrubal then requested that the next day be set aside for a meeting, at which, in a face-to-face discussion, terms for the surrender of the citadels in the various cities could be drawn up, and a date set for the garrisons in them to be withdrawn, and for the Carthaginians to remove their property from them (without penalty). His request granted, Hasdrubal immediately issued orders for his heaviest troops to make their way out of the pass, by any means they could, as soon as darkness fell and throughout the night after that. It was carefully arranged that not many leave that first night; smaller numbers would, by their silence, be more capable of eluding the enemy and, also, of slipping away along narrow and difficult pathways.

The two parties came to the meeting the following day, but since that day was consumed with inordinately long discussions, and the (intentional) documentation of irrelevancies, it was then adjourned to the next. The oncoming night gave Hasdrubal further time to send out even more men, and not even on the following day did the business come to a conclusion. So it was that several days were spent on an open discussion of terms, and several nights on a clandestine evacuation of Carthaginians from the camp. Then, when most of the army had been evacuated, there was no longer Carthaginian support even for provisions they had initially proposed, with agreement less and less forthcoming as their fear and honesty diminished in tandem. The time had now come when nearly all the infantry troops had left the pass when, at dawn one day, a dense mist covered the whole pass and the plains around it. Seeing this, Hasdrubal sent a man to Nero to put off the meeting to the following day, claiming that the present day was one on which religion forbade Carthaginians to conduct any serious business. Not even then was there any suspicion of dishonesty, and Hasdrubal was spared that day. He thereupon immediately left camp with his cavalry and elephants, and slipped quietly away to safety. By about the fourth hour the sun had dispersed the mist, and brought back the clear light of day; and the Romans set eyes on a deserted enemy camp. Only then did Claudius recognize the Punic trickery* and, when he realized he had been hoodwinked, he followed hard on the heels of the departing Hasdrubal, ready to face him in regular battle. The enemy, however, refused to engage, though there were some skirmishes between the Punic rearguard and the advance troops of the Romans.

18. In the meantime, the peoples of Spain who had defected after the defeat were not returning to the Roman alliance, although there were no new defections, either. At Rome, too, after the recovery of Capua, the Senate and people felt as much concerned about Spain as they did about Italy, and it was decided that the army there should be augmented and a commander sent out to it. But there was less agreement about whom to send than there was on the point that, when two top commanders had perished within a thirty-day period, extra special care was required in choosing the man to succeed them. Various candidates were suggested, but the expedient eventually settled on was that the people should hold an election to create a proconsul for Spain. The consuls then announced a date for that election.*

At first people had expected those who believed themselves qualified for such an important command to put their names forward; but such hopes proved groundless, and feelings of melancholy over the defeat, and grief for the lost commanders, reappeared. The state was in mourning, almost at a loss how to proceed, but on election day the people went down into the Campus. They turned towards the magistrates and scrutinized the faces of the leading citizens, who themselves simply looked at each other. And people started to murmur that things were so bad, and confidence in the state so low, that no one dared accept authority for Spain. Then, suddenly, Publius Cornelius—son of the Publius Cornelius who had fallen in Spain, and then about twenty-four years of age—declared his candidacy, and stood on higher ground so he could be seen. Everyone's gaze turned on him, and their shouts and cheers immediately predicted a happy and successful command for him. They were then instructed to cast their ballots, and it was not just the centuries that voted unanimously for command in Spain being vested in Publius Scipio; individuals were unanimous, as well. But, after the event, when their excitement and fervour had died down, silence suddenly fell as people silently reflected on what they had done. Had their positive feelings for the man counted for more with them than reason? It was his age that caused the greatest concern, but some also had morbid fears over the family's fortunes and the man's name. He would be proceeding from two ill-fated households, and into those provinces where his campaigns would necessarily be conducted amidst the tombs of his father and his uncle.

19. When Scipio detected people's concern and anxiety after such an impulsive act, he called an assembly and discussed his age, the command entrusted to him, and the war that had to be fought. This he did with such a magnanimous and noble spirit that he revived and renewed the enthusiasm that had died down, and filled men with higher expectations than trust in a man's promise or a rational assessment based on confidence in his success would usually inspire.

In fact, Scipio won admiration not simply for his unquestionable merits; from his early years he also had a talent for showcasing them.* In public speaking he would represent most of his actions as prompted by dreams at night, or divine inspiration. Perhaps he genuinely had a superstitious bent, or perhaps he sought unhesitating acceptance of his orders and plans by vesting them with some oracular authority. He had, moreover, been preparing people for this since the beginning, since his adoption of the *toga virilis*.* For since that time he had spent no day on any public or private business without first going to the Capitol where, entering the temple, he would take a seat and pass some time, usually on his own and in seclusion. This was a practice he kept up throughout his life, and in some it generated the belief in the story—perhaps deliberately put about, perhaps spontaneous—that Scipio was a man of divine origin. It also brought back into currency the rumour that earlier circulated about Alexander the Great, a rumour as fatuous as it was presumptuous. It was said that his conception was the result of sexual union with a snake, that this miraculous creature was often seen in his mother's bedroom, and that it slithered away and vanished from sight when people came in. Scipio himself never ridiculed people's belief in these supernatural tales. In fact, he actually strengthened it by developing a sort of knack for neither rejecting nor openly affirming anything of this kind. There were many other instances of this sort of thing, some genuine, some affected, that won this young man superhuman admiration; and these were what at that time gave the state the confidence* to vest such great responsibility, and so great a command, in a man by no means mature in years.

The forces from the old army in Spain, and those that had crossed from Puteoli with Gaius Nero, were now augmented by 10,000 infantry and 1,000 cavalry, and Marcus Junius Silanus was assigned to Scipio to assist him in the campaign. And so, with a fleet of thirty ships, all of them quinqueremes, Scipio set off from the mouth of the Tiber, skirted the coast of the Etruscan Sea, the Alps, and the Gulf of Gaul, and then rounded the promontory of the Pyrenees, putting ashore his troops at Emporiae, a Greek city, whose people also derive from Phocaea.* Ordering his ships to follow, he set off overland from there and came to Tarraco, where he held a meeting of all the allies; for delegations had flooded to him from every part of the province as soon as they got word of his coming. There he ordered the ships to be hauled ashore, sending back four triremes from Massilia that had, as a courtesy, escorted him from their home. Scipio then proceeded to give replies to the delegations, whose peoples were perturbed by the many changes of fortune they had experienced. This he did in a stately manner that derived from a great confidence in his own abilities, but without letting slip a single arrogant word, and there was, in everything he said, great conviction as well as great dignity.

20. After setting off from Tarraco, Scipio paid visits both to allied communities and the army's winter quarters. There he was fulsome in his praise of the soldiers: even after the blow of two serious and successive defeats, he said, they had still held on to the province. They had kept the enemy out of all the lands north of the Ebro, not allowing him to feel any of the benefits of his success, and they had steadfastly defended their allies.

Scipio kept Marcius with him, showing him such respect as to make it plain that he feared nothing less than anyone standing in the way of his own glory. Silanus then succeeded Nero, and the new recruits were led into winter quarters. Scipio had been swift in making all the obligatory visits and doing everything that was necessary, and he now retired to Tarraco. He enjoyed no less a reputation amongst the foe than amongst his fellow citizens and the allies; and the enemy also had some sort of premonition of what was to come that brought a dread that was all the more intense because of their inability to rationalize their blind fear. The Carthaginians had left for winter quarters in different directions, Hasdrubal son of Gisgo going as far as Gades on the Ocean, and Mago into the interior (specifically, above the pass of Castulo). Hasdrubal son of Hamilcar remained closest to the Ebro, wintering in the neighbourhood of Saguntum.*

At the end of that summer during which Capua was taken and Scipio arrived in Spain, a Punic fleet had been summoned from Sicily to Tarentum. In its efforts to cut off supplies to the Roman garrison in the citadel of Tarentum, this fleet had succeeded in blocking every approach to the citadel from the sea. The longer it stayed in place, however, the more acute it was making the problem of grain provisioning—not for their enemy, but for the Carthaginian allies! Grain could be shipped in for the townspeople along the shores that were secure, and through ports that were open under Carthaginian naval protection; but this was not as much as the fleet itself consumed, with its motley mixture of sailors of every kind. The upshot was that the garrison in the citadel, because of its small numbers, was able to survive on what had been stockpiled earlier, even without importing food, while even what was imported was insufficient for the Tarentines and the fleet. Eventually, the fleet moved off, leaving the townspeople more grateful than they were for its arrival, though this brought little relief to the food-supply since, with naval protection gone, grain could not be imported.

21. At the end of the same summer Marcus Marcellus, arriving in the city from his province of Sicily, was granted by the praetor Gaius Calpurnius an audience with the Senate in the temple of Bellona.* After giving an account of his achievements, Marcellus lodged a mild complaint—more on behalf of his men than himself—that he had not been allowed to bring his army home from the province on the

completion of his mission. He then asked permission to enter the city in triumph, and his request was denied. There had been a long discussion in the house about which of two courses made more sense. Should they refuse a man a triumph now that he was present when, during his absence, a period of public thanksgiving had been authorized in his name, and honour formally paid to the gods, for successes achieved under his command? On the other hand, should a man celebrate a triumph as though the war were terminated, when the senators had instructed him to pass his army on to his successor—a decree that would not have been passed were there not hostilities continuing in the province? And celebrate it, too, when the army was not there to bear witness to whether or not the triumph was merited? A compromise was reached: Marcellus should enter the city with an ovation.

With senatorial authorization, the tribunes of the plebs then brought before the people the proposal that Marcus Marcellus should retain his *imperium* on the day he entered the city with an ovation. The day before his entrance into the city, Marcellus celebrated a triumph on the Alban Mount* and, after that, in his ovation, he had large quantities of plunder brought into the city before him. Along with a model of Syracuse after its capture, catapults, ballistae, and a whole panoply of war engines were carried in the procession, and with them there were also the objets d'art amassed over a long period of peace thanks to the wealth of the Syracusan kings. There were heaps of silver and bronze artefacts, furniture, precious clothing, and many famous statues, Syracuse having been one of the Greek cities most richly endowed in such things. To mark the victory over Carthage, too, eight elephants were led along, and not the least impressive sight was that of the Syracusan Sosis and the Spaniard Moericus walking ahead of Marcellus wearing crowns of gold. One of these men had acted as guide during the night when entry was gained into Syracuse; the other had sold out the Nassus and its garrison. Both were granted Roman citizenship, and 500 *iugera* of land. Sosis' grant was of land in Syracusan territory that had belonged either to the king or to men who had been enemies of Rome, and a house in Syracuse—the choice was his—that had belonged to one of those punished under the rules of war. Moericus and the Spaniards who had seceded along with him were to be awarded a town in Sicily, along with its farmland, to be taken from one of those communities that had defected from the Roman people; and Marcus Cornelius was given the duty of assigning to the men the town and land where he thought suitable. Belligenes, the man responsible for Moericus' switch of allegiance, was also decreed 400 *iugera* in the same area of Sicily.

After Marcellus left Sicily, a Carthaginian fleet put ashore 8,000 infantry and 3,000 Numidian cavalry on the island. The cities of Murgentia and Ergetium defected to them, to be followed by Hybla, Macella, and some lesser-known towns. Furthermore, the Numidians, led by Muttines, roamed the length of Sicily, putting to the torch farmland belonging to the allies of the Roman people. In addition, the Roman troops were resentful, partly because they had not been taken home from the province with their commander, and partly because they had been ordered not to take winter quarters in the towns. Accordingly, they showed little enthusiasm for their duties, and it was lack of a leader, rather than lack of inclination, that staved off mutiny. Facing these difficulties, the praetor Marcus Cornelius used a combination of reassurance and punishment to calm the men, and he also brought back under his control all the communities that had defected. It was one of these communities, Murgentia,* that Cornelius awarded to the Spaniards who were owed a city and its lands, as specified by the senatorial decree.

22. Both consuls had Apulia as their area of responsibility, but by now there was less to be feared from the Carthaginians and Hannibal, and so they were instructed to proceed to a sortition for Apulia and Macedonia as their provinces. Macedonia fell to Sulpicius, who now became Laevinus' successor.

Fulvius was called to Rome for the elections, and when he was holding the meeting for the election of consuls, the junior members of the Voturia century, who had the first ballot, voted for Titus Manlius Torquatus and Titus Otacilius. The crowd then converged on Manlius, who was present at the meeting, to congratulate him, and there was no doubt that he had the unanimous support of the people. Manlius, however, with a multitude swarming all round him, proceeded to the consul's dais, where he appealed to the consul to hear the few words he had to say and to have the century that had voted called back. Everyone was now on tenterhooks, wondering what Manlius was going to ask for. He then requested exemption from office because of an eye ailment. It would be a brazen pilot, and a brazen general, too, that would ask for the lives and fortunes of others to be put in his hands when his every action depended upon the eyes of others, he explained. Accordingly, if Fulvius thought fit, he should order the junior members of the Voturia century to retake the vote, and bear in mind, when they were electing consuls, the war that was going on in Italy and the crisis facing the republic. Their ears, he said, had barely recovered from the uproar and commotion the enemy had produced when, a few months earlier, he had all but shaken the walls of Rome.

After this a majority of the members of the century loudly protested that their minds were unchanged, and they would appoint the same consuls as before, at which point Torquatus retorted: 'As consul, I shall be no more able to bear your conduct than you will be able bear my authority. Go back to the urn; and reflect that there is a war with Carthage in Italy, and that the enemy commander is Hannibal.'

The century was now swayed by the man's commanding presence and the murmurs of respect all round him. They asked the consul to call in the senior members of the Voturia century, for, they said, they wished to hold a discussion with their elders, and accept their authority in appointing the consuls. The senior members of the Voturia were then called, and time was granted for an in camera discussion with them in the voting enclosure.* The senior members declared that three men should be given consideration. Two, Quintus Fabius and Marcus Marcellus, had already been showered with honours, they said, but if they really wanted a new man elected consul to face the Carthaginians, there was Marcus Valerius Laevinus, who had brilliant land and sea operations against King Philip to his credit.

There followed discussion of the three men, after which the senior members were discharged, and the younger men proceeded to the vote. They declared elected, both of them *in absentia*, Marcus Claudius, now in the limelight after his conquest of Sicily, and Marcus Valerius, and all the other centuries followed the lead of the one that voted first.*

So much for those who ridicule admirers of the past! If there does exist a philosopher-state somewhere—a product of our scholars' imagination rather than their knowledge—I certainly would not believe its leaders could be more serious-minded or restrained in their political ambition, or the commons more principled, than in this case. That a century of younger men should have wanted to consult their elders about whom they should invest with power by their vote seems very implausible these days, when the influence that even parents have over their children is slight and ineffectual.*

23. Elections for the praetorship were held next, and the successful candidates were Publius Manlius Volso, Lucius Manlius Acidinus, Gaius Laetorius, and Lucius Cincius Alimentus.* As it happened, news arrived after the elections of the death in Sicily of Titus Otacilius, the man whom, in his absence, the people would apparently have made Titus Manlius' colleague, had there been no interruption in the electoral proceedings. The Games of Apollo had been staged the previous year and, when the praetor Calpurnius moved that they be again staged this year, the Senate decreed that a vow be taken making them a permanent institution.

That same year there were numerous sightings and reports of prodigies. The statue of Victory on the roof of the temple of Concord was struck by lightning. It was knocked down but became lodged amongst those statues of Victory amidst the antefixes, and fell no further. It was also reported that the wall and gates at both Anagnia and Fregellae had been struck by lightning; that in Forum Subertanum* streams of blood flowed for an entire day; that at Eretum stones fell as rain; and that at Reate a mule had given birth. Full-grown animals were sacrificed to expiate these prodigies, with a one-day session of prayer appointed for the people as well as the nine-day rite.*

A number of state-appointed priests died that year and were replaced by new ones. Marcus Aemilius Lepidus replaced Manius Aemilius Numida as decemvir for sacrifices; Gaius Livius replaced Marcus Pomponius Matho the pontiff; and Marcus Servilius replaced the augur Spurius Carvilius Maximus. Because the pontiff Titus Otacilius Crassus died after the end of his year, there was no nomination made for a replacement. The Flamen of Jupiter, Gaius Claudius, left office over a procedural oversight in placing the entrails.*

24. Marcus Valerius Laevinus had earlier held clandestine meetings with Aetolian leaders to gauge their sympathies, and it was about this time that he came, with a swift fleet of ships, to a council of the Aetolians which had been scheduled earlier to discuss the matter.* Laevinus pointed to the capture of Syracuse and Capua as

evidence of Roman success in Sicily and Italy, and added that he followed the traditional practice of the Romans, inherited from his ancestors, of dealing with allies. Some allies, he explained, the Romans had accepted as citizens in equal partnership with themselves; others they kept in such a prosperous condition that they actually preferred to be allies than citizens. And the Aetolians, he added, would find themselves all the more honoured for having been the first overseas nation to enter into friendship with Rome. As for Philip and the Macedonians, they were difficult neighbours for the Aetolians, but he had already curtailed their violent and haughty temper, and would in future bring them to the point not only of quitting the cities they had filched from the Aetolians but of finding Macedonia itself under threat. Then there were the Acarnanians, he said. The Aetolians resented the fact that these had been torn from their league, and he would bring them back to their old status, making them subject to Aetolian authority and control.

Such were the undertakings and promises given by the Roman commander. Scopas, the current praetor of the Aetolian people, and Dorimachus, a leading Aetolian citizen, endorsed them with their own authority, both of them praising the power and majesty of the Roman people in a less reserved, and so more persuasive, manner. But it was the prospect of gaining Acarnania that swayed the Aetolians most. And so terms were drafted on which they were to become friends and allies of the Roman people, and a rider was added containing the following conditions:

The Eleans and Lacedaemonians, as well as Attalus, Pleuratus, and Scerdilaedus, should enjoy the same treaty rights if such was their pleasure and wish (Attalus was king of Asia, Pleuratus and Scerdilaedus the kings of the Thracians and Illyrians respectively).

The Aetolians were to proceed immediately to war on land against Philip, and the Romans were to provide naval assistance in the form of no fewer than twenty-five quinqueremes.

With regard to the cities from Aetolia as far as Corcyra, the soil, buildings, walls, and agricultural lands would belong to the Aetolians, and all else that was taken would be the booty of the Romans. The Romans would also take steps to see that the Aetolians should have possession of Acarnania.

In the event of the Aetolians making peace with Philip, they were to add a clause to the treaty stipulating that the peace would have force only if Philip eschewed armed conflict with the Romans, their allies, and those subject to them. Likewise, in the event of the Roman people making a treaty with the king, they were to ensure that he would have no authority to make war on the Aetolians and their allies.

Such were the terms they agreed upon, and two years later they were copied and put on display, at Olympia by the Aetolians, and on the Capitol by the Romans, so they would have the sacred monuments to witness them.* The delay occurred because the Aetolian envoys were detained in Rome for a prolonged period, though this did not impede the implementation of the provisions. The Aetolians did, indeed, immediately open hostilities against Philip, and Laevinus captured Zacynthus, a small island close to Aetolia which has a single city bearing the same name as the island (Laevinus took the city by force, apart from its citadel). Laevinus also captured Oeniadae and Nassus,* two Acarnanian towns, and annexed them to Aetolia. He now also felt that Philip was well enough embroiled in a local war not to be able to turn his thoughts to Italy, the Carthaginians, and his pact with Hannibal, and he withdrew to Corcyra.

25. Philip was wintering at Pella when he was brought the news that the Aetolians had defected. His plan was to lead his troops into Greece in early spring; and so that Macedonia could count on the Illyrians, and the neighbouring towns to her rear, taking no action, he made a lightning raid on the lands of Oricum and Apollonia. When the people of Apollonia came out to face him, he drove them back within their walls in terror-stricken panic. After laying waste the closest parts of Illyricum, he just as speedily veered into Pelagonia and took Sintia, a Dardanian city that could have provided the Dardanians with a passage into Macedonia. These operations were speedily completed. Now, with the Aetolian War in mind, and the concomitant war with Rome, Philip went down into Thessaly by way of Pelagonia, Lyncus, and Bottiaea, for he believed that people there could be induced to join him in hostilities against the Aetolians. He then left Perseus* at the pass into Thessaly with 4,000 troops, to prevent the Aetolians from entering the district, and—before he should find himself preoccupied with more serious matters— brought his force back to Macedonia and marched on the Maedi in Thrace.* That people had made a practice of swooping down on Macedonia whenever it became aware that the king was engrossed in some foreign war, and his kingdom left without protection. To break

their power, Philip proceeded to lay waste their fields, and to assault Iamphorynna, the Maedic capital and stronghold.

When Scopas was told that the king had left for Thrace, and was engaged in a war there, he put all Aetolians of fighting age under arms, and prepared to invade Acarnania. The Acarnanian people were no match for the strength of the Aetolians, and they could see that Oeniadae and Nassus were lost and that, in addition, war with Rome was on the horizon. The Acarnanians, even so, put up a fight, though it was an angry reflex rather than a strategic move. Wives, children, and older men over sixty were sent to the closest parts of Epirus, and men aged between fifteen and sixty took an oath not to return home unless victorious. They framed a terrible curse against any of their own people who would receive in his city, in his house, at his table, or by his hearth a man who left the field in defeat, and they also made a most solemn appeal to their Epirot hosts to observe the injunction. They further begged the Epirots to bury under a single mound those of their men who fell in battle, and to set the following epitaph over their buried soldiers: 'Here lie the Acarnanians who met their end fighting for their country against Aetolian aggression and injustice.'

Their courage fired by this, the Acarnanians encamped right on their borders, facing the enemy. By sending messengers to Philip to inform him of their precarious situation, they obliged him to drop the war in which he was engaged, despite the surrender of Iamphorynna and the success of other operations. Word of the oath taken by the Acarnanians had at first caused a postponement of the Aetolian offensive, and then news of Philip's coming even made them fall back into the interior of their country. As for Philip, despite his forced marches to prevent the Acarnanians being overwhelmed, he did not advance beyond Dium. Then, when he heard of the Aetolian withdrawal from Acarnania, he too retired to Pella.

26. At the start of spring Laevinus sailed from Corcyra. Rounding the promontory of Leucas, and arriving in Naupactus, he declared that he would head for Anticyra, and he instructed Scopas and the Aetolians to meet him there. Anticyra lies in Locris, to the left as one enters the Corinthian Gulf, and getting there from Naupactus involves a short journey by land or by sea. An assault on the town, conducted from both sides, began some two days later, but the attack from the sea was the more intense because there was all manner of artillery and assault apparatus on the ships, and, in addition, it was the Romans who were attacking on that side. The result was that the city capitulated in a matter of days. It was handed over to the Aetolians, the booty falling to the Romans, as had been agreed. Meanwhile, Laevinus was brought a letter informing him that he had been declared consul during his absence from Rome, and that Publius Sulpicius was coming to succeed him. However, he then came down with a lingering illness, and was later coming to Rome than everyone had expected.

Entering his consulship on 15 March, Marcus Marcellus went through the formalities of convening the Senate that day, but declared that he would conduct no business pertaining either to state policy or the provinces in the absence of his colleague. He was aware, he continued, that there were large numbers of Sicilians housed near the city on farms belonging to his political opponents, and, so far from not allowing them to make public, in Rome, the charges brought against him by his personal enemies, he would personally have granted them an immediate hearing before the Senate. The problem was that these men pretended to be afraid to talk about the consul in his colleague's absence, but when his colleague arrived, he would permit no business to be discussed before the item of the admission of the Sicilians to the Senate. Marcus Cornelius, he continued, had been virtually recruiting people throughout Sicily to ensure that the maximum number came to Rome to complain about him; and, to tarnish his reputation, Cornelius had also filled the city with letters that falsely claimed a state of war existed in Sicily. The consul earned distinction for his self-restraint that day. He dismissed the Senate, and it looked as if there would be a suspension of all business until the other consul's return to the city.

The inactivity, as usually happens, gave rise to idle talk among the masses. There were complaints about the length of the war, about the devastation of farmlands around the city, wherever Hannibal had gone on the attack with his troops, about Italy being depleted by troop-levies, and about the armies cut to shreds almost on a yearly basis. People complained, too, that both men elected to the consulship were war-mongers who were too headstrong and aggressive, the sort who could stir up war in the midst of peace and tranquillity, and who would certainly not allow the state a breathing space in the midst of war.

27. Such talk was interrupted by a fire which, on the night preceding the Quinquatrus,* broke out around the Forum, and in a number of places simultaneously. The seven shops (which later became five), and the bankers' establishments that are now called the 'New Banks', all went up in flames at the same time. After that, private houses caught fire—there were no basilicas in that period—as did the Quarries district, the Fish Market, and the Royal Atrium.* The temple of Vesta was barely saved, thanks mainly to the assistance of thirteen slaves, who were afterwards bought with state funds and manumitted. The blaze continued for a night and a day, and no one doubted that it was a case of arson because it had broken out in several spots at the same time, and in different areas, too. The consul, therefore, on the authority of the Senate, publicly announced at an assembly that there would be a reward for anyone identifying to the authorities those responsible for the fire, monetary in the case of a free man, and freedom in the case of a slave.

A slave belonging to the Calavii family of Capua—his name was Manus—was induced by the reward to denounce his masters as well as five young noblemen of Capua whose fathers had been beheaded by Quintus Fulvius. He claimed they were responsible for the fire, and added that they were going to set others at various places if they were not arrested. Arrested they were, they and their slaves. At first some effort was made to discredit the informer and his information. He had been punished with a whipping the day before, they said, and had run away from his masters; and, being angry and irresponsible, he had fabricated this charge out of what was simply an accident. But when the charge was brought against them in the presence of their accuser, and when the process of interrogating their henchmen began in the Forum, they all confessed, and masters and their slave accomplices alike were executed. The informant was granted his freedom and 20,000 *asses*.

On his way past Capua, the consul Laevinus was surrounded by a crowd of citizens of the town. They tearfully begged for permission to go to the Senate in Rome to plead with the senators—if they could finally be moved to pity—not to allow the Capuan people to be utterly destroyed, and the Capuan name wiped out, by Quintus Flaccus.

Flaccus claimed to have no private quarrel with the people of Capua. His antipathy towards them was governmental policy, he said; his anger was directed against an enemy of the state, and would remain unchanged for as long as he was sure that the Capuans maintained their present attitude towards the Roman people. For, he said, there was no race, no people, on the face of the earth who hated the Roman name more than they. He had good reason for keeping them confined within their walls: any finding a way of getting out of there roamed the countryside like wild animals, mutilating and butchering whatever came in their way. Some had gone over to Hannibal, others had gone off to set fire to Rome—the consul would find traces of Capuan misconduct in the half-burned Forum, he said. Vesta's temple had been a target, along with her ever-burning fires and, hidden away in the inner sanctum, destiny's pledge of Roman imperial power.* He was very strongly of the opinion, he said, that it was unsafe to give the Capuans leave to enter the walls of Rome.

Laevinus made the Capuans swear an oath to Flaccus that they would return to Capua four days after receiving their answer from the Senate, and then bade them accompany him to Rome. Surrounded by this crowd, and with Sicilians streaming out to meet him and joining him on the road to Rome, Laevinus gave the impression of a man who was grieving for the overthrow of two renowned cities, and who was bringing the defeated peoples into Rome to accuse the city's most distinguished men. But the business that the two consuls first brought before the Senate focused on state policy and the provinces.

28. At the meeting, Laevinus gave an account of the situation in Macedonia and Greece, and of how matters stood with the Aetolians, Acarnanians, and Locrians; and he also reported on his own land and naval operations in the sector. Philip had been set to invade Aetolia, he said, but had been driven back into Macedonia by him, and had withdrawn deep into the centre of his realm. Accordingly, the legion there could be withdrawn: the fleet sufficed for keeping the king out of Italy.

After the consul's report on himself, and the sphere of responsibility that he had held, the question of future responsibilities was raised by both consuls. The senators decreed that one should have Italy, and the war with Hannibal, as his sphere; the other should assume command of the fleet formerly under Titus Otacilius and, jointly with the praetor Lucius Cincius, take over the administration of Sicily. The consuls were then assigned by the Senate the two armies in Etruria and Gaul, comprising four legions. The two city legions of the previous year were to be despatched to Etruria, the two formerly commanded by the consul Sulpicius to Gaul. Command of Gaul and its legions was to go to the man chosen by the consul whose area of authority would be Italy. Gaius Calpurnius was sent to Etruria after his praetorship, with a year's extension of his *imperium*. Quintus Fulvius was assigned Capua as his province, and his *imperium* was also extended for a year. Orders were given for the army made up of citizens and allies to be reduced in numbers, with a single legion of 5,000 infantry and 300 cavalry formed from the two then in operation, and the men with the longest service records being discharged. In the case of the allies, too, only 7,000 infantry and 300 cavalry were to remain operative, the same principle of length of service also being applied here in discharging veterans.

In the case of Gnaeus Fulvius, consul the previous year, no change was made in either the allocation of Apulia as his province, or in the army that he had been commanding; he merely had his *imperium* extended for a year. Fulvius' colleague, Publius Sulpicius, was instructed to demobilize his entire army, with the exception of his ships' crews. Likewise there were orders for the army under the command of Marcus Cornelius in Sicily to be demobilized on the consul's arrival in the province. The praetor Lucius Cincius was given the veterans of Cannae, representing about two legions, for the occupation of Sicily. For Sardinia the praetor Publius Manlius Volso was also assigned that number of legions; these were the legions that Lucius Cornelius had commanded in that same province the year before. The consuls were given orders to raise the city legions without enlisting anyone who had been in the army of Marcus Claudius, Marcus Valerius, or Quintus Fulvius and without the total number of Roman legions that year exceeding twenty-one.

29. After these resolutions of the Senate, the consuls proceeded to the sortition of provinces. Sicily and the fleet fell to Marcellus, Italy and the war against Hannibal to Laevinus. The Sicilians had been awaiting the sortition, standing in full view of the consuls, and this result came as a blow to them, like a second capture of Syracuse. The result was that their sobbing and tearful remarks immediately made people turn to look at them, and later on set tongues wagging. For these men went around to the homes of senators dressed as mourners, declaring that, if Marcellus went back there with *imperium*, every group in their delegation would leave Sicily altogether, and not just their own home towns. They had done nothing to deserve his implacable rancour towards them earlier, they said, and what would his anger drive him to now, when he knew that Sicilians had come to Rome to complain about him? Better for that island to be engulfed by the flames of Aetna, or swallowed up by the sea, than to be virtually surrendered to a personal enemy for punishment.

These grievances of the Sicilians first did the rounds of the homes of the nobility, and became a common topic of conversation that was generated partly by sympathy for the Sicilians, and partly by jealousy felt for Marcellus. They also came to the Senate. The consuls were then asked to discuss with the Senate the possibility of exchanging provinces. Marcellus at that point stated that, had the Sicilians already been granted a senatorial audience, his thoughts on the matter might possibly have been different. As it was, however, he was concerned about anyone being able to say that these men were inhibited by fear from freely complaining about an individual under whose authority they would shortly be, and so he was ready to exchange his province if it made no difference to his colleague. But he was petitioning the Senate not to make a formal judgement on the matter in advance, he said. For while it would have been unfair for his colleague to be given the right to choose his province without sortition, how much greater an injustice—no, insult, rather—it was for his own allotment in the sortition to be passed over to his colleague!

And so the Senate adjourned after making its wishes known, but without a formal decree. A private arrangement was then made between the consuls to exchange their provinces, as destiny swept Marcellus on to confront Hannibal. Marcellus would be the first man to have won from him the glory of a battle which, after all the failures, was not a defeat, and the last of the Roman generals to enhance the Carthaginian's reputation by falling in battle, and that just when the Romans were achieving military success.

30. The provinces were exchanged, and the Sicilians were brought into the Senate. They produced a lot of talk about the unfailing loyalty of King Hiero towards the Roman people, trying to turn that to the credit of their state. They claimed to have hated the tyrants— Hieronymus, and then Hippocrates and Epicydes who followed him—for various reasons, but most importantly because they had

left the Romans to join Hannibal. That was why Hieronymus had been killed by the leaders of Syracuse's youth after what was virtually a public resolution, they said. That was why a group of seventy of the most prominent young noblemen had formed a conspiracy to assassinate Epicydes and Hippocrates, only to be let down by Marcellus' tardiness: Marcellus had not brought his army to Syracuse at the appointed time, and the young men, betrayed by an informer, were all put to death by the tyrants.

And, they continued, it was Marcellus who, by his ruthless sacking of Leontini, was responsible for the tyranny of Hippocrates and Epicydes. But, after that, the leading citizens of Syracuse had never stopped going over to him with commitments to deliver the city to him any time he chose. At first, however, Marcellus preferred to take it by force, but then it turned out that, after trying everything, he could achieve this end neither by land nor by sea. At that juncture, he preferred to have Sosis the coppersmith and the Spaniard Moericus as his agents for the surrender of Syracuse rather than leading Syracusan citizens, whose numerous offers to do this for him only met with rejection. Marcellus' aim, evidently, was to have greater justification for massacring and pillaging the Roman people's oldest allies. Just suppose it had not been Hieronymus who had gone over to Hannibal, but the whole Syracusan people and their Senate. Suppose, too, that the Syracusans had, as a matter of public policy, closed the gates on Marcellus, and not their tyrants, Hippocrates and Epicydes, who had kept the Syracusans in subjection. And suppose the Syracusans had fought the Roman people with the resolve of the Carthaginians. Even then, what damage, beyond what he actually did, could Marcellus have inflicted on them to show his animosity towards them—short of actually destroying Syracuse? At all events, they said, the people of Syracuse had been left nothing but their city's walls and looted buildings, and the gods' temples which had been broken into and robbed, with the removal of the very statues of the gods and their ornaments. Many, too, had seen their property confiscated, to the point where they had not even bare land to support themselves and their families with the remnants of their pillaged fortunes. Their plea to the conscript fathers, they concluded, was that, if everything could not be returned, they should at least order what could be found and identified to be restored to their owners.

When they had finished their complaints, Laevinus told the

Syracusans to leave the temple so the senators could discuss their petition. 'No, let them stay,' declared Marcellus, 'so that I can give them my response face to face. For those of us fighting your wars for you, members of the Senate, are evidently required to face the accusations of those whom we have defeated in battle, and to have the two cities captured this year impeaching us—Capua Fulvius, and Syracuse Marcellus.'

31. The Sicilian embassy was therefore brought back into the Senate house, and the consul Marcellus spoke as follows:

'Senators: I have not so far forgotten the eminence of the Roman people and this *imperium* that I hold that I, a consul, would deign to defend myself before accusers who are Greeks—not if it were a matter of a charge being brought against me personally.* However, it is not what I myself did that is under investigation—in the case of an enemy my actions, whatever they were, are endorsed by the rules of war—but what those people ought to have suffered. If they were not our enemies, then it makes no difference whether my "violation" of Syracuse occurred just now, or in the time of Hiero. But if they defected from the Roman people, drew their swords for an armed attack on our spokesmen, closed up their city and fortifications, and used a Carthaginian army to defend themselves against us, who can protest against their suffering acts of aggression, when they have committed such themselves?

'I turned down an offer from leading Sicilians to surrender the city! I regarded Sosis and the Spaniard Moericus as better people to whom to entrust a matter of such importance! You people are not in the lowest order of Sicilian society, since you can criticize the humble condition of others. And yet who amongst you promised to open the gates to me? Who promised to let my armed forces into the city? You hate and abhor those who did it, and not even in this place do you leave off disparaging them—so far were you from taking any such action yourselves! Senators, the low status of the people in question —which those men use to denounce them—itself constitutes the most solid argument that no one wanting to serve our republic has been turned away by me.

'Besides, before I blockaded Syracuse, I attempted to establish a peace treaty by sending spokesmen to them as well as by going to parley with them. But then I saw they showed no reluctance to maltreat my spokesmen, and that I was getting no response despite going personally to meet their leaders at the gate. And that was the point at which I finally took Syracuse by armed force, after I had gone through many hardships on land and sea.

'As for what befell the Syracusans after the capture, they could more justifiably lodge that complaint with Hannibal, and his defeated Carthaginians, than with the Senate of the victorious people. As for me, senators, if I had been intending to deny that Syracuse was sacked, then I would never have used its spoils to beautify the city of Rome. In terms of individuals, I know that what I took from them, or gave them, as victor is justified by the rules of war, as well as the merits of each case. Whether or not you ratify these settlements that I have made is more a concern for the state than it is for me. *My* responsibility has been loyally discharged; but it is a matter of importance for the state that you not make other leaders more phlegmatic in future by failing to ratify my acts. And since you have now heard, in our presence, what both the Sicilians and I had to say, senators, we shall both leave the temple together to let the Senate discuss the issues more freely in my absence.'

With that the Sicilians were sent off, and Marcellus left for the Capitol to levy troops.

32. The other consul then put the matter of the Sicilian demands before the senators. Opinions were long divided, and most of the Senate were of the opinion, of which Titus Manlius Torquatus was the leading advocate, that they should have opened hostilities against the tyrants, who were the common enemy of both the Syracusans and the Roman people. The city's surrender should have been accepted, and it should not have been taken by force, they felt. Its surrender accepted, it should have been shored up by the restoration of its earlier constitution and independence, not crushed militarily when it was exhausted from a wretched despotism. A beautiful and famous city had perished, they said, set up as the victor's prize in the struggles between the tyrants and the Roman commander. It was a city that once had been the breadbasket and treasury of the Roman people and, thanks to her generous gifts, the Roman republic had on numerous occasions been aided and beautified, the last occasion being during this very war with Carthage. If King Hiero, the most loyal supporter of the power of Rome, should rise from the dead, how could anyone not feel ashamed when either Syracuse or Rome were shown to him? After looking upon the half-ruined and pillaged city that was his home, he would walk into Rome to set eyes on the spoils taken from that home in the approach to the city, practically at the city gate.

These and similar remarks were made with the purpose of arousing animosity against the consul and pity for the Sicilians, but the senators nevertheless showed discretion in their decree. The measures taken by Marcellus during his conduct of the war and after his victory were to be ratified, but in future the state of Syracuse was to be the concern of the Senate. The senators would, in fact, bid the consul Laevinus to promote the well-being of the state, as far as could be done without loss to the republic.

Two senators were sent to the consul on the Capitol to instruct him to return to the Senate house, and when the Sicilians had been admitted the senatorial decree was read out. Some congenial remarks were addressed to the envoys, who were then told to leave. These now flung themselves at Marcellus' feet. They begged him to pardon them for what they had said in bemoaning and trying to find relief for their catastrophic circumstances, and they begged him, too, to take them and their city under his protection and patronage. With the decree of the Senate now reassuring him, the consul sent them on their way with a few kind words.

33. The Capuan representatives then received their audience with the Senate, but their presentation was more emotional, and their case harder to make. They could not deny they deserved punishment, and there were no tyrants for them to blame. But they believed they had paid a sufficient penalty, with so many of their senators poisoned to death and so many beheaded. Few of the nobility had survived, they said, the few whom a guilty conscience had not driven to drastic measures for themselves, or the victor's anger had not condemned to death. And so they begged for freedom for themselves and their families, along with some portion of their belongings. They were Roman citizens, they said, several of them connected to Rome by marriage, and now even by blood relationships, too, thanks to the intermarriage they had long enjoyed.*

The Capuans were then removed from the temple. For a while the senators wondered whether Quintus Fulvius should be brought from Capua (for the consul Claudius had died after the city's capture) so the matter could be discussed in the presence of the commander responsible for the operation, as had been done in the case of

Marcellus and the Sicilians. Then they saw Flaccus' legates, Marcus Atilius and Gaius Fulvius, Flaccus' brother, present in the Senate, as well as Quintus Minucius and Lucius Veturius Philo, who were likewise legates of Claudius. These were men who had been present throughout the campaign, and the senators were reluctant to have Fulvius recalled from Capua, or the case of the Capuans left in abeyance. Then Marcus Atilius Regulus, the man who enjoyed the greatest prestige of all those who had been at Capua, was asked his opinion.

'I formally declare', Regulus replied, 'that I was on the consuls' advisory board when the question arose, after the capture of Capua, of whether there was anyone amongst the Capuans who deserved our republic's gratitude. It was found that there were two women in this category: Vestia Oppia, a lady from Atella living in Capua, and Faucula Cluvia, who had once earned her living by prostitution. Vestia had offered sacrifice every day for the security and victory of the Roman people; Faucula had secretly provided starving prisoners with food. But the rest of the people of Capua had the same feelings towards us as did the Carthaginians, and what distinguished the men beheaded by Quintus Fulvius from the others was their rank rather than their guilt.

'I do not see how senatorial action can be taken without authorization from the people in the case of Capuans holding Roman citizenship, and I also note that the following was the action taken in the case of the defection of the people of Satricum in the time of our ancestors. The plebeian tribune Marcus Antistius at that time presented the plebs with a proposal on the issue, and the plebs voted to leave to the Senate the right to judge the Satrican case.* In my opinion, then, we must discuss with the plebeian tribunes the possibility of one or more of them bringing a proposal to the plebs that authorizes us to decide the case of the people of Capua.'

The plebeian tribune Lucius Atilius, on senatorial authority, then brought before the plebs a bill, worded as follows: 'With regard to all the people of Capua, Atella, Calatia, and Sabatum,* who, by surrender to the proconsul Quintus Fulvius, have put themselves under the authority and power of the Roman people; and with regard to the persons they surrendered along with themselves, and to the property they surrendered along with themselves—land and city, objects divine and secular, implements, and whatever else they

surrendered—I ask you, citizens, what you wish done in this regard.'
The plebs decreed as follows: 'Our wish and command* is that the
decision reached, under oath, by the majority of the Senate, be put
into effect.'

34. Following this resolution of the plebs, the matter was put
before the Senate, which first of all restored to Oppia and Cluvia
their property and their freedom and instructed them to come to
Rome if they wished to claim further recompense from the Senate.
Decrees were passed for individual Capuan households,* but it is not
worth the while to list them all. Some faced expropriation of their
property, and being sold into slavery along with their wives and
children, exception being made for daughters who had married outside the community before they became subject to the jurisdiction of
the Roman people. Others were to be imprisoned, with discussion of
their eventual fate left until later. In the case of others, the senators
used classifications based on their property assessments to determine
whether or not they should be dispossessed. They also voted that
farm animals that had been captured, apart from horses, should be
returned to their owners; and the same was to apply to slaves, apart
from adults of the male sex, and to all property not attached to the
ground. They ordained that all citizens of Capua, Atella, Calatia,
and Sabatum were to have free status, apart from those who had
themselves served with the enemy, or whose fathers had done so. But
none was to be a Roman citizen, or have Latin status, and none of
those who had been present in Capua during the period when the
gates were shut was to remain in the city, or on the farmland of
Capua beyond a certain date.* These people were to be given a place
to live beyond the Tiber, but not on its banks.

As for those who, during the hostilities, had not been in Capua or
in any Campanian city that had defected from the Roman people, the
senators voted to have them removed to a point north of the River
Liris, in the direction of Rome. In the case of those who had gone
over to the Romans before Hannibal's arrival in Capua, they voted to
have them transferred to an area north of the River Volturnus, with the
proviso that none should possess land or a building within fifteen miles
of the sea. Those moved across the Tiber were—themselves and their
descendants—forbidden to acquire or possess land anywhere other
than in the territory of Veii, Sutrium, or Nepete,* and their holdings
there were restricted to a maximum of 50 *iugera* per person.

The Senate also ordered the property belonging to all senators and office-holders in Capua, Atella, or Calatia to be put up for sale in Capua; and the free persons, who they had decided should be sold into slavery, were to be sent to Rome and put on sale in the city. Art work and bronze statues allegedly taken from the enemy the senators referred to the College of Pontiffs for a decision on which were sacred and which unconsecrated. Thanks to these decrees, the Capuans, when the senators dismissed them, were rather more despondent than they had been on their arrival in Rome. And now their complaints were directed not at Quintus Fulvius' cruel treatment of them, but at the unfairness of heaven, and their own abominable fortune.

35. After the Sicilian and Capuan delegations had been dismissed, troop mobilization got under way. Then, once the army had been enrolled, the question of increasing the complement of oarsmen came up for discussion.* For this there was insufficient manpower available, nor were there at that time any funds in the public purse for buying rowers and providing their pay. The consuls therefore proclaimed that private individuals should (as had been done earlier) provide the oarsmen, along with their pay and thirty days' worth of food rations, and do so on the basis of their property rating and their class. This announcement met with such a howl of protest, and such indignation, that what was lacking for a riot was not so much the conditions as a leader. The consuls, people claimed, had now picked on the common folk of Rome,* after the people of Sicily and Capua, as their next victim for ruin and persecution. Drained year after year by tribute, they were now left with nothing but their land, and that was bare desert, they said. The enemy had burned their houses, and the state had appropriated the slaves that worked their land, buying them up cheaply for the army, or else commandeering them as oarsmen. All silver or bronze in anyone's possession had been taken from him to pay oarsmen and the annual taxes. And now there was no coercion, no authority by which they could be forced to give what they did not have. The state could sell their property, and maltreat their bodies—which was all that remained to them! They had nothing more with which they could even be ransomed!

People made these angry comments not in secret, but quite openly in the Forum, and before the eyes of the consuls, as they milled about them in a huge crowd. And the consuls, employing censure and solace in turn, simply could not calm them down. They then declared that they were giving the people a three-day period to think the matter over, and that time the consuls themselves employed to examine the problem and find a solution. The day after that interval they convened the Senate to consider the matter of bringing the oarsmen up to strength. After a long discussion in which they admitted that the people's refusal was reasonable, they changed the tenor of their remarks, going so far as to say that, reasonable or unreasonable, the burden had to be placed on private citizens. For with no money in the treasury, how were they going to provide naval crews? And without crews, how could Sicily be secured, or Philip kept away from Italy, or the coasts of Italy safeguarded?

36. It was a difficult moment, and practical thinking was bogged down, and a sort of paralysis had seized men's minds. Then the consul Laevinus spoke. The magistrates rank above the Senate, he said, and the Senate above the people, and a man's eminence morally obliges him to take the lead in assuming all tasks that involve hardship and difficulty.

'If you want to impose something on an inferior,' he continued, 'accept that as an obligation for yourself and your family first, and you will the more easily have everyone listening to you. And the expense is not burdensome for people when they see every one of their leading men accepting more than his fair share of it. So, do we want the Roman people to have fleets and to man them, and do we want private individuals to provide oarsmen without balking at the expense? Then let us first impose that burden on ourselves. We senators should tomorrow bring to the treasury all our gold and silver, and all our bronze coin. The following can be excepted: a ring for each man, his wife, and each child; a *bulla** for a son; and, in the case of those with a wife and daughters, an ounce of gold for each. As for silver, former occupants of curule offices may retain their horses' decorative emblems, and two pounds of the metal per person, so as to have the saltcellar and plate for their religious functions. The other senators should retain just one pound per person. And bronze coins—let us leave 5,000 *asses* to each family head. All other gold and silver, and all bronze coin, we should immediately deposit with the treasury officials,* before issuing any senatorial decree. Voluntarily making a contribution, and competing to give assistance to the state, may also inspire the equestrian order, and then the plebeians as well, to emulate us.

'We, the consuls, have long discussed the matter, and this is the only road we have found to follow. Start out on it, and may the gods lend you a helping hand. If the state is healthy, she easily safeguards the individual's property; but you would waste your time trying to save what is yours if you abandon the public cause.'

These words met with such an enthusiastic response that the consuls were actually thanked by the senators. After the Senate was adjourned, every member brought to the treasury his own gold, silver, and bronze; and so heated was their rivalry to have their names listed first, or amongst the first, on the public records that the treasury officials were incapable of taking the deposit, or the secretaries of recording them. The equestrian order responded with the same unanimity as the Senate, and the plebs followed the equestrian class. Thus, with no senatorial edict and no pressure from a magistrate, the republic was short of neither oarsmen to make up the complement, nor the money to pay them. When all the preparations for war were completed, the consuls left for their provinces.

37. There was no other point in the war at which the Carthaginians and Romans, both experiencing a variety of fortunes, were fluctuating so much between hope and fear. In the provinces, failure in Spain and success in Sicily had brought the Romans a mixture of dejection and elation. In Italy, too, Tarentum being taken from them was a sore loss, but unexpectedly holding on to the citadel had brought them joy. Likewise, there had been sudden panic and fear when Hannibal blockaded and attacked the city of Rome, but this turned to jubilation with the capture of Capua a few days later. Events overseas, too, saw a kind of balance in their oscillating fortunes. Philip had declared himself an enemy at what was hardly a favourable time, but the Aetolians and King Attalus of Asia were also enlisted as new allies, as though destiny were promising the Romans empire in the East.

It was the same with the Carthaginians. They felt their capture of Tarentum compensated for the loss of Capua and, while they prided themselves on having reached the walls of the city of Rome without resistance, they were galled by the failure of the enterprise. They felt embarrassed, too, at being regarded with such contempt that, while they were actually sitting at the walls of Rome, a Roman army was being led off to Spain through another gate. There were also the Spanish provinces, where two great Roman commanders and their armies had been slaughtered. The closer the Carthaginians had come to hopes of finishing the war in that theatre and driving the Romans from there, the greater their exasperation that their victory had been rendered null and void by Lucius Marcius, a stopgap commander. So fortune was evening things up, and everything hung in the balance on both sides, with hopes and fears as alive as if they were actually starting the war at that moment.

38. What vexed Hannibal above all was Capua which, blockaded by the Romans with greater resolve than he had shown in defending it, had lost him the support of many of the peoples of Italy. And all of these he could not hold in check with garrisons, unless he were prepared to split his army into many small sections, which was very much to his disadvantage at that time. He could not withdraw such garrisons as were in place, either, and leave the loyalty of his allies open to speculation or subject to intimidation. Temperamentally prone to greed and cruelty, Hannibal now leaned towards pillaging what he could not protect, so that his enemy would be left only devastated territory. That was a terrible plan initially, and had terrible results for him. For he alienated the sympathies of everybody, and not just of those subjected to the unwarranted destruction, since the example reached further than the actual danger. And the Roman consul lost no opportunity to probe the feelings of the cities wherever any hope was to be seen.

The two most prominent men in Salapia were Dasius and Blattius. Dasius sided with Hannibal; Blattius, as far as he safely could, espoused the cause of Rome, and he had, in clandestine messages, led Marcellus to hope that the town could be betrayed to him. In fact, however, that could not be achieved without the complicity of Dasius. Blattius waited a long time before approaching Dasius, and he did so then only because he lacked a better plan, not because he had hopes of success. Dasius, who opposed the idea, and also felt personal enmity towards his rival for power, revealed the matter to Hannibal. Hannibal had the two men summoned. He was, however, engaged in some business before his tribunal, and intended hearing the case of Blattius momentarily. As the two men stood there, accuser and accused, with the public removed, Blattius proceeded to bring up again with Dasius the matter of betraying the town. And indeed Dasius, thinking the truth was obvious, cried out that he was being propositioned to turn traitor right before Hannibal's eyes. To Hannibal and those present the very brazenness of such an act made the charge all the more implausible. It was simply a case of rivalry and personal hatred, they decided—and the charge was being brought because, inasmuch as there could be no witness, there was greater scope for fabrication.

The men were therefore dismissed. Blattius, however, did not abandon his bold design until, by continually drumming the idea into Dasius' ears, and explaining how it would benefit themselves and their homeland, he convinced him that the Punic garrison, comprising 500 Numidians, should be delivered to Marcellus, along with Salapia.

The delivery could not be brought off without great loss of life, for the Numidians were by far the bravest horsemen in the entire Punic army. Thus, although the move came as a surprise, and the Numidians could not make use of their horses within the city, they nevertheless took up their arms in the fracas and attempted a sortie. Then, unable to get out, they went down fighting to the bitter end, with no more than fifty of them falling into the hands of the enemy alive. Far more damaging to Hannibal than the loss of Salapia was the loss of this contingent of horsemen; never thereafter did the Carthaginian enjoy superiority in what was hitherto his greatest strength, his cavalry.

39. At this time, too, the food-shortages in the citadel of Tarentum were almost beyond endurance. The Roman garrison in place there, and Marcus Livius, who commanded the garrison and citadel, had all their hopes centred on provisions sent from Sicily; and to safeguard the transport of these along the Italian coastline a fleet of some twenty ships was riding at anchor off Rhegium. The man in charge of the fleet and the supplies was Decimus Quinctius, who was of undistinguished background but who, as the result of many brave exploits, had an outstanding reputation as a soldier. Initially, Quinctius had five ships, the largest of them two triremes that had been put under his command by Marcellus. Later, his energetic conduct being frequently in evidence, a further three vessels were given to him. Finally, by personally requisitioning from the allies—from Rhegium, Velia, and Paestum—ships due under treaty, he built up the fleet of twenty ships noted above.

This fleet had set off from Rhegium when, at Sapriportis, about fifteen miles from the city of Tarentum, Democrates confronted it with a like number of Tarentine vessels. As it happened, the Roman commander was advancing under sail, not suspecting a fight ahead. He had, however, taken on a full complement of oarsmen in the area of Croton and Sybaris,* and was now in possession of a fleet extremely well manned, and well armed, given the size of its vessels. And then, by chance, the wind dropped entirely at the very moment that the enemy came into view. This meant that Quinctius had time to stow the rigging,* and get his oarsmen and fighters ready for the forthcoming engagement.

Rarely have conventional fleets clashed with such ferocity, for they were fighting to decide something greater than their own fate. The Tarentines, who had, after nearly a century, recovered their city from the Romans, were now fighting to liberate the citadel as well; and they were hoping to cut their enemy's supply line by depriving him, with a naval battle, of his dominance at sea. The Romans, who had held on to the citadel, were fighting to demonstrate that their loss of Tarentum had nothing to do with strength and courage, but was the result of treachery and deceit.

The signal now went up on both sides, and the vessels charged each other with their prows. There was no backing water with the oar, no permitting the enemy to break free whenever they grappled a ship that they overtook. They engaged at such close quarters that it became almost hand-to-hand fighting, the battle fought as much with the sword as with projectiles. The prows remained locked together, the sterns being swung round by the oars on the enemy ship. So closely grouped were the ships that hardly any weapon thrown landed harmlessly in the sea between them, and, like lines of infantry, they pushed against each other front to front, with the fighting men able to move from ship to ship.

The engagement that stood out from all the others, however, was that between the two ships that clashed at the head of the lines. In the Roman vessel was Quinctius himself, and in the Tarentine was Nico, who was surnamed Perco. This man loathed the Romans, and was in turn detested by them; and this animosity was as much a personal as a public matter, for Nico belonged to the faction that had betrayed Tarentum to Hannibal. As Quinctius was fighting and simultaneously urging on his men, Nico took him by surprise and ran him through. When the Roman fell headlong over the prow, still holding his weapons, the victorious Tarentine leaped smartly over to the Roman ship, which was now in confusion after the loss of its leader. He pushed back the enemy, and when the prow was in Tarentine hands, and the Romans, crowded together, were having little success defending the stern, a second enemy trireme suddenly appeared astern. Caught between the two, the Roman vessel was captured. The sight of the flagship being taken struck panic into the others. Fleeing in all directions, some were sunk on the open sea, and others, hurriedly rowed to shore, soon became plunder for the people of Thurii and Metapontum. As for the freighters following with the supplies, only a small fraction fell into enemy hands; the others oriented their sails in different directions to catch the shifting winds, and sailed out to sea.

The Tarentines were nothing like as fortunate in the fighting at Tarentum during that period. Some 4,000 men who had gone out on a foraging expedition were roaming at large through the fields. Livius, who was in command of the citadel and the Roman garrison, was ever on the lookout for opportunities to strike the enemy, and he sent out against them from the citadel an energetic officer, Gaius Persius, with an armed force of 2,500. Persius attacked the foragers as they drifted widely dispersed about the fields, and for a long time he cut them down everywhere. The few survivors of that large enemy force he drove into the city in panic-stricken flight through the half-open gates, and in that same attack the city actually came close to being taken. Thus successes were balanced at Tarentum, the Romans victorious on land and the Tarentines at sea, but both were robbed of the hope that they glimpsed of taking possession of the grain.

40. It was at about this same time, with most of the year already gone, that the consul Laevinus, whose coming had been eagerly awaited by allies old and new, arrived in Sicily. His very first priority, he thought, was to settle the chaotic situation that still reigned in Syracuse in the early days of the peace. After that he led his legions to Agrigentum, which represented the last phase of the war and was occupied by a strong Carthaginian force. And fortune attended his enterprise.

The commander of the Carthaginians was Hanno, but they had all their hopes centred on Muttines and his Numidians. Muttines was on the move throughout Sicily, carrying off plunder from Roman allies; he could not be kept out of Agrigentum by force or any other means, nor could he be stopped from making forays from the town whenever he chose. The man's celebrity had for some time been putting even the commander in the shade, and eventually he aroused in Hanno such resentment that he took little pleasure even in Muttines' successes, because of who was responsible for them. Finally, Hanno transferred the man's command to his own son, believing that he would be taking away Muttines' authority among the Numidians along with his power.

Things, however, turned out very differently. Thanks to his own unpopularity, Hanno only increased the support Muttines had long enjoyed. Furthermore, Muttines refused to take the undeserved slight lying down, and he immediately sent undercover agents to Laevinus to negotiate the handover of Agrigentum. Through his agents, Muttines won Laevinus' confidence, and a plan of action was put in place. The Numidians then took control of the gate facing the sea, expelling or killing the guards, and let into the city some Romans sent expressly for that purpose. The Romans proceeded in a column towards the town centre and the forum, raising a great clamour, and Hanno, thinking it was merely the Numidian troops making a noisy protest, as had happened before, went forth to quell the disturbance. But there, in the distance, he caught sight of a crowd much too large to be the Numidians, and Roman shouts, with which he was not at all unfamiliar, came to his ears. He fled before he came within range of a weapon. Slipping out of the gate that lay on the far side of the city, and taking Epicydes as his companion, he came down to the sea with a few men. There, fortuitously, they came upon a small sailing vessel and, abandoning Sicily to their enemies, a prize for which they had fought for so many years, they crossed to Africa. The large numbers of Carthaginians and Sicilians left behind did not even try to put up a fight; they fled wildly and blindly, but found the exits blocked, and were killed close to the gates.

After taking possession of the town, Laevinus flogged and beheaded those in charge at Agrigentum, and the others he sold off along with the booty, sending all the money that he raised to Rome.

When word of the disaster that had overtaken the people of Agrigentum spread through Sicily, there was everywhere a sudden shift of sympathies in favour of the Romans. Twenty cities were soon sold out to them, and six more taken by force, while about forty came under Roman protection through voluntary surrender. The consul meted out to the leading men of these communities such rewards and punishments as they deserved, and forced the Sicilians finally to

lay down their arms and turn their attention to farming the land.*
His policy was designed not only to make their island sufficiently
fertile to support its inhabitants, but also to have it alleviate problems
of the grain-supply of the city of Rome and of Italy, as it had done on
many occasions in the past. After that Laevinus sailed over to Italy,
taking with him a disorderly crowd of men from Agathyrna.* There
were 4,000 of them, a ragtag bunch of all sorts of unsavoury individuals—exiles, debtors, and many who had committed capital
offences when they had been living in their own communities and
under their own laws. And after similar fortunes had, for various
reasons, concentrated these men at Agathyrna, they had been making a living by robbery and pillage. Laevinus did not feel it was
particularly safe to leave them behind on an island just beginning to
achieve unity under the new peace, as they would provide the fuel for
revolution. Moreover, they would be of use to the people of Rhegium, who were then searching for a gang of men with experience in
robbery for their raids on the territory of Bruttium. And that year
saw the end of Sicily's involvement in the war.

41. In Spain, Publius Scipio launched his ships at the start of
spring.* He then issued an edict summoning the allied auxiliaries to
Tarraco, and ordered the fleet and transport ships to head out from
there for the mouth of the River Ebro. He also gave orders for the
legions to muster in this same location on leaving their winter quarters, and then he personally set off from Tarraco with 5,000 allied
troops to join this army. On his arrival he felt he should make an
address, particularly to the veteran soldiers who had survived the
catastrophic setbacks. He called an assembly, and gave the following
speech:*

'No new commander before me has been able to give his soldiers
justified and well-merited thanks before actually making use of their
services. My case is different. Before I even set eyes on my province
or my camp, fortune put me in your debt. First there was your great
dedication to my father and uncle, during their lifetime and after
their deaths, and then your valour in keeping secure for me, their
successor, and for the Roman people, a province that was as good as
lost after their terrible defeat. Now, thanks to heaven's blessing, the
aim of our present preparations, and the steps we are taking, is not to
permit *us* to remain in Spain ourselves, but to make sure that the
Carthaginians do not. They are designed not to permit us to stand

before the banks of the Ebro to keep the enemy from crossing, but to allow us to cross it ourselves, and take the war over it. What I fear is that this plan might strike some of you as being too grand, and too adventurous, when you reflect on your recent defeats, and when you consider my age. No one is less able than I to expunge from his thoughts the battles lost in Spain. My father and my uncle were killed within thirty days of each other, our family visited with deaths piled one on the other. Being left on one's own with almost no family breaks the spirit, and yet the good fortune and valour of our commonwealth forbid me to lose all hope for the final outcome. Our lot, granted to us by some divine providence, is to emerge victorious after defeat in all our major wars.

'I ignore the examples of old—Porsenna, the Gauls, the Samnites—and I shall start with the Punic Wars. How many were the fleets, how many the generals, how many the armies that were lost in the first war! And what am I to say of this one? In all the defeats I was either present myself or, if I was not there, I more than anyone felt their repercussions. The Trebia, Trasimene, Cannae—what are these but a history of Roman armies and Roman consuls cut to shreds? Add the defection of most of Italy, of Sicily, of Sardinia; add, too, that sheer terror and panic at seeing a Punic camp set up between the Anio and the walls of Rome, at the sight of a victorious Hannibal almost at our gates. In this general collapse, only the courage of the people of Rome stood unimpaired and unshakeable, and it was this that resurrected and restored all that had fallen to the ground.

'After the disaster at Cannae, Hasdrubal was making his way towards the Alps and Italy—and had he joined up with his brother, the name of the Roman people would no longer be in existence. Men, it was you, led by my father and under his auspices, who were the very first to stand in his way. Your success *here* made up for failure *there*.

'Now, thanks to heaven's blessing, all goes well and successfully in Italy and Sicily, with the situation looking better and brighter every day. In Sicily, Syracuse and Agrigentum have been taken; the enemy has been driven from the entire island; and the province has once more been brought under the sway of the Roman people. In Italy, Arpi has been recovered and Capua taken. Hannibal has made his whole journey from the city of Rome in panic-stricken flight, and has been forced back into the farthest corner of Bruttian territory.

His prayers to the gods are now for nothing more than that he be granted a safe retreat and withdrawal from the land of his enemies. Men, when defeat followed hard on the heels of defeat, and the gods were virtually standing alongside Hannibal, you joined my parents here—let me honour them equally with that title—to hold up the tottering fortunes of the people of Rome. So what could be more irrational than that you, those very same men, should lack confidence when all goes well and successfully over there in Italy? I wish, too, that what happened recently were, for me, as free from grief <. . .>*

'The immortal gods, the protectors of Roman power, were responsible for the centuries unanimously authorizing that the command be vested in me, and these same gods are now, by augury, auspices, and even nightly visions, predicting that all will go successfully and well. And my mind, which has been my greatest foreteller of the future up to now, also has a presentiment that Spain is ours, that in a brief while the whole Punic race will be driven from here, covering sea and land in humiliating flight. What my mind spontaneously predicts is also suggested by rational analysis of the facts. Persecuted by the Carthaginians, their allies send delegations to beg for our protection; and their three commanders, wrangling almost to the point of mutiny, have drawn their armies away from each other in three directions, going into widely separated areas of the country. The bad luck that recently afflicted us is now descending on them. They, too, are being abandoned by their allies, as we were earlier by the Celtiberians, and they have also split their armies, which was what brought my father and uncle to grief. Their internal conflicts will not permit them to coalesce, and individually they will not be able to resist us. Men, simply give your support to the Scipio name, and to the offshoot of your former commanders, one growing again from the stump that was pruned. Come, veterans, take your new army and your new leader across the Ebro; take them over into lands through which you have often passed with many heroic deeds. You now see in me a face and expression resembling those of my father and uncle, and you recognize in me their physical features. Soon I shall see to it that I exemplify and reflect also their character, loyalty, and valour, making every one of you say that Scipio, his general, has come back to life, or has been born again.'

42. With these words Scipio sparked the enthusiasm of the men.

Leaving Marcus Silanus with 3,000 infantry and 300 cavalry to safe-guard the region, he crossed the Ebro with all the other troops, which amounted to 25,000 foot and 2,500 horse. Since the Punic armies had withdrawn into three widely separated regions, some pressed him to attack the one closest to them. Scipio, however, think-ing that there was danger that such a move might bring about the unification of the three armies, and that his single force would be no match for all of them, decided instead, as an interim measure, to launch an attack on New Carthage. This was a city that was in any case wealthy from its own resources, but it was also full of all manner of military equipment belonging to the enemy—it was there that he kept his arsenal, his treasury, and his hostages from all over Spain. In addition, the town was conveniently situated for a crossing to Africa, and it had the further advantage of overlooking a harbour large enough for a fleet of any size (and was possibly the only such port on the Mediterranean coastline of Spain).

No one knew the army's destination, with the sole exception of Gaius Laelius.* Laelius had been sent around the coast with the fleet, but had orders to regulate the speed of his vessels so that the fleet would be entering the harbour at the very moment that Scipio appeared with his army on land. The land and sea journeys from the Ebro to New Carthage were completed in six days.* A camp was then established on the side of the city that faced north, and an earthwork created to secure its rear, the front being protected by the natural features of the place.

In fact, the lie of New Carthage is as follows. There is a bay about halfway down the coast of Spain, facing mainly south-west, and receding inland about two and a half miles. It is slightly more than twelve hundred paces wide. At the entrance to this bay, a small island forms a barrier on the seaward side that shelters the harbour from all winds except the south-westerly. From the deepest recesses of the bay a peninsula runs out, and it is on this strip of elevated land that the city is built, its eastern and southern sections surrounded by the sea. To the west, access is blocked by a lagoon that also runs in a slightly northerly direction, its depth varying according to the rise and fall of the tide.* A causeway, some two hundred and fifty paces in width, connects the city to the mainland. The Roman commander did not throw up a protective barrier on this, although it would have taken very little effort to construct one. Either this was a brash display of confidence for the benefit of the enemy, or he wished to have an unencumbered line of retreat from his frequent forays to the city walls.

43. When he had completed all the necessary defence-works, Scipio went on to deploy his vessels in the harbour, as though making the point that there was also a naval blockade in force. Taken by boat around the fleet, he warned the ships' captains to maintain a strict vigil at night; an enemy under siege, he told them, made every kind of move, and at every possible opportunity, at the start of the operation. He then went back to camp to explain to the soldiers the reasoning behind his decision to commence his campaign with an offensive against the city, and also to give them hope of taking it by his words of encouragement. Calling an assembly, he made the following address:

'Men, if any one believes that you have been brought here only for an assault on a single city, that man's assessment is more accurate with regard to the effort you face than the advantages to be gained. You will, it is true, be attacking the walls of just one city, but in taking that one city you will be taking all of Spain. In it are the hostages of all the most important princes and peoples; and, as soon as these men are in your hands, they will put under your control everything now under the Carthaginians. In it lies all the money belonging to the enemy. Without it they cannot carry on a war—they maintain mercenary armies—and you will find that money *very* useful for winning the support of the barbarians. In it are their artillery, their arsenal, their weapons, all their military equipment. This will mean you being well provided with equipment, and the enemy deprived of it. In addition, we shall take possession of a city of great beauty and wealth, and one which, at the same time, has the great advantage of an excellent harbour, through which everything needed for the war can be supplied by land and sea. And while we shall ourselves enjoy these great assets, we shall also be depriving our enemies of much greater ones. This is their stronghold, their granary, their treasury, their armoury—this is where they have everything stored. The direct crossing from Africa is to this city, and this is their only anchorage between the Pyrenees and Gades. From here Africa threatens the whole of Spain* <. . .> But since I see you drawn up in formation, let us cross over to attack New Carthage with all our strength and with confidence.' And when all the men cried out in

one voice that this was what they should do, he led them to New
Carthage, and then ordered an assault by land and sea.

44. Mago,* the Carthaginian commander, had now armed <the
town's inhabitants>, and when he saw the preparations being made
for the land and sea assault, he proceeded with his own troop
deployment. He ranged 2,000 of the town's inhabitants as a buffer
on the side facing the Roman camp. He next placed a contingent of
500 of his men in the citadel, and set 500 more on a hill in the eastern
sector of the city. The large numbers remaining he ordered to be
ready for any contingency, and to rush to whatever quarter shouting
or an emergency might call them. He then threw open the gate and
sent forth the men whom he had deployed on the roadway leading
towards the enemy camp. On the instructions of their commander
himself, the Romans gave way a little so that they would be closer to
the reinforcements that were to be sent in during the actual combat.

At the start, in fact, the two lines stood their ground not unevenly
matched. Then continuous waves of reinforcements sent in from the
Roman camp not only turned the enemy to flight but put such
pressure on them as they fled that, but for the recall being sounded,
it looked as if the Romans would have broken into the city inter-
mingled with the fugitives.

The consternation on the battlefield was actually no greater than
that throughout the city. Many of the guard-posts had been abandoned in panic-stricken flight, and the walls had been deserted, their
defenders having leaped down by the shortest route they could find.
Scipio, who had mounted a hill that they call the Hill of Mercury,*
saw that the fortifications were at many points stripped of their
defenders. He ordered everyone to be summoned from the camp; all
were to advance to assault the town and bring ladders. Scipio himself
had three sturdy young men cover him with their shields, since
weapons of all kinds were now flying in large numbers from the
walls, and he pushed ahead towards the city. He shouted encouragement, and gave orders appropriate to the situation; but what best
served to fire the spirit of the men was that he was there to witness
and observe the courage, or the faint-heartedness, of every individual. As a result, the men rushed forward, facing wounds and
missiles, and neither walls nor the soldiers standing on them could
stop them racing each other to clamber up. And, at the same time,
the section of the city bordered by the sea also came under attack,

though there, rather than real pressure being applied, it was just a chaotic scramble. As the troops landed, and swiftly put ashore ladders and men, and as they hurried to clamber ashore by the quickest path, they simply got in each other's way, thanks to their haste and rivalry.

45. In the meantime, the Carthaginian commander had once more manned the walls with troops, and these had at their disposal a large quantity of javelins drawn from their immense arsenal. But neither men, nor their javelins, nor anything else, provided as effective a defence for the walls as did the walls themselves. Few were the ladders that were long enough to reach such a height, and the longer the ladders the weaker they were. The result was that, as the man at the top could not get over the wall, and others were nevertheless climbing up behind, the ladders would break simply from the weight placed on them. In some cases the ladders held firm, but the men still fell to the ground when the height produced dizzy spells.

Men and ladders were dropping all over, and the confidence and enthusiasm of the enemy were increasing with their success. Accordingly, the retreat was sounded, giving the beleaguered citizens hope, not only of an immediate break from their arduous struggle, but for the future, too. The city, they thought, could not be taken by scaling-ladders and encirclement, while siege-works were a difficult proposition—and one that would give the Carthaginian commanders time to bring them assistance.

The commotion of the first attempt had barely died down when Scipio ordered men who were fresh and uninjured to take the ladders from those who were by then exhausted and wounded, and to intensify the assault on the city. He now also knew that crossing the lagoon to the city wall on foot was easy, something he had learned from fishermen of Tarraco who had explored the length of the lagoon both on light boats and, when the boats ran aground, by wading through the shallows. So, when he was brought word that there was an ebb tide, Scipio personally led a band of 500 armed men to the lagoon.

It was about the middle of the day. The water level was dropping in any case, as the tide ebbed,* but in addition there was also a brisk north wind that had arisen and was helping to sweep the receding waters of the lagoon in the same direction as the tide. This had exposed the shallow areas, so much so that at some points the water came up to the navel, and at others barely to the knees. Scipio had worked this out by careful observation and reason, but he made it out to be a miracle and a case of divine intervention. The gods, he said, were turning back the sea to make a way over for the Romans; they were draining the lagoon and bringing into view paths on which man had never set foot. And he bade them follow the lead of Neptune, who would guide them on their journey, and reach the walls by taking a path right across the lagoon.

46. Those making the landward approach to the town were facing enormous difficulties. It was not simply the height of the walls that impeded the Romans' progress; the enemy also made sorties and had them under fire from both sides, so that as they pushed forward they faced greater danger from the flanks than from the front. By contrast, the 500 on the other side of the town found it easy crossing the lagoon, and then climbing to the top of the wall. The wall was not built up there as the protection offered by its very location on the lagoon inspired sufficient confidence, and the Romans were faced with no outpost of armed men and no sentries—everybody was concentrating on bringing assistance to where there was an obvious threat.

The men thus entered the city without opposition, and headed as quickly as they could for the gate at which all the fighting was concentrated. Everybody's attention was focused on this. In fact, the eyes and ears of the combatants, and of those watching and encouraging them, were so absorbed with it that none realized the city had been taken behind them until javelins came raining down on their backs, and they had the enemy attacking them front and rear. That threw the defenders into a panic. The walls were taken, and the breaking down of the gate got under way both inside and out. Soon, when the leaves of the gate had been cut down, and hacked to bits so as not to obstruct their passage, the soldiers mounted their charge. There were also large numbers scaling the walls, but these then veered off to butcher civilians, while the men who had entered by the gate advanced in battle formation to the forum, through the city centre, accompanied by their officers and preserving their ranks.

Scipio now observed that the enemy were fleeing in two directions. Some were heading eastwards towards the hill occupied by the 500-strong garrison; others were making for the citadel, to which Mago himself had also beaten a retreat with almost all the soldiers who had been driven from the walls. Scipio therefore sent some of his troops to storm the hill, and others he led in person to the citadel. The hill was taken with the first charge. Mago tried to hold the citadel but when he saw that the whole city had been overrun by the enemy, and that the situation was hopeless, he too capitulated, surrendering the citadel and its garrison. Until the surrender of the citadel the slaughter continued throughout the city, and no adult male meeting the Romans was given quarter. Then, the signal given, the bloodbath ceased, and the victors turned to the plunder—an enormous assortment of all sorts of things.

47. Approximately 10,000 free persons of male sex were taken prisoner. Of these Scipio released those who were citizens of New Carthage, restoring to them their city and such property as the war had left them. There were also about 2,000 men who were skilled tradesmen. These, he declared, would be state property of the Roman people,* and added that they could hope for early emancipation if they were diligent in their work of providing war materials. All the others, large numbers of young resident aliens and able-bodied slaves, he put in the service of the fleet, to make up the numbers of his oarsmen (and he had also increased the size of the fleet with eighteen captured vessels*). In addition to this mass of people there were also the Spanish hostages, and these were treated with as much respect as if they were the children of allies.

The quantity of military equipment taken was enormous. There were 120 catapults of the largest dimensions, and 281 smaller ones; 23 large-scale and 52 smaller-scale ballistas; a huge number of the larger and smaller scorpions, and of weapons and projectiles; and 74 military standards. Large amounts of gold and silver were brought to the commander. There were 276 golden dishes, nearly all of them a pound in weight; there were 18,300 pounds of silver, in bullion and coin, and a large number of silver vessels. All this was weighed and counted, and then put in the charge of the quaestor, Gaius Flaminius. There were 400,000 measures of wheat and 270,000 of barley. Sixty-three transport vessels were overpowered and captured in the harbour, some with their cargoes of grain and weapons, as well as bronze and iron, sail-linen, rope, and other materials for equipping a fleet. The upshot was that amidst all these riches taken as the spoils of war New Carthage represented the least significant prize of all.

48. That day Scipio instructed Gaius Laelius to stand guard over

the city with the marines;* he himself led the legions back to the camp. The men were exhausted after all the military operations they had packed into a single day. They had fought in the line of battle, faced extremes of hardship and danger in taking the city, and, after taking it, had done battle—and on unfavourable terrain, as well— with those who had taken refuge in the citadel. Scipio told them to take some rest and refreshment.

The following day Scipio called a meeting of the soldiers and the marines. He first of all offered praise and thanks to the immortal gods who had not only, in a single day, made him master of the richest of all the cities in Spain, but had also earlier ensured that nearly all the wealth of Africa and Spain was accumulated in that city. The result was that the enemy was now left almost nothing, he said, while he and his men had everything in abundance. He then went on to praise his men's courage. Nothing had deterred them from climbing over, or bursting through, all the obstacles that stood in their way—not the enemy counterattack, not the height of the walls, not the unexplored shallows of the lagoon, not the fort perched on a hill, or the citadel with its formidable defences. And while he owed his overall success to every single one of them, he added, the exceptional honour attaching to the 'mural crown'* belonged to the man who had been first to reach the top of the wall, and whoever thought he deserved that prize should claim it.

There were two claimants: Quintus Trebellius, a centurion of the fourth legion, and Sextus Digitius, a marine. But the competition between the two men was less heated than the fanatical support that each had generated in the other men of the corps to which he belonged. The marines had Gaius Laelius as their champion, the legionaries Marcus Sempronius Tuditanus. The dispute was verging on mutiny, and Scipio announced that he would appoint three judges to examine the case, hear witnesses, and render a decision on who had been the first over the wall into the town. Gaius Laelius and Marcus Sempronius represented their respective parties, and to them Scipio added Publius Cornelius Caudinus as a disinterested third. These three he ordered to sit as a board of judges and hear the case.

The affair, however, was rousing even greater antagonisms because both sides were now deprived of men of great influence, who had actually been restraining rather than championing their partisan fervour. At that point Gaius Laelius left the board and came to see Scipio at the tribunal. He told him that the matter was losing all semblance of moderation and propriety, and that the men were close to coming to blows. Even in the absence of a violent outcome, he said, it was a deplorable precedent that was being set by the affair, for duplicity and perjury were being employed in a contest for a prize for gallantry. The legionaries stood on one side, he continued, the marines on the other; and they were ready to swear, by all the gods, to what they wanted to be true, rather than what they knew to be true, and to make not just their own persons guilty of perjury, but their military standards, their eagles, and the sanctity of their oath of allegiance as well. He added that he was bringing this matter before Scipio on the advice of Publius Cornelius and Marcus Sempronius.

Scipio warmly commended Laelius, and called the men to an assembly. There he announced that he was reliably informed that Quintus Trebellius and Sextus Digitius had reached the top of the wall at the same moment, and so he was awarding 'mural crowns' to both men* for their valour. He then made awards to the rest in accordance with their service and bravery in the field. Gaius Laelius, admiral of the fleet, he honoured above all others with every kind of commendation, putting him on a level with himself, and awarding him a golden crown and a gift of thirty oxen.

49. Scipio then had the hostages from the Spanish communities summoned to him. The number of these I am reluctant to put on record, as I find it set at about 300 in one source and at 3,724 in another.* There is as much discrepancy between the historians on other items, too. One records that the Punic garrison was 10,000 strong, another that it was 7,000, and yet another that it was not more than 2,000. In one source I find the number of prisoners taken as 10,000, in another more than 25,000. If I follow the Greek author Silenus, I should put at about 60 the number of larger and smaller scorpions that were captured; if I follow Valerius Antias, then there were 6,000 larger scorpions and 13,000 smaller ones—so unbridled is the fabrication of historians!* There is no agreement even about commanders. Most claim that Laelius commanded the fleet, though some say it was Marcus Junius Silanus. Valerius Antias informs us that it was Arines who commanded the Punic garrison, and surrendered to the Romans; other writers say that it was Mago. No agreement is found on the number of ships captured, and none on

the weight of gold and silver taken, or the amount of money realized for it. If one must agree with some of these sources, figures halfway between the extremes seem closest to the truth.

When the hostages were summoned to him, Scipio first told them all to be of good cheer. They had, he said, come into the power of the Roman people, who preferred to secure people's support by kindness rather than fear, and to have foreign nations joined to them in a loyal bond of alliance, rather than downtrodden in wretched servitude. After that he took the names of their communities, and made an inventory of the prisoners, itemizing the numbers that belonged to each people. He then sent messengers to their homes, with instructions for persons to come to recover their relatives. In the cases where ambassadors of the communities were present in town, he restored the hostages to them on the spot. The others he put in the care of the quaestor Gaius Flaminius, who was told to treat them kindly.

As this was going on an elderly woman emerged from the midst of the crowd of hostages. She was the wife of Mandonius, who was the brother of Indibilis, chieftain of the Ilergetes. She threw herself in tears at the commander's feet, and proceeded to beg him to give stricter injunctions to the guards about caring for, and dealing with, the female hostages. When Scipio replied that the women would certainly go short of nothing, the woman replied: 'What you are talking about matters little to us—for how important, in a plight like this, is not having enough? It is another worry that torments me as I consider the tender years of these ladies, for personally I am now out of danger of such assault as is made on a woman.'

Surrounding the woman were the daughters of Indibilis, at the peak of their youth and beauty, and other women of similar high birth, all of whom respected her like a mother.

'Thanks to my own discipline, and that of the Roman people,' Scipio replied, 'I would in any case guard against the desecration of anything in our keeping that is considered sacred. But the courage and dignity of you ladies now make me even more scrupulous in this; even in misfortune you have not forgotten the respect due to a lady.' He then put the women in the care of a man of proven integrity, and instructed him to look after them with as much consideration and respect as if they were the wives and mothers of guests.

50. After this, a female captive was brought to Scipio by the

soldiers, a grown girl of such strikingly good looks that she caught the eyes of all wherever she went. Scipio made enquiries about her home and parents, and one of the pieces of information he received was that she was engaged to a chieftain of the Celtiberians, a young man named Allucius. He immediately had the parents and the fiancé summoned from her homeland, but meanwhile he was told that the young man was desperately in love with his intended bride. So, immediately on the fiancé's arrival, Scipio addressed him in terms more carefully chosen than he did the parents:

'It is as one young man to another that I address you,' he said, 'so that there may be less self-consciousness in this conversation between us. Your fiancée was brought to me as a prisoner by our soldiers, and I was told that you were very much in love with her, something which her looks made quite understandable. Now, I would myself like to be pardoned for loving a fiancée too deeply, if I were granted the opportunity to enjoy the pleasures appropriate to my age, especially a correct and lawful love, and if affairs of state had not taken up all my attention. Instead—something I *can* do—I give support to *your* love. Your fiancée has, in my care, received the respect that she would receive from her own parents, your future parents-in-law. She has been kept intact for you so that she could be given to you as a gift, inviolate, as befits my dignity and yours. In return for that gift I ask only this—be a friend of the Roman people! And if you think I am a good man, with the sort of personality that the tribes here earlier came to know in my father and uncle, then rest assured that there are many like us in the Roman state. Rest assured, too, that one could not cite a nation in the world today that you would like less to have as your enemy, or like more to have as your friend.'

The young man was overwhelmed with both embarrassment and delight. He took Scipio's hand, and called on all the gods to show him gratitude on his behalf, since he himself had nothing like the means to express his thanks as he would wish, or as Scipio's kindness to him deserved. After that, the girl's parents and relatives were summoned. Since the girl was being returned to them free of charge, and they had brought a weighty quantity of gold for her ransom, they began to implore Scipio to accept this as a personal gift from them. They would, they swore, feel no less grateful if he accepted than they were for his returning the girl undefiled.

Since they were so insistent, Scipio agreed to accept the gift, and gave orders for it to be set at his feet. Then, calling Allucius to him, he said: 'You will be receiving a dowry from your father-in-law, but in addition this will be yours from me as an extra wedding gift,' and he told him to pick up the gold and keep it. The young man was then sent home, delighted with the gift and with the honour paid to him, and there he filled the ears of his compatriots with well-merited eulogies of Scipio.* A young man had come who was very much like the gods, he said, a man who was victorious everywhere thanks to his generosity and kindness as much as his military power. Allucius then held a troop-levy amongst his dependants, and within a few days returned to Scipio with 1,400 handpicked horsemen.

51. Scipio kept Laelius with him for as long as he needed his advice on the disposal of the captives and hostages, and the booty. When all had been arranged to his satisfaction, he gave him a quinquereme, and put on board with him as prisoners of war Mago and about fifteen senators who had been taken along with him. He then sent him to Rome to announce the victory.

As for Scipio, the few days he had decided to remain in New Carthage he used for drills for his naval and land forces. On the first day the legions underwent armed manœuvres over a distance of four miles. On the second they were ordered to see to the servicing and cleaning of their arms before their tents. On the third they used wooden swords to fight a simulated pitched battle, and javelins tipped with a ball for throwing practice. On the fourth they were allowed to rest, and on the fifth they had armed manœuvres again. This cycle of work and rest they kept up the whole time they remained in New Carthage. The rowers and marines would put out to sea in calm weather, and test the manœuvrability of their vessels in mock naval battles.

These exercises, conducted on land and sea outside the city, honed the men for war both physically and mentally.* Meanwhile, artisans of all kinds had been shut up in a public plant, and the city itself rang with the noise of military equipment being prepared. The commander would supervise all these activities with equal care. At one moment he was with the fleet or in the dockyard; at another he was on manœuvres with the legions; on another occasion he was spending his time inspecting the works on which the hordes of tradesmen were everyday engaged, in keen competition, in the workshops, arsenal, and dockyards.

After these initial undertakings, and after repairing sections of the wall that had taken a battering, and posting troops to provide for the city's defence, Scipio set out for Tarraco. While still en route he was approached by numerous delegations. Some of these he responded to on the march, and sent on their way; in other cases he deferred the business until his arrival at Tarraco, where he had given notice of a meeting for all the allies, old and new. And, in fact, nearly all the tribes north of the Ebro assembled for the meeting, as did many from the further province, as well.

At first the Carthaginian leaders deliberately suppressed the news of the capture of New Carthage, but then the facts became too well known for the matter to be covered up or ignored, and they tried to make light of it in their announcements. A single town in Spain that had been taken from them on one day, they said, by the unexpected arrival of the Romans—a piece of trickery, almost. A young show-off, they added, elated by such a paltry gain, had, in his excessive euphoria, made this out to be a great victory. But when he heard that three generals and three conquering armies of his enemy were coming, then he would quickly be reminded of the deaths in his family.

Such were the bold comments the Carthaginians made in public; but in their hearts they knew full well what a weakening of their strength, in every respect, the loss of New Carthage represented for them.

BOOK TWENTY-SEVEN

1. This was how matters stood in Spain. In Italy, meanwhile, the consul Marcellus gained Salapia when the town was betrayed to him, and Marmoreae and Meles he took by force from the Samnites. Some 3,000 of Hannibal's men, who had been left to garrison these towns, were overpowered within them, and the plunder taken, which was considerable, was left to the Roman soldiers. Two hundred and forty thousand measures of wheat were also found, and 110,000 measures of barley.

However, the joy over this success in no way compensated for the disaster sustained within a few days of it, not far from the city of Herdonea.

The proconsul Gnaeus Fulvius was encamped in the area, hoping to recover Herdonea, which had defected from the Romans after the defeat at Cannae. He was not, however, in a very safe or well-secured position. Carelessness was ingrained in the general's nature, and his hopes were increasing it—for Fulvius had learned that the inhabitants' loyalty to the Carthaginian had been wavering ever since the news had arrived that, after losing Salapia, Hannibal had left the area for Bruttium. All this had been duly reported to Hannibal by messengers sent covertly from Herdonea, making him anxious to hold on to an allied city, and also giving him hope of making a surprise attack on the enemy. Taking a light-armed force, he hurried towards Herdonea by forced marches, so swiftly that he almost outran word of his coming; and to strike greater terror in his enemy he approached the town with a line deployed for battle.

The Roman, who was Hannibal's equal in daring, but not his equal in strategy and military strength, swiftly led out his troops and engaged, and the fifth legion and the allied contingent on the left vigorously entered the fray. Hannibal, however, had given a signal to his cavalry to ride around the battle when the lines of infantry had everyone's eyes and attention focused on the struggle in progress; some were to swoop down on the enemy's camp, others on their rear as they made their attack. Two years earlier Hannibal had defeated the praetor Gnaeus Fulvius in the same area, and now he uttered caustic remarks about this Gnaeus Fulvius having the same name, and declared that the battle would also have the same outcome.*

This proved no idle fancy on Hannibal's part. Many of the Romans had fallen in the hand-to-hand fighting during the clash of the two infantry lines, but the ranks were still holding their ground in formation. Then the uproar raised by the cavalry was heard to their rear, and so were the shouts of the enemy in their camp. The noise first of all made the sixth legion fall back—it had been stationed in the second line and so was the first to be thrown into disarray by the Numidians—and then the fifth and those at the very front. Some scattered in flight; others were killed in the thick of the action—and there Gnaeus Fulvius himself went down, along with eleven military tribunes. How many thousands of Romans and allies were killed in that battle one could not categorically state—not when I find 13,000 in one author, and no more than 7,000 in another!

The victor took possession of the camp and its spoils. Because he had information that Herdonea had been on the point of defecting to the Romans, and would not have remained loyal had he withdrawn from there, Hannibal removed the entire population to Metapontum and Thurii, and burned the town. Its leading citizens, who, it was discovered, had held clandestine discussions with Fulvius, he put to the sword. The Romans who had escaped the disastrous encounter sought refuge in Samnium with the consul Marcellus, to whom they came, poorly armed, by various routes.

2. Marcellus was not in the least perturbed by this disastrous defeat. He wrote a letter to the Senate in Rome to report the loss of the general and the army at Herdonea, but added that he himself was still the same man who, after the battle of Cannae, had crushed Hannibal when he was full of himself over his victory. He was now going to face him, he said, and would see to it that the Carthaginian's exhilaration and gloating were short-lived.

In Rome, at all events, there was deep melancholy over what had happened as well as fear for the future. The consul, however, marched from Samnium into Lucania, and pitched his camp on level ground at Numistro, in full view of Hannibal, while the Carthaginian established himself on a hill. Marcellus then gave a further indication of his confidence by being the first to deploy his troops in battle formation. And when he saw the standards issuing forth from the gates, Hannibal did not refuse battle. But they marshalled their battle lines in such a way that the Carthaginian had his right wing extended up the hill, while the Romans had their left close to the town. The troops first sent in by the Romans were the first legion and the allied right flank, and by Hannibal his Spanish troops and Balearic slingers, his elephants also being driven into battle once the engagement got under way.

For a long while the battle favoured neither side. They drew out the action from the third hour until nightfall, and, when the front lines were exhausted from fighting, the first legion was relieved by the third, and the allies on the right by those on the left. On the side of the enemy, too, fresh troops took over the battle from those who were spent. Thanks to this injection of fresh spirit and strength, a renewed and savage struggle suddenly flared up from one that had flagged, but night parted the combatants with victory unclear.*

The following day the Romans stood in the battle line from sunrise until well into the day, and, when none of the enemy came forward to face them, they took their time gathering up their spoils, and heaped their dead up in one spot and burned them. That coming night Hannibal quietly struck camp and went off into Apulia. When daylight revealed that his enemy had fled, Marcellus left his wounded lightly guarded at Numistro, with the military tribune Lucius Furius Purpurio in charge, and proceeded to dog Hannibal's footsteps. He overtook him at Venusia. There, over a number of days, charges were made from the forward posts on both sides that led to scrappy infantry and cavalry encounters rather than significant battles, nearly all of them favouring the Romans. After that the armies were marched through Apulia without any noteworthy engagement, since Hannibal would advance at night, looking for a site for an ambush, while Marcellus would follow him only in broad daylight, and after reconnoitring the route.

3. In Capua, meanwhile, Flaccus had been spending his time selling off the property of the leading citizens and renting out the farmland that had been appropriated by the Roman state, taking grain as rent in all cases. During this process—as if to make sure that Flaccus would not lack grounds for venting his wrath on the Capuans!—a fresh piece of villainy that had been secretly developing was brought to light through informers.

The Roman rank and file had been removed from the town buildings by Flaccus, who had forced them to build huts for themselves, at the gates and by the walls, after a fashion suitable for soldiers. The reason for this was partly so that the houses in the city could be leased along with the farmland, but also because Flaccus feared that the city, with its all too seductive charms, might soften his troops, too, as they had Hannibal's. Now, a number of the huts were made of wickerwork and planking, and some were of interlaced reeds covered with straw—everything being almost designed to feed a fire. A hundred and seventy Capuans, led by the Blossii brothers,* plotted together to set fire to all of these at the same time during the night.

The affair was divulged by slaves of the Blossius household, and on the proconsul's order the city gates were promptly closed. A signal was given, the soldiers rushed to arms, and all the guilty parties were arrested. Following an intensive investigation, these men were condemned and executed, and the informants were given their freedom and 10,000 *asses* each.

The people of Nuceria and Acerrae now complained that they had nowhere to live, Acerrae having been partly burned and Nuceria destroyed, and Fulvius sent them to the Senate in Rome. The people of Acerrae were given leave to rebuild what had been burned. The Nicerians were granted their preferred option of resettling at Atella, and the people of Atella were ordered to move to Calatia.

Amidst the many important items that were on the minds of people at this time, some of them positive, some negative, the citadel of Tarentum was not forgotten. Marcus Ogulnius and Publius Aquilius set off as a delegation into Etruria to purchase grain that was to be transported to Tarentum. In addition, 1,000 soldiers from the army in the city, an equal number of Romans and allies, were sent to that town with grain to serve in the garrison.

4. Summer was now at an end, and the time for consular elections was close at hand. However, a letter from Marcellus had caused the senators some concern. Marcellus claimed that it was not in the interests of state for him to move a single step away from Hannibal. He was now putting pressure on the Carthaginian, he said, who was running from him and refusing to engage. The senators thus faced a dilemma: taking a consul out of the war just when he was making headway, or else being short of consuls for the coming year.* The best option seemed to be to recall the consul Valerius from Sicily, despite the fact that he was outside Italy. On a directive from the Senate, a letter was then sent to Valerius by the urban praetor Lucius

Manlius, and it was accompanied by the letter from the consul Marcus Marcellus. From these Valerius would learn why it was he, rather than his colleague, whom the senators were recalling from his province.

At about that time representatives from King Syphax came to Rome with news of successful battles the king had fought with the Carthaginians. There was no people to whom Syphax was a more implacable enemy than the Carthaginians, they said, and none to whom he was a closer friend than the Romans. He had earlier sent representatives to Gnaeus and Publius Cornelius in Spain, they added, but now he had decided to seek friendship with Rome directly from the source, as it were. The Senate not only responded favourably to the representatives, but also sent its own representatives to the king with gifts. These were Lucius Genucius, Publius Poetelius, and Publius Popillius, and the gifts they brought were a purple toga and a purple tunic, a chair of ivory, and a five-pound golden bowl. The men had further instructions to proceed to the courts of other African kings, and they bore gifts that were to be presented to each of these, too, namely a *toga praetexta* and a golden bowl weighing three pounds. In addition, Marcus Atilius and Manius Acilius were sent to Alexandria as a delegation to the royal couple Ptolemy and Cleopatra* to remind them of their ties of friendship with Rome, and to renew those ties. As gifts they brought a toga, a purple tunic, and a chair of ivory for the king, and an embroidered wrap and a purple cloak for the queen.

During the summer that witnessed these events there were numerous prodigies reported from nearby towns and country areas. At Tusculum, it was said that a lamb had been born with its udder full of milk, and also that the top of the temple of Jupiter had been struck by lightning and its roof almost completely torn off. At Anagnia, at roughly that time, it was claimed that the ground before the city gate had been struck by lightning, and that it burned for a day and a night although there was nothing to fuel the fire. In addition, birds reportedly abandoned their nests in the trees in the grove of Diana at the crossroads of Anagnia. At Tarracina, in the sea not far from the harbour, snakes of amazing size were supposed to have jumped from the water like fish at play. It was said that at Tarquinii a pig had been born with a human face, and that, at the Grove of Feronia in the territory of Capena, four statues had sweated out copious quantities of blood for a day and a night. By decree of the pontiffs, expiation ceremonies for these prodigies were conducted with full-grown sacrificial animals, and one day of prayer was prescribed at all the couches in Rome, with a second day at the Grove of Feronia in the territory of Capena.

5. When he received his letter of recall, the consul Marcus Valerius delegated his province and army to the praetor Lucius Cincius and sent the commander of the fleet, Marcus Valerius Messalla, to Africa with a number of his ships. Messalla was to conduct raids there and, at the same time, gather intelligence on the activities and plans of the Carthaginian people. Valerius himself then set off for Rome with ten ships, and convened the Senate immediately on his arrival, after a successful voyage. He there gave a report on his achievements, observing that, after almost sixty years of Roman military involvement on land and sea in Sicily, which had often entailed dreadful defeats, he had now brought that province to heel. There was no Carthaginian left in Sicily, he said, and there was not a Sicilian still missing from it—the absentees who had been driven out by fear had all been restored to their cities and farms, where they were now ploughing and sowing. Deserted land was being worked again; it was at last bearing crops for its cultivators, and represented the Roman people's most reliable safeguard for the grain-supply in peace and war.

After that Muttines and any others who had served the Roman people well were ushered into the Senate, and, in fulfilment of the consul's promise, all had honours conferred upon them. Muttines was even made a citizen of Rome* after a bill, authorized by the Senate, was brought before the people by the plebeian tribunes.

During the time that this was going on in Rome, Marcus Valerius, reaching the coast of Africa with fifty ships some time before dawn, made a surprise landing in the territory of Utica. He plundered the area extensively, taking many prisoners along with other booty of all kinds. He then went back to the ships and made the crossing to Sicily, returning to Lilybaeum twelve days after he left it. The captives were interrogated, and from them a number of facts were ascertained; and a detailed and ordered transcription was made of them for the consul Laevinus, so that he could see how matters stood in Africa. Five thousand Numidians were in Carthage, it was learned, with a dynamic young leader, Masinissa son of Gala, and other fighting men were being hired throughout Africa to be shipped to Hasdrubal in Spain. The goal was for Hasdrubal to cross to Italy and link up with Hannibal with the largest possible army and at the earliest possible moment, and the Carthaginians believed that it was in this strategy that victory lay. It was further discovered that a huge armada was being constructed for the recovery of Sicily, and the prisoners believed that it would soon make the crossing.

This information was read aloud in the Senate by the consul, and it made such an impression that the house voted that he should not wait for the elections but appoint a dictator for the supervision of elections and immediately return to his province. But a disagreement held the matter up. The consul insisted that he would, when he was in Sicily, appoint as dictator Marcus Valerius Messalla, who was then in command of the fleet, but the senators informed him that the appointment of a dictator outside Roman territory, which was limited to the confines of Italy, was not possible.

The plebeian tribune Marcus Lucretius now formally laid the matter before the Senate for a ruling, and the Senate decreed that the consul should, before he left the city, put to the people the question of the man they wanted appointed dictator. The consul should then appoint as dictator whomsoever the people named. If the consul refused, then the praetor should put the question to the people, and, in the event of a refusal from him, too, the tribunes should refer the matter to the plebs. The consul did, in fact, refuse to put to the people a matter which, he claimed, was his to decide, and he instructed the praetor to do the same. The tribunes then put the question to the plebs, and the plebs decided that Quintus Fulvius, who was at Capua at the time, should be appointed dictator. But, on the night before the assembly of the plebs was to be held, the consul slipped furtively away to Sicily.* The senators were now left in the lurch, and they voted to send a dispatch to Marcus Claudius, ordering him to come to the assistance of the republic that had been abandoned by his colleague, and to declare as dictator the man who was the people's choice. So it was that Quintus Fulvius was appointed dictator by the consul Marcus Claudius, and, by the same resolution of the plebs, the *pontifex maximus* Publius Licinius Crassus was appointed master of horse by the dictator Quintus Fulvius.

6. On his arrival in Rome, the dictator dispatched his legate Gaius Sempronius Blaesus (whom he had had alongside him in Capua) to

the army in his province of Etruria, where he was to replace Gaius Calpurnius, and Calpurnius he summoned by letter to take charge of Capua and his own army there. Fulvius then announced the holding of the elections at the earliest possible date. The electoral process, however, could not be completed because of a dispute that arose between the tribunes and the dictator.

The right to vote first had fallen by lot to the junior members of the tribe Galeria, and they had declared Quintus Fulvius and Quintus Fabius their choice as consuls. The other tribes, too, would have been similarly inclined when called on in their routine order, but the plebeian tribunes Gaius and Lucius Arrenius intervened. They insisted that back-to-back offices were unconstitutional, and that the election of a man who was actually presiding over the vote set a much worse precedent still. So, they said, if the dictator accepted his own nomination, they would veto the election, but if other nominations, and not his own, were considered they would not obstruct the proceedings. The dictator justified the election by appealing to the authority of the Senate, to the decision of the plebeian council, and to various precedents. In the consulship of Gnaeus Servilius, he reminded them, the other consul, Gaius Flaminius, had fallen at Trasimene. Then, on senatorial authority, a proposal was brought to the plebs, which the plebs ratified, that the people should have the right, for as long as there was war in Italy, to elect whatever former consuls they pleased, and as often as they wished.* He also had precedents supporting the procedure, he said. An old one was the case of Lucius Postumius Megellus, who had been elected consul with Gaius Junius Bubulcus in elections over which he himself had been presiding as *interrex*. A recent one was that of Quintus Fabius, who would certainly not have permitted himself back-to-back consulships had this not been in the public interest.

After lengthy wrangling with arguments like this, an agreement was finally reached between the dictator and the tribunes to abide by the decision of the Senate. In the view of the senators, this critical moment for the republic called for affairs of state to be conducted by veteran commanders who had experience and skill in warfare, and so they declared that they did not favour any delay in the elections. The tribunes acquiesced, the elections were held, and Quintus Fabius Maximus and Quintus Fulvius Flaccus were elected, the former for the fifth and the latter for the fourth time. The praetors were elected next, and these were Lucius Veturius Philo, Titus Quinctius Crispinus, Gaius Hostilius Tubulus, and Gaius Aurunculeius. The magistrates for the year elected, Quintus Fulvius resigned his position as dictator.

At the end of the summer a Punic fleet of forty ships crossed to Sardinia under the command of Hamilcar. It first conducted raids on the farmlands of Olbia; then, when Publius Manlius Volso appeared with his army, it sailed to the other side of the island and plundered the lands of Carales, after which it returned to Africa laden with all manner of spoils.

A number of Roman priests died that year, and replacements were made. Gaius Servilius was made pontiff in place of Titus Otacilius Crassus; and Tiberius Sempronius Longus, son of Tiberius, was made augur in place of Gaius Atilius Serranus. Likewise Tiberius Sempronius Longus, son of Tiberius, replaced Tiberius Sempronius Longus, son of Gaius, as decemvir for sacrifices. The *rex sacrorum* Marcus Marcius and the chief *curio* Marcus Aemilius Papus also died, but were not replaced in their priesthoods that year.

That year saw the appointment of Lucius Veturius Philo and Publius Licinius Crassus, the *pontifex maximus*, as censors. Licinius Crassus had previously been neither consul nor praetor, but made the step from the aedileship directly to the censorship. However, these censors did not revise the roll of senators, or conduct any official business; the death of Lucius Veturius pre-empted this, and Licinius then resigned his post as censor. The curule aediles Lucius Veturius and Publius Licinius Varus repeated the Roman Games for a single day. The plebeian aediles Quintus Catius and Lucius Porcius Licinus made a donation of bronze statues, paid for out of money taken in from fines, at the temple of Ceres, and they put on the games with considerable grandeur for the resources available in that period.

7. At the end of this year,* Scipio's legate Gaius Laelius came to Rome, thirty-three days after leaving Tarraco, and he attracted large crowds when he entered the city with a train of captives. The following day he was brought before the Senate. There he recounted how New Carthage, capital of Spain, had been captured in one day, and how a number of cities that had defected had been recovered and some new ones drafted into an alliance. Information from the prisoners pretty well squared with that in the dispatch

that had been sent by Marcus Valerius Messalla. What particularly caused the senators concern was the threat of Hasdrubal's voyage to Italy, when the country could barely stand up to Hannibal and his forces. Laelius was also brought before the popular assembly, where he delivered the same information as he had in the Senate. The Senate proclaimed a single day of religious thanksgiving for Publius Scipio's successes, and instructed Gaius Laelius to go back to Spain as soon as possible with the ships with which he had come.

On the basis of many sources I have placed the capture of New Carthage in this year, though I am not unaware that some have recorded that it was taken the following year. It seemed to me less plausible that Scipio spent an entire year in Spain without actually doing anything.*

On 15 March, Quintus Fabius Maximus and Quintus Fulvius Flaccus became consuls, Fabius for the fifth time, and Fulvius for the fourth. On the day on which they entered office, the two were assigned Italy as their sphere of responsibility, but with their authority demarcated by region: Fabius was to operate around Tarentum, Fulvius in Lucania and Bruttium. Marcus Claudius had his *imperium* extended for a year. In the praetorian sortition of provinces, Gaius Hostilius Tubulus received the urban jurisdiction; Lucius Veturius Philo, the foreigners' jurisdiction together with Gaul; Titus Quinctius Crispinus, Capua; and Gaius Aurunculeius, Sardinia.

The distribution of armies amongst the provinces was as follows. Quintus Fulvius was assigned the two legions then under Marcus Valerius Laevinus in Sicily, and Quintus Fabius the legions that Gaius Calpurnius had commanded in Etruria. The army of the city was to move to Etruria, where Gaius Calpurnius would again have charge of that province and its army. Titus Quinctius would take charge of Capua and the army that had been under Quintus Fulvius. Gaius Hostilius was to assume from the propraetor Gaius Laetorius command of his province and army, which was then at Ariminum. Marcus Marcellus was assigned the legions with which the consul had been operating. Marcus Valerius and Lucius Cincius, who also saw their *imperium* extended in Sicily, were delegated the army that had fought at Cannae, and they were ordered to make up its numbers with soldiers surviving from the legions of Gnaeus Fulvius. The consuls sought these out, and sent them off to Sicily. The men were, in addition, to serve under the same humiliating conditions as the veterans of Cannae, and those troops of Gnaeus Fulvius who had been sent to Sicily by the Senate in its displeasure over a similar incident of flight in battle. In Sardinia, Gaius Aurunculeius was assigned the same legions with which Publius Manlius Volso had carried out his responsibilities there. Publius Sulpicius was given orders to keep watch on Macedonia with the same legion and fleet as before, with his *imperium* extended a year. Orders were given for thirty quinqueremes to be sent from Sicily to the consul Quintus Fabius at Tarentum, and the remainder of the fleet, it was decided, would be used for raids on Africa—Marcus Valerius Laevinus should either sail over in person or, if he chose, send Lucius Cincius or Marcus Valerius Messalla instead. In the case of Spain, no changes were made, apart from Scipio and Silanus receiving extensions of their *imperium*, not for a year but until such time as they were recalled by the Senate.* Such was the distribution of responsibilities and armies for that year.

8. Although attention was focused on more pressing matters, elections to the post of chief *curio*, in which a priest to replace Marcus Aemilius had to be chosen, nevertheless aroused an old quarrel. The patricians declared that the nomination of Gaius Mamilius Atellus, the sole candidate from the plebs, should be disallowed; for, they said, nobody outside the patrician order had held that priesthood before. An appeal was made to the tribunes, who referred the question to the Senate, and the Senate granted the people the authority to decide the case. So it was that Gaius Mamilius Atellus became the first man from the plebeian order elected chief *curio*.

The *pontifex maximus* Publius Licinius also obliged Gaius Valerius Flaccus to be inaugurated as Flamen of Jupiter, against his will, and Gaius Laetorius replaced Quintus Mucius Scaevola as decemvir for sacrifices on Scaevola's death.

I would have been glad to say nothing about the motive for a flamen being forced to accept his position had it not been a case of a bad reputation turning into a good one.* It was because of a youth of shiftlessness and dissipation that Gaius Flaccus was taken up as flamen by the *pontifex maximus* Publius Licinius, though the young man was hated by his brother and other relatives for these very shortcomings. When his religious and ceremonial duties became his preoccupation, he swiftly put aside his old character, to the point that none of the younger generation enjoyed greater esteem or approval amongst the leading senators, whether they were family relations or strangers. The general acceptance of his new reputation gave him a justifiable self-confidence, and that prompted him to reclaim a right that, thanks to the disreputable character of earlier flamens, had elapsed over the years, namely entry into the Senate. Flaccus went into the Senate house, only to have the praetor Publius Licinius usher him out, and he appealed to the plebeian tribunes. As flamen he was actually reclaiming a time-honoured right of his priesthood, which was, he said, granted to the office of flamen, along with the *toga praetexta* and curule chair. The praetor's position was that a right should be based not on outdated precedents from ancient history, but on recent practice relating to the matter in question, and no flamen of Jupiter had exercised that right in the time either of their fathers or their grandfathers. The tribunes ruled that, as the privilege had fallen into disuse thanks to the apathy of some flamens, the loss should fall on those individuals themselves, not on the priesthood. And so, with no opposition even from the praetor, the tribunes escorted the flamen into the Senate, to the great approval of the senators and plebs. All were of the opinion, however, that the flamen had gained his end more from the probity of his life than from the right of the office.

Before going to their provinces, the consuls raised two city legions to make up the numbers required for the other armies. The consul Fulvius assigned to Gaius Fulvius Flaccus, who was his brother, the responsibility of taking the old city army to Etruria and bringing back to Rome the legions then stationed in Etruria.

The consul Fabius, on his side, instructed his son Quintus Maximus to seek out the remnants of Fulvius' army (some 4,344 men) and lead them to the proconsul Marcus Valerius in Sicily, and then to take over from Valerius two legions and thirty quinqueremes. The removal of these legions from the island did nothing to weaken the defence of the province in terms of real, or perceived, strength. An excellent job had been done of bringing the two old legions up to strength, and Valerius also had a large force of Numidian deserters, both infantry and cavalry. In addition, he recruited Sicilians with fighting experience who had been in Epicydes' army or that of the Carthaginians. By adding these foreign auxiliaries to individual Roman legions, Valerius kept up the appearance of two armies. He

ordered Lucius Cincius to use one for the defence of the part of the
island which had represented Hiero's kingdom, and the other he
employed himself to defend the rest, once demarcated into Roman
and Punic spheres of power.* He also split his fleet of seventy ships so
that protection could be afforded to the entire length of the coastline.
Valerius made a point of travelling through the province with
Muttines' cavalry to visit farms and take note of what was cultivated,
and what was not, and using that as grounds for commending or
criticizing landowners. Thanks to such diligence on his part, the
grain-yield was great enough for him to send some to Rome, and also
transport some to Catina for provisioning the army that would be
spending the summer around Tarentum.

9. In fact, the soldiers shipped to Sicily, most of them of Latin
status or allies, nearly proved to be the cause of some serious unrest.
Great and critical events, it is true, often arise from the insignificant
ones.

Some grumbling had begun amongst the Latins and the allies
in their meetings.* For nine years, they were saying, they had been
drained by having to raise troops and supply their pay; almost
every year they faced some terrible defeat in battle; and their men
were either being killed in the field, or carried off by disease. A
compatriot conscripted by the Roman was more lost to them than
one captured by the Carthaginian, they said: by the enemy he was
sent home without ransom, but by the Romans he was taken out of
Italy into something more aptly termed exile than military service.
For seven years the soldier who had fought at Cannae had now been
growing old in that exile, and he would die before the enemy—right
now at the height of his strength—left Italy. With old soldiers not
coming home, and new ones being conscripted, there would soon be
no one left! So, they said, they should refuse the Roman people what
the circumstances were shortly going to refuse them anyway, and do
so now before reaching extreme depopulation and poverty. If the
Romans saw the allies in agreement on this, they would certainly
consider making peace with the Carthaginians; otherwise Italy
would never be free of war as long as Hannibal lived. Such were their
discussions at their meetings.

The Roman people then had thirty colonies.* Since all had delegations in Rome at the time, twelve told the consuls that they lacked
the wherewithal to supply fighting men and cash. The twelve were

Ardea, Nepete, Sutrium, Alba, Carseoli, Sora, Suessa, Circeii, Setia, Cales, Narnia, and Interamna.

The consuls were taken aback by this surprising turn of events, and they tried to dissuade the delegates from such a terrible idea. They thought they would have greater success with censure and reproaches than with a gentle approach, and they kept telling them that what the delegates had dared express to the consuls, the consuls could not bring themselves to utter in the Senate. For that would not simply be a refusal of military obligations, they explained, but outright defection from the Roman people. They told them that they should promptly return to their colonies and hold discussions with their people, behaving as if the subject had not been broached— for, so far, they had only discussed, and not taken, such a momentous step. They should remind their people that they were not Capuans or Tarentines, but Romans, that they were of Roman descent, and that they had been sent out from Rome into the colonies, and into land taken in war, in order to propagate the Roman race. They owed the Romans as much as children owed to their parents—if they had any sense of duty to, or any memory of, their mother city of old. So they should consider the matter afresh—for their earlier reckless deliberations would only lead to betraying Roman power and handing victory to Hannibal.

The consuls pressed these arguments in turn for quite some time, but the delegates remained unmoved. They had no suggestion to take home, they said, and their senate* had no new business to discuss—for they had neither soldiers for conscription, nor money to be given as soldiers' pay. The consuls saw they were adamant, and they reported the matter to the Senate. Here such panic struck the members that most said the empire was finished, that other colonies and the allies would follow suit, and that they had all banded together to betray the city of Rome to Hannibal.

10. The consuls encouraged and reassured the Senate. They said the other colonies would remain as loyal and reliable as before, and even those who had failed in their duty would be brought to respect Roman power, if envoys were sent around those particular colonies to chasten them rather than plead with them.

The consuls were then given senatorial leave to take any action or measure they thought to be in the interest of the state. After first sounding the feelings of the other colonies, they summoned representatives of those colonies, and asked if they had any soldiers mobilized from the register.* Speaking for the eighteen other colonies, Marcus Sextilius of Fregellae replied that there were indeed men mobilized from the register. In fact, he said, the colonies would supply more, if more were needed, and would also assiduously carry out any other instructions or wishes of the Roman people. They had no shortage of resources for that, he said, and of loyalty they had a superabundance. The consuls prefaced their reply by saying that they felt the praise the representatives would receive from them personally was insufficient, and that all the senators should offer them thanks in the Senate house; and they instructed them to follow them into the Senate. The Senate addressed to them a decree couched in the most respectful language, and directed the consuls to bring them before the popular assembly as well. There the consuls were to mention the many distinguished benefits these colonies had conferred upon them and their ancestors, and refer in particular to their recent service to the state.

Not even today, after the passage of so many generations, should these people be passed over in silence, or deprived of their meed of praise*. They were the peoples of Signia, Norba, Saticula, Fregellae, Luceria, Venusia, Brundisium, Hadria, Firmum, and Ariminum; on the Tyrrhenian Sea, Pontia, Paestum, and Cosa; and, inland, Beneventum, Aesernia, Spoletium, Placentia, and Cremona. As a result of the assistance provided by these colonies, the power of the Roman people stood firm at that time, and they were officially thanked in the Senate and the popular assembly. As for the twelve other colonies that refused to heed the requisition, the senators ordered that no mention be made of them; their representatives were not to be dismissed, held back, or addressed by the consuls. A silent reprimand of this kind seemed most appropriate to the dignity of the Roman people.

As the consuls were making all the other necessary preparations for the war, the decision was taken to withdraw the gold raised by the five-per-cent tax,* which was being kept in reserve in the inner treasury to meet emergencies. Approximately 4,000 pounds of gold were withdrawn, and from this sum the consuls, the proconsuls Marcus Marcellus and Publius Sulpicius, and the praetor Lucius Veturius (who had drawn Gaul as his province) were each given 500 pounds. A further 100 pounds was given to the consul Fabius to be transported to the citadel of Tarentum. The rest of the gold they used to contract out, for ready money, the provision of clothing for the army that was winning renown for itself and its commander in its operations in Spain.

11. It was further decided that, before the consuls left the city, there should be expiatory ceremonies for the various prodigies. The following had been struck by lightning: a statue of Jupiter and a tree close to the temple on the Alban Mount, a grove at Ostia, the city wall and temple of Fortuna at Capua, and the city wall and a gate at Sinuessa. There were also reports that the water of the Alban Lake had flowed with blood, and that at Rome, in the sanctuary of the temple of Fors Fortuna, a statuette on the goddess's garland fell of its own accord from her head into her hand. It was well established that at Privernum an ox had talked and a vulture had swooped down on a shop in the forum when it was crowded; and that at Sinuessa a child of indeterminate sex was born, part male, part female (gener-ally called 'androgynous', a Greek term, as often, Greek being easier for the formation of compound words*), milk had fallen as rain, and a boy had been born with an elephant's head. Full-grown victims were used for the expiation of these prodigies; and there was a proclamation enjoining public ceremonies at all the couches, and one day of public prayer. It was also decreed that the praetor Gaius Hostilius should promise games for Apollo in a vow, and celebrate them, just as they had been promised and celebrated in recent years.

At that time, too, the consul Quintus Fulvius held the voting assembly for election of censors. The censors elected were two men who had not been consuls, Marcus Cornelius Cethegus and Publius Sempronius Tuditanus. With senatorial authorization, a motion was brought to the plebs, which gave its consent, that the two censors should lease out the farmland of Capua.

Revision of Senate membership was held up by infighting amongst the censors over the selection of Senate leader.* The preroga-tive of choosing the leader fell by lot to Sempronius, but Cornelius insisted that they follow the practice handed down to them from their forefathers of choosing as leader the man who, amongst all the ex-censors still alive, had been the first to hold the office. That man was Titus Manlius Torquatus. Sempronius claimed that the gods had allotted him the right to choose, and they had thereby also given him the right to choose freely. He was going to exercise his own judgement in doing this, and would select Quintus Fabius Maximus whom he could conclusively prove—even to Hannibal's satisfaction—to be at that time the leading man in the Roman state. After a long war of words, Sempronius' colleague gave way and the consul Quintus Fabius Maximus was selected as leader in the Senate by Sempronius.

After that the rest of the Senate membership was revised, and eight men were struck off, including Marcus Caecilius Metellus, the man infamous for having advocated leaving Italy after the defeat at Cannae. That same issue was used in attaching censure to equestrians, too, though those touched by that particular scandal were very few. Knights who were former members of the legions at Cannae, and were then serving in Sicily—and they were numerous—all had their horses taken from them.* The censors also added a time factor to this harsh punishment, refusing to recognize past service in the case of individuals who had served with public horses, and stipulating that they must all serve ten seasons with their own horses. The censors also rooted out a large number who should have been serving in the cavalry, and they reduced to the grade of poll-tax payer all who had been seventeen years of age when the war started, but had failed to serve. After that they put out for contract rebuilding projects for the area around the Forum destroyed by fire—seven shops, the food market, and the Royal Atrium.

12. When all necessary business had been completed in Rome, the consuls left for the war. Fulvius left first, and went ahead to Capua; Fabius followed a few days later. Fabius pleaded with his colleague in person, and with Marcellus by letter, to detain Hannibal by putting the utmost pressure on him, while Fabius himself was mounting his attack on Tarentum. The enemy had now been driven back everywhere, Fabius told them, and had nowhere to make a stand and no secure base behind him; if Tarentum were taken from him, he would have no reason to remain in Italy. Fabius also sent a message to the commander of the garrison in Rhegium that had been stationed there by the consul Laevinus as a buffer against the Bruttii. The garrison was 8,000 strong, mostly men from Agathyrna, as noted above,* who had been shipped over from Sicily, and they were people who had been used to a life of larceny. To their numbers had been added Bruttian deserters from the locality, men just as reckless and

just as desperate. Fabius ordered the commander to take this band out, first to raid the lands of the Bruttii, and then to assault the city of Caulonia. The men carried out their orders with passion rather than zest, and after robbing and chasing off the farmers, they proceeded with an all-out assault on the city.

Marcellus was galvanized into action both by the consul's letter and by his conviction that no Roman general was as good a match for Hannibal as he. As soon as there was plenty of forage in the fields, he left his winter quarters and met Hannibal in the area of Canusium. The Carthaginian leader was trying to induce the citizens of Canusium to defect, but on hearing of Marcellus' approach he struck camp. The country here was open, with no cover for an ambush, and so Hannibal proceeded to fall back towards a wooded region. Marcellus dogged his footsteps, and kept pitching camp close to him; the work of establishing camp complete, he would immediately deploy his legions for battle. Hannibal would skirmish with him, using his cavalry only by individual squadrons, and only the javelin-throwers of his infantry, but he felt total engagement was unnecessarily risky. He was, however, drawn into the confrontation he was trying to avoid.

Hannibal had been marching by night, and Marcellus overtook him in an area that was flat and open. He tried to pitch camp, but Marcellus frustrated him by attacking the men engaged in the work on all sides. The result was a pitched battle, with all their forces engaged, and when night was approaching they parted on equal terms. The camps, just a short distance from each other, were hurriedly fortified before darkness fell.

At dawn the next day, Marcellus led his forces into the field, and Hannibal did not decline the fight. He addressed his men at length, telling them to remember Trasimene and Cannae, and smash the insolence of the enemy. They were constantly pressing and goading them, he declared, never letting them march on in peace or pitch camp, never letting them take a breath or look around. Every day they were obliged to see before them, with the rising sun, a Roman army on the plains. If the enemy left just one battle bloodied, he would be more tempered and restrained in his future operations.

Animated by these exhortations, and at the same time sick and tired of the insolence of a foe who, every day, was pressuring and provoking them, the Carthaginians went into battle with great spirit.

The fight went on for more than two hours. Then, on the Roman side, the allied troops on the right, and the elite contingent of allies,* began to falter. When Marcellus saw that, he brought the eighteenth legion into the front line. While some were falling back in fear, and others were slow in coming into line, the whole formation was thrown into turmoil, then quite clearly beaten back; and, fear vanquishing their sense of honour, they began to flee. In the action and the flight about 2,700 citizens and allies lost their lives, including four Roman centurions and two military tribunes, Marcus Licinius and Marcus Helvius. Four military standards were lost from the allied contingent that had begun the flight, and two from the legion that had come to the front when the allies were giving ground.

13. On his return to camp, Marcellus delivered an address to his men so biting and caustic that they found their angry commander's words even harder to take than a losing engagement that had lasted the entire day. 'In the circumstances, I can at least praise and thank the immortal gods for one thing,' he said. 'Our victorious foe did not actually attack the camp itself when you were making your panic-stricken dash for the rampart and the gates! I am sure you would have deserted the camp with as much terror as you quit the fight! What fear, what terror suddenly came over you to make you forget who you were, and against whom you were fighting? These are obviously the same enemies you spent last summer defeating in battle, and then chasing from the field after defeating them! The same men whose tracks you have dogged the last few days as, day and night, they fled before you! The men whom you wore down in skirmishes, and whom, yesterday, you would allow neither to march nor to pitch camp! I pass over the things on which you can pride yourselves, but I *will* mention something that ought to make you feel shame and regret. I mean, of course, that yesterday you broke off the fight when it was a drawn battle. What did last night do to you, or what today? Has there been some lessening of your forces, or some increase in theirs? For I do not seem to be talking to my own army, or to Roman soldiers—only your bodies and weapons are the same. Had your spirit remained the same, would the enemy have seen your backs, or robbed any maniple or cohort of its standards? Until now the enemy was priding himself on cutting Roman legions to shreds; but you, on this day, have for the first time given him the glory of actually putting a Roman army to flight.'

At this a cry went up, begging forgiveness for the day's performance, and asking him to put his soldiers' courage to the test again,
whenever he wished. 'All right, men, I *will* put it to the test,' he
replied. 'I shall tomorrow lead you out into battle so that, as winners,
not losers, you can gain the pardon you seek.'

Marcellus then ordered the cohorts that had lost their standards to
be kept on barley-rations,* and the centurions of the maniples whose
standards had been lost were instructed to stand to one side, swords
unsheathed and belts removed. He also called for everybody, infantry
and cavalry, to assemble, under arms, the following day. The meeting
was then dismissed, the men admitting that the tongue-lashing
they had received was well deserved, and that on that day none but
their commander had shown himself a man in the Roman battle line.
Now they must satisfy him, either dying themselves or winning a
superlative victory.

They next day, as ordered, they appeared armed and equipped.
The commander complimented them, and announced that he was
going to lead into the front line the men with whom the flight had
begun the previous day, and the cohorts that had lost their standards.
He was now making a formal declaration, he said, that they all had
to fight and win, individually and together doing their best to prevent the previous day's defeat being reported at Rome before that
day's victory. They were then ordered to take food to build up their
strength, so that they would have sufficient stamina if the battle were
prolonged. When all was said and done to boost the men's morale,
they proceeded to the field.

14. When Hannibal was brought the news, he declared: 'Clearly
we have an enemy who can tolerate neither good fortune nor bad.
Winning, he puts fierce pressure on his defeated foe; losing, he
renews the fight with his conquerors.' With that he called for the
trumpet-signal, and led out his troops.

The fighting was considerably fiercer on both sides than on the
previous day; the Carthaginians were struggling to secure the glory
won the day before, the Romans to wipe out their disgrace. On the
Roman side, the left allied contingent and the cohorts that had lost
their standards were fighting in the front line, and the eighteenth
legion was deployed on the right wing. The legates Lucius Cornelius
Lentulus and Gaius Claudius Nero commanded the wings, and
Marcellus kept the centre solid by his presence, giving encouragement

and taking note of performance. On Hannibal's side the Spaniards were in the front line, and these represented the main strength in the entire Carthaginian army.

After a long period of indecisive combat, Hannibal ordered elephants to be brought to the front, thinking that this might create havoc and panic in the enemy. And, indeed, the beasts did at first bring chaos to the troop deployment and the ranks; trampling down or else scattering in terror those in their vicinity, they had actually created an opening in the line at one point. In fact, the flight from there would have been more widespread had not the military tribune Gaius Decimius Flavus seized the standard of the first maniple of *hastati* and called upon the maniple under that standard to follow him. Decimius took the men to the point at which the beasts, crowded together, were causing the greatest trouble, and told them to hurl their spears at them. All their weapons stuck fast in their target, for it was not difficult, at close range, to hit such huge bodies so densely packed together. Not all the beasts were wounded, but those with weapons in their backs turned to run, and in doing so— such being their undependable nature—stampeded the uninjured animals as well.

At that point, it was no longer a matter of one maniple hurling javelins. Now every single soldier was doing so, as long as he was able to keep up with the herd of fleeing elephants. When an elephant is startled, its fear drives it on with a fury that cannot be controlled by the driver on its back; and the beasts now charged their own side with all the more force, creating greater carnage than they had amongst the enemy. The line was in chaos where the animals charged through; the Roman infantry pushed forward at that point; and it did not take much of a fight to force back the disordered and panic-stricken Carthaginians. Then Marcellus sent cavalry in pursuit of the fugitives, and the chase stopped only when these were driven in consternation back into their camp. For, apart from everything else that was causing panic and alarm, it so happened that two elephants had collapsed right in the gateway, and the Carthaginian soldiers' dash back to their camp had to be made over the ditch and the rampart. It was there that the enemy suffered the greatest loss of life, with some 8,000 men killed, and five elephants. But for the Romans it was no bloodless victory, either.* Roughly 1,700 men were killed from the two legions, and of the allies more than 1,300. The number of the wounded, citizens and allies, was very high. Hannibal struck camp the following night. Marcellus wanted to follow him, but the large number of his wounded prevented him from doing so.

15. Scouts were sent out to track Hannibal's column, and they brought news the following day that he was heading for Bruttium.

It was at about this time that the Hirpini, the Lucani, and the people of Vulceii* capitulated to the consul Quintus Fulvius, surrendering to him the garrisons of Hannibal in their cities. They were welcomed with kind words by the consul, who merely reprimanded them for their past mistakes. The Bruttii, too, were given similar hopes of pardon after the brothers Vibius and Paccius, who were by far the most distinguished members of their tribe, came with a request for the same conditions of surrender as the Lucanians had been given.

The consul Quintus Fabius stormed the town of Manduria in the territory of the Sallentini, taking about 4,000 prisoners, and a considerable amount of other booty, as well. From there Fabius left for Tarentum, where he established his camp right at the harbour entrance. Putting to use the ships that Laevinus had kept to safeguard his supplies, he loaded some with engines and the tackle used for assaulting city walls, and others he equipped with catapults, rocks, and every kind of projectile. He equipped the freighters in this way, too—and not just those propelled by oars—so that some of his men could bring the engines and ladders up to the walls, while others could, at long range, inflict wounds on the enemy defenders on the fortifications. These ships were equipped and readied for an attack on the city from the open sea, and, in fact, the sea was clear of the enemy, the Punic fleet having been transferred to Corcyra when Philip was preparing for his attack on the Aetolians. Meanwhile, in Bruttium, the forces besieging Caulonia, fearing a surprise attack from Hannibal, withdrew to some higher ground before his arrival. This safeguarded them from immediate attack, but offered them no other advantage.

During his siege of Tarentum Fabius was helped on his way to great success by a trivial circumstance. The Tarentines had a garrison composed of Bruttians that had been supplied by Hannibal, and the garrison commander was deeply in love with a young woman whose brother was in the army of the consul Fabius. In a letter from his sister, the brother was informed of her new relationship with a

rich foreigner, who was very well respected amongst his people. This
now made him hopeful that the lover could be driven to any lengths
by his sister, and he informed the consul of his hopes. Fabius
thought this was not simply wishful thinking, and the brother was
ordered to go over to Tarentum posing as a deserter. There, through
his sister, he struck up a relationship with the commander. At first
he discreetly probed the man's feelings, and then, when he had
evidence enough of his fecklessness, he used the woman's charms to
drive him into betraying the post he had been assigned to guard. A
plan of action and the timing were established, and a soldier, surreptitiously despatched at night from the city along a path between
the Tarentine outposts, reported to the consul what had transpired,
and what steps had been agreed on for the future.

At the first watch, Fabius gave the signal to the men in the citadel
and to those standing watch over the harbour. He himself made his
way around the harbour and, unobserved, took up a position in the
eastern area of the town. Then trumpets blared out simultaneously
from the citadel and from the harbour and ships that had been
brought to shore from the open sea; and shouting and an enormous
racket was deliberately raised at every point where the danger was
actually at a minimum. The consul meanwhile held back his men
in silence.

Now Democrates, the former naval commander, happened to be
in charge in that particular sector.* Democrates saw that all was quiet
around him, whereas there was a noisy commotion in the other
areas of town, with the shouting that sometimes goes up when a city
is taken. He feared that the consul was actually on the attack
and initiating combat while he was himself doing nothing, and so he
led his force over to the citadel, the source of the most alarming
noise of all. Fabius judged from the time that had elapsed, and the
silence that had fallen, that the defensive troops had been withdrawn
from that point—for whereas, shortly before, there had been the ring
of voices that were rousing soldiers and calling them to arms, now no
voice came from there at all. He therefore had ladders advanced to
the section of the wall at which, according to the report of the man
who had negotiated the betrayal, the Bruttian cohort was on guard-
duty. It was there that the wall was taken first, the Bruttii helping
and welcoming the Romans, who passed over the fortifications into
the city. After that the closest gate was broken down so the main

body of the troops could be admitted. Then, at about the break of day, a cry went up and the Romans, meeting no armed resistance, made their way to the forum. And now they drew upon themselves the combined onslaught of all who had been engaged in fighting in the area of the citadel or the harbour.

16. The fighting that broke out at the entrance to the forum was more violent than it was sustained. The Tarentines were not on a par with the Romans in courage, weaponry, and military expertise, or in vigour and physical strength. As a result, after simply throwing their javelins, they turned in flight almost before coming to close quarters with their foe, and slipped away, along city streets with which they were familiar, to their own homes or those of friends. Two of their officers, Nico and Democrates, went down fighting bravely. Philemenus, who had been responsible for the betrayal of the city to Hannibal, galloped away from the battle. His horse was shortly afterwards recognized wandering aimlessly through the city, but his body was nowhere to be found. It was commonly thought that he had fallen headlong from his mount into an open well. The commander of the Punic garrison, Carthalo, laid down his arms, but as he was coming to the consul to remind him of ties of hospitality between their fathers, a soldier met him and killed him.* There was indiscriminate slaughter of the armed and unarmed in every quarter, and of Carthaginians and Tarentines alike. Even the Bruttii were killed in large numbers throughout the city, perhaps by mistake, or possibly because of the long-standing hatred towards them; or perhaps it was to snuff out the rumour of betrayal, and make it look as if the city had rather been captured by force of arms.

After the carnage the Romans scattered to ransack the city. It is said that 30,000 slaves were captured; a huge quantity of silver, in plate and coin; 3,080 pounds of gold; and statues and paintings almost to rival the artwork of Syracuse. But Fabius showed more strength of character in passing up booty of that sort than Marcellus had. When a secretary asked him what he wanted done with some colossal statues (they were gods, each with his appropriate clothing, represented as fighting in battle), Fabius gave orders for 'the people of Tarentum to be left their angry gods'.* The wall separating the city from its citadel was then pulled down and demolished.

While this was taking place in Tarentum, Hannibal had accepted the surrender of the troops who had been blockading Caulonia.

Then, hearing that Tarentum was under attack, he drove his column along rapidly, day and night, but during the dash to bring assistance he heard of the city's capture. 'The Romans have *their* Hannibal, too,' he said. 'We have lost Tarentum the same way we took it.'

However, not to appear to have turned back with his force like a man in flight, Hannibal pitched camp just where he had halted, some five miles from the city, and after remaining there a few days he withdrew to Metapontum. From there he sent two Metapontine citizens to Fabius in Tarentum, with a letter from the leading men of the city. The men were to accept a guarantee from the consul that they would receive an amnesty for their earlier actions if they betrayed Metapontum to him, along with its Punic garrison. Fabius, assuming the offer they brought to be genuine, fixed a date for coming to Metapontum, and gave the men a letter to be taken to their leaders. The letter was then brought to Hannibal. Hannibal was pleased with the success of his trick, finding that not even Fabius had proven immune to his cunning, and he laid an ambush not far distant from Metapontum.

Fabius took the auspices before leaving Tarentum, and time and again the birds* would not give him favourable signs. He also consulted the gods with the sacrifice of an animal, and was told by the priest that he must be on his guard against treachery on the enemy's part, and against an ambush. When Fabius thus failed to arrive on the prearranged date, the citizens of Metapontum were sent back to him to coax him, if he hesitated to come. They were arrested on the spot and, fearing a more intensive investigation,* they revealed the trap.

17. In Spain, Publius Scipio had spent the entire winter trying to enlist the support of the natives, partly with gifts and partly by restoring their hostages and prisoners of war. Now, at the start of the summer* during which these events were taking place in Italy, a distinguished Spanish chieftain, Edesco, came to see him. Edesco's wife and children were in the hands of the Romans, but something quite apart from that had also brought him, namely that virtually spontaneous shift of sympathy that had turned all Spain towards the Romans, and away from the rule of the Carthaginian. It was the same thing that prompted Indibilis and Mandonius, undoubtedly the leading men in all Spain, to take all the forces of their countrymen, abandon Hasdrubal, and withdraw to the hills overlooking his camp,

from which a retreat could safely be made to the Romans along the unbroken chain of mountains.

Hasdrubal saw that his enemy's forces were increasing by leaps and bounds, while his own were only decreasing, and he also realized that, if he failed to bring off some bold stroke, his numbers would only continue their disastrous decline. He therefore decided to engage at the earliest opportunity. Scipio was even keener to fight. His successes had increased his confidence, and he also preferred to do battle with a single commander, and a single army, before the enemy armies could join up, than to face them together. However, even supposing he had to fight a number of armies simultaneously, he had found a way of increasing his troop-numbers. He observed that his ships were serving no purpose because the entire Spanish coastline was now clear of Punic fleets, and so, beaching his vessels at Tarraco, he combined their crews with his land forces. And he had plenty of weapons—those captured at New Carthage, as well as those that he had had manufactured by the large numbers of tradesmen whom he had kept interned after the city's capture.

Since Laelius, without whom he was unwilling to initiate any important action, had also returned from Rome, Scipio left Tarraco at the beginning of spring with these troops, and began to advance on the enemy. He was making his way over territory that was completely pacified, with allies escorting him or welcoming him as he passed through the lands of each tribe, when he was met by Indibilis and Mandonius and their troops. Indibilis addressed Scipio on behalf of the two, with no trace of the uncouth and crude language of a barbarian, but with modesty and dignity; and he was more inclined to justify their defection to Rome as being necessary than to boast about having seized the earliest opportunity for it. He knew, he said, that amongst one's old allies the word 'turncoat' aroused hatred, and amongst new ones suspicion, and he did not object to this general tendency amongst men, if it was the motive for the desertion, and not the term itself, that produced this twofold antipathy. He then gave an account of his and Mandonius' services to the Carthaginian commanders, of the Carthaginians' greed and arrogance, and of the injustices of all kinds inflicted on the two of them and their people. Up to that point, theirs had been merely a physical presence on the Carthaginian side, he said, but their heart had long been on the side on which they thought there was respect for what was just and right.

People who cannot endure the violence and injustice of men also seek refuge as suppliants with the gods, he added; and all they asked of Scipio now was that their defection be seen as neither unconscionable nor creditable. He should gauge the value of their service on the basis of the qualities he found in them from personal experience from that day on.

That was just what he was going to do, replied the Roman commander, and he would not regard as turncoats men who did not think an alliance binding when it was based on no respect for obligations human or divine. Their wives and children were then brought before them and restored to them, as they wept tears of joy; and that day the two leaders were offered Scipio's hospitality. The following day their assurances were accepted with the conclusion of a treaty, and they were sent off to bring up their troops. Following that, the Romans shared their camp with them until, under their guidance, they reached the enemy.

18. The nearest Carthaginian army, that of Hasdrubal, was close to the city of Baecula,* and here the Carthaginians had cavalry outposts stationed before the camp. The skirmishers, the advance troops, and the men at the head of the column attacked the outposts as they were coming off the march, and before choosing a spot for their camp, and they made the attack with such contempt that the level of morale on each side was readily apparent. The Carthaginian cavalry was driven back into the camp in panic-stricken flight, and the Roman advance almost reached the gates. In fact, that day, the Romans pitched camp with their appetite for the fight merely whetted.

During the night Hasdrubal pulled his troops back to a hill with a broad plateau on its summit. There was a river to his rear, and before him, and on his flanks, a kind of steep slope hedged his entire position. Below him there was another piece of even ground, with a gentle gradient, and that, too, was bordered by a second steep slope, no easier to climb than the other. The next day Hannibal saw the enemy line standing before their camp, and he sent his Numidian cavalry and his Balearic and African light infantry down to this lower flatland.

Scipio rode around his ranks and standards, pointing out to his men an enemy who, he said, had abandoned all hope of fighting on level ground, and were now trying to hold the hills. All that enabled them to stand in sight of the Romans was their confidence in their position, not in their fighting ability and weapons. But, he continued, New Carthage had had walls that were higher, and those the Roman soldier had scaled—hills had proved no barrier to his weapons, nor had a citadel or even the sea. The high ground they had taken would serve their enemies one purpose only—to make them jump over cliffs and precipices to achieve their escape! But that path of flight he would close off for them, too, he said. And he then gave orders to two cohorts, one to hold the entrance to the valley through which the river ran, and the other to maintain a blockade on the road that led from the city into the country along the hillside.

Scipio himself took the light-armed troops* that had driven back the enemy outposts the previous day and led them against the enemy light infantry, who were standing on the brow of the lower slope. At first they advanced over rough terrain, with nothing obstructing them but the difficulty of their path. Then they came within range of the enemy, and a huge mass of weapons of all kinds immediately poured down on them. They retaliated by hurling stones they found on the spot—they were scattered about in profusion, and nearly all of a size for throwing—and the soldiers were joined in this by the crowd of camp-followers who were amongst the fighting men.

The climb was hard, and the men were all but buried under the showers of weapons and stones, but thanks to their experience in scaling walls, and their sheer determination, those at the front reached the top. The enemy here were light-armed skirmishers, men protected by their distance from the foe, avoiding combat as they hurled their weapons from afar; but they were also undependable in fighting hand-to-hand at close quarters. So, as soon as the foremost Romans gained some level ground on which they could firmly plant their feet, they drove them from their position and forced them back against the battle line that was standing on the higher ground, causing severe losses in the process. Scipio then ordered his triumphant men to advance up the hill against the centre of the enemy line, and he divided the rest of his troops between himself and Laelius. Laelius he ordered to proceed to the right, moving around the hill until he found a way up with a gentler slope, and he himself advanced a short distance around to the left and attacked the enemy flank.

From the start the enemy line was thrown into disarray, the men trying to wheel the wings around, and turn the ranks to face the shouting that came from every side. In the midst of this chaos, Laelius came on the scene. As the enemy backed away to prevent damage being inflicted from the rear, their front disintegrated. That gave even the men in the centre the opportunity to climb to the top, though this they could never have succeeded in doing over such broken ground had the Carthaginian ranks remained solid, with the elephants positioned before the standards. There was slaughter on every side, and Scipio, who had charged the enemy's right wing with his left, was wreaking particular havoc on the now-exposed flanks. There was no room left at this point even for flight. Roman detachments had blocked the roads on both sides, to the right and left; and the camp gate had been shut by the commander and his officers as they made their escape. In addition, the elephants had been startled, and the Carthaginians were as afraid of the panic-stricken beasts as they were of the enemy. The result was that some 8,000 men lost their lives.

19. Before joining battle Hasdrubal had hurriedly amassed his war chest and sent ahead elephants, and now he headed along the River Tagus towards the Pyrenees, gathering up en route as many of the fugitives from the battle* as he could. Scipio took possession of the enemy camp, conferring on his soldiers all the plunder, apart from free persons, and, in making an inventory of the prisoners, he found the number to be 10,000 infantrymen and 2,000 cavalrymen. Of these he sent home all the Spaniards without ransom, but he instructed his quaestor to sell off the Africans. After that, a crowd of Spaniards began to swarm around him, men who had surrendered earlier as well as those taken prisoner the day before, and they of one accord hailed him as their 'king'. Scipio thereupon had silence proclaimed by a herald. The greatest name for him, he declared, was the one with which his own soldiers had hailed him—'general'.* The title of king, which had great prestige elsewhere, he explained, was anathema in Rome. As for his having the spirit of a king—if that was what they considered the noblest thing in a man's character—that was for them to judge in silence, but they should avoid the use of the word. They became aware then, barbarians though they were, of the greatness of the man's soul; this was a title at which all other human beings were agog with wonder, and he was looking down on it from a position of such superiority. After that, gifts were distributed amongst the Spanish chieftains and princes, and Scipio told Indibilis to choose any three hundred horses that he liked from the large number that had been captured.

When the quaestor, following his commander's orders, was putting the Africans on sale, he was told that there was amongst them a young male adult of strikingly good looks and of royal stock, and he sent him to Scipio. Scipio questioned the boy on his identity and nationality, and asked why he had been in military service at his age. He replied that he was Numidian, and his people called him Massiva, that he had been left an orphan by his father and then been brought up by Gala, king of the Numidians, his grandfather on his mother's side. He had crossed to Spain with his uncle Masinissa, who had recently come with his cavalry to assist the Carthaginians, but he had never before gone into battle, having been forbidden to do so by Masinissa on account of his age. On the day of the battle with the Romans, he had, behind his uncle's back, surreptitiously taken weapons and a horse and gone into the fight, but he had been thrown headlong when his horse fell, and had been captured by the Romans.

Ordering a watch kept on the Numidian, Scipio completed all the official business he had to do. He then withdrew to his headquarters, summoned the boy, and asked him if he would like to go back to Masinissa. With tears of joy in his eyes, the boy replied that he really would like to do that. Scipio thereupon presented him with a gold ring, a tunic with the broad stripe,* as well as a Spanish cloak, a golden brooch, and a horse with its trappings, and then sent him on his way with some horsemen, who were ordered to escort the boy as far as he wished.

20. A council of war was held after that. Some of those present advised immediate pursuit of Hasdrubal, but Scipio felt this was dangerous—he feared that Mago and the other Hasdrubal might join forces with him.* He therefore limited himself to sending a contingent to blockade the pass over the Pyrenees, and he himself spent the remainder of the summer accepting the submission of Spanish tribes.

A few days after the battle of Baecula, at the time when Scipio, returning to Tarraco, had left the pass of Castulo, the commanders Hasdrubal son of Gisgo and Mago reached Hasdrubal from Further Spain. This was assistance that came too late for Hasdrubal, the defeat having already been sustained, but their arrival was not at all inopportune for discussions on the conduct of the rest of the war. At their meeting, they exchanged intelligence on the sympathies of the Spaniards in each man's theatre of operations, and Hasdrubal son of Gisgo expressed the opinion that the farthest reaches of Spain—the area on the Ocean around Gades—had no experience of the Romans as yet, and so were still staunchly loyal to the Carthaginians. But only he thought this way; the other Hasdrubal and Mago were both agreed that the benefits Scipio had conferred had made a deep impression on all the Spaniards, tribes and individuals alike. They believed there would be no end to the desertions to the Romans until all the Spanish troops were either removed to the most remote parts of Spain, or led over into Gaul. So, they said, even without the decree of the Carthaginian senate,* it would have been necessary for Hasdrubal to go to Italy. That was where the whole war was centred, but Hasdrubal would, at the same time, be taking all the Spanish forces out of Spain, far from the reputation Scipio had established. His army, they said, had been depleted by desertions and also by the defeat he had suffered, and they felt its numbers should be supplemented with Spanish troops. They further proposed that Mago transfer his army to Hasdrubal son of Gisgo and cross in person to the Balearic Islands, with a large sum of money, to hire mercenary auxiliaries,* and that Hasdrubal son of Gisgo should withdraw deep into Lusitania with his army, and avoid engaging the Romans. Finally, they suggested that Masinissa should have a force of 3,000 horsemen, made up from the cream of the entire cavalry, and that he make a sweep of Hither Spain, bringing assistance to allies and plundering enemy towns and farms. After taking these decisions, the commanders separated to put them into effect. Such were that year's developments in Spain.

In Rome, Scipio's reputation was growing by the day. In the case of Fabius, although the capture of Tarentum was due to treachery rather than valour, it still redounded to his credit. Fulvius' reputation was on the wane, and Marcellus was even in disrepute—apart from his poor performance in his first battle, he had led his men off to their quarters in Venusia in midsummer, when Hannibal was still at large in Italy.

Marcellus had a personal enemy in the plebeian tribune Gaius Publicius Bibulus. Ever since that first battle which had gone badly for Marcellus, Bibulus had been continually making speeches that had discredited him and made him unpopular with the plebs. Now he was advocating the annulment of his *imperium*. However, Marcellus' relatives gained authorization for him to leave a lieutenant in Venusia and come to Rome to clear himself of the charges that his enemies were bringing against him, and they also prevented any debate, in his absence, of the annulment of his command. As it happened, Marcellus reached Rome to fend off the humiliation he faced at the same time as the consul Quintus Fulvius arrived for the elections.

21. The debate over Marcellus' *imperium* took place in the Circus Flaminius, before a huge gathering of plebeians and people of all classes. The tribune of the plebs brought his charges not only against Marcellus, but against the nobility as a whole. It was thanks to the nobles' treacherous and dilatory conduct, he said, that Hannibal had been, for nine years now, holding Italy as his own province, having spent more of his life there than in Carthage! The people of Rome were reaping the benefits of the extension of Marcellus' command, he added: his twice-beaten army was having its summer season quartered in Venusia!

By citing his achievements Marcellus so effectively rebutted this address of the tribune that not only was the bill to annul his *imperium* rejected but, the next day, all the centuries elected him consul with tremendous unanimity. As his colleague he was given Titus Quinctius Crispinus, who was praetor at the time. The next day saw the following men elected to the praetorship: Publius Licinius Crassus Dives (the *pontifex maximus*), Publius Licinius Varus, Sextus Julius Caesar,* and Quintus Claudius.

On the days on which the election took place there was concern in the community about a revolt in Etruria. According to a letter from Gaius Calpurnius, the propraetor with responsibility for that area, the unrest had begun amongst the people of Arretium. The consul designate Marcellus was therefore swiftly dispatched to the region to investigate, and, if the situation seemed to warrant it, he was to send for an army and transfer the theatre of operations from Apulia to Etruria. Fear of this checked and restored order to the Etruscans. Ambassadors from Tarentum also sought a peace settlement that would grant them their independence and their own constitution, and the Senate's reply was that they should return when the consul Fabius arrived in Rome.

Both the Roman and the Plebeian Games were that year repeated for a single day. Lucius Cornelius Caudinus and Servius Sulpicius Galba were the curule aediles, and Gaius Servilius and Quintus Caecilius Metellus were the plebeian aediles. Servilius, people said, had not had the right to be tribune of the plebs and had no right now to be aedile. For, although it had been believed for ten years that Servilius' father had been killed by the Boii near Mutina, while he was serving as one of the three land commissioners, it was now well established that he was still alive and in enemy hands.*

22. In the eleventh year of the Punic War, Marcus Marcellus and Titus Quinctius Crispinus entered the consulship, this being Marcellus' fifth time in the office (counting the consulship in which he did not actually serve because of irregularity in the electoral procedure). Both consuls were assigned Italy as their area of responsibility. They were granted the two armies of the previous year's consuls, and there was a third that was, at that time, at Venusia under the command of Marcellus. The consuls were to select the two they wanted out of the three, and the third would be put at the disposition of whichever commander would be allotted responsibility for Tarentum and the Sallentini.

The other responsibilities were distributed as follows. Of the praetors, Publius Licinius Varus received the urban jurisdiction, and Publius Licinius Crassus, the *pontifex maximus*, that over foreigners, and a further responsibility to be decided by the Senate. Sextus Julius Caesar received Sicily, and Quintus Claudius Tarentum. There was a year's extension of *imperium* for Quintus Fulvius Flaccus; his area of responsibility, to be held with one legion, was to be Capua, formerly under the praetor Titus Quinctius. Gaius Hostilius Tubulus also had his *imperium* extended, and he was to succeed Gaius Calpurnius as propraetor in Etruria, at the head of two legions. There was also an extension of Lucius Veturius Philo's *imperium*, and he was to have Gaul as his province as before, but now as propraetor, and with the same two legions with which he had held it as praetor. The Senate also decided that what was done for Lucius Veturius should also apply to Gaius Aurunculeius who, as praetor, had had Sardinia as his province, with two legions under his command, and the proposal to extend his *imperium* was brought before the people. Aurunculeius was further assigned, for the defence of his province, fifty warships that Publius Scipio would be sending from Spain.

Publius Scipio and Marcus Silanus were both also assigned the provinces they currently held in Spain, along with their armies, for a year.* Scipio was ordered to send over to Sardinia fifty of the eighty ships* now under his command that he had brought with him from Italy or captured at New Carthage. For there were rumours of intensive naval preparations in Carthage that year, and it was said that the Carthaginians would blockade the entire coastline of Italy, and of Sicily and Sardinia, too, with two hundred vessels.

In Sicily, the division of resources went as follows. Sextus Caesar was given the army from Cannae. Marcus Valerius Laevinus, who also had his *imperium* extended, was to take over the fleet of seventy ships lying off Sicily, and to that number he was to add thirty vessels that had been off Tarentum the year before. With this hundred-strong fleet, he would, if he concurred, cross to Africa on raiding expeditions. Publius Sulpicius also had his *imperium* extended for a year; with the fleet he already commanded he was to take responsibility for Macedonia and Greece. There was no change made in arrangements for the two legions stationed at the city of Rome, and the consuls were authorized to raise supplementary forces wherever necessary. The defence of the Roman empire that year rested on twenty-one legions.

The urban praetor Publius Licinius Varus was also assigned the task of refurbishing thirty old warships docked at Ostia, and furnishing twenty new ships with crews. He would thus have a fleet of fifty vessels to patrol the coastline in the vicinity of the city of Rome. Gaius Calpurnius was ordered not to move his army from Arretium before the arrival of his successor. Tubulus, like Calpurnius, was also instructed to be particularly on his guard against any subversive designs amongst people there.

23. The praetors now left to take up their assignments, but religious concerns detained the consuls: after a number of prodigies had been reported, they were having difficulty obtaining favourable omens. From Campania had come reports of lightning striking two temples in Capua—those of Fortuna and Mars—as well as a number of tombs. At Cumae it had been announced that mice had been gnawing at some gold in the temple of Jupiter—such are the trivialities in which misguided superstition sees divine intervention!—and at Casinum that a huge swarm of bees had settled in the forum. At Ostia, it was said that the city wall and a gate had been struck by lightning;

at Caere, that a vulture flew into the temple of Jupiter; and, at Volsinii, that the lake was suffused with blood. A day of public prayer was held because of these prodigies, and over a number of days full-grown victims were sacrificed without favourable omens being attained— it was a long time before the favour of the gods was regained. In fact, the deadly events thus prophesied actually came down on the consuls' heads, and the state remained out of harm's way.

The Games of Apollo had first been celebrated by the urban praetor Publius Cornelius Sulla, in the consulship of Quintus Fulvius and Appius Claudius. Since then all the urban praetors had celebrated them, but they made the vow for one year only and had no fixed date for the celebration. That year a serious epidemic broke out which spread through the city and the countryside, but it led to chronic rather than fatal illness. Because of the epidemic, prayers were offered at crossroads throughout the city and, in addition, the urban praetor Publius Licinius Varus was instructed to bring a bill before the people that a vow be made promising the games as a permanent fixture on a set date. Varus was the first to make the vow in these terms, and he celebrated the games on 5 July. That date was subsequently kept a holiday.

24. As for the people of Arretium, the reports grew daily more serious, and the concerns of the senators were increasing. Gaius Hostilius was therefore sent written orders not to put off taking hostages from the people of Arretium; and Gaius Terentius Varro, to whom Hostilius was to deliver them to be taken to Rome, was sent to the town with *imperium*. When Varro arrived, Hostilius immediately ordered one of the legions that was encamped before the city to advance into it, and he deployed armed units at strategic points. Then, after summoning the senators, he made his demand for the hostages in the forum. When the senate requested a two-day period to consider the matter, Hostilius proclaimed that they must hand them over immediately, or else he would take all the children of the senators the following day.

The military tribunes, allied officers, and centurions were then ordered to keep watch on the gates to prevent anyone leaving the city during the night. This was done in a rather slack and careless manner, however, and, before nightfall, seven leading members of the senate slipped away with their children before sentinels were posted at the gates. Their absence was noticed at dawn the next day, when there was a roll-call of senators in the forum; and their property was sold off. A hundred and twenty hostages were taken from the remaining senators, these being the senators' own children, and they were handed over to Gaius Terentius Varro to be escorted to Rome.

In the Senate, Varro made the whole situation look more threatening than it had seemed earlier. Accordingly, since an uprising in Etruria appeared imminent, Gaius Terentius himself was instructed to take a single legion—one of the two urban legions—to Arretium, and with it secure the city. It was also decided that Gaius Hostilius should make a sweep of the whole province with the rest of the army, and take measures to ensure that subversive elements were given no opportunity for insurrection.

When Gaius Terentius reached Arretium with his legion, he demanded from the magistrates the keys to the city gates, but the magistrates claimed the keys could not be found. Varro believed they had been dishonestly removed rather than lost through inattention, and he had different keys made for all the gates, and carefully saw to it that he had everything under his control. He warned Hostilius with some urgency that his only hope of avoiding an Etruscan insurrection lay in taking steps ahead of time to make insurrection impossible.

25. After that, the issue of the Tarentines became the subject of heated debate in the Senate, in the presence of Fabius. Fabius was himself defending the people he had actually captured in war, but others were hostile, many claiming that their crime was as great as the Capuans' and their punishment should be, too. A senatorial decree was passed, on a motion by Manius Acilius, that the town should be garrisoned, with all Tarentine citizens confined within the walls, and the whole question left in abeyance, to be considered afresh when Italy was in a calmer state.

There was as much dispute over Marcus Livius, the commander in the citadel of Tarentum. Some wanted to censure him in a senatorial decree, on the grounds that it was thanks to his negligence that Tarentum was betrayed to the enemy; others proposed rewarding him for having defended the citadel over a five-year period, and then being primarily responsible for Tarentum's recapture. Those between the extremes stated that it was to the censors, not the Senate, that responsibility for examining Livius' record belonged. And Fabius was of this opinion. He added, however, that he allowed that it was thanks to Livius that Tarentum was recovered, as Livius' friends had often declared in the Senate. For, he said, the town would not have had to be recovered if it had not been lost.

One of the consuls, Titus Quinctius Crispinus, set off for Lucania with supplementary troops to join the army that had been commanded by Quintus Fulvius Flaccus. As for Marcellus, religious problems arose in quick succession to prick his conscience and keep him in Rome. One such was the matter of his having promised a temple to Honos and Virtus* at Clastidium during the Gallic War, and its dedication now being regularly obstructed by the pontiffs. The pontiffs claimed that it was not proper for a single shrine to be dedicated to more than one god. In the event of a lightning-strike, or some supernatural phenomenon within it, they said, expiation would be a problem, in that one could not be sure to which deity sacrifice should be made; for, except in the case of certain gods, one victim could not properly be sacrificed to two deities. And so a shrine to Virtus was added, the work being hurriedly carried out, but the temples were not, in fact, dedicated by Marcellus himself. Marcellus then finally set off with reinforcements for the army he had left at Venusia the year before.

Because he believed that the recovery of Tarentum had earned Fabius a great reputation, Crispinus attempted to blockade Locri in Bruttium. He had sent for all kinds of artillery and siege-engines from Sicily, and he had had ships brought from there, too, to make an assault on the seaward part of the city. But the blockade was raised because Hannibal had moved his forces to Lacinium, and also because of a rumour that Crispinus' colleague, Marcellus, with whom he wished to join up, had already led his army from Venusia. Crispinus therefore moved back into Apulia from Bruttium, and at a point between Venusia and Bantia the consuls established their two camps less than three miles distant from each other. As the war had now been diverted from Locri, Hannibal also returned to this same region. Both consuls were impetuous by nature, and they deployed their battle lines almost on a daily basis, fully confident that the war could be brought to an end if the enemy engaged the two consular armies that were now united.

26. Hannibal had been both a winner and a loser in his two engagements with Marcellus the previous year. While, therefore,

neither hope nor fear was unreasonable on his part, if he had to fight the same man, he did think that he would be no match at all for the two consuls together. He therefore focused entirely on his old strategy, and began to search for a location for an ambush. There were, however, a number of skirmishes between the two camps, producing mixed results. The consuls believed the summer could be drawn out with such encounters, and, thinking that an offensive against Locri could also be mounted, they sent written instructions to Lucius Cincius to cross from Sicily to Locri with his fleet. To make an assault on the walls possible from the land, as well, they gave orders for part of the army that was garrisoning Tarentum to be brought to Locri.

Hannibal learned of this scenario from some people of Thurii, and he sent men to lie in ambush on the road from Tarentum. There, at the foot of the hill of Petelia, 3,000 cavalry and 2,000 infantry were placed in hiding. The Romans walked into them without conducting reconnaissance, and fell into the trap. Close to 2,000 men were killed, and about 1,500 taken alive. The rest scattered in flight and returned to Tarentum through the fields and woods.

A tree-covered hill lay between the Carthaginian and Roman camps.* At first neither side took possession of it: the Romans were unaware of the features of the side of the hill facing the enemy camp, and Hannibal had considered it better suited for an ambush than an encampment. Hannibal had therefore sent a number of Numidian squadrons there during the night for this purpose, and hidden them in the middle of the wood. In the daytime, none of the men would move from the position for fear that their arms, or they themselves, might be spotted from afar. In the Roman camp, the troops were noisily demanding that the hill be seized, and secured with a fort; otherwise, they said, if it were seized by Hannibal, they might have the enemy virtually at their throat. This made Marcellus sit up. 'Why do we not ourselves go and reconnoitre with a few horsemen?' he said to his colleague. 'Seeing for ourselves will give us a better idea of what to do.' Crispinus agreed, and they set off with 220 cavalrymen, 40 from Fregellae and the rest from Etruria.* Along with them went the military tribunes Marcus Marcellus, son of the consul, and Aulus Manlius, as well as the two allied officers Lucius Arrenius and Manius Aulius.

Some have recorded that the consul Marcellus conducted a

sacrifice that day, and that after the first victim had been slaughtered the liver was found to be lacking its 'head'.* In the second animal everything normally there was found in place, and there was in fact an enlargement in the 'head', but the priest was not at all pleased to find entrails simply too propitious appearing after those which were undersized and deformed.

27. In fact, the consul Marcellus was so eager to engage the enemy that he would say that their respective camps were never close enough to each other. And, on that occasion, as he emerged from his defence-works, he gave the signal for each man to be ready at his post; they were to gather up the baggage and follow should the hill that they were going to reconnoitre prove to their liking.

Before the camp lay a small stretch of flat ground, and from it a road ran up the hill, completely open to view from every direction. When the Numidians had been put in position, there was no expectation of a great opportunity like this coming their way; there was just the hope that they could intercept men who strayed too far from their camp looking for food or wood. But now their scout gave them the signal to emerge, all at the same time, from their hiding-places. Those who had to rise up from the brow of the hill, right in front of the Romans, did not let themselves be seen until men had made their way round to cut off the path to their rear. Then they all sprang out on every side, and attacked with a shout. The consuls were in a hollow, unable to climb the slope occupied by the enemy, and yet having no way to beat a retreat because they were surrounded at the rear. The engagement could, nonetheless, have gone on longer, had the Etruscans not started to flee, striking panic in the others. Even so, deserted though they were by the Etruscans, the Fregellan cavalry did not give up the fight, as long as the consuls were unwounded and kept things going, shouting encouragement, and themselves participating in the action. But then they saw both consuls receive wounds, with Marcellus run through by a lance and slipping from his horse, on the point of death. At that they, too, the very few still surviving, took to flight, along with the consul Crispinus, who had been struck by two javelins, and the young Marcellus, who was also wounded.

The military tribune Aulus Manlius fell in the battle, and of the two allied officers Manius Aulius was killed and Lucius Arrenius taken prisoner. Five of the consul's lictors fell into enemy hands alive, and the others either perished or made good their escape with the consul. Forty-three cavalrymen went down, either in the engagement or as they fled, and 18 were taken alive.

There had been uproar in the camp, the men clamouring to go to the consuls' aid, but then they saw the consul and the other consul's son, both of them wounded, and the meagre remains of the ill-starred expedition, return to camp.

The death of Marcellus was a matter for great regret in any case. But it was the more so because he had blindly thrown himself, his colleague, and, one might almost say, the entire republic into a reckless situation, and that was not in keeping with his age—he was then more than sixty—or the caution one would have expected from a seasoned commander.

It would involve me in many detours around a single episode were I to try to follow up in detail all the variant accounts of Marcellus' death. Let me pass over others and focus on Coelius, who gives three different sequences of action. One is the traditional version; the second comes from the text of the eulogy given by the son, who participated in the action; and the third is one that Coelius presents as having been researched and established by himself. But while there is variation in the story, most report that Marcellus left camp to reconnoitre, and all that he was caught in an ambush.

28. Hannibal felt the death of one of the consuls and the wounding of the other had truly terrified his enemy. Not to let slip any opportunity, he immediately moved his camp to the hill on which the engagement had taken place. There he found and buried Marcellus' body. Crispinus, daunted both by his colleague's death and his own wound, left the following night, when all was quiet, and encamped on the first mountains he reached, in an elevated spot offering protection on all sides.

The two commanders then revealed their ingenuity, one trying to set a trap, the other to avoid one. Hannibal had taken possession of Marcellus' ring when he found the corpse, and Crispinus, fearing the seal might be craftily used by the Carthaginian for some forgery, had sent messengers around the nearby communities to inform them that his colleague had been killed, and that the enemy had his ring. He warned them not to put their trust in any letter written in Marcellus' name. This message from the consul had reached Salapia slightly before a letter, written in Marcellus' name, was brought from

Hannibal.* This stated that Marcellus would be coming to Salapia the night of that very day, and the soldiers in the garrison should be at the ready in case he needed their services for anything. The people of Salapia saw through the trick. They thought Hannibal was look- ing for a way to punish them, angry not simply over their abandon- ing his cause, but also at the killing of his cavalrymen.* They sent back the messenger (who was, in fact, a Roman deserter) so that their soldiers could do what they wanted done without being observed. They then placed townspeople on watch along the walls and at stra- tegic points in town, put sentries and patrols on high alert for the night, and posted the strongest troops they had in the garrison at the gate by which they thought the enemy would come.

Hannibal approached the city at about the fourth watch, and at the front of his column were Roman deserters bearing Roman arms. When they reached the gate, these men, all speaking Latin, called out the watchmen and told them to open up since the consul was coming. Just as if they had been woken by the shouts, the watchmen bustled and scurried about, and strained to open the gate. The port- cullis had been lowered, and some now used crowbars, others ropes, to raise it, bringing it up to a sufficient height for men to be able pass under it standing up. No sooner was there enough room for them to pass than the deserters came racing through the gateway. When about 600 had entered, the rope holding it was released and the portcullis came down with a loud crash. A number of the Salapians then attacked the deserters who, anticipating a peaceable reception, had their arms nonchalantly slung from their shoulders after their march; others stood on the gate towers and the walls, and chased off the enemy with stones, stakes, and javelins.* So it was that Hannibal left the area, hoist with his own petard. He set off to raise the siege of Locri, which had now been started by Lucius Cincius, who was conducting an all-out attack with siege-works and all sorts of artillery that he had brought from Sicily.

By this time Mago felt little confidence in his ability to hold and defend the city of Locri, and his first glimmer of hope arrived with the news of Marcellus' death. Right after that came the message that Hannibal had sent ahead his Numidian cavalry and was himself mak- ing all possible haste to follow up with his infantry column. And so, as soon as Mago learned, from a signal from the watchtower, that the Numidians were approaching, he himself suddenly flung open the gate, and made a defiant sortie against the enemy. The battle at first hung in the balance, more because Mago had taken the Romans by surprise than because he could match them in strength. Then the Numidians arrived on the scene, and the Romans were struck with such panic that they bolted in disorder to the sea and their ships, abandoning the siege-works and equipment they had been using to pound the walls. So it was that the siege of Locri was raised by Hannibal's arrival.

29. When Crispinus discovered that Hannibal had left for Bruttium, he ordered the military tribune Marcus Marcellus to lead off to Venusia the army that had been under his colleague's command. He himself left for Capua with his own legions, barely able to stand the jolting of his litter, such being the severity of his wounds. He also wrote a letter to Rome about his colleague's death, and the great danger in which he now found himself. He could not, he said, come to Rome for the elections. He felt he would be unable to stand the rigours of the journey, and he was concerned about Tarentum— Hannibal might take his army there from Bruttium. He should, he added, be sent some representatives of the Senate, discerning individuals with whom he could discuss his wishes vis-à-vis state policy.

When this letter was read out, it brought deep sorrow over the death of one of the consuls and grave concern about the other. The Senate therefore sent Quintus Fabius the younger to the army in Venusia, and three senatorial representatives—Sextus Julius Caesar, Lucius Licinius Pollio, and Lucius Cincius Alimentus (who had returned from Sicily a few days earlier)—were sent to the consul. The representatives had instructions to inform the consul that, if he were unable to come in person to Rome for the elections, he should appoint a dictator, within Roman territory, to supervise them. They were also to say that, if the consul left for Tarentum, it was the will of the Senate that the praetor Quintus Claudius should lead his legions from the town to where he could offer protection to the greatest number of cities belonging to Roman allies.

During that same summer Marcus Valerius crossed from Sicily to Africa with a fleet of a hundred ships. Landing at the city of Clupea, he inflicted widespread devastation on the countryside, and met virtually no armed resistance. The marauding troops were then swiftly brought back to the ships because word suddenly came that a Punic fleet was approaching. The fleet numbered eighty-three ships, and the Roman admiral fought a successful engagement against them not far from Clupea. Eighteen ships were captured and the rest put to flight. Valerius then returned to Lilybaeum with ample spoils from his land operations and the sea battle.

That same summer* Philip answered an appeal for assistance from the Achaeans. Machanidas, tyrant of the Spartans, had been causing them great distress with a war on their border, and the Aetolians, too, had been conducting raids on them with forces that they ferried on ships across the strait between Naupactus and Patrae (locally called 'Rhion'). There was also a report that the king of Asia, Attalus,* was about to cross to Europe because, at their most recent council meeting, the Aetolians had conferred on him their people's highest office.

30. Philip therefore made his way down into Greece, and was met at the city of Lamia by the Aetolians. They were led by Pyrrias, who had been elected praetor for that year along with Attalus (who was elected in absentia), and they had with them auxiliary forces from Attalus, as well as about 1,000 men that Publius Sulpicius had sent them from the Roman fleet. Philip fought two successful battles against this general and these forces, killing about 1,000 of the enemy in each of them. Daunted by this, the Aetolians subsequently kept within the walls of the city of Lamia, and Philip therefore led his army back to Phalara. This is located on the Malian Gulf, and it was once heavily populated because of its excellent harbour, the safe anchorages in the vicinity, and other advantages for communication by sea and land.

Ambassadors from King Ptolemy of Egypt, and also from Rhodes, Athens, and Chios, came to Philip at Phalara, their mission being to bring an end to the conflict between him and the Aetolians. The Aetolians also invited Amynander, king of the Athamanians, and a neighbour of theirs, to the negotiations as a peace-broker. But everybody's concern was less for the Aetolians, a people more aggressive than Greeks usually are, than for keeping Philip and his kingdom out of the affairs of Greece, where they would constitute a serious threat to the states' independence. Discussion of peace was held over for the council meeting of the Achaeans, and a venue and date for that meeting was established, with a thirty-day truce obtained for the interval.

The king then left Phalara and came through Thessaly and Boeotia to Chalcis in Euboea. He had heard that Attalus was heading for Euboea with a fleet, and he wanted to keep him from its harbours or from landing on its coastline. Leaving a force in Chalcis to face Attalus, in case he made the crossing in the meantime, Philip then set off with a few cavalrymen and light infantry, and came to Argos. There, by the vote of the people of Argos, he was given charge of the Festival of Hera, and of the Nemean Games, because the Macedonian kings claim descent from that city-state. When the Festival of Hera was finished, he went straight from the event to Aegium for the council meeting of his allies, which had been scheduled quite some time before.*

At the meeting there was discussion of ending the Aetolian war so that neither the Romans nor Attalus would have reason to enter Greece. But, with the truce barely expired, all such plans were upset when the Aetolians heard that Attalus had reached Aegina, and also that a Roman fleet was anchored off Naupactus. Invited to attend the council of the Achaeans, at which the deputations involved in the peace discussions at Phalara were also present, the Aetolians at first complained only about some minor infractions of the agreement during the truce. They ended, however, by declaring that hostilities could not be terminated unless the Achaeans restored Pylus to the Messenians, and unless Antintania were given back to the Romans, and the Ardiaei to Scerdilaedus and Pleuratus.

Philip naturally felt it was outrageous that the conquered party should be offering terms to him, the conqueror. He stated that, even on the previous occasion, it was not from any hope of non-aggression on the part of the Aetolians that he had listened to peace proposals, and concluded a truce. He simply wanted to have all his allies witness that he had sought grounds for peace and the Aetolians grounds for war.

And so, without achieving peace, Philip adjourned the council. He left behind 4,000 troops as protection for the Achaeans, and accepted their offer of five warships. These, he had decided, he would add to the Carthaginian fleet recently sent to him and to the ships coming from King Prusias in Bithynia; and with this force he would challenge in a naval battle the long-standing Roman supremacy at sea in the region. Philip himself went back to Argos from the meeting. For now the date of the Nemean Games was close at hand and he wanted them honoured by his presence.

31. While the king was preoccupied with organizing the games, and was allowing himself more relaxation during the days of the festival season than he could on campaign, Publius Sulpicius set sail with his fleet from Naupactus, and put in at a point between Sicyon and Corinth. Here Sulpicius inflicted widespread destruction on farmlands renowned for their fertility, and the news called Philip away from the games. He set off swiftly with his cavalry, ordering the infantry to follow behind. He attacked the Romans as they wandered in disorder through the fields, heavily laden with plunder and with no fear of such an attack, and he drove them back to their ships. The Roman fleet then returned to Naupactus, not at all pleased with its haul of booty.

For Philip, the remainder of the games had been given added lustre by the circulating report of the victory he had won—slight though it was, it was over the Romans!—and the days of the event were celebrated with effusive joy. This was heightened all the more by a popularity-seeking gesture on the part of the king, who set aside his diadem, his purple robe, and the rest of his royal apparel, and put himself, in appearance, on a level with everybody else. Free societies love nothing more than this. In fact, he might, by such a gesture, have given people some sure hope for their personal freedom, had he not made the whole scene one of filth and degradation by his unconscionable debauchery. Day and night he would prowl around the homes of married men with one or two companions, and the less noticeable he was by bringing himself down to the level of a private citizen, the greater the licence he took. In fact, liberty, of which he had given others only the illusion, he had turned entirely to profligacy in his own case. For he did not always gain his ends by money or seduction, but went so far as to add violence to his scandalous behaviour, and for husbands and parents alike it was perilous to check the king's sexual appetite with an inconvenient moral firmness. Even one of the most important of the Achaeans, Aratus, saw his wife taken from him (her name was Polycratia) and whisked off to Macedonia with the promise of a royal marriage.*

After spending the Nemean Festival in such debauchery, Philip stayed on a few extra days and then set off for Dymae. His objective was to drive out from Elis an Aetolian garrison that had been invited, and subsequently admitted, into the city by the Eleans. The Achaeans, and their commander-in-chief Cycliadas, met the king at Dymae.

The Achaeans felt a passionate hatred for the people of Elis for distancing themselves from the other Achaeans, and were furious with the Aetolians who, they thought, had incited the Romans to war against them, as well. With their armies united, they set off from Dymae and crossed the River Larisus, which separates the territory of Elis from that of Dymae.

32. The first day of their entry into enemy territory they spent on looting. The following day they approached the city with their battle line formed up, having first sent ahead cavalrymen to provoke the Aetolians—a race ever ready to charge their enemy—by riding up to the gates.

What the aggressors did not know was that Sulpicius had crossed from Naupactus to Cyllene with fifteen ships, that he had set ashore 4,000 soldiers, and that he had entered Elis in the dead of night to prevent his column being sighted. As a result, the surprise at recognizing Roman standards and armour amongst the Aetolians and Eleans struck sheer terror into them. At first, the king wanted to pull back his troops. Then, seeing his men under pressure in a clash that had started up between the Aetolians and the Tralles, an Illyrian tribe, he himself charged a Roman cohort with his cavalry. In the process his horse was run through by a javelin, unseating the king and flinging him over its head to the ground. A struggle flared up, furious on both sides, with the king under attack from the Romans, and his own men trying to protect him. The king himself put up a remarkable fight, although he was obliged to go into battle on foot amidst his horsemen. Then, when the struggle became one-sided, and men were falling or being wounded in large numbers all around him, he was seized by his men and put on another horse, on which he fled the field.

On that day Philip encamped five miles from the city of Elis, and on the next he led out all his troops against a nearby stronghold of the Eleans, called Pyrgus, having heard that a crowd of peasants and their livestock had been driven there through fear of plundering expeditions. In the initial panic caused by his arrival he captured this unarmed rabble, and the plunder taken compensated for his humiliation at Elis. As Philip was dividing up the plunder and the prisoners (which totalled 4,000 men, and roughly 20,000 farm animals of all kinds), a message arrived from Macedonia. A certain Aeropus, he was told, had captured Lychnidus, after bribing the officer in command of the citadel and the garrison. The man was also in control of a number of the villages of the Dessaretii and was even rallying the Dardani to his cause. Philip therefore abandoned the Achaean/Aetolian conflict, though he left in place 2,500 fighting men of all categories, under the leadership of Menippus and Polyphantas, to provide protection for his allies. Leaving Dymae, he made his way through Achaea, Boeotia, and Euboea, and after a ten-day march reached Demetrias in Thessaly.

33. At Demetrias, other messengers met the king with news of more serious trouble. They told him that the Dardani had been streaming into Macedonia, that they were now occupying Orestis and had come down as far as the Argestaean plain. It was also rumoured amongst the barbarians, they said, that Philip had been killed. Now during the operation on which Philip fought the raiders near Sicyon, he had crashed into a tree when his horse bolted, and there he broke off, on a projecting tree-branch, one of the horns on his helmet. The horn had been found by an Aetolian, taken into Aetolia, and brought to Scerdilaedus, who was familiar with this decorative feature of the helmet. That was what spread the rumour that the king had been killed. After the king's departure from Achaea, Sulpicius set off with his fleet for Aegina, where he joined up with Attalus. The Achaeans fought a successful battle against the Aetolians and Eleans not far from Messene; and King Attalus and Publius Sulpicius went into winter quarters on Aegina.

The consul Titus Quinctius appointed Titus Manlius Torquatus dictator for the conduct of elections and the games, but then, at the close of this year, died as a result of his wound (some sources place his death in Tarentum, others in Campania). And so had arisen a circumstance unparalleled in any war to date: without fighting a battle of any consequence, two consuls had been killed, leaving the state parentless, as it were. The dictator Manlius appointed Gaius Servilius, then serving as curule aedile, as his master of horse. On the first day of its session, the Senate instructed the dictator to stage the same Great Games that the urban praetor Marcus Aemilius had put on in the consulship of Gaius Flaminius and Gnaeus Servilius, and which Aemilius had also promised in a vow would be celebrated five years after that time. The dictator then staged the games, and also made a vow that they would be celebrated again five years later.

However, two consular armies were now very close to the enemy and without leaders. All else was therefore put aside, and there was but one pressing concern for the senators and people: electing consuls as soon as possible, and electing men possessed of a valour that could resist Punic duplicity. Throughout the war, they reasoned, the impulsive and hot-headed character of the commanders had brought disaster, and in that very year the consuls had fallen into a trap they failed to see through being too eager to engage the enemy. But the fact is that the immortal gods had shown pity on the Roman people by sparing the guiltless armies and making the consuls themselves pay for their recklessness with their own lives.*

34. The senators were casting about for potential consuls, and one man, Gaius Claudius Nero, stood head and shoulders above the rest. The problem was finding a colleague for him. And though the senators considered Nero an excellent candidate, they also thought him rather too impetuous and volatile for the present military situation and an enemy like Hannibal. They thought his hasty character needed to be tempered by being paired with a cool-headed and prudent colleague.

A possibility was Marcus Livius who, at the end of his consulship many years before, had been convicted of a crime* by the popular assembly, a disgrace he had so taken to heart that he moved to the country and, for many years, avoided the city and all public gatherings. Some seven years after his condemnation, the consuls Marcus Claudius Marcellus and Marcus Valerius Laevinus had brought him back to town, but he wore old clothes, had long hair and a long beard, and in his demeanour and expression showed that he clearly remembered the humiliation to which he had been subjected. The censors Lucius Veturius and Publius Licinius forced him to have his hair and beard cut, and to put aside his rags; and they had him attend Senate meetings, and carry out other duties of public life. Even then, however, he would utter only one word in support of a motion, or silently vote for it. Until, that is, the time arrived when the case of his relative, Marcus Livius Macatus, came up, and the man's reputation was at stake. That made Livius stand up and give his opinion before the Senate. Being heard now, after such a long time, he had everybody's eyes riveted on him, and he became a topic of conversation. He had not deserved the wrong he had been done by the people, said the senators, and, in so dangerous a war, the state had suffered a grave loss in not availing itself of the help or advice of a man of such qualities. They further noted that Gaius Nero could be given neither Quintus Fabius nor Marcus Valerius Laevinus as his colleague, because the election of two patrician candidates was disallowed;* and the same argument applied in the case of Titus Manlius (who, in any case, had refused the consulship when offered it, and would do so again). They would have an excellent pair of consuls, they concluded, if they put Marcus Livius alongside Gaius Claudius as his colleague.

The people had no objection to this idea raised by the senators. The only man in the community against it was the one on whom the office was being conferred, and he accused his fellow citizens of capriciousness. They had not felt compassion for him as a defendant in rags, he said, and now they were offering him the white toga,* which he did not want. This meant offices and punishments being heaped on the same man! If they thought him a good man, why had they condemned him as a criminal and a lawbreaker? If they had found him guilty, why entrust him with a second consulship, after wrongly entrusting him with the first? When he produced these and similar arguments and criticisms, the senators reprimanded him. They reminded him of Marcus Furius Camillus, who was actually a recalled exile when he restored his native city to her erstwhile position from which she had been unseated.* One must soothe one's country's anger, like that of one's parents, they said, simply by patient acceptance of it. By their concerted efforts they were then able to make Marcus Livius consul alongside Gaius Claudius.

35. Two days later the praetorian elections were held, and Lucius Porcius Licinus, Gaius Mamilius, Gaius Hostilius Cato, and Aulus Hostilius Cato were elected praetors. When the elections were over, and the games had been held, the dictator and his master of horse resigned their positions. Gaius Terentius Varro was sent into Etruria as propraetor so that Gaius Hostilius, relieved of his responsibility there, could proceed to Tarentum and take over the army that the consul Titus Quinctius had commanded. Lucius Manlius had a diplomatic mission overseas in Greece, where he was to keep watch on developments. Also, the Olympic Games were to be held that summer, at which there would be large crowds of spectators from around Greece; and so Manlius was also to attend this meeting, if he could get a safe passage through the enemy. Thus he could urge any Sicilian refugees from the war who were in attendance, or any

citizens of Tarentum driven out by Hannibal, to return home, and make them aware that the Roman people were restoring to them all the property that they had owned before the war.

Since it looked as if the oncoming year would be fraught with danger, and there were no consuls in office in the republic, all eyes turned to the consuls designate. People wanted them to conduct a provincial sortition at the earliest opportunity; they wanted each of them to know ahead of time the province he would have, and the enemy he would face. There was also discussion in the Senate, initiated by Quintus Fabius Maximus, of reconciling the two. The animosity between them was well known, and in Livius' case his personal misfortune had made it even more bitter and acrimonious, believing as he did that, in his time of adversity, he had been treated with disdain. He was therefore the more unrelenting of the two, and he insisted there was no need of a reconciliation, that they would each pay greater care and attention to every detail so that a colleague with a grudge would not have the chance to profit from his mistake. Nevertheless, the Senate had its way: the feuding was set aside, and they carried out their public duties with harmony and cooperation.

Their provinces were not geographically connected as in previous years, but set apart at the two ends of Italy. One was assigned Bruttium and Lucania, to counter Hannibal, and the other Gaul, to counter Hasdrubal (who was, word had it, already approaching the Alps). The consul drawing Gaul as his province* was instructed to take his pick of the two armies located respectively in Gaul and in Etruria, along with which he would also be assigned the troops stationed in the city. The one to whom responsibility for Bruttium fell was to mobilize new city legions, and take over one of the two armies—the choice was his—of the previous year's consuls. The army remaining after the consul had made his choice was to be taken by the proconsul Quintus Fulvius, whose *imperium* was to run for a year. The Senate had already substituted Tarentum for Etruria as Gaius Hostilius' province, and now they substituted Capua for Tarentum. Hostilius was assigned one legion, which had been commanded by Fulvius the year before.

36. Concern over Hasdrubal's advance on Italy was growing by the day. First, Massiliot ambassadors had reported that he had made the passage into Gaul, and that his coming had created a flurry of excitement amongst the Gauls because he was said to have brought a

large amount of gold to hire mercenaries. Then came a communiqué from Sextius Antistius and Marcus Raecius, who had been sent on an official fact-finding mission from Rome along with the Massiliot ambassadors. The two had informed the Senate that they had sent men, along with Massiliot guides, to make a detailed report based on intelligence gathered from Gallic chieftains, who had ties of hospitality with the guides. And, they said, they were certain that Hasdrubal would cross the Alps the following spring with the huge army he had now assembled, and that the only thing stopping him at that time was the inaccessibility of the Alps in winter.

Publius Aelius Paetus was elected and installed as augur in place of Marcus Marcellus, and Gnaeus Cornelius Dolabella was installed as *rex sacrorum* in place of Marcus Marcius, who had died two years earlier. In this same year the census-purification was performed by the censors Publius Sempronius Tuditanus and Marcus Cornelius Cethegus. The number of citizens in the census came to 177,108, a figure considerably smaller than it had been before the war.* It is on record that, in that year, for the first time since Hannibal's invasion of Italy, the Comitium was provided with shade. It is further recorded that the Roman Games were repeated for one day by the curule aediles Quintus Metellus and Gaius Servilius, and also that the Plebeian Games were repeated by the plebeian aediles Gaius Mamilius and Marcus Caecilius for two days. These aediles also offered three statues at the temple of Ceres. There was, moreover, a feast to Jupiter to mark the games.

Gaius Claudius Nero and Marcus Livius then entered office as consuls, Livius for the second time. Having already held the sortition for their provinces as consuls designate, they ordered the praetors to hold the sortition for theirs. The urban jurisdiction fell to Gaius Hostilius, but he was further assigned the foreigners' jurisdiction so that the three other praetors could leave the city for their respective duties. Sardinia fell to Aulus Hostilius, Sicily to Gaius Mamilius, and Gaul to Lucius Porcius. A total of twenty-three legions was then apportioned amongst the magistrates' areas of responsibility, as follows. The consuls were to have two legions each, and Spain would be allocated four. The three praetors would take two each, to serve in Sicily, Sardinia, and Gaul respectively. Gaius Terentius would have two in Etruria, Quintus Fulvius two in Bruttium, Quintus Claudius two in the area of Tarentum and the Sallentini, and Gaius Hostilius

Tubulus would have one in Capua. Two city legions were also to be raised. The people elected tribunes for the first four legions so allocated, and the consuls sent tribunes to the others.

37. Before the consuls could leave there was a nine-day ceremony because a shower of stones had fallen at Veii. Following the mention of one prodigy, there was the usual phenomenon of others being reported. Lightning was said to have struck the temple of Jupiter and the Grove of Marica at Minturnae, and the city wall and a gate at Atella. To make their report more alarming, the people of Minturnae added that a stream of blood had flowed in a gateway of the temple. At Capua a wolf had come through a gate at night and badly mauled a guard. These prodigies were expiated with full-grown sacrificial animals, and, by decree of the pontiffs, there was a one-day period of public prayer. The nine-day ceremony was then held again because a shower of stones had been observed in the Armilustrum.*

No sooner was the public conscience quit of religious concerns than a report came to trouble it once more. At Frusino, it was said, a child had been born the size of a four-year old, and it was not its size that excited wonder as much as the fact that, as was the case at Sinuessa two years earlier, it was unclear at its birth whether it was male or female. Soothsayers brought in from Etruria declared it to be a foul and loathsome prodigy, that the child should be taken from Roman territory, kept from all contact with the ground, and sent to the bottom of the sea. It was then placed, alive, in a box, taken out to sea, and thrown in.

The pontiffs also decreed that three groups of nine young girls should proceed through the city singing a hymn. The girls were in the temple of Jupiter Stator familiarizing themselves with the hymn, which was a composition by the poet Livius,* when the temple of Queen Juno on the Aventine was struck by lightning. The soothsayers interpreted this as a prodigy affecting only married women* and said the goddess needed to be appeased with a gift. Accordingly, married women with homes in the city of Rome, or within ten miles of the city, were summoned to the Capitol by an edict of the curule aediles. The women then selected twenty-five of their number as those to whom they should bring a small contribution from their dowries. From the money collected, a golden bowl was made as a gift for the goddess; it was taken to the Aventine, where, with ritual purification and cleansing, sacrifice was offered by the married women.

A date for a second sacrifice to the same goddess was immediately fixed by the decemvirs, and the order of ceremonies was as follows. Two white cows were led into town, through the Porta Carmentalis,* from the temple of Apollo, and behind them were carried two statues of Queen Juno, made from cypress wood. Then came the twenty-seven young girls, dressed in long robes, singing the hymn to Queen Juno. In those days the hymn might, to the rude intellects of the time, have seemed to have some merit, but cited now it would be thought tasteless and uncouth. The train of girls was followed by the decemvirs wearing laurel garlands and the *toga praetexta*. The celebrants proceeded from the gate into the Forum, along the Vicus Iugarius. The procession halted in the Forum where the girls, passing a cord through their hands, moved forward beating their feet in time with their singing. Then, going by way of the Vicus Tuscus and the Velabrum, they came through the Forum Boarium as far as the Clivus Publicius and the temple of Queen Juno. There the two victims were sacrificed by the decemvirs, and the cypress-wood statues were carried into the temple.

38. With the gods ritually placated, the consuls held a troop-levy, and did so with greater vigour and intensity than anyone remembered levies being conducted in previous years. The fact was that the dread occasioned by the war had been doubled by the advance of a new enemy into Italy, and, in addition, the pool of young men from which they could enrol soldiers was smaller. Accordingly, they forced even the colonists on the coast to provide soldiers, though they were said to have an inviolable right to exemption. When the colonists refused, the consuls publicly announced a date on which each of them was to bring before the Senate the grounds for their exemption. On the appointed day the following peoples were represented at the Senate: Ostia, Alsium, Antium, Anxur, Minturnae, Sinuessa, and (from the Adriatic coast) Sena. They all read out their agreements granting them exemption, but in none of the cases, except those of Antium and Ostia, was the agreement considered valid while an enemy remained in Italy. Even in the case of those two colonies, men of fighting age were bound by oath not to spend more than thirty nights outside the walls of their colony for as long as the enemy remained in Italy.

The entire Senate thought that the consuls should take the earliest possible opportunity to go into battle. Hasdrubal had to be confronted during his descent from the Alps so that he could not foment unrest among the Cisalpine Gauls or in Etruria, which was already looking for a chance to rebel. Hannibal, too, had to be kept occupied with his own campaign so there would be no possibility of his leaving Bruttium and meeting his brother. Livius, however, was hesitant. He had little confidence in the armies assigned to his areas of responsibility, whereas his colleague could choose from two fine consular armies and a third which was under the command of Quintus Claudius at Tarentum. He had also raised the suggestion of recalling slave volunteers to service. The Senate gave the consuls carte blanche to draw supplementary troops from any source they wished, to select any troops they liked from all the armies, and to conduct exchanges and transfers from the provinces of any men they thought would serve the state well.

All these measures were put into effect by the consuls, who acted in perfect harmony. Slave volunteers were drafted into the nineteenth and twentieth legions. Some authorities state that, for this campaign, Marcus Livius was also sent powerful auxiliary forces from Spain* by Publius Scipio, and that these comprised 8,000 Spaniards and Gauls, about 2,000 legionaries and 1,800 cavalrymen, a mixture of Numidians and Spaniards. They add that Marcus Lucretius brought these troops by sea, and that Gaius Mamilius also sent approximately 3,000 archers and slingers from Sicily.

39. The alarm in Rome was heightened by a letter from the praetor Lucius Porcius in Gaul, reporting that Hasdrubal had moved from his winter quarters and was already making his way over the Alps. Hasdrubal had mobilized and put under arms 8,000 Ligurians, said Porcius, and these would join him once he had crossed into Italy, unless someone were sent into Liguria to keep them occupied with a war there. His own army was weak, he added, but he would advance as far as he thought he could in safety.

The letter obliged the consuls to complete their troop-levy post-haste, and leave for their provinces earlier than they had intended. Their plan was for each to keep the enemy bottled up in his province, and not permit them to meet up or join forces. They were greatly aided in this strategy by an erroneous assumption on Hannibal's part. Although he had expected his brother to cross into Italy that summer, Hannibal thought back on his own experiences—the Rhône crossing, and then the Alps, and five months of battling men and the terrain—and he did not anticipate that Hasdrubal's journey would be anything like as easy and swift as it turned out to be. And thanks to that, he was late moving out of his winter quarters.

In fact, everything went more quickly and easily for Hasbrubal than either he himself or anyone else had expected. For not only did the Arverni, and then other Gallic and Alpine tribes, welcome his coming, but they even went to war alongside him. Furthermore, he was leading his army along a path which, impassable earlier, had now, thanks to his brother's crossing, become a largely open thoroughfare.* And, in addition, their route lay through peoples whose character had now been softened, thanks to the Alps being regularly traversed over a twelve-year period. For, before that, having had no visits from outsiders, and not being accustomed to setting eyes on a stranger in their land, they were xenophobic towards the entire human race. At first, in fact, they had no idea of the Carthaginian's destination, and they had believed that his objective was their rocky homes and strongholds, and plunder in the shape of animals and men. Then word had reached them of the Punic War with which Italy had been ablaze for eleven years, making it clear that the Alps was merely a passageway, and that two mighty cities, separated from each other by a large expanse of sea and land, were in a struggle for power and dominion.

Such were the factors that had opened up the Alps for Hasdrubal. However, what he had gained by the speed of his march a delay at Placentia—on which he mounted an unsuccessful blockade rather than a direct assault—subsequently cancelled out. Hasdrubal had thought the town, lying on a plain, would be easy to take, and the renown of the colony had induced him to make the attempt. By destroying that city, he thought, he would strike terror in all the others. He not only slowed his own progress by the siege but he had also held up Hannibal, who was moving from his winter quarters after receiving news that his brother's crossing had gone much faster than he had expected. For Hannibal now began to take into account what a slow process the investment of cities was, and he also remembered how unsuccessful his own attempt on that same colony had been on his victorious return from the Trebia.

40. The consuls set off from the city, in opposite directions, for what were almost two simultaneous wars, and that only increased people's worries. For they recalled the disasters that Hannibal's initial arrival had brought on Italy, and they were also tortured by the question of what gods would be so kind to the city and empire as to grant the state success on both fronts at the one time. To that point, they had kept things going by compensating for reverses with successes. When Roman fortunes had taken a fall at Trasimene and Cannae, victorious campaigns in Spain had raised them again. Later, when successive defeats in Spain had partly destroyed two armies, and two fine commanders had been lost, numerous successes in Italy and Sicily had come along to support the shaken republic. Besides, the geographic separation—the fact that one of the theatres of war lay at the world's end—had given them some breathing space. Now, however, two wars had been brought into Italy; two famous commanders stood on different sides of the city of Rome, and it was on one spot that the whole brunt and burden of this perilous war had become focused. The first of the two to gain a victory would join forces with the other in a matter of days. They were also frightened because of the previous year, darkened by the deaths of the two consuls.

Such were the cares tormenting people when they sent off the consuls as they left for their assignments. It is recorded that Quintus Fabius gave a warning to Marcus Livius, still full of resentment towards his fellow citizens, as he left for the campaign. Fabius told him not to be hasty in engaging before he got to know the sort of enemy he was facing, to which Livius replied that he would take the field the moment he set eyes on the enemy's column. When asked why he was in such a hurry, Livius retorted: 'Either I shall acquire a brilliant reputation from the enemy, or I shall derive pleasure from the defeat of my fellow citizens—a pleasure well deserved, even if it is not honourable.'

Before the consul Claudius reached his province, Gaius Hostilius Tubulus attacked Hannibal with a number of light-armed cohorts as he was leading his army along the far edge of Tarentine territory* into that of the Sallentini. The Carthaginian's column was not in regular formation, and Tubulus struck terrible panic into it, killing roughly 4,000 men and capturing nine military standards. Quintus Claudius had had his troops billeted throughout the cities in the land of the Sallentini, and had moved out of winter quarters when he heard of the enemy's movement. Now, to avoid coming to grips with two armies at the same time, Hannibal struck camp from the area of

Tarentum by night, and withdrew into Bruttium. Claudius steered his army towards the Sallentini, and Hostilius, who was on his way to Capua, met up with the consul at Venusia. There, 40,000 infantry and 2,500 cavalry were selected from the two armies for the consul's operation against Hannibal. Hostilius was instructed to lead the remaining troops to Capua, where he was to hand them over to the proconsul Quintus Fulvius.

41. Hannibal now brought together all the troops that he had kept in winter quarters or in the garrisons in Bruttian territory. He then came towards Grumentum in Lucania,* hoping to recover the towns that had, out of fear, defected to the Romans. The Roman consul also marched to Grumentum from Venusia, taking care to reconnoitre the roads, and he encamped about a mile and a half from the enemy. The rampart of the Carthaginian camp seemed to be hard up against the walls of Grumentum, with a mere half-mile between them. Between the Punic encampment and the Roman lay some level ground, with treeless hills rising up to the left of the Carthaginians, and to the right of the Romans. The hills aroused misgivings in neither side, providing, as they did, no tree cover or hiding-places for an ambush.

In the middle of the level ground a number of forays from the two armies' advance posts precipitated skirmishing hardly worth the mention. It was apparent, however, that the Roman's one aim was to prevent his enemy's departure; Hannibal, on the other hand, in his eagerness to get away from there, reputedly took the field in full force. The consul Nero then resorted to the enemy's tactics, which were all the more appealing because there could be little fear of an ambush on such open hills. He ordered five cohorts, with an additional force of five maniples, to cross the mountain ridge at night, and position themselves on the far slope of the hills. Details of when the men were to emerge from ambush, and attack the enemy, he gave to the officers he was sending with them, Tiberius Claudius Asellus, a military tribune, and Publius Claudius, a prefect of the allies.

Nero himself led all his troops, infantry and cavalry, out to battle at dawn. Shortly afterwards Hannibal also put up his signal for battle, and shouting arose in the camp as his men rushed to arms. Cavalry and infantry then came racing from the Carthaginian camp and, all over the plain, they made a disordered charge at the enemy. When the consul saw their disarray, he ordered Gaius Aurunculeius, military tribune of the third legion, to send the cavalry of his legion against the enemy with all the force he could. The Carthaginians had scattered like animals all over the plain, said Nero, so much so that they could be mown down and crushed before they formed up.

42. Hannibal had not yet left the camp when he heard the shouting from the battlefield. The uproar sent him into action, and he rapidly led his other troops against the enemy. The cavalry charge had already struck panic in the closest of the Carthaginians, and the Roman infantry—the first legion and the left allied contingent—was also advancing into battle. In complete disorder, the enemy engaged with whatever chance put in their way, foot soldier or cavalryman. The battle spread as reinforcements came up, and gained intensity as more men rushed into the fray. Despite the uproar and panic all round, Hannibal might still have formed up his men as they fought—not an easy task for any but a seasoned force with a seasoned commander—had it not been for the shouting from the cohorts and maniples who came running down the hills. Hearing this behind them made the men fear that they might be cut off from their camp. They were panic-stricken, and a rout began all over the battlefield. Losses were diminished only by the camp's proximity, which made flight shorter for the demoralized Carthaginians—for the cavalry were hard on their heels, and the cohorts had attacked the flanks side-on, running downhill on a clear and easy path. Even so, more than 8,000 men were killed, and more than 700 taken prisoner, with the capture of nine military standards. The elephants had been of no use in such a swift and disordered battle, but four were killed and two captured. Losses for the triumphant Romans and their allies were around 500.*

The following day the Carthaginian made no move. The Roman commander led his troops out for the fight but, seeing no one come to face him, then gave orders for the spoils to be gathered up from the enemy dead, and for the bodies of his own men to be brought together and buried. After that, for several days in succession, Nero came forward so close to the enemy gates as to give the impression that he was making an assault. Finally, Hannibal simply left behind, on the side of the camp facing his enemy, a large number of fires and tents, and a few Numidians, who were to let themselves be seen on the rampart and at the gates. He then set off at the third watch and proceeded towards Apulia. At dawn, the Roman force came up to the rampart. The Numidians then followed the pre-arranged plan of putting in a brief appearance in the gateways and on the rampart, and, after duping the enemy for some time, they galloped off and joined their comrades on the march.

The consul now observed that all was still in the camp, and that even the few men who had been walking about at dawn were nowhere to be seen, and so he sent two horsemen forward into the camp to investigate. On learning that all was secure, he ordered the advance into the camp, and, after staying long enough only for the men to run off to gather spoils, he sounded the retreat, and led the troops back, long before the onset of night.

The next day he set out at dawn. He followed his enemy with forced marches, guided by reports and the tracks left by their column, and caught up with them not far from Venusia. There, too, there was a scrappy engagement, in which more than 2,000 Carthaginians were killed. The Carthaginian commander then headed for Metapontum, taking mountain roads by night so as to give the Romans no scope for battle. From Metapontum, Hanno, who had been the garrison commander there, was sent with a handful of men into Bruttium to put together a new army. After adding Hanno's troops to his own, Hannibal took the same roads back to Venusia by which he had come, and then went on to Canusium.* At no point had Nero relaxed his pursuit of the enemy, and when he himself was setting out for Metapontum, he had called Quintus Fulvius to Lucania so the region should not be undefended.

43. Meanwhile, after commencing the siege of Placentia, Hasdrubal had sent off four Gallic horsemen and two Numidians with a letter for Hannibal. They travelled practically the length of Italy through the midst of the enemy but, while they were following Hannibal during his withdrawal to Metapontum, they came upon roads they did not know, and ended up in Tarentum. They were then brought to the propraetor Quintus Claudius by some Romans who were out foraging in the fields. At first they tried to mislead Claudius with evasive responses, but then the threat of torture forced the truth out of them, and they told him that they were bearing a letter to Hannibal from Hasdrubal. The men and the letter, still sealed, were put in the charge of the military tribune Lucius Verginius, to be taken to the consul Claudius Nero, and an escort of two squadrons of Samnites was sent along with them.

When the company reached the consul, the letter was read, with the help of an interpreter, and the prisoners were interrogated. Claudius at that point decided that the crisis facing the state did not call for an operation based on conventional strategy, with each consul engaging the enemy assigned to him by the Senate, and functioning within his specific area of responsibility with his own army. There had to be some bold new stroke, something startling and unexpected, an enterprise that would terrify the citizens as much as the enemy, but which, successfully concluded, would turn great fear into great joy. Nero then sent Hasdrubal's letter to the Senate in Rome, and also explained his plans to the members. Since Hasdrubal was informing his brother by letter of his intention to meet him in Umbria,* Nero advised the senators to recall a legion to Rome from Capua, to hold a levy of troops in Rome, and to face the enemy at Narnia with the army from the city.

Such was Nero's letter to the Senate, but he also sent men ahead through the territory of Larinum, and that of the Marrucini, the Frentani, and the Praetutii, that is the lands through which he would be leading his army. The men were to instruct all these peoples to carry provisions from their farms and cities to the roadside, ready for his men to eat, and to bring out horses and other animals of conveyance so that there would be plenty of transport for those suffering from fatigue. Nero himself selected from his entire army the strongest citizen and allied troops, picking out 6,000 infantry and 1,000 cavalry. He announced that he intended to seize the closest city in Lucania, along with its Carthaginian garrison, and ordered this hand-picked force all to be ready for the march. He set off at night, and then veered towards Picenum. In fact, the consul was marching with all the haste he could muster to join his colleague, having left his legate Quintus Catius in charge of the camp.

44. In Rome the alarm and panic was no less than it had been two years earlier when a Carthaginian camp had been pitched before the walls and gates of the city. People were undecided whether to praise or condemn the consul's daring march, and what was most unfair was the obvious fact that judgement of it would depend on the outcome. A camp had been left without a leader close to an enemy like Hannibal, it was said, and left with an army which had been depleted of all its strength, all its elite troops. And the consul had made a show of heading into Lucania, while in fact he was making for Picenum and Gaul, leaving behind his camp whose security depended entirely on the enemy's misperception, on his ignorance of the fact that the commander and part of the army had left. What would happen, they asked, if that became known? What if Hannibal decided either to use his entire army to chase Nero and his 6,000 troops, or to attack the camp that was left wide open to looting, without strength, without supreme command, and without auspices?

The past defeats in that war, and the violent deaths of two consuls the previous year filled people with dread, and they noted that all those setbacks had occurred when there was only one enemy commander and one enemy army in Italy. Now there were *two* Punic wars in the country, two mighty armies and practically two Hannibals! For, like Hannibal, Hasdrubal was also the son of Hamilcar, and he was just as dynamic a leader as his brother. He, too, had had many, many years of training in warfare against the Romans in Spain, and he had made a name for himself through his twin victories, and the destruction of two armies with their famous commanders. In terms of the speed of his journey from Spain, at least, and his success in inciting Gallic tribes to war, he had more reason to boast than Hannibal himself! For Hasdrubal had put together this army of his in that same region where Hannibal had lost most of *his* soldiers to hunger and the freezing temperatures, which were the most wretched ways to die. Men well acquainted with the Spanish situation would make the further point that, in engaging with Gaius Nero, Hasdrubal would not be facing a commander unfamiliar to him. In fact, they said, when Hasdrubal happened to be caught in a difficult pass, he had duped and hoodwinked Nero, like a little boy, with a charade of framing terms of peace. People also assumed the enemy's military strength to be greater, and their own smaller, than was actually the case, for fear always leans towards a pessimistic analysis.

45. When he had put enough distance between himself and the enemy to be able to disclose his plan quite safely, Nero briefly addressed his men. No commander, he told them, had ever had a plan that looked more foolhardy, but was in fact more sound, than his. He was leading them to certain victory, he said. For his colleague had left for the campaign only after receiving from the Senate cavalry and infantry enough, and more, to meet his needs—forces stronger and better equipped than if he were going to face Hannibal himself—and now they themselves would tip the scale completely by whatever additional strength they brought to the fight. Once it was simply heard on the battlefield—and he would see to it that it was not heard earlier—that a second consul and a second army had arrived, that would certainly bring them victory. Hearsay decides the outcome of war, he continued, and insignificant factors push the mind towards hope or fear. And they themselves would reap nearly all the glory in the event of success—it was always the last factor in the equation that was regarded as decisive. They could see, he added, people's admiration and support for them as they marched by.

And it was indeed true that they were everywhere marching along amidst vows and prayers and words of praise from rows of men and women who had come pouring from all over the countryside. 'Defenders of the state' they called them, and 'champions of the city of Rome and her empire'. In those men's weapons and sword-arms, they declared, lay their own and their children's security and liberty. They prayed to all the gods and goddesses to grant the soldiers a prosperous journey, a successful battle and swift victory over the enemy. They prayed, too, that they would be obliged to repay the vows they had made on their behalf,* that, just as they were now anxiously sending them on their way, so, in a few days, they would come happily to meet them as they rejoiced in their victory. Then they all issued invitations, proffered gifts, and persistently entreated the men to take whatever could serve their own or their animals' needs, and take it from them rather than others. They showered everything on them without stint. The soldiers' restraint was equally impressive; they would not take anything beyond their needs. There was no dawdling, no stopping and breaking formation to eat. They marched day and night, barely giving themselves enough rest to meet the body's natural requirements.

Men had also been sent ahead to Nero's colleague to announce the army's coming and to ask whether he wanted them to arrive secretly or openly, by day or at night, and also to ask whether they would be housed in the same camp or another. Livius felt arriving secretly, during the night, was preferable.

46. The tablet had been circulated* in the camp by the consul Livius: tribunes were ordered to house tribunes, centurions to house centurions, cavalrymen cavalrymen, and foot soldiers foot soldiers. For enlarging the camp was a bad idea, Livius decided—the enemy might surmise that the other consul had arrived. In fact, packing more men into a small space to erect their tents was going to prove easier because Claudius' troops had brought with them for the operation almost nothing but their weapons. However, the column had been enlarged with volunteers as it moved along. Veterans, men whose service was over, had offered to join them, and so had younger men, who had raced to enlist. Claudius had enrolled any whose physique and bodily strength seemed to qualify them for fighting.

The camp of the other consul, Livius, was at Sena,* and Hasdrubal was only about half a mile away. So, as he drew near, Nero halted where he had cover from the mountains in order not to enter the camp before nightfall. Then the men filed in silently and were all taken to their tents, and offered hospitality, by soldiers of their own rank, amid enthusiastic rejoicing on everyone's part.

The next day there was a council of war, which the praetor Lucius Porcius Licinus also attended. Licinus had his camp beside that of the consuls, and before their arrival he had run the whole gamut of military tactics on the enemy, leading his force over the high country and seizing narrow passes to obstruct their passage, or else harassing their column with attacks to the flanks or rear. And so, on this occasion, he attended the council of war. Many at the meeting inclined to the opinion that engaging the enemy should be delayed. This would give Nero time to refresh his men, now exhausted from the journey and lack of sleep, and also allow him a few days to familiarize himself with his enemy. Nero, however, proceeded not simply to urge the other course, but abjectly pleaded with them—what had made his strategy sound was his speed, he said, and they should not now make it a risky one by delaying. It was a bluff that had left Hannibal virtually frittering away his time without attacking a camp that lacked its commander, or taking to the road to pursue him, and that bluff would not last long. But before Hannibal made a move, he explained, Hasdrubal's army could be destroyed, and they could return to Apulia. Delaying and giving the enemy time meant both betraying that camp of his to Hannibal, and also opening for him a path into Gaul, enabling him to join up with Hasdrubal at his leisure and wherever he wished. No, they should lose no time in giving the signal and going out to battle, he said. They must take full advantage of the bluff that had been pulled on the enemy who was absent and on the one who was present, while the one still did not know that he was facing fewer troops than he thought, and the other that he faced more and stronger ones. When the council adjourned, the signal for battle was put up, and they went forward immediately to battle stations.*

47. By now the enemy were standing in formation before their camp. What delayed the engagement was the fact that, as Hasdrubal rode forward before the standards, he picked out amongst the enemy old shields that he had not previously seen, and horses that were somewhat emaciated. In addition, the Roman numbers seemed unusually large. Guessing what was in fact the case, he quickly sounded the retreat. He also sent men to the river, from which the Romans were drawing their water, to take some prisoners who could be inspected for signs of more than usual sunburn, as would be found after a recent march. At the same time, Hasdrubal ordered men to ride around the Roman encampment, at a remove, and examine whether the rampart had been extended anywhere; these men were also to keep their ears open for whether there were one or two bugle-calls.

This was all duly reported back to Hasdrubal, and he was taken in by the fact that there had been no enlargement of the camps. There were two camps (just as there had been before the other consul's arrival), one belonging to Marcus Livius, and the other to Lucius Porcius, but in neither had there been any extension of the fortifications to accommodate more tents. Hasdrubal, however, was a veteran commander used to facing a Roman enemy, and the news the men brought that there had been one bugle-call in the praetor's camp, but two in the consul's, caused him some concern.* There must be two consuls there, he thought, and the question that tormented him was how one of them had slipped away from Hannibal. The last thing he could have suspected was what had actually happened, namely that Hannibal was the victim of such an enormous subterfuge that he had no idea of the whereabouts of the commander and the army that had been encamped right next to him. It must be, thought Hasdrubal, that his brother had not dared pursue the consul because he had suffered a serious defeat. In fact, Hasdrubal was very much afraid that things had gone badly wrong, that he himself had come too late to help, and that the Romans were now enjoying the same success in Italy as they were in Spain. Sometimes, though, the thought would cross his mind that his letter might not have reached Hannibal, that the consul had intercepted it and that he had now come with all speed to crush him.

Vexed by such worries, Hasdrubal had the fires extinguished, and at the first watch he gave the signal for the men to gather their equipment in silence. He then ordered them to move out. In all the consternation and confusion of the night, little attention was paid to the two guides, one of whom settled into a hiding-place, of which he had earlier made a mental note, while the other swam across the River Metaurus* at a point where he knew it was shallow. Deserted by the guides, the column at first drifted aimlessly through the country-side; and a number of men, exhausted and weary from lack of sleep, threw themselves down at various points, leaving only a few around the standards. Hasdrubal issued instructions for them to advance along the river-bank until the light should arrive to show the way. But he would double back when he lost his way along the twisting and turning banks of the winding river, and he made little headway. He decided, therefore, to cross as soon as dawn revealed a suitable fording point. But the further he retreated from the sea, the higher the banks became on both sides of the river, and he failed to find any shallow spots. Frittering away the day like this, he gave his enemy time to catch up with him.

48. Nero came on the scene first, at the head of the entire Roman cavalry; then Porcius followed with the light infantry. They harassed and charged the weary column from every direction, and the Carthaginian commander now abandoned his march, which resembled a flight, intending to lay out a camp on a knoll overlooking the river-bank. At that point Livius arrived with all the heavy infan-try, deployed and armed not for marching but for immediate engagement. The Romans then combined all their forces, and the line was arranged for battle, Claudius taking the right wing and Livius the left, with command of the centre assigned to the praetor.

Hasdrubal now gave up constructing his camp—he saw that he had to fight. He positioned his elephants in the front line before the standards. Next to them, on the left wing and facing Claudius, he set the Gauls—less because he had confidence in them than because he thought that they were feared by the enemy. The right wing, facing Marcus Livius, he took for himself and the Spaniards, and it was in these veteran troops that he placed his greatest hope. The Ligurians* were stationed in the middle, to the rear of the elephants. But the formation had depth rather than breadth, and the Gauls received cover from a hill projecting before them. The section of the front line held by the Spaniards engaged the Roman left wing, and the entire Roman right stood beyond the fighting, and for now remained out of it, the hill before them preventing them from making any frontal or flank attack.

There was a huge clash between Livius and Hasdrubal, with terrible loss of life on both sides. This was where the two commanders stood, and here stood most of the Roman infantry and cavalry, as well as the Spaniards—veteran troops acquainted with the Roman way of fighting—and the Ligurians, a tough race in battle. It was to this area, too, that the elephants were driven; with their initial charge they had caused havoc amongst the front lines, and had also made the standards give ground. Then, as the clash and shouting intensified, there was less of a possibility of controlling them, and they moved about between the two lines as though uncertain to which side they belonged, and not unlike rudderless ships.

Claudius called out to his men: 'So what was the point of covering so much ground at such speed?' as he tried, without success, to march his troops up the hill before him. When he saw it was impossible to get through to the enemy in that quarter, he withdrew a number of cohorts from the right wing, where he could see they would be standing around inactive rather than engaged in the fight. These he led around behind the fighting line, and made a charge on the enemy's left wing that surprised not only the enemy but his own side, as well. Such was the speed of the manœuvre that the cohorts made an appearance on the flank and then, at the next moment, were attacking the rear. So it was that the Spaniards and Ligurians were being cut down on every side, at the front, on the flank and at the rear, and by now the slaughter had reached the Gauls. In that quarter the fighting was the lightest. Most of the men had left their positions—they had slipped away in the night, and were lying asleep throughout the countryside—and those present were exhausted from the journey and lack of sleep, physically incapable of exerting themselves, and barely able to carry their weapons on their shoulders. And by now it was the middle of the day, and thirst and the heat left them gasping, ready to be cut down or captured in droves.

49. As for the elephants, more were killed by their own drivers than by the enemy. The drivers kept a workman's chisel and a mallet

at hand; and when the animals began to get out of control and charge their own side, the keeper would place the chisel between the ears, at the point where the neck joins the head, and drive it home with all his strength. That, it was found, was the swiftest way of dispatching a beast of such a size, once the animals left the drivers no hope of controlling them, and the first man to have instituted the practice was Hasdrubal, a leader with a great reputation for his other achievements, and above all for that battle. It was he who kept his men fighting by encouraging them, and facing the dangers with them. It was he who energized them alternating entreaties and reproaches, when they were worn out and giving up the fight from weariness and exhaustion. It was he who called back men in flight, and rekindled the battle where it had been abandoned at several points. In the end, when fortune clearly favoured his enemy, he refused to survive the great army that had followed the fame of his name, and galloped straight into a Roman cohort. There, fighting, he died a death that was appropriate for a son of Hamilcar, and brother of Hannibal.

At no time in that war were so many of the enemy killed in a single battle, and, with the loss of their commander and their army, the Carthaginians seemed to have been repaid for Cannae with a disaster of equal magnitude. The enemy dead totalled 57,000; 5,400 were taken prisoner; and there were large quantities of booty of all kinds, including gold and silver. More than 4,000 of the Roman citizens who had been prisoners in enemy hands were also recovered. That was some consolation for the soldiers lost in the battle, for it was no means a bloodless victory, with Roman and allied losses around the 8,000 mark.*

How far the victors felt they had had more than enough bloodshed and killing became clear the following day. Word came to the consul Livius that the Cisalpine Gauls and Ligurians who had either taken no part in the battle or had escaped the slaughter were retreating in a single column, with no recognized leader and no standards, and in no formation and with no system of command. They could all be wiped out if a cavalry squadron were let loose on them, he was told. 'No,' said Livius, 'let some of them survive to tell of the enemy's defeat and our courage.'

50. Nero left on the night following the battle and, moving the column along at greater speed than on his outward journey, he reached his base camp, and the enemy, in five days.* There were

smaller crowds along his route—no messenger had preceded him—but they welcomed his coming with such elation as to be almost beside themselves with joy.

As for Rome, words cannot be found to recount or describe either of its emotional states—neither that in which the city anxiously awaited the outcome, nor that with which it received the news of the victory. Throughout the days after the news arrived that the consul Claudius had left, at no time between sunrise and sunset did any senator leave the Senate house or the presence of magistrates, nor the people the Forum. Married women, unable to provide material assistance themselves, turned to prayer and appeals to heaven, roaming through all the shrines and urgently petitioning the gods with entreaties and vows.

While the city was gripped by such anxiety and tension a vague rumour arose that two riders from Narnia had reached the camp that had been set up to barricade the entrance to Umbria, and that they brought news of a massacre of the enemy. At first this merely went into men's ears without registering in their minds; the news was too great, too joyous, to be mentally absorbed or believed. Besides, the very speed of its arrival made acceptance difficult—the battle reportedly took place only two days earlier. Then a letter from Lucius Manlius Acidinus was brought from the camp, and its subject was the arrival of the two Narnian riders. That dispatch, borne through the Forum to the praetor's tribunal, brought the senators forth from the Senate house. And such was the rush and scramble with which the people converged on the doors of the Senate that the messenger could not get near it. Instead, he was pulled away by the crowds around him, who repeatedly asked him questions and noisily demanded that the letter be read out on the Rostra before it was read in the Senate. Eventually, these people were pushed aside and restrained by the magistrates, and the glad tidings could be dispensed to minds unable to cope with them. The letter was read aloud first in the Senate, and then in the popular assembly, and, depending on the individual's temperament, some felt unreserved joy, while others were going to withhold belief until they heard about it from the envoys, or a despatch from the consuls.

51. Then news came that the consular envoys themselves were coming. At that point people of all ages ran to meet them, every one of them wishing to be the first to drink in such joy with eyes and

ears, and there was one long line reaching all the way to the Mulvian bridge. The envoys were Lucius Veturius Philo, Publius Licinius Varus, and Quintus Caecilius Metellus. With crowds of people of every class milling about them, they came forward into the Forum while some asked the envoys themselves, and others their attendants, to tell them what had happened. And as each person heard the news that the enemy army and its leader were destroyed, that the Roman legions were unharmed, and that the consuls were safe, they would immediately go on to share their joy with others.

It was with difficulty that the envoys made their way to the Senate house, and with much greater difficulty that the crowd was pushed aside, to stop the public from intermingling with the senators. Then the letter was read out in the Senate, after which the envoys were taken over into the popular assembly. Once the letter had been read out there, Lucius Veturius himself gave a fuller account of the events, which was received with great approval, and finally even with noisy applause from the entire gathering—for people could barely contain their delight. Then they dispersed, some making the rounds of the temples of the gods to offer thanks, and others going home to share the happy news with their wives and children.

To mark Marcus Livius' and Gaius Claudius' destruction of the enemy commander and his legions, while preserving intact their own army, the Senate decreed three days of public thanksgiving. The praetor Gaius Hostilius made the announcement of that period of thanksgiving before an assembly, and the ceremonies were held by both men and women. All the temples saw the same large crowds throughout the three-day period, as women and their children, dressed in their finest clothes, and freed now from all fear, gave thanks to the immortal gods, as though the war were over. That victory also affected the state's financial workings; from then on people dared to carry on business as in peacetime, selling, buying, putting out loans and repaying them.

The consul Gaius Claudius had been careful to keep Hasdrubal's head, and bring it with him. When he returned to his camp, he ordered it to be tossed before the forward posts of the enemy. He also had his African prisoners put on display for the enemy, wearing their chains, and two he released, telling them to go to Hannibal and recount to him what had taken place.

Shaken by this great blow to his people as well as his family,

Hannibal is said to have stated that he now saw clearly the destiny of Carthage.* He struck camp, intending to gather together in Bruttium, in the furthest corner of Italy, all those supporting troops to whom he could not give protection if they were widely dispersed. He then moved all the people of Metapontum from their homes, along with all such Lucanians as were under his control, and took them over into Bruttian territory.

BOOK TWENTY-EIGHT

1. With Hasdrubal's crossing of the Alps, much of the war had been transferred into Italy, and there seemed to have been correspondingly less action in the Spanish theatre. Suddenly, however, hostilities again flared up here as serious as before.* At that point the Roman and Carthaginian occupation of Spain was as follows. Hasdrubal son of Gisgo had fallen back as far as the coastline of the ocean at Gades, and the shores of our sea* and practically all of eastern Spain was under the control of Scipio and Rome. A new commander, Hanno, had crossed from Africa with a fresh army to replace Hasdrubal Barca. He had joined up with Mago and had quickly put under arms large numbers of men in Celtiberia, which lies between the two seas. Scipio therefore sent Marcus Silanus to confront him with 10,000 infantry and 500 cavalry.

Silanus forced the pace of his march as much as he could, though the poor condition of the roads and narrow passes often hedged by forest—terrain frequently encountered in Spain—slowed him down. Even so he outran not only messengers who might report his arrival, but even any rumour of it, and reached the enemy guided by some local Celtiberian deserters.

When the Romans were about ten miles from the enemy, they learned from these same deserters that there were two enemy camps alongside the road they would be taking. On the left were the Celtiberians, a newly raised army of more than 9,000 men, and on the right was the Carthaginian camp. The Punic camp was well guarded, they were told, with outposts, sentries, and all the usual security features of military operations, but the other was poorly and carelessly defended, as one would expect from barbarians who were also new recruits, and whose fears were diminished because they were in their own lands. This was the one that Silanus thought should be attacked first, and he ordered his troops to keep to the left as much as possible so they would not at any point be spotted from the Carthaginian outposts. Then, sending ahead scouts, he advanced on the enemy at a rapid pace.

2. Silanus was about three miles away, and still none of the enemy had spotted him, thanks to the cover provided by the uneven terrain

and the shrub-covered hills. There was a hollow here that was deep and thus hidden from view, and in this he told his men to sit and take food. Meanwhile, scouts arrived confirming what the deserters had said. The Romans then threw all their baggage together in their midst, took up their weapons and advanced for the fight in regular battle order. They were a mile away when they were spotted by the enemy, and suddenly there was panic. Mago, too, came riding up at a gallop from his camp as soon as the shouting and uproar broke out.

There were in the army of the Celtiberians 4,000 heavy-armed troops and 200 cavalry. These constituted a full legion, and were the pick of their forces, and so Mago placed them in the front line, setting the rest, the light-armed troops, in reserve. He then led them all from the camp, formed up in this manner, and barely had they gone beyond their palisade when the Romans hurled their javelins at them. The Spaniards crouched down in the face of the enemy barrage, and then rose to hurl theirs in turn. The Romans, in their usual close formation, received them with shields locked tightly together; then they closed in and proceeded to fight with the sword. However, the broken ground rendered the speed of the Celtiberians, whose practice it was to run to and fro in the fight, ineffectual, while at the same time it did not disadvantage the Romans, who were used to stationary combat. (The only problem for the Romans was that the restricted space and clumps of bushes precluded keeping ranks and imposed a pattern of fighting individually, or two-on-two, as in a gladiatorial match.) And while the setting impeded the enemy flight, it also delivered them up, as though bound hand and foot, to slaughter. After nearly all the heavy-armed Celtiberians had been dispatched, it was the turn of the light infantry, and the Carthaginians who had come to their aid from the other camp, to be driven back and cut down. A contingent of no more than 2,000 infantry, and all the cavalry, fled the field with Mago when the battle had barely got under way. The other commander, Hanno, was taken alive, together with those who had arrived last on the field, when the battle was already lost. Almost all the cavalry, and the older men in the infantry, who followed the fleeing Mago, reached Hasdrubal in the area of Gades nine days later. The Celtiberians, the new recruits, slipped away into the woods close by and then scattered to their homes.

It was a timely victory. The war already stirred up was not terminated by it, it is true, but the makings of a future war *were* terminated, that is, the possibility that the Carthaginians, after rallying the Celtiberian people, could incite further tribes to arms. Scipio warmly praised Silanus, and now gained hope of finishing off the war, if he did not himself hold up the campaign by postponing action. He therefore marched on Hasdrubal in the furthest reaches of Spain, where the last vestiges of the conflict still remained. The Carthaginian general happened to have his camp in Baetica* to ensure the loyalty of his allies, but he now suddenly pulled out, taking his troops towards the ocean coast at Gades in what was more of a flight than a march. He decided that he would always be threatened with attack as long as he kept his army together, and so, before making the journey through the strait* to Gades, he sent off his entire army to various cities. Thus the men would have walls to defend them, and they could defend the walls with their weapons.

3. Scipio saw that the theatre of war was now widely fragmented and that taking his forces around to individual cities would be time-consuming rather than difficult, and so he turned back. But, in order not to leave the region in enemy hands, he sent his brother Lucius Scipio with 10,000 infantry and 1,000 cavalry to attack the wealthiest city in those parts, which was called Orongis by the barbarians.* The city lies in the lands of the Maesesses, a tribe of the Bastetani; it has fertile soil and there is also some silver-mining there. This served as Hasdrubal's base for his raids on peoples living in the interior of the country.

Scipio encamped close to the city, but before proceeding to the circumvallation he sent men to the gates to parley with the inhabitants at close quarters, to probe their feelings and urge them to try out the friendship, rather than the might, of the Romans. The response was not a friendly one, and so he surrounded the city with a ditch and a double rampart. He then split his army into three divisions, so as to have one always on the attack while the other two were resting. When the first division commenced the attack, there was a fierce fight which produced no clear result. Approaching the walls, and bringing up ladders, as weapons rained down on them, was no easy task. Even those who had managed to set up their ladders against the wall were thrust down with forks made especially for the purpose, or else had grappling irons thrown on them from above, so that they faced the danger of being hoisted up and dragged on top of the wall.

When Scipio realized that, because of his numerical inferiority, the chances of victory were about even, and that the enemy had the further advantage of fighting from their walls, he recalled the first division and assaulted the town with the two others together. The enemy were exhausted from fighting the first wave, and this tactic struck so much fear into them that the townspeople suddenly fled and abandoned the walls, while the Punic garrison, fearing the city had been betrayed, left their posts and gathered together in one spot.

At that point the fear came over the townspeople that, if the enemy entered the city, all those in their path would be indiscriminately butchered, whether they were Carthaginian or Spanish. And so they suddenly threw open a gate and rushed from the town in large numbers. They held out their shields before them for fear of being the target of missiles thrown at long range, but showed their empty right hands to make it clear that they had thrown their swords aside. Whether this could not be seen because of the space between them, or whether treachery was suspected is unclear, but the deserters came under attack, and were cut down just as if they were a regular battle line. Then, using the same gate, the troops took the fight into the city; and at other points, too, gates were being hacked down and broken open with axes and picks; and as each cavalryman entered, he would gallop forward, following prior orders, to secure the forum.* The cavalry had also been assigned a detachment of *triarii* as support; the legionaries made a sweep of the other areas of the city. They did not loot, and did not kill any they met, except when they met armed resistance. All the Carthaginians were put under guard, as were about 300 of the townspeople who had closed the city gates. The rest had the town put back in their hands and their property returned. In the assault on that city there were about 2,000 enemy casualties, and no more than 90 Roman.

4. Taking that particular town brought satisfaction to those involved in the operation, but it also brought satisfaction to the commander-in-chief and the rest of the army; and the men provided a fine spectacle as they arrived driving a huge crowd of prisoners before them. Scipio praised his brother in the most glowing terms, comparing the capture of Orongis with his own capture of New Carthage. But winter was now coming on, making it impossible for

him to launch an assault on Gades, or hunt down Hasdrubal's army, scattered all over the province as it was, and he therefore led all his forces back into Hither Spain. He then sent the legions off to their winter quarters, and dispatched his brother Lucius to Rome, along with the enemy commander Hanno and other prisoners of note. After that he himself withdrew to Tarraco.

That same year a Roman fleet was sent across from Sicily to Africa under the proconsul Marcus Valerius Laevinus, and this conducted widespread raids on the countryside around Utica and Carthage. Booty was actually taken off from around the very walls of Utica, on the fringes of Carthaginian territory.* As the Romans were sailing back to Sicily they were met by a Punic fleet of seventy warships. Seventeen of the Carthaginian ships were captured, and four sunk out at sea; the remainder of the fleet was driven back and put to flight. Victors on land and sea, the Romans headed back to Lilybaeum, carrying large quantities of plunder of every kind. The sea having now been made safe by this defeat of the enemy fleet, supplies of grain were shipped to Rome in large quantities.

5. The proconsul Publius Sulpicius and King Attalus passed the winter on Aegina, as noted above,* and, at the beginning of the summer in which these events occurred, they crossed from there to Lemnos with their fleets combined (there were twenty-five Roman quinqueremes and thirty-five belonging to the king). Philip also made a move. Wishing to be ready for any initiative on the part of his foe, whether he had to meet him on land or sea, he came down in person to the coast at Demetrias, and proclaimed a date for his army to muster at Larisa.

At the news of the king's coming, embassies from his allies converged on Demetrias from all parts. This was because the Aetolians had felt a surge of confidence thanks to their alliance with Rome, and also after the arrival of Attalus, and were making predatory raids on their neighbours. And the Acarnanians, Boeotians, and the inhabitants of Euboea were not alone in feeling great alarm; so, too, did the Achaeans who, apart from the Aetolian war, were also being intimidated by the Spartan tyrant Machanidas, who was encamped not far from the borders of Argos. All these allies gave an account of the dangers threatening their various cities by land and sea, and made a plea for assistance from the king.

Even the reports from Philip's own kingdom indicated no peaceful state of affairs there. Scerdilaedus and Pleuratus were up in arms, he was told, and some of the Thracian tribes, especially the Maedi,* would overrun the parts of Macedonia closest to them should the king be preoccupied with a long war. The Boeotians and peoples of the interior of Greece were also reporting that the pass at Thermopylae, at the point where the road is restricted in a narrow defile, was being blocked by the Aetolians with a ditch and a palisade in order to deny Philip passage to defend the cities of his allies.

Even a listless commander would have been galvanized to action by so many emergencies all round him. Philip dismissed the embassies with a promise to bring assistance to them all as time and circumstances permitted. Peparethus was, for the moment, the most pressing item on his agenda—word had come from there that Attalus had taken a fleet across from Lemnos and had laid waste all the countryside around the city—and he sent a garrison to protect the town. He also sent Polyphantas with a modest force into Boeotia, and to Chalcis he sent an officer of his royal guard, Menippus, with a thousand peltasts (the *pelta* is a shield not unlike the *caetra*). Menippus was given an additional force of 500 Agrianes to enable him to defend all areas of the island.

Philip himself left for Scotussa, and gave orders for Macedonian troops to be brought over to that town from Larisa. At Scotussa it was reported to him that a council meeting of the Aetolians had been scheduled at Heraclea, and that King Attalus would be coming to discuss with them the overall direction of the war. Philip then led his troops by forced marches to Heraclea in order to disrupt the meeting by suddenly appearing on the scene. The meeting had, in fact, been adjourned before his arrival; but the crops in the fields were close to ripeness, and, before leading his troops back to Scotussa, Philip made a thorough job of destroying them, especially along the Gulf of the Aenianes.* He then left his entire army at Scotussa, and withdrew to Demetrias with only his royal guard. After that, to enable him to counter any enemy move, he sent men into Phocis, Euboea, and Peparethus to pick out elevated locations from which beacons would be visible. Philip himself installed a lookout post on Tisaeus, a mountain with an enormously high peak, so that from fires raised at distant points he could in a moment receive intelligence on any of his enemy's operations.

The Roman commander and King Attalus sailed from Peparethus

over to Nicaea, and from there they moved the fleet across to the city of Oreus in Euboea. (When one leaves the Gulf of Demetrias heading for Chalcis and Euripus, Oreus is the first of the Euboean cities on the left-hand side.) An arrangement was made between Attalus and Sulpicius that the Romans would make the attack from the sea, and the king's forces would do so by land. **6.** It was three days after the fleet put in that they commenced their assault on the city; the intervening time had been spent on secret discussions with Plator, who had been put in command of the city by Philip.

The city has two citadels, one overlooking the sea and the other in the centre of town. From the latter a road leads down to the sea by an underground passageway, and at that time it was safeguarded where it reached the sea by a first-rate defence-work, a five-storey tower. It was in this sector that fierce fighting first broke out: the tower had been equipped with projectiles of all kinds, and in addition artillery and siege-engines had been put ashore from the ships for an attack on it. While the struggle diverted everyone's attention, and all were looking on, Plator let in the Romans through the gate of the citadel that was beside the sea, and the citadel was taken in a moment. The townspeople, driven back, headed for the other citadel in the city centre—and there men had been posted to close the gate on them. Shut out like that, they were cut down or captured between the two citadels. The Macedonian garrison stood massed together beneath the wall of the citadel; it had not run off in panic, but it had not joined the battle with determination either. With Sulpicius' permission, Plator put the men aboard some ships and set them ashore at Demetrium in Phthiotis.* Plator himself then went back to join Attalus.

Emboldened by his easy success at Oreus, Sulpicius immediately headed for Chalcis with his victorious fleet, but there the result in no way matched his expectations. Here the sea forms a channel, wide at both extremities but then becoming a narrow strait, giving anyone first looking at it the impression of a double harbour with two mouths at opposite ends—but one would be hard pressed to find a more inhospitable mooring for a fleet. From the high mountains on both sides sudden squalls come rushing down. In addition, the actual strait, the Euripus, does not ebb and flow seven times daily at regular intervals, as people say; rather, surging this way and that as capriciously as a wind, it hurtles along like a torrent on a sheer mountainside. As a result, night or day, there is no calm mooring for ships.

The fleet faced not only an inhospitable anchorage, but also a town that was unflinching in its resolve and impregnable. It was enclosed on one side by the sea, while on the landward side it was superbly fortified and well secured, thanks to its strong garrison and especially to its steadfast officers and dignitaries—so different from Oreus with its wavering and fleeting loyalties. It had been a foolhardy enterprise, and the Roman now showed good judgement. Taking account of the difficulties involved and not wishing to waste time, he swiftly abandoned the venture and moved his fleet across to Cynus in Locris. Cynus serves as the mercantile centre of the city of Opus, and lies a mile from the sea.

7. Philip had been sent warning of this move by the beacon signals from Oreus but, thanks to the treachery of Plator, they had been put up on the lookout too late for him to react; in addition, he was outclassed in naval strength, which made it difficult for his fleet to reach the island. Because of the time that had been lost, he abandoned the attempt, instead moving swiftly to relieve Chalcis, when he received the signal. Chalcis is also, in fact, a city on the same island, but the strait by which it is separated from the mainland is so narrow that it is linked by a bridge, which makes access to it easier by land than by sea.

Philip therefore advanced from Demetrias to Scotussa, and then left Scotussa at the third watch. He successfully dislodged and put to flight the Aetolian garrison blockading the pass at Thermopylae, driving his panic-stricken enemy into Heraclea, and then, in the space of a single day, he marched more than sixty miles to Elatia in Phocis.*

It was on that day, too, or thereabouts, that the city of Opus was being sacked by King Attalus after its capture. Sulpicius had conceded the rights to the booty from the city to the king because, a few days earlier, Oreus* had been sacked by the Roman soldiery, with the king's men having no part in it. The Roman fleet then retired to Oreus, but Attalus, unaware of Philip's approach, continued to fritter away time extorting money out of the important citizens of Opus. So unexpected was Philip's attack that Attalus might well have been overwhelmed but for a number of Cretans, who, it happened, had gone quite some distance from the city in search of forage, and had spotted the enemy column in the distance. Attalus' men were without weapons and out of formation. They made a disordered rush towards the sea and their ships, and, as they were trying to unmoor the ships, Philip came on the scene, causing great confusion among the sailors, even from the shoreline. Philip then returned to Opus, railing against gods and men for his having lost the opportunity of such a rich prize, an opportunity filched from him almost before his eyes. The people of Opus were also subjected to his resentful outburst. They could have held out against the siege until his arrival, he said, instead of practically conceding defeat at the first sight of the enemy.

After settling affairs at Opus, Philip left for Torone.* Attalus also left the area. Initially he went to Oreus, but when it was reported to him that King Prusias of Bithynia had invaded his kingdom, he abandoned his Roman venture and the Aetolian War, and sailed to Asia. As for Sulpicius, he withdrew his fleet to Aegina, his point of departure at the start of spring.

Philip had no greater difficulty taking Torone than Attalus had had in taking Opus. The town was inhabited by refugees from Phthiotic Thebes who, when their city had been captured by Philip, had thrown themselves on the mercy of the Aetolians. The Aetolians had then given them a home in this city, which had been laid waste and left deserted after an earlier war, also fought against Philip. After his recovery of Torone, which was just mentioned, Philip left the town, and took Tithronion and Drumiae, small towns of little consequence in Doris. He then came to Elatia, having already issued orders for representatives from Ptolemy and the Rhodians to await him there.

At Elatia there was some discussion of ending the Aetolian War; for the representatives had recently attended the council of the Romans and Aetolians at Heraclea. During the discussion news was brought that Machanidas had decided to attack the Eleans while they were preparing to celebrate the Olympic Games. Philip thought this should be his top priority, and so he dismissed the representatives with the accommodating answer that he had not been responsible for the war, and he would not stand in the way of peace, provided that it could be concluded on equable and honourable terms. After that he set off with a lightly equipped column, coming down through Boeotia to Megara and then Corinth. At Corinth he picked up supplies and headed for Phlius and Pheneus. Reaching Heraea, he heard that

Machanidas, alarmed at news of his coming, had beaten a retreat back to Sparta, and the king therefore withdrew to Aegium to attend the council of the Achaeans. Philip also thought that he would find at Aegium the Punic fleet that he had sent for in the hope of making some gains by sea. The Carthaginians had, however, left for the Oxeae Islands a few days earlier, and had then headed for the Acarnanian ports when they heard that Attalus and the Romans had set off from Oreus. They were afraid that, if they were attacked within the strait of Rhium (that is, the narrowest point within the Corinthian Gulf), they would be crushed.

8. Philip was upset and annoyed. He had moved rapidly in every case, he reflected, and yet had failed to be on time for any of these emergencies; and fortune had scoffed at his swiftness by sweeping away every opportunity out of his view. In the meeting, however, he concealed his bitterness and spoke with a confident optimism. He called gods and men to witness that in no place and at no time had he failed to head, as fast as was humanly possible, to wherever the clash of the enemy's weapons had been heard. In fact, he said, it was difficult to decide which was greater, his spirit for fighting the war, or his enemy's wish to flee from it. Hence Attalus' slipping through his fingers at Opus and Sulpicius at Chalcis, and now, in the past few days, Machanidas, too. But one does not always succeed in running away, and, anyway, a war cannot be considered arduous in which one achieves victory merely by coming into contact with the enemy. The most important factor, he said, was that he now had the enemy's admission that they were no match for him. He would soon have a clear victory, and the enemy would find their fight with him no more successful than they themselves expected.

His allies were pleased with the king's address. Philip then turned Heraea and Triphylia over to the Achaeans, but restored Aliphera to the people of Megalopolis because they provided adequate evidence that it had been part of their territory. After that he crossed to Anticyra with some ships furnished to him by the Achaeans (three quadriremes and the same number of biremes). From there he put to sea with seven quinqueremes and more than twenty skiffs—these he had earlier sent into the Corinthian Gulf to join the Carthaginian fleet—and landed at Erythrae, an Aetolian town close to Eupalius. He did not take the Aetolians by surprise. All the men in the fields, or in the nearby fortresses of Potidania and Apollonia, fled into the forests and hills, but in their haste they were unable to drive off with them their farm animals, which were taken as booty and put aboard the ships. Philip sent Nicias, the praetor of the Achaeans, to Aegium with the livestock and the rest of the plunder. He then proceeded to Corinth, and from there had his land forces taken overland through Boeotia.

Philip himself set sail from Cenchreae and, skirting Attica and rounding Sunium, arrived at Chalcis, virtually passing through the midst of enemy fleets. He had high praise for the townspeople's loyalty and courage—neither fear nor selfish hopes had swayed them, he said—and he urged them to remain committed to their alliance in future, if they preferred their lot to that of the peoples of Oreus and Opus. He next sailed from Chalcis to Oreus, where he put the government, and defence of the city, in the hands of those of its leading citizens who, when the city was taken, had chosen flight over surrender to the Romans. After that he crossed from Euboea to Demetrias, from which he had first set off to bring aid to his allies.

At Cassandrea Philip then laid down the keels for fifty warships, and assembled shipwrights in large numbers to complete the work. Attalus' departure and the timely assistance Philip had himself brought to his beleaguered allies had now left conditions tranquil in Greece, and so he retired to his kingdom to begin hostilities against the Dardanians.

9. At the end of the summer during which this took place in Greece, Quintus Fabius, son of Quintus Fabius Maximus, was sent by the consul Marcus Livius as his representative to the Senate in Rome. Fabius reported to the Senate that the consul believed Lucius Porcius and his legions were sufficient protection for his province of Gaul, and that he personally could leave the province and the consular army could be withdrawn. The senators then not only ordered Marcus Livius to return to the city, but ordered his colleague Gaius Claudius Nero to do so, as well. The only difference in the instructions for the two was that Marcus Livius' army was to be brought back, while Nero's legions that were facing Hannibal were to remain in his sphere of authority. The consuls had agreed through correspondence that, as they had one policy in their conduct of matters of state, so they would reach the city at one and the same moment, despite coming from opposite directions. Whoever reached Praeneste first was under orders to await his colleague there.

It transpired that the two men reached Praeneste on the same day. From there, they sent ahead official notification for the Senate to hold a plenary session at the temple of Bellona three days hence, and then they came towards the city, where the whole population came streaming out to meet them. It was not simply a case of people milling around them and greeting them; they all wanted to touch the victorious sword-arms of the consuls, some offering words of congratulation, others expressions of gratitude because, thanks to them, the state had been saved. In the Senate the consuls, following the practice of all commanders, gave an account of their achievements, and then requested, as their due for their energetic and successful conduct of state affairs, that honour be paid to the immortal gods, and that they be permitted to enter the city in triumph. The senators replied that they were certainly ready to grant their requests, in recognition of the services of the gods first of all, then of the consuls. And so public thanksgiving in the names of the two men, and a triumph for them, were officially sanctioned, but an arrangement was made between the consuls that, since their military operation had been a cooperative effort, they would not hold separate triumphs. The triumphant exploit, it was noted, had taken place in Marcus Livius' province, and the auspices also happened to be Livius' on the day of the battle. In addition, Livius' army had been brought back to Rome, while Nero's could not be taken out of his province. Accordingly the agreement was that the soldiers should follow Marcus Livius, who would enter the city in a four-horse chariot, and Gaius Claudius would ride in on a horse, and without soldiers.

The sharing of the triumph in this way enhanced the renown of both men, but more so that of the one who conceded recognition to the other while surpassing him in merit. That man on the horse, people would say, raced the whole length of Italy in the space of six days, and, on the day on which he fought a pitched battle with Hasdrubal in Gaul, he had Hannibal believing that he was encamped opposite him in Apulia. So, they reasoned, one consul had defended both halves of Italy and faced two commanders who were superb generals, using his strategy to combat one and meeting the other in the flesh. Nero's name had sufficed to keep Hannibal pinned down in his camp, they said, and what had overthrown and destroyed Hasdrubal if not that man's arrival on the scene? So the other consul could ride high in his many-horsed chariot if he wished, but it was on one horse that this triumphal procession was really travelling through the city. Even if he were on foot, it would be Nero who would remain in people's minds, they said, thanks to the glory he won in that war, or his disregard for it in that triumph.

Such were the comments from spectators,* who attended Nero all the way to the Capitol. The money the consuls brought to the treasury amounted to 3,000,000 sesterces and 90,000 bronze *asses*. Marcus Livius gave each of his soldiers 56 *asses*, and Gaius Claudius promised to give his own men, now absent, the same amount when he returned to his army. It has been observed that, when the soldiers engaged in their banter,* Gaius Claudius was on that day the butt of more songs than was their own consul. It has also been noted that the *equites* had high praise for the legates Lucius Veturius and Quintus Caecilius, whom they urged the plebs to make the following year's consuls, and that the consuls threw their weight behind this early recommendation of the *equites*. For the next day, at an assembly of the people, they commented on the courageous and loyal services that they had received from the two legates in particular.

10. As election time was approaching and it had been decided that the elections would be held by a dictator, the consul Gaius Claudius appointed his colleague Marcus Livius dictator, and Livius in turn appointed Quintus Caecilius master of horse.* Lucius Veturius and Quintus Caecilius, who was also master of horse at the time, were duly declared consuls elect by the dictator Marcus Livius. The praetorian elections were held next, and the men elected were: Gaius Servilius, Marcus Caecilius Metellus, Tiberius Claudius Asellus, and Quintus Mamilius Turrinus, who was at the time a plebeian aedile. The elections completed, the dictator resigned his office, disbanded his army, and, in accordance with a senatorial decree, left for Etruria, which was to be his sphere of responsibility. Here he was to hold enquiries into which peoples of Etruria and Umbria had considered seceding from the Romans to Hasdrubal when he was due to arrive in the area, and which had helped Hasdrubal with troops, supplies, or in any other way. Such were that year's events at home and abroad.

The Roman Games were repeated three times in their entirety by the curule aediles Gnaeus Servilius Caepio and Servius Cornelius Lentulus. The Plebeian Games were also once repeated in their entirety by the plebeian aediles Marcus Pomponius Matho and Quintus Mamilius Turrinus.

In the thirteenth year of the Punic War, the consuls Lucius Veturius Philo and Quintus Caecilius Metellus were both assigned Bruttium as their area of responsibility so they could continue operations against Hannibal. In the praetorian sortition that followed, Marcus Caecilius Metellus received the urban jurisdiction, Quintus Mamilius the foreigners' jurisdiction, Gaius Servilius Sicily, and Tiberius Claudius Sardinia.

The distribution of the armies was as follows. To one of the consuls went the army that Gaius Claudius* had commanded as consul the previous year, and to the other that which Quintus Claudius had commanded as propraetor—two legions, in each case. In Etruria, the proconsul Marcus Livius was to take over the two legions of slave volunteers from the propraetor Gaius Terentius (Livius had already received a year's extension to his *imperium*). It was further decided that Quintus Mamilius should transfer his jurisdiction to his colleague, and take over Gaul, along with the army that Lucius Porcius had commanded as praetor. Mamilius had orders to lay waste the agricultural lands of the Gauls who had defected when Hasdrubal arrived. Gaius Servilius was, like the previous governor Gaius Mamilius, assigned the task of defending Sicily with the two legions from Cannae. The old army that Aulus Hostilius had commanded was shipped out of Sardinia, and the consuls raised a new legion which Tiberius Claudius was to take over with him to the island. Extensions of *imperium* were accorded to Quintus Claudius and Gaius Hostilius Tubulo so that they could have Tarentum and Capua respectively as their spheres of authority. The proconsul Marcus Valerius, who had overseen the defence of the coastline of Sicily, was instructed to transfer thirty ships to the praetor Gaius Servilius, and return to the city with the rest of his fleet.

11. In the suspense that gripped the city at such a critical juncture of the war, people attributed every incident, favourable or unfavourable, to divine intervention, and portents were reported in large numbers. At Tarracina the temple of Jupiter was said to have been struck by lightning, at Satricum the temple of Mater Matuta. No less frightening for the people of Satricum were two snakes that slithered into the temple of Jupiter, actually entering by the door. From Antium came news that men harvesting wheat thought the

ears of wheat were bloodstained. At Caere a two-headed pig was born, and a lamb that was both male and female. At Alba, it was said, two suns had been seen, and at Fregellae daylight appeared during the night. In the area of Rome it was claimed that an ox had talked, that in the Circus Flaminius the altar of Neptune had sweated profusely, and that the temples of Ceres, Salus, and Quirinus had been struck by lightning.

The consuls were instructed to use full-grown victims to expiate these prodigies, and to hold a single day of public prayer, and this was carried out in accordance with a decree of the Senate. But what frightened people more than all the prodigies, whether reported from outside the city or seen at home, was the fire going out in the temple of Vesta (for which the Vestal who had been on watch that night received a flogging at the order of the pontiff Publius Licinus). Although this was the result of human negligence, and was not a divinely sent portent, it was still decided that atonement should be made with full-grown victims and that public prayers should be offered at the temple of Vesta.*

Before leaving for the war, the consuls were urged by the Senate to take measures to bring the plebeians back to the land. Thanks to heaven's blessing, said the Senate, the conflict had been removed from the city of Rome and from Latium, making it possible to live in the countryside without fear; and it was absurd to pay more attention to Sicilian agriculture than Italian.* But this was no easy matter for the people. Free farmers had been swept away by the war; there was a shortage of slave labour; livestock had been plundered; farmhouses had been destroyed and burned. Even so, under the pressure of consular authority, large numbers did return to the land. Discussion of the issue had been prompted by complaints made by delegations from Placentia and Cremona that their agricultural land was being raided and pillaged by their Gallic neighbours. Most of their colonists had disappeared, they said, and they were now left with sparsely populated cities and countryside that was a desolate wilderness. The praetor Mamilius was given the responsibility of protecting the colonies against the enemy, and in accordance with a decree of the Senate the consuls gave official notice that all citizens of Cremona and Placentia were to return to their colonies by a specified date.

Then, at the start of spring, the consuls themselves also left for the war. The consul Quintus Caecilius assumed leadership of Gaius

Nero's army, and Lucius Veturius that of the propraetor Quintus Claudius, making up its numbers with soldiers he had enrolled himself. The consuls marched their troops into the territory of Consentia. This they plundered far and wide, but the column, now heavily laden with booty, was set upon by some Bruttians and some Numidian javelin-throwers in a narrow pass, putting at risk not only the men with the plunder but anyone carrying arms as well.* However, it was more of a brawl than a battle, and after sending the booty ahead the legions reached cultivated land without losses. From there they set off into Lucania, where the entire population once more accepted its submission to the Roman people without a fight.

12. There was no encounter with Hannibal that year. After the recent blow that had fallen both on his country and on him personally, he did not offer battle, and while he remained inactive the Romans did not provoke him. Such were the powers they thought that one leader possessed, even if all else was falling apart around him! And I am inclined to think the man was more admirable in adversity than when things were going well for him.* He had been fighting a war in his enemy's country, so far from home, over a period of thirteen years, with mixed success. He had an army that was not made up of his own countrymen, but was a mixture scraped together from all nations with no shared features in terms of law, culture, or language; they were dissimilar in appearance and in dress, with different arms, religious rites and practices, and almost with different gods. But he fused them together with some sort of bond, so successfully that there was never any seditious behaviour, either amongst the men themselves or towards their commander, despite the fact that in enemy territory Hannibal was often short of money for their pay and short of provisions as well. In the First Punic War there had been atrocious incidents involving the commanders and the men because of the lack of such things. Hannibal's hope of victory had rested entirely in Hasdrubal and his army, and when they were wiped out, and Hannibal abandoned the rest of Italy, retiring into a corner of the country in Bruttium, who could not find it amazing that there was no mutiny in his camp? For, in addition to everything else, there was the further problem that the only way he could hope to feed his army was from the farmland of the Bruttii, and this, even were it all under cultivation, was too small to feed a force of such magnitude. Furthermore, most young men had been swept away from

agriculture by the war, which kept them otherwise employed, as had the inbred practice of their nation of merging their military activities with marauding. And no supplies were being sent to him from home, either, since the Carthaginians were preoccupied with maintaining their hold on Spain, as though all was proceeding well in Italy.

In Spain, things were in one way going much the same as in Italy, in another very differently. They were the same inasmuch as the Carthaginians had been defeated in the field with the loss of their commander, and had been pushed back all the way to the ocean on the farthest coast of the country. But they were also different in that Spain, thanks to its geography and the character of its people, was a country better fitted not just than Italy, but than any other part of the world, for reviving a flagging war. That is why Spain was the first of the provinces acquired by the Romans, at least on the mainland, but the very last to be totally subdued—which did not, in fact, happen until our day, under the command and auspices of Augustus Caesar.*

Hasdrubal son of Gisgo, who was the greatest and most famous Carthaginian leader after the Barcas, had at that time returned from Gades in hopes of renewing hostilities. With the assistance of Mago son of Hamilcar he held troop-levies throughout Further Spain and put under arms roughly 50,000 infantry and 4,500 cavalry. On the number of mounted troops there is pretty much agreement amongst the sources; some, however, record a total of 70,000 infantry being brought to the city of Silpia.* It was at Silpia that the two Punic commanders took up a position on the open plains, determined not to refuse the offer of battle.

13. When Scipio was brought the information that this enormous army had been assembled, he thought he would be no match for such overwhelming numbers with his Roman legions unless he offered at least a show of strength by putting his barbarian auxiliaries into the field against them. On the other hand, he felt he should not have to depend on them for so much of his strength that their switching sides would be a crucial factor—it was this that had been the undoing of his father and uncle. He therefore sent Silanus ahead to Culchas,* who ruled over twenty-eight towns, to obtain from him the cavalry and infantry he had promised to raise over the winter. Scipio himself left Tarraco and came directly to Castulo, picking up small groups of auxiliaries, as he went along, from allies living along his route. At Castulo he was met by the auxiliary troops that Silanus brought,

which numbered 3,000 infantry and 500 cavalry. From there he went ahead to the city of Baecula with his entire army, which now numbered 45,000 men, citizens and allies, infantry and cavalry.*

As Scipio's men were establishing their camp, Mago and Masinissa charged them with their entire cavalry force. They could have caused serious problems for the men engaged in the defence-works had it not been for the sudden appearance of some Roman cavalry who had been concealed by Scipio behind a hill that was conveniently situated for this purpose. These now charged the enemy cavalry, who were out of formation, and right at the start of the engagement drove off the most adventurous of them, those who had ridden up closest to the earthwork and even advanced amongst the men engaged in its construction. The fight with the others, however, who had come forward in formation and in marching order, was more drawn out, and long remained indecisive. But then light-armed cohorts were brought back from the Roman outposts and the men at work on the defences were withdrawn and ordered to take up their weapons. More and more appeared on the scene, fresh men relieving the exhausted, until there was a large body of soldiers charging into battle from the camp, and after that the Carthaginians and Numidians were quite clearly in retreat. They began by disengaging in squadrons, with no panic or haste disrupting the ranks, but then the Romans started to put greater pressure on their rear, and withstanding the assault became impossible. With no thought now for their formation, they ran off in all directions, taking the shortest possible route. The morale of the Romans was considerably raised by the battle, and that of the enemy correspondingly diminished, but even so for a number of days after that there were persistent sallies made by the cavalry and light infantry on both sides.

14. When the strength of the two sides had been sufficiently tested in such mêlées, it was Hasdrubal who first led his troops into the battlefield, and then the Romans also marched forward to face them. But the two lines simply stood in formation before their respective earthworks, and no attempt to engage was made by either side. And so, when the day was coming to an end, the commanders marched their troops back to camp, the Carthaginian first, then the Roman. This sequence of events repeated itself for several days. The Carthaginian would always be the first to lead his troops from camp, and the first to sound recall when they were weary of being on their

feet. There was no charge, no spear thrown, and no battle-cry raised on either side. In the one line the Romans formed the centre, in the other a mixture of Carthaginian and African troops, and in both armies the allies were on the wings (there were Spaniards on both sides). Before the wings of the Carthaginian line stood the elephants, which, from a distance, looked like castles.*

By now the word in both camps was that they were going to fight the battle deployed as they had stood. The two centres, composed respectively of Roman and Carthaginian troops, who were the people responsible for the war, would meet each other, with morale and strength evenly matched on the two sides. When Scipio saw that this notion had taken a firm hold, he deliberately changed his entire formation for the day on which he intended to engage. In the evening he passed a tablet through the camp, ordering men and horses alike to be prepared and fed before dawn. Cavalrymen, under arms, were to hold their horses bridled and saddled.*

Day had barely dawned when Scipio hurled his entire cavalry and light infantry against the Carthaginian forward posts. He then immediately advanced with his heavy-armed troops, the legionaries, but, contrary to what his own men and the enemy had been firmly expecting, he had strengthened the wings with Roman soldiers and drawn the allies away into the centre. Hasdrubal, startled by the shouting of the Roman horsemen, charged from his tent, and when he saw the mêlée before his earthwork, his own men in a panic, the legionary standards glittering in the distance, and the plain filled with the enemy, he unleashed his entire cavalry force against the cavalry of the enemy. He himself marched from the camp with his infantry column, but, in deploying his line, he made no change from the usual order.

The cavalry fight remained indecisive for a long while and in fact a decision could not be reached between them because as each side was driven back, which happened almost on an alternating basis, they could retire to safety in their infantry line. But when the infantry lines were no more than half a mile distant from each other, Scipio signalled the recall to the cavalry and, opening the ranks, brought all the cavalry and light infantry into the centre of his force. Making two divisions of them, he set them in reserve behind the wings.

After that, when it was now time to commence the battle, Scipio ordered the Spaniards, who formed the centre of the line, to advance at a measured pace. From the right wing, where he was in command, he sent a messenger to Silanus and Marcius to instruct them to lengthen their wing leftwards, as they saw him extend his to the right, and to engage the enemy with their light infantry and cavalry before the centres could meet. The two wings were accordingly extended by the addition to each of three cohorts of infantry,* and three cavalry squadrons, and of some skirmishers as well, and with these they advanced swiftly, the rest of the troops following at an angle. The line thus arched in the centre, where the Spanish troops were advancing more slowly.*

The wings had now come to grips with each other, but the veteran Carthaginians and the Africans, the strength of the enemy army, had not even reached the point where they could throw their spears. And yet they did not dare run to the wings to help their comrades there engaged since they were afraid of leaving the centre of the line open to those enemy troops heading straight for them. The wings meanwhile were under serious pressure on two fronts. The Roman cavalry, light infantry, and skirmishers had outflanked them, and were making side-on attacks; and the cohorts were bearing down on them in front, hoping to detach them from the rest of the line.

15. It was now a very uneven fight in every sector, mostly because a crowd of Balearic islanders and fresh Spanish recruits were pitted against Roman and Latin soldiery. In addition, as the day progressed, Hasdrubal's army began to lose strength. The men had been subjected to a lightning attack in the morning, and then had been forced to join the battle line quickly before they could take food to give them stamina. And indeed this was why Scipio had deliberately delayed matters to ensure that the fighting would take place late in the day, for it was only at the seventh hour that the infantry contingents charged from the wings. It was much later that the battle actually reached the centre, and the result was that the heat of the midday sun, the fatigue of standing under arms, and hunger and thirst all took their toll on the Carthaginians before they even came to grips with their enemy. So they simply stood there, supporting themselves on their shields. On top of everything else, there were also the elephants. These were driven to distraction by the cavalry, skirmishers, and light infantry with their frenzied manner of fighting, and they had moved from the wings into the centre.

As a result the Carthaginians, physically and psychologically exhausted, backed away, though they still preserved their ranks; it was as if the line were withdrawing, unbroken, at the commander's order. But when the victors observed that the battle had tilted in their favour, they piled on the pressure all the more fiercely from every side. Resisting these assaults was not easy, although Hasdrubal made every effort to try to hold the men back and stem their retreat by crying out that they had a safe haven in the hills to their rear if they withdrew gradually. Fear overpowered their sense of honour, however, and all those closest to the foe began to give ground; then suddenly they all turned and rushed off in flight. They halted first at the lower slopes of the hills, at which point the Romans hesitated to march their troops up a hill that was facing them, and the Carthaginian officers began to call their men back into position. But then the sight of the enemy standards advancing resolutely towards them made them resume their flight, and they were driven back in panic into their camp. The Romans were not far from the enemy earthwork and with their relentless thrust forward would have taken the camp, but for a downpour that followed a period of that blazing sunshine which emanates from gaps in clouds that are heavy with rain. So heavy was the rain that the victors had difficulty making it back to their own camp, and some were also prey to religious qualms about undertaking further operations that day.

The Carthaginians were weak from their exertions and their wounds, and the stormy night was calling them to a rest they sorely needed; but the fearful danger they faced permitted them no time to relax, as the enemy were sure to attack the camp at dawn. They built up their earthwork with stones that they accumulated from all the gullies in the surrounding area, hoping to defend themselves with fortifications, since they could not count on their weapons for adequate protection. But then the desertion of their allies made flight appear a safer prospect than staying where they were.

The defections began with Attenes, chieftain of the Turdetani,* who deserted with a large number of his people; then two fortified towns were betrayed* to the Romans, along with their garrisons, by the garrison commanders. Faced with this tendency to revolt, Hasdrubal wished to stop the rot spreading further and struck camp the following night when all was quiet.

16. When, at dawn, men in his forward posts reported that the

enemy were gone, Scipio sent his cavalry ahead and ordered the main force to get under way. The men were marched along at such a rapid pace that, had their pursuit kept strictly to the enemy's tracks, they would unquestionably have overtaken the fugitives. Instead, they accepted the assurance of the guides that there was a shorter route to the River Baetis which would enable them to fall on the enemy as they made the crossing.

Finding that his way over the river was shut off, Hasdrubal veered towards the ocean, and from this point the Carthaginians' disordered retreat resembled a flight, which put some distance between them and the Roman legions. But the Roman cavalry and light infantry kept harassing them and slowing them down by attacking their rear or flanks. The Carthaginians would halt to counter these repeated assaults, engaging the enemy cavalry at one moment, and their skirmishers and auxiliary infantry the next; and meanwhile the legions appeared on the scene. After that it was no longer a battle; it was more like animals being slaughtered—until their leader authorized flight by personally making off to the nearest hills with approximately 6,000 poorly armed men. The rest were cut down or taken prisoner.

The Carthaginian fugitives hurriedly fortified a makeshift camp on the highest of the hills, and from there they had little difficulty in defending themselves since the enemy's attempts to climb the steep incline came to nothing. But a siege of even a few days in the desolate and barren environment was impossible to endure, and this set off desertions to the enemy. Eventually, since the sea was not far distant, the commander himself had ships sent to him,* abandoned his army, and fled to Gades by night.

When told of the enemy commander's flight, Scipio left 10,000 infantry and 1,000 cavalry with Silanus to continue the siege of the camp, and himself returned to Tarraco with the rest of his troops. The march took seventy days,* as he was examining en route the cases of chieftains and communities, so that rewards could be assigned on the basis of an accurate assessment of their services. After Scipio's departure, Masinissa had a secret meeting with Silanus, and then, wishing also to have his people accept his new programme, he crossed to Africa with a few of his compatriots. The reason for his suddenly changing sides was not clear at the time; but that his actions did have reasonable motivation even at that point was subsequently demonstrated by the fact that he remained staunchly loyal to Rome right down to his last years. Mago then headed for Gades in the ships that Hasdrubal sent back; the others, abandoned by their leaders, either deserted or fled, and became dispersed amongst the neighbouring communities. No force of any significance in terms of numbers or strength now remained.

This was basically how the Carthaginians, thanks to Publius Scipio's leadership and under his auspices, were driven from Spain, in the fourteenth year from the commencement of the war, and the fifth from Publius Scipio's acceptance of the province with its army.* Not long afterwards, Silanus returned to Scipio at Tarraco with the news that his operation had been successfully concluded.

17. Lucius Scipio was sent to Rome, with a large number of noble prisoners of war in his charge, to report that Spain had been brought to heel. The reaction to the news was general jubilation and pride, except in the case of the man responsible for it. Scipio, who had an insatiable appetite for deeds of courage and true glory, thought the recovery of Spain was little compared with the goal on which his hopes and noble aspirations were focused. He already had his eyes set on Africa and the great Carthage, and he saw that campaign as the crowning glory that would assure him eminence and fame. Thinking therefore that he should do some preparatory work, and garner the support of kings and nations, he determined to sound out King Syphax first.

Syphax was the king of the Masaesulians.* The Masaesulians, a people situated next to the Mauri, face just that part of Spain where New Carthage lies. At that point the king had a treaty with the Carthaginians, but Scipio believed that he would consider this no more important or inviolable than barbarians generally would, their loyalty always being dependent on the vicissitudes of fortune. He therefore sent Gaius Laelius to Syphax as his spokesman, bearing some gifts. The barbarian was pleased with the gifts, and because the Romans were doing well in every sector, while the Carthaginians were doing badly in Italy and had completely failed in Spain, he agreed to accept a pact of friendship from the Romans. He added the stipulation, however, that the exchange of promises to ratify the pact had to be done with the Roman commander in person. Laelius therefore returned to Scipio having received from the king nothing more than the promise that Scipio should have a safe conduct.

For anyone contemplating an attack on Africa, Syphax was important in every respect. He was the wealthiest king in that part of the
world; he had already faced these very Carthaginians in war; and the
bounds of his kingdom were conveniently situated relative to Spain,
separated from it only by a narrow strait. Scipio therefore thought
the ends justified taking a great risk, since they could be gained in no
other way. He left Lucius Marcius in Tarraco, and Marcus Silanus in
New Carthage—Silanus had come there overland by forced marches
from Tarraco—for the defence of Spain, and he himself crossed to
Africa with Gaius Laelius. They left New Carthage with two quinqueremes, and relied mostly on the oar since the sea was calm,
though occasionally they were sometimes helped by a gentle breeze.*

Now, as it happened, Hasdrubal, after being driven from Spain,
sailed into the harbour of Siga* with seven triremes at that very same
time. He had dropped anchor and was bringing the ships to shore
when the two Roman quinqueremes were spotted. Nobody had any
doubt that they belonged to the enemy, and that they could be overpowered by the larger number of Carthaginian vessels before they
entered the harbour. However, the Carthaginians succeeded only in
creating consternation and alarm, as marines and sailors unsuccessfully attempted to get their weapons and ships in a state of readiness.
For a slightly stronger wind from the open sea hit the Roman sails and
brought the quinqueremes into the harbour before the Carthaginians
could weigh anchor; and then nobody dared make further trouble
since they were in a harbour belonging to the king. And so they
disembarked, Hasdrubal first, and Scipio and Laelius soon after him,
and went to the king.

18. Syphax felt it was truly marvellous—as indeed it was—to have
generals of the two richest nations of the time come to seek a peace
treaty with him on one and the same day. He offered the two men
hospitality and, as chance had decided on their being under the one
roof and in the same home, he made an effort to bring them
into conversation with a view to ending their disputes. Scipio, however, said that, while he felt no personal animosity towards the
Carthaginian that might be ended by talking, he could, in an official
capacity, have no dealings with an enemy without the Senate's
authorization. The king put considerable pressure on him to accept
an invitation to dinner along with Hasdrubal, so neither of his guests
would seem to have been unwelcome at his table, and Scipio did not

refuse. They then dined together in Syphax's palace, Scipio and Hasdrubal even sharing the same couch, since that had been the king's pleasure.

Indeed, such was Scipio's sociability and instinctive tactfulness in any given situation that he won over, with his smooth conversational manner, not only Syphax, a barbarian with no experience of Roman manners, but a deadly adversary, as well. Hasdrubal made it very clear that he had a greater admiration for the man from having seen him in the flesh than because of his military successes, and he said he did not doubt that Syphax and his kingdom would soon be in the power of Rome—such was the man's ability to win people over. Consequently Hasdrubal felt that the question for the Carthaginians now was not so much how Spain had been lost as how they could hold on to Africa. The great Roman general was not on a pleasure trip or a voyage to pleasant climes, he thought, not if he had left behind a province only recently subdued and left behind his armies, too. That was not why he crossed to Africa with two ships, putting himself at the mercy of a hostile land, and entrusting himself to a king's authority and his untested word of honour. No, he harboured ambitions of making himself master of Africa; and he had long been contemplating this and openly complaining that he, Scipio, was not at war in Africa the way that Hannibal was in Italy.

Scipio made a treaty with Syphax and then left Africa. At the mercy of shifting and generally tempestuous winds he reached the port of New Carthage three days later.

19. While Spain was now quiet as regards the Punic War, it was clear that certain communities, aware of their past wrongdoings, were quiet from fear rather than from any feelings of loyalty to Rome. The most important of these, both in size and the extent of their guilt, were Iliturgi and Castulo.* Castulo had been an ally when things were going well for Rome, but had defected to Carthage when the Scipios and their armies were crushed. The people of Iliturgi had betrayed and killed the men who had sought refuge with them after that disaster, thereby adding an atrocity to their defection. When Scipio first arrived, and Spain hung in the balance, severe measures against these peoples would have been justified, but impractical. However, now that there was peace, the time for reprisals seemed to have arrived. Scipio therefore had Lucius Marcius summoned from Tarraco, and sent him with a third of his

troops to launch an attack on Castulo. Scipio himself came to Iliturgis after a march of about five days. The gates were shut, and all measures had been taken and preparations made to counter an attack—their guilty conscience, their awareness of what they deserved, made a declaration of war redundant.

This became Scipio's exordium for his speech of encouragement to the men. By closing the gates, he said, the Spaniards had themselves shown they were aware of the fearful punishment they deserved. The war against them should therefore be conducted with much greater hostility than the war with Carthage: with the Carthaginians it was an almost dispassionate struggle for empire and glory,* but these men had to be punished for their treachery and brutal atrocities. The time had arrived, he said, for them to exact revenge for the unspeakable murder of their comrades, and for the trap that would have been set for them, too, had their flight taken them to the same place. The moment had also come, he concluded, to set a grim example that would ensure for all time that nobody could consider a Roman citizen and a Roman soldier, whatever his circumstances, a convenient target for mischief.

Inspired by these words of encouragement from their leader, the soldiers immediately distributed ladders amongst men who had been hand-picked from each of the maniples. The army was also split, so that Laelius could take command of one of the halves as a lieutenant, and they then simultaneously launched their attack on the city at two points, bringing terror on two fronts. It was not one leader, or a group of chieftains, who inspired the townspeople to a spirited defence of the city, but their own fear, which arose from a guilty conscience. They remembered—and they kept reminding others—that the enemy were not seeking victory over them but their punishment. What mattered, they said, was where they all met their end. Would they breathe their last fighting in the line of battle, where the dangers of war, equally shared, often raised up the conquered and struck down the conqueror? Or would they do so later, in a city burned and destroyed, after being whipped and chained, and suffering all manner of foul indignities before the eyes of their captive wives and children?

And so it was not simply men of military age and males who put their courage and strength into the effort. Women and children did so as well, supplying the fighters with weapons, and carrying stones to the fortifications for the working parties. It was not just a matter of their freedom, which fires the hearts only of the brave; before their eyes was the spectre of the worst tortures of all, and a disgraceful death. Their morale was fired, too, by competing with each other for their share of the work and the danger, and simply by looking at each other. And so, such was the force of the initial clash that an army that had conquered the whole of Spain was often repulsed from the walls by the fighting men of a single town, and fell back in panic in a battle that was not bringing them glory.

When Scipio saw this, he feared that all his men's failed efforts would raise the enemy's morale, and dampen his men's enthusiasm; and he felt he had to make a personal effort and take his share of the danger. He scolded the men for their faint-heartedness, ordered the ladders brought up, and threatened to make the climb himself if they held back. When he had already come close to the walls, at no small risk to himself,* a cry arose on every side from the men, concerned as they were for their commander, and ladders began to go up simultaneously at many points. In addition, Laelius put pressure on from the other side. With that the resistance of the townspeople was crushed, the defenders were thrown down, and the walls were taken.

20. In the uproar the citadel was also taken, on the side where it was considered impregnable, and this thanks to some African deserters then amongst the Roman auxiliary troops. The townsmen had directed their attention to the spots that seemed to be in danger, while the Romans kept moving up wherever access was possible. The deserters meanwhile noticed that the highest part of the city, because it enjoyed the protection of a precipitous cliff, was lacking any kind of fortification and was also without defenders. Some men of slight build, and agile from extensive training, then climbed up where the uneven projections of the cliff-face made it possible, and they carried with them iron spikes. Wherever they were faced with a stretch of rock that was too steep, or too smooth, they would drive the spikes into the rock a short distance from each other, and thus virtually made steps for themselves. The first men would then haul up with their hands those following them, while the men behind pushed up those ahead of them, and in this way they reached the top. From there they ran down with a shout into the city that had already been taken by the Romans.

It was then that the rage and loathing behind the attack on the city truly became apparent. Nobody considered taking captives alive; nobody thought about booty, though everything was open to plunder. It was a massacre, of armed and unarmed alike, and of women as well as men, the invaders' ruthless fury descending even to the massacre of infants. They then torched the buildings and tore down what the flames could not consume. Such was the delight they took in obliterating even the last traces of the city, in wiping out the memory of their enemies' home.

From there Scipio led his army to Castulo. This city was defended not only by people who had come from elsewhere in Spain, but also by the remnants of the Carthaginian army after its widespread flight. But news of the disaster that had befallen Iliturgi had reached there before Scipio's arrival, and terror and despair had swept through the city. And since the two parties' circumstances were different, and everyone was looking out for himself without thought for anyone else, there was at first unexpressed suspicion, and then open disagreement, creating a rift between the Carthaginians and the Spaniards. The Spaniards were under the command of Cerdubelus, who openly advocated surrender, and the Carthaginian auxiliaries were under Himilco. Secretly receiving assurances from the Romans, Cerdubelus betrayed to them the auxiliaries and the city. There was more clemency in this victory; there was less guilt on the part of the people and the voluntary surrender had done much to soothe the Romans' anger.

21. Marcius was then sent off to bring to heel any barbarians not yet completely subdued. Scipio returned to New Carthage to discharge his vows, and also to stage a gladiatorial show that he had prepared to commemorate the deaths of his father and his uncle. The gladiatorial show did not draw on the sort of men from whom the professional trainers usually take their combatants, that is, slaves off the vendor's platform, and free men who put their lifeblood up for sale. All the fighters provided their services voluntarily and without charge. Some were sent by their chieftains to exhibit their tribe's inbred valour; others readily declared they would fight to please the commander. Others again were driven by a competitive and combative spirit to challenge their comrades, and not refuse a challenge that was offered them. Some settled with the sword differences that they had not been able, or had not wished, to end through discussion, agreeing amongst themselves that the disputed property should go

to the victor; and these were not people of low birth, but men of rank and distinction.

Now two cousins, Corbis and Orsua, were in competition for the chieftainship of a community called Ide,* and they declared that they would fight for it with the sword. Corbis was the elder of the two, but the father of Orsua had been the last chieftain, having received the post from an elder brother on his death. Scipio wanted to settle the matter through discussion and soothe ruffled feelings, but both men said they had already told the family members they had in common that they would not do this, and they would accept no judge, divine or human, other than Mars. The elder man had confidence in his strength, the younger in his youth, and the two preferred to die in combat rather than be subjected to the other's authority. They could not be made to abandon such folly, and they provided the army with an outstanding show, and an illustration of how great a curse lust for power is amongst mankind. The elder man, by virtue of his experience with weapons and his artfulness, easily overcame the brute force of the younger.

Apart from the gladiatorial show there were also funeral games, which were celebrated as elaborately as the province's resources and the camp environment would allow.

22. In the meantime military operations were being conducted no less energetically by Scipio's legates. Marcius crossed the River Baetis, called the Cirtes* by local people, and accepted the surrender of two wealthy communities without a fight. Then came the city of Astapa,* which had always supported Carthage, though it was not this that merited Roman anger so much as the fact that its people had been nursing a particular resentment, beyond what the pressures of war might arouse, towards the Romans. They had a city that could rely neither on its position nor on its defences for protection enough to justify their confidence, but their natural predilection for marauding had driven them to make raids on the lands around them belonging to allies of the Roman people, during which they rounded up some straggling Roman soldiers, camp-followers, and traders. They had even ambushed a large caravan—large because travelling in small numbers was unsafe—as it was passing through their territory, catching it in an awkward spot and wiping it out.

The army was brought forward for an assault on this city. The townspeople, well aware of their guilt, felt there could be no safety in capitulation to such an embittered force, but they also could not hope to save themselves with their fortifications and weapons. They therefore decided to inflict on themselves and their families a deed abhorrent and barbaric. They marked off a spot in the forum for gathering together the most valuable of their possessions, and they told their wives and children to take a seat on the pile they made, heaping up wood around them and throwing on bundles of brushwood. Then they gave specific instructions to fifty armed men. As long as the outcome of the fight was in doubt, they were told, they were to keep their fortunes, and the persons more precious than their fortunes, under guard in that place. If they saw that the day was lost, and the city about to be taken, then they could be sure that all the men they saw marching out to battle would fall in the fight itself. They therefore begged them, they said, in the name of all the gods above and below, to bear in mind their liberty, which had to be terminated that day, either by death with honour or by ignominious servitude, and not leave behind anything on which a furious enemy could vent his rage. They had swords and torches in their hands— and friendly and loyal hands should eliminate what was bound to perish rather than leave it to the insults and arrogant mockery of the enemy. To these appeals was added a dreadful curse that was to fall on any one deflected from his resolve by hope or squeamishness.

After that, they flung open the gates, and rushed out in a swift and violent charge; and there was no Roman forward post strong enough to hold them, because the last thing to be feared was the enemy daring to emerge from their fortifications. Only a few cavalry squadrons, and some light infantry hurriedly despatched from camp to meet the situation, came to confront them. It was a battle characterized more by the courage of the combatants and the ferocity of the onslaught than by any regular order. The cavalry that had been the first to face the enemy were flung back, bringing panic to the light infantry; and the fighting would have reached the very edge of the rampart had not the cream of the army, the legionaries, formed a line of battle in the few moments they were given to deploy. Even amongst the legionaries there were a few moments of alarm in the front ranks, as the enemy in blind rage threw themselves with reckless abandon in the way of Roman sword thrusts. Then the seasoned soldiers, standing firm against these wild onslaughts, cut down the first-comers, bringing those who followed to a halt. Shortly afterwards, the veterans attempted to go on the offensive themselves, only to discover that none of the enemy would give ground, that all were firmly resolved to die where they stood. They then extended their lines to overlap the enemy flanks, an easy manœuvre, thanks to their numerical superiority, and killed them to the very last man as they fought in a circle.

23. In fact, these were the actions of an angry enemy taken in the thick of the fray against armed men who were fighting back, and they were in accordance with the conventions of warfare. Another, grimmer kind of slaughter was going on in the city. Scores of weak and defenceless women and children were being murdered by their own citizens, who were hurling bodies, most of them still breathing, onto a burning pyre, while streams of blood choked the rising flames. And eventually these men, too, exhausted from the pitiful slaughter of their own people, flung themselves and their weapons into the midst of the fire.

Only when the massacre was finished did the Romans came on the scene. The first sight of the grisly scene left them momentarily stunned and horrified. Then, with the greed inherent in human nature, the soldiers tried to snatch from the flames the gold and silver that glittered amid the pile of other articles. Some were engulfed by the flames, others burned by the blast of hot air for, with the huge crowd pressing forward from behind, there was no way for those at the front to step back. So it was that Astapa was destroyed by fire and the sword, with no plunder for the soldiers. Marcius accepted the surrender of the other peoples of the area who capitulated from fear, and then led his victorious army back to Scipio in New Carthage.

It was just at that time that deserters arrived from Gades with a promise to betray that city and the Punic garrison within it, along with the garrison commander and the fleet. (Mago had actually stopped in Gades after his flight, and had brought together ships on the Atlantic coast. Along with these, he had also assembled a respectable force of auxiliaries from the coast of Africa across the strait and, thanks to the assistance of his prefect Hanno, from the Spanish districts closest to him.) Assurances were exchanged with the deserters, and Marcius and Laelius were sent to Gades for cooperative action by land and sea, Marcius with some light-armed cohorts, and Laelius with seven triremes and a quinquereme.

24. Scipio himself came down with a serious illness, made worse

in the reports of it—people have an inherent love of deliberately exaggerating rumours, and everyone now added to what he had heard—and this unsettled the whole province, especially its outlying areas. It was clear from the furore that an idle rumour had raised just how much unrest would have been caused had the loss been a real one. Allies did not maintain their loyalty, nor the army its sense of duty.

Mandonius and Indibilis had counted on having the kingdom of Spain for themselves once the Carthaginians had been driven out, but nothing had happened to bring their hopes to fruition. Accordingly they spurred their countrymen (that is, the Lacetani) to revolt and, rousing to arms the Celtiberian youth, aggressively pillaged the lands of the Suessetani and Sedetani,* who were allies of the Roman people.

There was another violent outbreak, this time involving citizens, in the camp at Sucro.* There were 8,000 men in the camp, stationed there as a garrison to protect the tribes north of the Ebro. It was not the arrival of vague rumours about their commander's life being in danger that was the original cause of these men's wavering loyalty. That had been the indiscipline that usually results from a long period of inactivity, and a contributing factor was the straitened circumstances of peacetime facing men used to an easy living from plundering enemy territory. At first there were only surreptitious exchanges between them. What were they doing amongst a pacified people if there were hostilities in the province, they asked each other; and if the war was now over and their mission accomplished why were they not being taken back to Italy? There were, in addition, demands for pay more insistent than a disciplined soldier would normally make. Tribunes doing the rounds of the watch found themselves subjected to insults from the sentries, and there had been nightly pillaging expeditions into the pacified farmland round about. Finally, in broad daylight, men would openly quit the standards without leave. Everything was now proceeding at the whim and caprice of the rank and file, with no heed for military institutions and discipline, or the orders of those in command. Even so, the Roman camp kept its usual appearance, and for one reason only. The men felt that, as the madness spread, the tribunes would not refuse to join their mutinous insurrection; and so they allowed them to administer justice at the headquarters, and would ask them for the password, and take their turns on guard-duty and on watch. While they had effectively undermined the authority of the command structure, they still maintained a display of obeying orders, though they were really following their own.

Then the mutiny flared up. For the men observed that the tribunes were disapproving and critical of what was going on, and were attempting to take a stand against it, openly declaring they would not be party to such madness. The tribunes were chased from the headquarters and shortly afterwards from the camp, and, by unanimous agreement, command was put in the hands of the two common soldiers who were the ringleaders of the uprising, Gaius Albius of Cales and Gaius Atrius* from Umbria. Completely dissatisfied with the insignia of the tribunes, these men even presumed to take upon themselves the symbols of the highest authority, the *fasces* and axes. And it never entered their heads that the rods and axes that they were having borne in front of them to intimidate others were actually threatening their own backs, and their own necks. The erroneous belief that Scipio was dead was clouding their minds, and they had no doubt that as soon as word of it spread abroad, as it shortly would, war would flare up throughout Spain. In the ensuing turmoil, they thought, money could be extorted from the allies, and the neighbouring cities could be pillaged; and in the upheaval in which anyone could dare to do anything, their own actions would attract less attention.

25. Day after day they were now waiting for fresh news, not merely that Scipio was dead but even that he was buried! But none came, and as the groundless rumours began to dissipate, the search began for those responsible for first putting them about. One by one men began to fall back, hoping they could appear to have been gullible in accepting such a story rather than have been its inventor. The leaders, now isolated, began to shudder at the thought of their own insignia, and of the real and duly appointed power that would soon turn upon them, replacing the spurious authority they were wielding. And so the mutiny began to lose momentum. Then reliable informants reported first that Scipio was still alive, and presently even that he was in good health; and seven military tribunes came on the scene, personally sent there by Scipio.

There were ruffled feelings when the tribunes first arrived, but they were soon smoothed out when the officers began to placate personal acquaintances they met with conciliatory language. Then they first of all made the rounds of the tents, and later appeared in the headquarters and at the general's tent, where they had seen groups of men engaged in conversation. They would address the men and, instead of reproaching them for what they had done, would ask them what had been responsible for the sudden outbreak of madness and sedition. The grievance usually adduced was that they had not been paid on time, and they also brought up the atrocity committed by the inhabitants of Iliturgi. After two generals and two armies had been wiped out, they said, it was thanks to their courage that the Roman name had been defended at that time and a hold maintained on the province. Yet while the men of Iliturgi had received the punishment they deserved for their crime, there was nobody to recompense the Roman soldiers for the service they had rendered.

The tribunes replied that in lodging such grievances the men were asking only for what was their due, and that they would relay them to the commander. They were happy that the problem was not more severe or more difficult to remedy, they said and, thanks to the blessing of the gods, Publius Scipio and the republic could now show their gratitude.

While Scipio was well acquainted with warfare, he had no experience of mutinous outbursts. The situation had him worried: he wished to avoid excess, whether it be in tolerating the army's insubordination, or in punishing it. For the moment he decided to continue with the lenient course on which he had embarked and, by dispatching collection agents around the tributary states, he raised the prospect of early payment for the men. He also straight away issued an edict for them to come together in New Carthage for their pay, in units or in a body, whichever they preferred.

The mutiny was now flagging, anyway, but the sudden arrival of peace amongst the recalcitrant Spaniards brought it to a standstill; for Mandonius and Indibilis had, when brought the news that Scipio was alive, abandoned their enterprise and returned to their territory. Now the mutineers had no one, whether citizen or foreigner, with whom to share their insane programme. As they examined every possible course of action, they found the only chance left to them after their villainous schemes—and that a not very safe one—was to submit to the commander's justifiable wrath, or to his mercy, which they felt was not beyond the bounds of hope. Scipio had pardoned even enemies with whom he had fought with the sword, they told themselves, and their mutiny had struck no blow and shed no blood—it had not itself been brutal and did not merit a brutal punishment. So glib are human beings when it comes to playing down their own wrongdoings! There was some indecision over whether they should go for their pay as individual cohorts or as a body, and the scale tipped towards going as a body, which they felt the safer option.

26. On the very days the mutineers were considering all this, there was a meeting devoted to them at New Carthage. There opinions were divided on whether punishment should be restricted to the ringleaders of the mutiny, who were no more than thirty-five in number, or whether more should be disciplined, in order to penalize what was less a mutiny than an outright rebellion that set a terrible precedent. The more lenient view won the day, namely that punishment be applied to the source of the offence; it was felt that a reprimand would suffice for the majority.

The meeting was adjourned and, to make it look as if this had been the business discussed, the army at New Carthage was given notice of an expedition against Mandonius and Indibilis, and instructed to prepare several days' food rations. The seven tribunes who had earlier gone to Sucro to quell the mutiny were now sent to meet the army, and each was furnished with the names of five of the ringleaders of the mutiny. They were each to employ appropriate third parties to invite his five to a reception, with a friendly expression and words of welcome, and when the men were drowsy with wine they were to put them in irons.

The mutinous troops were not far distant from New Carthage when they learned from men they met on the road that the entire army, under the command of Marcus Silanus, was setting out against the Lacetani the following day. This not only freed them from all the dread that lurked at the back of their minds but also brought them great satisfaction, because now they would have the commander on his own, and not themselves be in his power.

Towards sunset they entered the city, and saw the other army making all the preparations for the march. They were welcomed with some well-chosen words; their arrival was propitious and timely for the commander-in-chief, they were told, because they had come just before the other army was setting out. With that, they went off to eat and relax. The ringleaders of the insurrection were taken away by the selected men to be entertained, and were then, with no trouble at all, arrested and clapped in irons by the tribunes.

At the time of the fourth watch the baggage-train of the army that was ostensibly marching off began to move out. At dawn, the troops set off, but the column was brought to a halt at the gate, and guards were then sent around all the other city gates to prevent anyone leaving. Next, the men who had arrived the previous day were summoned to a meeting, and they swiftly converged in a threatening manner on the commander's dais in the forum, intending to intimidate him with their noisy interjections. The moment that the commander climbed the dais, the soldiers were brought back from the gates, and they stood in a circle behind the unarmed assembly. With that, all the men's truculence vanished and, as they later admitted, nothing gave them such fright as the unexpected vigour and healthy complexion of the commander (whom they had expected to behold on his sickbed) and a look on his face they claimed they did not remember seeing even in battle. For a while Scipio sat in silence, until word came that the ringleaders of the mutiny had been brought into the ground, and that all was ready.

27. Then, when silence fell at the herald's signal, he spoke as follows:

'Never did I think I would find myself lost for words with which to address my army. That is not because I have ever made words rather than actions the subject of my training, but because, having been brought up in the camp almost from childhood, I was familiar with the soldier's character. But you are different, and I am at a loss for ideas and words on how to address you, and I do not even know the title to use. Shall I call you 'citizens'—when you have abandoned your country? Or 'soldiers'—when you have turned your back on authority and the auspices, and broken the sacred obligations of your oath? Or 'enemies'? I recognize the features, faces, dress, and bearing of my fellow citizens; but I see the actions, words, designs, and temperament of an enemy. For how are your wishes and aspirations different from those of the Ilergetes and Lacetani? And yet the leaders of *their* frenzy, the men they chose to follow, Mandonius and Indibilis, were of royal stock—*you* bestowed the auspices and supreme authority on the Umbrian Atrius and the Calenian Albius.

'Tell me, men, that you were not *all* involved in that, or that you did not all *want* to be involved, that it was just a few who were guilty of such delusion and lunacy. I shall willingly accept your denial of guilt! For such were the transgressions that, if the whole army was involved, atonement could be made only with enormous sacrifice.

'It is with reluctance that I touch on these matters, which are like wounds—but unless they are touched and handled they cannot be healed! Frankly, after the Carthaginians were driven from Spain, I could not believe that there was anyone in the whole province who hated the fact that I was alive—such had been my conduct vis-à-vis my enemies as well as my friends. How wrong I was! Look at it! In my own camp the report of my death was not only readily believed, but eagerly awaited! It is not that I have any wish to believe the guilt lies with all of you. In fact, if I believed my whole army had wished me dead I would die here before your eyes right now, and would take no pleasure in a life that was offensive to my fellow citizens and my men.

'No, the fact is that, like the sea, every crowd is naturally motionless. In you, too, there is the calm or there are tempests, according to the motion produced by the squalls and breezes. And the responsibility and cause of all your wild behaviour lies with the ringleaders. You caught the insanity from them, and it seems to me that not even today are you aware of how far your madness went, of the extent of the outrage you dared to inflict on me, your country, your parents and children, and on the gods who witnessed your oath. You seem unaware of how far you violated the auspices under which you fought, the military traditions and discipline of your forebears, and the majesty of our supreme command.

'About myself I say nothing. Let us attribute your belief in my death to thoughtlessness rather than a wish for it to be so, and let us assume I am the sort of man whose command an army could understandably find unsupportable. But your country—what had she done to deserve your betraying her by making common cause with Mandonius and Indibilis? What had the Roman people done to make you remove *imperium* from duly elected tribunes* and confer it on private individuals? And, not satisfied with merely having those men as your tribunes, how could you—a Roman army!—then award the *fasces* of your commander-in-chief to such men as had never even had a slave to give orders to? Albius and Atrius billeted themselves in the general's tent; it was at their quarters that the trumpet was sounded; it was they who were asked for the password; and they sat on the dais of Publius Scipio; a lictor attended on them; people were moved aside as they went forward and the *fasces* and axes were carried before them. Stones falling as rain, thunderbolts hurled from heaven, animals producing bizarre offspring—such are the things *you* consider to be portents. But this is a portent that can be expiated by no sacrificial victims and by no supplicatory offerings—only by the blood of the men who dared to commit such a heinous crime.

28. 'No crime has rational motivation, and yet I would like to know—as far as one can in the case of a fiendish act—what you were thinking, and what your plan was. A legion that was once dispatched to garrison Rhegium* committed the crime of killing the foremost members of the community, and holding that wealthy city in its control for a ten-year period. For that offence the entire legion— four thousand men*—were beheaded in the Forum in Rome. But they followed the lead of a military tribune, Decimus Vibellius, not someone who was practically a camp-follower, an Umbrian called Atrius, whose very name is a bad omen. And, in addition, they did not throw in their lot with Pyrrhus, or with the Samnites or the Lucanians. You made common cause with Mandonius and Indibilis, and were intending to join forces with them. Those legionaries were going to keep Rhegium as their permanent home, just as the Campanians kept Capua after taking it from its Etruscan inhabitants of old, and as the Mamertines kept Messana in Sicily.* And they had no intention of launching an attack on the Roman people or allies of the Roman people. Were you going to keep Sucro as your place of residence? If I had left you in the town when, on the completion of my mission, I was retiring as your commander-in-chief you would have been justified in protesting to gods and men that you were not returning to your wives and children!

'But let us suppose that you had driven from your minds all memory of these, along with the memory of your country and of me—I still want to follow the scenario for this criminal, though not absolutely crazy, scheme. Did you really intend to wrest the province of Spain from the Roman people? And to attempt that when I was still alive, and the rest of the army still in one piece—the army with which I captured New Carthage in a single day, and with which I routed and put to flight, and then chased out of Spain, four commanders and four armies of Carthage? And your numbers being only

8,000, all of you of inferior quality to Albius and Atrius, under whose authority you put yourselves?

'I pass over my reputation and leave it entirely out of the question, assuming the only wrong I was done by you was to have you too readily believe me dead. Now, suppose I had in fact died. Was the republic going to expire along with me? Was the empire of the Roman people going to fall with me? I pray that Jupiter Optimus Maximus not allow this to happen! I pray that the city that was founded to live for ever, founded with favourable auspices and the support of the gods, not be only as long-lived as this frail and mortal body of mine! Flaminius, Paulus, Gracchus, Postumius Albinus, Marcus Marcellus, Titus Quinctius Crispinus, Gnaeus Fulvius, my own family members the Scipios—all those fine commanders have been taken from us in this one war. And yet the Roman people lives on, and will continue to live on, though a thousand others die, whether by the sword or from disease. Would the republic then have been buried at the funeral of a single individual—me? Indeed, you yourselves, when the two commanders, my father and my uncle, were killed here in Spain—you still selected Septimus Marcius as your leader against the Carthaginians, elated by their recent victory.

'And I am talking as if, in the event of my death, the Spanish provinces would have been without a commander. Marcus Silanus was sent out with me to this sphere of command with the same authority, and the same powers,* and my brother Lucius Scipio and Gaius Laelius were my legates. Would these men have failed to champion the majesty of our empire? Could one army have been compared with the other, or one army's officers with the other's? Could there have been any comparison in terms of their status, or the justice of their cause? And had you been superior in all these respects, would you have shouldered arms against your country and against your own citizens? Would you have wanted to see Africa ascendant over Italy, and Carthage over the city of Rome? What wrong did your country do to deserve that?

29. 'An unjust conviction leading to a miserable and undeserved exile once drove Coriolanus* to launch an attack on his country, but his individual sense of duty to his family called him away from a crime against the state. In your case, what was the resentment or anger that spurred you on? Your pay was given to you a few days late because your commander was ill. Was that a sufficient reason for

declaring war on your country, for abandoning the Roman people to join the Ilergetes, for regarding nothing in the divine or human sphere as inviolably sacred?

'You were evidently in the grip of insanity, men, and the disease that assailed my body was no more severe than that which assailed your minds. I shudder at the thought of what men believed, what their hopes and aspirations were. Let forgetfulness sweep it all away and obliterate it, if such is possible; failing that, let there be some veil of silence over it.

'I would not deny that what I have just said may well have struck you as harsh and cruel, but how much more cruel do you think your actions were than my words? You think it fair that I should put up with what you have done; so will you not even resign yourselves to being *told* all about it? But even those actions of yours will not be cast up at you any more. I just hope that you can forget them as easily as I shall. So as far as you, as a whole, are concerned, I shall have satisfaction enough, and more than enough, if you regret your wrongdoing. The Calenian Albius and the Umbrian Atrius, and all the other ringleaders of this foul insurrection—they shall pay for their acts with their blood. So far from causing you pain, the sight of their punishment should bring you joy, if your sanity has returned. They have done nobody greater harm or injury than they have you.'

He had barely finished speaking when, as had been arranged, his audience's eyes and ears were subjected to all manner of horror. The troops that had cordoned off the assembly banged on their shields with their swords; the crier's voice was heard calling out the names of the men who had been found guilty in the council meeting; and these were dragged naked into the midst of the gathering, where all the instruments of punishment were brought into view. The men were tied to stakes, flogged, and beheaded. So paralysed with fear were all those present that there was not even a moan to be heard, much less any voice raised in protest against the harshness of the punishment. Then all the corpses were dragged from their midst, the ground was cleansed, and the soldiers were summoned by name before the military tribunes. They swore the oath of allegiance to Publius Scipio, and each was paid as his name was called. With that the mutiny of the troops that began at Sucro came to an end.

30. During this same period Mago's lieutenant Hanno, who had been sent out from Gades by Mago with a small detachment of

African troops, had put under arms, with the inducement of pay, some 4,000 young Spaniards in the area of the River Baetis. After that he saw his camp taken from him by Lucius Marcius and, in the turmoil of its capture, he lost most of his men, though there were losses incurred in the flight, too, when the Roman cavalry gave chase to the scattered fugitives. Hanno himself made good his escape with a handful of men.

In the course of these events at the River Baetis, Laelius sailed through the straits into the Atlantic Ocean and put in with his fleet at Carteia,* a city that lies on the Atlantic coast, at the point where the sea starts to open out after the narrows. Laelius had, as was noted above, entertained the hope of taking control of Gades through surrender and without a fight, and men actually came to the Roman camp of their own accord to make such a promise. However, the plot to betray the town came to light prematurely, and Mago arrested all involved and delivered them to the praetor Adherbal* for removal to Carthage. Adherbal put the conspirators aboard a quinquereme, which he sent on ahead because it was slower than a trireme. He then followed, a short distance behind, with eight triremes.

Just when the quinquereme was entering the straits, Laelius, who was himself in a quinquereme, came sailing out of the harbour of Carteia at the head of seven triremes. He made straight for Adherbal and his triremes, firmly convinced that the Carthaginian quinquereme, already caught up in the rapid waters of the strait, could not be brought back against the tide. Faced with this sudden turn of events the Carthaginian momentarily panicked, unsure whether to follow his quinquereme or swing round his prows to face the enemy. That very moment of hesitation robbed him of the option of declining battle; for now the Carthaginians were within weapon-range, and under enemy pressure on every side. In addition, the tide had removed all means of effectively steering the ships. It did not even look like a naval battle: there was no choice of movement, and no skill or tactics. The natural character of the strait and its tide took complete control of the entire struggle, bringing the combatants into collision with their own as well as the other side's vessels as they vainly attempted to row in the other direction. The result was that one could see a ship that was in flight spun round by a swirl of water, and carried against the victors, and one in pursuit turning as if to flee, if it hit a contrary current. In the battle proper a ship would be trying to ram an enemy vessel with its beak, only to be turned at an angle and be rammed itself by the other's beak; and another, presented broadside-on to the enemy, would suddenly spin round to charge prow-on. But while the battle of the triremes fluctuated since chance was in control of it, the Roman quinquereme was either more stable because of her weight, or else was the more easily managed because she had more banks of oars cutting the churning waters, and she sank two triremes, and sheared the oars off one side of a third, as she charged by. She would have wrecked all the others she overtook had not Adherbal raised the sails and made it across to Africa with his five remaining ships.

31. The victorious Laelius returned to Carteia. There he was told of events at Gades, how the plot had been exposed and the conspirators sent off to Carthage, frustrating the hopes with which they had come* to him. Laelius then sent a message to Lucius Marcius to tell him they should return to their commander-in-chief if they did not wish to waste time sitting before Gades. Marcius agreed, and they both returned to New Carthage a few days later.

With their departure Mago now had a respite from the pressure of facing a twofold threat from land and sea, and, in addition, when he heard about the uprising of the Ilergetes, he conceived a hope of recovering Spain. He therefore sent messengers off to the senate in Carthage to give an exaggerated account of the mutiny in the Roman camp, as well as of the uprising of the allies, and to urge the senators to send reinforcements so that their Spanish empire, the legacy of their fathers, could be regained.

Mandonius and Indibilis, who had withdrawn to their lands, for a time remained inactive, anxiously awaiting a reliable report of the decisions taken with regard to the mutiny. They were confident that, if Roman citizens were pardoned for their wrongdoing, then they, too, could be granted a pardon. When word spread of the severity of the punishment, however, they felt that their own transgression would rate a similar penalty. And so, recalling their countrymen to arms, and assembling the auxiliary forces they had had earlier, they took 20,000 infantry and 2,500 cavalry and crossed into the territory of the Sedetani, where they had maintained a base camp at the start of their insurrection.

32. By scrupulously paying all of the men, guilty and innocent alike, and by his conciliatory demeanour and language towards them

all, Scipio easily regained his soldiers' goodwill. Before moving camp from New Carthage, he called an assembly, and delivered a lengthy tirade against the treachery of the insurgent chieftains. His feelings as he was setting off to punish that villainy could not be compared with those he had when he recently corrected his compatriots' misdeed, he declared. Then it had been like cutting out his own guts, he said, when, with sighs and tears, he had taken the lives of 30 men to atone for the folly, or the guilt, of 8,000; but now he was happily and confidently proceeding to a massacre of the Ilergetes. For the Ilergetes were not born in the same land as he, nor was there any treaty binding them to him; the only ties they had with him, those of loyalty and friendship, they had themselves broken by their crime. In his army, he said, he could see men who were all citizens, allies, and Latins. But, in addition to that, he was also very moved to see that there was barely a single soldier who had not been brought from Italy either by his uncle Gnaeus Scipio—the first Roman to have come to the province—or by his father or himself. So all were now used to the name and the authority of the Scipios, and he wanted to take them back with him for a well-earned triumph in Italy. And he hoped that they would support his candidacy for the consulship, and consider that to be an honour that would be conferred on all of them alike.

As for the operation that lay before them, he continued, anyone who considered that to be a *war* was forgetting his own achievements. In fact, in his eyes Mago was a greater source of worry than the Ilergetes—Mago who, with a handful of men, had fled the world for an island surrounded by the Ocean.* For in that case at least they faced a Carthaginian leader, and a Punic force, no matter how small. In this one they faced bandits and bandit leaders. These might have some strength when it came to pillaging their neighbours' fields, burning houses, and stealing cattle, but in regular combat on the battlefield they had none; in the fight they would rely more on speed in flight than on their weapons! So it was not because he saw in them any danger, or the seeds of a greater conflict, that he had decided to crush the Ilergetes before leaving his province. No, it was, first of all, so that such an unconscionable uprising not remain unpunished, and, secondly, so that it could not be said that any foe still remained in a province so thoroughly brought to heel by great courage and good fortune. Accordingly, they should, with the gods' assistance, follow him, not to wage war—for this was not a fight against an enemy that was a match for them—but to make criminals pay for their crime.

33. After addressing them like this, Scipio dismissed the men, and ordered them to prepare to march the following day. Ten days after leaving New Carthage, he reached the River Ebro.* He crossed the river and three days later pitched camp within sight of the enemy.

Before him lay a plain ringed by mountains. Scipio now ordered some cattle, most of them taken from the enemy's own fields, to be driven into this valley in order to stimulate the barbarians' savage rapacity, and he sent some light-armed men to give them protection. Once the battle had been started with a charge from these light-armed troops, Laelius was under orders from Scipio to launch an attack with his cavalry from a place of concealment. There was a conveniently projecting hill that provided cover for the surprise attack of the cavalry, and so the fight was not delayed.

Spotting the cattle in the distance, the Spaniards swooped down on them, and the light-armed swooped down on the Spaniards while they were busy with their plunder.* At first they struck fear into them with their spears. Then, after hurling the light weapons—which could provoke fighting rather than decide the issue—they drew their swords, and the hand-to-hand fighting commenced. It was an evenly matched infantry engagement, and would have remained so but for the arrival of the cavalry. These not only trampled down the men before them with a head-on charge, but some also rode around the foot of the slope, and positioned themselves to the rear of the enemy, cutting off most of them. And so it turned into a greater massacre than is usually the case in skirmishes provoked by such attacks.

Rather than discourage the barbarians, the reverse infuriated them and, not to appear demoralized, they formed up for battle at dawn the following day. The terrain was, as noted above, a valley. It was narrow and could not hold all the enemy troops, so that only about two-thirds of the enemy infantry, and all their cavalry, came into battle. The remainder of the infantry took up a position on the side of a hill.

Scipio thought the restricted terrain favoured him: a battle at close quarters would better suit the Roman soldier than the Spaniard and, in addition, the enemy army had been drawn into a location that could not accommodate all his immense forces. He now turned his thoughts to a new strategy. While he could not himself use his cavalry to cover his flanks in such restricted terrain, the enemy, too, could not use the cavalry that they had brought down with their infantry-men. Scipio therefore instructed Laelius to lead the cavalry on a detour over the hills, by the most secluded route he could find, and to do his best to separate the cavalry battle from that of the infantry. He then brought all his infantry forces to face the enemy, and estab-lished a front of four cohorts* because he could not extend the line any further.

Scipio lost no time in engaging; he wished to use the battle itself to divert attention from the cavalry going over the hills. The enemy had no idea that the Roman horsemen had been taken on the detour until they heard the clamour of cavalry going into action behind them.

And so there were two separate battles under way, with two infan-try lines and two cavalry bodies locked in combat down the length of the plain, since the confined space would not permit combined action involving both kinds of fighting. But in the case of the Span-iards, the infantry could be of no assistance to the cavalry, nor the cavalry to the infantry; in addition, the infantry had been deployed, unwisely, on the level ground through confidence in cavalry support. They were, as a result, cut to pieces. The cavalry, too, who had now been encircled, were unable to resist the enemy foot soldiers before them—for their own infantry had been mown down—nor the enemy cavalry to their rear. Though they long resisted from their stationary mounts, whom they formed into a circle, they were killed to a man, and not a single foot- or horse-soldier fighting in the valley survived. There remained the third of their force that had stood on the hill, where they had a safe view of the engagement without taking part in it—these had both the room and the time for flight. Their chieftains also made good their escape along with them, slipping away in the turmoil before their army could be entirely surrounded.

34. That same day the Spaniards' camp was taken, and apart from the other booty some 3,000 men were taken as well. About 1,200 Romans and allies fell in that battle, and there were more than 3,000 wounded. The victory would have been less bloody had the battle been fought on a wider plain that offered an easier escape route.

Indibilis now abandoned his plans for combat. He felt that, in his predicament, there could be no safer course than an appeal to the integrity and clemency of Scipio, which he had already experienced, and he sent his brother Mandonius to him. Mandonius fell at Scipio's knees, and laid the blame for everything on the suicidal lunacy that reigned at the time, when not merely the Ilergetes and Lacetani, but the Roman camp as well, had been as it were infected by some deadly madness. Such was the plight in which he, his brother, and the rest of their people found themselves, he said, that they would return to Publius Scipio, if he felt it appropriate, the lives they had already been granted by him. Or, if they were twice spared, they would, in gratitude, for ever dedicate to him, and him alone, the existence that they owed him. Earlier, at a time when they had as yet no experience of his clemency, they had had confidence in their cause; but now they had all their hopes pinned on the compassion of the victor, and none in their cause.

The Romans had a long-standing custom in dealing with a people with whom they had had no friendly dealings through treaty, or an alliance on terms of equality. They did not accept authority over that people, and assume them pacified, until they had first surrendered all their possessions, religious and secular, given hostages, been disarmed, and had garrisons established in their cities. Now when Mandonius was before him, Scipio gave both him and the absent Indibilis a lengthy tongue-lashing, declaring that they really had deserved to die for their transgression, but that thanks to his own generosity, and that of the Roman people, their lives would be spared. In fact, he said, he was not even going to disarm them or demand hostages, since these were safety measures taken by men who feared further uprising. No, he would leave them the free use of their weapons, and set their minds at ease. But if they revolted, he added, he would vent his wrath, not on innocent hostages, but on them themselves, and he would seek retribution not from an unarmed foe, but from one under arms. Now that they had experience of both conditions, he was offering them the choice of enjoying the favour of the Romans, or facing their wrath.

With that Mandonius was sent off,* and the only demand made of him was for money so the troops could be paid. Scipio then sent Marcius into Further Spain, and Silanus to Tarraco. He himself waited a few days for the Ilergetes to pay up the entire amount of the money required of them and then, at the head of a light-armed force, caught up with Marcius when he was approaching the Ocean.

35. Negotiations with Masinissa had begun some time earlier but had been delayed on various pretexts because the Numidian wanted at all costs to meet Scipio face to face, and ratify their pact by clasping his right hand. That was the explanation for Scipio's long and circuitous journey on this occasion.

Masinissa was at Gades when he was informed by Marcius that Scipio was on his way. He began to claim that his horses were degenerating from being penned up on an island, that they were causing a shortage of provisions for everyone else, and themselves suffering from that shortage; in addition, his horsemen were losing their edge through inactivity. In this way he gained Mago's permission to cross to the mainland to conduct raids on the closest Spanish farmlands. On landing, Masinissa sent three leading Numidians ahead to fix a time and place for talks. He gave the order for two of these men to be held back by Scipio as hostages. The third was sent back to conduct Masinissa to the appointed rendezvous, and then the two men came to the meeting with a small retinue.

Thanks to the fame of Scipio's exploits, the Numidian had already been struck with admiration for the man, and he had formed a mental picture of an imposing and commanding physical presence. But a deeper awe took hold of Masinissa when he saw him in the flesh. Scipio was, indeed, possessed of great natural dignity, but his flowing locks enhanced it, as did a physical appearance that owed nothing to grooming and was, quite the reverse, that of a real man and a soldier. There was, moreover, his age, for he was at the height of his powers, which were magnified and highlighted by the bloom of his youth, which seemed to be revived after his illness.*

The Numidian was practically spellbound when they met. He thanked Scipio for sending back his brother's son; ever since then, he said, he had been searching for that opportunity which the immortal gods had now finally offered him, and which he had not let slip. His desire now was to devote his energies to Scipio and the Roman people, and in such a way that not a single foreigner would prove to have given greater assistance to the Roman state. He had long been wishing to give such assistance, he said, but he had had less opportunity in Spain, a land that was foreign and unknown to him. However, he would now easily provide it in the land in which he had been born and raised with the prospect of inheriting his father's throne. He added that, should the Romans send Scipio to Carthage, too, as commander-in-chief, he was quite sure that Carthage would not last long.

Scipio was pleased to see and listen to Masinissa; he knew that he represented the true strength of the enemy cavalry force, and the young man also gave clear indications of his mettle. Assurances were exchanged and Scipio began his return journey to Tarraco. With the consent of the Romans, Masinissa raided the fields in the neighbourhood so that he would appear to have had good reason for crossing to the mainland. He then returned to Gades.

36. Mago now despaired of success in the Spanish theatre, hopes for which had been raised first by the soldiers' mutiny and then by Indibilis' insurrection. As he prepared to cross for Africa, news reached him from Carthage that he was under orders from his senate to take to Italy the fleet he had under him at Gades. In Italy he was to hire as large a force of Gallic and Ligurian warriors as he could, join up with Hannibal and not allow a campaign that had started with great vigour, and even greater success, to lose its momentum. Money was shipped to Mago from Carthage for that purpose, and Mago himself wrested as much as he could from the people of Gades. He plundered not only their treasury but their temples, as well, and pressured all private individuals to contribute gold and silver to the public purse.

In the course of his journey along the Spanish coast, Mago set ashore some soldiers not far from New Carthage, and raided the farms in the vicinity. He then brought the fleet up to the city. There, after keeping his men on board during the day, he had them disembark at night and led them to the section of the wall that was responsible for the Roman capture of New Carthage. He felt that the city was not strongly garrisoned, and also that a number of the citizens would rise up in the hope of a change of regime. However, men had come in panic from the countryside with simultaneous reports of the Carthaginian raids, the flight of the farmers, and the approach of the enemy. Furthermore, Mago's fleet had been spotted during the day, and it was becoming clear that his choice of anchorage before the city had not been fortuitous. And so men were deployed with weapons and held in readiness inside the gate that faced the lagoon and the sea.*

When the enemy, a crowd of sailors interspersed with the soldiers, came up to the walls out of formation, and with more commotion than vigour, the gate was suddenly flung open and the Romans rushed out with a shout. They threw their foe into disorder, drove them back with their very first charge and volley of missiles, and inflicted heavy losses as they pursued them to the shore. In fact, had ships not been brought to land to take the panic-stricken men on board, there would not have been a single survivor from the rout or the battle. There was panic on the ships, as well. Men were pulling up ladders, trying to prevent the enemy from charging aboard along with their own fighters, and cutting through hawsers and cables so there would be no time lost in getting under way. Many met terrible deaths as they swam to the ships, unsure in the darkness of what to head for or what to avoid. The following day, when the fleet had beaten a hasty retreat back to the ocean, whence it had come, some 800 dead men, and about 2,000 weapons, were found between the wall and the shore.

37. On returning to Gades, Mago found that he was shut out of the town, and instead put in at Cimbii,* a place not far distant from Gades. He then sent a delegation to protest against the gates being closed to an ally and a friend. The townsmen made the excuse that it had come about because a mob, incensed over some pillaging by the soldiers as they disembarked the ships, had converged on the gates. Mago induced their sufetes* (a sufete is the chief magistrate amongst the Phoenicians) to come to a meeting, along with the town's financial officer, and had them all flogged and crucified.

After that Mago crossed with his ships to Pityusa,* an island lying roughly one hundred miles from the mainland and then inhabited by Carthaginians. The fleet was thus given a warm welcome, and was generously provisioned and also reinforced in terms of fighting men and weaponry. Their confidence bolstered by this assistance, the Carthaginians sailed over to the Balearic Islands, fifty miles from Pityusa.

There are two Balearic islands.* One is larger than the other and better endowed with armaments and fighting men. It also has a harbour, where Mago felt he could spend a comfortable winter, autumn being now at an end. But the fleet was given a reception that was just as hostile as if the island's inhabitants were Romans. Today, slings are the islanders' principal weapon, but in those days they were their only one; and no individual from another race possesses as much skill in their use as any single member of the Balearic peoples.

Stones fell like the thickest hail, hurled in such enormous quantities at the fleet as it approached the land that the Carthaginians, not daring to enter the harbour, instead turned their ships on a course out to sea.

They crossed to the smaller island of the Balearians, which was agriculturally fertile but less well populated and less well armed than the other. Disembarking, they established camp in a well-protected position above the harbour, and then took possession of the city* and its farmlands without a fight. They recruited 2,000 auxiliary troops and dispatched them to Carthage, and then drew their vessels ashore for the winter. After Mago's departure from the Ocean coastline, the people of Gades capitulated to the Romans.

38. Such were the operations conducted in Spain under Publius Scipio's command and authority.* Scipio himself now put the province in the hands of Lucius Lentulus and Lucius Manlius Acidinus,* and returned to Rome with ten ships. He was accorded a meeting with the Senate in the temple of Bellona outside the city, and there he gave an account of his achievements in Spain. He enumerated his pitched battles, and the towns he had taken by force from the enemy, and named the tribes that he had brought under the sway of the Roman people. He had gone to Spain to face four commanders and four victorious armies, he said, and had left not a single Carthaginian in the land. He then hopefully raised the question of a triumph for these achievements, but he did not pursue the matter earnestly, since it was well known that, to that day, no man who had not been in office at the moment of his success had ever celebrated a triumph. When the Senate adjourned, Scipio went into the city on foot where he had 14,342 pounds of silver, and a large quantity of coined silver, carried before him to the treasury.

Lucius Veturius Philo then presided over the consular elections. At these the centuries unanimously, and enthusiastically, declared Publius Scipio consul, and as his colleague Scipio was given Publius Licinius Crassus, the *pontifex maximus*. It is, in fact, on record that the attendance at these elections exceeded that of any election during the war. People had come together from all over, not only to vote, but just to get a glimpse of Publius Scipio. They converged in large numbers on his home and on the Capitol, where he was busy with his sacrifice, offering to Jupiter the hundred oxen he had promised in a vow in Spain. They silently assured themselves that, just as Gaius

Lutatius had finished off the earlier Punic War, so Publius Cornelius would finish off the one that was now upon them; and just as Scipio had completely driven the Carthaginians from Spain, so would he drive them from Italy. They were earmarking Africa as his province, as if the war in Italy were over.

The election of the praetors followed. The two current plebeian aediles, Spurius Lucretius and Gnaeus Octavius, were duly elected, and from candidates then holding no office Gnaeus Servilius Caepio and Lucius Aemilius Papus.

Publius Cornelius Scipio and Publius Licinius Crassus began their consulship in the fourteenth year of the Punic War. In the allocation of provinces, Sicily came to Scipio without sortition and with his colleague's approval—Crassus was *pontifex maximus* and his religious duties obliged him to remain in Italy—and Bruttium was then assigned to Crassus. After that, the praetorian provinces were assigned by sortition. The city jurisdiction came to Gnaeus Servilius, Ariminum (as Gaul was then designated*) to Spurius Lucretius, Sicily to Lucius Aemilius, and Sardinia to Gnaeus Octavius.

A meeting of the Senate was held on the Capitol. Here a senatorial decree was passed, on a motion from Publius Scipio, authorizing Scipio to put on the games he had vowed during the mutiny of the troops in Spain, and to finance them out of the moneys he had himself deposited in the treasury.

39. After that Scipio brought before the Senate some spokesmen of the people of Saguntum, and the eldest made the following address:

'Senators: While no misfortune can exceed what we have endured in our determination to maintain, to the very last, our loyalty to you, your services, and those of your generals, towards us have been such that we do not regret the calamities we have suffered. You undertook a war for our sakes, and having undertaken it you have prosecuted it for thirteen years, and with such tenacity that you have yourselves faced, and made the Carthaginian people face, the most dire of predicaments. In Italy you had a terrible war on your hands, and Hannibal as your enemy; and yet you sent a consul into Spain at the head of an army to gather together the debris, one might say, of our wreck. From the moment they arrived in the province, Publius and Gnaeus Cornelius never stopped doing whatever would help us and harm our enemies. First of all they restored our city to us; they sent men throughout Spain to search for our citizens who had been sold into slavery, and, delivering them from servitude, gave them back their freedom.

'We were on the verge of exchanging the most miserable lot for one that was desirable when your generals, Publius and Gnaeus Cornelius, perished, an event that brought almost more sorrow to us than it did to you. At that point we truly thought that we had been returned to our ancient homeland from faraway places only to face ruin once more and to see a second destruction of our native city. And, we thought, we certainly needed no Carthaginian general or Carthaginian army to bring about our undoing—we could be exterminated by the Turduli,* our oldest enemies, who had also been to blame for our earlier destruction. Then, suddenly, and to our surprise, you sent us Publius Scipio here, seeing whom makes us think ourselves the most fortunate of all the people of Saguntum! For we have seen him declared consul—the man who is our hope, our succour, our salvation—and we shall be reporting that sight to our fellow citizens. He captured a large number of our enemy's towns in Spain and, in every case, he set the Saguntines apart from the mass of prisoners and sent them home. Finally there was Turdetania, so implacable to us that Saguntum could not survive while that race of people remained intact. Scipio inflicted such a crushing defeat of them that not only do we ourselves have no reason to fear them but—if I may be forgiven for saying so—even our descendants do not, either. We see in ruins the city of the people for whose gratification Hannibal had destroyed Saguntum; and we take from their lands a tax, the income from which pleases us, but not us much as the revenge it represents!

'We could not have hoped or wished for more than this from the immortal gods, and the senate and people of Saguntum have sent us to you as a ten-man delegation to thank you. We are, at the same time, to congratulate you on your conduct of affairs in Spain and Italy over these years. Thanks to this, you now have Spain militarily under your control not just as far as the River Ebro, but to where the Ocean marks the ends of the earth, and of Italy you have left the Carthaginian nothing but the area enclosed by the rampart of his camp. We have been instructed not only to offer thanks for this to Jupiter Optimus Maximus, protector of the Capitoline citadel, but also, with your permission, to bear to the Capitol this gift of a golden wreath to commemorate your victory. We request your permission to do this, and request also, if you think it appropriate, that you ratify and, by your authority, make permanent the benefits your generals have conferred on us.'

Responding to the Saguntine delegation, the Senate declared that the destruction and subsequent rebuilding of Saguntum would remain an illustration to the whole world of the loyalty between allies that both had maintained. Their generals' actions in restoring Saguntum and delivering Saguntine citizens from servitude had been correct and appropriate, and in accordance with the will of the Senate; and all the other benefits the generals had conferred on them had been approved by the Senate. The senators added that they accorded the delegates permission to place their gift on the Capitol. Orders were then issued for the delegates to be provided with accommodation and hospitality, and for a gift of not less than 10,000 *asses* to be presented to each of them.

The other delegations were then brought before the Senate and granted an audience. The delegates from Saguntum requested permission to make a journey to see as much of Italy as they could in safety, and for this they were given guides, and letters were dispatched to the various towns with instructions that they give the Spaniards a warm welcome. There followed discussion of state policy, the raising of legions, and the distribution of provinces.*

40. It was now common gossip that Africa had been set aside as Publius Scipio's new province, without recourse to sortition, and Scipio himself, no longer satisfied with a modicum of fame, would say that he had been declared consul not simply to conduct the war but to finish it. And, he said, there was no way of achieving that end other than by his personally transporting the army to Africa, and if the Senate opposed him, he would quite openly declare, he would achieve his end through the vote of the people. This project found no favour at all with the most prominent senators, but all of them, from fear or self-interest, held their tongues—all, that is, except Quintus Fabius Maximus. When asked his opinion, Fabius spoke as follows:

'I realize, senators, that many of you think that what is under discussion today is a matter already decided, and that anyone who voices an opinion on Africa as an assignment, on the assumption that it is still open for debate, will be wasting his breath. But, personally, I cannot in the first place see how Africa is firmly established as the responsibility of our brave and stalwart consul when the Senate has not resolved, nor the people authorized, that it be an official assignment for the coming year. Secondly, if it *is* an official assignment, then I do not think any fault lies with a senator who, in his turn, states his opinion on a matter under discussion, but rather with the consul who makes a mockery of the Senate by pretending to bring up as business a matter already settled.

'And yet I am quite sure that, when I oppose this mad rush to cross to Africa, two things are sure to be thought of me. The first is that I have an inherent tendency to delay. Young men are welcome to call this fear or lethargy, as long as I can feel no regret that other people's strategy inevitably appears more appealing at first sight, but mine proves better in practice. The second thing is that I am spitefully critical and jealous of a gallant consul's celebrity that is increasing with every passing day. To check any suspicion of this, I can cite the life I have lived, my character and my dictatorship, plus five terms as consul, along with so much glory earned in battle, and in domestic affairs, that I am more tired than desirous of it. If this does not defend me against such suspicion, then at least my age entirely frees me from it! For how can I be in competition with a man who is not even as old as my son?

'When I was dictator, when I was still full of vigour and in the process of achieving great things, I was vilified by my master of horse. But nobody, either in the Senate or before the people, heard me raise any objection to the man's authority being made equal to mine, something unheard of up to that point. The man was, in certain people's judgement, on the same level as me, and I preferred to have actions, not words, bring him in short order to acknowledge freely that I was his superior. And now that I have held the offices of state I am certainly not going to set myself in competition and rivalry with a young man in his prime. And for what? To have Africa assigned to me as an area of responsibility if he is refused it, of course,* when I am now weary, not just of a public career, but simply of life! I must live and I must die with the glory that I have achieved: I prevented Hannibal's victory so that victory over him could go to you who now have the strength to win it.

41. 'It will be only fair for you to forgive me one thing, Publius Cornelius.* In my own career I never set what people thought of me above the interests of the state, and so I shall not put your glory ahead of the public good either. It would be different if there remained no struggle in Italy, or if the enemy were such that there was no glory to be won from his defeat. In that case, the man holding you back in Italy, even though he were doing that for the public good, might be regarded as having taken steps to remove, along with the war, the possibility of your winning glory. But Hannibal is an enemy who has been occupying Italy for thirteen years with an army that still remains intact. Will you, Publius Cornelius, be displeased with your renown if, as consul, you drive from Italy the enemy who has caused us so many funerals, and so many defeats, and if you win distinction for finishing this war, as Gaius Lutatius did for finishing the First Punic War? Unless, that is, Hamilcar is to be regarded as a better commander than Hannibal, or that war as being more important than this, or unless that victory is greater and more glorious than this one is going to be—provided that it falls to us to triumph during your consulship! Which would you prefer? To have pulled Hamilcar away from Drepana or Eryx,* or to have driven the Carthaginians and Hannibal from Italy? Although you cherish glory already acquired more than glory you hope to acquire, not even you would take greater pride in having freed Spain rather than Italy from the war.

'Hannibal has not yet reached the stage that anyone who chose another theatre of war would not be thought to have feared him rather than to have despised him. So why not get yourself ready for this effort? If your goal is the supreme glory of finishing off the Punic War, why not go straight from here and focus hostilities where Hannibal is located? Why not do that rather than take the circuitous route you propose of crossing to Africa and hoping that Hannibal will follow you there? It is also the natural way of doing things: you defend what is yours before you go on to attack what belongs to others. Let there be peace in Italy before there is war in Africa, and let us be rid of fear ourselves before we go on to inspire it in others. If both things can be achieved under your leadership and authority, then go on to storm Carthage over there after you have vanquished Hannibal here. If one of the two victories has to be left to fresh consuls, the earlier one will turn out to be the greater and more famous, as well as being the cause of the second. Set aside the fact that the treasury cannot support two armies operating independently in Italy and in Africa,* and set aside the fact that we are left with no reserves from which to keep our fleets maintained and to provide supplies. Even apart from that, everyone is aware of the huge risk involved.

'Publius Licinius will be fighting the war in Italy, Publius Scipio in Africa. Suppose Hannibal emerges victorious, and proceeds to march on Rome. I pray that all the gods avert the omen, and my heart shudders at the mere mention of it, but what has happened once can happen again. Is that the point at which we finally call you back from Africa, you the consul, just as we recalled Quintus Fulvius from Capua? And what if it turns out that the fortunes of war are evenly divided in Africa, too? Your own family should be a warning to you—your father and uncle cut down with their armies within thirty days of each other. And that after they had, by their magnificent achievements on land and sea over a number of years, added great lustre to the name of the Roman people, and to your family, amongst foreign races. I should run out of daylight if I tried to list the kings and commanders who brought terrible defeats on their armies through ill-considered invasions of enemy lands. The normally prudent state of Athens quit its war at home to cross to Sicily with a large fleet, on the advice of a young man whose energy was as impressive as his noble birth. In a single naval battle they inflicted abiding damage on their own prosperous community back home.*

42. 'But my examples are from abroad and too distant in time. Let us take as an illustration Africa, now under discussion, and Marcus Atilius, which provide a famous example of fortune cutting both ways.*

'When you catch sight of Africa from the sea, Publius Cornelius, you will certainly think your assignments in Spain to have been child's play. For what similarity is there between the two? Your journey was over a pacified stretch of water along the coastline of Italy and Gaul, putting in at the allied city of Emporiae. Disembarking your men, you led them to allies and friends of the Roman people in Tarraco, going through lands that were all perfectly safe. Then, after Tarraco, your route lay through Roman military positions. In the neighbourhood of the River Ebro were armies of your father and uncle, and after the loss of their commanders these, by virtue of that very tragedy, were all the more ready for the fray. Their leader was the well-known Lucius Marcius. True, his was an irregular appointment, and he was chosen to meet the needs of the moment by a vote of the soldiers; but while the famous generals had birth and regular state offices to commend them, he was their peer in the whole gamut of military skills. The attack on New Carthage proceeded at a very easy pace, and none of the three Punic armies came to defend their allies. As for everything else—and I do not belittle it—it simply is not to be compared with a war in Africa. There we have no harbour open to our shipping, no territory that has been brought to heel, no allied state, no friendly king, no place to establish a bridge-head, and no way to advance. Wherever you look, all is hostile and threatening.

'Are you relying on Syphax and the Numidians? It should be enough to have relied on them once. Hasty action is not always successful, and treachery attempts to win confidence in minor affairs so that, when the stakes are high, the duplicity is well rewarded. The enemy brought down your father and uncle in battle—but not before the Celtiberian "allies" had done so with their treachery. And you yourself did not face as much danger from Mago and Hasdrubal as you did from Indibilis and Mandonius, whose allegiance you had accepted. Having experienced a mutiny of your own soldiers, do you think you can trust Numidians? Syphax and Masinissa both want to see themselves rather than the Carthaginians supreme in Africa, but after them the Carthaginians rather than anyone else. At the moment, the rivalry between them and all manner of inducements to conflict are stimulating them, because the threat from without is far removed. Show them Roman arms, and a foreign army, and you will have them rushing together to put out what they consider to be a fire engulfing them all. The Carthaginians defended Spain in one man-ner; but it is in another that they will defend the battlements of their native city, the temples of their gods, their altars, and their homes, when the fearful wife sees them off to battle, and little children come running before their feet.

'Again, just suppose that the Carthaginians have enough con-fidence in a united Africa, in the loyalty of the kings allied to them, and in their own fortifications. Suppose they actually send a new army from Africa into Italy when they see the country divested of the protection supplied by you and your army. Or suppose that they order Mago to join up with Hannibal—for it is known that Mago has left the Balearics with his fleet, and is skirting the coastline of the Ligurian Alps. Naturally, we shall find ourselves in the same frightful situation that we were in recently, when Hasdrubal descended on

Italy. And you let Hasdrubal slip through your fingers into Italy—you who are going to quarantine not just Carthage, but the whole of Africa, with your army! He had been defeated by you, you will say. All the more reason for me to wish—as much for your sake as the country's—that a defeated man had not been allowed passage into Italy!

'Allow me to credit your strategy with all that turned out well for you, and for the empire of the Roman people, and to blame all that turned out badly on the shifting fortunes of war, and on bad luck. The fact is that the better and braver you are, the more your native city and all Italy wants to hold on to such a protector! And you yourself cannot conceal the truth that, wherever Hannibal is to be found, that is the centre and hub of this war—for you declare that your reason for crossing to Africa is to draw Hannibal there with you. So, whether it be here or over there, it is with Hannibal that your fight will be.

'Are you then going to be stronger on your own in Africa, or here with your army joined to that of your colleague? Does not the recent example of Claudius and Livius also serve to illustrate how important a difference that makes? And what, I ask you, is going to make Hannibal stronger in terms of arms and personnel? Being in a remote corner of Bruttian territory where he has long been vainly appealing for reinforcements from home, or having Carthage close by with all of Africa allied to her? What sort of idea is this, to want to decide the issue where your forces are halved, and your enemy's much greater, instead of where your two armies are to be fighting against one, and one worn down by so many battles and such long and arduous service?

'Keep in mind the contrast between *your* strategy and your father's. As consul he left for Spain in order to encounter Hannibal when he came down from the Alps, but then he returned to Italy from that assignment. When Hannibal is in Italy, *you* are preparing to leave the country—not because you think it serves the interests of the state but because you think it will promote your reputation and glory. It was the same when you left your province and your army without legal authority, and without the sanction of a senatorial decree.* A commander of the people of Rome, you entrusted to two ships the fortunes of the state and the majesty of our empire, the safety of which was staked on your life.

'My own opinion, senators, is that Publius Scipio has been elected consul not to serve his own personal interests, but to serve the republic and us. And I think that the armies have been raised for the protection of the city and Italy, not for consuls to take over to any part of the world they choose with king-like arrogance.'

43. The address was appropriate to the situation, and Fabius also had personal authority and a reputation for his inveterate sagacity. He therefore impressed most of the Senate, especially the senior members, and more people appreciated the older man's discretion than the younger's impetuous spirit. Then Scipio is said to have delivered the following speech:

'Senators: Quintus Fabius himself allowed at the beginning of his address that he might be suspected of spiteful criticism in presenting his opinion. I would not myself presume to make such a charge against so great a man, but such a suspicion has not been entirely erased, whether the problem lies in how he has presented his case or in the facts themselves. For, in his attempt to smother any charge of envy, he has been extremely fulsome in his praise of his own political career and famous exploits. It is as if the competition I risk facing must come from the lowest sort of people, and not from him— because he towers above everybody (and I do not conceal my attempts to rise so far myself), he would not countenance my being considered on his level. He has represented himself as an old man who has finished his career, and me as being younger even than his own son. The assumption is that thirst for glory is coterminous with human life, and that the most important element of it is not concerned with how we are remembered by posterity. I am certain that it is the case with all great souls that they compare themselves not only with men of the present, but with the luminaries of every age. I certainly do not hide my desire not only to achieve your renown, Quintus Fabius, but—if you'll forgive me for saying so—even to surpass it, if I can. Your attitude towards me, and mine towards my juniors, should not be such that we are unwilling to see any citizen achieve success similar to ours. For that would hurt not only those who are the objects of our envy, but the state as well, and almost the entire human race.

'Fabius expanded on the danger I would face in crossing to Africa, to the point of making me think that he was worried not just about the republic and our army, but about me personally. How did this sudden concern for me come about? Remember when my father and uncle were killed, when two of their armies had been practically exterminated, when the Spanish provinces were lost, and four Carthaginian armies and four commanders held the whole country in fear of their armed might. Remember how a general was sought for that war and nobody put himself forward apart from me, how nobody dared submit his name and how the Roman people conferred that command on me when I was twenty-four years old. Why was it that no one at that moment made any mention of my age, of the enemy's strength, of the difficulty of the war, or of the recent defeat of my father and my uncle? Has there now been some greater debacle in Africa than there was at that time in Spain? Are there now greater armies in Africa, and more and better commanders, than there were in Spain at that time? Did I have greater maturity for conducting the war then than I have now? Is Spain a more appropriate theatre for war with a Carthaginian enemy than Africa? Four Punic armies were defeated and put to flight; many cities were stormed or frightened into submission; the whole country was subdued as far as the Ocean, along with its droves of chieftains and barbarous tribes; all of Spain was recovered, with no trace of war left behind. After that it is easy to make light of what I have done—as easy, indeed, as to make light, if I return victorious from Africa, of those very things that are now being exaggerated and made to seem horrific, just to hold me back!

'Fabius says we have no access to Africa, that no harbours are open to us. He talks about Marcus Atilius' capture in Africa, suggesting that Marcus Atilius ran into trouble on first reaching the country. He does not remember, either, that the ill-starred commander *did* find African ports open to him, and that he fought a splendid campaign in his first year, and, in the eyes of the Carthaginian military leaders, remained unbeaten to the end. So you will have no success browbeating me with that particular example. If that defeat had been sustained in this war, not the first one—recently and not forty years ago*—why would I have less justification for crossing to Africa after Regulus' capture than for crossing to Spain after the Scipios fell in battle? I would not allow that the Spartan Xanthippus* was born to be a greater blessing to Carthage than I would be for my own country, and my confidence would only increase from knowing that so much importance can lie in the courage of one individual.

'But we also have to hear about the Athenians, and how they made their reckless crossing to Sicily, neglecting the war at home. Now since you have the time for Greek stories, why not rather tell of Agathocles, King of Syracuse?* When Sicily had long been aflame with a war with Carthage, he crossed to this same Africa and threw the war back to the source from which it had come.

44. 'But what is the point of using dated and foreign examples to illustrate how effective it is to take the offensive to intimidate the enemy and, removing the threat from oneself, to expose another to danger? Can there be a more important and more contemporary example than Hannibal? Seeing other people's territory being pillaged is very different from seeing your own torched and destroyed; and the aggressor has more spirit than the one fighting off the threat. In addition, there is the fear of the unknown; but as the invader you see up close the enemy's pluses and minuses. Hannibal had not expected to see so many peoples in Italy defect to him, and it was after the defeat at Cannae that they did so. How much less security and stability could the Carthaginians expect to find in Africa, faithless allies and domineering and arrogant masters as they are. In addition, even though we were abandoned by our allies, we still held out by virtue of our own strength—the Roman soldier. The Carthaginian has no might in his citizenry, using as he does African and Numidian mercenaries, intrinsically capricious peoples prone to switching allegiance.

'In this case, as long as there is no hesitation on our part, you will at one and the same time receive word that I have made the crossing, that Africa is aflame with war, that Hannibal is making his way out of this country and that Carthage is under siege. You may expect more encouraging and more frequent reports from Africa than you used to receive from Spain. Such hopes are raised in me by the fortune of the Roman people, by the gods who are witnesses to the treaty the enemy broke, and by the kings Syphax and Masinissa, on whose loyalty I shall rely, while also ensuring that I am well protected against duplicity.

'Many factors that the distance now renders unclear the war will clarify; and the mark of a soldier and a leader is not to miss any opportunity that presents itself, and to put to strategic use what he is offered by chance. Quintus Fabius, I shall have the adversary you tender—Hannibal, that is—but let me draw him after me rather than have him hold me here. Let me force him to fight in his own country—and Carthage, rather than some crumbling Bruttian forts, will be the prize of victory. And there is no question of the state suffering damage here while I make the crossing, set my army ashore in Africa, and advance my camp in the direction of Carthage. You were able to assure that, Quintus Fabius, when the victorious Hannibal flitted around all Italy, and you should avoid the insulting suggestion that the consul Publius Licinius, a man of great courage, cannot assure it now, when Hannibal has already been badly shaken and is all but spent. And the reason for Licinius' not participating in a sortition for such a distant province was simply so that the *pontifex maximus* should not be absent from his religious duties.

'But let us suppose, for heaven's sake, that the war were not brought to an end any earlier by the strategy I am advocating. Even then, being seen to have the courage not only to defend Italy, but also to conduct an offensive against Africa, would be in keeping with the dignity of the Roman people, and their reputation amongst kings and nations of foreign lands. It is important, too, to avoid having it believed and spread abroad that no Roman commander would dare to do what Hannibal dared to do, and that whereas, in the First Punic War, when the fight was for Sicily, Africa was frequently attacked by our armies and fleets, now, when the fight is for Italy, she is left in peace. Italy has been tormented for so long. Let her finally have some rest, and let Africa have her turn of burning and devastation. Let us have a Roman camp threaten Carthage's gates, rather than once more see the enemy's rampart from our own walls. Let Africa be the theatre for the remainder of the war. It is to that country that the terror, the flight, the pillaging of fields should be diverted, and the defection of allies and the other military disasters that have descended on us over a fourteen-year period.

'I have said enough about the interests of the state, the campaign now facing us, and the areas of responsibility in question. It would have to be a long speech, irrelevant to your concerns, if I wished to disparage Quintus Fabius' fine reputation and boost my own, just as he belittled my achievements in Spain. I shall do neither, members of the Senate, and then, if nothing else, the younger man will at least have surpassed the older in curbing and restraining his language. My life and achievements have been such that I am quite happy to hold my tongue and live with the opinion you have independently formed of them.'

45. Scipio's address was less favourably received: word had got round that, if he failed in the Senate to have Africa assigned to him as his area of responsibility, he would immediately bring a proposal before the people. And so Quintus Fulvius, who had held four consulships and had also been censor, demanded of the consul that he make a clear statement before the Senate. Would he leave it to the senators to determine the areas of responsibility, and accept their decision, or would he take the matter to the people? When Scipio replied that he would do whatever served the interests of the state, Fulvius said: 'When I put that question to you, I was not unaware of what your reply and what your reaction would be. For you make it clear that you are sounding out the Senate rather than consulting it, and that, if we do not immediately vote you the assignment you want, you have a proposal for the people already drawn up. Accordingly, tribunes of the plebs, I earnestly request that you stand by me when I refuse my opinion. For even if the division favours my proposal, the consul is not going to accept it as binding.'

And with that wrangling broke out, because the consul claimed it was unconstitutional for the tribunes to intervene in support of any senator refusing to state his opinion when asked to do so in his turn. The tribunes then delivered the following judgement: 'If the consul permits the Senate to decide on the assignment of responsibilities, it is our wish that the decision of the Senate be binding, and we shall not allow the matter to be brought before the people. If the consul does not so permit, we shall support a person refusing to voice his opinion on the matter.' The consul requested a day to discuss the issue with his colleague, and the following day the Senate had his permission.

The areas of responsibility were assigned as follows.* One of the consuls received Sicily together with the thirty warships that Gaius Servilius had commanded the year before. That consul was also given leave to cross to Africa if he felt it to be in the interests of the state. The other was given Bruttium and the war against Hannibal, with his own choice of army. Lucius Veturius and Quintus Caecilius were to decide by sortition, or by mutual agreement, which of the two was to continue operations in Bruttium with the two legions that the consul would leave there. The one given that assignment would have his *imperium* extended for a year. All others who were to take charge of armies and hold official responsibilities (apart from the consuls and praetors) also had their *imperium* extended. It fell to Quintus Caecilius by sortition to join the consul for the war against Hannibal in Bruttium.

The games vowed by Scipio were then put on, with large crowds of enthusiastic spectators in attendance. Marcus Pomponius Matho and Quintus Catius were sent on a mission to Delphi to take a gift from the spoils of Hannibal. They bore a golden crown weighing 200 pounds, and reproductions of the spoils made from 1,000 pounds of silver.

Scipio had not been granted a request to levy troops, but he had not been particularly insistent, either. He did, however, secure authorization to take volunteers with him and—because he had stated that the fleet would not involve state expense—to receive all allied contributions for the construction of new ships. The various peoples of Etruria were first to commit to helping the consul, according to the means of each.* The people of Caere promised grain for the crews and all manner of provisions. Populonia promised iron, Tarquinii sail-linen, and Volaterrae wax caulking for ships, and grain. Arretium made a commitment of 3,000 shields and as many helmets, and also a total of 40,000 javelins, Gallic spears, and long pikes, in equal numbers. It would also supply axes, shovels, scythes, basins, and grinders sufficient for forty warships, as well as 120,000 measures of grain, and a contribution towards the upkeep of naval officers and oarsmen. Perusia, Clusium, and Rusellae made a commitment of fir for the construction of ships, and a large quantity of grain. Scipio also availed himself of fir from the state-owned forests. The peoples of Umbria promised to supply fighting men, as did those of Nursia, Reate, Amiternum, and the entire Sabine area. Large numbers of Marsi, Paeligni, and Marrucini gave their names as volunteers for the fleet. The people of Camerinum, who had a treaty with Rome based on equal rights, sent an armed contingent of 600 men.

Keels were laid down for thirty ships, twenty quinqueremes and ten quadriremes. Such was the determination with which Scipio then attacked the work that the vessels were launched, fully equipped and rigged, forty-four days after the timber had been taken from the woods.

46. Setting aboard approximately 7,000 volunteer soldiers, Scipio left for Sicily with thirty warships, and Publius Licinius came to the two consular armies in Bruttium. Of these armies, Licinius took for himself the one that Lucius Veturius had led as consul, leaving Metellus in charge of the legions which he had already commanded, for he thought that Metellus would find it easier to operate with men accustomed to his authority. The praetors also left for their various spheres of duty.

Since the war was facing a financial deficit, the quaestors were instructed to sell off an area of Capuan farmland between the Fossa Graeca* and the coast. Moreover, people were allowed to lay information about lands that had belonged to any Campanian citizen, so that it could become the property of the Roman people. The informer's reward was fixed at a tenth of the value of the land about which he had provided the information. Furthermore, the urban praetor Gnaeus Servilius was assigned the task of ensuring that citizens of Capua settled only where they were allowed to do so by the senatorial decree, and of punishing those residing elsewhere.

That same summer Mago son of Hamilcar put a force of hand-picked fighting men aboard his fleet, and crossed to Italy from the smaller of the Balearic Islands, where he had spent the winter. He brought with him 11,000 infantry and roughly 2,000 cavalry on about thirty men-of-war and numerous freighters, and, thanks to the speed of his arrival, he captured Genua,* where there were no troops patrolling the coastline. Mago next landed on the shores of the Ligurian Alps, hoping to create some unrest in the area. The Ingauni, a Ligurian tribe, were at the time engaged in a war with the Epanterii Montani.* The Carthaginian therefore deposited his booty in the Alpine town of Savo and, leaving ten warships riding at anchor there to protect it, sent the rest of his warships to Carthage for the defence of the coast there, for there was talk that Scipio would be crossing over. Mago then struck a treaty with the Ingauni, preferring to have their support than their adversaries', and proceeded to launch an offensive against the Montani. His army was day by day on the increase as Gauls flocked to him from every direction, drawn by the fame of his name. This caused the senators great concern when they learned of it from dispatches sent by Spurius Lucretius. They feared that, should there be another war of similar proportions in that area, with only the enemy leader changed, then their joy two years earlier, when Hasdrubal and his army were wiped out, might prove to have been unfounded. They therefore instructed the proconsul Marcus Livius to move his army of slave volunteers from Etruria up to Ariminum. In addition, the praetor Gnaeus Servilius was instructed to have the two city legions put under the command of a man of his choosing (if he thought this to be in the interest of the state), and brought from the city. Marcus Valerius Laevinus led those legions to Arretium.

In that same period about eighty Carthaginian freighters were captured off Sardinia by Gnaeus Octavius, who had charge of that province. Coelius claims that their cargo was grain and other provisions destined for Hannibal, Valerius that they were taken as they were transporting to Carthage plunder from Etruria, and Ligurian and Montanian prisoners of war.*

In Bruttium nothing of any significance occurred that year. A plague had fallen on the Romans and the Carthaginians, hurting both sides equally, though the Carthaginian was afflicted with food-shortages as well as the disease. Hannibal spent the summer in the area of the temple of Juno Lacinia. There he built and dedicated an altar, adding a large inscription, written in both Punic and Greek, which listed his achievements.*

BOOK TWENTY-NINE

1. On reaching Sicily, Scipio formed his volunteers into ranks and centuries.* Three hundred of them, young men in their prime and of outstanding physical strength, he kept around him, unarmed, and he left them ignorant of why they were being kept in reserve and not put into centuries or given weapons. Then he assembled a 300-strong cavalry force to cross with him to Africa, selecting young men of superior family and means from all over Sicily, and he fixed a date on which they were to appear, equipped and furnished with horses and weapons. Such a campaign far from home struck them as a grim prospect, and they thought it would expose them to many hardships and much danger on both land and sea. And their parents and relatives, too, not just the conscripts, were prey to such anxiety.

When the appointed day arrived, the men appeared with their weapons and mounts. Then Scipio announced that he was receiving reports that a number of the Sicilian horsemen were alarmed at the thought of such a campaign, which they expected to be onerous and demanding. If that was how they felt, he said, he preferred them to say so right now rather than to find them grumbling later on, and turning out to be half-hearted soldiers of no use to the republic. They should therefore speak their minds, and they would get a sympathetic hearing from him. When one of the men found the courage to say that, given the choice, he certainly would not want to serve, Scipio said to him: 'Well, young man, since you have not concealed your feelings, I shall provide a replacement for you. You are to transfer to him your weapons, your horse, and all the other military equipment; you are to take him home with you from here right away, train him and see that he is schooled in horsemanship and armed combat.'

The man gladly accepted the conditions, and Scipio entrusted to him one of the three hundred men he was keeping unarmed. When the others saw the horseman freed from service with the commander's approval, they all asked to be excused, and all accepted a replacement. So it was that Roman horsemen replaced the 300 Sicilians, without state expense. The Sicilians took responsibility for their instruction and training, because the commander had ordered that anyone who failed to do this would have to take on the service himself. They say that the cavalry squadron turned out to be superb,* providing assistance for the republic in numerous battles.

Scipio then conducted an inspection of the legions, and selected from them soldiers with the largest number of campaigns to their credit, and especially those who had served under Marcellus. These, he believed, were the men who had received the finest training and who were, thanks to their long blockade of Syracuse, the most adept in besieging cities. For it was no minor operation that Scipio had in mind: he was already contemplating the destruction of Carthage.* He then distributed his troops amongst the towns, and requisitioned grain from the city-states of Sicily, making sparing use of that imported from Italy. He refurbished old ships and sent Gaius Laelius to Africa on raiding expeditions with them. His new ships he drew up on shore at Panormus to pass the winter on dry land, because they had been hurriedly put together from timber that was still green.

Having completed his preparations for war, Scipio came to Syracuse, which was still quite unsettled after the great upheavals of the war. Some Greeks were trying to reclaim property, which had been restored to them by the Senate, from people of Italian stock who were holding on to it with the same ferocity with which they had seized it during the hostilities. Feeling his first priority was to safeguard the integrity of the state, Scipio restored the property to the Syracusans by edict, and also by passing sentences on those who persisted in their unlawful possession. Such measures met with approval not only from the plaintiffs, but also from all the communities of Sicily who, as a result, assisted the war effort all the more assiduously.

That same summer a serious war arose in Spain. It was the Ilergetan Indibilis who fomented it, and the only reason he had for it was his admiration for Scipio, which led him to look down on other Roman commanders. Scipio, he felt, was the only leader the Romans had left, the rest having been killed by Hannibal. When the two Scipios had fallen, he reasoned, they had had no one to send to Spain apart from him, and when the war in Italy gained momentum they had called him back from there to face Hannibal. The Romans now had only nominal leaders in Spain and, apart from that, they had also withdrawn a seasoned army.* They had left behind a completely volatile situation, and a disorganized bunch of recruits, and there would never be another occasion like that for freeing Spain. To that day the Spaniards had served either the Carthaginians or the Romans, and not simply the one or the other in turn, but occasionally the two at once. The Carthaginians had been driven out by the Romans, and now the Romans could be driven out by the Spaniards, if they could form a united front. Thus Spain could be for ever liberated from all foreign control, and could return to her native culture and observances.

With such arguments Indibilis spurred not just his own tribesmen to action, but the neighbouring tribe of the Ausetani, and other peoples* in his and their vicinity, as well. So it was that within a few days 30,000 infantry and about 4,000 cavalry converged, following Indibilis' instructions, on the land of the Sedetani.

2. The Roman commanders, Lucius Lentulus and Lucius Manlius Acidinus, fearful of an escalation of hostilities through initial negligence on their part, also united their armies. They then led their troops through the lands of the Ausetani in a non-aggressive fashion, treating hostile soil as though it were pacified, and on reaching the position held by the enemy, they pitched their camp three miles away from theirs. They first sent envoys in an attempt, which proved futile, to persuade the Spaniards to lay down their arms. Then there was a lightning attack by the Spanish cavalry on a Roman foraging party. Horsemen were therefore sent out from a Roman outpost to assist the foragers, and this precipitated a cavalry engagement, but no significant advantage was gained by either side.

At sunrise the next day the Spaniards were all deployed under arms, their line visible about a mile from the Roman camp. The Ausetani were in the centre, with the Ilergetes holding the right wing, and some little-known Spanish tribes the left. Between the wings and the centre they left gaps wide enough to enable them to send out cavalry at the appropriate moment. The Romans followed their usual pattern of deployment, but followed the enemy configuration in one respect: they, too, left paths open for the cavalry between the legions. Lentulus realized, however, that only one side would actually profit from its cavalry, and that was the one that first sent its horsemen into the gaps in the enemy line. He therefore ordered a military tribune, Servius Cornelius, to command his cavalry to charge at a gallop through the wide passages in the enemy formation.

The infantry engagement did not begin well for the Romans; and the twelfth legion, positioned on the left wing facing the Ilergetes, was giving ground. Lentulus waited only long enough to bring up the thirteenth legion from the reserves to the front to support the twelfth, and then, with the fight once more evenly matched in that quarter, he came to Lucius Manlius, who was in the front ranks, shouting encouragement and bringing up reserve troops to points where they were needed. Lentulus informed Manlius that the left wing was now secured, and that he had despatched Cornelius to encircle the enemy with a brisk cavalry charge.*

Barely had Lentulus uttered these words when the Roman cavalry charged into the midst of the enemy, throwing the infantry ranks into chaos, and simultaneously closing the path the Spaniards intended using for their own cavalry charge. The Spanish horsemen therefore abandoned the cavalry fight, and dismounted. When the Roman officers saw the confusion in the enemy ranks, and observed their alarm, their panic and their wavering standards, they urged and entreated their men to attack the demoralized force, and not allow the line to reform. The barbarians could not have held out against such a furious charge but for their chieftain, Indibilis, who, along with his dismounted cavalry, threw himself in the enemy's path before the front units. The fighting in that quarter remained ferocious for some time. The king was half-dead, but still holding his ground. Then he was pinned to the ground by a javelin, and those fighting around him went down under a volley of missiles; and with that the flight began in every sector. Casualties were increased because the horsemen had no room to mount their horses, and also because the Romans were putting heavy pressure on a demoralized foe; and there was no turning back until they seized his camp, as well. Thirteen thousand Spaniards fell that day, and roughly 1,800 prisoners were taken. The Roman and allied dead numbered slightly more than 200, most of them on the left wing. The Spaniards who had been driven from the camp, or who had escaped from the battle, first of all scattered through the countryside, and then returned to their various communities.

3. The survivors were then called to a council meeting by Mandonius. There they deplored their disastrous losses and berated the men who had fomented the war; and they voted to send envoys to hand over their weapons, and negotiate terms of surrender. The envoys put the blame on Indibilis, whom they declared the prime mover of the war, and the other chieftains, most of whom had fallen

in battle, and they offered to give up their weapons and surrender. The answer they received, however, was that acceptance of their surrender depended upon their surrendering, alive, Mandonius and the other instigators of the war. Failing that, they were told, the Romans would bring their army into the land of the Ilergetes and the Ausetani, and then, in turn, into that of all the other tribes.

Such was the reply to the envoys, and it was duly reported to the council. At the meeting Mandonius and the other chieftains were then arrested and delivered up for punishment.* Peace was thus restored to the peoples of Spain, who were obliged to pay double taxation that year, and provide a six-months' supply of grain along with cloaks and togas for the army. In addition, hostages were taken from some thirty tribes.

And so unrest and rebellion in Spain had been whipped up, and put down, in just a few days, and with no serious upheaval; and now the threat of war focused entirely on Africa.

Gaius Laelius had reached Hippo Regius* under cover of night, and at dawn he led out his soldiers, in formation and supported by the crews of his ships, to conduct raids on the local farmland. Everyone here was calmly going about his business, as in peacetime, and the damage inflicted was heavy. People brought the alarming news to Carthage, filling the city with sheer terror: a Roman fleet had arrived, they said, and with it the commander Scipio (and there had already been talk of Scipio's crossing to Sicily). The Carthaginians had no idea how many ships these people had seen, or the size of the force raiding the fields, and under the influence of fear they over-estimated all reports. At first terror and panic gripped their hearts, and then a gloomy foreboding. Such was the change in their circum-stances, they reflected. Recently they had themselves been victors, and had had an army before the walls of Rome; they had mown down so many enemy armies, and accepted the capitulation or voluntary surrender of all the peoples of Italy. Now the fortunes of war had turned, and they would see Africa being plundered and Carthage under siege; and to face these ordeals they had nothing like the strength the Romans had possessed. For the Romans had their prole-tariat and they had Latium to give them an ever-burgeoning supply of young men to replace all their slaughtered armies. There was no military strength in their own urban, or agrarian, proletariat, they said—hence the mobilization of mercenary auxiliaries from the ranks of the Africans, a perfidious race that shifts loyalties with every prospect of gain.* Then there were the kings—Syphax alienated from them after his meeting with Scipio, and Masinissa, a deadly enemy who had openly abandoned them! There was no hope and no help to be found anywhere! Mago was neither fomenting unrest in Gaul, nor joining up with Hannibal, and Hannibal himself was weakening both in reputation and strength.

4. The Carthaginians had lapsed into these depressing reflections after the recent report, but fear for the present brought them back to consider how to deal with the perils they were now facing. It was decided that there should be a swift troop mobilization in the city and countryside, and that they would send men to hire mercenary auxiliaries from among the Africans. They would fortify the city, gather in grain, make ready arms and armour, and fit out ships and send them to Hippo to challenge the Roman fleet. They were involved in this when the message arrived that it was not Scipio, but Laelius, who had made the crossing, and with forces enough only for conducting raids on agricultural areas—Roman military activity was still mostly centred on Sicily.

The Carthaginians were thus given a breathing space, and a start was made on sending embassies to Syphax and other chieftains, with a view to establishing alliances. Men were also sent to Philip to promise him 200 talents of silver for an invasion of Sicily or Italy. There was also a delegation sent to the Carthaginian generals in Italy, instructing them to create all kinds of emergencies to detain Scipio. As for Mago, he was sent not only envoys, but twenty-five warships, as well, plus 6,000 infantry, 800 cavalry, seven elephants, and, in addition, a large sum of money to hire mercenaries. The thinking was that, with such support, Mago could move his army closer to the city of Rome and join up with Hannibal.*

Such was the preparation and planning taking place in Carthage. Meanwhile, Laelius was making off with huge quantities of plunder from farmlands that were unprotected and devoid of troops, and Masinissa, when he heard of the arrival of a Roman fleet, came to him with a few horsemen. Masinissa complained that Scipio's handling of operations was half-hearted: he had not yet brought an army over to Africa, although the Carthaginians were demoralized, and Syphax was embroiled in wars with his neighbours. He added that he was convinced that Syphax, given the leeway to arrange affairs to his satisfaction, would show no loyalty whatsoever in his future dealings with the Romans. Laelius should encourage and urge Scipio not to hold back, and he himself, despite having been driven from his throne, would assist the Romans with both infantry and cavalry forces not to be scoffed at. Laelius should not himself wait around in Africa, either, he said, for he believed that a fleet had set sail from Carthage, and engaging that fleet in Scipio's absence would certainly not be a safe move.

5. Following this conversation, Laelius sent Masinissa off, and the following day set sail from Hippo with his plunder-laden ships. He returned to Sicily and delivered Masinissa's communiqué to Scipio.

It was at about this time that the ships sent to Mago from Carthage put in at a point between the land of the Ligurian Albingauni* and Genua. Mago happened to have his fleet at anchor there at the time, and after hearing out the envoys, who relayed the orders for him to muster the largest armies he possibly could, he promptly held an assembly of Gauls and Ligurians, there being large numbers of both in the area. He told them that his mission was to champion their liberty. As they could see for themselves, he was now being sent reinforcements from home, but, he added, his strength, and the size of his army for waging that war, depended on them. He explained that there were two Roman armies in operation in the area, one in Gaul, and the other in Etruria, and he knew for sure that Spurius Lucretius was going to join forces with Marcus Livius. For effective resistance to two Roman commanders and two Roman armies, many thousands of men had to be put under arms.

The Gauls expressed the greatest enthusiasm for this, but observed that they had one Roman camp within their territory, and a second almost within sight of them in nearby Etruria. If it became known that the Carthaginians were receiving assistance from the Gauls, they would instantly have hostile armies invading their land from both directions. Mago should therefore request of the Gauls only such assistance as could be given covertly. The Ligurians were in a different situation, they said: with Roman camps a long way off from their farmland and cities, they could make their decisions freely, and it was only right that they should put their younger men under arms, and take their fair share of the war.

The Ligurians did not demur, requesting only a two-month period for recruiting troops. Meanwhile, Mago proceeded to hire Gallic mercenary soldiers by sending agents covertly through their territory, and he was also sent supplies of all kinds by the Gallic tribes in secret consignments.

Marcus Livius brought his army of slave volunteers from Etruria into Gaul. He joined up with Lucretius, and prepared to face Mago should he move out of Liguria and come closer to the city. If the Carthaginians remained inactive in that remote corner of the Alps, however, Livius would remain in position close to Ariminum, in order to protect Italy.

6. After Gaius Laelius' return from Africa, Scipio was aroused by Masinissa's words of encouragement. In addition, his men were fired with a desire to cross to Africa as soon as possible when they saw plunder from enemy territory being unloaded from an entire fleet. However, this major scheme was put on hold by a lesser one, namely the recovery of the city of Locri, which, during the Italian defections, had also gone over to the Carthaginians. A gleam of hope of attaining this goal arose from a very minor incident.

Marauding rather than regular warfare was now the order of the day in Bruttium. The Numidians had started this, and the Bruttii followed suit, as much because it suited their make-up as because of their alliance with Carthage. Finally, even the Roman soldiery became infected with the disease and, within the limits set by the officers, began to take pleasure in looting and making raids on enemy farms.

Now, a number of Locrians who had come out of their city were surrounded by the Romans and taken off to Rhegium. Amongst prisoners taken were a number of tradesmen who had been regularly hired by the Carthaginians for work in the citadel of Locri. The tradesmen were recognized by some prominent Locrian citizens who were at the time in exile at Rhegium, having been expelled by the opposing faction that had delivered Locri to Hannibal. These men put to them questions usually asked by people who have been long absent from home, and the tradesmen told them what was going on in Locri—and also gave them hope that they would deliver the citadel to them if they were ransomed and sent back. For, they said, they lived in the town, and the Carthaginians trusted them in every respect. The exiles, suffering severe homesickness and also feeling a burning desire for vengeance on their enemies, promptly redeemed the men and sent them back home. First, however, they came to an agreement with the tradesmen on a programme for bringing off the

coup, and on the signals these were to look for in the distance from
the citadel. They then went off to Syracuse to see Scipio, with whom
there were also a number of the Locrian exiles, and recounted what
the prisoners had undertaken to do. This gave the consul some hope
of its success, and so the military tribunes Marcus Sergius and Publius
Matienus were sent back with the exiles, under orders to take 3,000
soldiers from Rhegium to Locri. The propraetor Quintus Pleminius*
was also given written orders to take an active part in the operation.

The force set off from Rhegium carrying ladders specially constructed to the height of the citadel, and around the middle of the
night, from the agreed location, they gave the signal to the fifth
column in the citadel. The men were prepared and on the alert, and
they themselves lowered ladders that were custom-made for the job.
They took in the Romans, who scaled the wall at several points at
once, and before any cry could go up, an attack was launched on the
Carthaginian sentries who, naturally, fearing no such occurrence,
had fallen asleep. The groans of the dying men were the first thing to
be heard. Then came the sudden uproar and confusion as men were
awakened from their sleep without knowing what had caused the
alarm; but eventually things became clearer as they began to rouse
each other. At last they were all issuing calls to arms, shouting that
the enemy was in the citadel and the sentries were being killed. The
Romans, nowhere near as numerous as their enemy, would have been
overwhelmed but for a cry raised by the men outside the citadel; for
this rendered unclear the source of the alarm, and the confusion and
darkness only served to intensify every groundless fear.

As a result the Carthaginians were terror-stricken. They assumed
the citadel to be now full of the enemy, and they abandoned the
fight and sought refuge in the other citadel (for there are two, a short
distance from each other). The townspeople were then left holding
their town, which was set between the two sides as the victors' prize;
and, every day, light skirmishes would be started from the two citadels. Quintus Pleminius was in charge of the Roman force, Hamilcar
of the Carthaginian. They each augmented their troops by summoning reinforcements from the surrounding areas. Finally Hannibal
himself was en route for the town. The Romans could not have held
out against him had not the sentiments of most Locrians, embittered
by Carthaginian arrogance and rapacity, felt more sympathy for the
Roman cause.

7. When he was brought the news that the situation in Locri was becoming more dangerous, and that Hannibal himself was on his way, Scipio did not want the force there also to be put at risk (for its withdrawal from the town would not be easy). He therefore left his brother Lucius Scipio in command of the garrison at Messana and, as soon as the tide turned in the straits,* set off from there with ten ships, the flow now in his favour.

Hannibal meanwhile sent a message from the River Bulotus, not far from the city of Locri, ordering his men to engage the Romans and Locrians with maximum force at daybreak. In the meantime, he explained, while everyone's attention was focused on that confrontation, he would himself make an attack on the unsuspecting city from the rear. At dawn, Hannibal found the battle already under way. He was unwilling to confine himself to the citadel—with his numbers he would choke such a restricted area—and he had not brought ladders for scaling the walls. He therefore piled up the baggage and presented his army, in battle order, close to the walls, hoping to intimidate the enemy. Then, as ladders and other materials needed for an assault were being prepared, he began to ride around the city with his Numidian cavalrymen to see just where he should launch his attack. As he went up to the wall, the man who happened to have been standing next to him was struck with a projectile from a 'scorpion'. The incident, which had exposed him to great danger, unnerved Hannibal. He ordered the retreat to be sounded, and established a fortified camp out of missile-range.

The Roman fleet arrived in Locri from Messana when much of the day still remained. The men were all put ashore, and they entered the city before sunset.

The next day the Carthaginians started the fighting from their citadel, and Hannibal, who had by now finished preparing the ladders and everything else for the assault, began to move up to the walls. Suddenly—the last thing he feared—the gate opened, and Romans came charging out at him. The attack of the Romans took the Carthaginians by surprise, and left some 200 dead; and when Hannibal realized that the consul was present, he brought the others back to camp. He sent word to the men in the citadel that they should look out for themselves, and then struck camp during the night and left. The men in the citadel set fire to the buildings they occupied, hoping that the resulting confusion would slow down the enemy, and then—moving at the pace of fleeing men—caught up with the column of their comrades before nightfall.

8. When he saw that the citadel had been abandoned by the enemy, and that their camp was empty, Scipio called the citizens of Locri to an assembly and severely reprimanded them for their defection. He executed the ringleaders, and made their property over to the principal members of the faction that had opposed them, in recognition of these people's exceptional loyalty to Rome. He said that he was not officially in a position to give anything to, or take anything from, the Locrians. They should send representatives to Rome and accept whatever fate the Senate saw fit to impose on them. Of one thing he was sure, he said: despite their shoddy treatment of the Roman people, they would be better off facing the wrath of Rome than having the 'friendship' of Carthage. Scipio then left his legate Pleminius to defend the city with the force that had taken the citadel, while he himself crossed to Messana with the troops with which he had come.

After they abandoned the Roman cause, the Locrians had been treated by the Carthaginians in such a high-handed and ruthless manner that they found it possible to endure ordinary inequities not only with sangfroid but almost with cheerfulness. But, in fact, in terms of unscrupulous and rapacious conduct Pleminius so outdid the garrison commander Hamilcar, and the Roman occupying force so outdid the Carthaginians, that it seemed like a contest in villainy, not arms. Of all the things that make the weak hate the strength of the powerful, there was not one that was not inflicted on the townspeople by the commander or his men. Unspeakable abuse was inflicted on the men themselves, on their children, and on their wives. Soon the greed of the Romans did not shrink from the desecration even of the sacred, and it was not simply a matter of the violation of ordinary temples. Even the treasures of Proserpina suffered this fate, though they had remained inviolate throughout history—apart from the time when they were said to have been looted by Pyrrhus, who paid a heavy price in atonement for the sacrilege, and returned his spoils. On that occasion the ships of the king were shattered in a wreck, and they succeeded in bringing nothing to land undamaged, apart from the holy money of the goddess that they were transporting. It was the same on this occasion, even if the disaster was of a different kind. That same money brought madness on all the men tainted with that violation of the temple, turning officer against officer and soldier against soldier with furious acrimony.

9. Pleminius had overall command, and some of the troops—those that he had himself brought from Rhegium—were serving directly under him, while others were under the tribunes. A soldier of Pleminius had filched a silver cup from the home of one of the townspeople, and as he fled, pursued by the owners, he happened to run into the military tribunes, Sergius and Matienus. The man then had the cup removed from him at the order of the tribunes. This led to quarrelling and shouting, and finally a fight broke out between Pleminius' men and those of the tribunes, the numbers involved and the disorder growing as people happened to come on the scene to help one side or the other.

Pleminius' men took a beating, and they came running to Pleminius pointing to their bloody wounds; and they added cries of indignation and told him of insults that had been directed at him during the brawl. Pleminius was furious. He charged from his house, had the tribunes summoned, and gave orders for them to be stripped of their clothes, and for whips to be made ready. Some time passed while the tribunes were being stripped—they kept struggling and begging the men present to help—and suddenly their soldiers, flushed with their recent victory, came running from all directions, just as if they had been summoned to arms against the enemy. When they saw the injuries the tribunes had already suffered from the lash, they were instantly fired with a much more uncontrollable fury. With no consideration for the man's authority, or even for civilized behaviour, they first gave the lictors a shameful beating, and then turned their attack on the legate. They fenced him off and isolated him from his men, viciously mauled him, and left him almost dead, with his nose and ears cut off.

The incident was reported to Scipio in Messana, and a few days later he sailed to Locri in a *hexeris*.* After hearing the cases presented by Pleminius and the tribunes, he exonerated Pleminius of any culpability and left him in place, still in command. The tribunes he found guilty and he clapped them in irons to be sent to the Senate in Rome. He then returned to Messana, and from there to Syracuse.

Pleminius was in an uncontrollable rage. He felt that the wrong he had suffered had been negligently dealt with and underestimated by Scipio, and that the only person capable of assessing the penalty was

the man who had been on the receiving end of the outrage. He had
the tribunes hauled before him and, after mutilating them with every
torture that can be inflicted on a human body, put them to death.
Then, not satisfied with punishing them while they were alive, he
threw them out unburied. He was just as brutal with the most prominent burghers of Locri who, he heard, had gone to Publius Scipio to
protest against the wrongs he had done them. The earlier instances
of shameful abuse that he had inflicted on the allies from covetous-
ness and greed he now multiplied from anger, and brought oppro-
brium and hatred not merely on himself, but on his commanding
officer as well.

10. The date for the elections was now approaching when a letter
from the consul Publius Licinius was brought to Rome. Licinius
reported that he and his army were afflicted by a serious disease, and
that, had not the malady struck the enemy with the same or even
greater virulence, holding out against them would have been impossible. Thus, since he could not himself come for the elections, he
would, if the senators concurred, appoint Quintus Caecilius Metellus dictator for the purpose of holding them. Demobilization of
Quintus Caecilius' army was in the interests of the state, he added,
since at the moment it was serving no purpose. Hannibal had already
taken his men back to winter quarters, and so virulent was the plague
that had struck Metellus' own camp that, unless the army were
swiftly disbanded, it looked as though not a single man would survive. The consul was given leave to take whatever measures he
thought the public interest and his own sense of duty called for.

At that time there was a sudden onset of religious fervour amongst
the citizens after an oracle was discovered in the Sibylline Books,
which had been consulted because of an increase in the number of
showers of stones that year. The oracle declared that whensoever a
foreign foe should bring war upon the land of Italy, he could be driven
from Italy, and vanquished, if the Idaean Mother were brought to
Rome from Pessinus.* The oracle, which had been discovered by the
decemvirs, made all the greater an impression on the senators
because of the report of the envoys who had taken the gift to Delphi.
The envoys declared that everything had been favourable during
their sacrifice to Pythian Apollo, and that there had been an oracular
response promising the Roman people a victory, one far greater than
that whose spoils had provided the gifts they were bearing. The

senators felt these hopes were confirmed by Publius Scipio's request for Africa as his province, which suggested that he had some presentiment of the war's conclusion. Wishing therefore to accelerate the victory that was announcing itself through prophecies, omens, and oracles, they now proceeded to discuss and consider the logistics of transporting the goddess over to Rome.

11. The Roman people had, as yet, no states in Asia allied to them. Nevertheless, people remembered that Aesculapius* had at one time been brought from Greece to check an epidemic, when there was still no formal alliance with that country, whereas now friendly relations had already been established with King Attalus for the conduct of joint hostilities against Philip. (Attalus would, they thought, do all that he could to help the Roman people.) They decided to send to the king a delegation consisting of Marcus Valerius Laevinus, consul on two occasions and a former commander in Greece; a former praetor, Marcus Caecilius Metellus; an ex-aedile, Servius Sulpicius Galba; and two ex-quaestors, Gnaeus Tremelius Flaccus and Marcus Valerius Falto. To these men they officially assigned five quinqueremes so they could maintain the dignity of the Roman people when they approached those lands that needed to be impressed with the prestige of the Roman name.

On their way to Asia the delegates went up to Delphi. There they immediately approached the oracle with the question of what prospects it foresaw for them, and the Roman people, of accomplishing the mission on which they had been sent from home. The response, they say, was that they would gain their end through the help of King Attalus, and that, after transporting the goddess to Rome, they must ensure that the person giving the goddess a warm welcome should be the best man in Rome. The delegates then came to the king in Pergamum. After giving them a friendly reception, Attalus accompanied them to Pessinus in Phrygia, put in their hands the stone that the local people said was the mother of the gods, and told them to take it away to Rome. Marcus Valerius Falto was sent ahead by the delegates with the message that the goddess was in transit, and that the Romans had to seek out the best man in their city-state to welcome her with the appropriate forms of hospitality.

Quintus Caecilius Metellus was appointed dictator for overseeing the elections by the consul, who was in Bruttium, and his army was disbanded. Lucius Veturius Philo was appointed master of horse. The

elections were then held by the dictator, and the consuls elected were
Marcus Cornelius Cethegus and Publius Sempronius Tuditanus, the
latter *in absentia* as he was on assignment in Greece. The praetors
elected after that were: Tiberius Claudius Nero, Marcus Marcius
Ralla, Lucius Scribonius Libo, and Marcus Pomponius Matho. The
elections over, the dictator resigned his position.

There were three repetitions of the Roman Games, and seven of
the Plebeian. The curule aediles were Gnaeus Cornelius Lentulus
and Lucius Cornelius Lentulus. Lucius had Spain as his province,
and, elected in his absence, he was also absent from Rome during his
tenure of the post.* Tiberius Claudius Asellus and Marcus Junius
Pennus were the plebeian aediles. That year Marcus Marcellus dedicated the temple of Virtus at the Porta Capena, sixteen years after it
had been promised in a vow at Clastidium in Gaul by Marcellus'
father, during his first consulship. Also during that year the Flamen
of Mars, Marcus Aemilius Regillus,* died.

12. The Greek situation had received no attention during the past
two years. As a result Philip forced the Aetolians, who had been
abandoned by the Romans* (the one power on which they relied for
assistance), to sue for peace, and accept it on his terms. Had he not
made every effort to accomplish this quickly, the proconsul Publius
Sempronius might have surprised him while he was still at war with
the Aetolians. For Sempronius had been sent to succeed Sulpicius in
his command with 10,000 infantry, 1,000 cavalry, and thirty-five
warships, and he represented a not inconsiderable force for helping
the allies.

With the peace barely concluded, news reached the king that the
Romans had reached Dyrrachium, that the Parthini and other tribes
in the area had been roused to hopes of revolutionary change and
that Dimallum was under attack. The Romans had actually made a
diversion into that area. They had been sent to aid the Aetolians but,
furious with the Aetolians because they had concluded a peace with
the king, without Roman authority and in contravention of their
treaty, they had abandoned their mission. When he heard about this,
Philip feared that greater unrest might arise among the neighbouring
tribes and peoples, and he made swiftly for Apollonia with forced
marches. It was to Apollonia that Sempronius had withdrawn, having sent his legate Laetorius into Aetolia with a portion of his troops,
and twenty-five ships, to see how matters stood there, and to upset

the peace, if he could. Philip plundered the agricultural land of Apollonia and, bringing his troops up to the city, gave the Romans the opportunity to do battle. But he saw that they made no move beyond manning the walls, and he had insufficient confidence in his forces for an assault on the city. Besides, he wanted to make a peace with the Romans, if he could, as he had with the Aetolians or, failing that, at least negotiate a truce. So he avoided provoking them with fresh hostilities, and withdrew into his kingdom.

The people of Epirus were now growing tired of the prolonged hostilities and at about this time, having first sounded the feelings of the Romans, they sent a delegation to Philip to broach the subject of a general peace. They were certain this could be arranged, they assured Philip, if he came to a meeting with Publius Sempronius, the Roman commander. Their request that Philip cross to Epirus was readily granted since the king himself felt no aversion to peace. At Phoenice, a city in Epirus, the king first held talks with Aeropus, Derdas, and Philip, the praetors* of the people of Epirus, and later met with Publius Sempronius. Present at the meeting were Amynander, king of the Athamanians, and other magistrates of the Epirots and Acarnanians.

The praetor Philip opened the proceedings. He made a plea for an armistice simultaneously to the king and the Roman commander, and asked them to grant that as a favour to the people of Epirus. The conditions for peace that Publius Sempronius laid down were that the Parthini, Dimallum, Bargullum, and Eugenium should be under Roman authority, and that, if the king sent ambassadors to Rome and gained the Senate's approval, Atintania should be ceded to Macedon. The peace was then concluded on these terms. Prusias king of Bithynia, the Achaeans, the Boeotians, the Thessalians, the Acarnanians, and the Epirots were included in the treaty by the king, and the people of Ilium,* King Attalus, Pleuratus, Nabis tyrant of Sparta, the Eleans, the Messenians, and the Athenians by the Romans. The terms were put in writing and a seal affixed to the document, and a two-month truce was fixed to allow envoys to be sent to Rome so that the people might sanction the peace on these conditions. The tribes did sanction it, and unanimously, because with the war now focused on Africa they wanted, for the time being, to be released from all other wars. The peace concluded, Publius Sempronius left for Rome to take up his consulship.

13. In the consulship of Marcus Cornelius and Publius Sempronius, and the fifteenth year of the Punic War, Cornelius was assigned
Etruria as his province, along with its old army, while Sempronius
was assigned Bruttium and given orders to muster new legions. As for
the praetors, the urban jurisdiction came to Marcus Marcius, the
foreigners' jurisdiction, plus Gaul, to Lucius Scribonius Libo, Sicily
to Marcus Pomponius Matho, and Sardinia to Tiberius Claudius
Nero. Publius Scipio had his *imperium* extended for a year, and
retained command of his army and fleet. The same prerogative was
extended to Publius Licinius, to allow him to hold Bruttium with two
legions for as long as the consul felt it was in the public interest for
him to stay on in the province with *imperium*. Marcus Livius* and
Spurius Lucretius also saw their *imperium* extended, each commanding two legions (those which they had used for the defence of Gaul
against Mago); so, too, did Gnaeus Octavius, who was to pass Sardinia, and his legion, on to Tiberius Claudius, and himself patrol the
coastline, within bounds set by the Senate, with forty ships. In Sicily,
the praetor Marcus Pomponius was assigned the two legions of the
army that had fought at Cannae. Titus Quinctius and Gaius Hostilius
Tubulus were to have charge of Tarentum and Capua respectively
with propraetorian authority, as they had the year before, and with
the old army in both cases. As regards the Spanish command, the
judgement of the people was sought on the two men they wished sent
as proconsuls to that sphere of authority.* The tribes unanimously
called for the same two men to hold these areas of responsibility as
proconsuls as had held them the year before, namely Lucius
Cornelius Lentulus and Lucius Manlius Acidinus. The consuls proceeded to hold a troop-levy, which was aimed at raising fresh legions
to serve in Bruttium and also (in accordance with their orders from
the Senate) supplementary troops for the other armies.

14. Africa had not yet been publicly declared a formal sphere of
responsibility, for the senators were keeping the matter a secret, I
believe, to prevent the Carthaginians coming to hear of it too soon.
Even so, the hopes of the citizen body had been raised of a campaign
in Africa that year, and of an imminent end to the Punic War. This had
filled people's minds with superstition, making them predisposed
both to report and to accept paranormal phenomena. Accounts of
such phenomena therefore began to circulate in greater numbers.
Two suns had been sighted, it was said, and there had been moments

of daylight during the night; and at Setia a meteor was said to have been seen travelling from east to west. It was reported that at Tarracina a gate had been struck by lightning, and that at Anagnia a gate as well as many points on the city wall had been struck. In the temple of Juno Sospita at Lanuvium there was a crash accompanied by a horrific roar. A single day of prayer was held to expiate these divine manifestations, and the nine-day rite was also performed because of a shower of stones.

In addition to this, there was also discussion of the welcome to be given to the Idaean Mother. One of the delegates, Marcus Valerius, had come ahead of the others with the news that she would soon be in Italy, and a fresh report had also come indicating that she was already at Tarracina. There was now a question of no small importance exercising the Senate: who was the best man in the community? And everyone would have preferred to win an honest victory in that particular competition than to have any commands or public offices conferred upon him, whether by vote of the Senate or the people. The senators adjudged Publius Scipio*—son of the Gnaeus Scipio who had fallen in Spain, and a young man who had not yet held the quaestorship—to be the best of the good men in the entire community. The qualities in the man that led them to such a decision I would have been happy to pass down to posterity, had such an account been passed down to me by writers living close to the time of the event. But I shall not introduce my own views reached through conjecture about a subject now long buried in the past.

Publius Cornelius was instructed to proceed to Ostia with all the married ladies to meet the goddess. There he was to welcome her from the ship, bring her to land, and hand her to the married ladies to be carried to the city.

After the ship reached the mouth of the River Tiber, Scipio, following his instructions, put to sea and, receiving the goddess from her priests, brought her to shore. The leading married women of the community received her. Amongst these was one whose name is pre-eminent, Claudia Quinta,* whose dubious reputation in earlier days, it is said, added greater lustre to the purity for which she was known to posterity thanks to her solemn duty on this occasion. The ladies kept passing the goddess to each other, from hand to hand, on their journey, as the entire community poured forth to meet them, and there were censers placed before the doors along the route where she was borne. As incense burned and people prayed that she should enter the city of Rome with grace and favour, they carried the goddess to the temple of Victory on the Palatine. This was on 12 April,* which was thereafter a holy day. The people crowded the Palatine bearing gifts for the goddess, and there was a *lectisternium* and games that were called the Megalesia.

15. Discussions in the Senate now focused on bringing up to strength the legions in the areas of official responsibility, and a suggestion was made by certain members that a state of affairs that had somehow been tolerated in difficult times should no longer be endured, now that, thanks to heaven's blessing, the threat had been removed. At this the senators' ears pricked up. The members went on to say that the twelve Latin colonies which had refused to provide soldiers in the consulship of Quintus Fabius and Quintus Fulvius had now enjoyed almost five years of exemption from military service,* regarding it almost as an honour or benefit conferred on them. Meanwhile, they added, good and loyal allies had—in return for their faithful service to the Roman people—been drained by levies conducted every year without interruption, during that period.

The mention of this did not simply remind the senators of an issue now well-nigh forgotten, but actually roused them to anger. As a result, they would permit the consuls to raise no item of business before this, and they passed a decree instructing them to call to Rome the magistrates and ten leading citizens from each of the communities in question, which were: Nepete, Sutrium, Ardea, Cales, Alba, Carseoli, Sora, Suessa, Setia, Circeii, Narnia, and Interamna. The consuls were to demand from each of these colonies twice the largest total of infantrymen that it had supplied to the Roman people ever since the appearance of the enemy in Italy, and also requisition 120 cavalrymen from each of them. Any that was unable to reach the required number of cavalrymen should be allowed to provide infantrymen, on the basis of three infantrymen per cavalryman. Foot and cavalry soldiers selected should be the wealthiest members of their community, and they were to be sent anywhere that supplementary forces were needed outside Italy. It was also resolved that a refusal to comply would lead to the detention of the magistrates and representatives of that colony, and that any request for a senatorial hearing be refused until they had fulfilled their obligations.

The Senate further decided that the colonies in question should have a tax imposed on them at the rate of one *as* per thousand, to be charged annually. The tax-assessment in these colonies would be based on the list established by the Roman censors—for it was the Senate's will that the list conform to that used for the Roman people—and be brought to Rome by the censors of the colonies (who would be under oath) before they left office.

Following this decree of the Senate, the consuls called to Rome the magistrates and most prominent citizens of the colonies involved, and made the demand for the soldiers and the tax. This led to the colonists shouting each other down in their objections and protests. Raising such a force of soldiers was impossible, they said, and they would scarcely manage it even if the requirement were the original number in the register.* They begged and pleaded to be allowed to appear in the Senate and make their appeal, saying that they had done nothing to deserve ruin. But even if they had to face ruin, they added, neither their misdeed nor the anger of the Roman people could make them contribute more men than they had.

The consuls stood firm, ordering the delegates to remain in Rome and the magistrates to go home to raise the troops. Unless the requisite complement of fighting men were brought to Rome, they were told, no one would grant them a senatorial hearing. With that, all hope of appearing before the Senate and making an appeal now removed, a troop-levy was conducted in the twelve colonies concerned and, thanks to the increase in younger men as a result of the long exemption, it was completed without difficulty.

16. Another matter that had been neglected and left in silence for almost as long was also brought up by Marcus Valerius Laevinus. He stated that it was only fair that the individuals concerned should finally be repaid the financial contributions they had made* when he and Marcus Claudius were consuls. No one should be surprised that he was taking a particular interest in the financial obligations incurred by the state, he said. A consul of the year in which the contributions were made had some personal involvement; and, besides, it was he who had suggested such a contribution, at a time when the public purse was empty and the people unable to afford the war tax. The senators were pleased to be reminded of this. They instructed the consuls to put the matter to the house, and then decreed that the money should be repaid in three instalments, the first to be

disbursed immediately by the consuls of the current year, the two others by the consuls two and four years after that.

One issue then put all other concerns in abeyance. To that date nothing was known of the terrible fate that had overtaken the Locrians but now, with the arrival of a Locrian delegation, word of it spread. And what roused public animosity was not so much Pleminius' criminal activities as Scipio's partiality, or his negligence, in his case. There were ten Locrian delegates, shabbily dressed in soiled clothing, and they approached the consuls as they sat in the Comitium. In Greek fashion they held before them olive-branches, symbolizing their suppliant status, and with tearful cries they flung themselves to the ground before the tribunal. When the consuls asked them to explain themselves, they said that they were Locrians, and that, at the hands of the legate Quintus Pleminius and the Roman soldiers, they had suffered what the Roman people would not even want the Carthaginians to suffer. They were begging the senators to grant them leave to appear before them, they explained, and to tell the sad tale of their tribulations.

17. They were granted an audience with the Senate, and the eldest of the Locrians gave the following address:

'I am aware, members of the Senate, that the most important factor in how our grievances are to be assessed by you is a full understanding on your part both of how Locri was betrayed to Hannibal, and of how Hannibal's garrison was then expelled and the town restored to your authority. For if culpability for our defection cannot be attributed to public policy, and if it becomes clear that our return to your control arose, not only with our support, but also thanks to our own efforts and valour—then you would be all the more indignant at seeing such undeserved and atrocious injuries inflicted on good and faithful allies by your legate and soldiers. My own opinion, however, is that an explanation of both our defections should be held over for another time, and that for two reasons. In the first place, I feel the matter should be discussed in the presence of Publius Scipio, who took back Locri and who is witness to all that we have done, good and bad. Secondly, no matter what our conduct has been, we did not deserve to suffer what we have suffered. We cannot hide the fact, members of the Senate, that, when we had a Carthaginian garrison in our citadel, we suffered many foul indignities at the hands of the garrison commander Hamilcar and his Numidians and

Africans. But what are they when they are compared with what we are suffering today?

'Please listen with indulgence, senators, to what I must reluctantly say. All of humanity is now on tenterhooks, waiting to see whether it is to be you or the Carthaginians who will be rulers of the world. If Roman and Carthaginian domination must be judged on the basis of what we Locrians suffered from the Carthaginians, or what we are suffering at this very time from your occupying troops, then there is no one who would not prefer to have them rather than you as their masters. But, that said, consider the Locrians' attitude towards you. When we had injuries much less serious inflicted on us by the Carthaginians, we looked to your commander for protection; now that we are enduring, at the hands of your garrison, treatment worse than an enemy would mete out, we have brought our complaints to you, and you alone. Either you will show some concern for our wretched plight, members of the Senate, or there remains nothing that we can ask even of the immortal gods in our prayers.

'The legate Quintus Pleminius was sent with a body of troops to recover Locri from the Carthaginians, and he was then left in the town with that same force. Senators—for our extreme suffering gives me the courage to speak openly—in that legate of yours there is nothing of a human being beyond his shape and appearance. There is nothing of the Roman citizen beyond his demeanour, his clothing, and the tones of the Latin language. He is a scourge, a frightful monster of the sort that the myths tell us used to plague the strait dividing us from Sicily, in order to bring destruction on mariners.

'Now were he satisfied with being the only one to inflict his criminal, libidinous, and rapacious treatment on your allies, then we might resign ourselves and satisfy this one yawning maw. As it is, he has made all your centurions and all your soldiers a Pleminius—that is how far he has wanted the debauchery and immorality spread around! They are all given to robbery, pillage, assault, wounding, murder. They rape married women, girls, and free-born boys torn from their parents' arms. Every day our city suffers capture; every day it is pillaged. Day and night every corner of it rings with the wailing of women and boys being violated and carried off.

'Anyone aware* of our situation would be amazed at how we are managing to put up with it, or how the perpetrators have not yet grown tired of their gross abuses. I cannot give—and it is not worth your while to hear—every detail of our past sufferings, but let me give you a general summary. I tell you that there is no home in Locri, no single individual that has escaped abuse. I tell you that there is no crime, no lust, no greed in any shape or form that has not been inflicted on anyone on whom it could be inflicted. It is virtually impossible to calculate which is the more horrible a situation in which a community can find itself—when an enemy has taken the city in war, or when a murderous tyrant has crushed it with armed force. Everything that captured cities endure we have endured, and are enduring now more than ever, members of the Senate. All the crimes that the most ruthless and despotic tyrants inflict on the citizens they have crushed—all these Pleminius has inflicted on us, on our children, and on our wives.

18. 'There is one specific item about which our feelings for religion, which lie deep in our hearts, oblige us to make a specific complaint. Members of the Senate, we should like you to hear this and, if you agree, free your state from a religious obligation—for we have observed the regard with which you not only worship your own deities, but also accept those from outside. There is in our city a shrine of Proserpina, and I believe some report of the holiness of this temple reached you during the war with Pyrrhus. While he was sailing by Locri with his fleet, on his way back from Sicily, Pyrrhus committed a number of atrocities against our community because of our loyalty to you. In particular he looted the treasury of Proserpina, which had, until that day, remained untouched. After setting the money aboard his ships, he himself set off on an overland journey. And what happened then, members of the Senate? The next day his fleet was severely damaged by a terrible storm, and all the ships carrying the sacred money were driven aground on our shores. And the proud king, finally learning from his enormous loss that the gods do exist, gave orders for all the money to be gathered together and replaced in the treasury of Proserpina. Even so, no good ever came to him after that. Driven out of Italy he made a foolish attack on Argos by night and met an inglorious and dishonourable end.*

'Your legate and your military tribunes had been informed of this incident, and of a thousand others; and they were not being told stories fabricated to increase their religious awe, but things that we and our ancestors knew for a fact about the clear intervention of the goddess's power. But they still dared to lay their impious hands on those inviolable treasures of hers, and with that abominable plunder to defile themselves, their homes, and your soldiers, too. Members of the Senate, please—for your own sakes and for your honour's sake— do not use these men on any of your operations either in Italy or Africa before you have atoned for their crime! For they may pay for the sin they have committed not only by shedding their own blood, but also by bringing ruin on their state.

'In fact, even now, senators, the anger of the goddess has not been slow in visiting your officers or your men. On occasion they have clashed in armed combat, Pleminius the leader on the one side, and the two military tribunes on the other. They fought with the sword no more ferociously with the Carthaginians than they did amongst themselves, and but for the intervention of Scipio, who came at our request, they might well in their rage have given Hannibal the chance of recovering Locri. But I suppose you may think the fury of the god is focused on the soldiers tainted by the sacrilege, and that there has been no sign of the goddess's divine power in punishment being inflicted on the leaders themselves. Quite the reverse—that is where she is most at work! The tribunes were flogged by the legate. Then the legate was trapped and cut off from his men by the tribunes; in addition to receiving lacerations to his entire body, he had his nose and ears cut off, and was left practically dead. Then, when the legate had recovered from his wounds, he had the military tribunes clapped in irons, and put them to death after flogging them and inflicting on them every form of torture normally reserved for slaves, and after that would not allow the burial of their dead bodies.

'Such is the punishment the goddess metes out to the looters of her temple, and she is not going to stop plaguing those men with all manner of frenzy until her holy money has been restored to her treasury. At one time, our ancestors were involved in a serious war with Croton and, because the temple is situated outside the city, they wanted to bring that money into town. At night a voice was heard coming from the shrine telling them to keep their hands off—this was the goddess's temple and she would defend it! They were struck with religious awe, which deterred them from removing the money, and they then tried to surround the temple with a wall. The defensive structure had been brought up to a certain height when it suddenly collapsed. On this occasion, too, as then and on numerous other occasions, the goddess has protected her own home—her own temple—or has exacted heavy penalties from their violators. But as for the wrongs done to us, no one can avenge them but you, members of the Senate, nor would we want it otherwise. It is to you and your honour that we turn for help as suppliants. It is all the same to us whether you leave Locri under the command of that legate and that garrison, or whether you hand it over for punishment to an angry Hannibal and the Carthaginians. We are not asking you to believe what we say right away, when the man is absent and has not been given a hearing. Let him come here; let him hear the charges in person, and in person rebut them. If he has failed to commit any criminal act that man can inflict on human beings, then we have no objection to suffering over again, if we can, all those torments, and to his being exonerated of any crime against gods and men.'

19. After this address by the Locrian delegates, Quintus Fabius asked them if they had brought these complaints to Publius Scipio. They answered that a delegation had been sent to him, but that he was busy with preparations for the war, and had either already crossed to Africa or would be doing so in a few days. They added that they had had experience of the favouritism shown to the legate by the commander. After hearing the dispute between Pleminius and the tribunes, Scipio had put the tribunes in irons and left the legate, who was equally guilty, or even more guilty, than they, in the position of power he was holding.

The delegates were told to leave the temple,* and then not only Pleminius, but Scipio, too, received a scathing reprimand in the speeches of the senior members. Severest of all was Quintus Fabius, who claimed that Scipio was naturally predisposed to destroy the discipline of soldiers. Thus it was that, in Spain, he had almost lost more through a mutiny of his soldiers than he had through the war. Like a foreign potentate, he was in turn over-tolerant with the indiscipline of his men and ruthless with them. Fabius then followed up his address with an equally harsh motion, which went as follows:

'That the Senate resolve that the legate Pleminius be brought to Rome in shackles, that he plead his case in his chains and, if the complaints of the Locrians proved true, that he be executed in prison and his property be appropriated by the state.

'That, inasmuch as Publius Scipio had left his assigned command without senatorial authorization, he be recalled, and that discussions be opened with the tribunes of the plebs about bringing before the people a proposal to revoke his *imperium*.

'That the Senate give a response to the Locrians in their presence, stating that the injustices, which they complained had been inflicted on them, had the approval of neither the Senate nor the people. The Locrians must be declared worthy men, and allies and friends of Rome, and restitution must be made of their children, wives, and all else that had been taken from them.

'That a search be made for all the money removed from the treasury of Proserpina, and that money be replaced in her treasury to twice the amount. And there should be a sacrifice of atonement; in view of the fact that sacred treasures had been moved, opened, and violated, the question of the requisite expiatory ceremonies, the gods for whom they are to be held, and the animals to be sacrificed should be referred to the college of pontiffs.

'That the soldiers in Locri all be transported to Sicily, and four cohorts of Latin allies be brought in to garrison Locri.'

Passions were inflamed in support of Scipio and against him, and as a result not all opinions could be gathered that day. Apart from the question of Pleminius' misconduct, and the afflictions of the Locrians, there were even criticisms of the commander's personal appearance—not simply unlike a Roman, but unlike a soldier. He would saunter around the gymnasium in a Greek cloak and sandals, it was said, and spend his time on books and exercising—and his entire staff enjoyed as much idleness and easy living, tasting the delights of Syracuse. Carthage and Hannibal were gone from Scipio's mind, they said, and the whole army, ruined through lack of discipline—like the one in Sucro in Spain earlier and that in Locri now—was an object of fear more to the allies than to the enemy.

20. Some of these criticisms were valid, and some, being partly so, also rang true,* but nonetheless it was the view of Quintus Metellus that prevailed. Metellus agreed with Maximus on everything else, but he disagreed on Scipio. Here was a man, he said, whom the state had recently chosen, very young though he was, as its sole commander for the recovery of Spain, and then, when Spain was recovered from the enemy, it had elected him consul to bring the Punic War to an end. He was the man on whom the state had pinned its hopes of drawing Hannibal from Italy and bringing Africa to heel. How did it make sense to recall him peremptorily from his area of responsibility, virtually condemned, like Quintus Pleminius, before he had stated his case? And to do that when the Locrians stated that the atrocities committed against them took place when Scipio was not even there, and when the only charge that could be brought against him was that of showing leniency, or restraint, in sparing his legate? His own view, he said, was that Marcus Pomponius,* the praetor to whom Sicily had been allotted as his sphere of command, should leave for his province within three days. The consuls should use their own discretion to choose ten representatives from the Senate to send with the praetor, and they should also send two tribunes of the plebs and an aedile. With these as his advisory body, the praetor should conduct an enquiry, and if the events that were the basis of the Locrians' complaints proved to have taken place on the orders of Publius Scipio, or with his acquiescence, they should order him to quit his area of responsibility. If Publius Scipio had already crossed to Africa, the tribunes of the plebs and the aedile, and two of the senatorial representatives whom the praetor thought most suitable for the job, should leave for Africa. The mission of the tribunes of the plebs and the aedile would be to bring Scipio back from there, and that of the two representatives to take command of the army until such time as the new commander reached that army. If the findings of Marcus Pomponius and the ten representatives were that those actions had not been ordered or sanctioned by Publius Scipio, then Scipio should stay with the army, and prosecute the war as he had proposed.

A decree of the Senate was passed to this effect, and an agreement was reached with the tribunes of the plebs that they should arrange between them, or choose by sortition, which two should accompany the praetor and the legates. The matter of expiatory ceremonies relating to the items in the temple of Proserpina that had been touched, defiled and removed was referred to the college of pontiffs. Marcus Claudius Marcellus and Marcus Cincius Alimentus were the tribunes of the plebs who left with the praetor and the ten representatives. An aedile of the plebs was also assigned to them. Should Scipio still be in Sicily, and refuse to obey the praetor's command, or if he had already crossed to Africa, the tribunes were to order the aedile to seize him and (by the right conferred by their sacrosanct office) they were to bring him back to Rome. Their plan was to go to Locri before proceeding to Messana.

21. As for Pleminius, there are two versions of the story. Some record that, when he heard what had transpired in Rome, he went into exile in Neapolis, and that on the way he happened to bump into Quintus Metellus, one of the senatorial representatives, and was brought back to Rhegium under duress by him. Others claim that a legate and thirty horsemen of the noblest families were sent out by Scipio himself to clap Quintus Pleminius in irons, and the other prime movers in the troubles along with him. Whether it was on Scipio's orders given earlier, or the praetor's at that time, all the men were handed over to the people of Rhegium to be kept under guard.

The praetor and the representatives set off for Locri where, first of all, following their instructions, they looked into the matter of religion. They searched out all the sacred money that was in the possession of Pleminius and the soldiers, and put it back in the treasury, adding a sum that they had themselves brought with them. They also held an expiatory ceremony. The praetor then called the common soldiers to an assembly, and ordered them to march out of the city. He established a camp for them on the plain, and issued a strict injunction against any soldier either remaining in the city or taking out with him goods that were not his own. He declared that he was now allowing the people of Locri to take whatever each of them recognized as his property, and to make a formal claim for anything that did not come to light. Before all else, he said, it was his will that free persons be immediately restored to the Locrians, and anyone failing to restore them faced severe punishment.

Pomponius next held an assembly of the Locrians. He told them that the Roman people and the Senate were restoring to them their independence and legal system, and that if any of them wished to prosecute Pleminius, or anyone else, he should go with him to Rhegium. If they wished to lodge an official grievance about Publius Scipio, charging that the outrageous acts in Locri against gods and men had taken place on Publius Scipio's orders, or with his acquiescence, they should send spokesmen to Messana, and he would hold an enquiry there with his board of advisers. Thanking the praetor and his legates, and the Senate and People of Rome, the Locrians declared that they would make the journey to prosecute Pleminius. In the case of Scipio, however, although he had shown insufficient concern for the wrongs done to their community, he was still the sort of man they would rather have as a friend than an enemy, and they were quite sure that all the execrable crimes had not been committed on his orders or with his acquiescence. Scipio had either placed too much confidence in Pleminius, and too little in them, or else it was that natural tendency some people have of not wishing to see wrong done, but then not having the will to punish the wrongs when they have been done.*

The praetor and his advisory board were thus spared the not inconsiderable task of conducting an enquiry into Scipio's case. They found Pleminius guilty, and about thirty-two others along with him, and they sent them off to Rome in chains. They themselves proceeded to Scipio so they could, with their own eyes, verify the widespread rumours about the general's dress and idleness, and his slipshod military discipline, and then take their findings to Rome.

22. While the delegation was en route for Syracuse, Scipio prepared to clear his name, not with words but action. He gave orders for the entire army to muster in the city, and for the fleet to be made ready for action—just as though they had to fight the Carthaginians that day on land and sea. On the day of their arrival, Pomponius and his party were given a hospitable welcome; and the day after that Scipio put on a display of his land and sea armies, not simply drawn up in formation, but with the infantry performing their manœuvres, and the fleet also staging a mock naval battle in the harbour. Then the praetor and the legates were taken around to inspect the arsenals, storehouses, and other military preparations. So impressed were they by each feature, and by the whole ensemble, that they were convinced that the defeat of the Carthaginian people could be achieved by that general and his army, and by no other. With a wish that the gods grant him success, they bade him cross to Africa and bring to fruition, at the earliest possible moment, the hopes the Roman people placed in him on that day when all centuries declared him consul ahead of all others. Such was the joy in their hearts when they left Sicily that it was as if the news they would be taking to Rome was not merely of outstanding preparations for the conflict, but of victory already won.

On their arrival in Rome, Pleminius and the others charged along with him were immediately thrown in jail. When they were first haled before the people by the tribunes, they found no room for pity in minds that were already filled with the sufferings of the Locrians. Later on, as their appearances became more frequent, anger cooled and passions subsided, and Pleminius' own mutilated features, and the memory of the absent Scipio, began to generate some sympathy with the crowd. However, Pleminius died in jail before his trial before the people could be concluded.

In the third book of his Roman History, Clodius Licinus* records that this Pleminius, through the agency of some men whom he had bribed, attempted arson in several parts of the city during games that Scipio Africanus was, in his second consulship, staging in Rome in fulfilment of a vow. The aim was to give Pleminius an opportunity of breaking out of prison and making his escape. But the crime subsequently came to light, according to Licinus, and by decree of the Senate he was consigned to the Tullianum.*

The only proceedings taken with regard to Scipio were in the Senate. There everybody, legates and tribunes alike, spoke in praise of the fleet, the army, and the leader, prompting the Senate to vote for the crossing to Africa to be made at the earliest possible time. They also voted that Scipio be permitted his choice of the armies in Sicily—he could decide which he would take with him to Africa, and which he would leave to garrison his province.*

23. While this was taking place on the Roman side, the Carthaginians had passed a nervous winter; with observation posts established on all their promontories, they had been gathering intelligence and becoming perturbed with every piece of news that arrived. But they also added to their military preparations something of no little significance for the defence of Africa, namely an alliance with King Syphax—for, the Carthaginians thought, it was thanks to their confidence in Syphax that the Romans were about to cross to Africa.

As was observed above, Hasdrubal son of Gisgo had a bond of hospitality with the king, which dated from the occasion when Scipio and Hasdrubal both happened to come to him at just the same time. But there had also been some preliminary mention of a marriage connection, of the king marrying Hasdrubal's daughter.* To bring this to fruition, and fix a date for the wedding, the girl being already of marriageable age, Hasdrubal set off to visit the king. Now, Numidians are particularly sensual people, more so than all other barbarians, and when Hasdrubal noted that Syphax's libido was aroused, he sent for the girl from Carthage and pushed the wedding ahead. And so that a bond between the states could be added to the private pact, an oath was taken, amid the general exchange of congratulations, confirming the alliance between the people of Carthage and the king, with promises given on both sides that they would have the same friends and enemies.

Hasdrubal, however, kept in mind the fact that the king had also struck an alliance with Scipio, and that barbarians are by nature undependable and capricious, and he feared that, if Scipio crossed to Africa, the marriage would prove a flimsy connection. Accordingly, while he had the Numidian aflame with his new infatuation, he induced him—with some gentle coaxing from the girl, as well—to send envoys to Scipio in Sicily. Through these he was to advise Scipio that he should not make his crossing to Africa relying on Syphax's earlier assurances, for he now had a marriage connection with a Carthaginian citizen, a daughter of the Hasdrubal whom Scipio had seen as a guest in his home. In addition, he now had a formal pact with the Carthaginian people. His primary wish, therefore, was that the Romans conduct their war with the Carthaginians, as they had done to that time, far away from Africa, and not oblige him to become embroiled in their conflict, militarily supporting one side and reneging on his alliance with the other. If Scipio would not stay away from Africa, and if he brought his army up to Carthage, then he, Syphax, would be obliged to fight for the land of Africa, his own birthplace, and also for the fatherland of his wife, and for her father and her home.

24. The envoys sent by the king with these instructions met Scipio in Syracuse. Scipio was now robbed of important support for his African campaign and also of his high hopes for it, but before the matter could become common knowledge he quickly sent the envoys back to Africa with a letter for the king. In this he time and again advised Syphax not to forswear his obligations of hospitality with him, or of the pact he had entered with the Roman people, and not to violate his religious duty, his honour, his solemn pledges, and the gods who witnessed and oversaw covenants.

But it was not possible to keep the arrival of the Numidians secret—they had been wandering around the city, and had spent time at the headquarters—and by maintaining silence on the reason for their coming Scipio risked having the truth come out through the very act of concealment. There was also a danger that fear of having to fight the king and the Carthaginians at the same time would sweep through the army. Scipio therefore steered his men away from the truth by seizing their attention with a lie. He summoned the soldiers to an assembly, and said they could delay no longer, that the allied kings were insisting that he cross to Africa as soon as possible. Masinissa had earlier made a personal visit to Gaius Laelius, he said, complaining that time was being wasted through inaction. Now Syphax was sending envoys, for he, too, was wondering what reason there could be for the protracted delay, and he was demanding either that the army be finally taken over to Africa, or that he be informed of any change in plans, so that he could take appropriate steps for himself and his realm. And so, since all was ready and prepared, and since the situation would brook no further delay, he intended to take the fleet over to Lilybaeum. There he would concentrate all his infantry and cavalry forces, and on the first day that would permit the ships to sail, he would, with the favour of the gods, make the journey over to Africa.

Scipio then sent a letter to Marcus Pomponius requesting that, if he were in agreement,* he come to Lilybaeum so they could together discuss the specific legions and the size of the force Scipio would take over to Africa. He also sent word along the entire coast for all freighters to be commandeered and brought together at Lilybaeum.

When all the troops and ships in Sicily had mustered in Lilybaeum, the city could not hold all the men nor the harbour all the ships, and such was the general enthusiasm for crossing to Africa that they felt they were being led not to war but to prizes of victory that were already assured. This was especially so with the remaining soldiers from the army of Cannae. They believed that it was under Scipio, and no one else, that they could discharge their duty to the state, and bring to a close their ignominious conditions of service. In fact, Scipio did not disdain soldiers in this category. He was well aware that the defeat at Cannae was not the result of cowardice on their part, and that there were no soldiers in the Roman army as seasoned and as experienced as they in various forms of combat but especially in blockading cities. The legions of Cannae were the fifth and sixth. Scipio declared that he would take them over to Africa, and then inspected the soldiers in them individually. Leaving behind those he thought unsuitable, he replaced them with men he had brought with him from Italy, and he provided supplementary troops for those legions to the point where each had 6,200 infantry and 300 cavalry.

From the army from Cannae Scipio also selected Latin infantry and cavalry for the campaign.

25. There is wide discrepancy in the sources on the number of troops taken over to Africa. In one I find 10,000 infantry and 2,200 cavalry; in another 16,000 infantry and 1,600 cavalry; in a third I find more than double this number—that 35,000 infantry and 3,000 cavalry were put aboard the ships. Some authors have not given a figure, and I would prefer to be in their company since the question is moot.* While he avoids a precise figure, Coelius still exaggerates and gives the impression of huge numbers. He says that birds fell to the ground when the soldiers' shout went up, and that the numbers boarding the ships were so great that it appeared that no mortal was being left behind in either Italy or Sicily!

Scipio took personal responsibility for ensuring that his men boarded the ships in a disciplined and orderly manner. Gaius Laelius, admiral of the fleet, made the seamen embark first, and kept them on board. The praetor Marcus Pomponius was given responsibility for loading supplies; he had forty-five days' worth of rations, including fifteen days' worth of cooked provisions, put aboard. When all were now embarked on the vessels, Scipio sent some boats around them with instructions for helmsmen and captains, along with two soldiers from each ship, to come to a meeting in the forum to receive their orders. When these had gathered together, Scipio first asked them if they had put on board water for men and animals that would last as many days as would the grain. When they replied that there was a forty-five-day supply of water on the ships, he directed the fighting men to remain calm and obey their orders, providing the seamen with the silence they needed to go about their duties without interruption. He added that he and Lucius Scipio would, with twenty warships, offer the freighters protection on the right wing, and the same number of warships under Gaius Laelius, commander of the fleet, and Marcus Porcius Cato,* quaestor at the time, would protect them on the left. He then issued orders about lights on the ships: men-of-war were to have one each and freighters two, while the identifying feature of the flagship, in the dark, would be three lights.

Scipio told the helmsmen to steer a course for Emporia.* This was very fertile farmland, and so the area abounded in produce of all kinds, and also had a native population with little aptitude for war, as so often happens when the soil is rich. It therefore seemed likely these people could be crushed before help could be brought from Carthage. After issuing these instructions, Scipio ordered the men to return to their ships and, with a prayer for heaven's blessing on the enterprise, bade them set sail the following day when given the signal.

26. Numerous Roman fleets had set out from Sicily, and indeed from that very harbour, but no departure had provided such a spectacle as this, either in that war (which was not surprising, since most of the fleets leaving had only been on raiding expeditions) or even in the First Punic War. And yet, if one took into account only the size of the fleet, then, admittedly, two pairs of consuls with two armies had also made the crossing in the past,* and in their fleet the number of warships was as great as the number of freighters with which Scipio was then making his crossing—for, apart from the forty men-of-war, he was taking the army over on some four hundred freighters. But the second war seemed to the Romans more serious than the earlier one because the hostilities were taking place in Italy, and also because of the terrible losses of so many armies, with their leaders also being killed. In addition, the commander Scipio had a great talent for boosting his own reputation, and he had now become the talk of the town and focused men's attention on him, both by his brave deeds and his own personal good fortune. And then there was the very idea of the crossing, attempted by no other commander before him in that war, for Scipio had made it known that the purpose of his voyage was to draw Hannibal away from Italy, carry over the war to Africa, and finish it there.

Not only had all the inhabitants of Lilybaeum come running in droves to the harbour to witness the event, but so too had legations from all over Sicily. The latter had assembled to pay their respects, and see Scipio off on his journey, or had travelled there with Marcus Pomponius, the praetor of the province. In addition, the legions that were being left behind in Sicily had come to see their comrades off. But it was not just a case of the fleet providing a sight for the onlookers on shore—those on board also had the spectacle of the entire shoreline covered with milling crowds.

27. At daybreak Scipio had a herald call for silence, and from the flagship he offered the following prayer: 'Gods and goddesses who dwell in the seas and on the land, I pray and beseech you: whatever has been done, is being done, and will hereafter be done under my command, may that turn out well for me, for the people and plebs of

Rome, and for our allies and Latins who follow the lead, authority, and auspices of the Roman people and myself, by land, sea, and river. Kindly assist all these deeds of ours, and crown them with success. And, the enemy defeated, bring the victors home with me safe and sound, bedecked with spoils, laden with plunder and triumphant. Grant us the ability to take retribution from those who hate us and fight us, and give to me and the Roman people the opportunity to inflict on the state of Carthage the punishments that the Carthaginian people has endeavoured to inflict on ours.'

After this prayer Scipio followed the traditional practice of slaughtering a sacrificial animal and throwing its raw entrails into the sea. He then had the signal for departure sounded on a trumpet. Surging forward before a wind of some force, they were quickly swept out of sight of land. After midday a mist began to rise, so thick that the ships could barely avoid colliding with each other, and the wind became calmer on the open sea. The fog remained just as dense during the oncoming night, but with the sunrise it dissipated and the wind picked up. Now they began to sight land. Shortly afterwards the helmsman told Scipio that Africa lay no more than five miles away, and that he could see the promontory of Mercury.* If Scipio gave him the order to steer in that direction, he said, the entire fleet would be in port in no time. When he had land in view, Scipio prayed to the gods, asking them to make his sighting of Africa bode well for the republic and for himself, and he then gave the order to unfurl the sails, and head for another landing spot further along. They were now scudding before the same wind, but at about the same time as the previous day the mist arose to cut off all sight of land, and with the onset of the mist the wind fell. Night then increased the disorientation everywhere, and they dropped anchor to stop the ships from colliding with each other or running aground. With the break of day the same wind arose once more, unveiling a panorama of the coastline of Africa. Scipio asked the name of the closest headland and, when he was told it was called 'The headland of the Beautiful One',* he said: 'The omen pleases me. Head the ships towards it.' The fleet put in there and all the troops were set ashore.

In describing the voyage as being a fair one, free of panic and confusion, I have accepted the account of a large number of Greek and Roman authorities. Coelius alone differs.* While he stops short of having the ships submerged by the waves, he does bring in all the other terrifying phenomena that can come from sky or sea. He finally has the fleet driven away from Africa by a storm that brought it to the island of Aegimurus, where, with difficulty, it re-established its course. Then, with the ships on the verge of sinking, Coelius has the men take boats, without the commander's order, and make an absolutely chaotic landing without their weapons, just as if they had been shipwrecked.

28. When the troops had been put ashore, the Romans measured out their camp on some nearby hills. By now the sight of the fleet, first of all, and then the commotion of the men landing, had brought a frantic dread not merely to the farmlands bordering the sea but to the cities, too. Crowds of men, with columns of women and children among them, had clogged the roads everywhere, but in addition to that there were also peasants driving their animals before them—one might have said Africa was suddenly being abandoned! In fact, in the cities, these people were bringing panic greater than they felt themselves when they arrived, and the chaos in Carthage in particular was close to that of a captured city. For in the almost fifty years* since the consulship of Marcus Atilius Regulus and Lucius Manlius, its people had not set eyes on a single Roman army, with the exception of some marauding fleets from which raids had been conducted on the coastal farmland. And, in those cases, once the pillaging of whatever chance put in the marauders' way was completed, there had always been a dash back to the ships before the commotion could alert the rural population. Hence the heightened excitement and panic in the city on this occasion.

And there was, in fact, another consideration. They had at home neither a strong enough army, nor a strong enough commander, to field against the Romans. Hasdrubal son of Gisgo was by far the leading man in the community,* by virtue of his breeding, reputation, wealth, and, at that time, even a family connection with royalty. But people remembered that he had been defeated, and put to flight, by that very same Scipio in a number of battles in Spain, and they thought that as a commander he was just as unevenly matched with Scipio as their makeshift army was with the Roman force. And so, as if Scipio were on the verge of attacking the city, the call to arms went up; gates were hurriedly closed, armed men posted on the walls, and sentries and outposts put in place—and there was little sleep during the oncoming night.

The next day 500 horsemen were dispatched to the sea to reconnoitre, and also to harass the Romans as they disembarked, and these ran into some Roman outposts. For by now Scipio, having sent his fleet on towards Utica, had advanced a short distance from the sea, and seized the closest high ground. He had then positioned his cavalry on guard at suitable points, and sent others to raid the fields.

29. These men engaged the Carthaginian cavalry squadron, killing a few in the actual engagement, but a large number as they chased them off, including their captain Hanno, a young nobleman.* Scipio not only laid waste the fields in the area but also captured the closest city of the Africans, which was quite a prosperous town.* In addition to the spoils, which were immediately put aboard the freighters and shipped off to Sicily, 8,000 prisoners of war, both free men and slaves, were taken.

However, what most pleased the Romans at the start of this operation was the arrival of Masinissa. Some sources claim that he came with no more than 200 horsemen, but most say that he had with him a cavalry force of 2,000. Masinissa was by far the greatest of the monarchs of his day, and it was he who provided the greatest assistance for the Roman cause. A brief excursus on the chequered fortunes the king experienced in losing and regaining his father's throne therefore seems appropriate.

Masinissa's father, whose name was Gala,* died while Masinissa was fighting for the Carthaginians in Spain. The throne then passed, in conformity with Numidian tradition, to the late king's very aged brother Oezalces. Oezalces also died not much later, and the elder of his two sons, Capussa, inherited his father's realm, the other son being just a boy. However, Capussa was succeeding to the throne thanks more to tribal law than because of any authority he wielded amongst his people or any power he had, and a man called Mazaetullus now came on the scene. Mazaetullus was a blood relation of the royal family, but he came from a house that had always opposed it and which had, with varying degrees of success, disputed the throne with those in power at that time. He stirred up his compatriots, with whom he carried great weight because of the antipathy they also felt for the royal family, and he quite openly started a military campaign, forcing the king to take the field and fight for his throne. In that battle Capussa lost his life, as did many of his leading citizens. The tribe of the Maesulii then fell entirely under Mazaetullus' authority and power, but Mazaetullus avoided assuming the title of 'king'. Happy enough with the modest title 'guardian', he conferred that of 'king' on the boy Lacumazes, sole survivor of the royal line. He married a well-born Carthaginian lady, a daughter of Hannibal's sister,* who had recently been the wife of King Oezalces, hoping thereby to gain an alliance with the Carthaginians, and he also sent a deputation to renew his former ties of hospitality with Syphax. These were all means of support against Masinissa that he was putting in place in advance.

30. When he heard that his uncle had died, and that his cousin had been killed, Masinissa crossed from Spain to Mauretania, where, at the time, Baga* was king of the Moors. Petitioning Baga with the most wretched entreaties, he obtained from him a contingent of 4,000 Moors to assist him on his journey, though his appeal for military assistance failed. After sending ahead a messenger to his own friends and those of his father, he came with the Moors to the borders of the kingdom, where about 500 Numidians rallied to his cause. Masinissa then sent the Moors back to the king, as had been agreed. He was now left with a body of men considerably smaller than he had hoped for, and one insufficient for undertaking the great enterprise he had planned, but he thought that with a vigorous and energetic push he would accumulate forces enough to bring off something. He then encountered Lacumazes near Thapsus,* as the prince was setting out to visit Syphax. Lacumazes' army panicked, and fled back into the city, which Masinissa then took at the first assault, accepting the surrender of some of the prince's men and killing others as they prepared to resist. During the confusion, most of Lacumazes' force, including the boy himself, continued on their journey and reached Syphax. Minor though the victory was, news of it right at the start of the campaign drew the Numidians over to Masinissa, and veterans of Gala came streaming to him from all parts of the countryside and from all the villages, encouraging the young man to recover his father's throne.

Mazaetullus considerably outnumbered Masinissa. He still had the army with which he had defeated Capussa, and he also had some of Capussa's men whom he had taken on after the death of the king. In addition, the young Lacumazes had brought him enormous auxiliary forces from Syphax. In fact, Mazaetullus had 15,000 infantrymen and 10,000 cavalrymen when he clashed with Masinissa, who had nothing like as many of either. Nevertheless, the day was won by the fighting ability of the veteran troops, and the capability of a leader who had received his training in the Roman–Punic conflict. The prince fled into Carthaginian territory with his guardian and a small group of Masaesulians.

Masinissa had thus recovered his father's throne, but he could see that he was left with a struggle against Syphax that was of considerably greater proportions. Thinking it best, therefore, to make up with his cousin, he sent men to give the boy hope that, if he put himself in Masinissa's hands, he would be held in the same esteem as Oezalces had earlier been held in Gala's court. They were also to promise Mazaetullus that not only would he receive no punishment, but he would also have all his property faithfully restored to him. The two men preferred a modest estate at home to exile, and Masinissa, despite Carthaginian efforts to prevent it, won them over to his side.

31. It so happened that, while this was taking place, Hasdrubal was at the court of Syphax. Syphax believed that it made little difference to him whether the kingdom of the Maesulians was in the hands of Lacumazes or Masinissa, but Hasdrubal told him he was making a big mistake if he thought Masinissa would be satisfied with the same territory as his father Gala, or his uncle Oezalces. The man, he explained, was possessed of a much greater spirit and intelligence than had ever been seen in any member of his race, and in Spain he had exhibited, before allies and enemies alike, a courage rarely found in humankind. If they did not quench that flame as it was on the rise, both Syphax and the Carthaginians would soon be engulfed in a huge conflagration with which they simply could not cope. Up until that point, he said, Masinissa's power had been weak and fragile as he tried to nurture a kingdom that had only just begun to coalesce.

By pressing his point, and egging on Syphax, Hasdrubal convinced him to move his forces up to the border with the Maesulians and pitch his camp on land that he had not only disputed, but actually fought over, with Gala, and to do so as though it were his undeniable right. He told him that, if anyone tried to drive him off, he should fight him in pitched battle, which would be the preferred option; if the Maesulians should quit the area through fear, he should advance to the heart of their kingdom. The Maesulians would either submit to his authority without resistance, or would prove no match for him in battle.

Spurred on by such comments, Syphax opened hostilities against Masinissa. In the first encounter, he defeated the Maesulians and put them to flight, and Masinissa, along with a few horsemen, fled from the battlefield to a mountain called Bellus* by the natives. A number of families accompanied their king, taking with them their huts* and animals, the only property those people possess. The rest of the Maesulian population submitted to Syphax's authority.

The mountain occupied by the fugitives is grassy, with a good water supply, and because it was good for raising cattle it also afforded an abundant supply of food for men whose diet consisted of meat and milk. From that vantage point they began with clandestine forays at night, and then moved on to open marauding, rendering the whole surrounding area insecure. It was Carthaginian farmland in the main that went up in smoke, because there was more plunder to be had there than amongst the Numidians and also because marauding was safer there. Soon they acted with such unchecked effrontery that they were carrying their booty down to the shore and selling it to merchants, who brought their vessels to land for that purpose. And more Carthaginians were killed or taken prisoner than was often the case in regular warfare.

The Carthaginians lodged complaints about this with Syphax. They proceeded to urge him—and he was himself incensed at the situation—to finish the mopping-up operations of the war, but it seemed to him beneath his royal dignity to be chasing a vagabond robber in the hills.

32. One of the king's officers Bucar, a man of energy and action, was chosen for the task. He was given 4,000 infantry and 2,000 cavalry, and plied with promises of huge rewards if he brought back Masinissa's head or, something that would provide immense satisfaction, if he took him alive. The marauders were scattered and off their guard when Bucar made a surprise attack on them. He managed to cut a large number of cattle and men off from their armed escort, and he drove Masinissa himself, and a few of his men, to the peak of the mountain. Then, assuming the campaign to be now almost finished, he not only dispatched the booty, that is, the cattle and men he had captured, to the king, but also sent back some of his troops, feeling that he had considerably more than were needed for what remained of the war. When Masinissa came down from the high ground, Bucar gave chase with no more than 500 infantrymen and

200 cavalrymen, and cornered him in a narrow ravine which he blocked at both ends. In the ravine the Maesulians suffered terrible carnage, but Masinissa, with not more than fifty horsemen, extricated himself by taking some mountain passes that were unknown to his pursuers. Bucar, however, dogged his footsteps and overtook him in some open country near the city of Clupea,* and there he had him so completely surrounded that, with the exception of four horsemen, he killed all of Masinissa's men.

Masinissa himself was wounded, but in the confusion Bucar let him and the four slip through his fingers. The fleeing men were in full view, and a squadron of cavalry set off in pursuit of its five enemies, spreading over the plain, with some cutting across in an effort to head them off. A large river was what the fugitives encountered next—and they headed their mounts into it with no hesitation, driven as they were by fear of a greater danger. Gripped by the swirling current, they were swept downstream at an angle past their pursuers. Two were swallowed up in the rushing torrent before their enemies' eyes, and it was thought that Masinissa himself had perished. But the two remaining cavalrymen actually climbed out together with him amidst some bushes on the far bank.

That was the end of the chase for Bucar. He would not risk entering the river, and he believed he now had no one to pursue. He returned to the king with the erroneous report that Masinissa had perished; and men were dispatched to take this immensely joyous news to Carthage. The story of Masinissa's death was carried throughout Africa, prompting varied reactions.

As he tended his wounds with herbs, Masinissa lived for a number of days in a hidden cavern, on what the two horsemen could steal. As soon as the wound had scabbed over, and he felt he could stand the jolting of travel, he went on his way, with extraordinary bravado, to reclaim his throne. He picked up no more than thirty horsemen en route, and with them he came to the Maesulians, making no secret of his identity. He created great excitement thanks to his earlier popularity, and also because of the unexpected joy that people felt at seeing safe and sound a man they thought had perished. The result was that in a few days 6,000 armed foot soldiers and 4,000 cavalry came flocking to him, and he was now not simply in possession of his father's throne but was even plundering tribes allied to Carthage, and the lands of the Masaesulians, that is to say Syphax's kingdom.

After goading Syphax into war like this, Masinissa next took up a position between Cirta and Hippo, on some hills* that suited his purpose in all respects.

33. Syphax now felt the matter was too serious for him to handle through his officers. He sent off his young son, whose name was Vermina, with a section of his army, ordering him to take his column around the enemy, and launch an attack from the rear while their attention was focused on Syphax himself. Since he was going to be making a surprise attack, Vermina set out at night, and Syphax then struck camp in daylight, marching in the open, apparently intending to fight a regular pitched battle. When he felt enough time had elapsed for those executing the encircling manœuvre to have reached their position, Syphax embarked on a gentle slope that led to the enemy, and, relying both on his superior numbers and on the trap set to the enemy's rear, brought his battle line straight up the hill. Masinissa, relying mostly on his position, which would enable him to fight on ground much more favourable to him, also formed up his men.

It was a fierce battle that long remained indecisive, with his position and the valour of his soldiers aiding Masinissa, and numbers, in which he was overwhelmingly superior, aiding Syphax. And those superior numbers, which were in two parts, one putting pressure on the enemy in front and the other having moved around to attack the rear, gave Syphax a conclusive victory, and did not even leave a means of escape open to the enemy, who were blocked front and rear. And so the infantry and cavalry were all cut down, apart from about 200 cavalrymen. Masinissa gathered these in a body around him, and split them into three sections. He then gave orders to break through the enemy, and told them where to regroup after they became dispersed in their flight. Masinissa himself made his way through the midst of the enemy weapons by the route he had designated for himself, but the other two squadrons were brought to a halt. One, from fear, surrendered to the enemy, and the other, more determined in its resistance, went down under a hail of javelins.

Vermina stuck closely to Masinissa's heels, but the king gave him the slip by constantly turning off onto different roads and eventually forced him to abandon a pursuit that had become tiresome and discouraging. He reached the Lesser Syrtis* with sixty cavalrymen. There, proudly aware that he had on numerous occasions tried to reclaim his father's throne, he spent all his time between Punic

Emporia and the tribe of the Garamantes until Gaius Laelius and the Roman fleet arrived in Africa. This makes me incline to the view that it was with a modest force rather than a large one that Masinissa subsequently came to Scipio. Large numbers are more in keeping with a man who is on the throne; my suggestion of smaller numbers better suits the circumstances of an exile.*

34. After losing a cavalry squadron together with its commander, the Carthaginians raised other cavalry with a new levy, and put it under the command of Hanno son of Hamilcar.* They put out repeated summonses to Hasdrubal and Syphax, by dispatches and messengers initially, and finally even by embassies. They sent orders to Hasdrubal to bring aid to his native city, which was virtually under siege, and they pleaded with Syphax to come to the support of Carthage and the whole of Africa. At that point Scipio was at Utica, encamped about a mile from the city; he had moved it there from the coast where, for a few days, he had maintained a base close to the fleet.

Hanno had been assigned cavalry in no way strong enough to give the enemy any trouble, or even protect the countryside from depredation, and so he made raising his cavalry numbers with a troop-levy his very first priority. He did not reject other nationalities, but in the main he hired Numidians, theirs being by far the leading cavalry nation in Africa. When now he had around 4,000 cavalry in his force, he took over a town called Salaeca,* about fifteen miles from the Roman camp. Brought the news of this, Scipio declared: 'Horsemen passing the summer under shelter! Let there be more of them, as long as they have a leader of that calibre!'

Thinking the Carthaginians' lethargic performance was all the more reason for him not to waste time, Scipio sent Masinissa ahead with his cavalry, ordering him to ride up to the city gates and draw the enemy out to fight. When the enemy had come out in full force, and was too formidable in the engagement to be easily withstood, Masinissa was to give ground gradually, and Scipio would join the battle at the appropriate moment. Masinissa then went ahead, and Scipio waited only as long as appeared sufficient for him to draw out the enemy and then followed with the Roman cavalry. Thanks to the cover of some hills,* which very conveniently screened the winding road on both sides, his advance went unnoticed.

Masinissa now proceeded according to plan, affecting in turn to threaten the enemy, and to take fright himself. He would ride right up to the gates, or he would fall back and, building his enemy's confidence with simulated fear, draw them into foolhardy pursuit. They had not all emerged from the town, and their leader had his hands full coping with various tasks: some of the men, torpid from drink and sleep, he was forcing to take up their weapons and bridle their horses; others he was restraining from disorderly and unruly sorties from all the gates, out of formation and without their standards. Masinissa faced up to their first hasty onslaughts. Soon, however, more men came pouring out in a dense body from one of the gates, making it an evenly matched contest. Finally, their entire cavalry came into the battle, and resistance was no longer possible. But when Masinissa gave ground it was not in disordered flight; falling back gradually he would parry their assaults, until he drew them up to the hills that concealed the Roman cavalry.

The cavalry then emerged from the hills, their strength intact and their horses fresh, and surrounded Hanno and his Africans who were exhausted from the fight and the chase; and Masinissa, too, suddenly wheeling around his horses, returned to battle. About 1,000 men who had formed the head of the column, and for whom retreat was not easy, were cut off and killed, and along with them fell their commander, Hanno. The others fled in disorder, especially panic-stricken by their leader's death, and the victors chased them for thirty miles, capturing or killing a further 2,000 cavalrymen. It was a well-established fact that these included no fewer than 200 Carthaginian horsemen, a number of them noted for their wealth and noble birth.

35. It so happened that, on the very day that these events took place, the ships that had transported the plunder to Sicily came back with supplies. It was as if they had had a premonition that the point of their return was to pick up a second cargo of booty! Not all sources have an account of two Carthaginian commanders of the same name being killed in two separate cavalry engagements because, I suppose, they were afraid of making a mistake and producing a doublet of the same incident. Coelius and Valerius, in fact, even have Hanno taken prisoner.*

Scipio conferred gifts of honour on the officers and cavalrymen, according to the service provided by each, and above all on Masinissa. He then installed a strong garrison in Salaeca, and set out in person with the rest of the army. He not only laid waste the fields all along his route, but he also took a number of cities and villages by storm, spreading the terror of war far and wide. On the seventh day after his departure he returned to his camp, with large numbers of men, cattle, and all other sorts of booty in tow, and he sent off the ships laden once more with enemy spoils.

Scipio now abandoned minor operations and pillaging expeditions to concentrate all his military resources on an assault on Utica, which, if he captured it, he would use as a base for the rest of his campaign. The seamen from the fleet were brought up to the city on the side that was bordered by the sea, and at the same time the land forces were brought up at a point where a hill overlooked the very walls of the city. As for artillery and siege-engines, some he had brought with him; more had been sent from Sicily with the supplies; and new ones were under construction in an arsenal where large numbers of craftsmen, who specialized in such work, had been confined for this purpose.

Under pressure on every side from such a massive force, the people of Utica had all their hopes pinned on the Carthaginian people, and the Carthaginians had theirs pinned on Hasdrubal, that is to say, on his convincing Syphax to act. But all was proceeding too slowly for the liking of those needing the assistance. Hasdrubal had managed to raise about 30,000 infantry and 3,000 cavalry with an extremely energetic recruiting drive, but he still did not dare move his camp closer to the enemy before Syphax arrived. Syphax came with 50,000 infantry and 10,000 cavalry* and, after swiftly moving camp from Carthage, he took up a position not far from Utica and the Roman entrenchments. Their arrival did have one important result: it made Scipio withdraw from Utica, his venture a failure, after a siege of some forty days in which everything he tried came to nothing. With winter now coming on, he established fortified winter quarters on a promontory that runs some distance out to sea and is connected to the mainland by a narrow spit of land,* and within a single circumvallation he enclosed the naval camp as well. The legionary camp was placed in the centre of the isthmus; the northern section was taken up by the beached ships and their crews, and the lower ground to the south, that ran down to the other shore, was occupied by the cavalry. Such were operations in Africa up till the end of autumn.

36. Grain had been stockpiled from the raids on all the surrounding countryside, and there had also been supplies imported from Sicily and Italy. In addition, the propraetor Gnaeus Octavius had shipped in from Sardinia copious quantities that he had obtained from the praetor Tiberius Claudius, whose province it was. Not only were the granaries full that had been built earlier, but new ones were constructed, as well. The army was short of clothing, and Octavius was instructed to negotiate with the praetor to see what could be supplied and transported there from the province. The matter was promptly taken care of, and in no time 1,200 togas and 12,000 tunics were dispatched.

During the summer of these events in Africa, the consul Publius Sempronius, whose area of responsibility was Bruttium, fought a scrappy engagement with Hannibal in the region of Croton while the armies were actually on the march, and it was a fight between marching columns rather than a pitched battle. The Romans were driven back, and roughly 1,200 of the consul's army lost their lives in what could more accurately be termed a brawl than a battle. Sempronius' men retreated in panic to their camp, but even so the enemy did not risk attacking it. In fact, that night, when all was quiet, the consul left the camp and, after sending a messenger ahead to the proconsul Publius Licinius to tell him to bring up his legions, he then joined forces with him. Thus two commanders and two armies came back to face Hannibal, and the engagement was not put off since the consul was encouraged by the doubling of his strength, and the Carthaginian by his recent victory.

Sempronius brought his own legions into the front line, and Publius Licinius' legions were kept in reserve. At the start of the battle the consul made a vow of a temple to Fortuna Primigenia in the event of his routing the enemy that day, and he had his prayer granted. The Carthaginians were defeated and put to flight, with more than 4,000 soldiers killed, and slightly fewer than 300 taken alive, and with fifty horses and eleven military standards captured. Shaken by the defeat, Hannibal led his army away to Croton.*

Meanwhile, at the other end of Italy, Etruria had almost entirely transferred its support to Mago, hoping that a change of regime* could be effected through him, and the consul Marcus Cornelius maintained control less by armed force than by the dread generated by his judicial proceedings. Cornelius conducted his enquiries, which were mandated by a senatorial decree, with complete impartiality, and at the start there had been numerous appearances and condemnations of Etruscan noblemen who had either themselves gone to Mago, or corresponded with him, about the defection of their people. Later some opted for self-imposed exile through consciousness of their guilt, and were condemned *in absentia*. In this way they avoided the death penalty and offered only their property, which faced possible confiscation, as a security for their punishment.

37. Meanwhile, in Rome, during the time that the consuls were engaged in these operations in the separate regions, the censors Marcus Livius and Gaius Claudius* read out the senatorial register. Quintus Fabius Maximus was chosen leader of the house* for the second time, and seven men received the mark of disgrace,* though none was a holder of a curule chair. The censors conducted rigorous and absolutely thorough surveys of building repairs. They put out for contract the construction of a road from the Forum Boarium to the temple of Venus, bypassing the spectators' seats, and for a temple of the *Magna Mater* on the Palatine. They also imposed a new tax on the sale of salt. At Rome and throughout Italy salt was selling for a sixth of an *as*.* The censors put out contracts for it now to be sold at the same price as before in Rome, at a higher price in the market towns and administrative centres, and at various prices elsewhere, according to the locality. There was a widespread belief that it was just one of the censors who dreamed up this tax. He was angry with the people, it was said, over a wrongful conviction he had once received in court, and it was the tribes who had been responsible for his conviction who were burdened most by his adjustment of the price of salt. That was why he, Livius, was given the surname 'Salinator'.

The five-year purification ceremony took place later than usual because the censors sent agents through the provinces to report on the number of Roman citizens who were in the armies in the various locations. With these included, the census numbered 214,000 souls. Gaius Claudius Nero performed the five-year purification ceremony.

The censors then received the census of the twelve colonies, submitted by the censors of the actual colonies, which was an unprecedented procedure. Its purpose was to ensure that there was, in the public records, documentation of the colonies' strength in numbers of soldiers and financial resources. A census of the equestrian order was begun next, and it so happened that both censors were in possession of a public horse.* When they came to the Pollia tribe, in which Livius was enrolled, the herald baulked at calling out the name of the censor himself. 'Call Marcus Livius,' said Nero. Whether some of the old antagonism between them still remained, or whether it was a self-important, and untimely, demonstration of uncompromising principle, Nero commanded Marcus Livius to sell his horse because of his conviction by the people. Similarly, when they came to the Arniensis tribe, and the name of his colleague, Marcus Livius commanded Gaius Claudius to sell his horse, citing two reasons. In the first place, he said, Claudius had borne false witness against him, and secondly he had not been candid in his reconciliation with him.

At the end of their censorship, there was an equally disgraceful competition between the two to sully the other's reputation, which only did harm to the reputation of both. When Gaius Claudius took the oath that he had acted according to the laws, and had gone up to the treasury, he placed amongst the names of those whom he demoted to the status of poll-tax payers that of his colleague. After that, Marcus Livius came into the treasury. There, with the exception of the Maecia tribe, which had not participated in his conviction, but which had also refused to elect him either consul or censor after the conviction, he left with the status of poll-tax payers the entire Roman people, all thirty-four tribes. His reasoning, he said, was that the people had convicted an innocent man, but that, after convicting him, they had elected him consul and censor, and they had to admit now that they had either been mistaken once in their initial judgement, or twice in the elections. Livius went on to say that among the thirty-four tribes was Gaius Claudius, who would also become a poll-tax payer. Had he had a precedent for twice leaving the same man with poll-tax paying status, he declared, he would have left Gaius Claudius, by name, in that category.

This squabble between the censors over assigning the mark of disgrace was unbecoming; but the censorial condemnation of the fickleness of the mob was in keeping with the earnest nature of the times. The censors were now in bad odour and the plebeian tribune, Gnaeus Baebius, thinking that he had a chance to make political capital at their expense, served a summons for both to appear before the people. The procedure was blocked by a unanimous decision of the senators, for fear that the office of censor be put at the mercy of the whim of the people.*

38. That same summer, in Bruttium, Clampetia was taken by storm by the consul, and Consentia, Pandosia and other communities of little consequence submitted to him of their own volition.* Since the time for the elections was now approaching, the preferred choice was to have Cornelius brought back from Etruria where there were no hostilities. Cornelius oversaw the election of Gnaeus Servilius Caepio and Gaius Servilius Geminus as consuls. The praetorian elections were held next, and those elected were: Publius Cornelius Lentulus, Publius Quinctilius Varus, Publius Aelius Paetus, and Publius Villius Tappulus. The last two of these were elected to the praetorship while they were serving as plebeian aediles. The elections over, the consul returned to his army in Etruria.

Priests who died that year, and their replacements, were as follows. Tiberius Veturius Philo was elected and inaugurated as flamen of Mars to replace Marcus Aemilius Regillus, who had died the year before. To replace Marcus Pomponius Matho* in his positions as augur and decemvir, Marcus Aurelius Cotta was elected decemvir, and Tiberius Sempronius Gracchus was elected augur although he was very young* (and this very rarely occurred in the allocation of priesthoods in those days). A gilded four-horse chariot was that year set on the Capitol by the curule aediles Gaius Livius and Marcus Servilius Geminus. The Roman Games were repeated over a two-day period, and the Plebeian Games were likewise repeated for two days by the aediles Publius Aelius and Publius Villius. There was also a banquet for Jupiter held in honour of the games.

BOOK THIRTY

1. It was now the sixteenth year of the Punic War, and the consuls
Gnaeus Servilius and Gaius Servilius* raised in the Senate the
question of the state of the republic, the conduct of the war, and the
assignment of provinces. The senators decided that the consuls
should agree between them, or use sortition to decide, which of
them would have as his responsibility Bruttium and the operations
against Hannibal, and which Etruria and the Ligurians. The one to
whom Bruttium fell was to assume leadership of Publius Sempronius' army, and Publius Sempronius, who also received a year's
extension of his *imperium* as proconsul, was to succeed Publius
Licinius, who was to return to Rome. Licinius now enjoyed a good
military reputation, in addition to all his other qualities, in which
he was unrivalled by any of his fellow citizens—for all the advantages a man could have had been lavished on him by nature and
fortune. He was of noble birth and wealthy; he was remarkable for
his good looks and his physical strength. He was regarded as a
superb orator, whether he had to plead a case in court or whether
he had occasion to speak for or against a motion in the Senate, or
before the people. He was an expert in pontifical law. And, on top
of this, his consulship had now also given him a reputation as a
soldier.*

The same decision was taken for Etruria and the Ligurians as had
been taken for Bruttium. Marcus Cornelius was instructed to pass
command of his army to the new consul while he himself, with an
extension of his *imperium*, was to have Gaul as his area of responsibility, taking over the legions that Lucius Scribonius had commanded
the previous year. The consuls proceeded to a sortition for their
duties, and Bruttium fell to Caepio, and Etruria to Geminus.

The sortition for the praetorian responsibilities followed. Aelius
Paetus drew the urban jurisdiction, Publius Lentulus Sardinia,
Publius Villius Sicily, and Quinctilius Varus Ariminum, with two
legions under his command that had previously served under
Spurius Lucretius. Lucretius, too, had his *imperium* extended; he
was to rebuild entirely the town of Genua, which had been destroyed
by the Carthaginian Mago. The extension to Publius Scipio's

imperium was not defined in terms of time, but by the completion of his assignment—it would last until the war in Africa was ended.* A decree was also passed for the holding of public prayers to ask that Scipio's enterprise in crossing to Africa prove advantageous to the Roman people, to the commander himself, and to his army.

2. A force of 3,000 was raised for service in Sicily because all the crack troops in that province had been shipped off to Africa. It was further decided that the defence of the coastline of Sicily should be secured with forty ships, in case an enemy fleet should cross from Africa. Villius, therefore, took thirteen new vessels with him to Sicily; the others would be old ones overhauled on the island. This fleet was put under the admiralship of Marcus Pomponius, praetor the previous year, whose *imperium* was accordingly extended, and he had fresh troops brought from Italy and assigned to the ships. The senators decided on a fleet of the same number of vessels for Gnaeus Octavius, who had also been praetor the previous year,* for the defence of the Sardinian coast, and he was given the same extension of his *imperium*. The praetor Lentulus was instructed to provide 2,000 fighting men for these ships. Then there was the coast of Italy. Where the Carthaginians would send a fleet was unclear, though it seemed likely that they would head for some unguarded spot, and so Marcus Marcius, a praetor the previous year, was given the responsibility of patrolling the coast, again with forty ships. The consuls enrolled 3,000 fighting men for that fleet, in accordance with a senatorial decree, and they also enrolled two city legions to meet all the contingencies that can arise in war. Spain was officially assigned to its old commanders Lucius Lentulus and Lucius Manlius Acidinus, who kept their armies and their *imperium*. Roman operations that year were conducted with a total of twenty legions and a hundred and sixty warships.

The praetors were then ordered to leave Rome to assume their responsibilities, but the consuls were charged with staging the Great Games of Titus Manlius Torquatus before leaving. When he was dictator, Torquatus had made a vow that these games would be celebrated four years later, if the republic remained in the same condition as it was then.*

Reports of prodigies from several places aroused fresh superstition in the hearts of people. On the Capitol, it was believed, crows had not only torn away some gold with their beaks but had actually ingested it. At Antium some mice gnawed at a golden crown. A huge swarm of locusts covered the whole countryside around Capua, but how they got there was not known. At Reate, a foal was born with five feet; at Anagnia, there were shooting stars at various points in the sky, followed by a huge blazing meteor; at Frusino, a bow encircled the sun in a thin line, and then that circle itself was enclosed by a larger solar halo. At Arpinum, the soil in the countryside subsided, producing a huge hollow in the ground. When one of the consuls sacrificed his first animal the liver's 'head' was missing.* These prodigies were expiated with the sacrifice of full-grown animals, and the gods to whom sacrifices were to be made were announced by the pontifical college.

3. This business taken in hand, the consuls and praetors left to assume their responsibilities. All of them, however, had their attention focused on Africa, as though that were their allotted duty. Either they perceived that this was now the focal point of the whole war, or they wished to be obliging to Scipio, to whom the eyes of the entire state were now turned. As a result, clothing and grain were being shipped to him not just from Sardinia (as noted above), but from Sicily and Spain as well; and from Sicily he was also shipped weapons and all manner of supplies. And at no point during the winter had there been any let-up in the numerous military activities which Scipio had around him on every side. He was blockading Utica; the camp of Hasdrubal lay before his eyes; the Carthaginians had launched their ships,* and they had their fleet at the ready and equipped to intercept his supplies.

Meanwhile Scipio had not lost sight of his plan of making up with Syphax; and he wondered whether, with regard to his wife, there had been a cooling of his passion from too much enjoyment of her. But from Syphax came suggestions for peace-terms with the Carthaginians, based on the Romans quitting Africa and the Carthaginians Italy, rather than any prospect that he would switch loyalties if the war went on. For myself, I am inclined to the opinion—and such is the version of most of the sources*—that these negotiations took place through envoys rather than that, as Valerius Antias records, Syphax came in person to parley in the Roman camp. At first, the Roman commander paid hardly any attention to the terms he suggested. Later, however, he became less intransigent in rejecting the very same conditions, and held out the hope that an agreement on the matter might be reached by the frequent interchange of ideas. This would give his men an acceptable pretext for coming and going to the enemy camp.

The Carthaginian winter quarters had been built from materials indiscriminately brought together from the countryside, and so the structures were almost entirely of wood. The Numidians, in particular, were quartered in huts of interwoven reeds, most of them under roofs of thatch, and they were dispersed here and there in no particular order, with some of them even encamped beyond the ditch and the palisade, as happens when ground is occupied without regulations. When word of this was brought to Scipio, it had given him hope of gaining an opportunity to burn down the enemy camps.

4. Along with the envoys he sent to Syphax, Scipio would also send as their attendants some senior centurions of proven courage and good judgement, dressed as slaves. These men could therefore wander here and there about the camp while the envoys were parleying. They could thus gather intelligence on all entrances and exits, on the layout and plan of the camp as a whole and in its various sections, on where Carthaginians and Numidians were billeted, and on the distance between Hasdrubal's encampment and that of the king. At the same time they could find out how the outposts and sentries functioned, and whether night or day would be more favourable for a surprise attack. And as there were regular discussions, different parties of men would be sent along to increase the number who could be familiarized with the whole scene. The increasing frequency of the talks was every day raising more sanguine hopes of peace in Syphax, and through him in the Carthaginians, but the Romans then told him that they were forbidden to return to their commander unless they were given a clear response. So, they declared, if Syphax's mind was made up, he should express his opinion, or, if he had to discuss the matter with Hasdrubal and the Carthaginians, then he should do so. It was time now for peace to be established or else for an all-out war effort to be undertaken, they said.

While Hasdrubal's opinion was being sought by Syphax, and the Carthaginians' by Hasdrubal, the spies had the time to get a good look at everything, and Scipio had the time to make all the necessary preparations. Furthermore, a natural consequence of this talk of peace and the prospect of concluding it was to make the Carthaginians and

the Numidian less concerned with taking precautions against their
becoming, in the meantime, the object of any hostile act. Finally an
answer was brought back, containing a number of unreasonable conditions that had been deliberately added* because of the Romans'
apparent eagerness for peace, and these very conveniently gave Scipio
the excuse he wanted for ending the truce. He told the king's messenger that he would take the proposals to his advisory council, and
the next day he gave as his answer that he alone had, unsuccessfully,
advocated the peace plan—nobody else was in favour of it. So, he
said, Syphax should be informed that his only prospect of peace with
the Romans lay in abandoning the Carthaginians.

In this way Scipio ended the truce so that he would have the
latitude to carry out his designs honourably. He launched his ships—
it was already the start of spring—and placed on board war-machines
and catapults, giving the impression that he was going to attack
Utica from the sea. He also sent off 2,000 infantry to seize the hill,
which he had earlier held, overlooking Utica.* His plan was to distract
the enemy's attention from his undertaking by giving them something else to worry about, and also to prevent any sortie from the city
or an attack on his camp, which, when he himself left to take on
Syphax and Hasdrubal, would be left only lightly garrisoned.

5. After these preliminaries, Scipio summoned his advisory council
and instructed his spies and Masinissa, who had detailed knowledge
of the enemy, to produce the intelligence they had gathered. Finally,
he set before them his plan of action for the oncoming night, and
ordered the tribunes to lead the legions from the camp the moment
that the council was adjourned and the trumpets had given the signal.
Following Scipio's orders, the troops began to move out towards
sunset, and at about the first watch they formed up their column for
the march. It was a seven-mile journey, and, moving at an easy pace,
they reached the enemy camp around midnight.*

There Scipio put some of his troops, along with Masinissa and his
Numidians, under the command of Laelius, ordering him to attack
the camp of Syphax, and hurl fire-brands into it. He then took
Laelius and Masinissa aside, and appealed to each of them to be all
the more diligent and careful since the dark lessened the possibility
of planned action. He himself would launch an attack on Hasdrubal
and the Punic camp, he said, but would not begin until he saw the
fire in the camp of the king. And that was not slow in appearing; for

when the first huts were torched, the fire took hold and immediately engulfed everything around them, and then spread throughout the camp in an unbroken blaze. And such a widespread conflagration during the night inevitably caused great consternation. The Africans, however, thought the fire was an accident unrelated to the enemy and the war, and came streaming forth without weapons to douse the flames.* They ran into an armed enemy, and in particular the Numidians, whom Masinissa, thoroughly familiar with the camp of the king, had posted in opportune spots at the exits. Many of the enemy were consumed by the flames as they lay half-asleep in their beds; many rushed off in headlong flight, and were trampled under foot as they clambered over each other in the restricted gateways.

6. The shimmering flames were sighted first by the Carthaginian sentries, and then by others who had been awakened by the nocturnal commotion; and these, too, were similarly deluded into believing that the fire was accidental. In addition, the noise of men being killed or wounded made them unable to grasp what was really happening, for they were unsure whether the cries came simply from the turmoil in the dark. And so, unarmed, and each on his own initiative, inasmuch as they had no suspicion that they were under attack, they came rushing from all the gates, each taking what for him was the closest path and carrying only what could serve to douse the fire, and ran right into the Roman column. They were all killed, and that was not simply a matter of an enemy's hatred; it was also to prevent anyone escaping with news of what was happening. Scipio then lost no time in charging the gates, which, as one might expect in such confusion, had been left unguarded. Torches were hurled on the closest buildings, and flames leaped up. At first they seemed to flicker in several different places, but then, spreading stealthily and continuously, they suddenly consumed everything in a single blaze.

Severely burned men and animals choked the roads leading to the gates, first in their unruly flight, and then with their dead bodies. Those not killed by the fire fell by the sword, and the two camps were destroyed in a single disaster. The two commanders, however, made good their escape. From the many thousands of soldiers a mere 2,000 infantry and 500 cavalry got away, and these were poorly armed, and most of them wounded and badly burned. About 40,000 men were slaughtered or consumed by the flames, and more than 5,000 taken prisoner, many of them Carthaginian noblemen and eleven of them senators. A hundred and seventy-four military standards were captured, and more than 2,700 Numidian horses. Six elephants were taken, and eight died by the sword or in the fire.* Huge quantities of arms were captured. The commander dedicated them to Vulcan and burned them all.

7. After escaping the battle, Hasdrubal, accompanied by a handful of the Africans, had headed for the closest city,* and all who had survived the fight had, following in the steps of their leader, also converged on this town. Then, fearing that it might surrender to Scipio, Hasdrubal left. In a short while, the gates opened and the Romans were also admitted; and, in view of the voluntary surrender, there were no reprisals. Shortly afterwards two cities were captured and pillaged, and the booty from them was awarded to the men, along with all that had been rescued from the flames when the camps were burned. Syphax entrenched himself in a fortified spot some eight miles away,* and Hasdrubal hastened to Carthage to prevent the shock of the recent defeat causing any weakening of strategy.

In Carthage, there was at first such a state of alarm that people believed Scipio would abandon Utica and immediately lay siege to their city. The sufetes—amongst the Carthaginians they held the equivalent of consular power—accordingly convened the senate, and there it came down to a struggle between three points of view. One proposal was for sending a deputation to Scipio to discuss peace. A second was for recalling Hannibal to protect his country from a war that would be their undoing. The third showed a truly Roman resolve in time of crisis: it advocated rebuilding the army and encouraging Syphax not to abandon the war. Because it had the support of Hasdrubal, who was attending the meeting, and all members of the Barca faction, this was the proposal that prevailed.

After that a troop-levy got under way in the city and the country-side, and envoys were dispatched to Syphax, who was also vigorously preparing for a renewal of hostilities. It was Syphax' wife who had prevailed on him to do this, and no longer with sweet nothings, as before—though these were themselves powerful enough to sway the lover's heart—but with entreaties and appeals to his compassion. Her eyes swimming with tears, she would implore him not to let down her father and her country, and not to allow Carthage to go up in the same flames as had destroyed his camp. The envoys also brought with them some well-timed assurance. Four thousand

Celtiberians, men in their prime who had been hired in Spain by their own recruiting officers, had met them in the environs of a city called Oppa,* they said, and, in addition, Hasdrubal would very soon be there with a force that was not to be despised. As a result, Syphax did more than simply give the envoys a warm response; he actually brought to their attention a large number of Numidian peasants to whom he had in recent days given weapons and horses, and declared that he would call up all the young men in his kingdom. He was aware, he said, that the disaster they had suffered was the result of a fire, not a battle, and that the loser in war was the man defeated in the field.

Such was Syphax's reply to the envoys, and only days later* Hasdrubal and he once again joined forces. That army totalled about 30,000 men.

8. Assuming that, as far as Syphax and the Carthaginians were concerned, the conflict was at an end, Scipio was now pressing on with the siege of Utica. He was actually moving the siege-engines up to the walls when the news of their renewed hostilities drew him away from the operation. He left a small force merely to keep up the façade of a blockade being maintained by land and sea, and he himself proceeded against the enemy with the main body of his troops. At first he dug in on a hill about four miles from the king's camp, and the next day he went down with his cavalry into what are called 'The Great Plains',* which lie at the foot of the hill. There he spent the day approaching and harassing the enemy outposts with light skirmishing. Similarly, on the two days that followed, both sides in turn engaged in disorderly sallies here and there, without achieving any worthwhile result; but on the fourth day they both came out to do battle.

The Roman commander deployed his *principes* behind the *hastati*, whose maniples formed the front line, leaving the *triarii* in reserve,* and he placed the Italian cavalry on the right wing, and the Numidians and Masinissa on the left. Syphax and Hasdrubal positioned the Numidians facing the Italian horse, and the Carthaginians facing Masinissa; and they placed the Celtiberians in the middle of the line to face the maniples of the legions.

Such was the formation in which the two armies encountered each other. With the first charge, the enemy wings, the Carthaginians as well as the Numidians, were both driven back at the same time.

The Numidians, who were mostly peasants, were no match for the Roman cavalry; and the Carthaginians, new recruits themselves, were no match for Masinissa, a redoubtable figure, and especially so after his recent victory. Though shorn of both wings, the Celtiberian line still stood its ground. Ignorant of the land, they could see no prospect of safety in flight; and there was no hope of clemency from Scipio—they and their people had been well treated by him, and had still come to Africa as hired soldiers to fight him. And so, with the enemy completely surrounding them, they fought stubbornly to the end, falling over each other in heaps. While attention was entirely focused on the Celtiberians, Syphax and Hasdrubal gained some time to make good their escape; and night fell on the victors, exhausted from the bloodbath, which had gone on beyond the battle.

9. The next day Scipio sent Laelius and Masinissa, together with all the Roman and Numidian cavalry, and the lightest-armed of the infantry, in pursuit of Syphax and Hasdrubal. Scipio himself took the main body of the army, and proceeded to reduce the neighbouring cities, all of them under Carthaginian control.* In some cases he did this by giving them hope, in others by intimidation or the use of force. At Carthage there was sheer terror. People assumed that Scipio, moving around the country with his forces, would quickly subdue all their neighbours and make a sudden attack on Carthage itself. The walls were therefore being repaired and strengthened with buttresses, and everyone was bringing in from the country whatever he needed for facing a protracted siege. Peace was rarely mentioned; more often there was talk of sending envoys to summon Hannibal home. But most felt that the fleet that had been mobilized to intercept Roman supplies should be sent to Utica in order to catch the enemy ships anchored there off their guard with a surprise attack—it might even overwhelm the naval camp, which was left only lightly garrisoned.

This was the strategy they favoured most, but they nonetheless voted to send a deputation to Hannibal. They thought that even a completely successful operation by the fleet would lead only to limited relief of the siege of Utica, and for the protection of Carthage itself they were left with no commander but Hannibal, and no army apart from his. The ships were therefore launched the next day, and at the same time the envoys also left for Italy. And, under the stimulus of their plight, all was being done in a hurry, with everyone thinking that any slacking on his part was a betrayal of the safety of them all.

Scipio was in the process of trailing around an army that was now heavily burdened with spoils from many cities. He sent his prisoners of war and other booty to the old camp near Utica and, focusing now on Carthage, he seized Tynes,* some fifteen miles from Carthage, its garrison having fled and abandoned it. Tynes was a place enjoying protection from its geographical situation as well as defence-works; it was also visible from Carthage, and itself afforded a view both of the city and the sea around it.

10. From Tynes, just when the Romans were constructing their rampart, the enemy fleet was spotted heading from Carthage to Utica. The work was therefore abandoned and the order given to march. The troops began to move out at a rapid pace so that their ships would not be taken by surprise—for these were facing the shore to take part in the siege, and were in no way ready for a naval battle. The vessels had artillery and siege-engines on board, and had either been converted for use as transports or had been brought up so close to the walls that they could be used for scaling in place of the usual mound and bridges. There was no way they could have stood up to a fleet that could manœuvre swiftly and was fully equipped with nautical gear and weaponry.

On reaching his destination,* Scipio abandoned the strategy usually employed in a naval engagement. He set the warships, which could have given protection to the other vessels, in the rearmost position, close to shore, and he had four rows of freighters deployed to form a wall against the enemy. Fearing that his lines could be broken in the tumult of battle, he harnessed the freighters with a relay of masts and yardarms running from one ship to another, and with strong ropes that lashed them together in what was virtually an unbroken chain. He also set planks on them to form a path along the whole line of ships, and under the bridges so formed he left spaces to enable scouting boats to run out against the enemy, and then beat a retreat in safety. All of this was put in place as swiftly as circumstances allowed, and then about 1,000 hand-picked men were set aboard the freighters to defend them. A huge stock of weapons, mostly of the throwing variety, was also brought together, in numbers sufficient for an engagement of any length. Thus prepared, the Romans remained on the alert, awaiting their enemy's approach.

Had the Carthaginians moved quickly, they could have taken their enemy by surprise with their first onset, for confusion reigned everywhere and men were scurrying about in disorder. But they were shaken by their defeats on land, and after them they had little confidence even on the sea, where they were stronger than their enemy. They spent the day sailing around in a dilatory manner, and towards sunset they put in at a harbour that the Africans call Rusucmon.* At sunrise the next day they deployed their vessels out at sea, anticipating a regular naval engagement, and expecting the Romans to come out to face them. They held their position for some time, finally attacking the freighters only when they could see that there was no movement on the enemy's part.

What developed was very dissimilar to a naval engagement and, more than anything, looked like ships making an attack on walls. The freighters had the clear advantage in height. The Carthaginians were hurling their missiles from their warships at a point above them, unsuccessfully for the most part because of the upward trajectory; and those thrown from the heights of the freighters fell more heavily and, thanks to the weight, were more accurate. The scouting boats and other light craft that would sally forth through the spaces under the planked gangways were, at first, merely sunk by the enemy warships with their greater momentum and size. Later on they also proved to be an obstruction to their own defensive troops; for, becoming interspersed amongst the enemy ships, they often obliged these men to hold back their weapons for fear of hitting their own side with a poorly aimed shot. Finally, the Carthaginians proceeded to hurl poles tipped with an iron hook (*harpagones** in military terminology) from their vessels onto those of the Romans. The Romans found it impossible to hack through these instruments, or the chains on which they were slung. The result was that, as each Carthaginian warship backed water, dragging a freighter that was hooked, one could see the cables by which it was connected to the other vessels snapping, or a number of ships being dragged off in a row. By this particular process all the bridges were torn apart, barely giving the fighting men on them time to jump over to the second row of ships; and about sixty freighters were hauled off to Carthage by the stern. The euphoria this inspired in the Carthaginians was not justified by the action, but it was all the more gratifying since it appeared as a single unexpected gleam of joy, no matter how small, interrupting an unbroken sequence of disasters and misery. In addition, the Roman fleet had apparently come close to being destroyed, and this had been thwarted only by the hesitation on the part of the captains of their own ships, and the timely arrival of Scipio.*

11. It so happened that, at about this time, Laelius and Masinissa had arrived in Numidia after a march of about fourteen days, and there the Maesuli happily bestowed on Masinissa his father's throne, as being their long-lost king. Syphax, whose officers and garrisons were driven from the kingdom, now kept to his old realm, though he had not the slightest intention of remaining inactive. Lovesick, he was under constant pressure from his wife and father-in-law, and he possessed men and horses in such numbers that the very sight of the military resources of a kingdom that had prospered for many years could have inspired a spirit even less barbarous and unruly than his.

He therefore gathered together all his men who were fit for war, and distributed horses, armour, and weapons amongst them; and he also formed up his cavalry in squadrons and his infantry in cohorts, as he had learned to do earlier from the Roman centurions. He then went out to meet the enemy with an army no smaller than his former force, but one that was almost completely new and without training. He encamped close to them, and at first a few horsemen went forward from the outposts, reconnoitring at a safe remove, but then running back to their comrades when driven off by a shower of spears. After that there were minor sorties from both sides in turn, with more coming into the fray as men were driven back and roused to indignation. This is what usually prompts cavalry engagements, with the successful side's hopes, and the defeated side's anger, bringing comrades into the action.

So it was in this instance. The battle was started by a few, but then the wish to join the action eventually brought the entire cavalry of both sides pouring onto the field. While it was a cavalry engagement pure and simple, there was little possibility of resisting the Masaesulians' superior numbers, as Syphax sent his huge columns of men into action. Then the Roman infantry* made a sudden charge through the gaps that the cavalry squadrons left for them, and thereby brought stability to the battle line, stemming the wild onset of the enemy. At this, the barbarians first of all slowed their horses; then they came to a halt, and were almost thrown into disorder by this strange way of fighting. Eventually, they not only gave ground before the enemy infantry, but they also failed to withstand the cavalry, which was given fresh courage now by the assistance of the infantry. By this time, too, the legionary troops were coming up, and at that point it was not simply a matter of the Masaesulians not waiting for the initial onset—they could not even resist the sight of the Roman standards and weapons! So powerful was their memory of earlier defeats, or else their present fear.

12. Syphax then rode up to the enemy cavalry squadrons, hoping he could check the flight of his men by putting them to shame when he put himself in harm's way. But his horse received a serious wound, and he was thrown off. He was overpowered, taken prisoner, and brought alive to Laelius—a sight that would please Masinissa more than anyone.

The loss of life in that battle was lighter than the margin of victory might have suggested, because the fighting had been limited to cavalry. No more than 5,000 were killed, and less than half that figure were taken prisoner when an attack was launched on the camp, to which large numbers, dismayed at losing their king, had made their way.

The capital of Syphax's realm was Cirta,* and it was here that a huge body of men had come after the rout. Masinissa declared that nothing could be more gratifying at that moment than to tour his ancestral kingdom as victor, now recovered after such a long period of time, but he cautioned that it was just as important not to fritter away time when things went well as when they went badly. If Laelius would allow him to go ahead to Cirta with the cavalry, and with Syphax in irons, he said, he would bring about confusion and panic everywhere. Laelius could then follow with the infantry in easy stages.* Laelius agreed, and Masinissa went ahead to Cirta, where he had the leading citizens of the town summoned to parley. While these men were still unaware of what had befallen the king, Masinissa made no progress with them either by informing them of what had happened, or by threats or persuasion—until the king was brought, in irons, into their sight. The shameful spectacle provoked an outburst of lamentation. Some abandoned the walls in panic, and others, hurriedly agreeing they should try to win the victor's favour, flung open the gates. As for Masinissa, he first dispatched troops to make the rounds of the gates and suitable spots on the walls, to prevent any escape, and then galloped in to seize the palace.

As he entered the vestibule, Sophoniba,* wife of Syphax and daughter of Hasdrubal, met him right on the threshold. When she saw him surrounded by a body of soldiers, cutting a conspicuous figure with his armour and general appearance, she assumed—as was indeed the case—that he was the king. She flung herself before his knees and said: 'The gods, and your own valour and good fortune, have seen to it that you have absolute power over us.* But perhaps a captive may be allowed to make a suppliant plea before the man who can decide if she lives or dies, and to touch his knees and his conquering hand. If so, then I beg and entreat you by that royal majesty, in which we too lived until a short time ago, and in the name of the Numidian race, which provided a common bond between you and Syphax, and I beg you by the gods who preside over this palace— with a prayer that they welcome you with more favourable omens than those with which they sent Syphax from here—to grant a suppliant this favour, that you personally decide the fate of your captive, no matter what your feelings are in that regard, and not let me face the overbearing and ruthless judgement of some Roman. Had I been no more than Syphax's wife, I would still have preferred to rely on the honour of a Numidian, of a man born, as I was, in Africa, rather than that of a foreigner from overseas. But you can understand what a Carthaginian, and what a daughter of Hasdrubal, has to fear from a Roman. I earnestly entreat you, if you can achieve it in no other way, to save me from falling under the control of the Romans by letting me die now.'

Sophoniba was a woman of outstanding beauty and in her prime. She was now grasping Masinissa's right hand and begging him for an undertaking that she not be surrendered to any Roman, her language more that of love than of entreaty. The result was that the victor's heart succumbed to pity; but, more than that, thanks to the Numidian proclivity for sensuality, the victor was brought to his knees by passion for his own captive. He gave her his right hand as a guarantee that he would fulfil her request, and went into the palace.

Masinissa then began to puzzle over how he could honour the commitment he had made. Finding no solution, he was prompted by his infatuation to employ an ill-considered and shameless plan of action, and gave orders for a marriage ceremony to be hurriedly arranged for that very day. His intention was not to allow either

Laelius, or even Scipio himself, any leeway in deciding the case of a presumed captive, for she would by then be married to Masinissa.

Laelius appeared on the scene when the ceremony was over. Far from hiding his disapproval of what had taken place, his initial reaction was to try to tear her from the wedding couch, and send her off to Scipio, along with Syphax and the other prisoners. He was then overcome by the pleas of Masinissa, who begged him to leave it to Scipio to decide to which of the two kings' fortunes Sophoniba would be appended. Laelius accordingly sent off Syphax and the prisoners of war and, with Masinissa's assistance, reduced the other cities of Numidia* held by the king's garrisons.

13. Following the announcement that Syphax was being brought into the camp, all the soldiers poured out in a crowd, as if to view a triumph. Syphax was at the front, in chains, and a crowd of Numidian noblemen came after him. At that point all the soldiers did as much as they could to play up Syphax's importance, and the fame of his race, thereby aggrandizing their own victory. This was the king, they would say, whose grandeur was recognized by the two most powerful nations on earth, the Roman and Carthaginian. So much so, indeed, that their own commander Scipio had left his assignment in Spain, and his army, to sail to Africa with a couple of triremes to seek the man's friendship. And the Carthaginian commander Hamilcar had not merely visited Syphax in his kingdom—he had even given him his daughter in marriage! Syphax, they said, had at the same time had both generals, the Carthaginian and the Roman, under his thumb, and just as both sides had used sacrifices to seek the blessing of the immortal gods, so too Syphax's friendship had been sought by both. Such had been his power, in fact, that he had driven Masinissa from the throne, and brought him so low that his life was protected only by a report of his death, and by his evading detection, living in the woods, like a wild animal, on what he could catch.

Such was the praise Syphax received from the bystanders; he was then brought to Scipio in his headquarters. Scipio, too, was touched when he compared the man's earlier and present fortunes, and also when he remembered their ties of hospitality, the clasping of their hands, and the pact they had made on the official and private level.

These same reflections also came to Syphax, raising his confidence as he addressed his conqueror. For when Scipio asked him what he thought he would gain in not only rejecting a Roman alliance but in actually opening hostilities, Syphax admitted that he had been wrong and had acted irrationally—but this did not date only from the time when he finally took up arms against the Roman people. That, he explained, had been the culmination, not the beginning, of his madness. He had lost his mind, and cast from his thoughts all private and official compacts, at the time when he welcomed a Carthaginian woman into his home as his wife. Those wedding torches had sent his palace up in flames, he said, and that fury, that fiend, had resorted to all manner of wheedling to turn his head and make him crazy. She had not rested until she had, with her own hands, fastened on him his abominable armour, making him face a man who was his host and friend. Even so, he added, while he might be done for and ruined, he still had one thing to console him in his misery—he could see that that fiend and fury had now passed into the house and home of the greatest enemy he had in the world. And Masinissa had shown no more caution or resolve than Syphax— because of his youth he was even more thoughtless. His marriage to Sophoniba, at all events, was characterized by greater folly and abandon than his own had been.

14. These words came not only from hatred felt for an enemy; they were prompted, too, by the pangs of love felt by a man aware that his loved one was with a rival, and they brought Scipio no small measure of concern. The haste with which the marriage had been celebrated, virtually in the midst of battle, lent substance to the charges—Masinissa had not even consulted or waited for Laelius. He had been in such a feverish rush that he took the woman into his home as his wife, completing the wedding rites before his enemy's household deities, on the very same day as he had set eyes on her as a prisoner of war. And Scipio found this all the more offensive because, when he himself had been a young man in Spain, he had been tempted by the looks of no female captive. He was mulling over such thoughts when Laelius and Masinissa appeared.

Scipio welcomed both of them with a friendly expression, and lavished on them words of the highest praise in the presence of a large number of his staff. He then took Masinissa aside and addressed him as follows:

'Masinissa, I think it was because you saw some merit in me that you came to me initially, in Spain, to establish ties of friendship with me, and then later, in Africa, when you put yourself and all your hopes in my hands. But of those virtues for which you thought me worth seeking out I would pride myself on none as much as my restraint and self-control. I wish, Masinissa, that you too could have added this quality to your other exceptional virtues. At our age, believe me, there is not so much danger from an enemy under arms as there is from the pleasures that surround us everywhere. A man who by his own self-control has held these in check, and suppressed them, has won much greater glory and a greater victory than we have now in defeating Syphax. Your dynamic and courageous conduct in my absence I have been delighted to record publicly and to remember; your other behaviour I prefer to let you reflect on yourself rather than have you blush at my mention of it.

'Syphax was defeated and taken prisoner under the auspices of the Roman people. That means that Syphax himself, his wife, his kingdom, his towns with the men inhabiting them, in short all that belonged to Syphax, now belong to the Roman people as their spoils.* The king and queen would have to be sent to Rome, even if the queen were not a Carthaginian citizen, and even if we did not discern in her father an enemy commander. It should be for the Senate and People of Rome to judge and decide the case of a woman who purportedly turned an allied monarch against us and drove him headlong into war. Have some self-control. See that you do not mar your many good qualities with a single vice, and ruin the gratitude you have earned for all your services by an error of greater importance than what was responsible for the error.'

15. When he heard this not only did a blush of embarrassment spread over Masinissa's face but tears also welled up in his eyes. He would, he said, abide by his commander's decision, but he begged him, as far as circumstances permitted, to take account of the promise he had thoughtlessly made—he had given an undertaking not to let Sophoniba pass into anyone's hands. Then, in an agitated state, he left the headquarters for his own tent. There, after sending off any who might see him, he spent a long time sighing and moaning, which was easily audible to the men standing around the tent. Finally, he let out a loud groan and sent for a trusted slave, the man in whose keeping lay the poison that was to be used to meet the uncertainties of fortune—a regular practice with royalty. He ordered the man to mix the poison in a cup and take it to Sophoniba,* and at the same

time to announce to her that Masinissa would have been glad to carry out his first commitment to her, one which he, as a husband, owed to his wife. Now those with the power were taking that option from him, and so he was honouring his second commitment, namely to see that she did not fall into the hands of the Romans alive. She should think of her father the commander, of her country, and of the two kings to whom she had been married, and make her decision with them in mind.

The servant came to Sophoniba bearing this message, and the poison along with it. 'I accept this wedding gift,' said Sophoniba. 'It is not unwelcome, if my husband has found it impossible to give his wife a greater one. But tell him this: my death would have been more acceptable had my marriage not coincided with my funeral.' The resolve with which she spoke was no greater than that with which she took and, with no sign of perturbation, fearlessly drained the cup.

When the incident was reported to him, Scipio feared that the headstrong young man might be prompted to some reckless act by his chagrin. He immediately summoned Masinissa, and by turns consoled him and gently rebuked him for having committed one hasty act to pay for another, and making the whole affair more grievous than it needed to be.

The next day, in order to divert the man's thoughts from the pain he was suffering, Scipio mounted the tribunal and had an assembly called. There he first of all addressed Masinissa as 'king' and lavished extraordinary praise on him, and then conferred upon him a crown of gold, a golden bowl, a curule chair, and an ivory sceptre, along with an embroidered toga and a tunic with a palm motif. He did him further honour by explaining that, amongst the Romans, there was nothing more splendid than a triumph, and those celebrating a triumph had no more splendid finery than that which the people of Rome thought Masinissa, alone of foreigners, now merited. He then paid tribute to Laelius, whom he also presented with a golden crown, and other soldiers were given awards in proportion to their merits. The king's feelings were soothed by such honours, and his hopes were raised that, with Syphax out of the way, he would soon take possession of all Numidia.

16. Scipio sent Gaius Laelius to Rome with Syphax and the other prisoners of war, and envoys from Masinissa accompanied them. He then moved his camp back to Tynes where he completed

the fortifications he had started earlier. Thanks to the momentary success of their attack on the fleet, the Carthaginians were filled with an exhilaration that was not only of brief duration but practically groundless; but they were stunned by the report of the capture of Syphax, in whom they had placed more hope than they had in Hasdrubal and his army. They no longer paid attention to anyone advocating military action, and they sent their thirty leading elders to sue for peace. (This was a council that enjoyed considerable respect* amongst the Carthaginians, and had a very great influence on the decision-making of the senate.)

On their arrival in the headquarters in the Roman camp, the elders prostrated themselves before Scipio like men performing obeisance, a practice that I suppose derives from the area of their origin.* Their language suited such obsequious flattery. Instead of trying to excuse their own culpability they shifted initial responsibility for the war to Hannibal and those who supported his power.* They asked for pardon for a city-state that had now been twice brought low by the recklessness of its citizens, and whose future preservation would once more depend on the favour of its enemies. It was power the Roman people looked for from victory over its foes, not their destruction, they said, and Scipio could give them any orders he liked, as they were ready to follow them to the letter.

Scipio replied that the hope with which he had come to Africa— and his hope had been further raised by the successful outcome of his campaign—was that he would return home with a victory, not a peace settlement. However, despite almost having victory in his hands, he said, he did not reject a peace treaty, so that all peoples might be made aware that the Roman people were fair-minded both in undertaking and concluding wars. He then declared that the following were his peace-terms. The Carthaginians were to hand back prisoners of war, deserters, and runaway slaves. They were to remove their armed forces from Italy and Gaul. They were to stay out of Spain. They were to leave all the islands that lay between Italy and Africa.* They were to surrender all but twenty of their warships and hand over 500,000 measures of wheat and 300,000 of barley. As for the financial indemnity in Scipio's demands, there is little agreement on the amount.* In one source I find 5,000 talents, in another 5,000 pounds of silver, in a third a demand for double his men's pay.

'You will be given three days to consider whether you are willing to accept peace on these terms,' said Scipio. 'If you *are* willing, make a truce with me and send representatives to the Senate in Rome.' With that the Carthaginians were dismissed. As they were now playing for time* to allow Hannibal to cross to Africa, they felt that no terms of peace should be refused, and so they sent one group of representatives to Scipio to arrange the truce, and another to Rome to ask for a peace treaty. The latter group made a show of taking along a few prisoners, deserters, and runaway slaves, so that a peace treaty would be more easily attainable.

17. Many days before this* Laelius arrived in Rome with Syphax and the more important Numidian prisoners of war. He gave the senators an ordered account of operations in Africa, prompting great elation over the current situation and raising great hopes for the future. When the question was put on the matter, the senators voted that the king should be sent to Alba for imprisonment, and that Laelius should be kept back in Rome until the Carthaginian representatives arrived.* A decree was passed authorizing four days of public prayer.

The praetor Publius Aelius adjourned the Senate and then convened the popular assembly. There he mounted the Rostra with Gaius Laelius. The people were told of Carthaginian armies being routed, of an enormously famous king being defeated and taken prisoner, of all Numidia being overrun in a singularly successful campaign. The people could not contain their euphoria in silence; they made clear their extravagant jubilation with cheers and all the usual manifestations of joy of the masses. The praetor accordingly gave an immediate order for the temple-custodians to open up the holy places throughout the city, and for the people to be given the opportunity of doing the rounds of them, throughout the day, paying homage and giving thanks to the gods.

The next day Aelius brought Masinissa's envoys into the Senate. They first of all congratulated the senators on Publius Scipio's successes in Africa, and then expressed their gratitude to them for the fact that Scipio had not merely addressed Masinissa as a king, but had actually made him so by restoring him to his father's kingdom. Now that Syphax had been deposed, Masinissa would remain on the throne without fear, and without opposition, if such was the Senate's decision, they said. They also thanked the Senate for Scipio's commendation of Masinissa before an assembly of his army, and for

the presentation of splendid gifts that he had made to the king.
Masinissa had done his best, and would go on doing his best, to show
himself worthy of this treatment. They added that the king requested
that the Senate ratify by decree the royal title and other benefits and
gifts conferred on him by Scipio, and he further requested that, if it
did not displease them, they send back any Numidian prisoners in
custody in Rome. That, they explained, would very much redound
to the king's credit amongst his people.

The response given to the envoys was that congratulations for
successes in Africa that they offered to the Senate should be shared
with the king. Furthermore, they said, Scipio's action in addressing
Masinissa as a king was, in the Senate's opinion, correct and proper,
and the members fully approved of everything else Scipio had done
to gratify Masinissa. They also passed a decree authorizing gifts for
the envoys to bear to the king: two purple cloaks, each with a golden
clasp; two tunics with a broad stripe; two horses with their harness-
decorations; two sets of cavalry armour with cuirasses; and tents and
military paraphernalia of the kind usually provided for a consul. The
praetor was instructed to see that the gifts were sent to the king. The
envoys were each given a minimum of 5,000 *asses*, and their attendants 1,000 each; and two tunics were presented to each ambassador,
and one to the attendants and to the Numidians who were to be
released from custody and restored to the king. In addition, a decree
authorized the provision of free-of-charge accommodation and
entertainment for the envoys.

18. During the summer that these senatorial decrees were passed
in Rome and military operations were being conducted in Africa, the
praetor Publius Quinctilius Varus and proconsul Marcus Cornelius
clashed in pitched battle with the Carthaginian Mago in the land of
the Insubrian Gauls.* The praetor's legions were in the front line;
Cornelius kept his in reserve but he himself rode up to the front and
there, positioned before the two wings, praetor and proconsul both
urged on the men to mount an all-out attack on the enemy. They
were achieving no success with this, and then Quinctilius said to
Cornelius: 'As you see, the battle is losing momentum. The enemy's
fear is being hardened into stubbornness by a resistance that is succeeding beyond their expectations, and there is a risk of it developing
into boldness. We should get a brisk cavalry charge going if we want
to shake them and make them give ground. So either you must keep

up the pressure at the front, while I lead the cavalry into battle, or I shall look after matters here in the front line, while you unleash the cavalry of four legions on the enemy.'

The proconsul was prepared to accept whatever part of the task the praetor wanted him to take on. The praetor Quinctilius then went forward to the cavalry with his son, an intrepid young man (his *praenomen* was Marcus), and, ordering them to mount up, he unleashed them against the enemy.

The disarray caused by the cavalry was heightened by the shouts that arose from the legions, and the enemy line would not have held had it not been for Mago who, when the cavalry first made their move, immediately brought the elephants, which were kept ready for action, into the fight. The horses were terrified by their trumpeting, their smell, and their appearance, and this completely undermined the assistance brought by the cavalry. While the Roman cavalry were in the midst of the action, where they could use lance and sword at close quarters, they had the upper hand; but when they were carried away from the fight by the startled horses they became, at a distance, better targets for the Numidian javelins. At the same time, among the infantry, the twelfth legion had been mostly cut down, and was holding its ground more to avoid humiliation than by virtue of its strength. It would not have held on any longer had not the thirteenth, which was brought into the front line from the reserves, taken up the indecisive struggle. Mago, too, went to his reserves, bringing up some Gauls to face this fresh legion. But these were scattered without much of a fight, and the *hastati* of the eleventh legion then bunched together and charged the elephants who were by now wreaking havoc on the infantry line as well. The animals were massed together, and so when the Romans hurled their javelins at them hardly any missed the mark. They then drove them all back to their own battle line, four of them collapsing from the severity of their wounds.

It was at that point that the enemy line was first driven back, and when they saw the elephants turn to run all the Roman cavalry came pouring out to increase the panic and disorder. As long as Mago stood before the standards, however, the Carthaginians retreated only by degrees, preserving their ranks and orderly manner of fighting. But when they saw him fall, his thigh run through by a weapon, and being carried from the field virtually lifeless, they all immediately turned to flight.*

Approximately 5,000 of the enemy were killed that day, and twenty-two military standards were taken. But it was no bloodless victory for the Romans, either. Casualties in the praetor's army numbered 2,300, by far the greatest number coming from the twelfth legion. Two military tribunes, Marcus Cosconius and Marcus Maevius, were also lost from that legion, and from the thirteenth, which had been involved in the closing moments of the fight, another military tribune, Gaius Helvius, fell as he was re-establishing the battle. In addition, about twenty-two eminent knights, along with a number of centurions, were crushed to death by the elephants. The battle might have gone on, but the Carthaginians ceded victory when their leader was wounded.

19. Mago left that night, when all was quiet, and, marching in stages as long as his wound would permit him to bear, he came to the coast in the land of the Ligurian Ingauni.* Here delegates from Carthage, who had docked in the Gallic Gulf* a few days earlier, came to him with orders for him to cross to Africa at the earliest possible moment. His brother Hannibal would be doing the same, they told him, for a delegation had gone to him with the same orders—the situation in which the Carthaginians were now placed would not permit them to hold Gaul as well as Italy with their armed forces.

Mago was galvanized to action not only by the command from his senate, and the danger his country faced, but also by fear of an attack from the victorious enemy if he delayed. He was also afraid that, once they saw Italy being abandoned by the Carthaginians, the Ligurians themselves would go over to the side in whose power they would soon find themselves. At the same time he was hoping that his wound would be less severely jolted on a sea journey than on the road and that he would find everything at sea more conducive to his recovery. He therefore boarded his troops and set sail, but barely had he passed Sardinia when he died from his wound.* Furthermore, a number of the Carthaginian ships that had been driven off course on the high sea were captured by the Roman fleet lying off Sardinia. Such were land and sea operations in the area of Italy close to the Alps.

The consul Gaius Servilius had done nothing worthy of note in his area of responsibility, Etruria, nor in Gaul, into which he had also gone. He did, however, deliver his father Gaius Servilius, along with

Gaius Lutatius, after they had been enslaved for fifteen years, both men having been taken prisoner by the Boii near the village of Tannetum.* He then returned to Rome, flanked by his father and Catulus, his reputation enhanced by a splendid act that was personal rather than official in nature. A proposal was brought before the people freeing Gaius Servilius from any liability for having contravened lawful procedure in serving as plebeian tribune and plebeian aedile while his father, who had held a curule chair, was (unbeknownst to him) still alive.* The proposal passed into law, and Servilius returned to his sphere of duty.

In Bruttium, where the consul Gnaeus Servilius was then serving, Consentia, Aufugum, Bergae, Baesidiae, Ocriculum, Lymphaeum, Argentanum, Clampetia,* and numerous other communities of little importance came over to him when they saw the Punic war effort flagging. That same consul also fought Hannibal in pitched battle in the vicinity of Croton, but information on that engagement is unclear. Valerius Antias gives a count of 5,000 enemy dead, making it an event of such magnitude as to suggest either a shameless fiction on his part or a negligent omission on the part of others. It is a fact, however, that nothing more was achieved by Hannibal in Italy. Envoys from Carthage recalling him to Africa happened to come to him, too, at about the same time as they did Mago.

20. It is said that as Hannibal listened to the words of the envoys he was gnashing his teeth and groaning, and barely able to hold back his tears. When his orders had been delivered to him, he said: 'Those men who were long trying to drag me back from here by blocking the shipment of reinforcements and cash are no longer using devious means to recall me, but doing it openly. So Hannibal has not been defeated by the Roman people, who have been so often slaughtered or routed, but by the Carthaginian senate with its carping jealousy. And Publius Scipio will not feel as much delight and exultation over this ignominious departure of mine as will Hanno who, unable to effect it by other means, has crushed our house by bringing down Carthage.'*

Anticipating this very outcome, Hannibal had prepared his ships ahead of time.* He therefore sent off the mass of his unserviceable troops, ostensibly as garrisons, to the few Bruttian towns that had been kept in check more by fear than loyalty, and the real strength of his army he shipped over to Africa. A large number of men who were of Italic descent had refused to go to Africa with him. They had taken shelter in the shrine of Juno Lacinia, which had remained inviolate till that day, but they had been foully murdered within the temple itself.*

Rarely, they say, has anyone departing into exile from his own country displayed such distress as Hannibal did then as he left the country of an enemy. It is said that he often looked back at the coast of Italy, levelling accusations against gods and men and even invoking curses on himself and his own head for not having led his men straight to Rome when they were covered with blood from the victory at Cannae. Scipio, he said, had dared to march on Carthage—a man who as consul had never set eyes on a Carthaginian in Italy!—while he himself, after slaughtering 100,000 soldiers at Trasimene and Cannae, had merely grown old in the vicinity of Casilinum, Cumae, and Nola! With such words of recrimination and regret Hannibal was pulled back from his long occupation of Italy.

21. Mago's departure was reported in Rome at about the same time as Hannibal's. There were thus two reasons for rejoicing, but the joy was diminished by the fact that the Roman commanders had evidently lacked the determination, or the strength, to hold back the two men, although they had been ordered to do so by the Senate.* It was lessened, too, by anxiety over how things might turn out now that the entire weight of the war rested on one army and one commander.

It was at about this time that envoys arrived from Saguntum, bringing with them some Carthaginians who had allegedly crossed to Spain to hire auxiliaries. These men had been captured along with their money. The envoys deposited in the vestibule of the Senate house 250 pounds of gold and 800 pounds of silver. The men were taken in charge and incarcerated, but all the gold and silver was given back. The envoys were thanked and also presented with gifts and ships for their return to Spain.

The point was then made by senior members of the house that people recognize good fortune more slowly than they do bad. One remembered well the extent of the terror and panic when Hannibal crossed into Italy, they observed—what disasters and what sorrows that had brought! The camp of the enemy was sighted from the city walls—what individual and communal prayers had gone up then! How often, in meetings, men would stretch their hands towards heaven, and they were heard poignantly asking if that day would ever come when they would see Italy free of the enemy and living in peace and prosperity again! Now, in the fullness of time, after fifteen years of war, the gods had finally granted this prayer—and yet there was no one ready to move that thanks be offered to them. That only shows, they said, that men did not appreciate a blessing even as it came to them, much less cherish the memory of it once it was past. Shouting then broke out from every quarter of the house demanding that the praetor Publius Aelius put the motion to the members. The motion was then carried that a five-day period of thanksgiving be held at all the couches of the gods, and that a hundred and twenty full-grown victims be sacrificed.

Laelius and the envoys of Masinissa had already been dismissed* when it was reported that the Carthaginian delegation that was coming to the Senate to sue for peace had been sighted at Puteoli and that it would be coming overland from there. It was decided therefore that Gaius Laelius be recalled so that he could be present at the peace negotiations. Scipio's legate, Quintus Fulvius Gillo, escorted the Carthaginians to Rome and, since they were forbidden to enter the city, they were lodged in the state villa and granted an audience with the Senate at the temple of Bellona.

22. The Carthaginian delegates made substantially the same speech as they had in Scipio's headquarters, and placed all responsibility for the war on Hannibal rather than on state policy. It was without the order of their senate that he had crossed the Ebro, not merely the Alps, they maintained, and he had on his own initiative launched his offensive not just on the Romans but even on the people of Saguntum before that. On any fair assessment, they said, the Carthaginian senate and people had kept their treaty with the Roman people intact up to that day. Accordingly they had been instructed to ask for nothing more than that they be allowed to continue with the terms of peace of the last treaty, the one concluded with Gaius Lutatius.*

Then, following tradition, the praetor gave all the senators the opportunity of putting any questions they wished to the delegates. Older members, who had been present at the negotiation of the treaties, put various questions to them, but the delegates' response was that they did not remember because of their age (for they were almost all young men). With that there was uproar from every corner of the Senate house. Choosing individuals to ask for a renewal of the old treaty, of which the men themselves had no memory, was, they said, a case of Punic duplicity.

23. The envoys were then taken from the Senate, and members' opinions were solicited. Marcus Livius proposed that they summon Gaius Servilius, since he was the closer of the two consuls, so that he could be present for the discussion of the peace treaty. No topic for debate could be more urgent than this, said Livius, and, in his view, discussion of it in the absence of one or both of the consuls was not really in accordance with the dignity of the Roman people. Quintus Metellus, consul three years earlier and also a former dictator, observed that, by massacring their armies and laying waste their farmland, Publius Scipio had brought the enemy to such a pass that they were suing for peace. Absolutely no one, he said, could more accurately appraise the Carthaginian intentions in suing for peace than could the man who was fighting a war before the gates of Carthage, and when it came to accepting or rejecting their peace proposal they should follow Scipio's advice and nobody else's. Marcus Valerius Laevinus, who had been twice consul, claimed that the men who had come to them were spies, not envoys. They should be ordered to leave Italy, he said, with guards sent to escort them right to their ships, and Scipio should be given written instructions not to relax the military pressure. Laelius and Fulvius made the further point that Scipio, too, had premised his hopes of a peace accord on the expectation that Hannibal and Mago would not be recalled from Italy. In fact, they said, the Carthaginians would resort to all manner of deception while they waited for their armies and their generals, and would then continue the war with no thought for their treaties, however recent they were, and in defiance of all the gods. This made even more people vote in favour of Laevinus' proposal, and the envoys were sent off with no peace concluded and almost without being given an answer.*

24. At about this time Gnaeus Servilius, who was in no doubt that the credit for restoring peace to Italy belonged to him, crossed to Sicily. He was intending to proceed from there to Africa, in pursuit of Hannibal who, he imagined, had been driven out of Italy by him. When word of this spread through Rome, the senators had initially passed a motion authorizing the praetor to inform the consul by letter that the Senate felt it appropriate that he return to Italy. But

when the praetor declared that Servilius would pay no attention to any letter of his, Publius Sulpicius was appointed dictator* expressly to resolve the problem and he, by right of his higher authority, recalled the consul to Italy. Sulpicius spent the remainder of the year on a tour of Italy with Marcus Servilius, his master of horse, visiting the cities that had split from Rome in the hostilities, and trying the cases of each of them.

During the period of the truce* a hundred freighters were sent from Sardinia by the praetor Publius Lentulus. Carrying supplies, and escorted by twenty warships, they crossed to Africa on a sea free of danger from both the enemy and bad weather. Gnaeus Octavius, who made the crossing from Sicily with two hundred freighters and thirty warships, did not enjoy the same good fortune. He had had a favourable passage to the point where he was almost in sight of Africa but then, first of all, the wind dropped and then it later veered to the south-west, throwing him off-course and scattering his ships far and wide. Thanks to a superlative effort by his oarsmen, Octavius himself struggled through the contrary swell and made the promontory of Apollo with the warships. Most of his freighters were swept to the island of Aegimurus—this lies out to sea across the mouth of the bay on which Carthage stands, and is roughly thirty miles from the city—while the others were carried to Aquae Calidae, right opposite the city.

All this happened in full view of Carthage.* As a result, people converged on the forum from all over the city, and the magistrates convened the senate. In the forecourt of the senate building the people were in uproar, demanding that such rich plunder not be allowed to slip out of their sight and through their fingers. Some objected that the peace negotiations, or else the truce—for it had not yet expired—put them under a moral obligation. The agreement they reached, however, as the senate meeting virtually merged with that of the people, was that Hasdrubal* should take a fleet of fifty ships over to Aegimurus, and then gather up the Roman ships dispersed along the coastline or in the harbours. The freighters had been abandoned by their crews and they were towed to Carthage by the stern, first from Aegimurus, then from Aquae Calidae.

25. The envoys had not yet returned from Rome, and the Roman Senate's decision on war or peace was still not known.* In addition, the truce had not yet expired. Scipio felt the Carthaginians' offence

to be all the more outrageous in that hopes of a peace settlement, and the moral obligation of the truce, had been trampled underfoot by the very men who had sued for a peace treaty and a truce. He immediately sent Lucius Baebius, Lucius Sergius, and Lucius Fabius to Carthage as his spokesmen.* The Romans were almost manhandled by the crowd that quickly gathered around them, and since they could see that their return journey would be no safer, they asked the magistrates, through whose assistance the violence had been prevented, to send ships to escort them. They were assigned two triremes. The vessels came with them as far as the River Bagradas, from which the Roman camp could be seen, and then returned to Carthage.

The Punic fleet was anchored off Utica, and three of its quadri-remes suddenly launched an attack from out at sea as the Roman quinquereme was rounding the promontory. Either a message telling them to do this had been sent from Carthage or else the admiral of the fleet, Hasdrubal, had dared to take the step without official authorization. But the Carthaginians were unable to ram the Roman ship, her speed enabling her to scud away, nor were their marines able to jump over from what were lower vessels to a higher one. The ship was also brilliantly defended for as long as it had a supply of missiles. When the weapons began to run out she could not have been saved had it not been for the proximity of the land, and the crowd of men that came pouring from the camp onto the beach. Driving her with all the speed the oars could manage, the crew ran her aground, and, with the loss of only the ship, those on board escaped without harm.

And so, with one violation following another, there was no doubt that the truce had been broken, and now Laelius and Fulvius arrived from Rome with the Carthaginian delegation. Scipio let these men know that it was not only the obligations of the truce that had been violated by the Carthaginians; in the case of his representatives international convention had been violated, too. He declared, how-ever, that he would, in their case, take no action that was unworthy of the institutions of the Roman people, or beneath his own principles. He then dismissed the delegates and proceeded with preparations for war.

As Hannibal was approaching land, he ordered one of his crew to climb the mast to get a look at the area they were heading for. The man told him that the prow was set towards a ruined sepulchre, and Hannibal, with a prayer to avert the omen, told the helmsman to sail on past it. He put in with the fleet at Leptis,* and there disembarked his troops.

26. Such were that year's events in Africa, and what follows runs into the year of the consulship of Marcus Servilius Geminus (master of horse to that point) and Tiberius Claudius Nero.

At the end of the previous year delegates had come from allied cities in Greece protesting that their farmlands had been laid waste by the forces of King Philip, and that envoys sent into Macedonia to seek redress had not been granted an audience with him. At the same time they apprised the senators of reports that an armed force of 4,000 men had crossed to Africa, under the command of Sopater, to assist with the defence of Carthage, and that a sum of money had been sent with them.* The Senate then voted in favour of sending a delegation to the king to report to him that, in the members' view, this contravened their treaty. The delegates sent were Gaius Terentius Varro, Gaius Mamilius, and Marcus Aurelius, and they were assigned three quinqueremes.

The year was marked by a huge fire, in which the Clivus Publicius was burned to the ground, and also by flooding. It was notable, too, for the cheapness of grain. For, apart from the fact that, thanks to the peaceful conditions, the whole of Italy was now open,* large quantities of wheat had also been sent from Spain. The curule aediles Marcus Valerius Falto and Marcus Fabius Buteo distributed this to the people, district by district, at a price of four *asses* a measure.

That same year saw the death of Quintus Fabius Maximus, at an advanced age (if there is any truth in the statement of some historians that he was an augur for sixty-two years). He was certainly a man who deserved his impressive *cognomen*, even if it had been a new one that he was the first to bear.* He exceeded the number of public offices held by his father, and equalled those of his grandfather. His grandfather Rullus was famous for a greater number of victories and for battles on a larger scale than those of Fabius, but simply having Hannibal as an adversary can compensate for all that. Fabius has been regarded as a man of more caution than action, but while one may question whether he was by nature a 'delayer', or whether such tactics were simply very appropriate to that stage of the war, nothing is more certain than that 'one man restored our fortunes by delaying', as Ennius puts it.* His son Quintus Fabius Maximus replaced him as augur, and Servius Sulpicius Galba replaced him as pontiff (for Fabius held two priesthoods).

Under the supervision of the aediles Marcus Sextius Sabinus and Gnaeus Tremelius Flaccus, the Roman Games were repeated once in their entirety, and the Plebeian Games three times. Both these men were made praetors, and Gaius Livius Salinator and Gaius Aurelius Cotta along with them. Discrepancies in the sources make it unclear whether elections that year were held by the consul Gaius Servilius or by Publius Sulpicius, who was appointed as dictator by the consul when he was detained in Etruria on official business (holding Senate-authorized judicial investigations into conspiracy amongst the leading citizens).

27. At the start of the following year, Marcus Servilius and Tiberius Claudius convened the Senate on the Capitol and raised the matter of the allocation of provinces. Since both men had their heart set on Africa, they wanted to have Italy and Africa decided by sortition, but thanks mostly to the efforts of Quintus Metellus they were neither denied nor granted Africa. Instead, the consuls were instructed to take joint action with the tribunes of the plebs to have the question brought before the people—if the tribunes so agreed— of the man they wished to see in charge of the campaign in Africa. The tribes unanimously voted for Publius Scipio, but the consuls still proceeded to sortition—for so the Senate had decreed—for the province of Africa.* Africa fell to Tiberius Claudius, who was to cross with a fleet of fifty ships, all quinqueremes, and there hold command with the same authority as Publius Scipio. Marcus Servilius was allotted Etruria. In that same province, Gaius Servilius also had his term of command extended in case the Senate decided that the consul should remain in the city.

Of the praetors, Marcus Sextius was allotted Gaul, and Publius Quinctilius Varus was to turn over to him his two legions along with the province. Gaius Livius received Bruttium with the two legions that the proconsul Publius Sempronius had commanded the year before. Gnaeus Tremelius received Sicily, with instructions to take over the province with its two legions from Publius Villius Tappulus, praetor the previous year. Villius was made propraetor, and ordered to protect the coast of Sicily with twenty warships and 1,000 fighting men. With the remaining twenty ships Marcus Pomponius was to ferry 1,500 soldiers back to Rome. Gaius Aurelius Cotta was allotted the city praetorship. The other praetors saw their commands extended, with arrangements for their provinces and armies remaining the same in each case.

The defence of the Roman empire that year rested on no more than sixteen legions. To secure the favour of the gods at the start of, and during, all these activities, the consuls were ordered to stage some games before they set off for the war. These were games that, in the consulship of Marcus Claudius Marcellus and Titus Quinctius, the dictator Titus Manlius had promised in a vow, along with the sacrifice of full-grown animals, should the republic remain in the same condition over the following five-year period as it was at that time. The games took place in the Circus Maximus over a four-day period, and the victims were sacrificed to the gods to whom they had been promised in the vow.

28. Meanwhile, hopes and fears were both increasing with every day that passed. People could not be sure in their minds whether they should be pleased over the fact that Hannibal's departure from Italy, after sixteen years, had left the Roman people with free occupation of the land, or whether they should rather feel fear because he had crossed to Africa with his army intact. The venue had changed, they thought, but not the danger, and the recently deceased Quintus Fabius had been a prophet of this great struggle; with good reason, he used to predict that Hannibal would be a more fearsome enemy in his own country than he had been in another's.

Furthermore, they said, Scipio's struggle would not this time be with Syphax, a king of ill-disciplined barbarians, whose troops were usually under the command of Statorius,* who was little more than a camp-follower. Nor would it be with Syphax's father-in-law Hasdrubal, a leader who was quick to flee, or with makeshift armies hastily put together from a poorly armed horde of peasants. No, it would be with Hannibal, a man practically born in the military headquarters of his father, a leader of consummate courage, and then nurtured and brought up surrounded by arms. He had been a soldier in boyhood, a commander when he was barely a young man, and he had come to old age with multiple conquests, filling the Spanish and Gallic territories, and Italy from the Alps to the straits of Messina, with monuments to his great achievements. He was at the head of an army that had seen as many campaigns as he,* and one toughened through enduring hardships that one could scarcely believe humans capable of bearing. It had been drenched in Roman blood on a thousand occasions, and it was carrying along spoils taken not just from the rank and file but from generals, too. On the field of battle Scipio would meet many men who had, with their own hands, killed praetors, generals, and consuls of Rome. He would meet many who were decorated with crowns given for courage in scaling walls and earthworks, and who had moved freely through captured Roman camps and captured Roman cities. The magistrates of the Roman people did not on that day have as many *fasces* as Hannibal was able to have carried before him, having taken them from the commanders he had killed!

Such were the alarming thoughts people turned over in their minds, increasing their worries and fears. There was another concern, too. Over the years they had become accustomed to conducting a war, right before their eyes, in various areas of Italy, and they had entertained little hope of an early end to the conflict. But now they were all on tenterhooks at the thought of Scipio and Hannibal as leaders pitted against each other for what seemed to be the final struggle. Some had tremendous confidence in Scipio and high hopes of victory, but even in their case the more their thoughts focused on the victory that was now so near, the more their worries grew.

Feelings amongst the Carthaginians were little different. At one moment, when they looked at Hannibal and the greatness of his achievements, they would regret having sued for peace. At the next they would reflect that they had been twice defeated on the battle-field, that Syphax had been taken prisoner, and that they had been driven from Spain and driven from Italy. All that, they realized, had been brought about by the valour and strategy of Scipio alone, and now they lived in awe of this man who was destined* from birth to be the leader who would bring about their downfall.

29. Hannibal had by now reached Hadrumetum. After spending a few days there* to let his men recover from the rigours of their sea journey, he moved on swiftly to Zama by forced marches, galvanized to action by alarming reports that the entire area around Carthage was occupied by Roman forces. Zama is five days' march from Carthage.

Some scouts that had been sent ahead by Hannibal were surprised by the Roman sentries, and brought before Scipio. Scipio put them in the hands of a military tribune and, telling them to make a thorough inspection of everything without fear, gave orders for them to be taken wherever they wanted to go in the camp. Asking them later if they had had a good look at everything at their leisure, he gave them an escort and sent them back to Hannibal.

Hannibal was not pleased with any of their reports—for they also brought the news that Masinissa had happened to arrive that very day* with 6,000 infantry and 4,000 cavalry—but he was especially shaken by his enemy's confidence, which was evidently not unwarranted. And so, although he was himself the cause of the war, and although by his arrival he had also sabotaged a negotiated truce along with hopes of a peace treaty, he nevertheless thought more equitable terms could be obtained by suing for peace with his strength intact than after defeat. He therefore sent a message to Scipio asking permission to discuss matters with him. Whether he did this on his own initiative or on orders from the state I cannot confirm. Valerius Antias has it* that Hannibal was defeated by Scipio in an initial battle, in which 12,000 of his soldiers fell and 1,700 were taken prisoner, and that it was after this that he came to Scipio in his camp, along with ten others, as an official representative of Carthage.

Whatever the truth of this, Scipio did not refuse to parley with him, and the two commanders agreed to bring forward their camps so they would be close to each other for the meeting. Scipio took up a position not far from the city of Naraggara*—it was favourably situated in general, and water was also available within a spear's throw— and Hannibal selected a hill four miles away which was safe and convenient, apart from the fact that it was some distance from water. To eliminate any possibility of treachery, a meeting place that was open to view from all directions was chosen at a point between these two locations.

30. The men came together with one translator each,* and the armed escorts of both were kept back at an equal remove. They were the greatest generals not merely of their own day, but of the whole of history down to their time, and they were a match for any king, or any commander, from any nation in the world. At the sight of each other they remained silent for a brief moment, almost dazed in their mutual admiration. Hannibal spoke first.*

'Perhaps it was from the start ordained by fate that I should be the one coming to sue for peace,' he said, 'I, who first commenced the hostilities with the Roman people, and who so often had victory almost in my grasp. If so, then I am happy that it is you rather than anyone else whom fortune has given me to petition. You have many remarkable achievements to your name. But in your case, too, not your least claim to fame will prove to be that Hannibal, to whom heaven had granted victory over so many Roman commanders, capitulated to you, and that you brought to an end this war, which was noted in its earlier stages for *your* defeats rather than ours. Chance, too, will be found to have brought about a laughable twist of fortune. I took up arms when your father was consul, and he was also the first Roman general whom I met in battle—and now I come unarmed to that man's son to sue for peace.

'It would clearly have been best if our ancestors had been temperamentally disposed by the gods to feel satisfied with the dominion they held, you over Italy and we over Africa. For not even in your case are Sicily and Sardinia prizes that can adequately compensate for the loss of all those fleets of yours, all those armies, and all those fine commanders. But while one may criticize the past, one cannot set it right. We have both striven after the possessions of others only to end up fighting for our own, and the war has not been confined to Italy for us, nor to Africa for you. You have seen the standards and arms of your enemy almost at your gates and at your walls, and we in Carthage are listening to the commotion coming from a Roman camp. Accordingly (something we should have found abhorrent, and something you should have wanted before all else) peace is under discussion at a time when you are enjoying the greater success. We who are conducting the negotiations stand to benefit most from the peace, and our respective states will ratify whatever terms we negotiate. All we need is a frame of mind that does not reject discussing plans for peace.

'In my case, I am returning as an old man* to the country I left as a boy, and the passage of time as well as the ups and downs of my career have taught me to prefer to follow the path of reason rather than that of fortune. In your case, I harbour misgivings over your youth and your unbroken record of success, both of which are conducive to a hot-headedness ill-suited to plans for peace. The man fortune has never disappointed cannot easily reflect on the vagaries of chance. Today you are just what I was at Trasimene and at Cannae. You took command when you were barely of age to be a soldier, and in all your exploits, no matter how reckless, fortune nowhere let you down. You exacted revenge for the deaths of your father and your uncle, and drew from a calamity a wonderful reputation for courage and extraordinary filial duty. The Spanish provinces that had been lost you recovered, driving from them four Punic armies. After you were made consul, and all others had little spirit even for defending Italy, you crossed to Africa. Here you cut to pieces two armies, captured and burned two camps within the same hour, made a prisoner of the powerful King Syphax, and seized so many cities in his kingdom, and so many that were under our control! And so you dragged me back from Italy on which I had kept a grip for sixteen years.

'Your heart may be set on victory rather than peace. I have greater familiarity with the proud spirit than the practical—and fortune such as yours once smiled on me, as well. But if the gods granted us rational thought, too, in the midst of success, then we should be thinking about not only what happened in the past but also what could happen in future. Forget about everything else—I myself am proof enough of all fortune's vicissitudes. Recently I had my camp pitched between the Anio and your city, and you beheld me carrying forward my standards, and practically scaling the walls of Rome. Now you see me here as a man who has lost two brothers, the bravest of men and the most eminent of commanders, and you see me before the fortifications of my city, which is virtually under siege, begging for it to be spared the sufferings with which I terrified yours.

'It is the greatest luck that one should trust the least. In your hour of success, and our precarious situation, granting peace will bring distinction and glory to you, while for us, who are suing for it, it is a matter of necessity rather than honour. A guaranteed peace is better, and safer, than a hope of victory: it rests in *your* hands, while the other is in the hands of the gods. Do not risk the success of so many years on the outcome of a single hour. When you consider your own strength, consider too the power of chance, and the evenly balanced fortunes of war; on both sides you will find the sword and the physical strength of humans. But nowhere less than in war do results match expectations. The glory that victory in battle will add to what you can now have by granting peace is not as great as what you will have thrown away in the event of a reverse. Honours won, and those anticipated, the hazard of a single hour can wipe out. In arranging a peace accord, Publius Cornelius, you have everything under your control; in the other scenario, you must accept the fortunes the gods assign you. One of the rare examples of success combined with courage here, in this land, would have been that of Marcus Atilius*— had he, in his hour of victory, granted our fathers a peace treaty when they sued for one. Instead, he failed to limit his success, or place controls on the good fortune that was sweeping him along, and the higher he was elevated the more ignominious became his fall.

'Now it is for the man who grants the peace, not the one who sues for it, to dictate its terms, but perhaps we Carthaginians may be thought not unworthy of imposing the penalty on ourselves. We are not averse to everything falling to you that was the cause of our going to war: Sicily, Sardinia, Spain, and all the islands in the sea between Africa and Italy. Let it be the lot of us Carthaginians to be confined within the coastline of Africa, and to see you holding sway by land and sea even over territories outside yours, since such has been the will of the gods.* I would not deny that the integrity of Carthage has been called into question because we were disingenuous in seeking the peace accord, and because, recently, we did not wait for its implementation. Scipio, the scrupulous observance of a peace treaty depends largely on the character of the people through whom the request for it is made. Your senators, I am told, have even refused peace* partly because the members of the delegation were not of sufficient status. This is Hannibal asking for peace. I would not be asking for it if I did not think it to be in our interests, and I shall keep that peace because of those same interests for which I asked for it. The war was started by me, and because of that I saw to it that nobody should regret my action—that is, until the gods themselves became envious of me. Likewise, I shall do my best to see that nobody regrets a peace accord that was gained through my efforts.'

31. The Roman commander's reply was in the following vein:* 'It did not escape me, Hannibal, that it was anticipation of your arrival that led the Carthaginians to scuttle the existing truce (to which you had given your word) as well as hopes of peace. And, in fact, you yourself do not try to hide that, since you withdraw from the terms of the earlier treaty everything except what has long been in our power anyway! You are anxious to make your fellow citizens aware of the great burden that is, thanks to you, being taken from their shoulders; but I too must endeavour to see that those items to which they then agreed are not removed from the terms of peace for them to enjoy as the rewards of their treachery. You Carthaginians do not deserve to have the same terms available to you as then, and you are actually seeking to profit from your duplicity!

'Our fathers did not fight a war of aggression over Sicily, nor did we over Spain. On the earlier occasion it was the peril of our Mamertine allies that armed us for a war of duty and justice, and on this it was the destruction of Saguntum. That you took the offensive you yourself admit, and the gods are also witnesses to the fact—the gods who provided a result in the earlier war that was in line with justice and righteousness, and who are providing, and will provide, the same in this one.

'As for me, I am aware of the frailty of man, I think about the power of fortune and I know that all our actions are at the mercy of a thousand vicissitudes. Now I admit that it would have been an arrogant and headstrong reaction on my part if you had come to sue for peace before I crossed to Africa, and I had rejected your petition when you were yourself voluntarily quitting Italy, and had your troops embarked on your ships. But, as it is, I have forced you back to Africa, and you are reluctant and resisting almost to the point of fighting, so that I feel no need to show you any consideration. Accordingly, if something is actually being added to the terms on which it seemed probable that a peace could be concluded—some sort of indemnity for the forceful appropriation of our ships, along with their cargoes, during the truce and for the violation of our envoys—then I have something to take to my council. But if you consider even that to be excessive, prepare for war, for you have found peace intolerable.'

So it was that they left the meeting to rejoin their escorts; no peace had been concluded and they reported that the discussion had been fruitless. They had to decide the issue in battle, they said, and accept whatever fortunes the gods might give them.

32. On reaching their respective encampments, both commanders gave orders for their men to make ready their weapons and their courage for the final struggle, which, if success were theirs, would make them victors not for a single day, but for all time. They would know by the night of the following day whether Rome or Carthage would rule the world, for the prize of victory would be not Africa

and not Italy, but the four corners of the earth.* And, they added, for those for whom the battle turned out to be a defeat the danger would be as great as the prize. For, in fact, there was no escape-route open to the Romans in a land that was strange and unknown to them, and, once her last resources were spent, Carthage seemed to be facing imminent destruction.

The following day they went out to decide the issue, by far the two most famous generals and the two most powerful armies that the world's two richest peoples could field. That day they were going to crown the many glories they had already won, or else lay them in the dust. As a result, their feelings wavered between hope and fear. Looking first at their own line, then that of the enemy, the men weighed up the strength of the two with their eyes rather than by calculation, and bright and gloomy reflections would simultaneously beset their minds. Considerations that did not occur to them automatically their commanders would supply, as they encouraged them and roused them to action. The Carthaginian leader would call to his men's minds their sixteen years of exploits in the land of Italy, the many Roman commanders and armies that they had totally annihilated; and when he had come to a soldier who had distinguished himself in some battle, he would cite the man's famous deeds. Scipio recalled the Spanish provinces, the recent battles in Africa, and the enemy's admission of inferiority—they had been obliged by fear to sue for peace but, thanks to their inherent faithlessness, unable to abide by it.* Moreover, since his discussion with Hannibal had been held in private and so offered scope for invention, Scipio gave it the spin he wanted. He made the prediction that, as the Carthaginian were taking the field, the gods had given them the same omens with which their fathers had fought at the Aegates Islands. The end of the war and their efforts was nigh, he said, and they now had in their hands the spoils of Carthage, and their return home to their country, parents, children, wives, and household gods. He uttered these words with head held high and with an expression of such happiness that one might have thought that victory was already his.

Scipio then drew up the *hastati* in the first line, with the *principes* behind them, and the *triarii* closing up the rear. 33. However, he did not draw up the cohorts* in close formation before their respective standards. Instead, he placed the maniples at some distance from each other, so as to leave a space through which the elephants could be driven without disordering the ranks. He positioned Laelius on the left wing with the Italian cavalry, and Masinissa and his Numidians on the right. (Scipio had earlier made use of Laelius' services as a legate, but that year, in conformity with a senatorial decree rather than sortition, he had him as his quaestor.) The open lanes between the maniples of the troops in the front line Scipio filled with *velites*, which were the light-armed troops of those days.* These were under orders to fall back behind their battle lines when the elephants charged, or else run left and right, position themselves with the front-line troops, and leave an alleyway open for the beasts, along which they would, as they ran, be showered with weapons from both sides.

To strike terror into the Romans, Hannibal placed his elephants at the forefront of his army—eighty of them, a total greater than he had had in any previous battle—and behind them he positioned his Ligurian and Gallic auxiliaries,* combined with Balearic and Moorish troops. In the second line he placed his Carthaginian and African forces, and a Macedonian legion.* Then, a short distance behind these, he drew up a supporting line of Italian troops, Bruttians for the most part, men who had gone with him when he left Italy, more of them under duress than of their own free will. Like Scipio, Hannibal also set his cavalry on the wings; the Carthaginians took the right, and the Numidians the left.

Hannibal's army was composed of so many men who had nothing in common in terms of language, culture, law, weaponry, dress, physical appearance, and their reasons for fighting, and he varied his exhortations accordingly. For the auxiliaries it was a matter of pointing out the pay they were receiving, and how this would be multiplied by proceeds from the booty. The Gauls could be aroused by their own particular and instinctive hatred for the Romans. The Ligurians, who had been brought down from their rugged mountain homes, were inspired to hopes of victory by the prospect of the rich plains of Italy. The Moors and Numidians Hannibal frightened by telling them how brutal Masinissa's rule would be. He worked on the various races by inspiring different hopes and different fears. As for the Carthaginians, they were told to keep in mind the walls of their native city, their household gods, and the sepulchres of their ancestors, as well as their children and parents, and their trembling wives. It was to be destruction and slavery for them, they were told, or else mastery of the world—there was nothing to be feared or hoped for between the two.

Such were the addresses being delivered by the commander amongst the Carthaginians, and the leaders of the various races amongst their own people (mostly through interpreters since there were also foreigners amongst each of the nations). But just then trumpets and bugles rang out on the Roman side, and such a loud shout went up that the elephants turned on their own men, especially on the Moors and Numidians on the left wing. Masinissa had no difficulty in adding terror to their disarray, and he stripped the Carthaginian line of its cavalry support in that sector. A few of the beasts, however, maintained their composure and were driven into the enemy, causing great carnage in the ranks of the *velites*, though they also received many wounds themselves. For the *velites* darted back to their maniples, leaving a path for the elephants so they would not be trampled under by them, and proceeded to hurl their spears at the animals, who were now in a cross-fire, from either side. There was no let-up in the javelins coming from the front-line troops, either, until eventually these beasts, too, driven from the Roman line by weapons raining down on them from every direction, put to flight the Carthaginian cavalry on their own right wing. When Laelius saw the disorder amongst the enemy, he added panic to their confusion.

34. The Punic line had been deprived of its cavalry cover on both flanks when the infantry engaged, and they were no match for the Romans either in confidence or strength. There were also factors that seem trivial in the telling but which are of great importance in action. There was the battle-cry of the Romans which was in unison, and therefore louder and more terrifying; while on the Carthaginian side there were only dissonant cries, coming as they did from a plurality of races with different languages. There was also, thanks to their own weight and that of their arms, the firmness of the Roman assault as they pressed into the enemy; on the other side there was skirmishing characterized by agility rather than strength.* As a result the Romans immediately drove back the enemy line with their first assault. Then, smashing into them with the shoulder and their shield-bosses, and moving forward as they forced them back, they made considerable ground, almost as if they were meeting no resistance. Furthermore, as soon as they felt the enemy line give way,

those at the rear pressed forward on those in front, and that in itself added great momentum to the thrust into the enemy.

On the enemy side, the auxiliary troops, who were giving ground, received no support from the second line, which comprised the Africans and Carthaginians. Instead, these also fell back, fearful that the enemy might reach them by cutting down those who were firmly resisting at the front. The auxiliaries therefore suddenly turned to run, and faced their own comrades. Some found shelter in the second line, but others, given no assistance earlier by that line and now excluded from it, proceeded to cut down the men who would not let them in. And there were now virtually two battles blending into one, since the Carthaginians were obliged to fight hand-to-hand with the enemy and at the same time with their own comrades. They would not, however, accept these demoralized and angry men into the line. They closed ranks, and drove them towards the wings and out into the open country round about, outside the actual fighting; their line was intact and still in formation, and they did not want these panicking and wounded fugitives to join it.

However, there were so many corpses and weapons littering the ground, on which the auxiliaries had been standing moments before, that the Romans found it almost more difficult to wade through them than it had been to get through the serried ranks of the enemy. The *hastati*, who formed the front line, were now pursuing the enemy wherever they could over heaps of bodies and weapons, and through pools of blood, and this threw the standards and the ranks into disarray. The formation of the *principes* had also begun to falter when they saw the line before them losing its solidity. Observing this, Scipio swiftly gave the order for the retreat to be sounded for the *hastati*. He then brought the wounded back to the rear line, and led the *principes* and *triarii* to the wings, so that the *hastati* forming the centre would have more cover and support.*

And so the battle started afresh,* for the Romans had reached their real enemies, men who were a match for them in weaponry, military experience, and the renown of their exploits, and men who faced prospects, and dangers, as great as theirs. But the Romans had greater numbers and greater confidence: they had already routed the enemy's cavalry and his elephants, and were now directing their fighting against the second line, having driven back the first.

35. After pursuing the routed enemy cavalry for some distance,

Laelius and Masinissa made a timely return to attack the enemy formation in the rear. It was that cavalry charge that finally vanquished the enemy. Many were surrounded, and killed in action; many scattered in flight over the broad plain surrounding the battlefield, only to perish there, at various points, since the Roman cavalry had complete control of the area. More than 20,000 of the Carthaginians and their allies lost their lives that day, and about the same number were taken prisoner, with the capture also of a hundred and thirty-two military standards and eleven elephants. On the winning side there were about 1,500 casualties.*

In the turmoil Hannibal slipped away with a few horsemen and escaped to Hadrumetum.* Before he left the field, he had done all he could, both before the battle and in the fight itself, and even Scipio, and all the military experts, had to admit that he had deserved credit for his remarkably skilful deployment of the battle line that day.* He had put his elephants right up front, so that their random charging, and irresistible momentum, would make it impossible for the Romans to follow the standards and keep ranks, the style of fighting in which they had most confidence. Behind the elephants he had placed the auxiliaries, ahead of the line of Carthaginians. In this way a motley crowd of men, composed of the scum of all races and held together by pay and not loyalty, would have no easy way of running off. At the same time, by accepting the initial brunt of the enemy charge, they would tire the Romans and, if nothing else, blunt their swords by taking their wounds. Then came the Carthaginian and African infantry, in whom lay all Hannibal's hopes. Their enemy's equal in all other respects, they would have the advantage of being fresh to the field and facing troops suffering from exhaustion and wounds. As for the Italians, it was unclear whether they were allies or foes, and so Hannibal had banished them to the back line, and also left a space between them and the other troops.

After this final demonstration of his military prowess, Hannibal fled to Hadrumetum. From there he was summoned to Carthage, to which he now returned thirty-five years after leaving it as a boy. There, in the senate, he admitted his defeat, not just in the battle but in the war, and said that the only hope of safety lay in Carthage being granted a peace treaty.

36. After the battle Scipio immediately overran and pillaged the enemy camp. Then, having been brought the news that Publius

Lentulus had arrived at a point off Utica with fifty warships, and a hundred freighters with cargoes of supplies of all kinds, he returned to his ships on the coast with massive quantities of plunder. He felt that terror should be brought to bear on the shaken Carthage on every side, and so, after sending Laelius to Rome with the news of the victory, he ordered Gnaeus Octavius to lead the legions overland to the city, while he himself rejoined his old fleet, now strengthened by the addition of Laelius' new one. He then set out from Utica and steered a course for the port of Carthage. He was not far away from the city when a Carthaginian vessel decorated with woollen fillets and boughs of olive came to meet him. There were ten envoys aboard, leading men of the community, who had been sent on Hannibal's initiative to sue for peace. They approached the rear of the flagship, holding out the emblems of suppliants and earnestly begging for Scipio's protection and mercy. The only answer they received was that they should make their way to Tynes, to which, they were told, Scipio would move his camp. Scipio sailed on to inspect the layout of Carthage, not so much with a view to gathering intelligence on the spot as to discomfit his enemy. He then returned to Utica, to which he also recalled Octavius.

While the Romans were en route to Tynes, they were brought the news that Syphax's son Vermina was coming to help the Carthaginians, with a force made up of more cavalry than infantry. Some of Scipio's infantry and all of his cavalry were sent to face Vermina, and they attacked the Numidian column on the first day of the Saturnalia,* putting them to flight after a slight skirmish. The Numidians, completely surrounded by Roman cavalry, found every escape-route cut off, and 15,000 of their men were killed and 1,200 taken alive, with the capture of 1,500 Numidian horses and seventy-two military standards. In the confusion, the prince himself escaped with a few of his followers. The Roman camp was then established at Tynes, in the same location as earlier, and thirty spokesmen* came to Scipio from Carthage.

The approach of these men was perforce, given their more difficult situation, far more abject than on the previous occasion, but they were heard with considerably less compassion because the memory of their treachery was still fresh. In the meeting of the general's council there was a righteous indignation that prompted all present to advocate the destruction of Carthage. Then, however, they began to think about the size of such an undertaking, and the length of the siege needed to take such a well-fortified and powerful city. Scipio, too, had his own cause for concern, namely that he would have a successor coming to appropriate to himself the credit for terminating the war, when the way to this had already been prepared by the efforts and dangers of another. Accordingly, all were brought round to the idea of peace.

37. The next day the spokesmen were recalled. They were sharply rebuked for their treachery, and cautioned that their many disasters should now make them finally believe that the gods and oaths were to be taken seriously. The following peace-terms, under which the Carthaginians would live as a free people under their own laws, were then dictated to them:*

The Carthaginians were to retain possession of the cities and territory that they had held before the war, and with the same boundaries, and the Romans would that day put an end to their depredations. They were to return to the Romans all deserters, run-away slaves, and prisoners of war, and surrender all their warships with the exception of ten triremes. They were also to surrender any trained elephants in their possession, and not train any more.

They were not to make war within Africa or outside Africa without the authorization of the Roman people.* They were to pay compensation to Masinissa and strike a treaty with him.

They were to keep the Roman auxiliary troops supplied with grain and pay until the time when their envoys returned from Rome. They were to pay an indemnity of 10,000 talents of silver in equal annual instalments over fifty years.*

They were to hand over a hundred hostages, chosen by Scipio, who would be between the ages of fourteen and thirty.

Scipio would grant the Carthaginians a truce on condition that the freighters captured during the time of the previous truce were restored to him, along with everything that had been aboard these vessels. Failing that, there would be no truce, and no prospect of peace.

The spokesmen were ordered to take these terms home. When they presented them in a public assembly, Gisgo* came forward to speak against settlement, and he was receiving a favourable hearing from the crowd, which did not want peace but was incapable of war. Hannibal, furious at such a case being put forward and reaching an audience at this critical juncture, grabbed Gisgo with his hand, and pulled him down from the raised dais. The sight of this, unfamiliar in a free community, provoked a buzz of disapproval amongst the people; and Hannibal, a military man, was, in turn, very disturbed by this licence of city life. 'I was nine when I left you,' he said, 'and I have come back after thirty-six years.* I think I have a thorough acquaintance with the arts of war, which the fortunes of both my private and official life have taught me from boyhood; but it is for you to educate me in the conventions, laws, and customs of civil life and the forum.'

With this apology for his ignorance, he discussed the peace treaty at length, explaining how far it was from being unfair, and how essential. The greatest difficulty of all the terms related to the ships that were captured during the truce—nothing could be found beyond the vessels themselves, and any investigation was not easy since those who would be accused were men opposed to the peace. It was decided that the ships should be returned, and the men tracked down at all costs. Scipio was to be allowed to appraise the value of all else that was missing and the Carthaginians would pay cash in that amount.

Some claim that Hannibal came to the coast from the battlefield, and from there immediately sailed to King Antiochus on a ship that had been made ready for him beforehand. Then, when Scipio demanded before everything else that Hannibal be surrendered to him, he was given the answer that Hannibal was not in Africa.*

38. When the spokesmen returned to Scipio, the quaestors were instructed to itemize, on the basis of public accounts, what had been state property aboard the vessels, and owners were to declare what was private. As an indemnity for the total amount, a demand was issued for an immediate payment of 25,000 pounds of silver, and the Carthaginians were granted a three-month truce. A rider was added that during the period of the truce the Carthaginians were to send envoys to no place other than Rome, and they were not to dismiss embassies that came to Carthage without first apprising the Roman commander of their identity and their mission. Lucius Veturius Philo, Marcus Marcius Ralla, and Lucius Scipio, the commander's brother, were sent to Rome with the Carthaginian delegation.

At about that time supplies from Sicily and Sardinia made the price of grain so low* that the merchant would leave his cargo of wheat to the crew to pay the cost of its transport.

The first announcement of renewed hostilities with the Carthaginians had caused panic in Rome. Tiberius Claudius was instructed to take a fleet to Sicily post-haste, and cross from there to Africa; the other consul, Marcus Servilius, was to remain in the environs of Rome until the state of affairs in Africa became known. However, all the arrangements for bringing together and launching his fleet were made in a lackadaisical manner by the consul Tiberius Claudius, because the senators had voted that authority to decide the terms on which peace would be granted lay with Publius Scipio rather than the consul.

A number of prodigies reported just after the news arrived of the renewal of hostilities, had also caused alarm. At Cumae, there seemed to be a shrinking of the sun's orb,* and there was a shower of stones; and in the territory of Velitrae the earth subsided in huge chasms, with trees pulled down into the abyss. At Aricia, the forum and the neighbouring shops were struck by lightning; so, too, was the city wall (which was struck at several points) and a gate at Frusino. On the Palatine it rained stones. Atonement for that particular prodigy was made with the traditional nine-day sacrifice, and for the others with the sacrifice of full-grown animals. Amidst all these occurrences, there was some extraordinary flooding, which was also interpreted as supernatural. The Tiber was in such spate that the Circus Maximus was flooded and arrangements were made for staging the Games of Apollo in the area of the temple of Venus of Eryx outside the Porta Collina. However, on the very day of the games there was a sudden clearing of the sky. The procession had already started out for the Porta Collina, but when it was announced that the waters had receded from the Circus it was suddenly recalled and re-routed into it. The restitution of its traditional site to the solemn spectacle increased the pleasure of the people, and also the numbers attending the games.

39. When the consul Claudius finally did leave the city, a violent storm blew up between the ports of Cosa and Loreta, causing him great alarm. From there he reached Populonium, where he waited at anchor for the rest of the storm to spend its force, and then crossed to the island of Elba. From Elba he went over to Corsica, and from Corsica to Sardinia. There, as he was passing the Insane Mountains,* a much more severe storm overtook him in what was also a more treacherous location, and scattered his fleet. Many vessels were damaged and stripped of their rigging, and some were wrecked; and in this battered and mutilated condition the fleet put in at Carales. The ships were hauled ashore and, while they were being repaired, winter overtook the consul. The year then came to an end and, as nobody proposed an extension of his command, Tiberius Claudius brought his fleet back to Rome as a private citizen.

To avoid being recalled to the city to conduct elections, Marcus Servilius had, before setting out for his province, appointed Gaius Servilius Geminus dictator; and the dictator then appointed Publius Aelius Paetus master of horse. The elections were scheduled on several occasions, but storms prevented them from being held.* And so, when the outgoing magistrates left office on 14 March, there were no new ones elected to replace them, and the state was left without curule magistrates.

The pontiff Titus Manlius Torquatus died that year, and was replaced by Gaius Sulpicius Galba. The Roman Games were repeated in their entirety three times by the curule aediles, Lucius Licinius Lucullus and Quintus Fulvius. On evidence provided by an informer, some clerks and couriers of the aediles were convicted of secretly removing money from the treasury, and this also damaged the reputation of the aedile Lucullus. The plebeian aediles Publius Aelius Tubero and Lucius Laetorius resigned their offices because of a flaw in the electoral procedure. They had by then already put on the Plebeian Games, and the banquet for Jupiter that was celebrated for the games, and they had also set up on the Capitol three statues that were financed by money taken in fines. The dictator and the master of horse, in accordance with a decree of the Senate, staged the games in honour of Ceres.

40. The Roman and Carthaginian envoys arrived together from Africa, and the Senate then met in the temple of Bellona. There, to the immense pleasure of the senators, Lucius Veturius Philo delivered a report on the battle with Hannibal, which, he said, was the last struggle with the Carthaginians, and it had finally brought an end to a dreadful war. He added, too, that Syphax's son Vermina had been conquered, a small increment to a successful campaign. Veturius was then instructed to go to the popular assembly and impart the glad tidings to the people. After that, all the temples in the city were thrown open for prayers of gratitude, and a proclamation was issued for three days of public thanksgiving. The envoys from the Carthaginians, and envoys who had also come from King Philip, sought an audience with the Senate, and, on the authority of the members, they were given the answer by the dictator that the new consuls would grant them one.

After that the elections were held. Gnaeus Cornelius Lentulus and Publius Aelius Paetus were elected consuls. The praetors elected were Marcus Junius Pennus, to whom the urban jurisdiction came by sortition; Marcus Valerius Falto, who was allotted Bruttium; Marcus Fabius Buteo, who was allotted Sardinia; and Publius Aelius Tubero, who drew Sicily. With regard to the consular provinces, it was the will of the Senate that no action be taken before the envoys of King Philip and those of the Carthaginians had been heard. The senators foresaw the end of one war being followed by the start of another.*

The consul Gnaeus Lentulus had a burning desire to have Africa as his province—he was seeking an easy victory should the conflict continue or, if it were now at an end, the glory of terminating such a momentous war during his consulship. He therefore declared that he would allow no business to proceed until Africa was officially assigned to him. His colleague, a reasonable man of some foresight, was in agreement—he could see that Lentulus' competition with Scipio for that honour was not only unjust but would also be one-sided. The plebeian tribunes Quintus Minucius Thermus and Manius Acilius Glabrio observed that Gnaeus Cornelius' tactic had already been attempted the previous year by Tiberius Claudius, without success. On the authority of the Senate, they said, the matter of whom they wanted to have *imperium* in Africa had been brought before the people, and all thirty-five tribes had formally awarded it to Scipio.

There were many impassioned debates on the issue, both in the Senate and before the people, and the eventual result was that the decision was left with the Senate. The senators, accordingly, voted after swearing an oath (as they had earlier agreed to do) and decreed that the consuls should settle on their respective provinces between themselves, or else proceed to sortition to decide which would have Italy, and which the fleet of fifty ships. The consul to whom the fleet came was to sail to Sicily. If it had by then proved impossible to negotiate peace with Carthage, that consul would cross to Africa where he would direct sea operations, while Scipio, who would retain his command, would direct those on land. Should there be agreement on the peace-terms, the plebeian tribunes were to consult the people on whether they would instruct the consul or Publius Scipio to grant the peace treaty and, if the victorious army needed to be brought back from Africa, which man should bring it. If the people then ordered that the peace be granted by Publius Scipio, and also that the army should be brought back by him, the consul was not to make the crossing from Sicily to Africa. The other consul (the one to whom Italy came by lot) was to take over command of two legions from the praetor Marcus Sextius.

41. Publius Scipio had his *imperium* extended in Africa, his sphere of responsibility, and he retained command of his armies. The praetor Marcus Valerius Falto was officially assigned the two legions in Bruttium that had been under the command of Gaius Livius the year before. Publius Aelius was to take over from Gnaeus Tremelius command of the two legions in Sicily. For Sardinia, Marcus Fabius was assigned the single legion that Publius Lentulus had commanded as propraetor. Marcus Servilius, consul the previous year, had his *imperium* extended in Etruria, and he also retained command of his two legions.

With respect to the Spanish provinces, it was noted that Lucius Cornelius Lentulus and Lucius Manlius Acidinus had already been there for a number of years, and it was decided that the consuls should arrange with the tribunes, if that met with their approval, to put before the plebs the question of whom they authorized to have command in Spain. To secure the province, that man was to enrol, from the two armies, a single legion of Roman soldiers, and fifteen cohorts of Latin allies, and Lucius Cornelius and Lucius Manlius were to bring the veterans back to Italy.

The consul was assigned a fleet of fifty ships which was to be made up from two fleets, that of Gnaeus Octavius in Africa, and that of Publius Villius, which was patrolling the Sicilian coast, and he would have his choice of vessels. Publius Scipio was to retain the forty warships that had previously been under him. If Scipio wanted to have Gnaeus Octavius command them, as before, then Octavius was to have *imperium* for that year as propraetor. If Scipio put Laelius in command, then Octavius was to leave for Rome, and bring back with him the ships of which the consul had no need. Marcus Fabius was also assigned ten warships for Sardinia. In addition, the consuls were instructed to raise two city legions, so that affairs of state would that year be managed with fourteen legions and a hundred warships.

42. The next item of business was the envoys from Philip and from the Carthaginians, and it was decided that Macedonians should be brought in first. Their address varied in its content, ranging from self-justification in the matter of the protests lodged by the emissaries sent from Rome to the king, about his raids on Roman allies, to actual charges against the allies of the Roman people and, with much greater vitriol, against Marcus Aurelius.* Aurelius, they said, one of the three envoys that had been sent to them, had raised troops there and stayed behind, making attacks on the Macedonians in contravention of their treaty, and frequently engaging their commanders in pitched battle. There were also demands for the return of those Macedonians, along with their commander Sopater, who had fought as mercenaries in Hannibal's army, and who were at that time kept in irons as prisoners of war.

These points were countered by Marcus Furius, who had been sent by Aurelius from Macedonia expressly for this purpose. Furius explained that Aurelius had been left behind to ensure that nations which were allied to the Roman people were not exhausted by Philip's depredations, and driven to defect to the king by his violent acts of aggression. Aurelius had not left the territory of the allies, he said, and he had ensured that marauders did not cross over into their fields with impunity. Sopater, Furius added, was a courtier and relative of the king, and he had been sent recently to Africa with 4,000 Macedonians and a sum of money for the purpose of aiding Hannibal and the Carthaginians.

Tackled on these points, the Macedonians gave evasive replies, and the reply they received themselves was not at all pleasant—their king was looking for war, they were told, and if he kept on he would soon find it! The treaty had been violated by him in two ways: by the wrongs he had inflicted on, and the armed aggression he had directed against, allies of the Roman people, and then by the military and financial assistance he had given to enemies of Rome. Moreover, said the senators, Publius Scipio seemed to them to have acted, and to be acting, quite rightly and properly in keeping in irons as enemies men who had been taken prisoner while bearing arms against the Roman people. Also, Marcus Aurelius was acting in the interests of the state, for which the Senate was grateful, in giving armed protection to allies of the Roman people, since he could not rely on treaty rights to safeguard them.

The Macedonians were sent off with this stern reply, and the Carthaginian delegation was called in. When the senators observed its members' ages and rank (for they were by far the foremost men of their community) every one of them admitted that this was now a genuine peace conference. The man who stood out from all the others was Hasdrubal (his compatriots gave him the sobriquet 'Haedus'), who had always been a promoter of peace and opposed to the Barca faction.* Thus, on this occasion, he carried all the more weight when he proceeded to shift responsibility for the war from his state to a few greedy men. His address was wide-ranging, at one moment rebutting charges, and at the next making certain admissions, so that gaining forgiveness would not be made more difficult by a shameless denial of known facts. Then he would even admonish the senators to handle their good fortune with care and restraint. If the Carthaginians had listened to him and Hanno, he said, and if they had been prepared to take advantage of a favourable opportunity, then they would have been in a position to *grant* the peace-terms they were seeking at that moment! Rarely are men given good fortune and good sense at the same time, said Hasdrubal. The reason for the Roman people's invincibility, he declared, was the fact that they remembered to be sensible, and use their judgement in times of success. Indeed, it would have been surprising if they had acted differently. Those for whom good fortune was something new lost control, because they were unused to it, and went mad with joy; but for the Roman people the joy of victory was familiar and almost routine, and they had extended their sway almost more by sparing the conquered than by conquest.

The other envoys were more plaintive in their address, emphasizing the position of enormous affluence from which the state of Carthage had fallen, and to what depths. Recently they occupied practically the whole world with their arms, they said, and now they were left nothing but the walls of Carthage. From behind these walls, they could see nothing that was under their sway, either on land or sea, and even their city itself and their own homes they would occupy only if the Roman people chose not to take the final step and vent its wrath on them.

It was apparent that the senators were leaning towards compassion.

Then, they say, one of them, furious over the Carthaginians' perfidy, called out and asked which gods they would swear by to conclude the treaty, since they had proven faithless to the ones they had invoked for the earlier one. 'By the same ones,' replied Hasdrubal, 'since they are so hard on those who violate treaties.'

43. All were now disposed to a peace treaty, but the consul Lentulus, whose area of responsibility was the fleet, vetoed the senatorial resolution. The plebeian tribunes Manius Acilius and Quintus Minucius then brought to the people the question of whether it was their wish and command that the Senate pass a decree authorizing peace with the Carthaginians. They also asked for the people's instructions on who was to grant the peace, and who bring the army back from Africa. On the question of the peace, the tribes voted unanimously in favour of it, and they further voted that Publius Scipio should grant the peace and that he, too, should bring back the army. Following this decision of the people, the Senate decreed that Publius Scipio should make peace with the people of Carthage, on terms he considered appropriate and in consultation with a board of ten commissioners.

The Carthaginians then thanked the senators, and they requested leave to enter the city and speak with their fellow citizens who were incarcerated there by the state as prisoners of war. Some of them, they explained, were their relatives and friends, men of noble birth; for others they had messages from their families. This being granted, the Carthaginians further requested an opportunity to ransom a select number of these men, and they were told to supply the men's names. When they supplied about 200, a senatorial decree was passed authorizing the Roman commissioners to take to Publius Scipio, in Africa, the 200 prisoners whom the Carthaginians selected. The commissioners were to report to Scipio that, in the event of peace being concluded, he should restore these men to the Carthaginians without payment.

The fetials* were then instructed to proceed to Africa for the concluding of the peace treaty, and at their request a decree of the Senate was passed expressed as follows: the fetials were each to take with them a flint knife and a bunch of sacred herbs so that, when the Roman general ordered them to conclude the treaty, they might ask the general for the sacred plants. It is the practice for this type of vegetation to be culled on the citadel and given to the fetials.

With that the Carthaginians were dismissed from Rome, and when they reached Scipio in Africa they made peace on the terms given above. They surrendered their warships, their elephants, the deserters, the runaway slaves, and 4,000 prisoners of war, including the senator Quintus Terentius Culleo. Scipio had the ships taken out to sea and burned. Some authorities state they numbered five hundred, and included every kind of oar-propelled vessel, and that suddenly seeing them on fire was as painful for the Carthaginians as if it had been Carthage itself going up in flames. Punishment for the deserters was harsher than that for runaway slaves: Latins were beheaded and Romans crucified.

44. Peace had last been concluded with Carthage forty years earlier, during the consulship of Quintus Lutatius and Aulus Manlius. The war commenced twenty-three years after that, in the consulship of Publius Cornelius and Tiberius Sempronius, and was brought to an end seventeen years later, in the consulship of Gnaeus Cornelius and Publius Aelius. They say that, later on, Scipio frequently commented that it was the ambition of Tiberius Claudius in the first place, and then that of Gnaeus Cornelius, that held him back from finishing off the war with the destruction of Carthage.

In Carthage, people were drained by the protracted war, and meeting the initial payment of cash seemed difficult. There were sadness and tears in the senate house but, they say, Hannibal was seen with a smile on his face. Hasdrubal Haedus criticized him for smiling while the people were weeping, when Hannibal was himself the cause of their tears. 'If one's inner thoughts could be observed with the eyes like one's facial expression,' Hannibal replied, 'then it would be clear to you that this smile you are criticizing comes not from a joyful heart, but from one almost insane with suffering. Even so, my smile is nothing like as inappropriate to the occasion as those irrational and absurd tears of yours. The time for weeping was when our weapons were taken from us, our ships burned, and an interdiction placed on foreign wars—that was the blow that finished us off. And you have no reason to believe that Romans were concerned that you should have peace. No powerful state can remain peaceable for long; if she does not have an enemy abroad, she finds one at home, just as very strong bodies, though apparently safe with regard to external factors, can collapse under their own strength. It is so true that we feel public misfortunes only to the extent that they impinge on our private interests, and in them there is no sting more painful than the loss of money. And so there was no groaning when the spoils were being hauled away from defeated Carthage, and when you were watching her being left unarmed and naked amidst all those heavily armed African tribes. But now, because tribute must be gathered from private sources, you are in mourning, as though you were attending the funeral of our state. How I fear that you will soon realize that today your tears have been for the most trivial of misfortunes!' Such were Hannibal's words amongst the Carthaginians.

Scipio called a meeting at which he conferred on Masinissa, in addition to his ancestral kingdom, the town of Cirta and other cities and lands from the realm of Syphax that had fallen under Roman power. He ordered Gnaeus Octavius to take the fleet to Sicily and hand it over to the consul Gnaeus Cornelius. He also instructed the Carthaginian envoys to leave for Rome so that the measures that he had taken in consultation with the ten commissioners might be ratified by the authority of the Senate, and on the order of the people.

45. With peace established on land and sea, Scipio put his army aboard his ships and crossed to Lilybaeum in Sicily. From there he sent most of his men on by sea, but he personally took a route through Italy, which was now happily savouring the peace no less than the victory. Crowds poured from the cities to pay their respects to him, and crowds of peasants also blocked the roads until he finally reached Rome. There he rode into the city in the most illustrious triumph ever. He had 123,000 pounds of silver borne to the treasury, and from the spoils he distributed 400 *asses* to each of his men. Syphax's death meant that he was missing from the public spectacle, but it did not diminish the glory of the triumphing Scipio. Syphax had died shortly before at Tibur, to which he had been transferred from Alba; but his death did, in fact, receive public attention because he was given a state funeral. (Polybius, who is by no means a source to be disregarded,* attests that this king was led along in the triumphal procession.) Behind the triumphing Scipio came Quintus Terentius Culleo, the cap of freedom on his head, and throughout his life thereafter Culleo rightly honoured Scipio as the man responsible for his liberty.

As for the *cognomen* 'Africanus', I have been unable to verify whether it was Scipio's popularity with his men or the favour of the people that brought it into circulation, or whether it began as flattery with his cronies, like Sulla's name 'Felix' and Pompeius' 'Magnus' in our fathers' day. At any rate he was the first commander to be honoured with the name of a nation he had defeated. Following his example men who were not in his class with respect to their victories later left impressive inscriptions on their portraits, and distinguished *cognomina* for their families.

APPENDIX 1

LIST OF VARIATIONS FROM THE TEUBNER TEXT

	Teubner	*This edition*
23.3.2	in curiam	in curia
23.35.19	capti*et	capta sunt
25.12.9	vomica	vomicam
26.31.1	ut \<velut\> si	ut si
28.21.6	Ibem	Idem
29.17.17	qui nesciat	qui sciat

There are also a few misprints in the four Teubner volumes that make up
Books 21–30. In the hope that it may be of some use to those following the
Latin, I note those that I have detected: 21.4.3 read *discerneres* (for *diszer-
neres*) and *quid* (for *quit*); 22.54.3 *hospitaliter* (for *hopitaliter*); 23.17.5 *urbis*
(for *ur bis*); 23.18.1 *ubi* (for *idu*); 23.30.16 *Ti. Sempronius Gracchus* (for
T. Sempronius Gracchus); 23.44.6 *utraque pars avidi* (for *utraque, pars avidi*);
25.22.2 *exercituum* (for *exercitum*); 25.31.5 *quidem* (for *qui em*); 25.41.9 *res*
(for *es*); 27.28.5 *allatae* (for *allati*); 28.21.6 *homines* for *hominum* (my thanks
to Professor Walsh for pointing this last instance out to me).

J.C.Y.

APPENDIX 2

HANNIBAL'S ROUTE OVER THE ALPS

Polybius and Livy on the route

Hannibal crossed the Alps by one of the western passes, arriving in the territory of the Insubres according to Polybius (3.56), but the Taurini according to both Livy (21.38) and, it seems, Polybius himself later on (see below). Polybius does not identify the pass; Livy (ibid.) discusses the question briefly but only to dismiss the Poenine pass, or Great St Bernard, and the Cremo, or Little St Bernard. His arguments are sensible, but he does not then say which pass, if any, he himself thinks was the right one.

The Alps had not been mapped or even extensively visited by Greeks and Romans before 218. So we cannot say how precise were the accounts of the primary sources (on whom see Introduction). Our main authorities are Polybius and Livy. Polybius reports that he himself visited the area and questioned eyewitnesses (3.48); but such persons must have been very old by then, and relying chiefly or wholly on their memories. He must also be using some or all of the primary sources. Livy evidently combines Polybius' account with at least one other; or, less likely, reproduces a predecessor who did the combining. Both mention relatively few place names after Hannibal's crossing of the Rhône, and not all are readily identifiable. With no archaeological evidence available, every theory thus depends on interpreting these accounts and comparing them with existing topography. Unsurprisingly, theories abound (see Further Reading below) and none has won universal acceptance.

The crossing of the Rhône

Where Hannibal crossed the Rhône is the first, much-debated issue. Polybius equates his route to the Rhône with the later Roman road, the Via Domitia, built around 120 BC from northern Spain to that river (it followed, rather more smoothly, the ancient 'way of Hercules'). This was marked out with milestones (P. 3.39) and met the Rhône's west bank near Ugernum (Beaucaire), facing Tarusco (Tarascon) on the eastern. So if Hannibal crossed farther upriver, Polybius has made a mistake.

Polybius also locates Hannibal's crossing point 'at the undivided stream' (meaning before it branches into its delta) at 'four days' distance from the sea for an army' (3.42). This would be 50–60 miles, as normal marching-speed in good country was some 12–15 miles (20–24 km.) a day. If he means the sea at the mouths of the Rhône, uncertainty strikes.

River-silt seems to have pushed the coastline there as much as 12 miles further south since his time—in the fourth century AD Arelate (Arles) was about 18 Roman miles, just over 16 modern miles, from the sea (Ammianus Marcellinus, *Histories* 15.11), while now it is 25 miles. This averages 0.56 miles a century. Many moderns, therefore, place the army's crossing a good deal farther upriver, supporting the theory that 'the Island' was the Rhône–Isère triangle (see below).

This looks implausible, however. The Rhône delta, the famous Camargue marshes, was no place for an army, and it would have been useless to take measurements there of distances from the sea. One suggestion is that Polybius means the army reached the Rhône four days after its last sight of the sea near Lunel, west of Nîmes; but Lunel is only about 32 miles from Beaucaire—two and a half days' march. Polybius' four days 'for an army' is best explained as starting from the sea at Massilia (Marseille). In the 120s Roman armies operated extensively in southern Gaul against many tribes, including the Volcae west of the Rhône, the Vocontii, and the Allobroges. A settlement was founded at Aquae Sextiae (Aix) and the Via Domitia built. Massilia, an old ally and a beneficiary of the intervention, was a crucial reference point for these operations. It lies 60 miles (96 km.) from Tarusco: four days' march.

The problem of 'the Island'

From the crossing, a four-day march took Hannibal to a triangle-shaped district called 'the Island', where he settled a succession dispute, befriended the inhabitants, and resupplied his army (P. 3.49; L. 21.31). The Island lay between the Rhône and a river which Polybius' manuscripts call the Skaras or Skoras, Livy's Sarar or Arar or Bisarar. A widely accepted view identifies the 'Skaras/Sarar' as the River Isara, today's Isère, while another possibility is the shorter River Eygues further south, which flows into the Rhône at Orange. Its ancient name is otherwise unknown, but in medieval times it was varyingly called the Araus, Escaris, and other forms— names possibly descended from 'Skaras/Sarar'.

It is likely that the Island lay at this confluence. From Tarascon to Orange is only some 27 miles by road, but Hannibal had further to go. Polybius does not name the Island's inhabitants, while Livy—or a predecessor of his—thinks they were the Allobroges, because these 'live close by' (21.31). But this is unconvincing, as Allobrogan lands lay beyond the Isère, while the Vocontii lay in between—north and south of the River Drôme. Beside the Rhône, between the Eygues and modern Montélimar, dwelt the Tricastini: the district is still called *le Tricastin*. If they were not the tribe Hannibal befriended at this stage, it was the Vocontii whose centres included Noviomagus (Nyons) halfway up the Eygues. At all

events, Polybius and Livy imply that Hannibal went further than the river
confluence, and on departing later 'he veered to the left into the lands of
the Tricastini' (L. 21.31).

From Tarascon via Orange to Nyons, for instance, is a reasonable four-
day march of some 53 miles (27 + 26). The difficulty is that 53 miles equal
only 445 stades: a 'stade' (*stadium*) was 210 yards long, thus 8.4 to the mile.
Polybius (3.39) implies the distance was 600 stades, 71 miles: but this is
surely too much for a four-day march—especially with elephants—even
on level ground. The '600' needs another explanation (see below).

An objection to identifying this triangle as the Island is its small area,
for Polybius compares the Island to the Nile delta in size as well as fertility. Nor is it bounded by 'almost impassable' mountains on its third side,
another Polybian feature, but by high uplands like the Massif du Diois.
Still, on its third (northern and eastern) side, the district does have the
upper Drôme as a boundary, with only a narrow gap between it and the
upper Eygues; and more high ground lies there, pierced by the 1,180-
metre Col de Cabre.

The Rhône–Isère triangle is often preferred as the Island because it is
larger and its eastern side is partly bounded by the Grande Chartreuse
ridges (and the Lac du Bourget). All the same, these hardly amount to an
impenetrable boundary, nor of course is this region the size of the Nile
delta either, which is as large as the southern half of Provence. Polybius is
plainly writing, or over-writing, for dramatic effect. Moreover, the region
begins 90 miles (about 760 stades) from Hannibal's Rhône crossing—a
distance hard for an army (including elephants) to cover in half a week;
while to look for a more northerly Rhône crossing causes still other
difficulties (see above). Again, this district was the heartland of the
Allobroges, who were not friendly.

In the whole region, the only difficult mountains are the Vercors massif,
but these lie between the Drôme and the Isère. The Drôme meets the
Rhône 74 miles north of Tarascon—600 stades indeed, and in Vocontian
land, not Allobrogan. But, as just noted, that is too far for a four-day
march; nor is Druma, the ancient name for the Drôme, corruptible into
'Skaras', 'Skoras' or 'Sarar' by the worst of copyists. Besides, this district
leaves the Tricastini well to the south. An army north of the Drôme and
making for the Alps would not pass through them.

The march 'along the river' and the question of the Durance

On leaving the Island, escorted initially by Island warriors, the army
marched 'along the river' for ten days and 800 stades (about 95 miles),
according to Polybius, to reach 'the ascent of the Alps' (P. 3.50), where the
Allobroges unsuccessfully attacked it. Then it was another 1,200 stades to

the pass (3.39). Along which river does Polybius mean? Clarifying this item of Polybian vagueness requires first a study of the puzzles thrown up by Livy.

Livy adds non-Polybian details for this march-sector (21.31–2). Hannibal 'veered to the left', passed through the Tricastini, then moved 'through the border territory of the Vocontii into the lands of the Trigorii', and so to the River Druentia (Durance), which he describes. These tribal names and relative positions are genuine: the Tricastini along the Rhône as mentioned above, the Vocontii farther east (the Vercors preserves the name of a Vocontian sub-tribe, the Vertamocori), and, east of them, the Trigorii in the River Drac valley with the Alps on their east side.

Livy's puzzles are these. Why the initial left turn, which sent the army, at least for a short time, in a direction generally away from the Alps? Again, why does he vividly describe the *lower* course of the Druentia, with its multiple, shifting, and gravelly branches—features of the southern half of the river—when his own account requires the upper, Alpine Druentia beyond the Trigorii? Third: why does he write (21.32) that 'from the Druentia' Hannibal moved over 'a mostly flat route', 'after being granted a safe passage by the Gauls inhabiting those parts', until he and his men reached the Alps? There was no safe-passage agreement in the Alps, and the implication that the army could leave the upper Durance *behind* them is a topographical absurdity. If its upper valley was their route, they had to follow the river to reach the pass.

These statements have produced very varying interpretations. For example, that Hannibal and the army marched up the Durance, not the Rhône, to reach the mountains; or their march 'along the river' was in fact along the Drôme to the middle Durance, then upstream; or the march ignored the Durance and followed the Isère and its tributaries to one of the more northerly passes, like the Little St Bernard, the Mont Cenis, or the Col du Clapier; or the army advanced in two or even three divisions by different (unidentifiable) routes, joining up again in Italy—even though such a division would have incurred catastrophic risks and is totally unattested.

The first puzzle is the simplest. Moving from the Island to the Tricastini meant (schematically at least) a left turn for an army that had marched up the Rhône and encamped, say, near Nyons. The Tricastini, too, may have had useful supplies available, or Hannibal perhaps wanted the latest word from downriver about the movements of the Roman army under the consul Scipio, for he may have expected a Roman pursuit. His next stages (via Vocontii to Trigorii) were north-eastwards, which would certainly bring him near the Allobroges along and beyond the generally westward-flowing Isère.

The Durance is the crucial Livian puzzle. The first thing to note is that Hannibal had indeed crossed its lower reaches en route to the Island, for the Rhône–Durance confluence near Avignon is only a short distance above Tarascon. Secondly, past Avignon the region is mostly flat and open (in contrast to hillier terrain between Tarascon and Avignon). But neither Livy nor Polybius mentions these details at the appropriate point. It has often been suggested that an inept later copyist managed to detach and misplace Livy's details, which suit the lower Durance, into two separate places on the Alpine sector of the march. But it is hard to see how this could happen, particularly with the brief second item about the flat country and the safe-passage. Both misplacements look like Livy's own ineptitude.

It is reasonable to infer that one or more non-Polybian writers had recorded Hannibal crossing the lower Durance, and at that point had described the river in terms suited to its southern half (there are two or more channels over lengthy stretches below Sisteron, for instance). They had also mentioned the flat peaceful march after Hannibal crossed it. But Livy simply hurries him to the Island, like Polybius. Then, conceivably, one or more writers reported that, after passing through the Trigorii, Hannibal reached the Durance (again): this would be its upper course, well north of Sisteron. But Livy seems not to have realized that the description he had available would no longer suit, and it seems no source named a different river being crossed in the Alps; therefore he did not stop to take stock. He may have been in a hurry here, interested less in topography than in the drama, bloodshed, and excitement of the march, to which he devotes much more space (21.32–7).

In Polybius, 'along the river' can hardly mean along the Eygues or Drôme. These would eventually lead to the middle Durance valley and so up to the Montgenèvre pass, far from contact with the Allobroges: a route from Island to pass moreover involving a maximum of 140 miles—1,176 stades, whereas Polybius' figures for the same march, though obviously rounded, total 2,000 (800 + 1,200). That the Isère was 'the river' is widely supposed instead. If so, and if Hannibal was advancing via *le Tricastin*, he would not have reached the Isère immediately, though Polybius taken literally might imply this; Polybius would be compressing the details, as often. But most likely, as often suggested too, Polybius means the Rhône itself.

For if Livy is right about the Tricastini, the army marched from the Island west or north-west through *le Tricastin*—thus along the Rhône again for some distance—before turning towards the Vocontii. If so, Polybius is treating a short initial advance along the Rhône as though it lasted the entire 800 stades. But the same part-for-the-whole treatment would apply to the Isère theory, if Hannibal reached that river via *le Tricastin*. (The theory that the Island lay between Rhône and Isère, making the 800 stades run entirely along the Isère, is unworkable: see above.) As to the Rhône, Polybius in fact sees it as flowing from north-east to south-west, and Hannibal as moving eastwards overall (3.47)—so from this viewpoint, even a brief march along it was towards 'the ascent'.

With any of these scenarios, it must be noted, Polybius does not contradict (or contribute to) Livy's implication that, after the Trigorii, Hannibal marched to the upper Durance.

Once Hannibal reached the western edge of the Vercors, he must have crossed this massif itself. For, before modern roadworks, the south bank of the Isère would have been too narrow for an army and he is not recorded as crossing to its farther and broader bank (Allobrogan territory). The Allobroges avoided attacking while he was on level ground, but did so as soon as he started 'the ascent of the Alps' (P. 3.50). This was not in their territory, for Hannibal then forced them to flee 'to their own land' (3.51) which Polybius implies was not far off. The attack itself took place in a pass (3.50). These items, as J. Lazenby has very plausibly suggested, suit the spectacular pass of Gorges de la Bourne in the northern Vercors. Its eastern end rises to a plateau which then gives a descent to the Drac–Isère confluence at Culare (Grenoble), which was Allobrogan (Cicero, *Letters to his Friends* 10.23). Hannibal then captured the town which the enemy had used as their base, seizing welcome cattle and grain (P. 3.51): very likely Culare.

Polybius' 800 stades for this sector is another rounded figure. The actual distance looks more like 86 miles or 722 stades, which we can round off to 750 (see below).

The route through the Alps

The next sector would be up the valley of the Drac, where the Route Napoléon now runs. A new attack was launched by 'the people dwelling around the pass' (P. 3.52)—therefore not the Allobroges but the Trigorii—in 'a difficult and steep gorge' (3.52–3; L. 21.32–3). Polybius reports that Hannibal came into great danger 'on the fourth day' (3.52), for the deceitful natives came pretending to be friendly guides, only to launch their attack 'after a march of two days'. This should not point to the attack occurring on the sixth day, but 'on the fourth day', for the previous deceitful offer did not itself put the army in great danger. The locals had probably made it on the first or second day.

The army's speed in the Drac's winding valley can hardly have been faster than the previous sector's 80-stades daily average. This would put the new attack in the 'difficult and steep gorge' at most 320 stades south of

Cularo—38 miles—somewhere along the Drac. Hannibal, with half the army, became separated from the rest and spent the night 'around a strong position of bare rock'—not necessarily on a bare high crag, as sometimes supposed and sought for (P. 3.53; L. 21.34 leaves out the rock). Certainly this attack site should not be sought far up the valley of the Durance, as often suggested (e.g. at L'Argentière-en-Bessée, 12 miles from the Montgenèvre). For, after the attack, it was still several days—punctuated by hit-and-run harassments—to the summit of the pass: the army reached it 'on the ninth day' (P. 3.53; L. 21.35). We cannot reckon this ninth day from the start of 'the ascent of the Alps': it would mean that, in under a week and a half, the army had advanced from Cularo along 120 or more miles (see below) of often very difficult country, fighting off severe attacks yet doing a minimum average of 13 miles a day, a normal rate on good terrain.

Beyond the Drac valley the route would be along the line of the later Roman road: over the Col Bayard at 1,248 metres, then 25 miles or so of relatively open plateau along the middle Durance—a noteworthy feature, this—via Vapincum (Gap) and Caturigomagus (Chorges) to Ebrodunum (Embrun) where the upper Durance valley begins to narrow. If Livy's non-Polybian source(s) mentioned the relatively open terrain here, that would help explain how he confused it with the earlier open country past the *lower* Durance. They had, moreover, been 'granted a safe passage' by the Gauls back there, whereas safe passage did not occur along this later sector. But very carelessly Livy inserts that detail here too.

From Embrun it is 30-odd miles northwards to the pass, whether the Montgenèvre or one of its neighbours, most notably the Col de la Traversette and Col Agnel (respectively north and east of Monte Viso) via the Durance's tributary the Guil, and the Col de Larche via the Ubaye. The road distances today from Grenoble to the Montgenèvre, the Traversette or Agnel, and the Larche are about 127, 120, and 143 miles respectively (206, 194, and 230 km.), and therefore 1,067, 1,008 and 1,201 stades. Polybius' distance from the start of Hannibal's ascent is 1,200 (3.39). We must look at his figures overall.

Polybius' distances and times

From the Rhône to the start of Hannibal's 'ascent of the Alps' Polybius gives as 1,400 stades, and for 'the crossing of the Alps' the 1,200 just mentioned. From the Island to the start of 'the ascent' he reports as 800 stades.

But from the Rhône to the Island is some 445 stades (53 miles), not 600 as the above figures would imply. Then from Nyons to the Rhône at (say) Montélimar, ancient Acunum, is about 30 miles. Next, if the route went upriver to around Valence for 27 miles and then via the south bank of the

Isère for 29 (open country nearly all the way) to the start of the Gorges de la Bourne at Pont en Royans, the total is 86 miles. This is only 722 stades: if so, Polybius' '800' rounds the total up. Yet, with one sector totalling 445 and the other 722, we are left—even if the figures are rounded to 450 and 750—with a shortfall of 200 stades (1,400 claimed but 1,200 actual).

What then of 'the crossing of the Alps', claimed as 1,200? Through the Gorges and over to Cularo is 35 miles (297 stades). Then (as noted above) from Grenoble to the Montgenèvre area is at least 120 miles or 1,070 stades. Thus 'the crossing of the Alps' took at least 1,367 stades. Rounded off, this makes 1,400: an excess of 200.

Hannibal, Sosylus, and Silenus cannot have taken careful measurements all the way. In the mountains especially, they were otherwise occupied; and in any case they are hardly likely to have taken complex measuring instruments with them. Nor were most Alpine routes surveyed and measured until well after Polybius' time, unlike the milestones on the Roman highway from the Rhône to Emporiae in north-east Spain, which gave that distance as 1,600 stades (P. 3.39). So Polybius' calculations must owe much to estimates, dead-reckonings and roundings by informants (verbal and written) and himself.

It may be mere chance that the rounded 'real' distances just arrived at—1,200 from Rhône to 'ascent' and 1,400 for 'crossing'—are the mirror-opposites of Polybius' 1,400 and 1,200. After all, there can be no certainty of the precise roads or paths followed by the army; even on fairly flat terrain, its progress may often have been more zigzag than most Roman or modern roads. Thus few distance-reckonings for it, ancient or modern, can claim precision. But if there is more than coincidence involved in the mirror-opposites, it may simply be that Polybius mistakenly reversed his totals when writing them in (particularly if he wrote them as numerals, for each would consist only of two Greek letters).

He also gives fifteen days for 'the crossing of the Alps' (3.56). The Trigorii attacked 'on the fourth day' from the captured town (day four), and arrival at the pass was 'on the ninth day' thereafter (day thirteen). Two days camping there make days fourteen–fifteen. There followed three of arduous road-repair (3.53–5; L. 21.37), so many moderns see eighteen as the figure Polybius meant or should have meant—or even twenty-one, as it took another three days to reach the plains. Still, with the army now technically in Italy, he may simply have excluded these further six days from his fifteen.

Characteristics of the pass

What we are told of the pass itself is not a great help in identifying it. Its most famous reported feature is that it gave a panorama of Italy. Again, it had enough flat ground for the army to camp for two days, while its descent on the Italian side was steep, partly broken off, and made more dangerous by having old and hard ice beneath a covering of newly fallen snow. It seems surprisingly difficult to find one western pass that combines such a panorama with ground for thirty thousand-odd troops, thousands of horses and pack-animals, and dozens of elephants. Nor is it encouraging that experienced modern visitors differ on what constitutes a view or non-view of Italy, for instance from the Montgenèvre, Traversette, or Clapier.

In reality, none of these supposed features is helpful. It is entirely possible that the 'view' was a dramatic exaggeration by Hannibal's historian-admirers—or an outright invention. In Greek and Roman historiography, a general preparing to lead his army into the land of their enemies was virtually obliged to give them a rousing speech full of vivid imagery; or at any rate historians were virtually obliged to compose one for him. Silenus and Sosylus surely did not fail their friend and patron.

The evidence of ice and snow is no help either. For one thing, experts differ on whether the climate in the Alps of 218 BC was more rigorous than today, and therefore whether ice and snow could be present in lower-level passes, like the Montgenèvre and the Larche, or only on much higher ones like the Traversette or Clapier. But in any case the state of the weather in late 218, and of the ice and snow on any pass, depended on the nature of that particular half-year. This holds true whether Hannibal crossed around the beginning of November as Polybius indicates (near the time of the setting of the Pleiades: 3.54), echoed again by Livy (21.35), or in late September—a widespread but unconvincing revisionist view.

Polybius wrote elsewhere, as cited by Livy's contemporary the geographer Strabo (P. 34.10 = Strabo 4.6.12), that there were four western Alpine passes, all of them steep: a pass by the Mediterranean coast (the Col de Tende), 'the pass through the Taurini which Hannibal crossed' (and even though the last three words are not in every MS, none of the other three passes would qualify as Hannibal's), one through the Salassi (who inhabited the Aosta valley; thus the Little or Great St Bernard), and the fourth through Rhaetia (western Austria). These descriptions are not topographically precise. In similar vague fashion, Cicero's scholarly contemporary, Varro, listed five passes (according to a late Roman commentator on Virgil: Servius on *Aeneid* 10.13)—the coastal pass, the one 'by which Hannibal crossed', another used by Pompey the Great en route to Spain in 78 BC, one that brought Hannibal's brother Hasdrubal to Italy in 207, and a fifth through the Graian Alps (thus the Little St Bernard).

According to Livy's older contemporary Sallust (*Histories* 2, fragment 98), Pompey claimed that his pass was different from Hannibal's and more convenient. But which pass he used, and which other pass was Hannibal's, remains unclear. We do not even know whether his claim was justified or merely a boast. The Montgenèvre was certainly used for the later Roman road, and being one of the lowest passes was a convenient one, so Pompey may well have used it. Meanwhile, for Hannibal's pass, quite possibly, he was relying on Coelius Antipater's recent history of the war—and Coelius implausibly took Hannibal via the *iugum Cremonis*, that is, the Little St Bernard or another northerly crossing route (L. 21.38).

Conclusions

Hannibal most likely crossed the Rhône near Tarascon, and it is best to identify the Island as the district between the Rhône and Eygues. The Allobroges, it seems, attacked the army in the Vercors; and we may reckon 'the ascent of the Alps' as via Cularo up the valley of the Drac, and over to the upper Durance valley. The second wave of attacks was probably by the Trigorii in the Drac valley; and the pass into Italy was—in order of probability—the Montgenèvre, the Traversette or Agnel, or the Larche. Polybius' distance-reckonings look like broad estimates, when not guesstimates.

These conclusions depend not only on interpreting how far Polybius' and Livy's accounts correspond with known geographical facts but, as much or more, on assessing the way they construct narratives, what their priorities in writing are (literary and moralizing, as well as factual), and the oversights and slips that could occur. Until a suitable Carthaginian cache (or graffito) is found, all these criteria will remain essential.

We may note how important Livy's non-Polybian contribution is. From the Rhône-crossing to the descent into Italy, Polybius supplies three names: Island, Skaras, and Allobroges. It is Livy's range of tribe- and place names, despite the faults, that makes practicable any attempt to reconstruct Hannibal's route over the Alps.

Further reading

In a short Appendix, footnotes and detailed modern references would be cumbrous. Distances are from the *AA Big Road Atlas of Europe* (4th edn.: Basingstoke, 1984), *France Routière et Touristique: Motoring Map* (Geographia series: London), both on the scale 1 : 1,000,000 and marking kilometre-distances on roads; and *Guide Bleu France 1974* (Paris, 1974).

The literature on Hannibal's route is huge. The careful bibliography in J. Seibert, *Forschungen zu Hannibal*, 195–7, starts with an Oxford work of 1820 and runs for more than two pages of small print. Among significant recent studies are:

P. Connolly, *Greece and Rome at War* (London and New York, 1981), 153–66.

G. de Beer, *Hannibal's March* (London, 1967).

E. de Saint-Denis, 'Encore l'itinéraire transalpin d'Hannibal', *Revue des Études Latines*, 51 (1973), 122–49.

G. de Sanctis, *Storia dei Romani*, 2nd edn., vol. 3, part 2 (Florence, 1968), 64–81.

S. Lancel, *Hannibal* (Paris, 1995), 98–133.

J. Lazenby, *Hannibal's War: A Military History* (Warminster, 1978), 34–48.

D. Proctor, *Hannibal's March in History* (Oxford, 1971).

A. L. F. Rivet, *Gallia Narbonensis: Southern France in Roman Times* (London, 1988).

J. Seibert, 'Der Alpenübergang Hannibals: Ein gelöstes Problem?', *Gymnasium*, 95 (1988), 21–73.

—— *Forschungen zu Hannibal* (Darmstadt, 1993), 193–213.

—— *Hannibal* (Darmstadt, 1993), 96–113.

F. W. Walbank, *A Historical Commentary on Polybius*, vol. 1 (Oxford, 1957), 361–95.

EXPLANATORY NOTES

The numbers in the left-hand column refer to the chapter numbers set in bold type in the text.

BOOK TWENTY-ONE

1 *an enemy . . . at the earliest opportunity*: Polybius' version is 'never to be on friendly terms with the Romans' (P. 3.11), a much less bellicose promise, and less satisfying to Roman tradition. L. produces the Polybian version only much later (35.19).

upheavals in Africa: after losing the First Punic War in 241, the Carthaginians had to cope with a mutiny of their unpaid foreign mercenaries, who were joined by large numbers of the much-oppressed native Libyan population of Punic Africa. The savage 'Truceless War' lasted from 241 to 238 (L. in ch. 2 rounds it up to five years) and Carthage's survival was chiefly due to Hamilcar, who became its effective ruler.

2 *the war he was fighting*: in 237 Hamilcar went to Spain and built a large and wealthy Carthaginian province in the south, perishing in battle in late 229 or early 228.

would retain its independence: in 225 (some think 226) the Romans struck an agreement with Hasdrubal that he would not lead an army north of the Ebro. In effect, this recognized Punic interests over the rest of Spain. Roman writers after 201 also insisted, contrary to all likelihood, that it exempted Saguntum from Punic interference. Saguntum was a small but wealthy Spanish town on the Mediterranean coast, not far north of Valencia; its Roman ruins survive. There is no sound evidence for its being an ally of Rome, but this did not deter later writers from claiming it.

3 *summoned him by letter*: a bogus story, set in 224, and by 30.37 L. has forgotten it (see note there). Hannibal went with his father to Spain in 237 and returned home only in 203.

Hanno, who led the opposing faction: Hanno, for some reason called 'the Great' in some sources, had been the dominant figure in Carthaginian affairs during the 240s, but lost primacy to Hamilcar Barca and Hamilcar's successors as generals-in-chief. See Introduction.

5 *a people south of the Ebro*: just where is debated. Somewhere in east central Spain seems likely.

the Vaccaei: a tribe living on the plains around the middle River Duero; Hermandica is modern Salamanca. The Carpetani, meanwhile, were a powerful people of Old Castile, who often supplied professional fighting men to Punic armies.

6 *in order to provoke a war*: L. must be wrong about the name Turdetani for the Saguntines' neighbours, as it applied to most of the peoples of the

Baetis (Guadalquivir) river valley in modern Andalusia—far from the east coast. Later he calls the neighbours 'Turduli' (28.39), another misnomer. Very near Saguntum was a town called Turis or Tyris (the river is still called the Turia), and its people—probably 'Turitani'—seem the likeliest neighbours to be involved.

6 *the infraction of the treaty*: Roman tradition dated this embassy to 219, during Hannibal's siege of Saguntum, but in following this L. gets himself into chronological confusions that he later only partly recognizes (ch. 15). Polybius reports an embassy in 220 and none during the siege: this is almost certainly correct. The envoys' names can be accepted all the same. Valerius (Flaccus) was probably a consul of 227, Baebius (Tamphilus) an ex-praetor. According to Polybius (3.15), they urged Hannibal to respect the Ebro treaty and not molest Saguntum; he flew into a rage and dismissed them.

7 *even when faced with destruction themselves*: the loyalty (*fides*) of the Saguntines to Rome became proverbial—an irony, since they were not formal allies at all. L.'s account of the siege is entirely from non-Polybian sources, for Polybius (3.17) merely reports that Hannibal took seven months to capture the town. Some of L.'s details, notably the speeches, are free compositions but others (e.g. Hannibal's wound, his later absence, episodes of the assaults) may cautiously be accepted.

8 *some 150,000 under arms*: a fantastic exaggeration from some Roman annalist (the egregious Valerius Antias comes to mind). In 218 Hannibal's entire military strength in Spain, with the expedition to Italy being planned, barely exceeded 100,000 men (ch. 38 and note).

10 *the one with right on its side*: the Romans' final victory in the earlier war with Carthage was the naval battle by the Aegates Islands, just offshore from Drepanum (Trápani), in 241. During the previous three years, Hamilcar as commander of Punic forces in Sicily had occupied nearby Mt. Eryx (Monte San Giuliano) to harass the besieging Romans. The 'Tarentum incident' occurred much earlier, in 272, when a Punic fleet briefly turned up outside that city when it was about to capitulate to the Romans: this was afterwards claimed to be a violation of a treaty of friendship between Rome and Carthage, so as to put the Carthaginians in the wrong even before the First Punic War broke out.

11 *the Oretani*: a tribe living between the Baetis and Anas rivers (today's Guadalquivir and Guadiana); their notable towns were Castulo, where Hannibal himself had found a wife (24.41 and note), Ilugo, Mentisa, and Oretum. Castulo, south of the Sierra Morena, may not have been involved in this brief insurgency.

15 *returned to his army in its winter quarters*: second- and first-century BC Roman historians misdated the siege of Saguntum from 219 to 218, thus creating the chronological dilemma L. describes. He himself accepted it in ch. 9; having now realized it is unworkable, he contents himself with acknowledging this but does not trouble to revise the earlier statement.

16 *before their city walls*: this depiction of gloomy alarm is hardly supported by the Romans' leisurely preparations for war, and their clear expectation of fighting it in North Africa and Spain. At this moment war had not yet been declared; still less had Hannibal started his march from New Carthage. But for dramatic purposes L. wants to have the Romans foreseeing what afterwards did happen.

18 *Quintus Fabius ... and Quintus Baebius*: the leader of the war embassy of 218 was almost certainly not Quintus Fabius Maximus (the later Cunctator) but Marcus Fabius Buteo, as the later historian Cassius Dio states (fragment 55.10). It was not official practice to provide the third names (*cognomina*) in such lists, but Livius and Aemilius were probably the consuls (Salinator and Paulus, respectively) of the previous year, Licinius (Varus) a consul of 236, and Baebius one of the two earlier envoys in 220.

19 *no such escape clause*: typically, Roman historical tradition sought to base its case for the Second Punic War on legalisms. This, however, suffered the basic flaw that at no time were the Saguntines formal allies of Rome (at best they were 'friends', *amici*)—although the war embassy plainly sought to make the Carthaginians think they *were* allies. L. draws much of his argumentation from Polybius, who is equally fuzzy (3.29–30).

to dissuade them from joining the Carthaginians: these further journeyings of the Roman envoys are generally disbelieved, partly because our sources are not clear on when they got back to Rome. But there is no good reason why Roman historians should have invented the account (the envoys receive mostly hostile replies) or pro-Punic writers should be interested. One possibility is that some envoys made this trip while others returned to Rome, a nuance afterwards lost on historians.

22 *fitted out and furnished with crews*: though L. does not acknowledge it, the military details in chs. 21–2 go back to Hannibal himself, via Polybius who affirms that he read them in an inscription put up by the general at Cape Lacinium in southern Italy (3.33; Livy reports this memoir later, in 28.46).

There is a tale: told by Hannibal's friend Silenus, later his historian, according to Cicero who gives Coelius' version of it (*De divinatione* 1.49). There is an obvious resemblance to the myth of Orpheus and Eurydice, but this is not enough to disprove that Hannibal had—or at least claimed to have—such a dream. 'Jupiter' would then equate to a principal Carthaginian deity, perhaps Ba'al Hammon ('Hercules' was Melqart, Carthage's protector). Onussa is usually identified with Peñíscola on the Spanish coast just south of the Ebro.

23 *at the foot of the Pyrenees*: as usual, Spanish names in L. raise problems. Certainly the Bargusii were friendly to Rome (ch. 19); but Hannibal had left an Ilergetan unit with Hasdrubal (ch. 22), which implies the Ilergetes were already pro-Carthage, and so does other evidence; while the Ausetani and Lacetani are found resisting Roman forces later in the year (chs. 60–1). Polybius (3.35) has Hannibal subdue the Bargusii, Ilergetes, Aerenosii, and

Andosini—the last two tribes otherwise unknown, and whose names perhaps baffled Roman annalists and so were replaced arbitrarily by ones better known. In turn, the Ilergetes now subdued may well have been, not the powerful people inland whose name survives in Ilerda (modern Lérida/Lleida), but a coastal people between Tarraco (Tarragona) and Barcino (Barcelona): interestingly, a coast town there bears the name Olérdola.

25 *and Gaius Papirius Maso*: later L. shows that Servilius at any rate was one of the other triumvirs (27.21 and note; 30.19). Here he fails to make clear whether the spokesmen seized by the Gauls were one or more of the land-commissioners or were other persons entirely. At least one commissioner, Servilius, seems to have gone out as a spokesman but not necessarily all three, and this could account for the later discrepancies.

were manhandled: or possibly, 'whether these men were roughly handled when they were on a mission to protest to the Boii', as Polybius has no mention of a separate delegation to the Boii: see Walsh's note (translator's note).

Tannetum: between Mutina and Parma.

27 *Hanno son of Bomilcar*: Appian terms him Hannibal's nephew (*Hannibalica* 20), which may or may not be correct. He was a reliable and energetic lieutenant but, when commanding a secondary army in Italy later on, too liable to suffer defeats at Roman hands.

at the first watch of the night: the night was divided into four watches (*vigiliae*) of three hours each, midnight being at the end of the second and start of the third watch. As night- and day-lengths vary with season and latitude, the first watch in this episode can be only roughly estimated as between 6 and 7 p.m.

had larger vessels: the text is perhaps unsound at this point: see Walsh's note (translator's note).

28 *how it was accomplished*: L.'s second, 'more reliable' description is a shortened and simplified version of Polybius' (3.46), and certainly seems likelier.

was disconnected from the other: the Latin actually says 'from the others', *ab ceteris* (translator's note).

31 *have been given the name 'the Island'*: see Appendix 2.

33 *The pass had precipitously steep cliffs on either side*: L. writes, and perhaps thinks, confusingly. He visualizes the pass as a road cut along the side of a steep mountain, for it has cliffs on either side, one of them falling into an abyss. Yet Hannibal is able to swoop down to the rescue from a higher position with armed support. L. is retelling Polybius' version (3.51) in more dramatic, but less lucid, form; Polybius shows that the Gauls could attack from the upper slopes (not a cliff) until Hannibal, up ahead of his column, came back to drive them off.

35 *he pointed out to them Italy . . . at the foot of the Alps*: it was probably now

late October or early November, though many scholars prefer September. The setting of the Pleiades (that is, when it sank below the horizon just after sunset) occurred around late October/early November in 218. The site of this famous panorama is even more debated, probably a pointless effort: see Appendix 2.

37 *by pouring vinegar on them*: a measure often seen as Livian fantasy, but now accepted by many scholars; the practice is also mentioned by the architect-writer Vitruvius (8.3.19).

38 *he lost 36,000 men . . . after crossing the Rhône*: Cincius became a prisoner of Hannibal's in or after 208; the general evidently found his conversation agreeable (both spoke Greek). But debate and disbelief bedevil assessment of L.'s and Polybius' figures for Hannibal's forces. L. avoids mentioning that the lowest figure here is Hannibal's own (recorded by Polybius, 3.56); he sees Cincius as a more 'authoritative' source than the general himself. In turn, the highest looks like an earlier source inflatedly estimating Hannibal's original forces in Spain and then blithely assuming that all of them were with him in Italy. It has occasionally been suggested that Hannibal had a propaganda interest in under-reporting his arrival-strength; but this is not obvious and his figure is at any rate consistent with those reported down to Cannae in 216. L. has followed Polybius in giving him 102,000 at New Carthage (ch. 23); Polybius reports 59,000 crossing into Gaul (3.60) after losses, detachments, and desertions; and then up to the Rhône there was no fighting. Hannibal's figure for losses after the Rhône is thus—very roughly—compatible with his figure for the forces reaching Italy.

the Taurini Semigalli: the Romans added the term 'Semigalli' (half-Gallic) to denote the mixed origin of this Alpine folk.

was given its name on that account: the Poenine Alps are now called the Pennine Alps (highest peak Monte Rosa), crossed by the Great St Bernard pass. The Taurini 'Semigalli' lived at the foot of the Alps farther south; their name survives in modern Turin (Torino); the other peoples mentioned dwelt in the Alpine valleys to their west and north. The Cremo ridge was the Little St Bernard.

39 *with the following harangue*: the consul's address to his men is matched by one of Hannibal's (chs. 43–4). The symbolism of this pairing is important: it marks the war's opening combat between Carthaginians and Romans, minor as this was (L. ignores the skirmish of ch. 29). Similarly to mark the last battle, in 202, L. will give Hannibal and Scipio Africanus, this consul's son, speeches in their turn, in reverse order (30.30–1): thus a Scipio opens, and a Scipio will close, the rhetorical accompaniment of the war's battles. Again, although not Hannibal's first speech in L. but his third (see chs. 21, 30), the new one is his first full-length oration in direct speech. It is noticeable that all three are made to his army: they make vivid L.'s picture of Hannibal as charismatic leader and bold commander.

40 *as prizes of war*: this is rhetoric; the Carthaginians had ceded only Sicily at the peace of 241—Sardinia was taken from them years later—and the war-indemnity (in rhetoric, 'tribute') finally agreed was for ten years.

46 *ran back amidst the supporting troops to the second line*: perhaps, with Walsh, we should read *inter subsidia ac secundam aciem* ('between the reserves in the second line') (translator's note). The text as translated is at odds with L.'s preceding report that Scipio's Roman and Italian allied cavalry were 'in reserve', i.e. were the supporting troops, for if so *they* were the second line. But in any case, L. misinterprets Polybius (3.65). The latter reports that the javelineers, given no time to throw their weapons—a point not in L.—retreated hastily 'through the gaps between their own squadrons' to avoid being trampled. L., trying to clarify this, ends up seemingly confusing himself and certainly baffling the reader, not to mention his later copyists.

an account . . . entrenched in popular tradition: L.'s criterion for preferring the younger Publius Scipio (later Africanus) as his father's rescuer is illuminatingly subjective. When Polybius tells the same story later (10.3) he cites Africanus' close friend Laelius as the source; L. does not, whether because he may not yet have read that far into Polybius and got the story elsewhere, or because he was uninterested in mentioning Laelius. That Laelius was entirely trustworthy on such a topic is not guaranteed; on the other hand, Coelius' source for his version is equally unknown, and Africanus did later have plenty of critics eager to deny him glory wherever possible.

47 *under Mago's leadership*: L., himself north Italian, uses his acquaintance with the area to help judge between Coelius' version and others'. The historians with the alternative account included Polybius (3.66).

48 *bribed with 400 gold pieces*: in L.'s day this would be equivalent to 10,000 *denarii*—a year's pay for nearly 50 ordinary legionary soldiers—and in 218 BC the value was probably much greater; so by rating the bribe as 'not high' he must be thinking of it in comparison with the value of capturing Clastidium.

49 *conducted by the consul Sempronius*: these operations, ignored by Polybius, are nevertheless detailed and plausible.

Hiero of Syracuse: Hiero had made himself leader of the city around 274, then king (265); after a short war with Rome (264–263) he aligned himself with the republic and remained a loyal ally until his death in 215 aged over 90. Syracuse and its surrounding territory were exceptionally prosperous under his rule. His chief scientist was Archimedes.

51 *sent it up the Adriatic to Ariminum*: Polybius has Sempronius dismiss the army under oath to reassemble in forty days' time at Ariminum (3.61), but then he reports it and him coming to Rome en route and heartening the city (3.68). Perhaps part of the army did so, or this may be a dramatic invention by Polybius. As the time was late autumn (roughly November 218: see Appendix 2), L.'s sea journey does seem unlikely.

52 *or else there was simply no hope*: a good example of dramatic interpretation by L. He is clearly visualizing what he feels was in the Romans' thoughts, though he presents it as a statement of fact. Literary colouring of this sort is common in ancient historians, including the normally prosaic Polybius (see previous note), and may occasionally mislead.

54 *Select from your entire force*: according to Polybius (3.71), Hannibal himself had earlier selected these men and now he put Mago in command of them. L., who is otherwise following Polybius closely, adds vividness to the story—and to his depiction of the brothers—by having Hannibal leave it to Mago to select the initial force.

the winter solstice: thus 21 December, or thereabouts. Sempronius must have been sent his recall notice before Hannibal crossed the Alps in October–November. Most scholars see him reaching the north then, but a junction with Publius Scipio even as late as 10 December would still leave enough time for the skirmish (ch. 52), the consuls' wrangling (ch. 53), and then the battle.

56 *to barely experience the joy of victory*: again, L. seeks to dramatize matters, this time the victors' psychology. Whether he draws on a different source for this or follows his own intuition, his picture is the opposite of Polybius' (3.74), who reports them being overjoyed at the completeness of their victory and their small losses.

57 *an act of sheer bravado on his part*: L. is hard on Sempronius, who plainly thought it his duty to return to Rome to hold the elections, and who then returned—presumably through the same dangers—to his troops in the north.

the Gallic War: the operations in Cisalpine Gaul after the defeat of the great Gallic invasion of 225.

58 *Hannibal . . . struck out into Etruria*: this dramatic account of a failed effort to cross the Apennines is unique to L., and it is hard to decide whether he should be believed. As it is not in Polybius and is followed by a certainly fictitious winter battle with Sempronius (ch. 59)—besides being reminiscent of the Alpine-crossing narrative in its carefully described torments—it must be doubted. Conceivably Hannibal did send out some exploratory units to scout the Apennine passes but decided that the weather was too violent for a winter's move; this could readily be magnified by an annalistic writer into a full-scale thwarted attempt.

59 *Luca*: modern Lucca, south of the Apennines; yet Sempronius' troops are afterwards reported wintering at Placentia (ch. 63), whence in March 217 they are summoned by the new consul Flaminius to meet him at Ariminum (Rimini), across the Apennines and by the Adriatic. Flaminius then advanced to Arretium (Arezzo) in Etruria (22.3). It is most unlikely that the troops were moved back and forth, from Placentia to Luca, then back to Placentia—all this during bitter winter weather—and afterwards to Ariminum. Sempronius may have betaken himself to Luca while leaving the army at Placentia; more likely this report is a Roman annalistic

mistake. Whether the new consul summoned the troops to Ariminum or, as some have suggested, to Arretium is another debated question.

60 *putting in at Emporiae*: Emporiae (a site today called Ampurias) was an old Greek colony, founded by Massilia. At some date it had established friendly relations with the Romans. L. describes it more fully in 34.9 (195 BC).

Cissis . . . was also taken by storm: this Iberian town was either the same as, or very near to, Tarraco (Tarragona) on the coast; Iberian coins stamped *Cese* are from there. L. does not mention that one of the 'important people' captured was Indibilis, king of the inland Ilergetes (Polybius 3.76, calling him Andobales); but he soon got away and would cause much trouble to the Romans until 206.

61 *imposing a fine on them as well*: this operation is generally judged a bogus annalistic confection, because the Ilergetes are thought of as those dwelling around Ilerda, who were Punic allies. But Atanagrus is a distinctive name and there were other Ilergetes on the coast (ch. 23 note); these were Hasdrubal's likely targets.

The details of the campaigns by Gnaeus and Publius Scipio in Books 21–5, from 218 to 211, are much doubted by moderns, in the belief that they involve improbable or impossible place names and are largely unmentioned by Polybius (whose history survives, however, only in excerpts after 216 BC). In this interpretation, the campaigns were largely invented by L.'s annalistic predecessors. Yet they include many items which are not intrinsically improbable, even though annalists—and L. himself—clearly had trouble correctly identifying place names or under- standing the course of events. Coelius Antipater, we know, drew on Hannibal's friend and historiographer Silenus (see note to ch. 22); we know, too, that Hannibal's other confidant Sosylus narrated Spanish events in detail (a papyrus fragment shows this). At least indirectly, then, L. had access to good materials on these campaigns.

returned to their winter quarters at Tarraco: Polybius and Appian (in his *Iberica*) say nothing of this operation; but Appian leaves out much else that is well attested, and Polybius himself can be selective about events (ch. 49 note). With Hannibal firmly subduing Spain's north-east earlier in the year, including the Ausetani and Lacetani (ch. 23), Gnaeus Scipio's forces need not have been so imposing as to lure these into revolt. Amusicus, a unique and possibly Celtic name, is hard to account for as just a Roman annalistic invention.

62 *at Caere the oracular lots had shrunk*: the lots (*sortes*) were wooden tablets with ancient prophetic writings, as also at Falerii (see 22.1) and Praeneste (Cicero, *De divinatione* 2.85–6). If they shrank, it was a bad omen.

Juventas: abstract divinity of Youth.

the Sibylline Books: three ancient scrolls which prescribed rituals for consulting and, when necessary, placating the gods; reportedly they also contained prophecies. They were under the care of the decemvirs.

63 *at Ariminum by 15 March*: because L. has the consul Sempronius retire to Luca at year's end.

gained him a second consulship: Flaminius was a vigorous and popular leader whose feisty style did not endear him to much of the ruling elite. As consul in 223 he had helped to complete the conquest of northern Italy (then called Cisalpine Gaul), but his championship of popular interests—for instance, land-grants to poorer citizens when tribune in 232—had made him a suspect demagogue to most politically powerful aristocrats. Many of these belonged to families with long pedigrees of consulships (the 'nobles'—*nobiles*, an unofficial term): for instance, Quintus Fabius Maximus, one of his severest critics, had consular ancestors going back to 485. As a result all our sources, Polybius included, are disparaging towards him. But Flaminius was able to exploit a mood of intermittent assertiveness among voters (22.34 note). Claudius' law seems just such an example: an effort to curb senators' supposed proclivity towards looking after their personal wealth at the expense of devotedly serving the *res publica*.

the Alban Mount: now the Colli Albani, 12 miles south-east of Rome, where the great Latin Festival in honour of Jupiter was celebrated annually by the consuls (see also 26.21 note).

the vote for recalling Flaminius . . . was unanimous: L. had presumably also told the story of the earlier attempted recall in 223; it does not strike him as odd that almost exactly the same thing should happen now, and clearly his feelings are with the outraged Senate. It is much likelier that this alleged recall is just a recycling of the earlier one by a hostile annalist.

BOOK TWENTY-TWO

1 *changes of clothing and headgear*: by headgear L. means wigs. The same story is in Polybius (3.78; Cassius Dio's abbreviator Zonaras (8.24) offers even more imaginative details) but it is hard to visualize how Hannibal could remain unrecognizable and still direct the army day by day. The Gauls, all the same, may well have been growing restive.

entered office in Rome: until late in the third century BC, consuls seem to have entered office on or around 1 May, but L. often notes 15 March as the date from here on. The change may have been made to enable campaigning to start as early as possible in spring; it is thought to date from around 222. In 153 the entry-date for consuls would become 1 January.

2 *went blind in one eye*: Nepos, *Hannibal* 4, has his sight damaged, not lost, in the right eye; the ailment must have been ophthalmia.

3 *as once they did Camillus from Veii*: Marcus Furius Camillus, exiled from Rome around 391, was urgently summoned home to take charge after raiding Gauls captured and sacked the city (cf. ch. 14, and note to ch. 50). L. is economical: Camillus had been at Ardea, but then collected what was left of the defeated Roman army at Veii.

4 *would then be shut in between the lake and the mountains*: L.'s and Polybius' descriptions of the site (close but not identical) and Hannibal's dispositions show that the Trasimene battlefield lay by the north shore of the raggedly oval lake. Neither makes the site clearer, and the difficulty is sharpened by Polybius' view (3.83–4) that the ambush took place, not along the shore, but in a valley at right angles to it. There is in fact such a valley at the north-west corner of the lake, by the village of Tuoro. If Polybius means something else, he has expressed it very opaquely (notably in an opening sentence (3.83) eighteen lines long!). L., utilizing at least one other source and, possibly, personal acquaintance with the area, locates the battle along Trasimene's northern shore; this has become the accepted view. Even so, the shore is a good 10 miles long and debate continues over whether the battle was along its western half or the much narrower eastern half. Burial-pits found near Tuoro have been both claimed as stemming from the battle (cf. ch. 7 on burials) and rejected as medieval. Current opinion inclines to the north-eastern half, around the lakeside town of Passignano.

5 *considerable composure in such a precarious situation*: L.'s picture of Flaminius in this crisis is much friendlier, despite his past criticisms, than Polybius', who has him shattered and desperate (3.83); Plutarch, *Fabius* 3, echoes L.

legion, cohort, or maniple: the cohort, as a unit of a Roman legion, seems to have been devised in this war for greater flexibility; previously it was only used in Latin and Italian allied contingents. In a legion it consisted of one maniple each of *hastati*, *principes*, and *triarii*, so there were ten cohorts to a legion. This seems L.'s first mention of it as a legionary formation; though here it may be just a rhetorical touch, there are many more to come: notably 23.18 (though this too may be L.'s own choice of term); 27.13, 18, 32, and 48–9; 28.14, 25, and 33.

there was an earthquake: not in Polybius, but the report was in Coelius (Cicero, *De divinatione* 1.78). Given Coelius' penchant for dramatizing events (see note to 29.27), this is no guarantee of factualness. L. does not record any measures afterwards by the Senate in reaction to the supposed calamity or its religious import, careful though he is as a rule about such items: a clue that, if there was any earthquake, it was much exaggerated in the later telling. The date by the Roman calendar was 21 June (Ovid, *Fasti* 6.767–8), but it is not certain that the calendar was correct at this period (cf. 30.29 note).

7 *contemporary with this war*: on Fabius Pictor, see Introduction. Though L. names him only here as a source, it hardly follows that he knew him solely via Coelius' history (he does not mention Polybius, one of his major sources, until 30.45). His use of Fabius here is a sensible one; Polybius too has 15,000 killed, perhaps from Fabius again. L. gives no figure for prisoners, but his report of 10,000 men getting away looks improbable; the 6,000 who did break though (ch. 6) were afterwards taken by Maharbal.

Polybius has 15,000 captured and it seems clear that Flaminius' army was virtually wiped out.

Romans he put in irons: but Campanians, who were Roman citizens too, though of a special kind (see Glossary: 'Campanian citizens'), were released (ch. 13).

8 *the hitherto unprecedented step of appointing a dictator themselves*: it was normal for one of the consuls to nominate a dictator for an emergency. Fabius had been consul in 233 and 228, Minucius in 221, so both were of high rank, and had been sound though hardly brilliant performers. Fabius' earlier dictatorship was around 221, not for war but for a civilian task (and his master of horse had been Flaminius, according to a late source). Later on L. finds himself unhappy with this account of Fabius being elected dictator by the people and argues he can have been only a 'provisional' one (*pro dictatore*: ch. 31), but this view is not supported by other evidence. That Minucius too was elected, to be master of horse, is again significant, for normally this officer was nominated by the dictator.

9 *as far as Spoletium*: Hannibal's attempt on Spoletium (Spoleto) is not in Polybius, who has him reach the Adriatic coast ten days after Trasimene (3.86). Roman tradition may have wanted to account for his not marching directly on Rome by inventing this claim of a heroic town's resistance. Spoletium was a Latin colony (see Glossary: 'colony').

11 *had forgotten the authority it carried*: the last time there had been a dictator for war (*rei gerundae causa*) had been in 248 during the First Punic War.

a Carthaginian fleet: what was this fleet doing in that area? Polybius states that it had expected to link up with Hannibal (3.96). Possibly he had originally intended to march on Rome, supported by the fleet, but changed his mind after Trasimene; by then it was too late to get word to the fleet at Carthage.

12 *felt unspoken concern*: this is patriotically imaginative colouring by L. Only pro-Hannibalic writers, like Sosylus and Silenus, could give him an idea of Hannibal's thinking, and they would scarcely depict the general in this light.

13 *'Casilinum' rather than 'Casinum'*: Casilinum stood on the River Volturnus just north of Capua, whereas Casinum (modern Cassino) lay 30 miles to the north-west. Casinum would indeed control the main route from Latium into Campania, but for Hannibal, with Fabius' army coming up behind him, moving thither was hardly sound strategically; nor would so distant a position do much to encourage the Campanians to defect. The tale seems invented, perhaps as an excuse to tell a tale of Hannibal's alleged cruelty.

into the plain of Stellas: the eastern part of the fertile Falernian plain, on the north side of the River Volturnus. The route L. describes includes Caiatia or (in the manuscripts) Calatia, neither of which fits a march via Allifae and Cales; it represents some early copyist's error. Because manuscripts were copied by hand, and our surviving manuscripts date to the

Middle Ages at the earliest and thus are at several removes from L.'s original, such errors can crop up at times—and then become perpetuated (or worse ones creep in).

14 *knights*: that is, men of the equestrian order (see Glossary; cf. note to 27.11).

would have chosen Minucius . . . over Fabius: Minucius is the third head-strong Roman in succession who revolts against more cautious and—for L.—wiser counsels. Sempronius vs. Scipio, and Flaminius vs. the Senate, have preceded, and Varro vs. Aemilius will follow. Polybius offers a rather similar (though not identical) picture, and some of this must be historically based (cf. ch. 25 note). But for literary and moral impact L. stylizes the picture with rhetorical and dramatic scenes, as here. These clashes bring to life the Romans' path to wisdom in Hannibal's war: to defeat this enemy, they must accept the ironic and painful paradox of discarding their normal aggressive élan and embracing caution and procrastination.

17 *and encamped in the region of Allifae*: the area of this famous ruse was north-eastern Campania, but it is not clear which heights are L.'s Callicula (Polybius calls them Mt. Eribianus: 3.92).

20 *set sail for Onussa*: this naval raid down Spain's Mediterranean coast is not widely believed because Polybius does not report it, the distances seem too ambitious, and 'Longuntica' is unknown. Yet the Carthaginian fleet had just been destroyed, so there could be little immediate opposition. 'Longuntica' is very possibly a copyist's error for Lucentum (today's Alicante), where the locally grown esparto could well have been stored as L. states. A mistake by a copyist is conceivable, because in the manuscripts *ad rem nauticam* ('for the use of the fleet') comes soon after the words *ad Longunticam*; an early copyist's eye could thus have miscopied *ad Lucentum* as *ad Longunticam*. Ebusus, modern Ibiza, was an old Carthaginian possession.

the pass of Castulo: an impossibility, for the area is over 300 miles in a straight line from the Ebro, and lies far inland, near Linares. A pass into the interior behind Tarraco may be meant, for the inland Ilergetes (around Lérida) soon reacted against the Romans. Years later the Scipio brothers did reach the Castulo area, where they met with disaster (24.41 note); an annalist who knew the name might carelessly suppose it was also reached in 217.

21 *Mandonius and . . . Indibilis*: these inseparable brothers were leaders of the inland Ilergetes and had been pro-Carthaginian enthusiasts even before 218. Indibilis had been captured at Cissis the previous year (21.60 note), hence his being here termed the 'former' chieftain; but clearly he was again free, maybe thanks to Mandonius. Gnaeus Scipio's inferred demonstration against the Ilergetes may have been an effort to thwart his return to them.

Ilergavonenses . . . Nova Classis: the latter ('New Fleet') is unknown but looks coastal; the Ilergavonenses or Ilercavonenses dwelt near the mouth of the Ebro, with Dertosa (Tortosa) their chief town, and were perhaps kin to the coastal and inland Ilergetes.

22 *Tarraco*: this town was built up into a major base by the Scipio brothers, and would become the capital of the later Roman province of Nearer Spain.

25 *the same constitutional powers*: Fabius had been elected by the people as dictator, not nominated by a consul (ch. 8). It was therefore open to the people to grant equal powers to Minucius, though it is unlikely he also received the title. On a dedicatory inscription he does term himself 'dictator', but he seems to have held the post earlier (ch. 8 note).

Marcus Atilius Regulus: he had been consul in 227. Not until 27.6 does L. mention that after Trasimene, and so around this time, a law was passed permitting the re-election of ex-consuls as often as the people wished.

family background was . . . downright sordid: Varro suffered a very bad press from ancient writers, including Polybius, both because he was in command at Cannae and because of his non-elite origins (even more so than Flaminius'). On the sequence of military 'hotheads' in 218–216 see note to ch. 14. Roman historiography was created, unluckily for Varro *et al.*, more by writers with connections to Fabius and the Scipios than by writers friendly to the hotheads. But the blame is exaggerated rather than invented, for disasters did occur under their commands.

30 *under your command and auspices*: Minucius' manly remorse is not in Polybius and is clearly dramatized by L. for moralizing impact. Such episodes may well have formed the scenarios of verse history-plays at Rome (*praetextae*) and a current view, notably urged by T. P. Wiseman (*Roman Drama and Roman History* (Exeter, 1998)), is that these heavily influenced later Roman historiography. As we lack any surviving Republican-era *praetextae*, this remains a hypothesis. But at times L. does seem to shape an episode in such a way: see notes to 23.4 and 30.12.

31 *island of Meninx . . . inhabitants of Cercina*: Jerba and Kerkenna lie just off the Tunisian coast in the Gulf of Sirte. Many Greeks, Polybius among them (1.39), identified Jerba as the *Odyssey*'s fabled isle of lotus-eaters.

had actually been dictator: see note to ch. 8.

32 *Geminus Servilius*: Roman authors sometimes reverse the usual order of second and third names for literary variety.

33 *20,000 full asses*: L. literally has '20,000 of heavy bronze' (*aeris gravis*), i.e. coins of *aes grave*, the original Roman currency, and he means the old standard of ten bronze *asses* to the later *denarius*—thus equivalent to 2,000 *denarii*, a handsome sum (cf. 21.48 note). A few years later the 10 *asses* were increased to 12 and then 16 to the *denarius*, so L. is careful to indicate he means the original standard.

payment of his indemnity: the Illyrians' country is more or less modern Albania; after wars with Rome in 229–228 and 219 they had been forced to pay a yearly indemnity. Demetrius of Pharus, an Illyrian princeling whose activities had prompted the Romans into the war of 219, had fled to Philip V, and was reportedly urging the king to mischief.

33 *a dictator . . . to hold the elections*: a civilian function of the dictatorship. Only a consul could normally appoint a dictator, which could lead to complications (see 27.5 for a notable example). Presumably the present consuls' objections were overcome somehow. In turn, irregularities of formal procedure or in omens—even an inopportune mouse-squeak on one occasion before 218—could vitiate an appointment to office.

34 *antagonism between the senatorial party and the plebeians*: there had been intermittent tensions, since at least the 230s, between the ruling elite (followed no doubt by supporters in the citizen body) and a vocal element of other citizens who wanted policies more socially assertive—and, at times, more militarily so as well. But in Roman historical writings the details became contaminated by the still more virulent political tensions (and sometimes actual violence) after 150 BC, which makes it now hard to identify fully the factors existing in the late third century.

The idea that it was a simple case of Senate vs. commoners (as ancient writers often claim) must be rejected, for consuls were elected by the *Comitia Centuriata*, the format of which gave preponderance to well-off and at least comfortably off citizens: men worth 100,000 *asses* and above. We should think, rather, in terms of contests between a well-established, though always evolving, elite of birth and wealth long used to enjoying most offices of state, and generally deferred to by the electorate, and more newly affluent and ambitious men seeking to become part of this 'in' group. Successful incomers then tended to take on the ethos of the established elite, to the exasperation of their former friends and associates, as L. notes (and as proved true even of the vilified Varro, whose descendants were mostly paragons of aristocratic mediocrity).

35 *almost went up in flames*: in the year after the Second Illyrian War of 219, fought by both consuls, one consul—Marcus Livius—was convicted of peculating booty (see 27.34 and note); the other, Paulus, had his reputation blasted even though he escaped a conviction.

Marcus Pomponius Matho: not the same as the praetor of the same name in 217 (ch. 7). There were several Pomponii about in these years and L. does not, perhaps could not, clearly distinguish between them.

36 *87,200 men . . . when the battle was fought at Cannae*: the figures are much debated, with estimates based on Polybius' and L.'s evidence ranging from 50,000 to 87,200. L.'s later piecemeal figures for casualties, prisoners, and survivors total 82,000 (chs. 49, 50, 52, 54, 62). What is clear is that the Romans created as large an army as possible in order to overwhelm their enemy by simple force.

38 *for the troops . . . to arrive*: on allies and Latins see Glossary: 'Latins'. The chronology of the campaign is not entirely clear. Consuls assumed office on 15 March (ch. 1), but Cannae was fought on 2 August, by the Roman calendar anyway—only a few days, L. writes, after Paulus and Varro took

over command of the army (ch. 40). Some scholars have argued that the calendar was inaccurate in 216; their proposals for the 'correct' date range from early March to July. Polybius has Hannibal staying at Gereonium until the crops were ready (3.107), and some date during summer is acceptable. Even so, the large army enrolments must have taken quite a while, and Polybius also reports that in the interim the proconsuls in Apulia were ordered not to take offensive action, and that great care and time were devoted to training the army (3.106). Only when the Senate decided on a pitched battle did it send the consuls to Apulia (3.107–8). L. regrettably finds no room for these clarifications: he wants to get on to the battle.

decuries: the smallest units of a cavalry squadron, each consisting in principle of ten horsemen and commanded by a decurion. Thirty decuries constituted the Roman cavalry of a legion.

the following words: nothing suggests that this is a genuine tête-à-tête. L. covers himself with the caveat, 'is *said* to have addressed him'. Its real aim is literary: to re-emphasize the superior insight and moral quality of Fabius and the need for the Romans to adopt the difficult but essential policy of Fabian tactics.

40 *long enough for them to do so*: L. lays the entire blame for seeking a pitched battle on Varro, but Polybius more carefully blames him for choosing to fight when he did. The Greek historian does makes it plain that the decision to seek out Hannibal and overwhelm him with unprecedentedly huge forces had been made by the Senate (3.107–8); the battle was awaited at Rome with great anticipation (3.112).

42 *the chickens refused their approval*: a coop of sacred chickens accompanied generals to war to give the auspices. If they ate when offered food by their keeper, especially if they let some of it fall from their beaks, this was an omen of victory; their refusing food was a divine warning (cf. 27.16). In 249 an impatient consul disregarded the chickens' refusal to eat (allegedly he threw them overboard: 'then let them drink'), attacked the Carthaginian fleet at Drepana in Sicily, and met with suitable disaster.

the dignity of his office: none of this detailed account in chs. 41–2 is in Polybius, and L.'s language is censorious and emotional. Yet the precision about Statilius (the name was Lucanian) and the two escaped slaves is surprising if the episode is wholly imaginary.

43 *with destiny thrusting them on*: a phrase famously adapted by the historian Tacitus in prophesying Rome's possible fall to German invasions— '*urgentibus imperii fatis*, with the destinies of the empire thrusting us on' (*Germania* 33).

the Volturnus wind: the sirocco, which blows from the south or south-east. Not mentioned by Polybius, but Fabius Pictor or Cincius could have recorded it.

46 *Hannibal . . . with his brother Mago*: Polybius does not mention Maharbal but gives command of the right wing to Hanno (3.114). Earlier the cavalry

supremo had been Carthalo (ch. 15), who reappears in ch. 49. Perhaps Hannibal varied his appointments from time to time, and if Maharbal was not commanding the right wing now, he was somewhere else in the army; later historians—or even Hannibal's friends Silenus or Sosylus—might be confused.

48 *commenced with a Carthaginian trick*: 'Carthaginian' in the charged sense of 'deceitful'. The trick is not in Polybius. L. reports the rest of the Numidians as being 'in the centre of the line', fighting listlessly, then being given fresh orders by Hasdrubal, the 'commander in that quarter'; but the Numidians had been on the Punic right, Hasdrubal on the left (ch. 46). L. has not fully understood proceedings and has also incorporated this dubious tale. The Numidian wing had neutralized the Italian allied left, and Polybius then reports Hasdrubal coming around from his wing after routing the Roman citizen cavalry there. Now the Italian cavalry fled and he sent the Numidians to pursue the Roman horse, while with his own he struck the rear of the legions. What had become of the Numidians' own commander, whether Hanno or Maharbal? Neither was killed or wounded, both were energetic, yet this initiative came from Hasdrubal.

49 *taken prisoner in the battle*: L.'s Roman dead, 48,200 in all, are many fewer than Polybius' 70,000 (3.117). But L.'s total of 19,300 for prisoners taken in battle and then at the Roman camps is virtually twice Polybius' figure of 10,000. Polybius gives only 3,370 survivors who got away, whereas L. claims 14,550 did. These figures are not really reconcilable, but two legions—of Romans plus Italian allies—were afterwards formed from the Cannae survivors who got away, which suggests that L.'s figure for them is more or less accurate. So too Polybius' total of prisoners, for Punic sources, including Hannibal himself in his Cape Lacinium inscription (for which see Introduction), could have recorded the prisoner count. By contrast, Polybius' high figure for the slain is not preferable to L.'s. All the same, many modern historians estimate lower totals again for Roman dead, arguing that the sources' figures were physically impossible to achieve by Hannibal's army of fewer than 50,000.

50 *disaster at the Allia*: in 390 BC (or more likely 387) an invading army of Gauls had shattered the Romans at the River Allia north of the city, captured Rome, and exacted a heavy ransom (cf. note to ch. 3). It was after this disaster that Camillus had been recalled (ch. 3 and note).

51 *'you do not know how to use the victory!'*: this famous story has been widely disbelieved, as Cannae is over 300 miles from Rome and not even cavalry could have raced from one to the other in four or even five days (Maharbal says 'on the fifth day', *die quinto*)—yet Maharbal promises the banquet to Hannibal and the infantry by then. Yet the tale is at least as old as Cato the Censor's history (Cato had been born in 234), and all our versions insist on the same time-span. Possibly Maharbal's advice was really given after Trasimene in 217, for that region is four to five days' reasonable march by an army; then he repeated it after Cannae or, in later memories (even his

own?), it got transferred to the more crushing victory. Compare also 30.12 and note.

the salvation of the city and the empire: L.'s view is usually rejected by moderns, on the grounds that Hannibal could not have captured heavily fortified Rome, in any case had an exhausted army, and was therefore right to stay in southern Italy to consolidate his victory by winning over defecting Roman allies. Still, he could have done this as effectively, or more so, from outside Rome; and could have disrupted all Roman efforts at recovery by blockading the city. There were few Roman troops left to prevent him. The alarm he caused when he made his famous, but totally ineffective, march on Rome in 211 (see Book 25) suggests how much greater panic would have erupted in summer 216.

52 *300 quadrigati*: coins of silver worth two Greek drachmas each; equivalent to two *denarii*, the famous Roman silver coin introduced later in this war (23.15 note). Purchasing conditions differed from today, but the *denarius* was approximately worth £20–25 ($US30–40) in early twenty-first-century money and so a *quadrigatus* would be double that.

some 8,000 of his finest soldiers: Polybius' figures total 5,700, of whom 4,000 were Gauls (3.117). L. obviously prefers a more optimistic source.

53 *Publius Scipio, who was just a young man*: this is not young Scipio's first appearance in the story (see 21.46) but it is even more romanticized than the earlier one. The detail of the names does suggest that these tribunes were indeed at Canusium and it may also be true that they chose Scipio, now 20 years old, as unofficial leader; but the story looks very embroidered beyond that. Incidentally, L. later gives young Metellus' first name as Marcus (24.18).

54 *made them abandon Sicily and Sardinia*: L. knows perfectly well (21.1) that the peace of 241 did not require the Carthaginians to cede Sardinia, but he often lets rhetoric have its head (cf. 21.40). The 'tax-paying and tributary status' is likewise loaded language for the war-indemnity the Carthaginians had had to pay over ten years.

57 *charges of sexual misconduct*: the Vestal Virgins, the only Roman priestesses, were custodians of the sacred fire that guaranteed the existence of the city, so loss of a Vestal's virginity (or the quenching of the fire) sacrilegiously imperilled Rome itself. Cf. 28.11.

an end to their great disasters: Fabius Pictor was later the first Roman historian (see ch. 7 note). Sending embassies to consult the Delphic oracle was an old custom; L. tells of one sent by Tarquin the Proud, last king of Rome (1.56), and another in 398 (5.15–16).

the Books of Fate: the Sibylline oracles (see 21.62 note).

58 *a struggle for honour and power, he told them*: this statement is at odds with the popular Roman view of Hannibal as hater and would-be destroyer of Rome (cf. 21.43), but it sounds authentic, chiming as it does with the implications of his agreement the following year with King Philip V of

Macedon (see note to 23.33). Hannibal's effort to reach a settlement with the Romans directly after his greatest victory itself fits this address to his Roman captives. For the theme of honour and power, cf. 28.19 and note.

59 *to ransom prisoners of war*: ransoming prisoners was a standard feature of warfare up to modern times. The ransom paid to the Gauls who captured Rome in 390 is recorded with some embarrassment by L. and others— some claimed that the recalled hero Camillus (ch. 3 note) had arrived in the nick of time to cancel it. Tarentum, in 280, had called in King Pyrrhus of Epirus to aid it in its war with Rome.

61 *the following peoples defected to the Carthaginians*: L.'s list, for impressive- ness' sake, covers all those who defected from 215 to 212, save of course the Gaulsa who had gone over to Hannibal in 218 and, more oddly, the Campanians of Capua, Hannibal's most important gain. Their omission (though condoned in Dorey's edition of the text) is likely to be a later copyist's error. The Hirpini were one of the four Samnite cantons, along with the Caudini, Caraceni, and Pentri. Nor did all of Bruttium and Luca- nia join Hannibal. The notice given to the Uzentini is odd; Uzentum was a little town in the Sallentine peninsula, the heel of Italy, and presumably defected in 213 along with others even more obscure (L. 25.1). In late 213 and 212 so did Tarentum and Metapontum; Locri and Croton, like several towns in nearby Bruttium, had gone over to Hannibal as early as 215.

BOOK TWENTY-THREE

1 *a coastal city in his possession*: holding a port would greatly ease Hannibal's communications with Carthage (and Spain), a need all the more important as he was both the commander-in-chief of Carthage's operations and the leader of the governing group at home.

2 *a rogue, but not totally unscrupulous*: strangely for so powerful and estab- lished a leader as L. makes Pacuvius out to be, he never reappears after his city's change of alliance, though apparently he was among the leaders put to death after Capua surrendered to the Romans in 211 (see 26.27). He may have lost dominance to Vibius Virrius (ch. 6 below), who was still influential until Capua surrendered to the Romans in 211 (26.13–14). But the entire Pacuvius story may be a highly worked-up account, focusing exaggeratedly on only one out of several leaders (ch. 4 note).

3 *'People of Capua'*: the Latin actually says 'Campanians' or 'People of Campania' (*Campani*). Capua was the chief city of the region of Campania, around modern Naples, and often the term 'Campanian' is used specific- ally of the Capuans (as it is by Livy throughout this section). Where the reference is clearly to the people of Capua, I have used 'Capuan' rather than 'Campanian' (translator's note).

4 *everybody deferred to him*: Pacuvius' saving of the Capuan senators seems a very contrived story. To judge by it, Pacuvius had been the sole senator trusted by the Capuans, with few or no other senators as his allies—a very unlikely situation for a leading politician. It is worth noting how the

account of Pacuvius' intrigues and Capua's defection could almost fall into five sections like a play (chs. 2–3, 4–6, 7, 8–9, 10). Like some other episodes in L., for instance the memorable story of Lucretia's rape (1.57–60) and the tale of Sophoniba and Masinissa (30.12–15), it shows his strong feeling for dramatic scenes—and, perhaps, his use of actual Roman historical plays (*praetextae*) for inspiration, as T. P. Wiseman has suggested for other episodes.

5 *disdain for him and his plight*: this miserable performance by the defeated Varro continues L.'s hostile portrayal from Book 22. It is hardly compatible with the consul's continuing efforts to pull together the remnants of the army of Cannae, or his many responsible posts, by Senate appointment, in the years to come.

to feed on human flesh: a glancing allusion to an accusation that L. otherwise ignores. Polybius (9.24) tells a story of one of Hannibal's close friends, also named Hannibal but nicknamed 'the Gladiator' (Monomachus), warning him that the arduous march to Italy could succeed only if he accustomed the troops to cannibalism; but, Polybius adds, Hannibal refused to act on this. The story of Hannibal using a bridge of corpses to cross a torrential stream is widely told in later writers (e.g. Appian, *Hannibalica* 28), but L. alludes to it only via Varro, a clear sign that he does not believe it.

6 *about recording it as a fact*: L. reported the Latins' demand of 338 BC in 8.4–6, and his refusal to believe it of the Capuans is sound. See also ch. 22. 'In some sources' (*in quibusdam annalibus*) very likely means L. found the claim in later annalists like Quadrigarius and Antias.

7 *asphyxiation in the searing heat*: a very similar atrocity story in Cassius Dio's *History* (fragment 57.30) tells of Hannibal later treating the senators of nearby Nuceria thus. Both may be invented, or the Capua event may have been transferred by later writers to Nuceria, and Hannibal, as a piece of propaganda.

Marius Blosius: sometimes spelt Blossius; for the family, see note to 27.3.

10 *onto a ship and sent off to Carthage*: L. does not indicate where on the coast this usefully available ship was. Capua lay over 20 miles inland, and all the ports were in Roman allies' hands. Possibly there was a prearrangement with Carthage for ships to approach the coasts from time to time: cf. note to ch. 11.

Ptolemy in Alexandria: King Ptolemy IV Philopator (222–204 BC); Egypt was on friendly terms with both warring powers.

11 *the Bruttian and <. . .> communities*: Dorey believes the name of an Italian people has dropped out of the text at this point (translator's note).

his brother's exploits in Italy: how did Mago, in turn, find passage to Africa? With the Italian and also the Sicilian coasts hostile, ancient ships needing regular land-stops to resupply, and the Roman navy on patrol, it was quite risky. Mago probably embarked from a Bruttian or Apulian shore, and on a waiting Punic ship—another hint that Hannibal was keeping up contacts with home. Compare the arrangements for Philip V's envoys to Hannibal (chs. 33–4).

12 *Himilco*: this may have been Maharbal's father (cf. 21.12).

13 *and a dictator*: the text is corrupt at this point. Rather than 'dictator', probably a Carthaginian officer's name has been corrupted ('Hannibal son of Bomilcar'?—cf. ch. 49) as well as the amount of the silver. Probably a line in an early manuscript was omitted by oversight. In ch. 32, L. has Mago still at Carthage, and assembling now 13,500 troops, 20 elephants, and 1,000 talents for Italy. This must be from a different source, so the missing figure for silver here may not be '1,000' as sometimes suggested.

14 *in no sphere for which he was responsible*: a somewhat backhanded compliment for Varro.

to mount a horse: in archaic Rome the dictator led the infantry legion, and the master of horse (his subordinate) the cavalry. It had become normal for the dictator to seek this permission, as Fabius too had done (Plutarch, *Fabius* 4).

were all for change: see note to 24.2 on such claims.

15 *was sacked and put to the torch*: cf. note to ch. 7 above.

500 denarii: the *denarius* was not introduced until later in the war; L.'s source (or L.) may have used the term by mistake for *quadrigati* (on which see 22.52 note) or *victoriati*. The *victoriatus* was a silver coin, struck early in the war, worth half a *quadrigatus*; sometime around 215–213 it was replaced by the *denarius*, with the same value but on a more reliable standard.

16 *possibly the greatest of that war*: L. allows patriotic pride to sway him for a moment, despite just having indicated that even 2,800 alleged Punic dead was a clear exaggeration.

17 *with a few Romans and Latin allies*: L.'s phrasing is odd in relation to the 500 Praenestines, for Praeneste itself was a Latin town. He may mean that the other Latin allies were much fewer and from various towns.

massacred the town's population at night: not all, but probably those who showed pro-Carthaginian sympathies. Some at least of the townspeople were still there, holding out along with the garrison, the next spring (ch. 19).

18 *Isalca*: the Gaetulians were nomad Berber people of southern Tunisia and Algeria. This is their unit's only mention; probably they were part of the Numidian cavalry, for Isalca was a prefect *(praefectus)*, a cavalry officer.

a column of elephants in their way: all of Hannibal's elephants had now perished save one (22.2) and reinforcements were yet to arrive (ch. 41 below), so this 'column' looks like a later writer's fancy; possibly most of the details of the assaults, too. Whether Hannibal really had all these siege-machines is particularly questionable.

its former discipline: L.'s own account, not to mention those of other historians, gives the lie to this complacent but widespread claim. It may have arisen from rancour more at the faithless Capuans than at the invaders.

19 *in the temple of Fortune*: this temple at Praeneste (Palestrina), as rebuilt around 80 BC, remains one of the most grandiose architectural structures of the republican era.

22 *all mention . . . was stifled*: if so, one wonders how L. could have a record of it. Yet the report in itself seems plausible—it may even have inspired the less trustworthy story of the Latins in 338 demanding it (see note to ch. 6 above)—not to mention being eminently sensible. Fabius Pictor, a senator himself, may well be L.'s direct or indirect source.

Marcus Fabius Buteo: probably the oldest living ex-consul (having been consul in 245) as well as oldest ex-censor, and probably he had been the leader of the war embassy to Carthage in 218 (21.18 note).

23 *the civic crown*: one of the highest Roman honours, a wreath of oak-leaves awarded to a man who had saved a fellow citizen in battle.

26 *the Tartesii*: seemingly a Spanish people dwelling in the south-west of the peninsula; their name recalls that of legendary Tartessus (Tarshish in the Bible), famed for its precious metals, generally located in the Río Tinto area. Some scholars suppose 'Tartesii' to be Roman historians' mistake for Turdetani, but that was the general name for most of the peoples of the broad and fertile Baetis valley (see note to 21.6). Greek and Roman writers are all too often vague about Spanish names and places: thus L. in the next paragraph is uninterested in, or ignorant of, what 'city' the rebels were besieging. Ascua (ch. 27) must be one of the towns called Oscua or Osca in the River Baetis (Guadalquivir) region in Andalusia.

28 *Hibera*: probably Dertosa (modern Tortosa) near the mouth of the Ebro; in imperial times it bore the extra titles 'Hibera Iulia Ilercavonia' as it was chief town of the Ilercavonenses (cf. 22.21 note).

29 *were placed on the right wing, however*: possibly (but less likely), 'Those on the right wing, however, were not all Numidians; there were also those whose practice etc.' (so Jal, Budé edn. of Book 22, p. 49) (translator's note).

sacked the enemy camp: from L.'s description, the stages of the battle of Hibera look almost like Cannae's. The difference was that, even though the armies were equal in size and the Roman centre was surrounded by Hasdrubal's crack troops, these were beaten back, and his cavalry, soon routed, could not repeat the envelopment by Hannibal's cavalry which had decided Cannae.

30 *Petelia . . . in Bruttium*: first mentioned in ch. 20.

Croton: the operations around Croton, Locri, and Rhegium are reported more fully, and rather differently, in 24.1–3.

repeated three times: if some flaw occurred in these ritual games, the entire activity had to be repeated, as the gods would accept nothing flawed.

31 *Castra Claudiana*: a large fortified encampment established by Marcellus the previous year, on a westward spur of the Campanian mountains roughly halfway between Capua (to the west) and Nola to its east.

to be replaced by Quintus Fabius Maximus: either an example of Roman piety even in the midst of war and at the cost of a much-desired appointment (compare ch. 36); or, as many suspect, a cunning manipulation of religious forms by the long-serving augur Fabius to his own advantage.

32 *Porta Capena*: the Capena gate in the south-eastern city wall, close to the Circus Maximus.

Mago . . . sixty warships: see note to ch. 13 above.

33 *a treaty of friendship with the Carthaginian*: Polybius (7.9) quotes verbatim the Greek version, drafted by Hannibal in the form of a sacred oath. The contrast with L.'s summary is striking. Hannibal's text says nothing of Philip invading Italy, or of Italy and Rome becoming possessions of the Carthaginians, or of Hannibal and his forces then joining Philip as allies in Greece. In fact, it provides that, should the Romans *in future* make war again on either signatory, the other will assist against them: a plain sign that Hannibal expected the Roman state to survive and to act independently after the war. L. of course knew Polybius' account—but has chosen to follow a grotesquely inaccurate but patriotic rival version, no doubt Roman (Fabius Pictor's? a later annalist's?).

34 *Calvus*: Latin version of his nickname, 'the Bald'. Many Carthaginians had nicknames, as the range of names among the political elite was narrow.

35 *thirty-four military standards <. . .> were captured*: reading *capta sunt signa* (translator's note).

36 *not easy to obtain*: a striking example of Roman (and not least Fabius') punctiliousness in religious observance even in such a crisis.

37 *near Grumentum in Lucania*: Longus was the consul of 218 defeated at the Trebia. Hanno seems to be the one whom another writer (Appian) calls Hannibal's nephew and who had been the hero of the crossing of the Rhône (21.27). As an independent general he was less brilliant.

Vercellium, Vescellium, and Sicilinum: these places, like the three taken later by Fabius (ch. 39), were small; the correct name of the third was probably Vicilinum.

40 *the Pelliti-Sardinians*: 'skin-clad Sardinians', the hardy population of the mountainous interior.

42 *the following address to the Carthaginian*: the appeal of the Samnites to Hannibal, and his rather testy reply, encapsulate the difficulties that the Carthaginian leader faced despite his successes. His new Italian allies expected him to protect them, resented having to provide him with recruits, and found themselves being harried in his absence by the ever-growing Roman military forces in central and southern Italy. If he tried to protect all of them, he would fatally disperse his field forces; but if he failed to help, he risked losing them.

43 *the Hirpini and Samnites*: an odd expression, for both groups were Samnites (Hirpini and Caudini).

reinforcements . . . and a number of elephants: these must be the forces voted at Carthage (ch. 13).

46 *fewer than a thousand*: it is hard to treat this account of Marcellus' battle at Nola as accurate, consisting as it does of two sizeable speeches and only a fuzzily brief battle account. It, and perhaps the alleged previous day's fight, may be annalistic exaggeration of skirmishing sorties by Marcellus' men. But the 272 cavalry deserters from Hannibal look genuine, and possibly too his loss of six elephants (see 26.5 note).

spolia opima: the arms and armour taken by a general from the opposing general's body after slaying him in personal combat; Marcellus himself had won them against a Gallic king in northern Italy in 222. Here Vibellius Taurea is speaking metaphorically, for neither he nor Claudius Asellus held a command.

47 *passed down as a country proverb*: the sense of the proverb (in Latin: *minime, sis, cantherium in fossam*) is obscure. It seems to mean 'don't put your nag into a ditch' (Taurea describing his warhorse ironically), as such a confined spot would hamper a horse's movements.

49 *The scrupulousness with which the contracts were fulfilled*: L. later tells a quite different story about certain contractors (25.1, 3–4). Here he settles for the patriotic picture.

the operations in Spain that summer were far more impressive than those in Italy: again Livy's use of annalistic sources makes these hard to follow. The only Iliturgi known was in the far south, on the upper River Baetis, whereas Intibili lay about 20 miles south of Dertosa. So 'Iliturgi' is probably an error for a nearby town, perhaps Dertosa Ilercavonia (cf. ch. 28 note). The same sources also seem to have turned one moderate Roman victory into two shattering ones.

BOOK TWENTY-FOUR

1 *the Carthaginian Hamilcar*: though evidently a Carthaginian, he is mentioned only in this chapter. Why L. should take the trouble to term him a Carthaginian (*Poenus*) is not obvious; so some editors of the text attach the adjective to 'his cavalry'. But one feels a need for some term explaining Hamilcar; maybe L. termed him a 'Carthaginian officer' (*Poenus praefectus*) and the noun got overlooked by a later copyist.

clear unanimity: in 23.30, L. wrote briefly that 'the common people [had] been betrayed by the aristocrats' at Locri. This present account must draw on a different source, and L. presumably overlooks his earlier report.

and Locri Carthage: as with Capua, Hannibal bound himself to respect the independence of the city. Continuing control of their port assured the Locrians of its harbour-dues and returns from trade.

2 *infected all the city-states of Italy*: L. is still echoing his strongly opinion-ated source (it seems unlikely this was Polybius, though his account of these years is largely lost). The evidence for a sharp commons-vs.-aristocrats divide is far from being so clear-cut. If L. himself is to be believed, Capua was taken over to Hannibal's side by a combination of its leading aristocrat (who had ties to the Roman aristocracy: 23.2), aris-tocratic allies of his like Vibius Virrius, and the ordinary people. At Arpi in Apulia, which defected about the same time, the ordinary citizens were able to convince the Romans, when they retook it in 213, that the town's treachery had been due to its own aristocrats (ch. 47 below). Tarentum was to be betrayed to Hannibal in late 212 by a group of young nobles (25.7–10). The Samnites who defected are not reported as doing so against the wishes of their local notables either (cf. 23.1). In Etruria later in the war, it was again to be aristocrats who came under Roman suspicion (27.24, 29.36, 30.26). L.'s facile generalization has had the serious further consequence of encouraging many admirers of Han-nibal to judge him as promoting democracy in Italy, a quite inaccurate notion.

Roman dominance was less than three generations old over much of Italy, and even younger in the south. Discontent with its constraints and demands was natural from time to time, and could be expected at more than one level of society—especially when (after Cannae) it seemed to be leading nowhere save to disaster and when a self-proclaimed rescuer was at hand. (Etruscan cities, whatever their dissatisfactions, were much more circumspect because Hannibal was elsewhere.) This was also a signal for regional, and sometimes domestic, dissensions to break out: Trebii versus Mopsii at Compsa (23.1), Pacuvius Calavius and friends versus Decius Magius at Capua, the Bruttii thirsting for revenge—and loot—against Greek cities like Croton, Locri, and Rhegium, and even against their kinsmen of Petelia (23.20). But when it was all over and passions had calmed, later writers—most of them aristocrats or with aristocratic patrons—could easily slip into the comforting generalization that it had all been the common people's fault.

3 *the temple of Juno Lacinia*: this stood on Cape Lacinium, now Capo Colonna (one column of the temple survives there). See also 28.46.

Dionysius, tyrant of Sicily: in reality of Syracuse, ruling 405–367 BC, but he did extend his power over much of Sicily and parts of southern Italy. He took Croton in 379.

4 *Hieronymus*: son of the deceased Gelo (23.30). He was about 14 on his accession. L.'s narrative of Sicilian, and particularly Syracusan, affairs down to the Roman siege is remarkably detailed—almost too much so for a Roman history—and well balanced. Surviving extracts from Polybius show that L. used him as almost his exclusive source for the events, to the point of mere paraphrase at times, though typically he does add colour and moralizing in places: for instance, a more hostile depiction of the young king.

6 *a young nobleman, also called Hannibal*: perhaps Hannibal's close friend Hannibal 'the Gladiator' (on whom see 23.5 note).

   These two had been born in Carthage: L. thus interprets Polybius' statement (7.2) that Hippocrates and Epicydes 'had lived as citizens among the Carthaginians' or 'had adopted Carthage as their country'. Perhaps he modifies Polybius from some other account, as often.

7 *before help could be brought*: Hieronymus reigned for thirteen months (Polybius 7.7), so his assassination must date to 214, probably the summer as campaigning was about to start. L. includes it under 215 to make a single connected account of the reign.

   the right to vote first: it was chosen by lot to be the *praerogativa tribus*; see Glossary: 'tribes'. Fabius' intervention in these elections was altogether extraordinary, consul though he was—and all the more so as Otacilius was his own kinsman by marriage and was Marcellus' half-brother (Plutarch, *Marcellus* 2). L. tries to explain it favourably in ch. 9.

8 *Flamen of Quirinus*: later (29.11) Regillus is called Flamen of Mars; here, in a speech composed by L., 'Quirinus' is probably a slip.

9 *Marcellus for the third*: Fabius' re-election for 214 was the second irregular consular election in as many years: see 23.30 for the first. Otacilius' election to a second praetorship was plainly a consolation prize. Fabius' criticism of his handling of the fleet makes it surprising that this was entrusted to him once more—but Fabius had perhaps been disingenuous.

   Maximus Rullus: actually Quintus Fabius Maximus Rullianus, a noted ancestor of the Delayer and the first to bear the *cognomen* Maximus, five times consul between 322 and 295. The event mentioned is the war of 295 which resulted in a great victory at Sentinum, at the cost of Decius' life, over a coalition of Gauls, Etruscans, and Samnites. Lucius Papirius Cursor and Spurius Carvilius Maximus achieved great things as consuls together for the second time in 272.

10 *Vicus Insteius*: a street running up the western side of the Quirinal hill.

11 *eighteen legions*: eighteen legions of Romans and allies would amount to some 200,000 men; in fact the total was probably twenty legions (J. Lazenby, *Hannibal's War: A Military History* (Warminster, 1978), 100). The fleets must have required another 45,000–50,000 as crews. For an ancient state, even Rome, this was a gigantic military effort.

12 *ostensibly to offer sacrifice*: the deep and sulphurous crater-lake Avernus (Lago d'Averno), west of Naples, was believed to have one of the entrances to the underground world of the dead (most famously depicted in Virgil, *Aeneid* 6).

13 *than hope of taking the city*: it is noteworthy how often Hannibal failed in his efforts to capture cities and even small towns, even though supposedly he had siege equipment (23.17, 18, 37).

16 *a painting of that festive day*: L. seems to be describing the scene of festivities shown in this painting. Hanno's losses, however, must be seriously

exaggerated (something quite a few of L.'s sources were happy to do); he was active in Lucania later (ch. 20), although like Gracchus he may well have replenished his army with levies.

17 *sent for the propraetor Pomponius*: Pomponius was last reported as propraetor in Cisalpine Gaul (ch. 10) and he would end the year there (ch. 44). Probably another Pomponius is involved, perhaps as a legate, even if L. and his source failed to realize this; several—all named Pomponius Matho—were active in these years (22.35 note).

Battle . . . reprimand by the consul: whether this battle really happened, or is a much exaggerated version of a brief Roman sortie, is hard to determine. That Gaius Claudius Nero should be the officer supposedly sent out with a picked force to work round the enemy army and then attack it unexpectedly, only to fail in his assignment, might look like a hostile writer's parody of his famously successful manœuvre at the battle of the River Metaurus in 207 (27.48), but the point of so laboured an invention would be hard to see.

18 *More than 2,000 such names were found*: if accurate, a remarkable example of the administrative information available, through the periodic censuses, to Roman officials in the third century BC, even if bureaucratic limitations meant that still others were missed.

20 *from the rock*: a cliff on the south-west side of the Capitoline Hill, named the Tarpeian Rock after a legendary traitress. (Soon after Rome's foundation, a girl named Tarpeia had betrayed the Capitoline, its citadel, to enemies.) From it, traitors and murderers were thrown. The enemy prisoners would be sold as slaves.

21 *had secured the Island with armed guards*: the Island (Ortygia) was the original, and is the heart of the modern, city, with its citadel facing the mainland; the mainland comprised the suburbs of Achradina, Tycha, and Neapolis. The broad plateau beyond these was called Epipolae and was surrounded by a long wall; the Hexapylon ('six-door') gate was halfway along this wall's northern face (cf. 25.24), it seems, at the northern end of Viale Scala Greca, where the highway to Lentini slopes downhill out of the modern city.

23 *praetors*: L. uses Roman titles, as he and other Latin writers often do for foreign states. At Syracuse the title was 'generals' (*strategi*); the 'quaestor' would be the *tamias*, the finance magistrate.

24 *not dishonourable in Greek society*: at Rome the profession of actor was legally of ill-repute (*infamis*) and subject to restrictions, even though some actors attained high respectability.

26 *they fell lifeless to the ground*: L.'s vivid narrative of this frenzied slaughter of former rulers, including womenfolk, has affinities with Polybius' account of a coup and similar massacres at Alexandria in 202 after the death of Ptolemy IV (15.24a–36). Polybius is probably his source here, as he certainly is for the account of the ensuing siege (P. 8.3–7).

33 *the Olympium, a temple of Jupiter*: the ruined remnants of this temple stand about 4 miles south-west of Syracuse.

34 *Archimedes*: a native Syracusan, he was now about 73 years old.

35 *Himilco*: either another Punic officer of this name, or just possibly Hannibal's subordinate of 23.30, now on a new and independent mission (he is not heard of again in Italy). Heraclea Minoa lay more than 120 miles west of Cape Pachynus.

to meet any eventuality: Marcellus had two, or perhaps three, legions besieging Syracuse; he must have drawn off at least one, with some Italian allied contingents, in his effort to save Agrigentum, but these were too few against Himilco's powerful army. They were more than a match, though, for Hippocrates' 10,500.

36 *Panormus*: modern Palermo (this legion was numbered 'I'). It is hard to account for the legion disembarking at the diagonally opposite end of Sicily from its destination (the siege of Syracuse). An advance 'through the coastal areas' to Pachynum is equally baffling, whether L. means it went along the west and south coasts via Drepana, which was Roman-held, then past the Punic-held cities of Heraclea and Agrigentum (a needlessly risky route); or along the north-east and east coasts via Messana and Tauromenium (a peculiarly roundabout route). 'Panormus' may be a mistake for Phintias (Licata) on the south-east coast—for Himilco, already outside Syracuse, tried to intercept the legion. He must have expected it to be marching cross-country to join Marcellus, and not eastwards along the coast.

39 *an act . . . heinous, or necessary*: L. seems to think both, but is clearly embarrassed at the amorality of Pinarius' action; cf. the following paragraph.

40 *war with King Philip also broke out*: Philip's operations suggest that he meant to exploit the Romans' preoccupation with Hannibal to establish his own hegemony over Illyria and the Greek cities on the Adriatic east coast, rather than any idea of joining in the war as such. He was completely unprepared for the vigorous Roman response.

41 *routed huge forces of the Spaniards*: presumably the rebel Tartesii, last heard of in 215 when they 'did not long abide by the terms of surrender'; but no details are given (23.27). According to L., the Scipio brothers' response to this Punic victory in 214 was an advance into south-east Spain. But that almost certainly dates to 212. Were L. correct here, then the brothers' successful advance was followed by two years (213 and 212) of inactivity—as he asserts in 25.32—followed by a renewed southern push the year after. Yet this renewed push he narrates under the year 212 itself. Much more likely, L.'s chronology as well as his geography is confused. He or one of his sources may have misdated these events through wrongly inferring that the defeat of the Tartesii imperilled all the Roman alliances in southern Spain and so forced the Scipios to come south. There cannot, in reality, have been many (or any?) such alliances yet. L. optimistically depicted

much or most of the Spanish peoples as joining the Romans' side in 215 (23.29), and earlier supposed that Gnaeus Scipio had advanced briefly from the Ebro to the environs of Castulo in 217 (22.20 note), but none of this is plausible. The years 214–213 are much likelier to have been the inactive ones, followed by a drive south in 212 which L. has misdated to this point. His and his source's, or sources', indistinct awareness of Spanish geography has much to answer for.

41 *Mt. Victory*: these places seem to have lain in inland south-eastern Spain, beyond the vast and wild mountain ranges north-west of Cartagena and around the upper reaches of the River Baetis (Guadalquivir). L. mentions that Hamilcar had perished there on campaign in winter 229–228, and this is plausible (the problems with his present chronology do not affect it). The river may have been the Segura, probably the one in which Hamilcar was drowned.

Castulo: a wealthy silver-mining city close to modern Linares. The later epic poet Silius Italicus (*Punica* 3.97–107) names Hannibal's wife as Imilce and claims she was descended from a king named Milichus. These are Punic names, but 'Imilce' could reflect the Phoenician and Carthaginian cultural influences that L. implies. Iliturgi(s) (Mengíbar) was on the River Baetis 12 miles further south; Bigerra is not otherwise known.

42. *Munda*: the name must be incorrect, for the only Munda known lay inland from Málaga; but, as it happens, an obscure town named Unda or Undi stood near the upper Baetis (Pliny, *Natural History* 3.10). Here again L.'s annalistic sources, seconded by L. himself, seem to have made an uncritical guess about a place name which they did not recognize, just as some sources happily expanded alleged enemy losses.

Auringis: possibly an annalist's version of Aurgi (modern Jaén), as probably also is the Orongis of 28.3, for neither of L.'s place names is otherwise known and Aurgi would be in the right area.

But the Spanish people: most translators here take the Latin *gens* to refer to Hannibal's family, but see Weissenborn–Müller's note (translator's note).

seven years in enemy hands: L. puts Saguntum's restoration too in the year 214, but Saguntum had fallen five years before then, in 219. This is one of the clues that the Scipio brothers' campaign should in reality be dated to 212.

the Turdetani: more likely the Saguntines' neighbours the Turitani; see note to 21.6.

43 *prevented from performing the ceremony*: the *lustrum*, which was both a five-year period from one censorship to the next (see Glossary: 'censors') and, more precisely, the purification ceremony (*lustrum*) with which each pair of censors closed their magistracy. This was a sacred procession, with ritual implements, around the boundary of the city. It could not be held if one censor had died in office.

45 *he burned them alive*: it is hard to see why Hannibal should have been so

savage, unless it was to frighten other possible defectors; by contrast, it is easy to see why Roman propagandists might want to plant on him another atrocity story that could not be too readily checked (see 22.13 note).

47 *was razed to the ground*: fires were all too common in crowded cities, and Rome was particularly vulnerable. The Salinae was a space (originally for storing salt from Ostia's salt-pans) beside the Tiber at the foot of the Aventine Hill, and the Porta Carmentalis was near the river at the foot of the Capitol. Near this, below the Capitol, was the Aequimaelium (a stretch of open ground) and the Vicus Iugarius which linked the riverside to the Forum. The temples of Fortuna and Mater Matuta stood on the Sant' Omobono site close by. Beyond the gate lay the Campus Martius, then a broad meadowland still barely encroached on by buildings.

48 *to include Africa as well*: this development more likely dates to 212, like the events earlier discussed (ch. 41 note).

confined to horses: Numidia was a very large but thinly peopled region, extending over the coasts and mountains between Carthage's territories and Mauretania about 800 miles westward. It thus covered much of northern Algeria as well as north-western Tunisia. Its people formed a number of fluctuating kingdoms and were famous for their cavalry skills. Syphax was in the process of uniting them under one rule, which did not please some of his fellow kings.

Gala: thus L., but his name (known from Numidian inscriptions in Punic) was actually Gaia. The Maesuli, or Massyli, dwelt near the territories of Carthage, Syphax's people (Masaesuli/Massaesyli) further west.

49 *seventeen years old*: Masinissa died in 149 aged 90 or more (Polybius 37.10; Livy, *Epitome* 48), so in 213 he should have been about 27. 'Seventeen' is, all the same, L.'s intended figure, for he judges Masinissa's leadership qualities unusual for his age, and in Book 30, recording events a decade later, L. still depicts him as youthfully ardent. A copying slip—'XVII' misread for 'XXVII'—may have been in the text of L.'s source here, assuming he was following a Latin author like Coelius.

Carthaginian legions: as often, L. uses a Roman technical term for a foreign item (cf. ch. 23 for Syracusan 'praetors').

BOOK TWENTY-FIVE

1 *went over to him*: the Sallentine peninsula is the heel of Italy. The only city known to have defected is Uzentum (part of L.'s list in 22.61).

superstition . . . permeated the citizen body: L. has already commented caustically on this phenomenon (24.10), but now gives examples of it at some length; there is more in chs. 12–13. Roman authorities, and the educated elite, viewed unsupervised—especially ecstatic—religious practices with deep misgivings. The strains of war, and later the widening contacts with the Mediterranean world, encouraged a steady stream of new cults; L. records an officially sanctioned example in 29.10 and 14, and for a famous furore in 186 BC over a new religion see 39.8–20.

2 *legal age to seek office*: Scipio was born in 235 or maybe 236. There was a convention that a man did not seek office until he had served ten campaigns, starting from the age of 16 or 17.

with a single day's repetition: see 23.30 note.

3 *separate portfolios*: this was the norm (one praetor for each), but the state of the war required as many praetors as possible to serve as field commanders.

twenty-three: the size of forces in the field was steadily growing; L. seems to omit the two legions of slave volunteers again, which would make the real number twenty-five—a total of at least 75,000 Roman citizens in arms (and this only if many legions were under strength) and as many or more Latins and Italian allies. There were 30,000–40,000 men (mostly allies) in the fleets as well. With half of southern Italy on Hannibal's side, the pressure on the remaining Roman and allied manpower was immense.

Pyrgi: a small seaport on the Etruscan coast, not far north of Rome.

They would put . . . than they really were: this revelation of some tax-collectors' skulduggery, and the support they received from other collectors (ch. 4), comes as a surprise after the glowing words about the scrupulous honesty of the tax companies in 23.49. It may well be that L. had not yet come across this episode when he was researching for Book 23.

4 *Most simply went into exile*: exile, by which a citizen lost his citizenship, was the legal equivalent of capital punishment and was often resorted to by offenders, but (as L. implies) it was hardly a satisfactory penalty for serious crimes.

5 *Publius Cornelius Calussa*: *pontifex maximus* around 332 BC. Crassus proved an outstanding *pontifex maximus*.

two triumviral boards were established: a triumviral board was simply a board, or commission, of three men set up for a specific task. The term was adopted by Mark Antony, Octavian, and Lepidus in 43 BC to cover their dictatorial control of the state.

6 *members of the Senate?*: L.'s rhetorical bent leads him to direct nearly all the rest of this speech, not to Marcellus, but to the Senate far away in Rome. He is thinking, of course, of it being read out via Marcellus' despatch to the house.

the Caudine Forks: in 321, a Roman army invading mountainous Samnium had been bottled up in an enclosed plain and forced to capitulate (see Livy 9.1–11 for the story). On the Allia, see 22.50 note.

7 *the fire of the previous year*: see 24.47 and note.

Hall of Liberty: attached to the Temple of Liberty on the Aventine hill (cf. 24.16). The rock shortly afterwards mentioned was the Tarpeian Rock (see 24.20 note).

9 *fourth watch of the night*: roughly between 3 and 6 a.m.

The Roman commander's reaction: one Marcus Livius (24.20, 26.39). At no point in his account of the capture, though, does Livy mention this incompetent's name.

11 *an earthwork was erected behind it*: so Nicolet-Croizat suggests in the Budé edition, rather than the alternative 'inside it'. Nicolet-Croizat cites Polybius' description of the defence works (8.33.1–6) (translator's note).

from Metapontum: these forces came by sea, as Polybius states (8.34); L., as often, follows his account closely though omitting some details and, conversely, adding a few from other sources.

most . . . place it in this year: the capture of Tarentum is indeed best dated to early 212, perhaps March or April; a less likely alternative is near the end of 213.

12 *the prophecies of Marcius*: see note to ch. 1 above. Marcius, who evidently lived before this time, was a famous soothsayer mentioned also by Cicero (e.g. *De divinatione* 1.89, giving him a brother as well), Pliny the Elder (*Natural History* 7.119), and Macrobius (*Saturnalia* 1.17).

the River Canna: no such river is known, but (as L. implies) believers assumed the seer meant the Aufidus and the battle of Cannae.

the tumour: reading *vomicam* (translator's note).

after the Greek manner: with the head uncovered (the only detail known).

13 *from seeding their fields*: in contrast to what was done in 215 (23.48). The pressure was being increased on Capua.

had fallen by sortition: in ch. 3, L. stated that both consuls had been assigned to the front against Hannibal; and he shows them now operating jointly near Bovianum in Samnium, across the mountains from Capua. So either L. changes to a different source here, or he thinks that the consuls themselves now drew lots to decide who should move into Campania. The latter seems rather likelier.

Hanno's quaestor: another use of a Roman term; presumably Hanno's quartermaster.

14 *Paelignian cohort*: an allied unit from central Italy.

the first centurion of the principes: centurion of the first maniple of the *principes* of a legion (see Glossary: 'legion').

15 *Mago*: not Hannibal's brother, who was in Spain, but his good friend Mago 'the Samnite' (cf. ch. 16 below; he is described by Polybius, 9.25).

to some ships on the shore: this recalls the similar escape, by the townfolks' good graces, of Lucius Atilius from Locri in 215 (24.1).

17 *met his end*: the story of Gracchus' death by the treachery of the outwardly loyal Flavus is widely told (the post-Livian sources probably draw on L.) and was also Polybius' version as a fragment shows (P. 8.35.1). It may come from a pro-Carthaginian writer like Silenus or Sosylus, who were with Hannibal on campaign, for it includes the report of Hannibal's full-scale

funeral for the fallen Roman leader. The less flattering account of how Gracchus died (ch. 17) is still compatible with treachery.

18 *strong ties of hospitality*: on such ties, cf. 23.4 and 46. This Crispinus was not the officer under Marcellus' command in Sicily (24.39)—he was still there (ch. 26 below)—but perhaps was his son. The officer in Sicily, who became consul in 208, must be the older man. This hospitality-bond, as often, probably bound the two families into a whole.

19 *the initial cavalry attack*: this fight is doubted by some scholars, but it seems too inconsequential to have been worth some annalist's inventing. More likely a skirmish is all that occurred.

perished ... by one means or other: another item often doubted, partly because it seems strange for so substantial a force to have been entrusted to a centurion, partly because the name Centenius was also that of the cavalry officer whose force had been destroyed after Trasimene by Hannibal (22.8). But some other such corps are heard of in southern Italy during the war, e.g. Pomponius Veientanus' (ch. 1 above) and another in 209 (27.12 and 17). None enjoyed much success. Hannibal may not have been led astray by Appius Claudius as thoroughly as L. supposes: he took the opportunity to annihilate Paenula.

21 *not more than 2,000 got away*: this first battle of Herdonea, too, is rejected by some scholars as improbable or even invented. But it is hard to see why Roman sources would invent a Roman disaster; and, if pro-Carthaginian writers did so and were the only ones to tell of it, why L. would accept it— or how such sources would know the details of the later successful prosecution of the defeated praetor (26.2–3). All the same, the victory did Hannibal little good.

22 *written orders from the praetor Publius Cornelius*: Cornelius must have been transmitting an order from the Senate; as a praetor he could not himself issue one to the consuls, who held superior *imperium*.

before 15 March: it was now the second half of the year, so this seems rather a long interval of grace; but there is no basis for emending the text.

23 *the Aetolians*: on this powerful Greek state see note to 26.24.

Galeagra: at a small cove, now Santa Panágia, on the coast just north of, and below, Epipolae not far from the Hexapylon gate.

Diana: in Greek she is Artemis; Livy gives the Roman equivalent.

24 *Nassos*: local form of Greek *nesos*, 'island' (its formal name was Ortygia). Later L. seems to Latinize the word to 'Nassus'.

He was reminded ... ablaze and reduced to ashes: Marcellus was recalling the great Athenian siege of Syracuse (415–413 BC), under two generals, which had ended in the annihilation of the besiegers at sea and on land (Thucydides, books 6–7). The tyrant Dionysius I had made Syracuse a major power and so it had remained until the First Punic War. The motif of generals weeping at the prospect of slaughter and destruction is recurrent: supposedly Xerxes did so when reviewing his expeditionary forces in

480 (Herodotus 7.45–6) and Scipio Aemilianus, destroying Carthage in 146, wept at the thought that the same fate might befall Rome (Polybius 38.21–2).

25 *interconnected house-walls*: the Latin text is uncertain, but, as the army was now at the walls around Neapolis and Tycha, perhaps it or part of it was quartered in suburbs or buildings just outside.

27 *had taken over* <. . .>: at least two names are missing from the manuscripts. One such village was probably Dascon, on the shore of the Great Harbour south of Syracuse; the other perhaps the little town of Bidis (cf. Cicero, *Against Verres II* 2.53–60). The forces holding them are not mentioned again, and probably fled after Syracuse fell.

a hundred and thirty warships and seven hundred freighters: this was the largest fleet put to sea by Carthage during the war. Its miserable performance was typical of her naval effort in the conflict.

28 *the Sicilian camp*: this must mean the forces at the villages just outside Syracuse (ch. 27).

freed from a high-handed tyranny <. . .>: there is another lacuna in the text at this point.

30 *the Arethusa fountain*: this still rises in the southern sector of the Island (Nassos). L. visualizes it in Achradina on the mainland—plainly he had never visited Syracuse—but this must be a misunderstanding, and his own narrative eventually sets the record straight. In myth, the nymph Arethusa fled to Sicily to escape the amorous river-god Alpheus, and was transformed into this fountain.

32 *after leaving their winter quarters*: L. records these Spanish events under the year 212, but his account of the Scipio brothers' earlier activities in the south, supposedly in 214, is almost certainly misdated from 212 (see notes to 24.41–2). In ch. 36 below he dates the brothers' disaster, in this new campaign, to 'the eighth year' since Gnaeus' arrival (cf. ch. 38 also), thus to 211. It is likely that the Scipios had wintered in southern Spain after their earlier campaign in 212 (as Appian states, naming Castulo as one of their bases: *Iberica* 16). If so, it was the two years 214–213 that had seen 'no significant development'.

Amtorgis: an unknown name; perhaps an error for Iliturgi(s) (Mengíbar) on the upper Baetis, or for another town, in Roman times called Iliturgicola, known to have lain nearby. A Greek source, perhaps even Silenus or Sosylus, may well have been one of those consulted by L. or by his own source. The Greek letters for ILIT- could be miscopied as AMT- while the form *-urgi(s)/orgis* was variable in renditions of Spanish place names.

33 *Roman commanders will always have to be circumspect in this regard*: this piece of sententiousness from L.'s armchair he may really owe to Polybius; the latter's account of these events does not survive, but he regularly offers helpful object lessons of this and many other kinds to readers.

34 *with 7,500 Suessetani*: Indibilis, former ruler of the Ilergetes in northern

Spain, is here reported leading a corps from their neighbours the Suessetani; L. does not explain why.

36 *twenty-ninth day after his brother's death*: this chronological item is plausible. The eighth year since Gnaeus' arrival in 218 BC would be 211: see notes to ch. 32 and to 24.41. If he and his army were crushed four weeks after Publius (a chronology reiterated in 26.18), the events in ch. 35 cannot have happened as swiftly as L. suggests in his narrative—the two Roman armies must have been far apart, and the Carthaginians' pursuit of Gnaeus must have lasted several days, not just one or two. L. preserves the chronological data (which he may have found in Polybius or even Fabius Pictor) while lavishing much more attention and empathy on the dramatic features of the brothers' catastrophes. Their error in dividing their forces in the face of three Punic armies is ignored.

Gnaeus' disaster can plausibly be located in the region around Castulo (Linares); Publius' somewhere to the west in Andalusia. With the disaster Pliny the Elder associates a town Ilorci, which stood not far from the upper Baetis (*Natural History* 3.9) and is probably identical with the 'Ilurgia' later punished for its treachery to survivors of Gnaeus' army (28.19 and note).

37 *the town-garrisons*: the first and only mention of these.

camp . . . north of the Ebro: L. fails to mention (or realize?) that, if this camp is factual, the survivors of the two disasters must have retreated from eastern Andalusia across hundreds of miles back to north-east Spain—a remarkable achievement by them, and a no less remarkable indicator of how sluggishly the Carthaginian generals handled their victory. L.'s account of how the surviving Romans repelled the enemy's attack is, at best, heavily embroidered for patriotic effect (see note below).

39 *two enemy camps were attacked*: this story of the Roman survivors decisively turning the tables on their foes must be plain invention, with some borrowing from Scipio Africanus' destruction—by night again—of two enemy camps outside Utica in 203 (cf. 30.5–6).

Claudius: this translator-historian, mentioned also in 35.14, is not otherwise known (he was not Claudius Quadrigarius); see note to 29.22.

who counterattacked from his camp: the Latin is unclear as to who actually made the counterattack. It could possibly have been Marcius (counterattacking from the first camp when Hasdrubal appeared on scene) (translator's note).

Piso: as an annalistic historian writing about eighty years after the war, he may have some better reliability if he recorded simply a victorious Roman ambush, though his 5,000 enemy dead still look exaggerated. These Roman claims presumably arose from the fact that the survivors did make it back to the Ebro, and from Roman writers' wish to palliate somehow the extent of the Scipios' disaster. But the Carthaginians' sluggish follow-up seriously limited the disaster's benefit to them.

40 *things sacred and profane*: L. bases his comments on similar (much longer) reflections by Polybius (9.10). Polybius judges the transfer of art works to Rome a political, rather than a moral, miscalculation. But Roman writers and thinkers, at least as early as Cato the Censor, were gravely exercised about their fellow citizens' moral slide from primeval rugged virtue, a slide so far gone by L.'s own day—so he declares in his 'Preface'—that 'we can bear neither our vices nor the remedies for them'. Opinions varied over when it began: another favoured date was 187 (booty from Asia Minor), but the favourite was 146 (after the sack of Carthage). Significantly, in all these cases the ensuing moral atrophy was ascribed to massive quantities of corrupting war-booty. Admiring works of art was a particularly degenerate habit (cf. the pained remarks of Sallust, *Catiline* 11).

of Libyphoenician nationality: Hippacra, later named Hippo Diarrhytus, is modern Bizerte on the coast 40 miles north of Tunis. 'Libyphoenicians' were a mixed group in the North African population, through intermarriage between Carthaginians and native 'Libyans'. It was highly unusual for a non-Carthaginian officer to hold authority equal or superior to Carthaginian commanders, and when it happened it could arouse jealousy. Xanthippus the Spartan, whose generalship saved Carthage from the invading Romans in 255, soon afterwards found it politic to depart elsewhere.

41 *6,000*: a conjectural figure, as a numeral is missing from the manuscripts.

if he saw fit: see 26.16 note on this standard formula (*si ei videretur* or, at times, *si ita videretur*).

BOOK TWENTY-SIX

1 *refused to grant discharge*: see 24.18, 25.5–7.

twenty-three Roman legions: L.'s breakdown involves only thirteen, while modern calculations give a total of twenty-one rather than twenty-three.

2 *At the beginning of the year*: L.'s year is 211, but the events concerning the Spanish command really occurred in 210: see notes to 24.41–2, 25.32.

'From the propraetor to the Senate': a propraetor was, properly, an ex-praetor whose *imperium* had been extended by the Senate after his year in office expired (see Glossary: 'magistrates'). The Senate's almost too lively sensitiveness to protocol is clearly illustrated; nor did it thank Marcius for his outstanding services to the republic—contrast the thanks to Varro after Cannae (22.61).

losing his army in Apulia: the technical term was *perduellio*, treachery in time of war; L. uses it in ch. 3 ('treason').

4 *light infantry amongst the legions*: the light infantry (*velites*) already existed (the 'skirmishers' of 21.55). Navius' innovation was, it seems, to have skirmishers mount up with cavalrymen as occasion demanded; L., no military expert, slightly misunderstands this.

5 *thirty-three elephants*: Polybius, here extant (9.3), does not mention elephants in Hannibal's subsequent actions. This need not mean they were invented by later writers; Polybius also ignores the presence of a much more important figure, Fulvius Flaccus. Bomilcar had brought forty elephants in 215 (23.13 and 41); six may afterwards have been lost (23.46 and note). A seventh might have been lost, or incapacitated, by 211. L.'s emphasis on Hannibal's speed can be judged merely relative.

he took . . . Calatia: surprising, for this town, west of Capua, near modern Maddaloni, had joined his side after Cannae (22.61). The manuscripts read *Galatiam*, but no such place is known around Capua.

6 *nothing like as momentous*: Polybius (9.3) narrates Hannibal strenuously but unsuccessfully assaulting the Romans' outer siege-lines, much like L.'s first version, but has no Capuan sortie or combat details. Appian (*Hannibalica* 38) echoes Polybius in even vaguer terms, but later (*Hann.* 41) has elephants and Latin-speaking troops unsuccessfully attacking Fulvius Flaccus' camp during Hannibal's return from the march on Rome: a fairly typical Appianic muddle. L.'s details of the fighting look broadly trustworthy, if exaggerated—especially the enemy's casualty counts, always optimistic in annalists.

then being a minor: or, possibly, 'without a father' (translator's note).

8 *a dispatch to the Senate in Rome*: Polybius by contrast (9.5) has Hannibal appear unexpectedly outside the city, causing general panic; this seems improbable. Hannibal allowed up to ten days for his march (ch. 7) and, even if L. is wrong about Flaccus' despatch, communities along and near Hannibal's route must have sent word ahead, as Fregellae supposedly did (ch. 9). Polybius' account dramatizes the elements of unexpectedness and coincidence (cf. next note); it need not be accepted uncritically.

crossed the Volturnus with about 15,000 infantry and 1,000 cavalry: whether this is factual is much debated, for Polybius continues to ignore the existence of Fulvius Flaccus. As he tells it (9.6–7), the consuls just happened to be enrolling two legions at this time, and they conducted the defence. L. obviously prefers the more dramatic version of Flaccus marching with might and main to save Rome, but it need not be pure fiction. Could the Senate and consuls feel secure that recruits just coming in would withstand Hannibal on their own? Besides, Flaccus surely sent word as soon as he learned of Hannibal's plan, or at least departure. He and Appius Claudius may indeed have been ordered to detach a force to Rome if at all possible. But it remains uncertain when this order reached them, and whether Flaccus did then march all the way to Rome—or turn back en route if, for instance, he learned of Hannibal's retreat. If the latter, it was a detail quickly lost in the various tellings.

9 *to retard his progress*: L. describes the route along the Via Latina, one of the great highways between Rome and the south. Coelius reported a different route (ch. 11 and note).

on a par with that of the consuls: another carefully recorded example of constitutional niceties. Ordinarily, a proconsul or propraetor forfeited his *imperium* if he crossed the sacred boundary (*pomerium*) of the city.

10 *Porta Esquilina and the Porta Collina*: the Esquiline and Colline gates were in the eastern and northern sectors, respectively, of the city wall. The areas outside the wall on these sides were relatively open ground at this time, though built over in later ages.

Clivus Publicius: a street crossing the Aventine Hill north-westwards and coming down (*clivus* means 'slope') to the Forum Boarium, site of the famous round temple, near the Tiber.

11 *bright and tranquil weather*: these thwarted battles must be suspect, but the Roman troops did march out of the city and fortify a camp (Polybius 9.6–7).

According to Coelius . . . from the city: Coelius' route is commonly accepted by scholars, because Polybius writes of Hannibal marching 'through Samnium' (9.5) and—although the communities mentioned by Coelius were not Samnites—Polybius' phrase would fit it better. Yet Coelius' route is astoundingly zigzag: first northward, skirting the Monte Matese massif, next through the central Italian valleys almost up to the Gran Sasso mountains, then westwards and finally southwards. Following this route, Hannibal could have no hope either of achieving a surprise arrival or, worse, of outdistancing possible reinforcements from Capua to the city. A retreat that way, on the other hand, lessened the risk of the Romans attempting to cut him off, or catching up with him.

12 *the suddenness of his appearance*: most of southern Italy was held by Hannibal's garrisons or allies, so an unexpected arrival outside Rhegium (the one major place not so held) is easier to account for than one outside Rome. Yet such a march will have taken weeks, for Rhegium (Reggio) lies some 420 miles from Rome. Hannibal in effect consigned Capua to its fate, as the letter from his officers there bitterly pointed out; we can accept its authenticity.

13 *razed to its foundations*: Alba, the city in Latium traditionally founded by Aeneas and ruled over by his descendants, fell fatally foul of the third king of Rome, Tullus Hostilius, in the seventh century BC.

15 *the chief magistrate*: literally 'the Sidicinian magistrate' (*magistratum Sidicinum*), the Sidicini being the people whose chief city was Teanum.

placed it unopened in the breast fold of his robe: Flaminius, who had similarly ignored a Senate decree in 223 when recalled before a battle in north Italy, was virulently attacked for it, a hostility L. plainly shares (21.63 and note). Fulvius Flaccus, a successful hero, gets much milder treatment.

Taurea Vibellius, a Capuan citizen: the braggart cavalier last heard of in 215 (23.46–7).

16 *if the proconsul sees fit*: the standard formula used by the Senate in instructing magistrates and promagistrates (also in 22.33, 25.41, 29.24, 43.14, and

elsewhere). Fulvius treated the formula literally as giving him the decision, whereas in practice it was meant simply as a courtesy.

laudable in every respect: L.'s detailed report of the punishment of Capua is followed later by a second one, still more detailed and differing on various items, which he dates to the following year 210 (chs. 33–4). Not all Capuan citizens, for example, were in fact enslaved.

17 *assigning troops to Gaius Nero*: Gaius Claudius Nero, last heard of in Campania the previous year (25.22). His activities more likely belong to 210, as the disaster to the Scipios should be dated to 211.

between the towns of Iliturgi and Mentisa: more annalistic confusion over Spanish geography. Nero's advance was southwards, whereas the Ausetani dwelt near the Pyrenees and had no places called Iliturgis or Mentisa. Very likely 'Ausetani' is a mistake for the Oretani, who dwelt between the Baetis and Anas rivers, and whose towns included Mentisa (21.11 note). Iliturgi(s) on the Baetis was not Oretanian, but here it could be a mistake for Ilugo, north of Castulo, which was. If so, Nero must have marched far into southern Spain to confront the Carthaginians. A nugget of truth may be concealed—a flying raid into the south by Nero, perhaps via the restored Saguntum.

the Punic trickery: this tale of Carthaginian cleverness outwitting Roman ingenuousness is improbable at best, and at worst may be invented. Yet the otherwise unknown name Black Rocks could be genuine; an inventor would more likely use a name he and his readers already knew.

18 *announced a date for that election*: another unconventional measure, comparable to the people's electing Fabius as dictator in 217 and Minucius later as co-dictator. Its outcome, the election of a 24-year-old junior senator to a major proconsular command, proved to be the turning point of the Second Punic War. L. dramatizes suitably.

19 *showcasing them*: L. draws partly on Polybius (10.2–5) for this account, but, as often, uses only some of his details while adding others, like Scipio's rumoured divine origin. Like Polybius, L. underlines both Scipio's charisma and the careful calculatedness that underlay it.

his adoption of the toga virilis: the adult *toga* was ceremonially put on when a boy turned 16.

gave the state the confidence: it is hardly likely that one reason for people choosing Scipio was a belief that his real father was a god. Polybius, who knew the family personally, more prosaically writes of Scipio's ability to convince others that his *plans* were divinely inspired (10.2, 5, 9); and of course he says nothing about divine parentage, a tale L. himself disdains. It was in fact a very much later—first-century BC—addition to the Scipio legend. Why does the sceptical L. bring it into his narrative? For literary effect: it adds colour both to the picture of religious fervour which he has more than once stressed (25.1 and 12) and also—even if he himself sees it as spurious colour—to his introductory pen-portrait of one of Rome's greatest leaders.

also derive from Phocaea: Phocaea, a Greek town in Asia Minor on the Aegean Sea, had sent out colonists to the western Mediterranean centuries earlier; Scipio's route took in Massilia, as the escort of Massiliot ships shows, and it was the most famous such colony.

20 *The Carthaginians . . . wintering in the neighbourhood of Saguntum*: here there is a startling contrast with Polybius' account (10.7). He locates Hasdrubal son of Gisgo near the mouth of the River Tagus (i.e. by the Atlantic Ocean); Mago in the far south-west of the peninsula; and Hannibal's brother Hasdrubal besieging 'some city' among the Carpetani, i.e. in Castile. L.'s location for the first Hasdrubal is—very roughly—near where Polybius puts Mago, but the other locations are irreconcilable. Possibly 'Saguntum' in L. is an error by him, or a source, for Segontia (a stronghold in central Spain): this would make his location for the other Hasdrubal compatible with Polybius'. Possibly too, the other two Punic armies moved around during winter trying to keep troops and animals properly supplied, and L. may reflect locations found in a different source. As often, when diverging from Polybius he does not indicate why he prefers an alternative.

21 *temple of Bellona*: at the foot of the Capitoline hill, near the later Theatre of Marcellus. Bellona was the goddess of war; her temple stood just outside the city boundary (*pomerium*), a convenient venue for meeting with promagistrates, whose *imperium* would lapse within the *pomerium*.

a triumph on the Alban Mount: this could be celebrated, unofficially, by a general who was denied, or not entitled to, a formal triumph in the city.

Murgentia: this town, also spelled Murgantia, lies inland at modern Serra Orlando between Catania and Enna.

22 *the voting enclosure*: this area of the Campus Martius was termed 'the Sheepfold' (*Ovile*), presumably a memory of the site's original use; rebuilt under Augustus as the Saepta Iulia (with the Pantheon alongside).

the one that voted first: this was the *centuria praerogativa*; see Glossary: 'centuries'. Another result of Torquatus' self-denial was that the hapless T. Otacilius, formerly denied a consulship due to his kinsman Fabius the Delayer's intervention (24.7–9), was yet again thwarted.

slight and ineffectual: an illuminating outburst by L., revealing both his sentimental admiration for the virtuous Rome of old and his conservative temperament's dissatisfaction at the disrespectful ways of modern youth.

23 *Cincius Alimentus*: praetor in 208, later a prisoner of Hannibal (cf. 21.38) and historian of Rome.

Forum Subertanum: a little Etruscan town (modern Suvereto, inland from Piombino?); cf. Pliny, *Natural History* 3.52. L.'s text may really mean 'in the forum of Subertum'.

the nine-day rite: showers of stones, and there were a lot of them in this war (e.g. 21.62, 23.31, 27.37), called for this particular ritual.

oversight in placing the entrails: the Flamen of Jupiter (*F. Dialis*) was

attended by a large and varied roster of ritual requirements and constraints. The rite involving a sacrificial animal's entrails was elaborate; to
get any of it wrong showed that the Flamen no longer enjoyed Jupiter's
favour.

24 *Marcus Valerius Laevinus . . . discuss the matter*: the Aetolian League was a
federal state in north-west Greece, formed during the previous century.
The Aetolians were aggressive, enthusiastic for plunder, and often at odds
with their neighbours, especially Macedon to their north and the Achaean
League (Polybius' homeland) in the Peloponnese. The Romans wanted
them as allies to counter Philip V's alliance with Hannibal.

they were copied . . . to witness them: part of the Greek text of this treaty,
Rome's first with a Greek state, survives in a damaged inscription. It
deals chiefly with how to treat cities that surrendered to the Romans and
Aetolians, and so corresponds roughly to L.'s third treaty-paragraph but
with several differences of detail. A fragmentary reference at its end to 'the
peace' may, in turn, correspond to the fourth paragraph. Possibly L.
includes items from Laevinus' original understanding with the Aetolians
that were omitted from the final version; but his performance with better-
attested treaties (cf. 23.33 and note) may point to his using a garbled source
for this one. Polybius' report of the treaty has not survived.

Nassus: Acarnanian Nassus should not be confused with the Nassos, or
Island, that formed the oldest part of the city of Syracuse (see 25.24 note).

25 *Perseus*: not Philip's son (born in 212) who succeeded him as king in 179,
but a Macedonian general.

Thrace: this country covered roughly the area of modern Bulgaria; its
peoples were warlike and still largely untouched by Greek civilization. The
Maedi, in the middle and upper valley of the River Strymon (Struma),
were still giving trouble to Macedonia's Roman rulers in 120 BC. Perhaps
the most serious difficulty for every Macedonian king was that he was
chief general as well as ruler, and virtually every military frontier claimed
his personal attention (often simultaneously).

27 *the night preceding the Quinquatrus*: 18 March, for this festival in honour of
Minerva was celebrated on the 19th (later it ran to several days).

the Quarries district . . . and the Royal Atrium: these sites and buildings were
in and around the northern part of the forum; for the bankers' establishments cf. ch. 11. The fire of 213 had been by the Tiber just to the west of
this (24.47).

destiny's pledge of Roman imperial power: the Palladium, an immemorially
ancient sacred image of Pallas Athena, believed to have been brought from
Troy to Italy by Aeneas and then lodged at Rome as a guarantee of the
city's integrity.

31 *brought against me personally*: reading *ut si de meo* (omitting Walsh's
addition of <*velut*>) (translator's note).

33 *had long enjoyed*: see 23.2 for examples.

the Satrican case: in 319 Satricum, in the River Liris valley near modern Frosinone, had been punished for defecting from its Roman alliance; interestingly, L.'s account of this (9.16) does not mention Antistius' intervention.

Sabatum: unknown but presumably another satellite town of Capua.

Our wish and command: cf. 21.17 for this formula, used in enactments of the people. L.'s very detailed account here ignores his earlier report (ch. 16) of the decisions supposedly made the year before. The simplest explanation, though not the only one possible, is that he has uncritically drawn on two sources: one dating the decisions to 211 and presenting them in the harshest light (perhaps with the implacable consul of 211, Fulvius Flaccus, in mind), the other recording them in 210 and offering a text of the Senate's decrees. The fuller details here *may* indicate they are reasonably trustworthy. A rather less likely explanation might be that these decrees superseded a harsher set of decisions that Flaccus had previously instigated.

34 *individual Capuan households*: the context implies this affected those of high status.

beyond a certain date: this proviso seems not to have been rigorously enforced. Some decades later, in 188, Capua and its satellite towns were restored to citizen status (L. 38.28 and 36).

Veii, Sutrium, or Nepete: towns in southern Etruria not far from Rome.

35 *came up for discussion*: for an earlier expedient to fund naval crews, see 24.11. It had either been discontinued or now had to be supplemented further. These new contributions were repaid in instalments between 204 and 202 (29.16).

picked on the common folk of Rome: not very plausible, even if good populist rhetoric. The complainants owned or had owned slaves and silver- or bronzeware; this suggests fairly sizeable property. Moreover, the damage done by Hannibal outside Rome in a few days' raiding cannot have been total, and this was the only time an enemy army came within 100 miles of the city.

36 *bulla*: a Roman child wore a leather or metal locket round the neck until the age of manhood at 16, or, for girls, the age of marriage. It contained an amulet with religious properties.

treasury officials: the *triumviri mensarii*, the special board created in 215 (23.21) to superintend the state's war-finances.

39 *Sybaris*: this city had been destroyed by Croton in 510 BC, and in 443 Thurii had been founded nearby; L. or his source, maybe for sentimental reasons, uses the old name for the newer.

to stow the rigging: ancient sea battles involved manœuvring the ships using oars, so sailing tackle had to be taken down and stowed when a battle loomed (cf. 21.49).

40 *farming the land*: Laevinus' measures and the restoration of peace had long-lasting beneficial effects on Sicily, which suffered no more disturbances until the slave revolts of the 130s BC.

Agathyrna: a town on the north coast of Sicily, east of Cephaloedium (modern Cefalù) and probably at or near Capo d'Orlando.

41 *at the start of spring*: L.'s time-indicators, even apart from the year, have difficulties; see note to 27.7.

gave the following speech: Polybius (10.6) gives Scipio an oration of half a page, which L. uses for parts of his own composition.

as free from grief <. . .>: there is a lacuna at this point; indeed the chief Livian manuscript, the Puteanus, has a lacuna extending to the end of ch. 43. The text in between is preserved in some later manuscripts' text of the next book (27): they got it from a now-lost manuscript. At some earlier stage, the section had been somehow transposed. Editors have restored it to its correct position.

42 *Gaius Laelius*: Scipio's closest friend and associate. Polybius became friendly with him forty years later, and Laelius may have given him a copy of the letter that Scipio wrote, around 190, to Philip V of Macedon detailing the events (P. 10.9). The Roman fleet numbered 35 warships (P. 10.17) plus a number of transports.

were completed in six days: L. relies extensively, though as usual not solely, on Polybius, whose own account of the capture of New Carthage survives (10.6–20). Both have the Romans reach New Carthage on the seventh day (thus P. 10.9). But Scipio's army would have had to march 50 miles a day for all six days, a quite impossible speed, for from the mouth of the Ebro the distance, even by modern roads, is about 290 miles (480 kilometres); Polybius (3.39) makes it 2,600 Greek *stadia*, about 310 miles. L. reports Scipio in 206 covering the same distance, in reverse, in ten days, hardly more plausibly (28.33 note). Various problematic solutions have been offered: that Polybius' Greek text reads 'seventh' erroneously and he really wrote 'seventeenth' (but this incurs manuscript objections); that the transports (ch. 41) carried the entire army (but this contradicts the sources' statements); or that the six days were counted from a spot nearer to New Carthage (but it is hard to see why).

the rise and fall of the tide: the lagoon lay on the northern—not western—side of the city (it was drained in the eighteenth century). Polybius' and L.'s compass points are out by 90 degrees. On the supposed tide, see ch. 45 note.

43 *from here Africa threatens the whole of Spain . . .*: the lines that follow here in the manuscripts are bracketed as spurious by most editors, but not by Walsh. The translation follows his text in assuming that something has dropped out after 'the whole of Spain' but that the rest of the speech is genuine (translator's note).

44 *Mago*: in his pre-battle speech, Scipio also told his men that Neptune, the god of the sea, had given him the attack plan in a dream and promised him

victory (P. 10.11). Mago the commandant of New Carthage (this is not Hannibal's brother) had hastily armed able-bodied citizens to supplement his 1,000 soldiers, as L. mentions just below.

the Hill of Mercury: by the eastern wall of the city; today called Castillo de los Moros. The Roman camp was on this side.

45 *as the tide ebbed*: Polybius (10.8) does not specify that Scipio's fishermen informants were from Tarraco, or that a tide caused the outflow; L. must draw on another source for this. It is again instructive how he blends this into a narrative largely based on Polybius. But both writers' accounts are full of difficulties: most crucial of all, the Mediterranean lacks tides (L. seems unaware of this), so the daily rise and fall of the lagoon's level—if genuine—must have had another cause. L.'s mention of a 'brisk north wind' may be that cause, for Polybius is inaccurate to insist (10.9) that hardly any breezes blow over the city and harbour. Many other theories have been put forward. A further question is why Mago had taken no steps to hold that side of the city wall, when he must have known of the daily recession of the lagoon, whatever its cause. A lesser issue is L. having the phenomenon occur around midday, while Polybius (10.13) makes it late in the day.

47 *state property of the Roman people*: these 2,000 craftsmen must have been resident non-citizens of New Carthage, perhaps including some skilled slaves. Capture made them Roman slaves; and instead of selling them off as normal, Scipio declared them 'state slaves' and left them to carry on their work, now for the Roman forces (see 27.17).

eighteen captured vessels: the manuscripts read 'eight' (*octo*) but Polybius 10.17 has the higher figure and a manuscript error is quite possible. The statistics that follow may also come from Polybius (but cf. ch. 49), but his account breaks off at this point to resume with the events that L. reaches in ch. 49.

48 *the marines*: the forces of the naval allies, who were not Roman troops. Polybius does not mention them, or the ensuing dispute over the mural crown, at all.

'mural crown': a gold crown awarded to the first man to scale the wall of an enemy city (P. 6.39). Polybius has Scipio promise it (10.11) but his surviving account does not include its award. The emotional outburst of soldiers and marines over who should have it, if genuinely recorded, is testimony to the stress they had all been under since the start of this immensely hazardous expedition.

to both men: Digitius' mural crown and Scipio's lavish commendation of Laelius might be read as attesting that the marines had taken the city's sea-wall, and scholars largely follow this view. Yet on both L.'s and Polybius' showing, the fleet had played a minor role in the assault (ch. 44 'rather than real pressure . . . just a chaotic scramble'; Polybius 10.12 restricts the fleet to hurling missiles), and the heaviest fighting had been at the gate facing the Roman land camp. This should be accepted. With no accurate

time-pieces or synchronization available, it would be impossible to establish whether a marine was first on the sea-wall or a centurion first on the
lagoon-wall (on opposite sides of the city)—still more whether they were
simultaneous. More probably both were in Scipio's picked 500-strong
force crossing the lagoon. Elite *allied* soldiers (*extraordinarii*) formed a
Roman general's crack force (cf. 27.12 note); Digitius may well have been
one. Laelius' commendation can be seen as reward for distracting the
defenders on the seaward side and a further diplomatic gesture to placate
the naval allies, as well (no doubt) as for being Scipio's closest collaborator
(cf. 27.17).

49 *3,724 in another*: the modest total of 300 is Polybius' (10.18); the inflated
one could be Valerius Antias' since L. then notes other excessive Valerian
statistics and variant items. L.'s difficulties in sorting through his varied
and conflicting predecessors are vividly illustrated, though his rather
desperate solution, to take the mean between the extremes, is not to be
recommended.

the fabrication of historians!: or possibly, 'so unbridled is his [i.e. Antias']
fabrication'. Antias is elsewhere criticized by Livy for his inflation of
numbers (33.10: 'Valerius, who is guilty of gross exaggeration of numbers
of all kinds') (translator's note).

50 *well-merited eulogies of Scipio*: L.'s dramatized, if rather stilted, account of
these tactful dealings by Scipio aim at bringing to life his nobility of
character and its impact on the Spaniards. L. develops Polybius' matter-
of-fact reports (10.18–19) using direct 'quotations' and significant elaboration: for instance, Polybius says nothing about returning the gold to
Allucius. Some of the additions must be taken from other sources (e.g.
Allucius' name) but much no doubt arises from L.'s own imagination.

51 *both physically and mentally*: these commendable tasks, also highlighted by
Polybius (10.20), mark the beginning of Scipio's remarkable training of his
forces in Spain to reach a level of skill and manœuvrability perhaps
unmatched in the ancient world.

BOOK TWENTY-SEVEN

1 *would also have the same outcome*: the battle of 'first Herdonea' is disbelieved by many scholars, but not all; see note to 25.21.

2 *with victory unclear*: a later writer (Frontinus, *Stratagems* 2.2) claims
Hannibal defeated Marcellus; but even if Frontinus is right—which is not
guaranteed—it seems clear that Hannibal did then withdraw, in effect
conceding the field to Marcellus.

3 *the Blossii brothers*: Marius Blossius had been the pro-Carthaginian *medix
tuticus* of Capua in 216 (23.7) and probably paid for this with his property
and his life when the city capitulated in 211. The Blossii brothers may
have been his sons or nephews, and been among the 300 young aristocrats
who had joined the Romans in 216 (23.31) or the 112 who did so in 213
(24.47).

4 *consuls for the coming year*: another example of procedural punctilio; cf. 22.8, 23.36, 26.9, and further wrangles in chs. 5–6 below. A praetor, whose *imperium* was inferior to the consuls', could not conduct elections to the consulship.

Ptolemy and Cleopatra: Ptolemy IV of Egypt (cf. 23.10) and his sister-wife Arsinoe; why L. calls her 'Cleopatra' is not clear, but perhaps it is just a mistake. Polybius (9.11a) records a Roman embassy to Egypt, between 215 and 211 or 210, on an urgent mission to procure grain; this hardly looks like L.'s, but L. records no other Egypt-bound embassy, and his report, deriving ultimately (it seems) from official records, looks preferable to the fairly woolly—and perhaps rephrased—excerpt from Polybius.

5 *made a citizen of Rome*: 'Marcus Valerius Mottones' and his four sons, all with Roman names, were later honoured at Delphi; the dedicatory inscription survives. Muttines added his patron Laevinus' personal and family names to his own, the usual practice for enfranchised foreigners.

furtively away to Sicily: just what the sticking-point was in this procedural merry-go-round is far from plain, or why Laevinus obstinately wished to appoint his (not close) kinsman Messalla dictator for holding the elections. If he favoured particular men (including himself?) for the consulship of 209, and needed Messalla for success, there is no sign of it in our evidence.

6 *as often as they wished*: L. did not mention this enactment in his narrative of 217, but there is no reason to doubt it.

7 *At the end of this year*: the year 210, by L.'s faulty chronology. Here there is a further oddity, for why should it take Laelius so long, thirty-three days, to reach Rome?

without actually doing anything: L.'s puzzlement goes back to his misdating of the elder Scipios' disasters to 212 instead of 211 (see 25.36 note). He ignores a separate puzzle, as do most moderns: if Scipio took New Carthage early in the year, why did neither he nor his Carthaginian opponents do anything noteworthy for the rest of that year?

recalled by the Senate: yet in ch. 22 (see note) L. reports each having his command extended in 208 for one more year.

8 *turning into a good one*: L. likes tales of moral regeneration—but this one quickly turns into yet another item on legal and constitutional usages.

into Roman and Punic spheres of power: no such line existed; once the Romans took over Sicily in 241, there was no Punic sector. 'Roman and Punic' is either a careless slip of L.'s or a manuscript miscopy. 'Greek and Punic' would make more sense, for Sicily had indeed once been partially under Greek and partially under Punic rule.

9 *in their meetings*: L. does not say where these meetings were held. It is not at all likely that the allies had formal gatherings without Roman envoys being present, a step the Romans would have considered subversive. The simplest explanation may be that Latin and allied delegates, sent to Rome perhaps to discuss their grievances, or simply work out their next required

quota of men and munitions, held discussions—discussions no doubt informal and unobtrusive. L. shows that only some allies, Latins, dared to act.

9 *thirty colonies*: loose phrasing again; L. means Latin colonies, not those of Roman citizens (see Glossary: 'colony'). Most of the twelve defaulters were relatively close to Rome, while most of the rest lay further afield; the 'inner' group, paradoxically, may have been more provoked because it was geographically easier for the authorities at Rome to call repeatedly on their resources and manpower.

their senate: L. means the senate in each colony.

10 *mobilized from the register*: the register (*formula*) of reciprocal services agreed upon by the colony and Rome, including a list of men of the colony eligible for military service.

their meed of praise: most of these colonies were in or near war zones, and so had a strong interest in keeping the war effort up to strength.

the five-per-cent tax: levied on the value of a slave set free by his or her owner. The 4,000 pounds of gold would be equivalent to about 5 million *denarii*.

11 *formation of compound words*: a touch of inverse snobbery. Latin, too, could form complex compound words (especially in epic verse), but Greek ones had greater cachet.

Senate leader: the honorary but highly prestigious position of *princeps senatus*, who would always be called on first to speak.

their horses taken from them: 'knights' proper (*equites Romani*) were supplied with horses by the state; other men of means who served in the cavalry had to provide their own mounts, but informally could be called *equites Romani* too. Why such ongoing punishment—if not mistreatment—of the survivors of Cannae? Our sources offer no reason save a rather self-satisfied glow about ancestral severity (cf. ch. 7 above; also 25.7; Plutarch, *Marcellus* 13).

12 *as noted above*: 26.40 and note.

elite contingent of allies: these were called *extraordinarii*. A Roman consul or proconsul in the field selected the best of the allied cavalry and infantry of his army as a crack corps (Polybius 6.26); these troops were thus 'outside the [normal] ranking' (*extra ordinem*).

13 *barley-rations*: that is, barley instead of the usual wheat for baking their bread.

14 *no bloodless victory, either*: this victory retrieved from a defeat looks dubious, and later L. reports a tribune of the plebs blaming Marcellus for *two* costly defeats (ch. 21), but in a partisan speech; and then Marcellus was elected consul for 208. So this second combat, bloody on both sides, may have occurred but on a smaller scale, later to be exaggerated by Roman historians. Once again Hannibal left the area, as he had after Numistro (ch. 2): if he could not inflict a disastrous defeat, he had to keep his forces

in being for a later try. But it looks as though Marcellus had worked out a technique of sharp, indecisive, but draining clashes which, in effect, steadily wore Hannibal's army down—an attrition-war which the Romans could sustain far better. Again, Hannibal's withdrawal to Bruttium to save Caulonia left the field clear to Fabius Maximus to attack Tarentum, just as Fabius had designed (ch. 12).

15 *Vulceii*: this town was itself Lucanian, near Samnium and Campania, so it is odd that L. mentions it separately. Moreover, other Lucani stayed loyal to Hannibal (ch. 51). Possibly L. wrote, or should have written, 'the Lucanian Vulceientes' (i.e. not *Lucani et Vulceientes*, but *Lucani Vulceientes*), to distinguish them from the famous Vulci in Etruria, whose citizens were 'Vulcientes'.

in that particular sector: that is, where Fabius had installed himself.

16 *met him and killed him*: Hannibal had left a modest Punic force at Tarentum (25.11), while Carthalo may have been the officer mentioned in 217 and 216 (22.15, 58). His inherited link with Fabius' family strikingly illustrates social ties between upper-class Carthaginians and Romans even amidst intense war.

left to their angry gods: i.e. the gods of Tarentum must have been angry with its people to allow the city to be captured.

the birds: the sacred chickens (22.42 note).

a more intensive investigation: that is, under torture.

17 *the start of the summer*: in reality summer 208 (see ch. 7 note). But some lines later, L. declares it the beginning of spring! Spring seems likelier if Scipio was keen on an early battle. Edesco was, it seems, a local Sedetanian king (see note to 28.24).

18 *Baecula*: near Castulo (Polybius 10.38) and usually identified with modern Bailén, but not attested otherwise. For the ensuing battle L. again follows Polybius closely. Scipio outnumbered Hasdrubal, though the gap usually estimated (35,000–40,000 versus only 25,000) looks too wide.

took the light-armed troops: here L. diverges from Polybius, but implausibly. Scipio in fact stayed with the legions who then climbed the hill to attack Hasdrubal's right flank—as L. gets round to mentioning near the end of this chapter. Polybius (10.39) also explains that Hasdrubal was still drawing up his main battle line when Scipio and Laelius fell on his flanks with the main Roman forces.

19 *fugitives from the battle*: some of the Carthaginian army did get away in good enough order to be reconstituted but, if 20,000 were killed or captured, the fugitives must have been relatively few. Even if L.'s and Polybius' figures for the captives really include the slain as well, as is sometimes (not very convincingly) suggested, Hasdrubal's army was effectively shattered.

'general': in Latin, *imperator*; the first recorded acclamation of a title voluntarily accorded to a victorious general by his troops. It was taken over by

Augustus and his successors as the imperial title. The first Spaniard to acclaim Scipio as 'king' was Edesco (cf. ch. 17), echoed by the irrepressible Indibilis (Polybius 10.40).

19 *a tunic with the broad stripe*: the broad purple stripe (*latus clavus*) on a garment was reserved for senators and their sons, and so was a gift that flattered the recipient's status.

20 *might join forces with him*: Scipio had feared this earlier (Polybius 10.38), but in fact, as Polybius notes, this Hasdrubal's antagonisms towards both his colleagues kept them away (10.37). Even so, their ensuing inactivity during Scipio's consolidation of his victory is dumbfounding.

decree of the Carthaginian senate: passed seven years earlier (23.27–8), unless more recently renewed.

to hire mercenary auxiliaries: but Mago next appears in Celtiberia, the following year, hiring troops (28.1); perhaps L. changes to a different source, or Mago's mission was changed in the interval—due to Mediterranean storms?

21 *Sextus Julius Caesar*: reportedly the first member of the family to bear the third name 'Caesar' (Pliny, *Natural History* 7.47).

alive and in enemy hands: the reason for this objection, which L. fails to explain, was that the son of a still-living father who had held a curule office (curule aedileship, praetorship, or consulship) was barred from a plebeian, i.e. non-curule, one. See also 30.19.

22 *assigned the provinces . . . for a year*: contrast ch. 7. L.'s source for this statement perhaps mechanically assumed a yearly renewal, in contrast to the source for the ch. 7 item.

eighty ships: contrast notes to 26.42 and 47; Scipio had 53 ships after taking New Carthage.

25 *Honos and Virtus*: 'Honour' and 'Courage', qualities worshipped as divine.

26 *between the Carthaginian and Roman camps*: these are the main armies' camps, near Venusia in Apulia.

the rest from Etruria: the consuls' escort seems to have been some of their own bodyguard of *extraordinarii* (see 27.12 note). Polybius, extant again, reports two cavalry squadrons and 30 light-armed troops with them (10.32); so either the two squadrons were very unequal in numbers or L.'s figures are faulty. The details of the combat are also divergent in the two accounts, while later on Plutarch, *Marcellus* 29, draws on Livy, and Appian (*Hannibalica* 50) has a brief and, typically, quite different version.

lacking its 'head': one of the organ's lobes was defined as its 'head'. For this to be missing was a very bad sign from heaven. There is a similar ill-omen in 30.2.

28 *a letter . . . was brought from Hannibal*: reading *allatae* for Walsh's *allati* (misprint?) (translator's note).

the killing of his cavalrymen: see 26.38.

stones, stakes, and javelins: for stakes as weapons, cf. 23.37.

29 *That same summer*: these events in Greece really date to 209, the correct year for the Nemean Games, celebrated in July near Argos (chs. 30, 31; F. W. Walbank, *A Historical Commentary on Polybius*, 3 vols. (Oxford, 1957, 1967, 1979), 2.15).

the king of Asia, Attalus: in fact of the small kingdom of Pergamum in western Asia Minor, which in 129 became the Roman province called 'Asia' (is L., then, drawing here from Coelius? He was writing later than this). Attalus reigned from 241 to 197 and greatly built up his kingdom's power, especially in later years through an astute alliance with the Romans.

30 *the council meeting . . . scheduled quite some time before*: i.e. the council of the Achaean League, as the previous paragraph shows.

31 *promise of a royal marriage*: Polycratia's husband Aratus was son and namesake of the famous statesman who had led the Achaean League from 245 until his death in 213.

33 *with their own lives*: a sound comment; the consuls had been eager to fight (ch. 25) and, had this happened, Hannibal quite possibly would have won. Such a victory, with Hasdrubal soon to start his own march from Spain to Italy, might have revolutionized the war.

34 *convicted of a crime*: a fine in 218 for peculation of war booty (see 22.35 and note). Livius, despite returning to the Senate, remained embittered and acerbic, with a particular animus, L. says, against Claudius Nero who supposedly had borne false witness against him (so we learn later, in 29.37).

was disallowed: it had been legally forbidden in the fourth century, though there remained a strong convention that one consul should be a patrician (see 23.31).

the white toga: candidates for office wore a brightly whitened toga (*toga candida*; so they were *candidati*).

had been unseated: see 22.3 note; Camillus had been exiled—the story went—because of the same kind of accusation levied against Livius.

35 *drawing Gaul as his province*: L. only later (ch. 38) shows that this province fell to Livius.

36 *smaller than . . . before the war*: according to Polybius (2.24), the census total in 225 was 273,000; similarly Livy, *Epitome* 20, for the census of 223. But it is not certain that all citizens were registered who were serving in the legions (21 under arms in 208, rising to 23 for 207), especially those abroad.

37 *the Armilustrum*: an area on the Aventine Hill, close to the Tiber, where every October a ceremony was held to purify the weapons of war.

the poet Livius: Livius Andronicus (284–204 BC), the earliest Roman poet. Brought a captive to Rome when Tarentum surrendered in 272 at the end of Pyrrhus' war, he adapted Greek tragedies and comedies into Latin (the first was produced at the *Ludi Romani* in 240 BC), and a translation/adaptation of Homer's *Odyssey*. As L. then remarks, later ages thought his works 'tasteless and uncouth' (and so L. refuses to quote anything from the hymn); only a small number of quotations survive.

37 *affecting only married women*: Juno, like her counterpart Hera in Greek myth and religion, was a goddess particularly associated with marriage and women.

the Porta Carmentalis: close to the Tiber (see 24.47 note).

38 *forces from Spain*: almost certainly incorrect; Scipio could hardly afford to detach forces from his theatre, nor do the alleged contingents appear in the record of the Metaurus campaign.

39 *a largely open thoroughfare*: L. believes both that Hasdrubal followed Hannibal's route through the Alps and that the Arverni (in modern Auvergne) welcomed him. L.'s grasp of Gallic geography, at this stage of his *History*, seems nearly as vague as his grasp of Spain's—unless 'Arverni' is an error for a more southerly people, e.g. the Volcae Arecomisci by the Rhône or the tribe whose king Hannibal had appointed (21.26, 31). His point about regular Carthaginian(?) communications via the Alps is mistaken, too: Hannibal had had none. L. is further mistaken, below, about a supposed attempt on Placentia by Hannibal in 218: the general had tried and failed to take a nearby depot (21.57).

40 *Tarentine territory*: a plausible emendation for the manuscripts' 'Larinum's territory' (that is, *agri Tarentini* for their *agri Larinatis*). Larinum is topographically impossible, for it lay over 150 miles north of the Sallentini. They too are odd here, for such a move took Hannibal still further away from the north. Attacking and capturing pro-Roman strongpoints in the Sallentine peninsula would hardly help him to join forces with his brother. Conceivably, Hannibal's real hope was to take Brundisium, something he had failed to do five years earlier (25.22); it would give him a major port for contact with Carthage and even, perhaps, with Hasdrubal.

41 *Grumentum in Lucania*: this town lay about 90 miles due west of Tarentum, in hilly country.

42 *Losses . . . were around 500*: at best, L.'s source or sources have magnified a small clash into a big Roman victory. Hannibal, despite the supposed heavy loss of life in his army, soon was able to slip away by a simple ruse. The figures for enemy dead and captured are suspiciously out of proportion too (but see next note).

went on to Canusium: Hannibal's zigzag movements are a puzzle. It has been suggested that some (like the one to Metapontum) are Roman inventions; but the reason for such invention is hard to see and, in any case, he certainly got no further north than Canusium in the end, wherever he had been. He may well have lost a lot of men in the intermittent clashes, for he spent time recruiting fresh troops. His activities suggest either indecision—the last thing he could afford at this crucial stage—or such unrelentingly close Roman attentions that his freedom of action was half-paralysed. The tactics that Marcellus had, perhaps, worked out (see note to ch. 14) were being used by his successors.

43 *to meet him in Umbria*: Hasdrubal's dispatch cannot have been just deliberate disinformation meant to fall into Roman hands, as sometimes supposed, for it was the only message he sent south; nor do we know of any message at all to him from Hannibal. The brothers had to make contact somehow, and as no other missive is heard of, this one probably was genuine.

45 *vows . . . made on their behalf*: in Greek and Roman religion a petitioner always promised an offering to the god(s) in return for the granting of the prayer. Once the prayer was granted the petitioner was obliged or 'condemned' (Latin *damnatus*) to make good on the promise.

46 *The tablet had been circulated*: the *tessera*, a wooden tablet bearing the orders of the day, that was circulated through the maniples of the army.

at Sena: many scholars judge Livy, and all other ancient writers who mention it, as wrong about Sena (today's Senigallia) and locate the camps 11 miles further up the coast near Fanum (Fano) on the River Metaurus, where the Via Flaminia to Rome began. This stems from the view that Sena lay too far south if Hasdrubal expected to meet Hannibal in Umbria, for he needed to swing inland along the Via Flaminia. But such a reinterpretation makes it very hard to understand the ensuing movements leading to the battle, especially Hasdrubal's desire to cross the Metaurus—on such a view, from its northern bank to its southern—which would lead to him ultimately being cornered, in front by the legions at Narnia and in Etruria, and in his rear by the pursuing consuls. In reality, from Sena too he could also strike inland if he wished (Lazenby, *Hannibal's War*, 183); nor is it obvious that Hasdrubal meant to cross the Apennines to meet Hannibal.

went forward immediately to their battle stations: this seems close to incredible for an army that had just made a 250-mile forced march from Apulia. The immediacy of the battle after Nero's arrival may be exaggerated for effect; on the other hand it cannot have been long delayed, for the very reasons Nero is then reported as giving.

47 *caused him some concern*: thus Roman punctiliousness over protocol—and perhaps the frosty relations between Livius and Nero—nearly cost them their advantage. Fortunately for them, and maybe for Roman history, Hasdrubal's clumsiness as a general was more pronounced than ever.

swam across the River Metaurus: L., as often, is unclear about topography. If the Carthaginians and Romans were encamped near Sena, their water-supply came from the River Misa or, 4 miles further north, the Cesano. The Metaurus lies another 7 miles further north again. Hasdrubal thus had to ford at least one of these rivers, unmentioned by L., before reaching the Metaurus.

48 *The Ligurians*: not mentioned by Polybius in his surviving excerpt on the battle (11.1–3). L. soon joins them to the Spaniards on Hasdrubal's right; and it seems likelier that there was no Punic centre, but only the Gallic corps on the left and these troops on the right. Nor does the praetor Porcius Licinus, in the supposed Roman centre, play any part.

49 *the 8,000 mark*: L.'s figures for the slain are dubious. Polybius has 2,000 dead on the Roman side, 10,000 on Hasdrubal's (11.3). The 5,400 prisoners are more plausible, for they could be counted. According to Ovid, the battle was fought on 22 June (*Fasti* 6.770).

50 *in five days*: an entirely impossible time-span for 250 miles (see note to ch. 46), least of all the day after a fierce battle. Supposedly they brought some prisoners with them, too (ch. 51). A dose of Roman propaganda can be diagnosed.

51 *saw clearly the destiny of Carthage*: Horace, in a splendid ode, celebrates this event (*Odes* 4.4).

BOOK TWENTY-EIGHT

1 *as serious as before*: L.'s chronology is now correct, as he reported no Spanish operations under 208.

our sea: the Mediterranean.

2 *Baetica*: the valley of the River Baetis (modern Guadalquivir) and surrounding uplands and coasts; Augustus so renamed the southernmost Spanish province, until then called Further Spain.

through the strait: of Gibraltar.

3 *called Orongis by the barbarians*: not otherwise known, and probably a variant form of Aurgi, modern Jaén (24.42 note). The 'Maesesses' are unknown; the word looks like an annalist's or copyist's error.

to secure the forum: i.e. the town's marketplace.

4 *on the fringes of Carthaginian territory*: Utica, only 30 miles north of Carthage, was a small independent ally with its own prosperous territory. Its sparse ruins are now inland, because alluvial build-up from the River Bagradas (Mejerda) has caused the Mediterranean to recede quite a distance.

5 *as noted above*: see 27.33.

the Maedi: see 26.25 and note.

Gulf of the Aenianes: another name for the Malian Gulf, the narrow waters with Thermopylae on their southern shore.

6 *Demetrium in Phthiotis*: on the mainland to the north; the fortress city of Demetrias stood nearby.

7 *to Elatia in Phocis*: within 24 hours Philip and his troops cannot have marched from Scotussa in Thessaly, have a fight with the Aetolians at Thermopylae, pursue them westwards to Heraclea, and then push on to Elatia. But from Heraclea to Elatia, first along the coast and then turning

inland, the road is about 25 miles, which is just possible in 24 hours and which L.'s source (Polybius?) may really have meant.

Oreus: in the Latin at this point the town is actually called Oreum, but elsewhere it is Oreus (translator's note).

Philip left for Torone: thus the manuscripts, but Thronium is meant (a town just east of Thermopylae). The real Torone was a northern Aegean town, something L. perhaps did not realize.

9 *comments from spectators*: their lavish praise in L. for Claudius Nero, and comparative downplaying of his fellow consul (despite him being a Livius), may not be entirely unconnected with the eminence of the Claudii Nerones in Augustan Rome—the emperor's wife Livia and her sons, including the future emperor Tiberius, all belonged to that family and L. knew them well.

banter: in triumphs soldiers were allowed to sing rude, and sometimes quite obscene, songs about their general (notorious examples in Suetonius, *Caesar* 49, 51); the aim was to avert any divine wrath over the general's unusual glory.

10 *dictator . . . master of horse*: it was very unusual, if not unique, for a dictator to be nominated to hold elections when both consuls were at Rome, and equally striking that Nero should nominate his colleague who, supposedly, disliked him intensely. The simplest explanation would be that it was an effort to perpetuate a harmony brought about by their joint victory (more complicated theories also exist).

Gaius Claudius: it is striking that the co-victor of the Metaurus did not have his *imperium* extended, unlike his colleague Livius. He is not heard of again until 204 (29.37).

11 *temple of Vesta*: on the importance of Vesta's sacred fire, see note to 22.57.

to Sicilian agriculture than Italian: a reference to Valerius Laevinus' successful measures in Sicily some years before (26.40, 27.5). L.'s report is a noteworthy though brief statement of agricultural conditions by 206 BC.

not only the men with the plunder but anyone carrying arms as well: reading *praedatores* with Walsh. If we accept the variant *praeda*, as most editors do, it would translate: 'putting at risk not just the booty, but the soldiers, too' (translator's note).

12 *than when things were going well for him*: the first half of L.'s discussion of Hannibal's leadership is based on Polybius' own admiring comments (11.19); the second half, with interesting remarks about Hannibal's finances and logistics, presumably from a different source.

Augustus Caesar: having indirectly highlighted the eminence of the Claudii Nerones (ch. 9 and note), L. now manages a complimentary mention of the emperor. The north-west of Spain, the last unconquered region, was subdued in a series of wars from 26 to 19 BC.

to the city of Silpia: Polybius gives 70,000 infantry and 4,000 cavalry (11.20), so L. is drawing on some other source for the figures he prefers.

Scipio had some 50,000 men (ch. 13 and note), and his complicated manœuvres at the ensuing battle imply that he was much outnumbered.

'Silpia' is an error, whether L.'s or a later copyist's; but manuscripts of Polybius too have an otherwise unattested name, *Elinga* (11.20). In Greek letters this could be a copying mistake for the known name Ilipa; L.'s 'Silpia' in turn looks like a misreading of 'Elinga'; and Ilipa is generally accepted as the right name. There were several Ilipas in southern Spain: the best-known lay upriver from Hispalis (Seville) and was later called Ilipa Ilia. But an Ilipa near the river south of Castulo, much further east, is another possibility: for Polybius, followed by L., almost certainly locates the battle there, and there is some independent evidence for such a town.

13 *Culchas*: this ruler (Kolichas in Polybius) must have built up a lordship somewhere in eastern Spain; but if his twenty-eight 'cities' could supply only 3,500 men, the realm was of no great size.

45,000 men . . . infantry and cavalry: L. understates the numbers of the Roman army if the manuscripts are correct. Polybius reports 45,000 infantry and about 3,000 cavalry; the latter figure may have been accidentally left out of L.'s original text by a later copyist. Similarly, nearly all manuscripts omit the numeral '500' just above, despite its being in Polybius.

14 *looked like castles*: at least some elephants had crenellated towers strapped to their backs, from which marksmen could throw or shoot missiles (see also L. 37.40; Pliny, *Natural History* 8.22, 27).

horses bridled and saddled: proper saddles had not yet been invented (though they existed in imperial times); a cloth or cloths, strapped to the horse's back, served instead.

three cohorts of infantry: Polybius (11.23) writes 'three maniples (this grouping of infantry is called by Romans a cohort)', using the respective terms *speirai* and *koortis*; but L. misreads him. On the cohort in this period, see 22.5 note.

advancing more slowly: Scipio's tactics at Ilipa are hard to follow, and L. does not help by heavily compressing Polybius (11.22–3). Scipio advanced but then held back his centre, consisting of the Spanish allied units; and put the Roman and Italian troops on his left and right wings through a complicated sequence of manœuvres which brought them obliquely onto the flanks of Hasdrubal's corresponding wings. Despite Polybius' detailed account—or maybe because of it—just how the Roman wings manœuvred is still debated. Even more worth asking is why Hasdrubal son of Gisgo simply stood in position and allowed all this to be done in front of him, instead of launching his own attack or attacks: for instance, against Scipio's complexly manœuvring wings—which at one point were marching away from the Roman centre, leaving gaps and exposing their flanks to the Carthaginians—or against Scipio's relatively weak centre. But on all the evidence Hasdrubal son of Gisgo was a hopeless general.

15 *Attenes, chieftain of the Turdetani*: 'Turdetani' was the general name for the many peoples of the Baetis region, who at the local level were known by

their town names or regional names. Attenes must have been one of the regional lords, and hitherto a vassal of the Carthaginians (as Culchas too possibly had been).

two fortified towns were betrayed: if news of the battle reached them, and their handover occurred, within a few hours of Scipio's victory and before Hasdrubal retreated, these towns must have been very close by. L. may be compressing for dramatic effect. Unfortunately Polybius' excerpt on the battle breaks off with the torrential downpour.

16 *had ships sent to him*: since L. gives no place names here except Gades, the geography of events is hard to clarify. If the battle *was* fought at Ilipa near Hispalis, and the Carthaginians—when prevented from crossing the Baetis southwards—'veered towards the ocean', they had to march due west towards the Río Tinto district, over 60 miles away; for the coast country north of Gades was (and is) a vast flat marshland, agreeable for nature-walkers but lethal for a fleeing army. Besides, L. writes that the remnants of the army camped on a high and barren—i.e. waterless—ridge not far from the sea.

It would make more sense of his account, probably drawn mainly from Polybius, if we infer that the Ilipa of the battle lay in eastern Baetica (see ch. 12 note) and that the beaten army retreated for some days westward down the Baetis valley until the Romans caught up with it. They then cornered its last remnants on a dry ridge not far from the Baetis (a river navigable far inland), at which point Hasdrubal and then Mago deserted their men to escape by water. L. does make the retreat seem to last only a day or two, but he similarly compressed into a seeming few days the disastrous four-week retreat of Gnaeus Scipio in 211 (see 25.36 note).

took seventy days: if true, this causes difficulties. Much more happened between the battle—notably, further military operations in various parts of Spain, Scipio's trip to Africa, a serious illness of his, and a dangerous mutiny by some Roman troops (chs. 16–38)—and Scipio's return to Rome to seek the consulship for 205. This has caused some scholars to date Ilipa to 207, not 206. The problem of 206 eases, but does not entirely disappear, when we note that Polybius implies the battle was fought early in spring (11.20). Scipio's visit to Syphax cannot, in turn, have needed more than a number of days; it took at most three days' travel either way (ch. 18). It has been suggested, too, that Scipio travelled not all the way back to Tarraco, but to New Carthage, taking less than seventy days (if so, these would be mistakes by L. or his source); and that the consular elections might have been delayed at the end of the year to enable him to stand. Cf. next note also.

the province with its army: 'the fourteenth year' would be 205, but L. here contradicts ch. 10 ('thirteenth', and cf. ch. 38). The slip is perhaps due to counting the war as starting with the attack on Saguntum in 219. By contrast, the year 206 was indeed the fifth year from Scipio's appointment, which had occurred in 210 (though L. put it in 211: see notes to 24.41–2). Rather than supposing that L. switches from one source for 'fourteenth' to a separate one for 'fifth', we can infer faulty reckoning by the man himself.

17 *Masaesulians*: a large, or at least very spread-out, Numidian people whose western border was with Mauretania.

helped by a gentle breeze: this suggests summer weather, a useful indication. The distance in a direct line is about 160 nautical miles. This smooth outward trip should have taken less than the more difficult three-day return journey that L. afterwards reports.

the harbour of Siga: 'of Siga' is added for clarity; it was Syphax's capital, now in western Algeria, a short distance inland.

19 *Iliturgi and Castulo*: the first town is named Ilurgeia in a brief Polybian excerpt (11.24) and Ilurgia by Appian (*Iberica* 32); both fit Pliny the Elder's Ilorci (25.36 note), but L.'s presumably Roman source(s) found 'Iliturgi(s)' again irresistible. The place is best identified with Ilugo, about 30 miles north-east of Castulo, a town attested on inscriptions (Appian writes of 'Ilurgia' and 'Castax' as the treacherous towns). Many scholars identify it, instead, with either Lorquí or Lorca near Cartagena, because L. has Scipio march from New Carthage to 'Iliturgi' in five days; but no believable reconstruction of the disastrous campaign of 211 fits this, while Lorquí and Lorca are too close to Cartagena. And for implausibly accelerated marching-times, we need look no further than Scipio's 'six-day' march to New Carthage in 209 (26.42 and note).

struggle for empire and glory: for this theme (here *de imperio et gloria*), compare 22.58, where Hannibal after Cannae speaks of it as 'a struggle for honour and power' (*de dignitate atque imperio*).

at no small risk to himself: according to Appian he was wounded on the neck; but it was clearly a minor injury.

21 *Ide*: site unknown, but perhaps in the mountains north of Córdoba, for an 'Idiensian' is attested on a late Roman inscription found in that region. The correction to 'Ibes' by most editors is not substantiated by evidence.

22 *Cirtes*: as a local name for the river, this is mentioned only here.

Astapa: inscriptions and Pliny (*Natural History*, 3.10) call it Ostippo; it is modern Estepa on the plains about 45 miles south of Córdoba. It is not clear how the Romans came to have allies in that district, as mentioned by L. in this paragraph, but most probably some communities had joined the plainly winning side after Ilipa and thus prompted reprisals from the still pro-Carthaginian Astapans.

24 *Lacetani ... Suessetani and Sedetani*: the Lacetani, rather misleadingly termed 'countrymen' of the Ilergetan brothers (L. probably means neighbours), dwelt between the Pyrenees and the Ilergetes of Ilerda, as did the Suessetani. L. only afterwards mentions (chs. 27, 31, etc.) that Mandonius and Indibilis had also stirred up their own people.

The Suessetani had once supplied troops to Indibilis (25.34) but—like the two brothers—must have sided with the Romans after Baecula. The

Sedetani, in later times spelt Edetani, occupied country south of the Ilergetes from the middle Ebro, including the later city of Caesaraugusta (Saragossa), to the hinterland of Saguntum where their centre was Liria (Llíria today). Edesco (27.17) may have been ruler of one or more Sedetanian towns. If L.'s naming them is correct, the brothers were trying to raise the whole of the east and north-east against the conquerors. What had become of Edesco is not known.

Sucro: a town on the river of the same name, today the Júcar, which enters the Mediterranean 25 miles south of Valencia. Livy describes its garrison as protecting the tribes 'on this side [i.e. north] of the Ebro' (*cis Hiberum*), but this is another geographical error; no Sucro is known in those parts. L.'s account fairly closely follows what survives of Polybius' (11.25–30), but Scipio's speech (chs. 27–9) is lengthier than, and largely independent of, Polybius' version (11.28–9).

Gaius Albius . . . and Gaius Atrius: the names are often doubted, as *albus* means white and *ater* black (Scipio plays on the latter point in ch. 28). But both do occur elsewhere; the Augustan poet Tibullus' family name was Albius, for instance. (In Australia in the 1980s–1990s, two successive leaders of a national political party were named, respectively, Blunt and Sharp.)

27 *duly elected tribunes*: i.e. military tribunes (see Glossary: 'tribunes, military').

28 *to garrison Rhegium*: in 280 a legion of Campanian citizens was sent there to protect the city against Pyrrhus, but seized control of it, expelled the menfolk, and ruled there until 270, when a Roman army retook the place and restored it to its citizens.

four thousand men: Polybius also tells this story (1.7) but gives a figure of 300 executed. 'Four thousand' merely generalizes from the theoretical strength of a legion of the period.

kept Messana in Sicily: Samnites had taken Capua around 425 and became Campanians; a body of Campanian mercenaries, serving in Sicily around 288, had taken over Messana, where they remained for ever (unlike their imitators at Rhegium). In 264, by agreeing to help them against their Sicilian enemies, the Romans managed to bring about the First Punic War against Carthage.

the same powers: rhetorical licence, for Silanus took his orders from Scipio. But both men held *imperium*, and in Scipio's absence or death Silanus could have taken charge. On his visit to Syphax Scipio had left him in charge at New Carthage and Laelius at Tarraco (ch. 17).

29 *Coriolanus*: in the very early Roman republic, Gnaeus Marcius, an attractive but arrogant patrician, won glory by capturing the nearby city of Corioli (hence his honorific *cognomen*), but opposed the plebeians' demands for social justice and was forced into exile, supposedly on false charges. He offered his services to the Romans' recent enemies and put Rome itself under siege in 488, only to be shamed into retreating when his

mother and wife came out to appeal to him in his camp. Shakespeare's play is based on Plutarch's biography, not L.'s account in Book 2 of *From the Foundation of the City*.

30 *Carteia*: L. counts the Atlantic as beginning immediately outside Gibraltar; Carteia stood near or at Algeciras. In 171 it became the first place outside Italy to be granted the status of a Latin ally, after 4,000 illegitimate sons of Roman troops in Spain sought recognition from the Senate and were settled there.

the praetor Adherbal: one of Gades' chief magistrates, it seems, though later on L. uses their correct title 'sufetes' (ch. 37). Roman authors often translated foreign institutions by supposed Roman equivalents (thus 'Carthaginian legions': 24.49 and note). Adherbal's remaining colleagues or successors themselves soon began to plan on delivering Gades to the Romans (ch. 37).

31 *the hopes with which they had come*: or perhaps 'the hopes with which he and his men had come . . .' (translator's note).

32 *an island surrounded by the Ocean*: Gades stood on a small island just off the Spanish coast, though silting-up has since joined it to the mainland.

33 *reached the River Ebro*: a few years earlier Scipio, reportedly but improbably, had marched from this river to New Carthage in six days (26.42 note). The present alleged ten days' march, again taken from Polybius (11.32), is also improbably fast—all the more so as L. has just had Scipio tell his men that the campaign is not a crucial one. We may wonder whether Laelius in old age exaggerated the speeds with which his friend and hero moved to confront foes.

L. has reported the Spaniards crossing into Sedetanian territory (ch. 31), and this lay south of the Ebro (ch. 24 note); yet now he, like Polybius, has Scipio crossing the river himself, thus to its northern side. The simplest explanation would be that, at word of his advance, the Spaniards had retired to Ilergetan territory—something neither Polybius in his surviving excerpt (11.31–3) nor L. notes.

busy with their plunder: L. does not make it fully clear that these Spaniards were only skirmishers from the main army (Polybius does rather better).

a front of four cohorts: on cohorts, see note to 22.5; here L. does echo Polybius correctly. Four cohorts, all the same, amounted to little more than 1,400 men, a very small force to take on supposedly 20,000 Spanish infantry. At some stage the rest of Scipio's infantry must have joined in (some 1,200 Roman and allied troops were killed, and 3,000 wounded: ch. 34), but even Polybius fails to mention this.

34 *With that Mandonius was sent off*: the brothers were incorrigible; a year later they were in arms again (29.1–3).

35 *revived after his illness*: Scipio was now 28 years old (see 26.18). Interestingly, a gold signet ring of around 200 BC from Capua, and a later coin struck at Canusium in Italy, bear the profile of a young man with hair to

the nape of the neck: portraits which have tentatively been identified as young Scipio (H. H. Scullard, *Scipio Africanus: Soldier and Politician* (London, 1970), 249–50, and plate 1).

36 *the gate that faced the lagoon and the sea*: L. seems to misunderstand his source (and to forget his own account in 26.44–6), for the two bodies of water were on opposite sides of the city. Mago may have been outside the eastern gate, which Scipio had attacked in 209 and which could be described as *between* both lagoon and sea; this would also allow the defenders to pursue his men to the shore.

Cimbii: unknown, but plainly a haven on the Ocean. The mainland opposite Gades is called 'the Curum coast' by Pliny (*Natural History* 3.7), perhaps a variant name for the place.

sufetes: see note to ch. 30. For 'financial officer' L. uses the Roman term *quaestor*.

Pityusa: later called Ebusus (modern Ibiza due east of Valencia); in fact there are two main islands (Ibiza and Formentera) plus islets, and they were more often termed, in the plural, the Pityussae. The town of Ebusus was an old Carthaginian colony.

two Balearic islands: Mallorca and Menorca.

took possession of the city: Port Mahón, the chief town of Menorca, was called Mago in Roman times, reputedly because it was settled (or resettled) by Mago, though no ancient writer seems to claim this.

38 *under Publius Scipio's command and authority*: only Appian (*Iberica* 37) records that Scipio also settled a number of convalescing Roman and Italian veterans at a new town he named Italica—the first Roman city outside Italy, though without official status until much later. Italica, just north of Hispalis (Seville) at modern Santiponce, was the home town of the emperors Trajan and Hadrian, who lavished attention on it.

Lucius Lentulus and Lucius Manlius Acidinus: Lentulus and Manlius (praetors in 211 and 210 respectively) had been vested with special *imperium* and sent out to relieve Scipio. L., usually so detailed in his record of appointments, is surprisingly abrupt in announcing these. Yet the appointment of Lentulus and Manlius must have been made some weeks or months earlier, for they were plainly at hand to take over from Scipio. This reveals that he had, for quite some time, been intending to leave Spain.

as Gaul was then designated: L. means Cisalpine Gaul, i.e. northern Italy.

39 *Turduli*: L. called the Saguntines' hostile neighbours 'Turdetani' earlier (21.6) and refers to Turdetania a few lines below. But 'Turduli' is not correct either. Various communities of Turduli dwelt in western Spain, none in the east. On the neighbours' likely name, Turitani, see 21.6 note.

discussion of . . . the distribution of provinces: L. is either careless or has changed his source without checking back, for he reported this distribution just above (ch. 38). The real issue, of course—as he goes on to clarify—was whether Scipio should invade Africa. Yet in giving him Sicily without sortition, the Senate had virtually agreed to invade; there was no point otherwise in sending the republic's best general to an island at peace. Raising the issue now looks like a last-ditch effort by the opponents of invasion to scuttle it—and indeed L. makes Fabius more or less admit this at the start of his speech. Fabius and his supporters certainly felt genuine concern at the risks, and they would have been proved correct if Hannibal had shown some of his old military energy. L., in turn, uses the well-established literary device of contrasted speeches to offer his readers an analysis of the pros and cons of the project. In this the two speeches are brilliantly effective.

40 *to me . . . if he is refused it, of course*: this is ironically meant.

41 *Publius Cornelius*: in the Senate, senators were addressed by first and family names only.

Drepana or Eryx: see 21.10 and 21.41.

cannot support two armies . . . in Italy and in Africa: Fabius exaggerates rhetorically. In 205 there were still eighteen legions under arms—including six in south Italy, four in Cisalpine Gaul, two in Sicily and four in Spain—and sizeable fleets, accounting for 20,000–40,000 more men on active service.

The normally prudent state of Athens . . . their own prosperous community back home: a very potted version of the Athenian expedition to Sicily of 415–413 BC. The nobly born 'young man' must be Alcibiades, who had instigated it but lasted only a few weeks as one of its generals before being recalled.

42 *fortune cutting both ways*: Marcus Atilius Regulus' initially successful invasion of Punic Africa in 256 ended the following year in disaster, and he himself was captured.

without the sanction of a senatorial decree: the visit to Syphax (ch. 17); another example of constitutional punctilio, here used in a dig at Scipio. It is a neat literary touch that L. makes Fabius grow more heated, and more critical of Scipio personally—despite earlier compliments—as he nears the end of his speech. Scipio then alludes to this at the start of his.

43 *forty years ago*: in fact, fifty.

the Spartan Xanthippus: unable to cope with Regulus themselves, the Carthaginian generals allowed Xanthippus, a seasoned mercenary officer who had recently joined them, to direct operations, with stunning success.

Agathocles, King of Syracuse: this resourceful and unscrupulous leader (who in fact took the royal title only later) invaded Africa in 310 and, as Scipio says, brought the Carthaginians to their knees—though Scipio does not mention that he too was ultimately unsuccessful, abandoning his army and his son in a hurried return to Sicily when the situation turned against him in 307.

45 *assigned as follows*: this denouement is abrupt. The dispute in the Senate

has reached its height—then suddenly the Senate gives Scipio what he wants. He must have used the day's grace to good effect behind the scenes. L. is more interested in the constitutional and procedural issues arising from the dispute than in the dispute itself. More broadly still, what interests him is the emblematic opposition between young, charismatic vigour and old, perhaps weary caution—rather than (for instance) who supported Scipio's position and who Fabius', or what the relative strength of the two sides in the debate was. Scipio's abrupt victory suggests, despite L., that he had a majority all along, partly perhaps because he promised to recruit volunteers only and otherwise cut costs.

the means of each: what follows is a noteworthy, even though limited, register of the economic capacities of Etruria's communities at this time. What munitions other parts of Italy contributed L. does not detail, or who built the fleet (no doubt the naval allies like Naples and Paestum). His source's interest, or his own, lessens after the Etruscan entries.

46 *Fossa Graeca*: a channel near Cumae, dug in earlier centuries to drain marshland in the coastal area.

captured Genua: and destroyed it, according to 30.1.

the Epanterii Montani: this and the other warlike Ligurian peoples dwelt in the mountains between Genua (Genoa) and Massilia. The Ingauni, or a section of them, are called Albingauni in 29.5 (see note there). 'Alpine' Savo is on the coast (modern Savona), at the foot of the Maritime Alps.

Coelius claims . . . prisoners of war: it is preferable to believe Coelius against Valerius Antias, not only on principle but because it is hard to see how Mago, just arrived from the Balearic Islands, can have acquired Etruscan booty. This, then, was another of the Carthaginians' infrequent efforts to send Hannibal supplies. That it consisted of foodstuffs (if Coelius' claim is correct) fits L.'s ensuing report of food-shortages in Hannibal's army, which recalls his statement (ch. 12) that the general could not obtain enough for his army from the ravaged lands he still occupied. That the effort failed is typical, in turn, of the Carthaginians' feckless naval performance throughout the war.

listed his achievements: on this famous, unfortunately lost, inscription, see 21.22 note. Hannibal set it up on a bronze column (Polybius 3.33, 56), probably one of those around the altar area. For his knowledge of Greek, see Nepos, *Hannibal* 13; Cassius Dio, fragment 54.

BOOK TWENTY-NINE

1 *into ranks and centuries*: this was the process of forming them into legions, first by assigning men to the three ranks of *hastati*, *principes*, and *triarii*, then distributing each rank into its ten *centuriae*.

to be superb: this measure of Scipio's resembles one by the Spartan king Agesilaus: during a campaign in Asia Minor in 396, he required each of the local rich to supply a fully equipped horse and cavalryman, or be conscripted themselves (Xenophon, *Hellenica* 3.4). So the story has been judged an annalist's invention. Yet some details are different; and it is better to judge the story as an annalist's elaboration of a real act (Scipio finding a way to equip his 300 without cost to the republic). It is also possible, of course, that Scipio himself got the idea from reading Xenophon (cf. ch. 19 on his interest in Greek books and culture at this time).

1 *contemplating the destruction of Carthage*: rhetorical flourish. Nothing suggests that Scipio or the Romans had this goal in mind, then or later. Meanwhile, many if not most of the seasoned legionaries were the long-suffering survivors of Cannae.

withdrawn a seasoned army: this is L.'s first mention of such a withdrawal, but Scipio did send two legions back to Italy, leaving the new governors with the remaining pair. These were hardly 'a disorganized bunch of recruits', but Indibilis is of course trying to arouse support.

the Ausetani, and other peoples: the Ausetani dwelt near the Pyrenees, so the other rebels were probably also neighbours—'little-known' tribes according to L. (ch. 2).

2 *a brisk cavalry charge*: L.'s description of this battle bears some notable (and, to some scholars, suspicious) resemblances to a later one in Italy; see note on 30.18.

3 *delivered up for punishment*: the Latin term here for 'punishment' (*supplicium*) implies execution.

Hippo Regius: this town (Annaba/Bône in eastern Algeria) lay over 200 miles from Carthage, with difficult country in between, and over 300 miles by sea from western Sicily; it was also in the territory of Masinissa's people the Maesuli or Massyli, not in Carthage's. Though most modern historians accept L.'s report, it is likelier that he or his source has confused Hippo Regius with Hippo Diarrhytus (also called Hippacra; today's Bizerte), about 40 miles north of Carthage. Like Utica, raided in 207 (28.4), this was a Phoenician sister-city and ally of Carthage; its nearness would much better account for the panic there, including the belief that Scipio's invasion had begun.

Masinissa, who came to meet Laelius, thus had to ride through Carthaginian territory from his refuge near the Emporia region (ch. 32). But if Laelius' landfall was Hippo Regius, then he would have had to ride a still greater distance, and through lands patrolled by his victorious enemy Syphax.

shifts loyalties with every prospect of gain: this is rhetorical, inaccurate, and quite unfair to the native 'Libyan' population of Punic Africa, whom the Carthaginians had ruled and conscripted for centuries. Hannibal's, and other generals', best troops during the war were Africans (of course, once recruited they had to be paid, though this often failed to happen). L. may be drawing on an excited source—pro-Carthaginian or Roman—or composing rhetoric of his own.

4 *join up with Hannibal*: Mago, like their brother Hasdrubal two years earlier, had effectively thrown away any strategic advantage from his descent on Italy by putting himself 700 miles away from Hannibal, with twelve fully alerted Roman legions in between. Some thousands more troops sent his way would make little difference to this losing equation.

5 *Albingauni*: for the Ingauni, see 28.46 and 30.19; this looks like a variant name, taken from the town Album Ingaunum on the Ligurian coast.

6 *The propraetor Quintus Pleminius*: L. compresses for convenience; Pleminius had not been a praetor but, as a *legatus* of the consul Scipio (ch. 8), he held *imperium* equivalent to a praetor's.

7 *The tide turned in the straits*: the regularly alternating south-to-north and north-to-south currents in the Straits of Messina (which inspired the myth of Scylla and Charybdis) are very strong. To reach Locri, Scipio needed the north-to-south flow.

9 *a hexeris*: a 'sixer' warship, with groups of six men at the oars (a quinque-reme or 'fiver' had groups of five), but how the oars and the grouping were arranged is unknown.

10 *from Pessinus*: the goddess Cybele or Great Mother (*Magna Mater*), the eastern deity of fertility, was worshipped at Pessinus, in central Asia Minor, in the form of a sacred stone (ch. 11). She also had a noted shrine on Mt. Ida, near Troy, and thus was of interest to the Romans, who claimed Trojan descent via Aeneas. Once established at Rome, Cybele's rites were far more decorous than in her homeland, where orgiastic dancing was practised, and self-castration by male enthusiasts (immortalized in Catullus' remarkable Poem 63).

11 *Aesculapius*: worship of this Greek god of healing (in Greek, Asklepios) had been brought to Rome in 293; his temple was on the Tiber island.

his tenure of the post: the point of electing someone already holding an official commission elsewhere, who could not therefore exercise his new functions, is hard to see. It is worth noting that Lucius Lentulus and his brother Gnaeus (later consul in 201) were elected together. Perhaps it was a step agreed on to enable Lucius to advance towards a consulship later, as a reward for his services in Spain (he was consul in 199).

Marcus Atilius Regillus: earlier termed Flamen of Quirinus, probably in error (24.8 and note).

12 *abandoned by the Romans*: a piece of welcome, if shortlived, candour. After operations in 208 (28.5–8), the proconsul Sulpicius Galba had passed two inactive years, leaving the Aetolians to cope with Philip V on their own. A vigorous raid by the king into Aetolia in 207 (Polybius 11.7) broke their resistance—something L. does not mention until 36.31! The Romans nevertheless viewed the Aetolians' peace with Macedon as a faithless act, for the Aetolians had not insisted on Philip also making peace with Rome as the treaty of 211 required (26.24).

the praetors: as usual, meaning the *strategi* of a Greek state.

12 *the people of Ilium*: Ilium was the city on the site of Troy, its people honoured by the Romans as kinfolk. All the states listed were 'associated' (*adscripti*) with the treaty, a form of international recognition. Some scholars suspect that a number of the alleged 'associates' are Roman annalists' additions; but, that issue apart, this treaty's details seem accurately reported.

13 *Marcus Livius*: proconsul in Cisalpine Gaul, afterwards appears as censor in this year (ch. 37), which may explain why one of the new praetors, Libo, was also assigned Gaul as a sphere of duty.

that sphere of authority: L. writes *eam provinciam*; then in the next sentence he uses the plural *eas provincias* for 'these areas of responsibility', no doubt being aware that at this period Spain was technically one military theatre but that, in 197, the Roman-held east and south were demarcated into two formal provinces, Hither and Farther Spain (32.28).

14 *Publius Scipio*: cousin of the great Publius Scipio; perhaps to distinguish between them, he acquired the nickname Nasica ('Bignose'), afterwards passed on to his descendants. He was to become consul in 191.

Claudia Quinta: other versions of the event (e.g. Suetonius, *Tiberius* 2) tell a miraculous tale of how Claudia, suspected of adultery, proved her innocence by drawing the goddess's ship off a Tiber mudbank by herself. L. is plainly unimpressed by this detail. A rival tradition, meanwhile, named the chief matron as one Valeria.

12 April: thus the manuscripts (*pridie idus Apriles*, the day before the Ides of April). But inscriptional evidence shows that the correct date was 4 April (*pridie nonas Apriles*, the day before the Nones). The festival was named the Megalesia because the goddess's temple at Pergamum, Attalus' capital, was the Megalesium ('Great Mother' in Greek being *Megale Meter*).

15 *exemption from military service*: since 209; see 27.9–10.

the register: see 27.10 note.

16 *the financial contributions they had made*: in 210 (see 26.36).

17 *Anyone aware*: reading *qui sciat* (Walsh reads *nesciat*) (translator's note).

18 *an inglorious and dishonourable end*: in 272 Pyrrhus assaulted Argos, but in confused street-fighting lost his helmet and was killed by a tile flung from a rooftop.

19 *to leave the temple*: the Senate may have been meeting in the Curia, since the Locrian envoys had approached the consuls in the Comitium outside (ch. 16). The Curia was also a temple, in its strict sense of a consecrated space.

20 *rang true*: according to Plutarch (*Cato Maior* 3), complaints about Scipio were made by his own quaestor, the acerbic Marcus Porcius Cato (cf. ch. 25), later famous as Cato the Censor. L. does not mention this, but his careful comment about criticisms implies that he found them in at least

one respectable source—possibly Cato's own later history, the *Origines*, or a work that drew on it. Polybius, incidentally, also knew Cato.

Marcus Pomponius: Scipio's mother was a Pomponia, and this praetor was Scipio's cousin. Metellus' choice was no doubt deliberate—and so was the Senate's acceptance of his proposals. Note too that the consuls then selected Metellus himself as one of the senators to accompany Pomponius (ch. 21).

21 *Scipio had either . . . wrongs when they have been done*: this is a reasonably just verdict on Scipio's less than admirable behaviour in the Pleminius case, whether the Locrians themselves put it thus or L. does it for them.

22 *Clodius Licinus*: there were two historians named Clodius, one around 100 BC who may also be the translator Claudius (mentioned in 25.39), the other named Clodius Licinus, who was contemporary with Livy and consul in AD 4. The former may or may not have been a Licinus too. It is very rare for L. to cite another historian so specifically, and he names Clodius Licinus only here: this implies a particular alertness to his version, perhaps because L. may only recently have read it. Which Clodius is meant, all the same, is not clear.

the Tullianum: the death-prison at the foot of the Capitoline, not far from the Curia (still accessible today). Scipio's second consulship was in 194.

his province: i.e. Sicily.

23 *Hasdrubal's daughter*: the beautiful Sophoniba ('Safonba'al' in Punic), whose tragedy is famously told in 30.12–15. One Greek version of the name is Saphonis, and as 'Sophonisba', a spelling in some fifteenth-century manuscripts, she became a favourite heroine of seventeenth- and eighteenth-century tragedy, including plays by Corneille, Voltaire, and James Thomson. (The latter was responsible for the much-derided line 'Oh! Sophonisba! Sophonisba! Oh!')

24 *if he were in agreement*: standard polite formula (26.16 note); Scipio's authority outranked his cousin Pomponius', so this was really a command.

25 *the question is moot*: L., working with a number of sources, is trying unsuccessfully to make sense of all of them. Which, if any, of the three totals he gives might be Polybius' is unknown, as the latter's account does not survive. That each of the 'Cannae legions' had as many as 6,200 infantry (ch. 24) has been doubted, but is conceivable given the importance of the expedition, even though similarly sized legions are not heard of again until the Third Macedonian War of 171–167. If so, their total of 13,000 Roman infantry and cavalry would imply, in turn, at least as many Latin and Italian troops and probably more. An army totalling around 30,000 men made sense, especially as Scipio could not now be sure of strong Numidian help. How L.'s various sources arrived at their varying totals can only be guessed.

Cato: see ch. 20 note.

a course for Emporia: Emporia (to be distinguished from Emporiae in north-east Spain) was the name for a fertile coastal district, later named

Byzacena, south-east of Carthage and on the western shore of the Gulf of Sirte. Whether Scipio really meant this as his destination, or used it as disinformation, is debated.

26 *had also made the crossing in the past*: in 256 (Regulus and Manlius, invading Africa with 330 warships) and again in 255 (Fulvius Nobilior and Aemilius Paulus, with 350, to rescue what remained of the shattered invasion army).

27 *the promontory of Mercury*: Cape Bon, 90 miles west of Sicily. The island of Aegimurus, Zembra today, lies near its western side.

The headland of the Beautiful One: in Latin, *promunturium Pulchri*, also sometimes called the Promontory of Apollo. This cape, today's Cap Farina or Ras Sidi Ali el Mekki, is farther west than Cape Bon, with the Gulf of Tunis lying between them (see also 30.10 and note). Carthage now lay directly south of the fleet, whereas the route to Emporia lay on the other side of the Cape Bon peninsula.

Coelius alone differs: a short quotation from 'Coelius' Book 6', in a Roman lexicon, reports an orderly landing somewhere by an army, and so some view L.'s résumé as a falsification of his account. But the fourteen-word quotation lacks a context and may refer to a different army's landing: e.g. Laelius' earlier raid (cf. ch. 3) or Mago's in Liguria (ch. 5).

28 *the almost fifty years*: in fact, fifty-two.

the leading man in the community: this Hasdrubal son of Gisgo was not a relative of Hannibal's family, so far as we know. But the disasters to Carthage since 209 seem, not surprisingly, to have weakened that family's virtual monopoly of political power at home and enabled Hasdrubal, no doubt with friends and supporters like the young cavalry captain Hanno (ch. 29), to reach this pre-eminence. Nevertheless, his circle and that of the Barcid family collaborated in defending their country (cf. 30.7).

29 *Hanno, a young nobleman*: a bigger cavalry defeat, again under a Hanno who is killed with many of his men, is narrated in chs. 34–5. This prompted some of L.'s sources (ch. 35), not to mention many scholars, to infer that there was only one battle, which got a double mention. But that is not convincing. The Carthaginians needed to reconnoitre the invasion force as soon as they could, while Masinissa—who played a leading role in the bigger battle—did not join Scipio right after the Romans landed. Again, Hanno was the commonest male name at Carthage.

quite a prosperous town: L. unhelpfully fails to give the name, but the likeliest town is Membrone, a small centre only 4–5 miles north of Utica. A possible alternative is Uzalis (El Alia today), about 8 miles north.

Gala: actually Gaia (24.48 note). L. may well draw on Polybius for this lengthy digression (chs. 29–33), as the Greek historian had conversed with Masinissa when he visited Africa in the king's old age (P. 9.25). No doubt the exciting account of his adventures lost nothing in Masinissa's telling half a century later.

a daughter of Hannibal's sister: another item of evidence that Hannibal had older sisters. His vigorous lieutenant Hanno, son of Bomilcar, may have been a nephew (21.27 note); and his father Hamilcar, to gain support from a Numidian prince—perhaps another brother of Gaia's—during the 'Truceless War' (21.1 note), had promised him a daughter as wife. But neither L. nor any other source records the name of any of the sisters.

30 *Baga*: interestingly, a hundred years later the Mauretanian king was named Bocchus, and in Julius Caesar's time he was named Bogud—very likely, variants of the same (royal?) name.

Thapsus: this cannot be the Punic town in Emporia where Caesar won a Civil War victory in 46 BC. Here it looks like an annalist's or a Livian mistake for Tipasa or maybe Thagaste, both of them Numidian towns on routes to the Masaesulii in the west.

31 *a mountain called Bellus*: unidentifiable, but it was near the sea as the next paragraph shows, and near fertile Carthaginian territory too. Somewhere in north-east Numidia is likely, not far from Thabraca (modern Tabarka); there is plenty of mountainous country south of this, and in Roman times even an inland town called Belalis.

their huts: huts of thatch and branches, easily portable by shepherds and nomads.

32 *Clupea*: the only Clupea known is a city on Cape Bon, in the heart of Carthage's own territory, so this must be another annalistic misnomer. If these events took place in eastern Numidia, the 'large river' that Masinissa then crossed was the River Bagradas (Mejerda) or a tributary, and its rushing torrent points to the season being spring (of 205).

on some hills: between Cirta (modern Constantine) and Hippo (i.e. Hippo Regius/Annaba) stretches the range called Monts de Constantine. Cirta was Syphax's inland capital, on a formidable site almost surrounded by the River Ampsaga's deep ravines.

33 *the Lesser Syrtis*: the Gulf of Gabès, south of the Emporia region, 200 miles in a straight line from the Monts de Constantine (previous note)—but much further by land, much of it across semi-desert or, nearer the coast, real desert. Inland from the Gulf dwelt the desert people, the Garamantes.

Large numbers . . . of an exile: a variant account, in later authors (Appian, and Dio via Zonaras), has Masinissa patch up an agreement with Syphax and Hasdrubal, and march with them against Scipio, only to change sides then. If L. knows this version he plainly and rightly disbelieves it, as did Polybius who, later on, also stresses the small force Masinissa brought to Scipio (P. 21.21).

34 *Hanno son of Hamilcar*: not a brother of Hannibal's; Hamilcar was one of the handful of names frequently used by Carthaginian aristocrats.

Salaeca: unknown. Scholars usually site it west of Utica, but there is no evidence of an ancient town at that distance. South-west of Utica, meanwhile, the area was a vast marshland; this rules out Salaeca being in that direction, for Masinissa afterwards rode back from there, under pursuit, towards the Roman camp outside Utica—something hardly possible across marshes. Salaeca may have lain close to the Lake of Bizerte to the north-west: the distance would be right (15 Roman miles = 12 modern), and the Carthaginians there could look for supplies from Hippo Diarrhytus at the head of the lake.

34 *the cover of some hills*: Appian (*Libyca* 14) mentions a tower at the spot, supposedly built by Agathocles during his invasion, 30 stades or about 3.5 miles from Utica. So the site has been identified with the range of hills stretching south-west from Utica, where an ancient ruin stands in a saddle between two of these hills (cf. 30.4 and note). Still, this would mean Masinissa had to conduct a dangerous fighting retreat over 15 Roman miles (see previous note) while Scipio waited comfortably for him outside the Roman camp. Quite possibly, instead, the battle site was nearer to Salaeca, wherever that lay.

35 *Hanno taken prisoner*: this is the version in Appian and Dio, who add that Masinissa used him in an exchange to free his own mother, a captive of Hasdrubal son of Gisgo. This pious detail may thus have been in Coelius and Valerius too—which does not make it more believable. For L. to pass over the opportunity to record such a commendable act strongly indicates that Polybius did not mention it, and that L. was not convinced by those who did.

50,000 infantry and 10,000 cavalry: these seem fantastic numbers (despite being from Polybius 14.1). Together Syphax's and Hasdrubal's armies would have totalled 93,000 (not to mention the garrison in Utica), even if Scipio may not have been too worried about Syphax's Numidian infantry. Scholars estimate that the two allies really had about 30,000 foot and 3,000–5,000 horse, but by contrast this estimate seems too low. For if Hasdrubal and Syphax had numbers only just superior to Scipio's 30,000 or so (see ch. 25 note), and many of them new and inexperienced troops at that, they would hardly have moved so close to him. Roughly 50,000 is a likelier total for the two men's armies (cf. 30.6 note). All the same, the two did not feel strong enough to launch an attack on the Roman camp.

a narrow spit of land: this is now a long and narrow ridge amid fields, with a village called Kalaat el-Andaless at its northern end. On Utica, see 28.4 note.

36 *led his army away to Croton*: the Roman victory looks very exaggerated, for Hannibal retired unmolested. L. records another supposed battle near Croton in 203 (30.19), probably a doublet of this one. The temple to Fortuna Primigenia was indeed dedicated (in 194: 34.53), but, as the strategic situation remained the same after the supposed battle, a large skirmish—favouring the Romans—seems more plausible.

a change of regime: the disaffection of Etruria seems overstated, too, though the ongoing investigations by the consul show that the Romans were suspicious, and perhaps had reasons to be. Still, Etruscan communities were not penalized after the war (contrast the fate of Capua and its associates);

we do not hear that they even received treatment like that meted out to the recalcitrant twelve Latin colonies (ch. 15). Such punishments as did occur must have been inflicted on individuals.

37 *Marcus Livius and Gaius Claudius*: these were the victors of the battle of the Metaurus, elected censors for 204–203. L. seems both pained and amused at their increasingly unseemly behaviour.

leader of the house: see 27.11 note on 'Senate leader'.

mark of disgrace: in the census register the censors placed a mark (*nota*) beside the name of a citizen whose conduct they judged disgraceful to the community; they had very wide discretion over what acts qualified for this. A senator thus marked out was thereby deprived of his membership of the house.

a sixth of an as: presumably per Roman pound. Saltworks belonged to the Roman state, but salt-collection was done by private contractors, who paid a sum for their contract and then sought their profit by selling the product itself to the public. By raising the price of those contracts applying outside Rome, the censors increased revenues, while no doubt permitting the contractors in turn to charge a higher retail price—a blow to consumers. The tale L. then tells, of Livius' resentment being the cause of the increase, smacks of whimsical hindsight based on his *cognomen* Salinator ('salt-seller'): in reality he was not the first to bear this. Incidentally the Maecia tribe, mentioned below as the only tribe in 219 not voting to convict him, was one of the rural tribes hit by the new prices.

a public horse: citizens of means, if registered in the eighteen centuries of cavalry, were granted a horse by the state for them to ride in war. In a review of these centuries, each member had to present himself with his horse for inspection; unsatisfactory cavalrymen could be made to sell their mount. This spat seems (and plainly seemed at the time) ridiculous, but—unlike the claimed motive for the increased salt-tax—there is little reason to doubt it.

whim of the people: this unseemly affair appears to have been allowed to die away, nor can the censors' decisions about poll-tax payers have stood for long.

38 *of their own volition*: Clampetia and Consentia are also reported submitting voluntarily to the next consul in Bruttium (30.19). L. must be drawing on two different sources, who gave the event in differing years with variant details.

Pomponius Matho: not the praetor in Sicily; on the plurality of Pomponii Mathones in these years, see 24.17 note.

he was very young: son of the Gracchus who was killed at the River Calor in 212 (25.15–16); he would marry Scipio's daughter Cornelia and himself be twice consul, in 177 and 163. Their sons were the reformers Tiberius and Gaius Gracchus. Fabius Maximus, too, had been appointed to a priesthood when fairly young, in 265: see 30.26.

BOOK THIRTY

1 *Gnaeus Servilius and Gaius Servilius*: the two consuls were not closely related (if at all); Gnaeus Caepio was a patrician, Gaius Geminus a plebeian. On Geminus, see 27.21.

a reputation as a soldier: a surprising claim, for Licinius had no military successes to his credit, either as consul in 205 or proconsul in 204. L.'s eulogy is unusually placed, for it embodies the sort of praises normally put into obituaries. Licinius did not die until 183 (39.46), but L. seems impatient to bring this character sketch into his account; perhaps he had just unearthed it in his researches.

until the war in Africa was ended: yet later on L. reports further renewals in 202 (ch. 27) and 201 (ch. 41). He may be drawing on conflicting sources; or else, quite possibly, other would-be conquerors' efforts to take command in Africa—consuls in 203, 202, and 201 all tried to do this (chs. 24, 27, 40)—made it necessary to reconfirm Scipio's commission each year after all.

2 *praetor the previous year*: in fact the year before (205), then propraetor in 204 (29.13).

same condition as it was then: a standard formula. The games were not, in the end, put on until 202 (ch. 27), so these consuls of 203 must have been distracted.

the liver's 'head' was missing: see 27.26 note.

3 *had launched their ships*: not out to sea, a rash act during winter; L. means they had them in commission, as he clarifies at once.

the version of most of the sources: Polybius is one of these (we have his account for these events: 14.1), and as usual L. is following him fairly closely. Scipio's position was in fact a difficult one, despite L.'s claim of lavish supplies from abroad. The winter will have slowed, or even stopped, these as well as immobilizing his relatively small fleet; two enemy armies were confronting him; nor could he be sure that, when spring came, Hannibal would stay on in Italy instead of returning—with his veterans— to join the confrontation.

4 *unreasonable conditions . . . deliberately added*: this is later Roman obfuscation. Polybius (14.2) reports Syphax successfully persuading Hasdrubal and the Carthaginians to accept the terms that he and Scipio had agreed on. He sees nothing wrong in Scipio's ensuing withdrawal from talks, but Romans obviously felt uncomfortable at this sharp dealing. The new 'unreasonable conditions' were thus invented, possibly quite early in the tradition.

the hill . . . overlooking Utica: of the two hills usually identified as the area of the battle of Agathocles' Tower (29.34 and note), this is the closer to the town. But L. has subtly modified Polybius' order of events. Polybius reports Scipio making these renewed moves at the start of spring—during the negotiations with Syphax. L., unlike the Greek historian, is anxious not to ascribe any more duplicity to his Roman hero than he absolutely must, so the moves are reported after the break-off of talks. But Polybius, too, seeks to put Scipio in the clear in his own way (14.3): after the break-off of talks, he writes, Syphax and Hasdrubal were eager to bring Scipio to battle. This may, of course, be true.

5 *around midnight*: in Polybius (14.4), 'towards the end of the third watch', roughly 3 a.m., but L. is not too fussy over such details. On the first watch, see 21.27 note.

to douse the flames: it seems clear that neither Syphax's troops nor Hasdrubal's had maintained proper vigilance, though sentries in the Punic camp are mentioned (ch. 6). The lengthy negotiations had relaxed their vigilance—hence Scipio's urgency in launching his attacks as soon as the talks were broken off (not a point L. labours).

6 *From the many thousands of soldiers . . . died by the sword or in the fire*: L. may have drawn these figures from Polybius, whose excerpted account of the events is incomplete. Polybius has the enemy generals escaping with just a few cavalry (14.6), but reports that, a day later, Hasdrubal son of Gisgo had 2,500 foot and horse at a town nearby; thus, as L. records (ch. 7), other escapees had rallied to him, and the same is implied for Syphax. Of course if the two had really had Polybius' earlier total of 93,000 men, over half their armies must still have survived—but an original 50,000 is much likelier (29.35 and note). Even if 40,000 dead is an optimistic Roman exaggeration, the other numbers look plausible; and the 40,000 might include survivors who failed to rally later and so were added to the tally of men lost.

7 *the closest city*: only Appian gives it a name, Anda (*Libyca* 24), but—as often with Appian—this is not known otherwise. Appian is quite capable of confusing it with Abba, where Syphax rallied some troops (see note below). Hasdrubal's city may have been Uzalis, 8 miles north of Utica (if this was not the town Scipio had captured earlier: 29.29 and note), Thizica 20 miles west, or Ad Gallinacium, the later Roman name for a village 10 miles to the south, across the River Bagradas. Just west of this last stood Cigisa and (on the other side of the Bagradas) Ucres, two small towns which might be termed 'cities', often an unrigorous term in ancient authors. The Carthaginians' consternation is all the more understandable if Scipio was now operating within a couple of days' march of their city.

Syphax . . . some eight miles away: Polybius names his halting-place Abba (14.6) and terms it 'nearby'; L. must get the measurement from another source. The name is not known otherwise, but a town called Thubba lay 20 miles south-west of Utica, beyond the marshland, and this may—with a little difficulty—count as 'nearby'. L.'s numeral would then be wrong. (If perhaps he had the distance rather underestimated as 18 Roman miles, a numeral 'XVIII' could have been corrupted in manuscripts to 'VIII', for the preceding word is 'Syphax'.)

a city called Oppa: in some manuscript 'Obba', and so perhaps L.'s name for Abba. But in contrast to L.'s account, Polybius (14.7) reports Syphax himself meeting the new mercenaries near that town. A few other details not in Polybius, like the Numidian peasants and the time-phrase 'only days later', show that L. is combining Polybius' version with someone else's. An Obba is known in the interior, some 120 miles south-west of Carthage, but how and why mercenaries from Spain should end up there is hard to see.

7 *only days later*: Polybius specifies 'in thirty days' and L. can hardly imply less time; even 30 days seems a very brief span in which to march inland, gather up fresh forces, and equip them in more or less battle-worthy fashion (Scipio had captured most of the earlier armies' armament: ch. 6). L.'s and Polybius' figure of 30,000 has been questioned; but the Carthaginians' forces back on the coast must have been few, if Scipio could leave behind only a small Roman force outside Utica, while the new area of operations was close to Syphax's kingdom. On the other hand, the 4,000 Celtiberians plainly were the most—and maybe the only—battle-hardened unit. According to Polybius, it was given out that they were 10,000 strong.

8 *'The Great Plains'*: Syphax and Hasdrubal had moved 80 miles further west, to broad plains around the River Bagradas near Bulla Regia, about 30 miles north-west of Thugga and between today's Bou Salem and Jendouba. Polybius (14.8) records that the Romans reached the area 'on the fifth day', which is feasible for an army in light array; L. may not fully realize the distance involved. The risk Scipio was taking was immense: a defeat so far inland would mean destruction on the scale of Regulus' disaster in 255.

leaving the triarii in reserve: this was the normal battle formation of a Roman army, including having the cavalry on either wing. Neither L. nor Polybius is helpful enough to tell us where the enemy infantry units stood. If they were with their cavalry comrades on either wing, Scipio was confronting all of the enemy army except the Celtiberians with just his cavalry, which would show how low he now rated the Africans' fighting capacity. All the same, since he used his second and third lines to surround the Celtiberians during the battle (a detail Polybius gives: 14.8), he could have brought those lines out, had need arisen, to back up the cavalry wings. A few moderns infer that he actually did this; others think that his cavalry had only the enemy horse to deal with, and place Hasdrubal's and Syphax's infantry in the centre alongside the Celtiberians. Neither supposition matches what Polybius and L. report. The enemy generals' hope may have been to overpower Scipio's cavalry with sheer numbers, then surround the legionaries while these were held by the Celtiberians.

9 *under Carthaginian control*: the logic of the ensuing events shows that Scipio now marched back towards the coast, no doubt down the populous and wealthy Bagradas valley. The Carthaginians had not had time to launch their attack on his fleet outside Utica before he reached Tynes.

Tynes: modern Tunis, which lies 11 miles (18 km.) from Carthage (L.'s 15 Roman miles and Polybius' 120 stades are a little exaggerated). Rather like New Carthage, it had the sea on one side (the Gulf of Tunis) and a lagoon on the other.

10 *On reaching his destination*: Utica and its environs lie 24 miles by road from Tunis, a distance requiring at the very least a day's forced march, though in this emergency Scipio very probably rode ahead with an escort. Still, the dilatoriness of the enemy fleet is striking, for the distance by sea was about the same and yet Scipio, on reaching his fleet, had time for elaborate countermeasures.

Rusucmon: next to the 'headland of the Beautiful One' (29.27 and note), it was in early modern times the pirate stronghold of Porto Farina. It lay 15 miles across the gulf, north-east of Utica and Scipio's beachhead.

harpagones: 'grappling irons', a Greek word (related to the name Harpies) meaning 'grabbers'; hence Molière's choice of it for the title-character in *L'Avare*.

the timely arrival of Scipio: a graphic illustration of the risks he took in his African campaigns.

11 *the Roman infantry*: L. means the light-armed troops, for only afterwards do the legionaries enter the fray.

12 *Cirta*: see note to 29.32.

with the infantry in easy stages: an interesting parallel to Maharbal's advice to Hannibal after Cannae—or maybe Trasimene (22.51 and note).

Sophoniba: first named here, though mentioned since 29.23. L.'s famous account of her tragedy (chs. 12–15) again has a drama-like structure and plenty of vivid confrontations: (i) the capture of Cirta, and Masinissa meeting and falling in love with Sophoniba, (ii) their marriage and Laelius' reaction, (iii) the return to Scipio's camp and Syphax's interview with the general, (iv) Scipio's counsel to Masinissa and its effects, (v) Sophoniba's suicide. It is quite unlikely that such elaboration came from Polybius, whose account of these events we lack: if L. has drawn on him for the basic facts, he has worked them up very imaginatively, and may have had one or more Roman historical plays (*praetextae*) to inspire him (cf. 23.4 note).

absolute power over us: i.e. Sophoniba and Syphax.

the other cities of Numidia: the kingdom's size, roughly equivalent to northern Algeria, means that, despite L.'s generalization, the cities directly subdued by Laelius and Masinissa must have been those between Cirta and the Punic frontier as their forces made the return march to Scipio's camp at Utica. Masinissa still had much trouble, over the next eighteen months or so, bringing Syphax's territories properly under control.

14 *now belong to the Roman people as their spoils*: this pronouncement may have come as rather a shock to Masinissa. It is not at all likely that Scipio had stated it in earlier times, when he needed the king's help.

15 *take it to Sophoniba*: we are meant to understand that she had come with Masinissa to the coast. Some later writers, like Appian, leave her in Cirta and Masinissa has to return there with the poison.

16 *enjoyed considerable respect*: apparently an 'inner' council of senior members of the Carthaginian senate (ex-sufetes?), but its formal functions—if any—are not known.

the area of their origin: alluding to Carthage being a colony of Tyre in Phoenicia, and to the practice, originally Persian, of *proskynesis*, self-prostration before a ruler (equivalent to the kowtow in imperial China). Polybius later censoriously mentions the same act (15.1), adding that the envoys also kissed the Romans' feet. In reality this, and possibly another ambassadorial prostration after Zama (ch. 36), are the only such actions ever recorded of Carthaginian envoys, and should not be supposed typically 'Punic'. The impression the envoys obviously made with it was surely intended.

supported his power: this is not evidence (though it is sometimes taken to be) that the Carthaginian aristocracy as a whole had always been against Hannibal. In the circumstances of 203 and with him far away, it was the best the spokesmen could do. See also notes to chs. 20 and 22.

islands . . . between Italy and Africa: this must mean those besides Sicily, Sardinia, and Corsica, which the Romans already held; the others would include the Balearics and Ebusus (though these properly lie between Italy and Spain).

little agreement on the amount: Polybius later (15.8) gives the 5,000 talents figure, whereas 5,000 pounds of silver would be equivalent to little more than 60 talents, a ridiculous amount unless L. is following a miscopied text. (The late Roman writer Eutropius (3.21) has 500,000 pounds.)

they were now playing for time: this seems a fair comment, for Hannibal's recall had been voted (ch. 9) and was not now rescinded or amended. Scipio was surely aware of this: his gamble was that Hannibal would be held in Italy until the terms were ratified.

17 *Many days before this*: the talks between Scipio and the Carthaginians, and the measures ensuing, must have taken two or three weeks at least, allowing Laelius and his group plenty of time to reach Rome.

until the Carthaginian representatives arrived: if this item is correct, L. is implicitly recording that word had already arrived from Africa that the envoys were on their way; for Laelius had set out before the peace-terms were agreed.

18 *the land of the Insubrian Gauls*: western Lombardy. Mago was last reported destroying Genua on the coast (ch. 1), so he must have moved north over the mountains, no doubt seeking to rally the Gauls in those parts.

turned to flight: L.'s account of this Roman victory over Mago has some close resemblances to his account of the victory over Indibilis in Spain in 29.2. For (i) when either battle is in the balance, one of the two Roman commanders calls on the other for 'a brisk cavalry charge' (*procella equestris*, the same term each time) to decide it; (ii) each battle has a faltering twelfth legion rescued by a thirteenth; (iii) each enemy leader is struck down, causing his men to lose heart. Yet not all the details are similar, and it is not to be doubted that both battles occurred. The likelihood is that full details were not available for one, so it was livened up by Livy (or one of his sources) with items from the other. If so, the present battle is probably the more accurate one, as it was fought in north Italy and against a brother of Hannibal himself, and L. gives some precise names and figures including quite heavy Roman losses. But a lead sling-bullet of 205 or so, found recently in Andalusia, mentions a *legio XIII*: so not all the coincidences should be judged fictions.

19 *the Ligurian Ingauni*: see 28.46, 29.5 and notes.

the Gallic Gulf: the Gulf of Genoa.

died from his wound: more fanciful accounts keep Mago alive, explaining his absence from the Zama campaign either by denying he left Italy in 203 (Appian, *Libyca* 49, 54) or by claiming that he was promptly sent back to Italy from Africa (so Dio's abbreviator Zonaras); and Hannibal's biographer Nepos has Mago perish in 193 (*Hannibal* 8). In reality, Mago left an officer, Hamilcar, behind to cause trouble for the Romans in Cisalpine Gaul over the next several years and Dio probably confused him with his chief. If a Mago related to Hannibal did perish in 193, it was probably a more distant kinsman: one such—a cousin?—was mentioned in 23.41.

near the village of Tannetum: L. writes from memory. In his report of the capture he gives the site as Mutina (21.25 and note); the Roman army that marched to the rescue was ambushed near Tannetum.

still alive: see 27.21 and note.

Consentia ... Clampetia: these communities were reported in 29.38 as deserting Hannibal the year before. The supposed 'pitched battle' with Hannibal that L. then mentions was also reported in 204 (29.36 and note); if Valerius Antias was L.'s sole source this time round, the item can safely be disregarded.

20 *by bringing down Carthage*: Hanno the Great (on whom see 21.3) is reported by Appian as still alive at this time (*Libyca* 34); L. may imply it too in ch. 42. But no one—not even L. apart from rhetorical flights like this—claims that he had had any influence over Carthaginian affairs for decades. L., in fact, admits the opposite all over again in ch. 42. If this alleged exclamation of Hannibal's is based on anything better than Roman imagination, L. is probably utilizing later efforts by pro-Hannibalic sources (like his friends Sosylus and Silenus) to shift blame for losing the war from him onto a supposed hostile power-clique at Carthage. The same effort, in reverse, was already being tried by the Carthaginians in 203: see ch. 16.

ahead of time: it is quite a surprise to find Hannibal possessing a transport fleet. Either it was sent from Carthage or (as L.'s words imply and Appian (*Hannibalica* 58) affirms) he had it built locally.

foully murdered within the temple itself: this atrocity is asserted, in varied versions, by many writers, claiming up to 20,000 victims. But the bulk of the army Hannibal took with him must itself have consisted of Italians, for not many of his original 26,000 (21.38 and note) can have survived. This army of Italy was his most reliable division at Zama (ch. 34 note), which makes it very unlikely that the general had previously massacred thousands of their comrades (in a sacred place, at that). The origin of the tale may be the 3,000 horses slaughtered because they could not be taken along (Diodorus 27.9); conceivably, too, a number of mutinous Italian troops were executed for refusing to leave Italy.

21 *ordered to do so by the Senate*: an item L. mentions almost casually, yet a very significant one. The Senate had realized (and so had Scipio: ch. 23) that the brothers, in Italy, were all but irrelevant to the outcome of the war; but allowing them to return to Africa had the potential to change that outcome. This makes it still more strange that no efforts are recorded of Roman attempts to obstruct Hannibal's collecting a transport fleet, his embarking, or his journeying to Africa.

had already been dismissed: here begins a very strange episode in L. Earlier, but not much earlier (ch. 17), he recorded the Senate deciding that Laelius should stay in Rome until the Carthaginian representatives arrived. Here we find Laelius first dismissed and then recalled. There follows a report, circumstantial and yet unconvincing, of the Senate rejecting the peace-terms agreed in Africa. The Punic envoys behave provocatively, senators are alienated, Laelius speaks in equivocal language, and the terms are rejected.

Such an outcome of the debate is improbable in itself, is contradicted by Polybius' surviving excerpts (especially 15.1 and 8) and by later writers like Appian and Dio (despite oddities in their versions, too)—and does not fit even L.'s own later narrative (e.g. ch. 38: alarm at Rome at the news of resumed hostilities). Plainly he has chosen to follow a source or sources which did not wish to record a ratification. One likely culprit would be a pro-Hannibal writer. For to record the Senate ratifying Scipio's terms, but the war still going on after Hannibal's return, would clearly suggest bad faith by the Carthaginians. Many details of the senatorial debate itself, however, point to a Roman source of information. L., then, seems to be using a Roman writer who had consulted pro-Hannibalic as well as Roman sources, and who was also (moralizingly?) keen to have the Senate reject a deceitful and arrogant enemy's overtures. The likeliest candidate would be Coelius Antipater.

22 *with Gaius Lutatius*: the Punic envoys may well have sought to saddle Hannibal alone with the blame for the war, a misinformation-campaign already begun (ch. 16 and note), and they may have spoken of the peace of 241. But they could scarcely hope to avoid mentioning the terms agreed on with Scipio, especially if the Senate knew about these already (see note on ch. 17).

23 *given an answer*: some of the details of the Senate debate may be genuine— Salinator's and Laevinus' grumpy interventions, the comments of Scipio's good friend Metellus, and even those by Laelius and Fulvius. In L.'s own

report, Laelius and Fulvius do not in fact oppose peace but instead warn against letting the Carthaginians play for time. If this is accurate, their comments thus amounted to urging swift ratification, contrary to L.'s claim that they influenced the vote in favour of rejection.

24 *appointed dictator*: Publius Sulpicius Galba was appointed by the other consul, Gaius Servilius Geminus, as L. only later (ch. 26) tells us. There, however, L. writes that it was the consul Geminus who was pursuing the investigations in Etruria and who, therefore, appointed Sulpicius to hold the elections. The official magistracy lists (the *Fasti Capitolini*) also give Sulpicius this function. All the same, Sulpicius may have acted, at the Senate's behest, to recall the consul Caepio as L. states; for Caepio did not persist in his bid to go to Africa. Marcus Servilius, the master of horse, was the consul Geminus' brother and was himself elected to the consulship for 202.

the period of the truce: L. is vague about the time; hardly during winter 203–202, a season when sailing was highly dangerous. The supply-fleets perhaps sailed in spring 202, for Scipio had demanded provisions from the Carthaginians for the truce period (ch. 16); but autumn 203 is also possible.

in full view of Carthage: on Aegimurus, see 29.27 and note. Aquae Calidae was the Roman name for a hot-springs spa, still in use today, near the town of Carpis (now Korbous) on the coast of Cape Bon opposite Carthage. Ships beached at Aegimurus can hardly have been seen from the city 30 miles away, but those at Aquae Calidae could, and word of the others would soon get around.

Hasdrubal: this seems to be a naval commander who, in Appian's account (*Hannibalica* 58), had led the warships escorting Hannibal's transports from Italy. He is less likely to be identified with Hasdrubal son of Gisgo.

25 *Senate's decision … was still not known*: on this L. directly contradicts Polybius (15.1), whose narrative survives from here up to Zama. Polybius states that Scipio had just received word from Rome of the treaty's ratification. To defend his story about the Senate rejecting it, L. has to maintain that no word at all had arrived; for to report that word of the rejection had come in would necessarily imply that the Carthaginians were free to resume hostilities. This burdens his account with difficulties, since otherwise he follows Polybius closely. In reality the Senate and people had ratified the peace, and this made the attacks on the Roman convoy and envoys genuine breaches of faith by the Carthaginians. L. wants to stress this while yet maintaining that the peace terms had been rejected.

his spokesmen: but even though Polybius gives a detailed summary of what the envoys said, L. includes none of it. Perhaps he dislikes the insulting and rather overbearing tone of their remarks in Polybius (and other sources?). As L. soon mentions, the envoys went to Carthage and back by sea, in a quinquereme.

25 *Leptis*: Leptis Minor (called 'Leptiminus' in later times, today's Lamta), on the southern edge of the fertile Emporia region, about 20 miles down the coast from Hadrumetum (Sousse) and some 110 miles south of Carthage. L. has Hannibal arrive before the end of 203, but the chronology of events—not only his, but that found in all sources—is very unclear: see note to ch. 29.

26 *sent with them*: this is all but certainly Roman propaganda fiction. No such troops figure in Polybius' account, though L. has them in Hannibal's second line at Zama (ch. 33) and later as prisoners (ch. 42). Perhaps a small body of Macedonian *mercenaries* signed up for service in Hannibal's field army, for he did have some mercenaries (ch. 33; P. 15.11) although Polybius' listing does not mention Macedonians. If afterwards they fell into Scipio's hands, they might have become the basis of Roman historians' much-inflated claim.

The named embassy to Philip V looks circumstantial, but its real mission has been lost or covered up. The complaints from Greek allies are very vaguely stated, but it is possible that Philip V had been encroaching in Illyria again. Yet when L. later reaches the preliminaries to the Second Macedonian War, it is Philip's aggression against Athens and across the Aegean that becomes the *casus belli* (31.1–3 etc.). L.'s report here looks like annalistic invention or exaggeration, preparing the reader for the coming war. See also ch. 42.

Italy was now open: a valuable indicator of the start of economic recovery, at least in areas accessible to the city of Rome; the measures authorized in 206 (28.11) were having an effect.

the first to bear: Maximus means 'greatest'; L. knows that Fabius the Delayer (Cunctator) was not the first to bear the name, but means that, had he been, it would have been thoroughly justified. The first Quintus Fabius Maximus had been his grandfather (or great-grandfather, in another account), surnamed or nicknamed Rullus or Rullianus, who had held five consulships between 322 and 295. His father (or, less likely, grandfather) had held three between 292 and 265. Fabius the Delayer must have been at least close to 80 when he died, even though his own first consulship had been in 233.

as Ennius puts it: a famous quotation (*unus homo nobis cunctando restituit rem*) from the epic verse-history of Rome, called *The Annals*, by this south Italian poet (239–169 BC). Ennius' rough-hewn and powerful epic became one of the cornerstones of Roman literature. The praise is deliberately paradoxical, for delaying—the Latin can also mean 'hesitating'—is not usually a decisive virtue, and gave rise to Fabius' later nickname 'Cunctator'.

27 *the province of Africa*: 'province' in the original sense of sphere of responsibility. These unseemly, and possibly unconstitutional, squabbles vividly illustrate how avid consuls in office could be for the glory of completing a great war and humbling an enemy; more squabbles ensued in 201

(ch. 40). Tiberius Claudius no doubt felt himself just as capable as Scipio of crushing Hannibal.

28 *Statorius*: the centurion sent to train Syphax's army in 214 or maybe 212 (24.48; on the date, see 24.41 note), but it is hardly plausible that he had stayed in his job after the king fell out with the Romans in 206.

as many campaigns as he: L.'s imaginative rhetoric should not be taken literally. Fifteen years of warfare cannot have left intact the bulk of Hannibal's original army, which by now must have been largely Italian (ch. 20 note).

man who was destined: the same expression (*fatalis ... dux*, 'destined leader') was used of Scipio in 22.53.

29 *a few days there*: the date of the war's final battle is even harder to fix than the site (on which see below), as there is only scattered evidence. Carthage accepted terms soon after it and the peace was ratified in 201, which makes a battle-date in the first half of 202 unlikely. A later skirmish was fought, according to L., on 17 December not long after the battle (ch. 36 and note). Again, Dio's abbreviator Zonaras (9.14) has an eclipse of the sun during the battle panicking the Carthaginians, and an eclipse is calculated to have occurred on 19 October—but one barely noticeable in North Africa's latitudes, nor does it figure in L.'s and Polybius' narratives.

The difficulty with a late 202 date is Hannibal's inactivity between landing at Leptis in 203 and marching to confront Scipio; but he lacked cavalry until Numidian allies joined him (Polybius 15.3; L. unhelpfully omits this) and also had to gather more infantry to bulk up his army. L. obscures the situation by having him move against Scipio seemingly only 'a few days' after landing and reaching Hadrumetum. He misunderstands Polybius (15.5): it was a few days after appeals to Hannibal from Carthage to take action that he moved from Hadrumetum, where he had evidently been building up his new army. The appeals were sent because Scipio was looting and laying waste the countryside (P. 15.4), another detail L. quite culpably omits.

The eclipse, in turn, may not have been very notable as such but could have been noted by other observers (at Carthage, and maybe Alexandria?), who afterwards reckoned it as occurring at or near the time of the battle. Exaggerating its impact would then be tempting for some writers, even if not L. and Polybius, leaving such exaggeration for Dio to pick up later. The Roman calendar, in turn, was notoriously erratic before its reform in 46 BC; so a *Roman* 17 December 202 could quite possibly have been an earlier real date (e.g. in early November). This inference is strengthened by the arrival, around that time again (ch. 36), of a fresh supply-fleet from Italy and by Laelius' trip to Rome—movements unlikely to be risked in midwinter.

that very day: L. cannot resist this dramatic touch, but Polybius (15.5) more credibly records Masinissa arriving the day after Scipio agreed to Hannibal's request for a face-to-face interview.

29 *Valerius Antias has it*: plainly one of Antias' best efforts in historical fiction.

Naraggara: recorded in Roman geographical sources as 30 Roman miles west of Sicca (Le Kef), and thus 50 or so miles (80 km.) west of the best-known of several towns called Zama. Polybius' text has 'Margaron', an unknown name but maybe a corruption, or Graecizing, of Naraggara. The name 'Zama' for the battle was erroneously inflicted by Hannibal's biographer Nepos (*Hannibal* 6) and has irrationally stuck. As Scipio was anxious to link up with Masinissa, the location is plausible; and, to prevent this if he could, Hannibal had to march across country from Hadrumetum. Since the country around Naraggara is hilly, the generally accepted view is that the armies then advanced to face each other on the broad plains a few miles south-west of Sicca. (If this is correct, the 'battle of Zama' arguably should be called the battle of Sicca.) This meant that the Roman army had moved even farther inland than the Great Plains—these lay 40 miles north-east—and the sole alternative to victory would be its annihilation (as L. notes in ch. 32).

30 *one translator each*: both men knew Greek, and may even have used it, but it was native to neither. For dignity's sake they would speak (at least to start with) in their own language.

Hannibal spoke first: on the symbolic significance of these two speeches, see 21.39 note. L. crafts them in his own rhetorical style at much greater length than Polybius' versions, borrowing, developing, and adding to items in those. Both historians' versions may be free compositions, though still perhaps including points that really were made; Sosylus and Silenus, in Hannibal's entourage, and Laelius in Scipio's camp quite probably recorded the gist of either man's words sometime afterwards. Hannibal's speech masterfully portrays a wearier, still proud, but wiser man—who yet succeeds in being a little patronizing towards his younger opponent.

as an old man: rhetorical exaggeration; he was 45.

Marcus Atilius: Regulus, in 255, on whom see notes to 28.42 and 43.

Let it be the lot . . . the will of the gods: Hannibal's geographical proposals do not differ much from the terms Scipio had set in 203 (ch. 16), or even from the situation afterwards created by the peace of 201. But in neither Polybius nor L. does he refer to the other demands put by Scipio (as L. has Scipio note at the start of his reply), notably an indemnity and a minimal Punic navy. It is likely enough that Hannibal kept to geopolitics, taking for granted that such additional provisos were inevitable.

have even refused peace: on this falsehood—L.'s, not Hannibal's—see note to ch. 21. L. did not there state anything about the status of the envoys.

31 *in the following vein*: Polybius, too, gives Scipio a briefer speech (15.8), and again L. borrows and enlarges on points from it. Scipio is more business-like than Hannibal and, understandably, more dismissive.

32 *the four corners of the earth*: this echoes Polybius (15.9); but the latter is stating his own view of the stakes involved, whereas L. artistically puts the

claim into the mouths of the two opposing leaders themselves. It is not, in fact, plausible that Scipio and Hannibal did have any such view. Certainly the outcome would decide who would dominate the western Mediterranean, but the many great powers in the east were a different matter. Or so, at least, they seemed to be in 202. Just fourteen years later, the situation would be dramatically different.

unable to abide by it: here again L. offers a view at odds with his earlier report that it was the Romans who had rejected the peace-terms.

33 *the cohorts*: L. does not make his point clear. Polybius (15.9) more lucidly explains that the *maniples* of the three Roman lines were deployed each behind the other so as to leave clear passageways through the infantry formation (maniples were normally arrayed like chessboard pieces). As three maniples, one from each line, formed a legionary cohort (perhaps as early as in this war: see 22.5 note), L. means to state that Scipio's cohorts were not formed up in the usual array. But he either fails to understand Polybius' description or else fails to convey it properly.

the light-armed troops of those days: cf. 26.4 note.

Ligurian and Gallic auxiliaries: these were Mago's men from north Italy (ch. 19). According to Polybius (15.11), this front line was 12,000 strong. Hannibal seems to have had rather more than 40,000 men (ch. 35 note). According to Appian (*Libyca* 41), Scipio had 23,000 Roman and Italian infantry and 1,500 cavalry, and this is plausible as he had to leave troops to hold his camp outside Utica and guard his fleet. But to Appian's figure we need to add the 6,000 Numidian foot and 4,000 horse whom Masinissa brought in (ch. 29).

a Macedonian legion: see ch. 26 and note. The Carthaginian and African forces must have been recruited recently, but L. thinks that *they* are the veterans from Italy described in chs. 28 and 32: for he makes the third line an untrustworthy one of Bruttian conscripts, and leaves it out of his battle narrative (ch. 34; cf. 35 and note). In reality, the army from Italy formed Hannibal's third line, as Polybius records (15.11).

34 *agility rather than strength*: by contrast, Polybius reports 'the mercenaries' of the front line gaining an initial advantage 'through their skill and daring' (15.13), and indeed L.'s own vivid detail—not Polybian but from some other source—of the Roman ranks using their shoulders and shield-bosses to force them back indicates a much closer combat.

more cover and support: by now L. has lost any clear idea of what was going on. For him, the Romans' 'real enemies' are the Carthaginians and Africans of the second line, but in reality these had fallen apart when attacked both by some of the panic-stricken first line and by the advancing Romans (P. 15.13)—leaving the third line, the veterans of Italy, face-to-face with the survivors of Cannae.

the battle started afresh: Scipio's leadership skill, and the expertise of his troops, in redressing the Roman battle line and opening it out—so that what had been the normal three-line formation now consisted of a single

very long line—have always been admired. It is, however, worth questioning why Hannibal was standing by with his veterans, while the rest of
his army was cut to pieces. Up till then, with most of the Roman army
occupied and indeed in some difficulties, and their cavalry still off the
field, it should have been the time for a potentially decisive counter-stroke,
using his third line of entirely fresh and superbly experienced veterans.
Scipio's *triarii*, though fresh too, would have been outnumbered. Leaving
the initiative to the Romans, and then accepting an old-fashioned face-to-
face battle of attrition, showed a sad decline in Hannibal's legendary talent
for manœuvres and stratagems.

35 *More than 20,000 of the Carthaginians . . . about 1,500 casualties*: all L.'s
figures are from Polybius (15.14). Hannibal's army presumably totalled
rather more than 40,000; Scipio's about 34,500 (ch. 33 note).

Hadrumetum: this town (modern Sousse on the coast) lay about 120 miles
from Naraggara and, if the battle was fought south of Sicca (see ch. 29
note on Naraggara), about 100 miles from the field. According to Nepos
(*Hannibal* 6) and others, Hannibal covered the distance in two days and
two nights. Like Polybius, whom he echoes (see next note), L. does not
dwell on what amounted to the general's abandonment of his surviving
troops, but prefers to laud his generalship up to the moment of defeat.

skilful deployment of the battle line that day: L. here compresses Polybius'
laudatory remarks (15.15–16), but blends them with others; thus his
ensuing words about the Carthaginian and African second line ('in whom
lay all his hopes'), not to mention his unmilitary notion that, *because* the
third line was supposedly untrustworthy, Hannibal had stationed it in his
own rear. (From which, incidentally, it must have evaporated by the time
Laelius and Masinissa returned with the cavalry—a point L. does not
notice.) Just as with the tale of the Senate rejecting Scipio's peace-terms,
we can only guess at why L. should ignore some details in Polybius (even
when otherwise following him closely) in favour of stuff from elsewhere
which fits neither the remaining Polybian material nor common sense.

36 *first day of the Saturnalia*: 17 December. Polybius' account is not extant
here, but this is a Roman date, so L. must be drawing on a Roman source.
This explains the unreliably huge claim of enemy slain and, perhaps, the
vagueness of location, but we may cautiously accept the victory itself and
its Roman date (though by the correct calendar the date may well have
been earlier: see ch. 29 note on 'a few days there'). The Saturnalia lasted
from the 17th to the 19th (and later from the 17th to the 21st), com-
memorating the ancient Italic god Saturn: it involved merrymaking,
exchanges of gifts, and a day's reversal of roles for masters and slaves—
slaves were set free and were waited on at table by their masters.

thirty spokesmen: the same number as in 203 (ch. 16), and probably again
the members of the inner council. See also ch. 42 note.

37 *dictated to them*: a few other provisos are stated by Appian (*Libyca* 54), for
instance a ban on enlisting foreign mercenaries and a Roman promise to

leave Africa in a hundred and fifty days; both may be genuine, for Polybius, whom L. copies, says he is recording only the major clauses (15.18).

without the authorization of the Roman people: in Polybius' version, warfare outside Africa was totally forbidden. This restriction on making war within Africa was, in practical terms, another ban, hence L.'s simplified wording. Next, L. deliberately tones down the proviso about Masinissa, which in reality required the Carthaginians to restore to him everything he 'or his ancestors' had ever possessed—a generalization exploited repeatedly by that wily king to annex more and more Carthaginian territory over the coming half-century.

10,000 talents . . . over fifty years: i.e. 200 a year, a smaller annual amount than the one levied in the peace of 241 (220 a year for ten years); just as the 25,000 pounds of silver required immediately (ch. 38; about 350 talents) was smaller than the lump sum required in 241 (1,000 talents). The Carthaginians, in fact, were able to offer full payment of the remaining indemnity as early as 191, an inconvenience the Romans declined.

Gisgo: unknown; a connection of the indefatigable, but now dead, Hasdrubal son of Gisgo? L. names him from a source other than Polybius, who speaks only of 'a senator' (15.19).

after thirty-six years: thus exploding the bogus story of him being sent to Spain in 224 (21.3 and note).

not in Africa: Hannibal did flee—in 195—to Antiochus III, the Great King, after machinations by his political foes with complicity from the Romans (see 33.47–8). This story, no doubt by some uninformed annalist, predates the event by seven years.

38 *price of grain so low*: L. means at Rome. His ensuing (obscurely put) point is that the merchant could not make enough profit from his grain cargo even to pay off his crew, so gave it to them in lieu of pay. L. may well be generalizing from one or two talked-about instances; it can hardly have happened often.

a shrinking of the sun's orb: presumably a partial eclipse of the sun is meant; but the only eclipse known was that of 19 October (ch. 29 note), too late to fit the period L. indicates and, anyway, barely if at all visible as far north as Italy.

39 *the Insane Mountains*: in Sardinia's north-east, supposedly so called from the frenzied squalls they produced.

prevented them from being held: storms were not just an inconvenience, but were ill-omened. Clearly it was a very bad winter.

40 *by the start of another*: war with Macedon did duly follow in 200.

42 *against Marcus Aurelius*: on the mission of Aurelius and his fellow-envoys, see ch. 26 and note.

opposed to the Barca faction: this is Hasdrubal Haedus' first appearance in L., despite his supposedly long opposition; Appian (*Libyca* 34) has him protecting Scipio's envoys to Carthage the year before, then leading the thirty senators to Scipio after Zama and making an even more florid speech (*Libyca* 49–53). He disappears again after ch. 44. Haedus means 'the Kid' (i.e., young goat), but the reason for the nickname is unknown. His effort to pin the whole blame for the war on the Barcid faction was the current Carthaginian line, and was what the Romans wanted to hear: Fabius Pictor followed it in his *History*.

43 *the fetials*: *fetiales*, an ancient priestly college (note their flintstone knives). They performed the rituals for duly opening and closing Roman wars, and in so doing had to act on enemy soil, or else a substitute for it by the temple of Bellona at Rome. To avert the unfriendly attentions of the foreign land's gods, they also bore sacred herbs from the Capitol. L. carefully uses the appropriate archaic Latin terms in this decree, including '*praetor*' in its old sense of 'general'.

45 *by no means a source to be disregarded*: a notorious piece of faint praise, given that Polybius has been probably L.'s single most important source for these books, and will continue to be in the following fifteen books. Later on, in 33.10, he is more complimentary to his Greek predecessor. For Syphax's death, L. seems to draw, even if indirectly, on an official record (the pontifical annals?), and he may be correct. Polybius' report (16.23) of Syphax being in Scipio's triumph could reflect the Scipionic family's wishful distortion, for it would have been grander to display the fallen king in person than merely show a picture of him, the usual alternative.

GLOSSARY

aediles two colleges of middle-ranking MAGISTRATES. The plebeian and curule aediles supervised various amenities and activities, such as markets, temples, streets, and festival games; they could impose fines. Only plebeians (see PATRICIANS, PLEBEIANS) could hold the plebeian aedileship, which was the older. A successful aedileship was often a springboard to higher office.

assemblies citizens were members of a variety of official assemblies which met when convened by appropriate MAGISTRATES to carry out specific functions. There were three chief ones. The Centuriate Assembly, in which citizens belonged to 193 'centuries', arranged mainly in five '*classes*' according to economic worth, elected senior magistrates, and passed laws. The Tribal Assembly, representing the 35 districts of Roman territory (see TRIBES), elected curule aediles and quaestors, and it too could legislate. The Council of the Plebs, formed on the 'tribal' basis again but open only to plebeian Romans, elected TRIBUNES OF THE PLEBS and plebeian aediles—and it could legislate as well, by passing resolutions (*plebiscita*) valid for the whole state. Centuries and tribes were very unequally distributed but, in every assembly, voting was counted by the unit; individual citizens' votes determined the vote of their unit. Roman women did not have the vote.

asses see MONEY.

augurs a senior college of priests who observed and interpreted omens from the behaviour of birds, such as the sacred chickens (22.42 note) and the flight of wild birds.

auspices before a major undertaking, consuls and other senior magistrates had to ascertain the will of the gods through a number of rituals (*auspicia*), such as observing the flight of birds and the behaviour of the sacred chickens (see 22.42 note). Action could not be taken until the auspices were favourable, as interpreted by the priests in attendance. Delegated officers, like LEGATES and PREFECTS, acted under the auspices of the magistrate who appointed them.

caetra a light, round shield with a leather cover, used by Spanish troops.

Campanian citizens in 343 BC the people of Capua and other Campanian cities were granted an associate form of Roman citizenship. They kept their own communal institutions but could also exercise most citizen rights at Rome (though not the vote); and vice versa. In practice, Rome controlled all foreign relations. As time passed, Capua and its satellite towns found this subordination irksome, and after Cannae they defected to Hannibal. As a result they lost their autonomy for a quarter of a century (see PREFECTS).

censors every five years, two MAGISTRATES were elected for eighteen months to bring the administrative condition of the republic up to date. Censors let out contracts for public buildings, roads, drains, and other infrastructure, scrutinized the membership rolls of the Senate and equestrian order to expunge moral delinquents (widely defined), carried out a census of all citizens including their financial and economic (and moral) status, and performed a solemn purification ceremony (*lustrum*). Normally, ex-consuls were elected as censors.

centuries (*centuriae*) see also ASSEMBLIES and LEGION. The same term was used in both the Centuriate Assembly and the legion because the former had originally been the citizen-soldiery readied for war. In the assembly, the first century to be asked its vote on a matter was selected by lot (the *centuria praerogativa*; see SORTITION) as the choice of the gods, and its lead was commonly followed by most or all of the others.

cognomen a Roman man's third name. This was not the family surname, as is often supposed; for that was the second name (*nomen*), such as Fabius or Cornelius. Many Romans had no third name, only a first name (*praenomen*, such as Gaius or Publius) and the *nomen* (e.g. Gaius Flaminius); but Romans of the social elite often—not always—had three, and customarily passed the third as well the second on to their sons. A fourth name was sometimes given as a nickname (Quintus Fabius Maximus was at first derisively, later admiringly, nicknamed Cunctator, 'the Delayer') or for military glory (so Publius Cornelius Scipio received the extra name Africanus: 30.45). Roman women normally had only a single name, the feminine form of the *nomen* (e.g. Cornelia, Claudia).

cohort an army unit of three maniples (see LEGION); it may have come into existence during Hannibal's war (see 22.5 note).

colony (**Roman** or **Latin**) a town-settlement of Roman or Latin citizens, planted by the Roman state on a strategically important site; colonists received grants of surrounding land. Roman colonies, composed of Roman citizens only, were small; Latin colonies, drawn from Roman citizens and LATINS, were larger and had more surrounding territory. Each colony was self-governing but enjoyed a close bond with Rome. The thirty Latin colonies were the most important group of Roman allies in Italy: their military manpower, together with Rome's, made the Roman state practically invincible.

Comitium the open space on the north side of the Forum, before the Senate house (Curia), where citizens could gather and be addressed by a magistrate standing on the speakers' platform, the ROSTRA. The Centuriate Assembly, however, met in the Campus Martius.

consuls the chief MAGISTRATES of the Roman republic. Two were elected each year, and entered office on 15 March (later changed to 1 January). The year was named after them: thus 'in the consulship of Publius Cornelius and Tiberius Sempronius' dated an event to 218. The consul's *IMPERIUM* was superior to a PRAETOR's and, in war, he commanded a larger army. Consular responsibilities were very wide; in practice, and in consultation with the Senate, they directed foreign affairs and attended to the main domestic concerns of their term; they were also the chief military commanders. Only a consul could nominate a DICTATOR. If one or both consuls were killed or had to abdicate office, replacement ('suffect') consuls were elected (see *INTERREX*). Members of leading patrician and plebeian families attained consulships far more often than other Romans in public life, and ex-consuls enjoyed immense prestige and influence.

curio a very ancient office though not a MAGISTRACY. Originally the spokesman of one of the *curiae*, the earliest groupings of Roman citizens, in historical times he had religious functions surviving from this role, and the position carried prestige. The chief *curio* (*curio maximus*) was elected by the people.

curule magistrate and **chair** CONSULS, PRAETORS, and one group of AEDILES conducted civil business on a folding chair with ivory inlay, called a *sella curulis*.

decemvirs, duumvirs, triumvirs officials appointed to particular areas of administrative work. The decemvirs (the 'board of ten for sacred rites') performed the rituals to expiate omens and prodigies, duumvirs (two officials) might be appointed to oversee the building of a promised temple, and triumvirs ('boards of three') were appointed to allocate land-grants at new colonies or for many other tasks—for example, supervising the coinage, judging serious cases (the *triumviri capitales*: 25.1).

denarius, quadrigatus, sestertius see MONEY.

dictator in a military emergency, or when neither consul was available at Rome for an important task like holding elections, one of the consuls could nominate a dictator. The dictator's legal authority (see *IMPERIUM*) overrode all others but he, and the master of horse he in turn nominated as his deputy, could hold office for six months at most. Fabius Maximus was the last dictator for military purposes until Sulla in 82 BC.

duumvirs see DECEMVIRS.

equestrian order, rank Romans of means who were not senators were expected to be available to serve as cavalrymen (*equites*), an expensive task, which is why they are often termed 'knights' in English. In the Centuriate Assembly (see ASSEMBLIES), eighteen centuries were reserved for such citizens, with precedence over the other centuries. Other wealthy men who were not registered in them came to be termed 'cavalrymen' too (*equites Romani*). Eventually this became a social and not strictly a military ranking. Senators' sons, if not senators themselves, were of equestrian status. Men of similar rank in other states and cities were also called *equites* ('knights') by Roman writers.

Fabius the *nomen* (see COGNOMEN) of one of the most eminent families at Rome from the earliest days of the republic. Its most famous member was Quintus Fabius Maximus, consul five times between 233 and 209, whose cautious resistance to Hannibal after the battle of Trasimene as DICTATOR, and in ensuing years, earned the nickname 'the Delayer' (Cunctator). Another Fabius, Marcus Fabius Buteo (consul in 245), was probably the famous envoy who declared war on the Carthaginians in 218 by letting fall a symbolic fold in his toga. Quintus Fabius Pictor, also a senator, later composed the first history of Rome (see Introduction).

fasces a Roman magistrate was attended by a body of lictors, each carrying a bundle of rods and axes (the *fasces*) symbolizing his authority to punish and to put to death. A consul or dictator had twelve lictors with *fasces*, a praetor six. In the city, the axes were removed and the *fasces* were dipped before the people in assembly.

flamen (Latin plural *flamines*) certain gods, notably Jupiter, Mars, and Quirinus, had a special priest (*flamen*) each for his personal rites. The flamen of Jupiter (*flamen Dialis*) was restricted by an elaborate and ancient network of taboos—for example, he was not permitted to see a dead body, and his hair- and nail-clippings must be ceremonially buried—which much restricted the public life of the appointee.

games many religious celebrations were accompanied by shows and entertainments (*ludi*), put on at state (and sometimes private) expense by the aediles. Notable were the Apollinine Games (in July), the Great or Roman Games (September), and the Plebeian Games (November). There were others of lesser scope, and after 200 BC further major *ludi* were instituted. Entertainments included horse-racing, athletics, gladiatorial contests, and performances of plays, both tragedies and comedies. But the slightest error in prescribed ceremonial, being offensive to the gods, meant that the entire games had to be repeated.

Hanno the commonest name among the Carthaginian aristocracy. Two men of this name play a noteworthy role in *Hannibal's War*: (1) Hanno 'the Great', one-time colleague of Hamilcar Barca, later the chief critic and political opponent of the Barcids. (2) Hanno son of Bomilcar, described by the later writer Appian as Hannibal's nephew, was one of his most trusted lieutenants; he commanded an independent army in southern Italy for some years, but did not enjoy great success, and is not heard of after 207. It is not absolutely certain that Hanno son of Bomilcar was the same as the southern army commander, but it looks very probable. Other names in the very limited range used by leading Carthaginians included Bomilcar, Carthalo, Hannibal, Himilco, Mago, and Maharbal.

Hasdrubal one of the most often used Carthaginian names. In *Hannibal's War*, the most notable are these: (1) Hamilcar Barca's son-in-law and second-in-command in Spain, who took over as general and effective leader of the Carthaginian state in 228, made the Ebro agreement with Rome in 225, and enjoyed great success until his assassination in 221. (2) Hannibal's brother, whom he appointed governor of Spain in 218. A skilful organizer but not a very good general, he was killed when he invaded Italy in 207. (3) An energetic cavalry officer in 218–216, who helped to win Cannae but is not heard of afterwards. (4) Hasdrubal, son of Gisgo, a leading aristocrat allied with the Barcids; co-commanded in Spain from 213 to 207, then was general in North Africa until 203; a vigorous and able man, but repeatedly defeated by the Romans in both theatres, though he helped to destroy the elder Scipios in 211. Father of the beautiful Sophoniba, whom he married to Syphax, the Numidian king, he was reportedly driven to suicide by his ungrateful fellow-citizens in 203 or 202.

hastati see LEGION.

imperium a CONSUL, PRAETOR, and DICTATOR held *imperium*, the power to command in peace and war. If the Senate chose, it could extend (*prorogare*) this for a further year or years after his term of office expired (see PROCONSUL) but, as a 'promagistrate', he could not re-enter Rome without losing it. The lawful civil authority of other magistrates, for example, that of the tribunes, was termed *potestas*, the general word for 'power'.

interrex an institution going back to the ancient kings of Rome. If both consuls died, or resigned office, the Senate appointed first one *interrex* and then up to four more, for five days each, to secure the proper AUSPICES and hold elections for new consuls. An *interrex* must be a patrician senator.

iugerum (plural *iugera*) a Roman measure of land, equivalent to 0.625 acres or 1.54 hectares.

knights see EQUESTRIAN ORDER.

Latin Festival an annual ceremony, dating from ancient times when Rome was a member of the Latin League, the religious and military association of the cities of Latium. By 338 BC many of these had been absorbed (or destroyed) by the Roman state, but the festival continued under the presidency of the consuls (see 21.63 note).

Latins people of the thirty Latin COLONIES in Italy and of the remaining Old Latin cities, notably Praeneste, and Tibur. Collectively, they are always referred to as The Latin Name (*nomen Latinum*), distinct from the other Italian allied states (*socii* or *socii Italici*).

lectisternium a solemn ceremony honouring a god or several gods as banqueting-guests; their effigies were set on couches in public and tables of food laid out before them.

legate a senior officer appointed by a magistrate or promagistrate to depute for him, e.g. as a divisional commander or a city governor.

legion the largest structural unit of a Roman army, consisting of heavy and light infantry, and cavalry. In the third and second centuries BC, its average strength was 4,200 infantry and 300 cavalry, but the infantry could be increased (as apparently at Cannae). Citizens were liable for service from the ages of 16 to 46, but many served for longer. There were 1,200 light infantry, called *velites*, recruited from those who could not afford heavy armour. The heavy infantry was distributed into three groups, each forming one line in battle-formation: 1,200 *hastati* (the youngest men) at the front, 1,200 *principes* (maturer soldiers) in the middle and 600 *triarii* (the oldest and most experienced) in the rear. Each line consisted of ten maniples (*manipuli*) which in turn consisted of two centuries each (*centuriae*); the commander of a century was a centurion. The names *hastati* ('spearmen') and *principes* ('front-liners') reflected an older array. By the third century, a legionary in the first two lines had two javelins for hurling and a sword, while only the *triarii* ('third-liners') retained thrusting-spears (*hastae*). Maniples were drawn up in chessboard array and could manœuvre flexibly, unless forced to fight in densely packed ranks (as at Cannae). The cavalry were stationed on one or both wings. A legion was accompanied by Latin and Italian allied contingents, normally larger in numbers, so a legion with allies was equivalent to a strong modern division. A consul commanded two such legions, a praetor one. See also COHORT.

lictors see FASCES.

magistrates the elected executive officials of the Roman state. They held office (unsalaried) for twelve months, CENSORS and DICTATORS excepted. In descending order of rank they were: two consuls, four praetors (later increased in number), two plebeian and two curule aediles, ten tribunes of the plebs (equal in rank to the aediles), and eight quaestors (more numerous in later times). Some junior elected offices, like military tribunes (see TRIBUNES, MILITARY) and *triumviri capitales* (see

DECEMVIRS), were technically magistrates too, but the term is rarely used of them. Each group of magistrates was termed a college (*collegium*)—cf. the word 'colleague'. It was normal for a young man to seek the lesser offices at the start of his career, hoping eventually to attain a praetorship or even a consulship; naturally, only a small number succeeded to senior levels. Only consuls and praetors, and dictators, held IMPERIUM; the authority of the rest was termed *potestas*. Magistrates in office could not be prosecuted, so it was uncustomary to hold the same office two years running or to seek another magistracy while holding office. By 218 BC, men who had reached the consulship enjoyed the highest political and social status of all citizens, and were often termed 'notables' (*nobiles*).

maniple see LEGION and COHORT.

master of horse a dictator's deputy, appointed by him (except in 217 when, unprecedentedly, Minucius Rufus was popularly elected to the position).

medix tuticus the chief magistrate of a Campanian town, especially Capua.

Mens abstract divinity, 'right thought' or 'right intellect'.

money (Roman) Roman coinage proper began early in the third century BC, modelled on various Greek forms. Previously, money-exchange was by weighed and stamped pieces of 'heavy bronze' (*aes grave*). This was replaced by the bronze *as* (plural *asses*), and by 218 a silver coinage also existed, related to the Greek drachma. Silver coins included *quadrigati* and *victoriati* (cf. 22.52 note). Around 211 a new silver coin, worth ten *asses*, was struck as the *denarius* (the 'ten-*asses* coin', but later retariffed at sixteen). This and its subordinate the *sestertius* (four per *denarius*) formed the basis of Roman silver coinage for the next five hundred years. In 203, a year of plentiful grain, four *asses* per measure of grain was a cheap price (see 30.26). The highest level centuries in the Centuriate Assembly consisted of citizens worth at least 100,000 *asses*. In 211, senators were reckoned as each worth well over a million (see 24.11).

ovation see TRIUMPH.

patricians, plebeians a formal distinction between Roman citizens. A small number of ancient families ranked as patrician; the origins of this status are debated, but it conferred social prestige, and patricians alone could hold the post of *interrex* and a few priestly positions. All other citizens, rich and poor, were plebeians, i.e. members of the PLEBS. Defeated in efforts, early in the republic, to monopolize office, patricians nevertheless continued to enjoy a disproportionate number of magistracies (not until 172 were both consuls plebeians, for instance), even though only some patrician houses, like the Cornelii, Fabii, and Valerii, maintained their centuries-long prominence; others—like the Julii—fell into relative obscurity for long periods. A few family names (Claudii and Servilii, for instance) occur in both patrician and plebeian elite houses: the great Marcus Claudius Marcellus was of the plebeian house.

plebs the Latin term for all citizens who were not patricians; the word in archaic times seems to have meant 'the many' or 'the majority' (like Greek *hoi polloi*). See TRIBUNES OF THE PLEBS.

poll-tax payers (*aerarii*) a punishment-ranking for peccant Roman citizens, imposed by the censors. For moral or other failings, *aerarii* had to pay a higher level of tax and could be transferred from their birth-tribe to one of the four city tribes, which were less prestigious.

pomerium the sacred boundary of the city of Rome, marked by boundary-stones and not always coinciding with the city walls (until 80 BC, for instance, the Aventine Hill was outside it).

pontifex maximus chief of the College of Pontiffs, and in a general sense the most senior priest of the Roman state. Like members of all priestly colleges, he was a man in public life and could hold magistracies, though he was not supposed to go abroad on campaign (28.38).

praetexta see TOGA PRAETEXTA.

praetors the second most senior magistrates (see MAGISTRATES); praetors held *IMPERIUM* and were normally assigned (by SORTITION) judicial duties at Rome or the administration of a PROVINCE. The urban praetor heard cases between citizens, the 'foreign' praetor those between citizens and non-Romans; Sicily and Sardinia-Corsica, the only provinces existing in 218, were governed by the other praetors. A praetor could also command an army, and this was a duty often given to them during the Second Punic War. From 197 their number was raised to six because two new Spanish provinces had been established.

prefects officers in command of a body of troops or a squadron of warships, or in some position of subordinate authority (*praefectus* means 'one put in charge' of something). The commanders of Latin and allied army contingents (see LATINS) were prefects. After Capua and the other rebel Campanian cities capitulated in 211, their affairs were administered by prefects appointed by the Roman state.

priesthoods there were numerous and varied priesthoods at Rome, from individual FLAMENS to colleges like the pontiffs (see *PONTIFEX MAXIMUS*), AUGURS, and fetials (see 30.43 note), all with specific functions though the *pontifex maximus* exercised a broad supervisory religious authority. Priesthoods were held for life and were normally held by senators, who in turn could combine them with magistracies (this was difficult for a special priest like the *flamen Dialis*, however). Appointment was by co-option.

principes see LEGION.

proconsul, propraetor, promagistrate a consul or praetor whose year of office expired while in military command might have his *IMPERIUM* extended or 'prorogued' for another year or years by the Senate and people. He was then described as acting *pro* ('in place of' or simply 'as') *consule* or *pro praetore*; the terms later became single words.

province (*provincia*) originally this term covered the sphere of duty of a senior magistrate, assigned to him by the Senate (if the two were at serious odds, he might find that his *provincia* was 'forests and pathways in Italy'). Theatres of war were designated by their territorial name, within and outside Italy ('Apulia', 'Sicily'), so the term eventually took on a geographical meaning apart from special contexts.

quaestors the most junior magistracy (see MAGISTRATES), by 218 some eight in number annually. The quaestorship was the first step in an official career, and despite their relative youth quaestors had important financial and related administrative duties. Two were attached to the consuls as their finance officials, four performed their tasks at home (e.g. managing the treasury) under the Senate's supervision, and two went to Sicily to administer taxes and levies. As the number of provinces increased after 201, more quaestors were elected for the same tasks (one per province).

quinquereme the standard third-century warship, with a larger crew than a trireme (though not necessarily much larger in size). The name seems to mean 'a five-rower [ship]', but the arrangement of oars and rowers in quinqueremes is debated. There were also 'four-rowers' (quadriremes). Still larger craft up to 'sixteen' and even a 'forty' are heard of, but these were more for show than for use. A Roman quinquereme had a crew of about 300, all citizens of maritime allies of Rome and sometimes Roman citizens too; it would also carry between 40 and 120 armed marines. Carthaginian warships were crewed by citizens of Carthage and her maritime allies. Quadriremes, triremes, and smaller ships like skiffs were used in support roles.

rex sacrorum this priest had replaced the early kings in several religious functions and sacrifices; he had to be a PATRICIAN and, unusually, was barred from all other offices.

Rostra the speakers' platform in the Comitium, at the northern end of the Forum. In 338 it was adorned with the beaks (*rostra*) of captured warships, and kept this name through many later rebuildings.

Saturnalia the great winter festival at Rome in honour of Saturn, originally on 17 December and later extended over several more days; see 30.35 note.

Scipio the *COGNOMEN* of one branch of a distinguished Roman family, the Cornelii; this branch was exceptionally successful and widely spread in the third and second centuries BC. During Hannibal's war the most notable members were: (1) Gnaeus Cornelius Scipio, consul in 222, who in collaboration with his brother Publius commanded Roman operations in Spain from 218 until his defeat and death in 211; he was an abler general than his brother; (2) Publius Cornelius Scipio, consul in 218, proconsul in Spain 218–211, and father of (3) Publius Scipio the younger, consul in 205 and 194, given the 'triumphal' *cognomen* 'Africanus' for his victory over Hannibal and the Carthaginians.

scorpion a small artillery machine (Latin *scorpio*), powered by twisted ropes, that shot iron bolts or arrows; its range could be several hundred yards.

seers, soothsayers (Latin *haruspices*) originally Etruscan, these priests interpreted omens from the organs of sacrificed animals, and portents like lightning-strikes and unnatural births.

senate, Carthaginian officially named The Mighty Ones (*h'drm*), this seems to have consisted of leading men, many or most of them former magistrates and generals, who were members for life. It decided most matters in consultation with the current SUFETES, but where there was a disagreement the issue had to be put before the citizen assembly of Carthage. An inner council of thirty had great prestige, but its functions are unclear. The Mighty Ones were some hundreds in number, for from their ranks were appointed the members of the powerful court of One Hundred and Four, which tried disgraced generals.

Senate, Roman this consisted of ex-magistrates and other individuals deemed worthy of appointment by the CENSORS; membership was for life. Properly the advisory council to the magistrates, as it had been to the ancient kings, the Senate's moral authority brought it the dominant role in the affairs of the Roman republic, especially during and after the Second Punic War. The Senate was convened by a magistrate, normally a consul, tribune, or praetor: former consuls (*consulares*) had precedence in speaking and were the most influential group of senators. Next in precedence were the former praetors, tribunes, and aediles; junior senators (*pedarii*)—those who had held no magistracy, or perhaps only up to the quaestorship—were not called on to speak but voted with the rest on resolutions. The honorary position of Senate Leader (*princeps senatus*) could be conferred by the censors on a distinguished ex-consul, who would always be the first called on to speak (27.11 note). In debating an issue, senators could not formally put a motion, but the presiding magistrate, who did so, in turn had to use one of the formal 'opinions' (*sententiae*) offered. The Senate also had certain residual powers such as appointing *interreges* (see *INTERREX*).

senators, local cities and towns in Italy, and in many other lands, were self-governing states, usually with executive magistrates, a senate, and a people's assembly (whatever the differences in details). As at Rome and Carthage, and in the Greek world, local senators and magistrates tended to belong to the affluent social strata of their communities.

socii Italici see LATINS.

sortition lots (Latin *sortes*) were used for selecting which century or tribe in the assemblies should vote first, and also for allocating particular areas of responsibility to even the highest-ranking magistrates. This meant that the choices were left to the gods' wisdom. The process was termed *sortitio*.

sufete the title of the two annual chief magistrates at Carthage; a Punic word, etymologically the same as the Hebrew *shophet*, 'judge'. Latin writers often call the sufetes 'praetors' or 'consuls', and Greek sources say 'king'.

toga praetexta the toga was a large woollen garment worn over the tunic by Romans doing public business. It was the distinctive garb of a citizen; white and essentially an extended half-moon in shape, it had to be carefully draped over the body. The *toga praetexta* had a crimson (Latin *purpureus*) cloth border sewn to it, and was worn by boys under 16 and by magistrates (cf. 21.63). Roman historical plays, always in verse, were termed *praetextae*, as one or more magistrates invariably appeared in them as characters. One such, for instance, was Naevius' *Clastidium*, a famous play about Marcellus' Gallic victory in 222 and put on not long after it.

triarii see LEGION.

tribes by 241 Roman citizen territory was distributed into 35 districts (*tribus*) of which four were in the city while the oldest rural tribes were near to Rome and very small. The rest lay further away and were larger, but each tribe formed one unit of the Tribal Assembly (see ASSEMBLIES) and its members' internal voting determined its single vote. On an issue or in an election, the tribe asked to vote first, the *praerogativa tribus*, was selected by lot (see SORTITION) and its choice was often followed by most or all of the rest.

tribunes, military the six senior officers of a legion. For the first four legions levied in a year, the military tribunes were elected by the Roman people (until 218 it had been unusual for more than four legions a year to be levied). Those of the other legions were appointed by the consul or praetor in command. Military tribunes were usually young men of equestrian status, including sons of senators.

tribunes of the plebs ten annual officials who in practice, though not technically, were MAGISTRATES. They entered office on 10 December. The tribunate was open only to plebeians (see *PATRICIANS, PLEBEIANS*), and was attained by men of both elite plebeian families and lesser ones. Originating in the early republic's struggles between the patricians and plebeians, and elected to protect the latter against arbitrary treatment, tribunes became accepted as integral to the proper working of the republic. Their extensive *potestas* (see *IMPERIUM*) included the right of intervention to protect any distressed citizen and, resulting from this, to veto any act or proposal of any magistrate or of the Senate. A tribune could propose legislation to the Council of the Plebs or Tribal Assembly (see ASSEMBLIES) and convene the Senate. The person of a tribune in office was sacrosanct: if struck, he could punish the offender even with death. Even a consul who obstructed him was liable to imprisonment (as would happen in 151 and 138). Tribunes did not command troops and were forbidden to leave the city during their term of office. They were seen as the most immediate recourse for citizens in trouble, especially poor citizens; and many holders of the office continued to take this role seriously.

triumph a religious and ceremonious procession by a general returning victorious with his army to Rome, dating back to very early times. It was authorized by the Senate to a magistrate or promagistrate (a proconsul or propraetor) acting under his own AUSPICES; a promagistrate needed an exemption to enter the city on that day without losing his *IMPERIUM*. Booty and prisoners were exhibited, the troops sang cheerful songs often insulting to their commander so as to ward off any divine displeasure at his glory, and the triumphator rode in a chariot, representing Jupiter himself (a slave therefore stood behind him to remind him that he was a mortal). The triumphal procession moved from the Campus Martius into the city and through the Forum up to the Capitoline Hill, where a share of the booty was dedicated to Jupiter in his temple. The prisoners were then sold as slaves or executed. A triumph was the zenith of pride and accomplishment for a Roman leader; if refused one, he might hold a private one on the Alban Mount. It was a slap in the face for Marcellus that, because of political antagonisms, he was granted only an ovation after his conquest of Syracuse (26.21). An ovation, granted for smaller victories, was less spectacular: the general went to the Capitol on foot or horseback.

INDEX

Note: Frequently occurring names, such as Carthage, Hannibal, Rome, and Italy, are not indexed.

A SELECTION OF OXFORD WORLD'S CLASSICS

ANN RADCLIFFE	The Italian
	The Mysteries of Udolpho
	The Romance of the Forest
	A Sicilian Romance
SAMUEL RICHARDSON	Pamela
FRANCES SHERIDAN	Memoirs of Miss Sidney Bidulph
RICHARD BRINSLEY SHERIDAN	The School for Scandal and Other Plays
TOBIAS SMOLLETT	The Adventures of Roderick Random
	The Expedition of Humphry Clinker
	Travels through France and Italy
LAURENCE STERNE	The Life and Opinions of Tristram Shandy, Gentleman
	A Sentimental Journey
JONATHAN SWIFT	Gulliver's Travels
	A Tale of a Tub and Other Works
HORACE WALPOLE	The Castle of Otranto
MARY WOLLSTONECRAFT	Mary and The Wrongs of Woman
	A Vindication of the Rights of Woman

The Oxford World's Classics Website

www.worldsclassics.co.uk

- Information about new titles
- Explore the full range of Oxford World's Classics
- Links to other literary sites and the main OUP webpage
- Imaginative competitions, with bookish prizes
- Peruse the Oxford World's Classics Magazine
- Articles by editors
- Extracts from Introductions
- A forum for discussion and feedback on the series
- Special information for teachers and lecturers

www.worldsclassics.co.uk

American Literature

British and Irish Literature

Children's Literature

Classics and Ancient Literature

Colonial Literature

Eastern Literature

European Literature

History

Medieval Literature

Oxford English Drama

Poetry

Philosophy

Politics

Religion

The Oxford Shakespeare

A complete list of Oxford Paperbacks, including Oxford World's Classics, Oxford Shakespeare, Oxford Drama, and Oxford Paperback Reference, is available in the UK from the Academic Division Publicity Department, Oxford University Press, Great Clarendon Street, Oxford OX2 6DP.

In the USA, complete lists are available from the Paperbacks Marketing Manager, Oxford University Press, 198 Madison Avenue, New York, NY 10016.

Oxford Paperbacks are available from all good bookshops. In case of difficulty, customers in the UK can order direct from Oxford University Press Bookshop, Freepost, 116 High Street, Oxford OX1 4BR, enclosing full payment. Please add 10 per cent of published price for postage and packing.